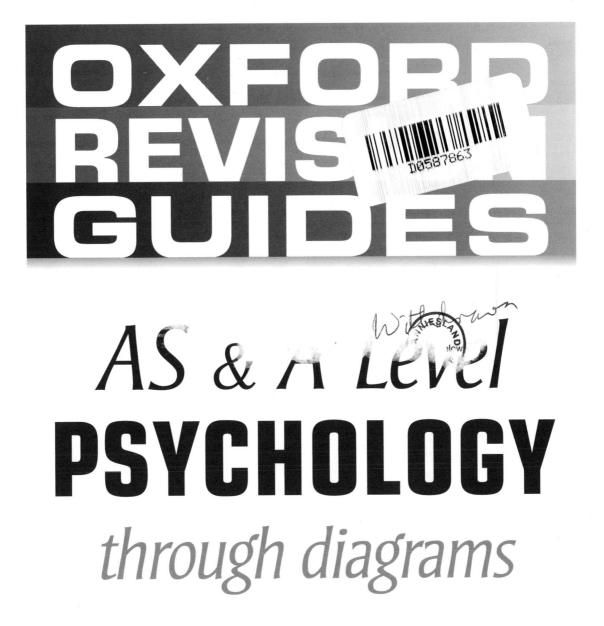

OXFORD REVISION GUIDES

AS & A Level
PSYCHOLOGY
through diagrams

Grahame Hill

OXFORD
UNIVERSITY PRESS

OXFORD
UNIVERSITY PRESS

Great Clarendon Street, Oxford OX2 6DP

Oxford University Press is a department of the
University of Oxford. It furthers the University's objective
of excellence in research, scholarship, and education by
publishing worldwide in

Oxford New York

Auckland Cape Town Dar es Salaam Hong Kong Karachi
Kuala Lumpur Madrid Melbourne Mexico City Nairobi
New Delhi Shanghai Taipei Toronto

With offices in

Argentina Austria Brazil Chile Czech Republic France Greece
Guatemala Hungary Italy Japan Poland Portugal Singapore
South Korea Switzerland Thailand Turkey Ukraine Vietnam

Oxford is a registered trade mark of Oxford University Press
in the UK and in certain other countries

British Library Cataloguing in Publication Data

Data available

ISBN-13: 978-0-19-915070-0

10 9 8 7 6 5 4 3 2

Typesetting, design and illustration by Hardlines, Long Hanbourgh, Oxon

Printed in Great Britain by Bell & Bain Ltd, Glasgow

Contents

Contents (cont.)

Contents (cont.)

Specification Contents (AQA A)

Specification Contents (AQA A cont.)

Specification Contents (AQA A cont. and AQA B)

AQA SPECIFICATION B

Because of space restrictions *complete* coverage of the AQA B AS and A2 specification is *not* provided. The following content, however, is related to the AQA B AS and A2 level specification and may be of use. Note that choices are required in the A2. *(Material in italics indicates useful links or background reading.)*

AS LEVEL

A2 LEVEL

Specification Contents (AQA B cont. and Edexcel)

EDEXCEL SPECIFICATION

The following content is relevant to the Edexcel AS and A2 level specification. Note that choices are required in some areas and that you may sometimes have covered different theories, studies or issues from those below. (Material in italics indicates useful links or background reading.)

AS LEVEL

The Cognitive Approach

The Social Approach

Cognitive Developmental Approach

The Learning Approach

Specification Contents (Edexcel cont.)

A2 LEVEL

Clinical Psychology

Specification Contents (Edexcel cont. and OCR)

OCR SPECIFICATION

Because of space restrictions *complete* coverage of the OCR A2 specification is *not* provided. The following content, however, is relevant to the AS level of the specification and some may be of use for the A2. Note that choices are required in the A2. *(Material in italics indicates useful links or background reading.)*

AS LEVEL

Specification Contents (OCR cont.)

Specification Contents (OCR cont.)

Overview

Introduction. What is psychology?

DEFINITIONS

The word 'Psychology' is derived from two Greek roots: 'Psyche', meaning 'mind' or 'soul' and 'Logos', meaning 'study of'. Psychology, therefore, literally means 'study of the mind'. However, a more recent definition by Atkinson et al (1991) suggests that psychology is:

'The scientific study of behaviour and mental processes'

Just giving this simple definition, however, is a bit misleading, since psychologists now and throughout their history have not only disagreed about the definition of psychology, but have also strongly disagreed about *what* should be studied in the subject and *how* it should be studied.

THE HISTORY OF PSYCHOLOGY

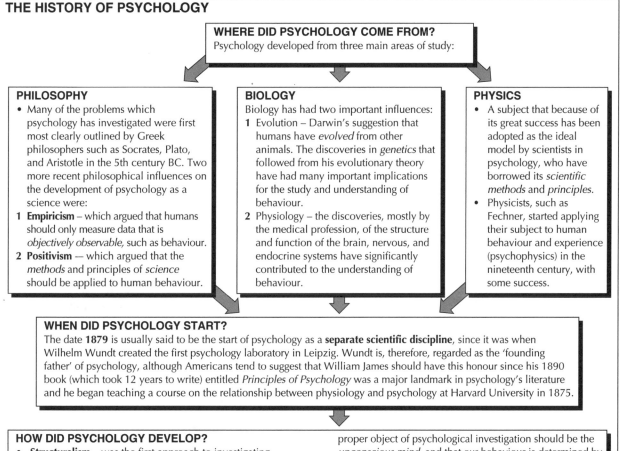

WHERE DID PSYCHOLOGY COME FROM?
Psychology developed from three main areas of study:

PHILOSOPHY
- Many of the problems which psychology has investigated were first most clearly outlined by Greek philosophers such as Socrates, Plato, and Aristotle in the 5th century BC. Two more recent philosophical influences on the development of psychology as a science were:
1 **Empiricism** – which argued that humans should only measure data that is *objectively observable,* such as behaviour.
2 **Positivism** — which argued that the *methods* and principles of *science* should be applied to human behaviour.

BIOLOGY
Biology has had two important influences:
1 Evolution – Darwin's suggestion that humans have *evolved* from other animals. The discoveries in *genetics* that followed from his evolutionary theory have had many important implications for the study and understanding of behaviour.
2 Physiology – the discoveries, mostly by the medical profession, of the structure and function of the brain, nervous, and endocrine systems have significantly contributed to the understanding of behaviour.

PHYSICS
- A subject that because of its great success has been adopted as the ideal model by scientists in psychology, who have borrowed its *scientific methods* and *principles.*
- Physicists, such as Fechner, started applying their subject to human behaviour and experience (psychophysics) in the nineteenth century, with some success.

WHEN DID PSYCHOLOGY START?
The date **1879** is usually said to be the start of psychology as a **separate scientific discipline**, since it was when Wilhelm Wundt created the first psychology laboratory in Leipzig. Wundt is, therefore, regarded as the 'founding father' of psychology, although Americans tend to suggest that William James should have this honour since his 1890 book (which took 12 years to write) entitled *Principles of Psychology* was a major landmark in psychology's literature and he began teaching a course on the relationship between physiology and psychology at Harvard University in 1875.

HOW DID PSYCHOLOGY DEVELOP?
- **Structuralism** – was the first approach to investigating psychology, pioneered by Wundt himself, who thought that the object of psychological investigation should be the *conscious mind,* and that it should be studied by *introspection* (looking inwards at one's own mental experience) in order to *break it down* into its component parts (such as images, sensations and feelings) like the science of chemistry had done with chemicals. One structuralist, Titchener, claimed there were a total of 46,708 basic sensations that combined to form the structure of the human mind, but the approach was very limited in its ability to explain and was replaced by functionalism.
- **Functionalism** – the approach William James advocated. James was influenced by Darwin's views and argued that the workings of the mind are functional, to survive and adapt, so we should investigate *what behaviour and thoughts are for.* Many of James's insights remain valid today, but functionalism was superseded by the next two very powerful approaches that both started around the turn of the century.
- **Psychoanalysis** – was in fact a method of *therapy* developed by Sigmund Freud in Austria, but in many major books, such as *The interpretation of dreams* (1900), Freud began describing in detail an underlying theory of the human mind and behaviour that has had an enormous (and controversial) impact on psychology. Freud argued that the

proper object of psychological investigation should be the *unconscious mind*, and that our behaviour is determined by processes of which we are not aware.
- **Behaviourism** – Behaviourists, such as John Watson, were extremely critical of all the approaches that concerned themselves with 'minds', and proposed that psychology should only investigate *observable behaviour* if it wanted to be an objective science. This approach dominated experimental psychology until the 1950s, when a strong resurgence of interest in the 'mind' developed in the form of the cognitive and the humanistic approaches, which suggested that behaviourism ignored all the most important and interesting things that go on in our heads.
- **Cognitive psychology** – aims to investigate the mind by using *computer information processing* ideas to arrive at testable *models* of how the brain works, and then applying *scientific methods* to confirm these models. The cognitive approach has enjoyed much success and is a very dominant one in psychology today.
- The **Humanistic approach**, however, has had less of an impact on psychology, since it has deliberately adopted a *less scientific* view of the human mind by arguing that psychology should focus on each *individual's conscious experience* and *aims* in life.
- The **Biological approach** has advanced *evolutionary, physiological,* and *genetic* explanations for human behaviour throughout the history of psychology.

The psychodynamic approach to psychology

ORIGINS AND HISTORY

- The psychodynamic approach was mainly initiated by *Sigmund Freud*, a Viennese doctor who specialised in neurology. Freud became interested in hysteria - the manifestation of physical symptoms without physical causes - and became convinced that *unconscious mental causes* were responsible not just for this disorder but for many disorders and even 'normal' personality. Freud developed psychoanalysis – a set of techniques for *treating* the unconscious causes of mental disorders and built up an underlying explanatory *psychoanalytic theory* of how human personality and abnormality develop from childhood.
- Freud's theory and approach were influenced by the ideas and society of his time, particularly by his early work with Charcot, the Parisian hypnotist, and Breuer the pioneer of the cathartic method. Freud's psychoanalytic approach had a great impact on psychology and psychiatry, and was developed in different ways by other *psychodynamic* theorists (those influenced by psychoanalytic assumptions) such as Jung, Adler, Klein, Anna Freud (his daughter) and Erikson.

Sigmund Freud (1856 - 1939)

"...I set myself the task of bringing to light what human beings keep hidden within them.....the task of making conscious the most hidden recesses of the mind is one which it is quite possible to accomplish".

ASSUMPTIONS

Psychoanalysis, as developed by Freud, had a very fixed set of assumptions that later psychodynamic theorists agreed with to differing extents. The most common shared assumptions of the approach are:

- *Unconscious processes* – many important influences on behaviour come from a part of the mind we have no direct awareness of, the unconscious.
- *Psychodynamic conflict* – different parts of the mind are in constant dynamic struggle with each other (often unconsciously) and the consequences of this struggle are important in understanding behaviour.
- *Emotional drives* – Freud believed behaviour is motivated by sexual and aggressive drives. The drives create psychic energy that will build up (like steam in a steam engine) and create tension and anxiety if it cannot be released in some form. While not all psychodynamic theorists agree with Freud's view, they do see emotional motivation as important.
- *Development* – personality is shaped by relationships, experience and conflict over time, particularly during childhood.

METHODS OF INVESTIGATION

- Freud used the *case study* method when treating his clients (seeing them individually and investigating them in detail), often using the clinical interview method to probe their past and question their behaviour. He *deeply* analysed and *interpreted* the *symbolism* of all they said and did. These methods remain the norm for most psychodynamic theorists.
- Two particular techniques Freud used were: *Free association* – the uninhibited expression of thought associations, no matter how bizarre or embarrassing, from the client to the analyst. *Dream analysis* – the 'royal road' to the unconscious, the analyst attempts to decode the symbols and unravel the hidden meaning of a dream from the dreamer's report.

CONTRIBUTION TO PSYCHOLOGY

Freud used his theory to explain a vast number of topics, such as:
- *Personality development* – due to fixation / defence mechanisms.
- *Moral / gender development* – the result of the Oedipus complex.
- *Aggression* – caused by hydraulic drives and displacement.
- *Abnormality* – the consequence of early trauma and repression.
- *Memory* – Forgetting caused by repression.
+ Slips of the tongue, the shaping of civilisation and customs, etc.

CONTRIBUTION TO SOCIETY

- The purpose of psychoanalysis was as a therapy to treat mental disorder. Once the unconscious cause of disorder was identified through dream interpretation etc., then a cure could be effected by getting it 'out in the open' to be discussed, resolved and controlled.
- Psychoanalysis can be applied to art and literature.

STRENGTHS

- Freud's ideas made a large impact on psychology and psychiatry and are still discussed and used today, around a 100 years after he started developing them.
- Freud thought case studies like 'Little Hans' and 'Anna O', his belief in determinism and his detailed collection of data provided scientific support for his theory.
- Psychodynamic therapies drew attention to the psychological causes of mental disorder.
- Psychoanalysis has enormous explanatory power and has something to say on a huge variety of important topics.
- Later psychodynamic theory tried to deal with the weaknesses of psychoanalysis and develop the strengths.

WEAKNESSES

Psychodynamic psychology has been accused of:
- Having vague concepts that can be used to explain anything but which can predict very little.
- Having concepts that are difficult to test and verify scientifically. Experimental research that has been conducted often fails to support psychodynamic ideas, and that which does seem to support them can often be attributed to alternative causes.
- Using unrepresentative samples and techniques that were not fully objective and therefore open to bias.
- Being linked with unsuccessful psychodynamic therapies.
- Having many concepts that can be explained by more scientific approaches such as cognitive psychology.

The learning theory approach to psychology

ORIGINS AND HISTORY

- The learning theory approach in psychology was initiated mainly by the behaviourists, who were influenced by the philosophy of **empiricism** (which argues that knowledge comes from the environment via the senses, since humans are like a 'tabula rasa', or blank slate, at birth) and the physical sciences (which emphasise scientific and objective methods of investigation).
- **Watson** started the behaviourist movement in 1913 when he wrote an article entitled 'Psychology as the behaviourist views it', which set out its main principles and assumptions. Drawing on earlier work by Pavlov, behaviourists such as Watson, Thorndike and Skinner proceeded to develop theories of **learning** (such as classical and operant conditioning) that they attempted to use to explain virtually **all** behaviour.
- The behaviourist approach dominated experimental psychology until the late 1950s, when its assumptions and methods became increasingly criticised by ethologists and cognitive psychologists. The behaviourist theories have been modified to provide more realistic explanations of how learning can occur, for example by psychologists such as Bandura with his social learning theory.

John Watson
'Give me a dozen healthy infants... and my own specified world to bring them up in and I'll guarantee to take any one at random and train him to become any type of specialist I might select - doctor, lawyer... and yes, even beggarman and thief.'

ASSUMPTIONS

The behaviourists believed:
1. the majority of all behaviour is **learned** from the **environment** after birth (behaviourism takes the nurture side of the nature-nurture debate), and so
   a psychology should investigate the **laws** and **products** of learning
   b behaviour is **determined** by the environment, since we are merely the total of all our past learning experiences, freewill is an illusion.
2. only **observable** behaviour not minds should be studied if psychology is to be an objective science, since we cannot see into other people's minds, and if we ask them about their thoughts they may lie, not know, or just be mistaken. Most learning theorists still adopt this scientific approach.

METHODS OF INVESTIGATION

The behaviourists adopted a very scientific approach, using strict laboratory experimentation, usually conducted on animals such as rats or pigeons. Animals were tested because the behaviourists believed:
- the laws of learning were universal
- there was only a quantitative difference between animals and humans
- animals are practically and ethically more convenient to test

CONTRIBUTION TO PSYCHOLOGY

The behaviourists' discoveries concerning the laws of learning were vigorously applied to explain many aspects of behaviour, such as:
- **Language acquisition,** e.g. Skinner's theory.
- **Moral development,** e.g. conditioned emotional responses of guilt and conscience.
- **Attraction,** e.g. Byrne & Clore's reinforcement affect model.
- **Abnormality,** e.g. the classical conditioning of phobias and their treatment.
+ aggression, prejudice, gender role identity, etc.

CONTRIBUTION TO SOCIETY

- The behaviourist learning theory approach has produced may practical applications for education (such as programmed learning) and the treatment of those suffering behavioural disturbances (such as systematic desensitisation for phobias, behaviour shaping for autism, and token economies for institutionalised patients).
- Operant conditioning principles have been used in training animals to perform tasks, from circus animals to guide dogs.
- Watson applied behaviourist theory to both child rearing and advertising, while Skinner offered many suggestions regarding the large scale manipulation of behaviour in society in his books such as *Beyond Freedom and Dignity* and *Walden Two*.

STRENGTHS

Behaviourism contributed to psychology in many ways:
- Behaviourism was very scientific and its experimental methodology left a lasting impression on the subject.
- It provided strong counter-arguments to the nature side of the nature-nurture debate.
- The approach is very parsimonious, explaining a great variety of phenomena using only a few simple (classical and operant) principles.
- Behaviourism has produced many practical applications, some of which have been very effective.
- Social learning theory has overcome some of the weaknesses of the behaviourists' theories.

WEAKNESSES

Behaviourist views have been criticised by other approaches for a number of reasons.
- Ethologists argued that the behaviourists ignored innate, built-in biases in learning due to evolution, but also disagreed with the behaviourists' use of animals and laboratory experimentation, saying that there is a biologically qualitative difference between humans and other animals and that experiments only demonstrate artificial, not natural learning.
- Cognitive psychologists think that behaviourism ignores important mental processes involved in learning; while the humanistic approach disliked their rejection of conscious mental experience.

The cognitive approach to psychology

ORIGINS AND HISTORY

- The cognitive approach began to revolutionise psychology in the late 1950s and early 1960s, to become the dominant paradigm in the subject by the 1970s. Interest in mental processes had been gradually resurrected through the work of people like Tolman and Piaget, but it was the arrival of the **computer** that gave cognitive psychology the terminology and metaphor it needed to investigate human minds.
- Cognitive psychology compares the human mind to a computer, suggesting that we too are **information processors** and that it is possible and desirable to study the **internal mental processes** that lie between the stimuli we receive and the responses we make. Cognition means 'knowing' and cognitive processes refer to the ways in which knowledge is gained, used and retained. Therefore, cognitive psychologists have studied perception, attention, memory, thinking, language, and problem solving.
- Cognitive psychologists believe these internal mental processes (our programming) can be investigated scientifically by proposing models of psychological functions and then conducting research to see, when people are given an input of information, whether their output of behaviour/verbal report matches what the models would predict.

E. Loftus

'...cognition refers to all those processes by which sensory input is transformed, reduced, elaborated, stored, recovered and used... cognition is involved in everything a human being might possibly do.'
Neisser (1966)

ASSUMPTIONS

Cognitive psychologists assume that:
1. The study of **internal mental processes is important in understanding behaviour** – cognitive processes **actively** organise and manipulate the information we receive – humans do not just passively respond to their environment.
2. Humans, like computers, are **information processors** – regardless of our hardware (brains or circuits) both receive, interpret and respond to information – and these processes can be modelled and tested **scientifically**.

METHODS OF INVESTIGATION

Cognitive psychologists mostly use:
- **Experimentation** – usually conducted in the laboratory, e.g. memory experiments conducted under strictly controlled conditions, where independent variables such as the time delay before recall are manipulated to find the effect on the amount of information retained.
- **Case studies** – for example the study of brain damaged patients such as those with anterograde amnesia in memory research.

CONTRIBUTION TO PSYCHOLOGY

Cognitive psychologists have sought to explain:
- **memory,** e.g. Atkinson and Shiffrin's multi-store model of the input, storage and loss of information, etc.
- **perception,** e.g. Gregory's theory on the role of mental processes in influencing/organising visual stimuli
- **attention,** e.g. Broadbent's filter model
- **artificial intelligence,** e.g. Rumelhart and McClelland's parallel distributed network models
- **social cognition,** e.g. the effects of stereotypes on interpersonal perception
- **abnormality,** e.g. Beck's ideas on the errors of logic and negative thinking of depressed patients

CONTRIBUTION TO SOCIETY

Cognitive psychology has had a broad range of applications, for example to
- **memory** – to help improve memory through mnemonic devices or to aid the police in eyewitness testimony
- **education** – Information processing theory has been applied to improve educational techniques
- **therapy** – such as the use of Ellis's rational emotive therapy to restructure faulty thinking and perceptions in depression, for example. When combined to form cognitive-behavioural techniques, effectiveness is improved
- **health promotion** – e.g. the health belief model and the following (or not) of health advice

STRENGTHS

Cognitive psychology is probably the most dominant approach today:
- It investigates many areas of interest in psychology that had been neglected by behaviourism; yet, unlike psychoanalysis and humanism, it investigates them using more rigorous scientific methods.
- In contrast to the biological approach, it bases its explanations firmly at a functional, psychological level, rather than resorting to reductionism to explain human behaviour.
- The approach has provided explanations of many aspects of human behaviour and has had useful practical applications.
- Cognitive psychology has influenced and integrated with many other approaches and areas of study to produce, for example, social learning theory, cognitive neuropsychology, social cognition, and artificial intelligence.

WEAKNESSES

Cognitive models have been accused of being
- over simplistic – ignoring the huge complexity of human functioning compared to computer functioning
- unrealistic and over hypothetical – ignoring the biological influences and grounding of mental processes
- too cold – ignoring the emotional life of humans, their conscious experience and possible use of freewill

The humanistic approach to psychology

ORIGINS AND HISTORY

- The humanistic movement developed in America in the early 1960s, and was termed the third force in psychology since it aimed to replace the two main approaches in the subject at that time, behaviourism and psychoanalysis. Influenced by gestalt psychology's idea of studying **whole units,** and existential philosophy with its belief in **conscious free will,** humanists argued that behaviourism's artificial and dehumanising approach and psychoanalysis's gloomy determinism were insufficient to provide a complete psychology.
- The humanistic approach aimed to investigate all the uniquely **human** aspects of **experience** such as love, hope, creativity, etc. and emphasised the importance of the individual's interaction with the environment. Humanists, such as **Maslow,** believed that every individual has the need to **self-actualise** or reach their potential, and **Rogers** developed client-centred therapy to help individuals in this process of self-actualisation.

Carl Rogers
'Humanistic psychology has as its ultimate goal the preparation of a complete description of what it means to be alive as a human being.' Bugental (1967)

ASSUMPTIONS

Bugental (1967), the first president of the American Association for Humanistic Psychology, described some of its fundamental assumptions:

- A proper understanding of human nature can only be gained from **studying humans,** not other animals.
- Psychology should research areas that are **meaningful** and important to human existence, not neglect them because they are too difficult. Psychology should be **applied** to enrich human life.
- Psychology should study **internal experience** as well as external behaviour and consider that individuals can show some degree of **free will.**
- Psychology should study the **individual** case (an idiographic method) rather than the average performance of groups (a nomothetic approach).
- In general, humanistic psychologists assume that the **whole person** should be studied in their environmental **context.**

METHODS OF INVESTIGATION

Humanists take a phenomenological approach, investigating the individual's conscious experience of the world. For this reason they employ the idiographic case study method, and use a variety of individualistic techniques such as

- flexible open ended interviews.
- the Q-sort technique, where the participant is given one hundred different statements on cards, such as 'I don't trust my emotions' or 'I have an attractive personality' which they have to sort into piles for personal relevance

CONTRIBUTION TO PSYCHOLOGY

The humanistic approach has been applied to relatively few areas of psychology compared to other approaches. The main areas of explanation have been in

- **personality/self identity,** e.g. Rogers's self theory
- **motivation,** e.g. Maslow's hierarchy of needs and self-actualisation
- **abnormality,** e.g. due to imposed conditions of worth by others or the inability to accept the true self. Humanists are against the nomothetic classification of abnormality

CONTRIBUTION TO SOCIETY

The humanistic approach's primary application has been to therapeutic treatment for anybody suffering 'problems with living'. Some humanistic therapies include

- client-centred therapy – whereby the client is encouraged to develop positive self-regard and overcome mismatch between their perceived self, true self, and ideal self
- gestalt therapy – developed by Fritz Perls, the aim is to help the client become a 'whole' (gestalt) person by getting them to accept every aspect of themselves

STRENGTHS

The humanistic approach has contributed to psychology by

- re-emphasising the need to study consciousness and human experience for a complete study of the subject
- serving as a valuable agent of criticism against the extremes of the earlier major approaches
- highlighting the value of more individualistic and idiographic methods of study, particularly in the areas of personality and abnormality
- emphasising the importance of self-actualisation, responsibility, freedom of choice, and social context in therapy

WEAKNESSES

Humanistic psychology has not, however, had the significant impact on mainstream academic psychology that the other approaches have. This is probably because humanists deliberately take a less scientific approach to studying humans since

- their belief in free will is in opposition to the deterministic laws of science
- they adopt a more idiographic approach, seeking the more unique aspects of individuals, rather than producing generalised laws of behaviour that apply to everyone
- the issues they investigate, such as consciousness and emotion, are amongst the most difficult to objectively study

The physiological approach to psychology

ORIGINS AND HISTORY

- Sometimes known as the biological, biopsychological, neurophysiological, nativist (considering nature rather than nurture) or innate approach.
- The biological approach to psychological matters has integrated with and run parallel to the rest of psychological thought since early Greek times – the Greek physician Galen suggested that personality and temperament may be linked to the levels of body fluids such as blood and bile in the body.
- As knowledge of human anatomy, physiology, biochemistry, and medicine developed, important insights for human behaviour and experience were gained. Penfield, for example, mapped the role of various areas of the cerebral cortex through microelectrode stimulation with conscious patients. Sperry investigated the effects of splitting the cerebral hemispheres on consciousness and psychological function.
- The field will progress still further as the technology to isolate the effects of genes and scan the living brain develops.

Roger Sperry
'All that is psychological is first physiological' Anon.

ASSUMPTIONS

Biologically orientated psychologists assume that
- all that is psychological is first physiological - that is since the mind appears to reside in the brain, all thoughts, feelings and behaviours ultimately have a physical/biological cause
- human genes have evolved over millions of years to adapt physiology and behaviour to the environment. Therefore, much behaviour will have a genetic basis
- psychology should, therefore, investigate the brain, nervous system, endocrine system, neurochemistry, and genes
- it is also useful to study why human behaviour has evolved in the way it has, the subject of evolutionary/sociobiological theory

METHODS OF INVESTIGATION

Common techniques include
- laboratory experimentation – e.g. stimulating, giving drugs to, or removing parts of the brain to see what effect it has on behaviour
- laboratory observations – controlled observations of physical processes, e.g. sleep or the scanning of the structure and activity of the brain.
- correlations – e.g. between twins and adopted family members to discover the genetic influence on intelligence or mental disorders.

CONTRIBUTION TO PSYCHOLOGY

Physiological researchers have contributed to an understanding of
- **gender development** – e.g. the influence of genetic and hormonal predispositions on gender behaviour and identity
- **aggression** – e.g. investigating the role of the limbic system
- **abnormality** – e.g. the dopamine hypothesis and enlarged ventricle theory of schizophrenia
- **memory** – e.g. brain scans of areas involved during memory tests or the effect of brain damage on memory
- **motivation** – e.g. the role of the hypothalamus in homeostasis
- **awareness** – e.g. biological theories of sleep, dreams and body rhythms
- **localisation of function** – e.g. the effect on behaviour of brain damage to certain areas

CONTRIBUTION TO SOCIETY

Physiology's main applications have been to
- **therapy** – e.g. drug treatment, psychosurgery, or electroconvulsive therapy for mental disorders such as schizophrenia or depression
- **health** – e.g. research on the causes, effects and management of stress
- **industry** – e.g. research on jet lag and shift work
- **sport** – e.g. the effect of arousal on performance
- **education** – e.g. the genetic basis of ability

STRENGTHS

Physiology has contributed to psychology in many ways:
- The approach is very scientific, grounded in the hard science of biology with its objective, materialistic subject matter and experimental methodology.
- It provides strong counter-arguments to the nurture side of the nature-nurture debate.
- Physiology's practical applications are usually extremely effective, e.g. the treatment of mental disorder.
- The physiological approach has contributed to psychologists' understanding of a very wide range of phenomena.

WEAKNESSES

- Reductionism – the biopsychological approach explains thoughts and behaviour in terms of the action of neurones or biochemicals. This may ignore other more suitable levels of explanation and the interaction of causal factors.
- The approach has not adequately explained how mind and body interact – consciousness and emotion are difficult to study objectively.
- Over simplistic – biopsychological theories often over-simplify the huge complexity of physical systems and their interaction with environmental factors.

The social psychological approach to psychology

ORIGINS AND HISTORY
- Researchers can be said to adopt a social psychological approach when they focus their research on *social behaviour* (**between** individuals or groups) and tend to regard *other people* and *social contexts* as just as, if not more, important as influences upon people as their dispositions and personality characteristics.
- Social behaviours include those most important to us such as attraction, helping, prejudice and aggression, while the influences studied include those of individuals (e.g. leadership and obedience), groups (e.g. conformity and crowding), societies (e.g. social norms and expectations) and culture (e.g. history, politics and language).
- Social psychology has a long history within scientific psychology, e.g. Triplett's (1898) social facilitation experiment. Like most psychological research, social psychologists began by investigating social processes and influence as they applied to the *individual*. Most of this research came from America and dominated social psychology, but a more sociological and European approach was gradually incorporated to take more account of social, historical and political contexts and collective/shared representations and identities.
- Social constructionism has taken the social approach one step further by suggesting our society, culture and language affect the very way we define psychological concepts and the process of scientific investigation itself – making unbiased study difficult if not impossible.

Stanley Milgram
Social psychology can be defined as 'the scientific investigation of how the thoughts, feelings and behaviours of individuals are influenced by the actual, imagined or implied presence of others' G. Allport (1935)

ASSUMPTIONS
Social psychologists assume that, for anyone who has been raised in a society:
1. All behaviour occurs in a social context, even when nobody else is physically present.
2. A major influence on people's behaviour, thought processes and emotions are other people and the society they have created.

METHODS OF INVESTIGATION
Social psychologists have used a very wide range of methods, e.g.
- Field experiments – e.g. Piliavin and others changed the type of victim requiring help in the everyday environment of a subway.
- Laboratory experiments – e.g. Milgram changed various social variables to affect obedience under controlled conditions.
- Surveys – e.g. questionnaires have been used on many people to measure the frequency and reasons for prejudiced attitudes.
- Observation / content analysis – e.g. to record discrimination.

CONTRIBUTION TO PSYCHOLOGY
Social psychologists have sought to explain:
- *Social influence* e.g. conformity, obedience, leadership, social facilitation and crowd behaviour.
- *Social cognition* e.g. social identity / categorisation, attitudes, attribution, stereotyping and emotion.
- *Social behaviour* e.g. inter-personal and inter-group aggression, discrimination, attraction and helping.
- *Social development* e.g. gender, self, attachment and intellectual development over time as a result of changing roles, social expectations, social circumstances and cultural influences.

CONTRIBUTION TO SOCIETY
Social psychology has had a broad range of applications, for example to:
- *Criminology* – e.g. attribution theory and jury decision-making.
- *Education* – e.g. the labelling and stereotyping of students' educational performance.
- *Industry* – e.g. in leadership/management selection and group productivity.
- *Sport* – e.g. team and audience effects on performance.
- *The Environment* – e.g. the effects of architecture and crowding on behaviour or attitude change towards the environment
- *Health* – e.g. social factors affecting the exposure and reaction to stress.

STRENGTHS
Social psychology is still an important approach today.
- Social influences have been shown to be involved in, and have a strong effect upon, people's behaviour, thinking and emotions – often stronger than dispositional influences.
- The approach has provided explanations for a great many phenomena.
- The approach has had many useful practical applications in a wide range of areas.
- The approach has provided evidence for its concepts and theories using a wide range of methods, often conducted in a scientifically objective manner.

WEAKNESSES
At times the social psychological approach has:
- Underestimated what people bring with them into social situations – individual differences (whether inherited or learnt) do affect the results of social psychological studies but are sometimes explored less.
- Provided only 'superficial snapshots of social processes' (Hayes, 1995), ignoring their development over time and the broader social, political, historical and cultural context that the research takes place in. For example American researchers measuring what their students find attractive in a photograph of a face in laboratory conditions at a particular time in history.

Psychology and science 1

To fully investigate whether psychology, despite its problems, is justified in calling itself a science, we must first outline what a science consists of, and then see how well psychology matches these criteria.

A science consists of various components:
- A **subject matter**
- Good **theories** and **hypotheses**
- Scientific **methodology**

THE SCIENTIFIC METHOD

Within a paradigm

PARADIGM

hypotheses are derived

from theories

to be tested in scientific ways

against the world/reality

to support or refute those theories

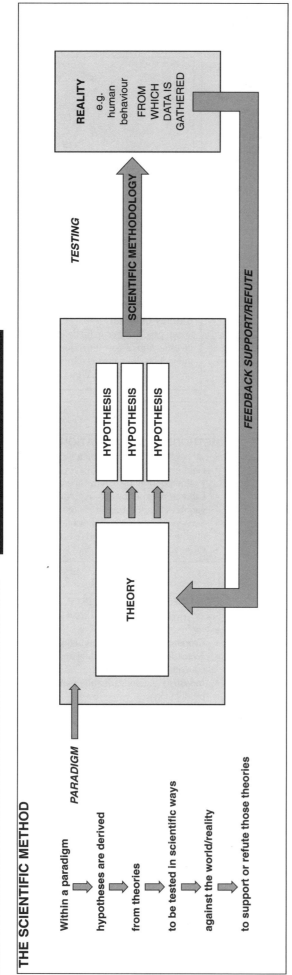

A SUBJECT MATTER

- The subject matter of a science is what the science is about. There should be agreement amongst researchers about *what* should be studied and *how*. **Kuhn** (1962) used the term 'paradigm' to describe this **shared set of assumptions, methods and terminology.**

- According to Kuhn's theory of the progression of science, paradigms go through changes over time, through three historical stages:

  a **Pre-science**, where there is no universally accepted paradigm.
  b **Normal science**, where researchers work sharing the same paradigm.
  c **Revolution**, where conflicting evidence becomes so overwhelming that a *paradigm-shift* occurs to a new perspective.

- Thus, the majority view at one time was that the earth was flat and was the centre of the universe, but this view became more and more criticised until it was superseded. Similarly, the Newtonian paradigm of physics was replaced by Einstein's which better fitted the facts of, for example, planetary motion.

PSYCHOLOGY'S SUBJECT MATTER

Does psychology have a unified subject matter and paradigm?

Kuhn argues that psychology is in a state of **pre-science**, because there are so many conflicting approaches to the subject that there is **no overall paradigm**. However, it could be argued that psychology has already gone through **several paradigm shifts**, from structuralism, to behaviourism, to cognitive psychology. Perhaps psychology is in the process of selecting the best set of approaches to form an integrated paradigm. Certainly most psychologists accept the definition of Psychology as the study of mind **and** behaviour.

Valentine (1982) proposes that **behaviourism** is the closest psychology has come to having a unified **paradigm,** since it had a clear subject matter (observable behaviour), assumptions (environmental determinism, learning, etc.), methods (strict laboratory experimentation), and terminology (conditioning, reinforcement, etc.). This paradigm dominated psychology for many years.

Other philosophers of science, such as **Feyerabend** (1975), argue that **science** does **not** progress in an **orderly** way through paradigms, but does and should progress **anarchistically** – as each researcher sticks tenaciously to their own theories, often in the face of opposition from others. Feyerabend argues that conforming to paradigms may limit creativity and progress, 'The only principle that does not inhibit progress is anything goes'. This view seems much more realistic of how psychology has developed, with many psychologists working as individuals or in small teams to defend their own particular area of research in the subject.

Psychology and science 2

THEORIES AND HYPOTHESES

A science should involve theories which should provide hypotheses to be tested in order to support or refute the theories. The theories themselves should provide *general laws* or principles to fulfil the aims of science – **understanding, prediction,** and **control.**

1 **Understanding** – Theories should provide understanding by being
  * **orderly** (theories should organise facts and find regularities and patterns to generate laws).
  * **internally consistent** (different parts of the theory should not contradict each other).
  * **parsimonious** (provide the greatest possible explanation in the most economic way).
  * **true!** (theories should correctly explain reality).

2 **Prediction** – A good theory should generate lots of **bold, precise hypotheses** to stimulate research to support or refute the theory.
  * According to **Karl Popper** (1959) scientific theories should be **refutable** (able to be shown wrong) and research should aim to falsify rather than support theories – since it is all too easy to find support to fit your theory, especially if you expect to find it. **Falsification** is best achieved by advancing bold and precise hypotheses, and if a theory is falsified then it should be rejected. Thus Popper is suggesting that science advances through refutation rather than support. This is why we ensure that we include a null hypothesis.
  * Another philosopher of science, **Imre Lakatos,** suggests that theories should be given a chance to prove themselves first, so they can develop. Lakatos proposes that theories or paradigms should have a **hard core** of crucial assumptions and a **protective belt** of auxiliary hypotheses – this belt can support being falsified to a certain extent (perhaps the first experiments made type 2 errors) but the hard core should remain unfalsified for the theory to remain credible. Good theories, he added, should also provide a **positive heuristic** – a future research program to generate new hypotheses and to produce unexpected findings.
  * Theories provide laws and principles to predict the future, but this can only occur if
    a a **deterministic/nomothetic** view is taken, rather than a freewill or idiographic approach.
    b **induction** is accepted, i.e. that we can generalise from a limited number of observations to general laws. Induction can **never prove** anything 100%, however, because it is impossible to observe all possible data at any one time and we can never prove that our next observation will not refute our law. Induction is the basis for inferential statistics which talk about the **probability** of chance factors causing the results.

3 **Control** – Theories should be **useful** and have **practical implications,** such as solving problems and improving the human condition. However, complete control may be , impossible in practice, due to the complexity of situations and the probabilistic nature of scientific laws. Knowing the high probability that something will occur 99/100 will not guarantee that it will occur on a certain occasion. Ethical issues are also raised concerning control – who should have it and whose purposes should it serve?

SCIENTIFIC METHODOLOGY

* A science should test its hypotheses in fair and objective ways, meaning its terms should be operationalised and its methods should be standardised, controlled and replicable.

PSYCHOLOGICAL THEORIES AND HYPOTHESES

The different approaches to psychology fulfil these principles to varying degrees:

1 **Psychoanalysis** has **great explanatory power** and understanding of behaviour, but has been accused of only explaining behaviour after the event, **not predicting** what will happen in advance and of being **unfalsifiable**/unrefutable. Some have argued that psychoanalysis has approached the status more of a religion than a science, but it is not alone in being accused of being unfalsifiable (evolutionary theory has too – why is anything the way it is? Because it has evolved that way!) and like all theories that are difficult to refute – the possibility exists that it is actually right. Kline (1984) argues that psychoanalytic theory **can** be broken down into testable hypotheses and tested scientifically. For example, Scodel (1957) postulated that orally dependent men would prefer larger breasts (a positive correlation), but in fact found significantly the opposite (a negative correlation). Although Freudian theory could also be used to explain this finding (through reaction formation – the subjects were showing exactly the opposite of their unconscious impulses!), Kline has nevertheless pointed out that theory would have been refuted by *no significant correlation*.

2 The **humanistic approach** in psychology deliberately steps away from a scientific viewpoint, **rejecting determinism** in favour of freewill, aiming to study the **individual** to arrive at a unique and in depth understanding. The humanistic approach does not have an orderly set of theories (although it does have some core assumptions) and is not interested in prediction and controlling people's behaviour – the individuals themselves are the only ones who can and should do that. **Miller** (1969) in 'Psychology as a Means of Promoting Human Welfare' criticises the controlling view of psychology, suggesting that understanding should be the main goal of the subject as a science, since he asks who will do the controlling and whose interests will be served by it?

3 **Behaviourism** had **parsimonious** theories of learning, using a few simple principles (reinforcement, behaviour shaping, generalisation, etc.) to explain a vast variety of behaviour from language acquisition to moral development. It advanced **bold, precise and refutable hypotheses** (such as Hull's drive theory equations) and possessed a **hard core of central assumptions,** such as determination from the environment (it was only when this assumption faced overwhelming criticism by the cognitive and ethological theorists that the behaviourist paradigm was overthrown). Behaviourists firmly believed in the scientific principles of **determinism** and orderliness, and thus came up with fairly consistent **predictions** about when an animal was likely to respond (although they admitted that perfect prediction for any individual was impossible). The behaviourists used their predictions to **control** the behaviour of both animals (pigeons trained to detect life jackets) and humans (behavioural therapies) and indeed Skinner, in his book *Walden Two* (1948), described a whole society controlled according to behaviourist principles.

4 Cognitive Psychology – adopts a scientific approach to unobservable mental processes by advancing precise models and conducting experiments upon behaviour to confirm or refute them.

* Full understanding, prediction and control in psychology is probably unobtainable due to the huge complexity of environmental, mental and biological influences upon even the simplest behaviour.

PSYCHOLOGICAL METHODS

* Behaviourist, cognitive and biopsychological approaches have used the most objective method, the laboratory experiment. Humanists point out many problems of using this method for human study.

Gender bias in psychological theory and research

THEORETICAL BIAS

Hare-Mustin and Maracek (1990) distinguish between alpha and beta bias in theories:

- **Alpha bias** exaggerates differences between men and women, serving to reinforce gender stereotypes.
- **Beta bias** minimises real differences between men and women, causing important parts of women's life experiences to be ignored.

These biases exist because **androcentric** (male biased) views are used as the standard or norm to explain the psychological experiences of both sexes. If women show different behaviour from the male norm, it is seen as inferior, and what does not concern the androcentric world view is not investigated.

REPORTING BIAS

- **Interpretation of results**
  Results that show gender differences may be reported in a way that emphasises female stereotypes or inferiority, e.g. concluding that women are more 'field dependent' rather than 'context aware' in visual perception, or have less self-confidence, rather than saying men are over-confident (Tavris, 1993).
  Gender differences in results are only average differences – variation in male and female scores means that, for example, some women will be superior to some men.
- **Selection of material to be published**
  Male biased editors and reviewers of psychology journals and books may filter out research on women, and studies that report no differences or findings contrary to male opinion (e.g. those that report very little pre-menstrual syndrome in women).
- **Use of results**
  Those studies that report genuine difference between men and women should not be used to discriminate against whichever sex seems weaker, but should be used to support the argument for increased training opportunities.

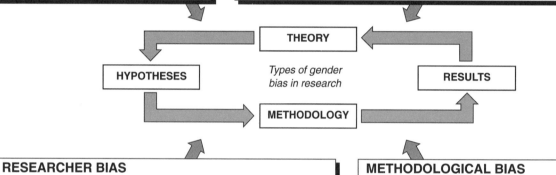

Types of gender bias in research

THEORY

HYPOTHESES

RESULTS

METHODOLOGY

RESEARCHER BIAS

Gender bias in research is likely to be caused by

- **lack of researchers**
  Researcher bias may occur because women are not appointed to, or promoted in, academic positions in male dominated universities. Alternatively, female academics may find themselves marginalised into areas outside mainstream psychology.
- **nature of researchers**
  Androcentric researchers are likely to propose hypotheses that
  a investigate stereotypical differences rather than real ones or similarities.
  b do not investigate important issues to women, such as pregnancy or female harassment and discrimination.
  c perpetuate biased ideas by, for example, searching for causes within women for different or abnormal behaviour (e.g. pre-menstrual syndrome) but in the environment for men (e.g. violent upbringing).

METHODOLOGICAL BIAS

Gender bias in the methodology of studies is found in

- the biased sampling of subjects – many famous studies in psychology (e.g. by Asch, Sherif, Kohlberg, Erikson) only used male subjects and generalised the results to women.
- the use of 'male preferred' techniques, such as the laboratory experiment with its 'manipulation' and 'control' of 'subjects'. Many feminists prefer less distant and hierarchical techniques, such as interviews where the emphasis is on personal experience and joint participation.
- the lack of controls to distinguish differences that are innate from those that are the product of gender socialisation or biased stereotypes (Weisstein 1993).

CONSEQUENCES OF GENDER BIAS

Feminists suggest that although gender differences may be minimal or non-existent, they are used against women to maintain male power. Judgements about an individual woman's ability are made on the basis of average differences between the sexes or biased sex role stereotypes, and this also has the effect of lowering women's self-esteem; making them, rather than men, think they have to improve themselves (Tavris, 1993).

VALIDITY OF GENDER BIAS

Maccoby and Jacklin (1974), in a thorough review of the research into sex differences, concluded that in the majority of areas no significant differences were found, and where they were found they were very small. The gender biased views of famous figures in psychology, such as Freud and Bowlby, have been disproved.

REDUCING GENDER BIAS

Equal opportunity legislation and feminist psychology have performed the valuable functions of reducing institutionalised gender bias and drawing attention to sources of bias and under-researched areas in psychology. More and more women are becoming psychologists and gender bias should be redressed as they become the majority in academic psychology.

Cultural bias in psychological theory and research

Social influence – Cross-cultural replications of obedience and conformity studies have revealed wide differences in resistance to influence.
Interpersonal relationships – Cultural bias in Western research on this topic, is revealed by its focus on
- brief, new acquaintances, rather than long term, kin relationships.
- the idea that marriage on the basis of romantic love is more desirable than on the basis of companionate love.
Helping behaviour – Western economic theories on the costs and rewards of helping behaviour may not be suitable for other cultures.
Abnormality – The increased diagnosis of mental disorder in immigrants may reflect prejudice or misunderstanding by a native diagnoser.
Psychometric testing – IQ and personality tests have been culturally biased in terms of content, phrasing, application, and assessment.

THEORETICAL BIAS

Cultures differ in many important ways from each other, for example in terms of their values, norms of behaviour and social structure - such as whether they emphasise individualism or collectivism, masculine or feminine values, etc. (Triandis, 1990).

Since cultural values strongly shape the construction of theories, a major problem is **ethnocentrism**, which involves
- inappropriately generalising the values and research findings of one culture to another without bothering to test other cultures. This limits the validity of theories and neglects important cross-cultural differences.
- imposing those values upon other cultures when conducting cross-cultural research. This distorts the validity of research, over-emphasises differences and can lead to unfavourable comparisons being made.

Nobles (1976) points out that the 'Eurocentric' approach (based on concepts such as 'survival of the fittest', 'competition' and 'independence') to the study of African people (who believe in 'the survival of the tribe', 'co-operation' and 'interdependence') amounts to an act of scientific colonialism.

REPORTING BIAS

- **Interpretation of results**
  Results that show cultural differences may be reported in a way that make non-American/European cultures appear deviant from the 'norm' or inferior.
- **Selection of material to be published**
  The predominantly white establishment in American and European psychology has filtered out research on black psychology, leading to the need to publish journals and books specifically for black psychology. Around two thirds of psychology in the world is North American.
- **Use of results**
  Results may be interpreted to fit political ideology and thus 'scientifically sanction' racist policies such as the eugenics driven policy of restricting immigration into the USA during the 1920s and 1930s based on the results of (biased) IQ tests.

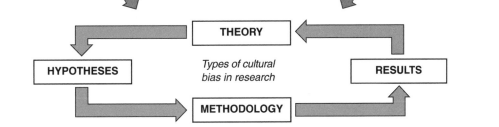

Types of cultural bias in research

THEORY — HYPOTHESES — METHODOLOGY — RESULTS

RESEARCHER BIAS

Cultural bias in research is likely to be caused by
- **lack of researchers**
  Researcher bias may occur because researchers from other cultures are not appointed to, or promoted in, academic positions in universities. 'Token' black psychologists in a predominantly white department, for example, may find themselves marginalised into areas outside mainstream psychology.
- **nature of researchers**
  Culturally biased or racist researchers are likely to propose hypotheses that
  a investigate stereotypical differences between 'races' (arbitrary and over-simplified categories based on skin colour) which may ignore cultural influences and perpetuate the stereotypes.
  b do not investigate important cross-cultural differences or similarities.

METHODOLOGICAL BIAS

Cultural bias in the methodology of studies is found in
- the biased sampling of subjects - the vast majority of the most famous studies in American and European psychology only used white subjects. Reviews of research in these countries frequently reveal less than 5% of subjects tested are not white.
- the use of Eurocentric scientific methods (based on 'control over nature', objective 'separateness' from the subject, and the investigation of individual 'differences' and 'uniqueness'), such as the laboratory experiment, is alien to the African concepts of 'oneness with nature', 'groupness' and 'similarity' (Nobles, 1976). These methods represent an imposed 'etic' (the study of a culture from the outside) when ecologically valid data can only be gained from an 'emic' study (from within the culture). Imposed 'etics' can lead to very culturally biased tests such as those on IQ described by Gould (1982).

CONSEQUENCES OF CULTURAL BIAS

Nobles (1976) argues that western psychology has been a tool of oppression and dominance. Cultural bias has also made it difficult for psychologists to separate the behaviour they have observed from the context in which they observed it.

VALIDITY OF CULTURAL BIAS

Culturally biased views have been exposed as false in many areas of psychology.

REDUCING CULTURAL BIAS

Equal opportunity legislation aims to rid psychology of cultural bias and racism, but we must be aware of merely swapping old, overt racism for new, more subtle forms of racism (Howitt and Owusu-Bempah, 1994).

'A nation of morons' Gould (1982)

AIM

To describe one part of the early history of intelligence testing as a way of discussing the following issues in psychology:

- The problematic nature of psychometric testing in general and the measurement of intelligence in particular.
- The problem of theoretical bias influencing research in psychology, in particular how psychological theories on the inherited nature of intelligence and the prejudice of a society can dramatically distort the objectivity of intelligence testing.
- The problem of the political and ethical implications of research, in this case the use of biased data to discriminate between people in suitability for occupation and even admission to a country.

THE HISTORY OF YERKES' TESTING OF INTELLIGENCE

What did Yerkes aim to do?

Yerkes aimed to

- show that psychology could prove itself as a respectable science by using intelligence testing to aid recruitment, and
- find support for the hereditarian view of intelligence (that intellectual ability was inherited through the genes).

How did Yerkes test intelligence?

Yerkes tested 1.75 million army recruits during the First World War, using three intelligence tests:

- Army alpha – a written exam for literate recruits
- Army beta – A pictorial exam for illiterate recruits and those who failed the alpha
- Individual exam - for those who failed the beta

Every individual was given a grade from A to E (with plus and minus signs), for example:

C- indicated a low average intelligence, suitable for the position of ordinary private in the army

D indicated a person rarely suited for tasks requiring special skill, forethought, resourcefulness or sustained alertness

What did Yerkes find?

- White American adults had an average mental age of 13, just above the level of moronity.
- Nations could be graded in their intelligence based on immigrants' intelligence test scores - people from Nordic countries scored higher than those from Latin or Slavic countries, with American 'Negroes' at the bottom of the scale.

What was wrong with Yerkes' findings?

Lots - they were a methodological, ethical, and practical disaster!

Methodological problems:	• Validity errors - the tests did not measure innate intelligence, since questions were often based on American general knowledge that recent immigrants would be unlikely to know, e.g. 'The number of Kaffir's legs is – 2, 4, 6 or 8 ?' (Army alpha test) The Army beta asked often poor and illiterate immigrants to spot errors in pictures of things they had probably never seen before (e.g. a tennis match without a net) and then write their answer.
	• Reliability errors – unstandardised procedures were followed, with individuals being given the wrong test, being rushed, and not given the appropriate re-tests - especially during the testing of black subjects.
Interpretation of findings errors:	• Ignored experience issue – the finding that immigrants scored higher the longer they stayed in America
	• Ignored education issue – the finding that there was a positive correlation between number of years in education and the IQ test scores - Yerkes interpreted causation from this by arguing that intelligent people chose to stay longer in education.
Negative implications of faulty conclusions:	• Intelligence can be objectively measured – therefore, people were assigned military positions and tasks according to their scores.
	• Intelligence is inherited – therefore, providing illegitimate evidence for those who advocated eugenics (selective breeding in humans), racist politics, and immigration restriction (the tests were influential in denying the immigration into America of up to 6 million people from Southern, Central, and Eastern Europe, many seeking political refuge, from 1924 to 1939).
	• IQ tests can predict future performance – thus providing biased support for the argument that special educational measures were a waste of time and money.

EVALUATION

Methodological:	Gould's criticism is based primarily on a methodological and theoretical critique of Yerkes' testing without presenting any empirical support for his own views.
Theoretical:	Contributes to an evaluation of an area of psychology which has many important implications. IQ tests have improved in sophistication, although there is still debate over their validity.
Links:	The ethics of socially sensitive research, the nature-nurture debate in intelligence, the validity and reliability of psychometric testing, bias in cross-cultural testing (see Deregowski).

The nature-nurture debate in psychology

NATURE **NURTURE**

APPROACH

Roots of the approach – nativist philosophy, biology (physiology and genetics), evolutionary theory.
Causes of behaviour – genetic determinism, inherited influence, maturational blueprint, neurochemical and hormonal influences, brain activity.
Methods employed – gene/chromosome mapping, twin and adoption studies, brain scanning, brain stimulation or damage studies, drug testing.
Implications – due to biological determinism, behaviour can only be changed through physical means, such as selective breeding (eugenics), gene therapy, brain surgery, or drugs.
Criticisms – reductionist, may neglect environmental influences.

Roots of the approach – empiricism philosophy, behaviourism, social psychology.
Causes of behaviour – the mind is regarded as a 'tabula rasa' (blank slate) at birth; therefore, knowledge and behaviour are the result of experience and learning from the environment.
Methods employed – use of classical and operant conditioning techniques to affect behaviour, manipulation of social environment to change behaviour.
Implications – due to environmental determinism, behaviour can be easily changed through manipulating reinforcement and environmental conditions. Anybody could be trained to do anything.
Criticisms – reductionist, may neglect innate influences.

AREAS OF EXPLANATION

Perception – Research conducted by Fantz, Bower, and Gibson and Walk on new-born babies indicated pattern detection, size constancy and depth perception are innate abilities.
Aggression – The ethologist Lorenz and psychoanalyst Freud believed aggression is an innate drive. Bio-psychologists have examined the role of hormones and brain areas in aggression.
Sex-role behaviour – Bio-psychologists propose gender identity is a direct result of genetic and hormonal influences.
Abnormality – The biomedical approach has isolated genetic and neurochemical causes of mental disorders.
Language acquisition – Chomsky proposed language is gained through the use of an innate language acquisition device.

Perception – Research into perception by Hebb on cataract removal and Turnbull on cross-cultural differences indicated that perceptual identification is a learnt ability.
Aggression – Social learning theory argues that aggression is learnt from the environment through observation and imitation. Social psychologists study conformity to aggressive norms.
Sex-role behaviour – Cultural relativism and learning theory argue that gender is socially constructed and reinforced.
Abnormality – The environment plays a role in the development of phobias, post-traumatic stress disorder, and anorexia.
Language acquisition – Skinner argued that language is learnt from other people via natural behaviour shaping techniques.

While some researchers have aimed to investigate the relative contributions of innate and environmental factors in psychology, it is now accepted that the two influences form a **continuum** and interact so thoroughly with each other that they are virtually inseparable. Even seemingly direct genetic influences, such as those on the physical development of the brain, are affected by environmental factors, from the inside of the womb to the pollution of the atmosphere. Many genes could impose a **susceptibility** to develop in certain ways or provide a 'norm of reaction' – a genetic potential that may or may not be realised by environmental circumstances. In a similar way, environmental experiences are **mediated** by not only innate abilities but even by the physical structure of the body, e.g. what gender or skin colour it has.

EXAMPLES OF NATURE-NURTURE INTERACTION IN PSYCHOLOGY

Perception – Blakemore and Cooper showed restricted environmental experience could physically affect the visual cortex of the brain.
Cognitive development – Piaget suggested that innate schemata develop and expand through interaction with the environment to adapt the child to its surroundings, although development was always limited by biological maturation.

Abnormality – Many mental disorders, such as schizophrenia, may have a genetic predisposition – those with an inherited susceptibility may be more likely to develop the disorder if they experience certain stressful environmental conditions. Animal studies have looked at the effect of aversive environmental stimuli upon the brain's neurotransmitters to explain depression.

Sex-role behaviour – The Biosocial approach proposes that factors such as the physical sex and innate temperament of a new born baby elicits sex typing behaviour from the people around it, leading to a self-fulfilling prophecy in terms of its gender identity.

THE STANDING OF THE DIFFERENT APPROACHES IN PSYCHOLOGY

NATURE ←—————————————————→ **NURTURE**

BIOPSYCHOLOGY
Focuses on genetic, physiological, hormonal and neurochemical explanations of behaviour.

PSYCHOANALYSIS
Focuses on instinctual drives of sex and aggression, expressed within the restrictions imposed by society via the ego and superego.

COGNITIVE PSYCHOLOGY
Focuses on innate information processing abilities or schemata that are constantly refined by experience.

HUMANISM
While accepting basic physiological needs, the focus is upon the person's experience of their social and physical environment.

BEHAVIOURISM
Focuses on the acquisition of virtually all behaviour from the environment via conditioning.

The reductionism debate in psychology

REDUCTIONISM	HOLISM & INTERACTIONISM

ASSUMPTIONS

Reductionism involves explaining a phenomenon by **breaking** it **down** into its **constituent parts - analysing it.** Reductionism works on the scientific assumption of **parsimony** – that complex phenomena should be explained by the **simplest underlying principles** possible.	Holism looks at same/higher level explanations. Interactionism shows how **many aspects** of a phenomenon or **levels** of explanation can **interact together** to provide a **complete** picture. Both approaches involve taking a gestalt approach, assuming that *'the whole is greater than the sum of its parts'.*

EXAMPLES IN PSYCHOLOGY

There have been many reductionist attempts to explain behaviour in psychology, for example:
- Structuralism – one of the first approaches to psychology pioneered by Wundt and Titchener involved trying to break conscious experience down into its constituent images, sensations, and feelings.
- Behaviourism – assumed that complex behaviour was the sum of all past stimulus-response learning units.
- Biopsychology – aims to explain all at the psychological or mental level in terms of that at the physiological, neurochemical or genetic level. Ultimately, psychology would be replaced by biology and the other natural sciences lower down on the reductionist ladder.

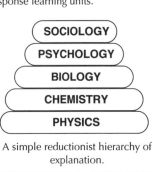

A simple reductionist hierarchy of explanation.

Other approaches have proposed higher level holistic and/or interactionist explanations of human behaviour, for example:
- **Humanistic psychology** – investigates all aspects of the individual as well as the effect of interactions between people. Gestalt therapy developed by Fritz Perls aims to enable people to accept and cope with all aspects of their life and personality.
- **Social psychology** – looks at the behaviour of individuals in a social context. Group behaviour may show characteristics that are greater than the sum of the individuals which comprise it (or *less* in the case of social loafing!).
- **Psychoanalysis** – Freud adopted an interactionist approach, in that he considered that behaviour was the result of dynamic interaction between id, ego, and superego.
- **Abnormal psychology** – mental disorders are often explained by an interaction of biological, psychological, and environmental factors. Schizophrenia may be due to a genetic predisposition triggered by environmental stress. An eclectic approach to therapy is often taken using drugs and psychotherapy.
- **Perception** – illusions show that humans perceive more than the sum of the sensations of the retina.

FOR

- Reductionist explanations in psychology adopt a very **scientific** and **analytical** approach, which has worked very well with the natural sciences.
- By breaking phenomena down into smaller simple components (as behaviourism did with stimulus-response units) these constituent parts are often more **easily tested.**
- By explaining behavioural phenomena in terms of their underlying physical basis, psychology gains the scientific **support** and **credibility** of these well established and robust sciences, and **unifies** with them to provide a **consistent** picture of the universe.

- The interactionist approach can **integrate** many **different levels** of explanation to provide a more **complete** and **realistic** understanding of behaviour.
- Holism does **not ignore** the **complexity** and the **'emergent properties'** of higher level phenomenon. For example, there may be aspects of crowd behaviour that could not be explained in terms of the individuals in that crowd.
- **Functional** explanations are only possible at higher levels – examining the social reasons **why** we show a certain aggressive behaviour is often more useful than providing a detailed neuronal, hormonal and physiological explanation of the act.

AGAINST

- **Oversimplification** – reductionist explanations often ignore many important interactions and the emergent properties of phenomena at higher levels. The whole may be greater than the sum of its parts.
- **Value of explanation** – higher level explanations may be less detailed and more useful than lower level ones. The **meaning** of an action, such as a hand wave, is only gained from its situation (e.g. greeting or drowning) not its underlying physiological description.
- **Validity of reductionism** – Rose (1976) argues that different levels of discourse cannot be substituted for each other. This raises the problem of the relationship between the **mind** and the **brain** - is a feeling of pain the same as the activation of nerve cells in a particular part of your brain? A neurologist may follow the 'neuronal path' of a pin prick up the arm and into a reception area of the brain, but the neurologist would have to rely on your conscious (psychological level) verbal report to know whether you *felt* pain or not.

- There is a great **practical difficulty** in investigating the integration of explanations from different levels. Research into mental disorders is beginning to understand the interaction of environmental, psychological, and biological explanations of disorders like depression.
- Holistic explanations of psychological phenomena that assume the mind is not the same as the body, tend to **ignore** the huge **influence** of biology on behaviour.
- Holistic explanations tend to get more **hypothetical** and divorced from physical reality the higher they go up the reductionist ladder. Higher level theories appear to **lack** the **predictive** power of the physical sciences (although there is a corresponding increase in the complexity of the systems investigated).

The freewill vs. determinism debate in psychology

FREEWILL

DETERMINISM

ASSUMPTIONS

The freewill approach assumes that humans **are free to choose their behaviour,** that they are essentially **self-determining.** Freewill does not mean that behaviour is uncaused in the sense of being completely random, but assumes that influences (biological or environmental) can be rejected at will.
Soft determinism (William James, 1890) suggests that freewill is not freedom from causation, but freedom from coercion and constraint – if our actions are voluntary and in line with our conscious desired goals then they are free.

The determinism approach assumes that **every physical event is caused,** and, since human behaviour is a physical event, it follows that it too is caused by preceding factors.
If all events are caused and perfect knowledge is gained of the current state of the universe, it follows that future events are entirely **predictable.**
Determinism, with its emphasis on **causal laws** is, therefore, the basis of science, which aims to reveal those laws to provide prediction and **control** of the future.

EXAMPLES IN PSYCHOLOGY

Humanistic psychology, proposed by the likes of Rogers and Maslow, is the strongest advocate of human freewill, arguing that we are able to direct our lives towards self-chosen goals. The emphasis on freewill is most apparent in humanistic based therapies, where the terms client and facilitator are used to indicate the voluntary nature of the situation, and the idea that the individual has the power to solve their own problems through insight. Humanistic therapies are usually non directive.
Cognitive psychology appears to adopt a soft determinism view considering problem solving and attentional mechanisms as the 'choosers' of thought and behaviour. While it seems that we select what we pay attention to, these mechanisms operate with the parameters of their innate capabilities and our past experience (just as a computer cannot choose to do something it was not built or programmed for) e.g. 'perceptual set' suggests that we are not free to choose what we see. However, language and metacognitive abilities may allow humans to choose from among many possible influences (Johnson-Laird,1988).

The majority of approaches in psychology adopt a fairly strict deterministic view of human behaviour.
Behaviourism took an extreme environmental determinism approach, arguing that learning from the environment 'writes upon the blank slate of our mind at birth' to cause behaviour. Watson's belief that the deterministic laws of learning could predict and control the future were reflected in his claim that he could take any infant at random and turn them into any type of specialist he might select. Skinner argued that freewill is completely an illusion created by our complexity of learning.
Psychoanalysis took the view of unconscious determinism - that our behaviour is controlled by forces of which we are unaware - the reasons for our actions are merely rationalised by our conscious minds. Later psychoanalysts, such as Erikson, looked at more conscious ego processes than Freud, however.
Biological approaches to psychology look at the deterministic influence of genetics, brain structure and biochemistry. Sociobiologists investigate evolutionary determinism.

FOR

- **Introspection** upon our decisions when many possible and equally desirable options are available often seems to indicate free choice. Subjective impressions should be considered.
- Even if humans do not have freewill, the fact that **they think they do** has many implications for behaviour. Rotter (1966), for example, has proposed that individuals with an external locus of control who feel that outside factors (e.g. chance) control their life, suffer more from the effects of stress than those who feel they can influence situations (an internal locus of control). Brehm (1966) argued people react if their freedom is threatened.

- The illusion of freewill is shattered very easily by **mental disorders** (obsessive compulsives lose control of their thoughts and actions, depressives their emotions) and psychoactive drugs (which can produce involuntary hallucinations and behaviour).
- Determinism is one of the key assumptions of **science** – whose cause and effect laws have explained, predicted and controlled behaviour (in some areas) above the levels achieved by unaided commonsense.
- The **majority** of all psychologists, even those sympathetic to the idea of freewill, accept determinism to some degree.

AGAINST

- It is **difficult to define** what freewill is and what the 'self' that 'does the choosing' consists of. Philosophers such as Descartes regarded it as the non-physical soul or spirit, while the existentialist philosopher Sartre preferred to think that freewill was a product of consciousness.
- The **evidence** for the existence of freewill is mostly **subjective** – where 'objective' studies have been conducted the results are a little disturbing – Libet (1985a) claims that the brain processes that initiate the movement of a hand occur almost half a second *before* the moment a subject reports choosing to move it!
- A pure freewill approach is **incompatible** with the deterministic assumptions of **science.**

- Determinism is **inconsistent** with society's ideas of self-control and responsibility that underlie all our moral and legal assumptions. Only extreme examples of determinism are taken into account (e.g. insanity).
- Determinism can never lead to complete prediction, due to
  a The vast complexity of influences upon any behaviour
  b The nature of induction – never being able to prove 100%
  c The notions of unpredictability (e.g. Heisenberg's 'uncertainty principle') and non-causality that physics has produced
- Determinism is **unfalsifiable** since it always assumes a cause exists, even if one has not been found yet.

Ethical guidelines for conducting research

ETHICAL GUIDELINES FOR THE USE OF ANIMALS IN RESEARCH

The Experimental Psychology Society (1986) has issued guidelines to control animal experimentation based on the legislation of the 'Animals (Scientific Procedures) Act' (1986). In general all researchers should:

1 Avoid or minimise stress and suffering for all living animals.
2 Always consider the possibility of other options to animal research.
3 Be as economical as possible in the numbers of animals tested.

However, before any animal is tested a Home Office Licence to conduct animal research has to be acquired. The Home Office provides legislation for and monitors:

- **The conditions under which animals are kept** – cage sizes, food, lighting, temperature, care routine etc. all have to be suitable for the species and its habits.
- **The researchers conducting the research** – all involved have to demonstrate they have the necessary skills and experience to work with the particular species they wish to study in order to acquire their personal licences.
- **The research projects allowed** – applications must be submitted outlining the project's aims and possible benefits as well as the procedures involved (including the number of animals and the degree of distress they might experience). Projects are only approved if the three requirements above are met and the levels of distress caused to the animals are justified by the benefits of the research. The conditions of the licence have to be strictly adhered to regarding the numbers, species and procedures (e.g. limits on the maximum level of electric shock) allowed. Research on endangered species is prohibited unless the research has direct benefits for the species itself, e.g. conservation.

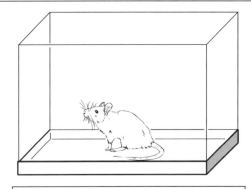

Bateson (1986) has specified some of the factors involved in deciding on the viability of animal research. Often the decision will involve a trade off between
a. The certainty of benefit from the research.
b. The quality of the research.
c. The amount of suffering involved for the animals.
Home Office licences are most likely to be awarded if factors 'a' and 'b' are high, and factor 'c' is low.

ETHICAL ISSUES IN HUMAN RESEARCH

The aim of Psychology is to provide us with a greater understanding of ourselves and, if required, to enable us to use that understanding to predict and control our behaviour for **human betterment**. To achieve this understanding psychologists often have no other choice but to investigate human subjects for valid results to be obtained. Humans, however, not only experience physical *pain* and *anxiety* but can also be affected mentally – in terms of *embarrassment* or *loss of self-esteem* for example. Humans also have **rights** of *protection* and *privacy* above the levels granted to other animals, and so this leads us to ethical dilemmas:

- How far should psychologists be allowed to go in pursuing their knowledge?
- Should humankind aim to improve itself by allowing people to be dehumanised in the process?
- Do the **ends** of psychological research **justify** the **means**?
- Can we ever know whether a piece of research will justify abusing the rights of individuals before we conduct it?

The existence of ethical constraints is clearly a serious but necessary limitation on the advancement of Psychology as a science and the major professional psychological bodies of many countries have published ethical guidelines for conducting research. In Britain, the British Psychological Society (1993) has published the "***Ethical Principles for Conducting Research with Human Participants***", which guides psychologists to consider the implications of their research (e.g. by asking members of the target population if they would take offence to the research) and deals with a number of methodological ethical issues such as:

CONSENT – Researchers are obliged, whenever possible, to obtain the participants' *informed* consent – *all* aspects of the research that might affect their willingness to give consent should be revealed. Consent is especially an issue when testing involves children or those unable to give it themselves, e.g. people with serious brain damage. Authority or payment must not be used to pressure participants into consent.

DECEPTION – The BPS Ethical Principles (1993) states that "Participants should never be deliberately misled without extremely strong scientific or medical justification. Even then there should be strict controls and the disinterested approval of independent advisors". Many psychology studies would not achieve valid results due to demand characteristics if deception was not employed, and so a cost-benefit analysis of the gains vs. the discomfort of the participant must be considered.

DEBRIEFING – Involves clarifying the participants' understanding of the research afterwards and discussing or rectifying any consequences of the study to ensure that they leave the study in as similar a state as possible to when they entered it. This is especially important if deception has been employed and the procedures could cause long term upset.

WITHDRAWAL FROM THE INVESTIGATION – Any participant in a psychological study should be informed of their right to withdraw from testing whenever they wish.

CONFIDENTIALITY – Under the Data Protection Act (1984) participants and the data they provide should be kept anonymous unless they have given their full consent to make their data public. If participants are dissatisfied after debriefing they can demand their data is destroyed.

PROTECTION OF PARTICIPANTS – Participants should leave psychological studies in roughly the same condition in which they arrived, without suffering physical or psychological harm. The risk of harm should not be greater than that found in everyday life.

OBSERVATIONAL RESEARCH – Hidden observational studies produce the most ecologically valid data but inevitably raise the ethical issue of invasion of privacy.

The arguments for and against testing animals

THE REASONS FOR CONDUCTING ANIMAL RESEARCH IN PSYCHOLOGY

- **Ethical reasons** – Many experiments that psychologists want to conduct are deemed unethical for human testing, but important enough to be justified for animal testing. Such experiments might involve controlled interbreeding, deprivation studies, brain surgery, or the trial testing of drugs.
- **Evolutionary continuum** – Some psychologists, such as the behaviourists, claimed that animal research was justified because humans have evolved from other animals and so the difference between them is only quantitative. Since humans are just more complex animals, it makes sense to study simpler organisms first, and then generalise to humans by 'scaling up' the results.
- **Convenience** – Animals are 'good subjects'. They do not try to understand the purpose of the experiment, are more controllable, and their faster breeding cycles allows tests to be conducted on the influence of heredity and environment on behaviour.

THE ETHICAL DEFENCE OF ANIMAL RESEARCH

Humans have a moral obligation to help humans first (a rather 'speciesist' assumption!) and the alternatives to animal research are either ethically undesirable (i.e. testing humans) or practically undesirable (using less reliable methods such as non-experimental observations or computer simulations).
2 Anti-vivisectionists have been accused of only drawing attention to a minority of the most vivid cases of animal suffering in psychology (although many would argue that such a minority of cases is still ethically unjustifiable).
3 There are now many safeguards in place to prevent the unnecessary use of animal research in psychology based on the legislation of the 'Animals (Scientific Procedures) Act' (1986).

THE CONTRIBUTION OF ANIMAL RESEARCH TO PSYCHOLOGY AND SOCIETY

Theoretical knowledge – Animal studies have contributed to our understanding of many topics in psychology, for example:
- Learning theory – e.g. from Skinner's rats and pigeons.
- Parental deprivation – e.g. from Harlow's rhesus monkeys.
- Perception – e.g. from Held and Hein's 'Kitten Carousel'.
- Language Acquisition – e.g. from chimp and gorilla studies.
- Aggression – e.g. from ethological and physiological studies.
- Abnormality – e.g. from Seligman's work on the preparedness of phobias and the role of learned helplessness in depression.

Practical applications of animal findings – for example:
- Behavioural treatments based on the principles of operant and classical conditioning, such as the systematic desensitisation of phobias derived from Wolpe's work on cats.
- Education – again based on the behaviourist's discoveries of learning using animals.

Practical uses of animals – for example as:
- Animal helpers, e.g. guide dogs, monkey home helps, airsea rescue pigeons, police drug-detecting dogs – all trained using learning theory principles.
- Military tools, e.g. the use of trained dolphins to deliver mines to the hulls of enemy ships or pigeons to deliver messages.

REASONS FOR NOT CONDUCTING ANIMAL RESEARCH IN PSYCHOLOGY

The two key ethical arguments against animal testing in psychology are:
1 The animals tested often **suffer** greatly. There is little doubt that a number of objective and behavioural measures indicate that animals can be said to suffer stress, pain and anxiety. Inflicting suffering upon another creature is morally objectionable. In many cases the suffering of animals (the means) has not been justified by the knowledge gained from the studies (the ends).
2 The suffering inflicted upon animals is often **unnecessary** for a number of practical and methodological reasons.
  a Humans are **physically qualitatively different** to other animals – for example, in terms of brain structure, complexity and specialisation (e.g. the human areas for language) and may react differently to drugs. Although there is only a 1.6% difference in the DNA of humans and chimpanzees, this 1.6% may be the most crucial for understanding human uniqueness.
  b Humans are **mentally qualitatively different** to other animals – for example, the humanists would regard human consciousness as a key difference. Superficial similarities in behaviour between rats and humans may lead to faulty over-generalisations of rat findings to humans ('ratomorphism') while the projection of human-like traits onto animals (anthropomorphism) may also lead to an exaggeration of similarity.
  c Laboratory studies on animals are often even more likely to **lack ecological validity** than those conducted on humans, and so these invalid findings are even less useful for generalisation to human behaviour.

EXAMPLES OF ANIMAL SUFFERING IN PSYCHOLOGICAL RESEARCH

Electric shocks
- Sheridan and King's (1972) later variation of Milgram's obedience study involved subjects being instructed to give real electric shocks to puppies. As usual, high levels of obedience were shown.
- Seligman and Maier (1967) found a 'failure to escape traumatic shock' in dogs by repeatedly administering unavoidable electric shocks. One of the dogs died.

Surgery
- Lashley (1929) removed parts of rats' brains in order to monitor later behaviour
- Delgado (1969) implanted electrodes into animals' brains to stimulate behaviour.

Deprivation studies
- Harlow raised rhesus monkeys in complete social deprivation. Their later behaviour was extremely maladaptive, being unable to properly interact with other monkeys or look after their young.
- Riesen (1950) raised chimps in complete darkness and then tried to condition them to fear a visually presented object by pairing it with an electric shock to find out if they could see.

Naturalistic observations / field studies
- Although these do not necessarily involve confinement, nevertheless stress may be caused to the animals and their natural behaviour disrupted through tagging and/or disturbing their feeding, mating and care for offspring.

Ethical issues and human psychological research

CONSENT

Milgram (1963) – The subjects in Milgram's study had volunteered to participate in a study of learning, not obedience. Having not been told of the researcher's objectives, they did not give their informed consent.

Bystander intervention studies – Such as those conducted by Darley and Batson (the 'Good Samaritan' study) or Piliavin (subway studies) where subjects were not asked for their consent at all. However, one could argue that people see the plight of others every day without consent.

Zimbardo et al (1973) – The subjects in the prison simulation experiment signed a formal 'informed consent' statement specifying there would be a loss of some civil rights, invasion of privacy and harassment.

DECEPTION

Milgram (1963) - The subjects were led to believe they were giving real electric shocks to another in an experiment on learning rather than obedience. Orne and Holland (1968) suggested that the subjects were involved in a 'pact of ignorance' with the experimenter – they did not really believe they were harming anyone.

Rosenhan (1973) – In the study 'On being sane in insane places' eight 'normal' people gained admission to psychiatric hospitals merely by pretending to hear voices and faking their name and occupation. One might argue that this case of deception was one that the victims were able to avoid.

Drug testing – Often involves the use of placebo control groups. Patients may be given either the real drug or pills that have no effect, but are not told which they have been given. Perhaps a necessary case of deception but what about the patients' rights to receive the best care?

Craik and Tulving (1975) – Tested Levels of Processing ideas by using incidental learning – subjects were not told they would be tested on their memory. A minor case of deception.

CONFIDENTIALITY

Confidentiality is of particular importance in case studies, especially involving data gained as part of a client–patient relationship. There are many examples in psychology of pseudonyms used to maintain anonymity, e.g. Genie, H.M., Anna O, etc.

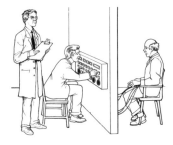

Milgram's experiment

OBSERVATIONAL RESEARCH

Hidden observational studies produce the most ecologically valid data but inevitably raise the ethical issue of privacy. The importance of this issue will be greater in certain areas of psychology (e.g. intimate behaviour in interpersonal relationships) than others (e.g. crowd behaviour).

WITHDRAWAL

Milgram (1963) – The study abused the right of subjects to withdraw from a psychology study – those wishing to leave were told 'you have no other choice, you *must* go on'. However, subjects had the right to leave and they were not physically restrained.

Zimbardo et al (1973) – Stopped their prison simulation study after just six days instead of the two weeks it was meant to run because of extreme reactions shown by the participants.

DEBRIEFING

Milgram (1963) – All subjects were fully debriefed and reassured after the experiment. They were shown that the learner was unharmed and had not received any shocks.

PROTECTION OF PARTICIPANTS

Milgram (1963) – Baumrind (1964) criticised Milgram's study as being unethical because it caused distress and anguish to the subjects. One had a seizure and all subjects could have suffered psychological damage. Milgram himself commented that 'In a large number of cases the degree of tension reached extremes that are rarely seen in sociopsychological laboratory studies'.
However, the results obtained were completely unexpected (Milgram asked for estimates beforehand), and although the subjects appeared uncomfortable with their obedience, Milgram concluded that 'momentary excitement is not the same as harm'. Milgram argued that it was the shocking nature of his findings that provoked a moral outrage.
A follow-up opinion survey conducted a year later found that 84% were 'glad to have been in the experiment', 15% were neutral, and only 1.3% were 'sorry or very sorry to have been in the experiment'. Around 80% of the respondents said there should be more experiments like Milgram's conducted, and around 75% said they had learnt something of personal value from their experience. The subjects were examined one year after the experiment by a psychiatrist who found no signs of harm.

Zimbardo et al (1973) – Zimbardo's prison simulation procedures were more stressful than the volunteer students playing the prisoner role expected. A surprise city police arrest and processing was followed by brutal treatment from the students playing the role of the guards, which caused psychological stress in the form of crying, rage and depression, and even the development of a psychosomatic rash.

Watson and Rayner (1920) – Conditioned a phobia of rats into an emotionally stable 11-month-old infant, 'Little Albert', by repeatedly startling the child with a loud noise every time a white rat was presented. The fear response generalised to other objects including rabbits, fur coats and even facial hair (including that on a Santa Claus mask!) but was never removed from the subject.

Bandura et al (1961) – Showed how aggression could be learnt in children through observational learning in their Bobo Doll experiment. However, is it right to produce aggression in children experimentally, even if they may acquire it from their own environment anyway?

Ethical issues in human behaviour change in psychology

If the aim of psychological understanding is to provide prediction and control for human betterment, then several issues need to be raised:

1 Should behaviour be controlled?

2 Who should do the controlling?

3 What behaviour should be controlled?

4 How should behaviour be controlled?

SHOULD BEHAVIOUR BE CONTROLLED?
The answer to this question often depends on the approach taken to psychology.

- Miller (1969) in 'Psychology as a means of promoting human welfare' argued that the primary goal of psychology should be to provide understanding and prediction only and, by making psychological knowledge available to the public, allow individuals to apply it to their own lives. This disagreement with the controlling aspects of psychology is in accord with humanist principles and assumptions of **self-actualisation**, but was opposed by behaviourist orientated psychologists such as Skinner who argued that, since freewill is an illusion and all behaviour is controlled by the environment anyway, it makes sense to have experts (psychologists!) doing the controlling.

- Clearly the issue of whether behaviour should be controlled is dependent on which side of the freewill vs. determinism debate one takes – the degree to which self-responsibility is bestowed on humans. If a degree of determinism is accepted, however, then the issue of whether behaviour should be controlled then revolves around the issues of **who** is doing the controlling and **how far** behaviour should be controlled.

WHO SHOULD DO THE CONTROLLING?
This concerns the issue of who is doing the controlling and for what purpose.

- **What should the ratio of power be between the individual and their society?**
  If we consider the area of abnormality then clearly there is a range of possible power arrangements depending upon the approach taken to treating disorders and the seriousness of the disorder itself. Humanist therapists would aim to clarify the client's problems with living in order to provide insight and encourage **self** improvement, whereas cognitive psychologists and psychoanalysts would take a more **directive** approach, aiming to persuade the subject to change their thinking/accept unconscious truths. At the other end of the continuum, the medical model approach would hold the majority of power with serious psychoses, and may insist on administering physiological treatments, which they could **enforce** if the patient was sectioned under the Mental Health Act (1983) – thereby assuming complete responsibility, even over the rights of the nearest relative if necessary. Thus the control of society can range from giving advice, to persuasion, to enforced treatment. The main ethical problem with social control of behaviour is deciding who controls the controllers.

- **Whose goals is behaviour being changed for – the benefit of the individual or society?**
  The goals of the therapy and the extent to which the individual can decide when therapy has been completed again depend upon the approach taken – psychology is not 'value-free'. Humanists such as Laing and Szasz are rather pessimistic about the seemingly caring approach of the medical model to abnormality, suggesting that society uses medical labels as a form of social control based on motives of fear and prejudice, and that institutionalisation and treatment merely perform the function of reducing atypical individuals into passive and 'model citizens'. The behaviourist Skinner firmly believed behaviour should be engineered and controlled by expert state psychologists.

WHAT BEHAVIOUR SHOULD BE CONTROLLED?
The issue of control crops up many times in psychology, and again represents a continuum in the desirability of behaviour change.

- Abnormality is generally accepted as an area in which behaviour change is accepted and often desired, even if mistakes have been and still are occasionally made (e.g. the former use of aversion therapy on homosexuals).

- Other areas of psychology such as education, advertising, social influence, attitude change and the reduction of prejudice and aggression all have ethical problems with the behavioural changes they wish to bring about. Most would agree, for example, that discrimination should be controlled, but what about prejudiced attitudes/opinions?

HOW SHOULD BEHAVIOUR BE CONTROLLED?
- Biological approaches – such as drugs, ECT, psychosurgery, or even gene therapy. Often these techniques are used before we have attained a proper understanding of how they work and what their effects might be. The techniques and the changes produced may often benefit society more than the patient in the long run, e.g. drugs controlling rather than curing, but we should not underestimate how anti-schizophrenic and anti-depressant drugs have changed many people's lives for the better.

- Behavioural techniques – such as flooding and aversion therapy. These can produce effective changes, usually on a voluntary basis, but can involve some trauma in the process. As with all types of therapy, a cost-benefit analysis on the benefits vs. side-effects should be considered. The use of electric shocks has controlled childhood eating disorders that might otherwise have killed their victims.

The ethics of socially sensitive research

Many of the studies conducted and topics researched in psychology have wider implications for those who are investigated and society as a whole. The ethics of socially sensitive research involves the psychologist being aware of:
- The implications of investigating certain controversial topics.
- The possible uses to which their research findings will be put.
- The amount of influence the psychologist has on public policy.
- The basis or validity of their research findings in controversial areas.
- The availability, understanding and interpretation of the data they provide.

DECIDING WHAT TO RESEARCH
Even the very act of phrasing hypotheses – deciding who and what is to be investigated – has ethical implications.
- Investigating potentially socially sensitive areas, such as race and its effects on IQ or the genetic basis of homosexuality, may serve to legitimise or perpetuate socially constructed differences and prejudices. Alternatively, one might argue that the only way to dispel such prejudices or tackle genuine difference is to investigate them objectively and scientifically to reach the truth. Avoiding controversial topics just because they are controversial (and may involve stress to the researchers) could be regarded as an avoidance of social responsibility.
- Whether objectivity in the phrasing and investigation of research hypotheses is possible is debatable. As the humanist psychologist Rogers (1956), in his debate with the behaviourist Skinner, commented 'In any scientific endeavour – whether "pure" or "applied" science – there is a prior subjective choice of the purpose or value which that scientific work is perceived as serving'.
- We must remember that what is investigated, even in seemingly pure academic research, is subject to social values. Much psychology, especially in the USA, has been (and still is) funded by the military and large businesses, for example Zimbardo's research into the psychological effects of imprisonment was funded by the US navy.

THE USE OF KNOWLEDGE
Psychologists should consider how their findings will be used and who will be affected by them.
- Knowledge is rarely neutral in practice, it can be used to improve the human condition or worsen it. The application of psychological knowledge to warfare is a good example. Watson (1978) has commented 'Psychology can be a worrying science in the hands of the military' – research on deindividuation and attitude change can be used to train soldiers to kill or brainwash prisoners of war, yet psychological research on intergroup conflict and post-traumatic stress disorder can also help prevent war or treat the victims of it.
- Even the same research findings, such as those on the operant conditioning of animals, can be applied to train animals to help the disabled, e.g. guide-dogs, or to deliver explosive weapons, e.g. 'Project Pigeon' (Skinner, 1960).

THE INFLUENCE OF THE PSYCHOLOGIST IN SOCIETY
The impact of socially sensitive research depends upon the influence the psychologists have in a society. Segall (1976) in 'Human Behaviour and Public Policy' identifies three main ways in which psychologists could affect political and social policies, by acting as:
- expert witnesses, e.g. giving evidence in court cases. The problem with this role for psychologists is that they lose control of their knowledge – policy makers can use or reject psychological expertise and knowledge at will. On the plus side, opposing psychological views can be presented for judgement, reducing the possibility of biased views influencing outcomes, e.g. alternative views on the value of testimony retrieved under hypnosis.
- Policy evaluators, e.g. helping research the impact of proposed political and social measures, such as new laws. Psychological research on the harmful effects of American school segregation for blacks and whites was influential in causing desegregation laws. The problems of this role for psychologists are that it is dependent upon the quality of research and prevailing social conditions of the time.
- Social-psychological engineers - to devise ways of ensuring desirable behaviour. Skinner (1971) advocated this view for psychologists in his book *Beyond Freedom and Dignity*. The problems with this role for psychologists are those of behavioural control in general (Who decides what behaviour is desirable? Who controls the controllers? etc.) and the possible unreliability of psychological research.

It follows that the potentially harmful effects of socially sensitive research become magnified with the power of psychologists in society.

THE BASIS OF PSYCHOLOGICAL KNOWLEDGE
With socially sensitive research, the psychologist must be particularly careful to avoid bias and error, and thus must make clear their **theoretical background**, the **limitations of their research** and the **generalisability of their findings.** Howitt (1991) argues that, since it is impossible to be objective and value free, psychologists should always be cautious when applying their findings. There are many examples of biased or faulty psychological research influencing social views and policies.
- Bowlby's (1951) maternal deprivation research drew attention to the adverse effects of early disrupted child-care but wrongly added support to the social view that it was the role of the woman to care for children.
- Gould (1981) in 'The Mismeasure of Man' describes how biased IQ tests carried out by Yerkes on immigrants to the USA led to eugenicists limiting immigration from Europe for people wanting to escape Nazi persecution.
- Cyril Burt's questionable view that 80% of IQ was genetically determined, influenced ideas on selective education at age 11.
- Gerard (1983) argued that the Social Science Statement supporting the 1954 Brown vs. Board of Education U.S. Supreme Court Decision which led to school desegregation was based on 'well meaning rhetoric rather than solid research'.

Although the premature application of psychology to political issues diminishes public confidence in the social sciences, all knowledge is relative to the time and decisions have to be made on currently available knowledge.

THE AVAILABILITY OF RESEARCH
In the case of socially sensitive research, psychologists have a responsibility to clarify the communication of findings to the media, public and policy makers to minimise any distortion or abuse of findings (they may only want to hear findings that confirm their own prejudices or policies). Miller (1969) argues that psychological knowledge should be freely given away to the public to prevent its exploitation.

Contemporary issue - genetic research and behaviour

The inherited basis of human behaviour has long interested philosophers, genetic biologists, psychologists, politicians and the general public, and has caused a good deal of debate and controversy. An understanding of the assumptions and methods of the physiological approach in this area can help explain the implications of research into the genetic basis of behaviour and the controversy it has generated.

ASSUMPTIONS OF GENETIC RESEARCH

Some genetic researchers have attempted to discover the influence of inherited factors on behaviour and mental abilities, assuming that genetic factors must influence such characteristics to some extent, since they are produced by bodies which are constructed based on the instructions contained in our DNA. Unfortunately, however, researchers have differed in their assumptions over exactly how strong genetic influences are and have often leapt to conclusions based on a faulty understanding of how genes express their influence. These conclusions have important implications and have caused strong disagreements between psychologists who favour the importance of nature and those who champion nurture. A more variable influence of inherited factors in combination with environmental ones has gradually become accepted as research revealed that:

- genes can only build bodies based on the environmental resources available, and environmental factors can influence the genes themselves
- human characteristics may be influenced by many genes (pleiotropy) , not all of which will necessarily be inherited
- some genes, e.g. those involved in Huntingdon's disease, have more direct and inevitable effects than others, e.g. those involved in Alzheimer's disease
- genes express their effects in many different and often subtle ways

Genetic research now implicitly investigates how genes interact with environmental factors to create behaviour and tries to determine the balance of influences for specific characteristics.

GENETIC RESEARCH METHODS

Two techniques used to investigate genetic influences include:

- Family resemblance correlations – these measure the degree of similarity in characteristics between genetically related (e.g. parents and offspring, siblings, cousins, etc.) and unrelated individuals on the assumption that the closer the genetic relationship the greater the similarity. Genetically identical (monozygotic) twins in particular have been compared with non-identical (dizygotic) twins, while adoption studies have helped control for the similar environments related individuals are more likely to share.
- Molecular genetics – modern technology now allows researchers to extract genetic material from individuals with a certain characteristic and see how it differs from that of people without the characteristic. This can reveal the coding of the genes correlated with the characteristics and their location amongst the 23 pairs of human chromosomes.

There are many problems with these methods however, so results gained from them have to be carefully interpreted. For example since adoption studies are natural experiments, they can never completely control for environmental effects. Molecular genetic research has found that individuals can possess the genes associated with a characteristic, without necessarily developing it themselves. At the moment, the possession of most human behaviour and abilities cannot be predicted with 100% certainty by either of the above methods.

IMPLICATIONS OF GENETIC RESEARCH

Given the variable effects of genes upon behaviour and the methodological problems involved in assessing them, particular care needs to be taken in how knowledge of genetic influences is used and interpreted.

In the past genetic research has been used for selection purposes based on faulty assumptions and methodology, for example research into the genetic basis of intelligence. The application of genetic research by society to control the selection of 'desirable' characteristics is known as eugenics and has led to horrific social injustice and genocide.

With improving technology, such as genetic screening and gene therapy, further ethical implications regarding the use of genetic knowledge for selection and control purposes will have to be considered. Employers may want to select their employees, insurance companies their customers, and parents their children (through abortion or gene therapy), based on the results of genetic screening. Some argue that just because the choice to genetically screen and control is placed in the hands of individuals rather than society does not make it any less 'eugenic'.

However, resistance to the idea that genes affect behaviour is often based on the mistaken assumption that genetic inheritance dictates our fate. For the reasons expressed above it is very unlikely that psychological characteristics are determined by genes in such an inevitable way, in most cases genes seem just as 'deterministic' as environmental influences. The positive effects of genetic screening and gene therapy should also not be ignored.

Genetic research on intelligence

Much early research on the inheritance of intelligence was:

- politically motivated by eugenic beliefs, often carried out by researchers biased towards discovering innate causes
- conducted using poorly controlled family resemblance studies and culturally biased IQ tests on different 'races'

Unsurprisingly it revealed that IQ was largely (around 80%) inherited, and was used to justify the selection of naturally bright individuals for jobs, special education at an early age and right of immigration into the USA. In some countries those thought genetically doomed to mental deficiency were sterilised to prevent them spreading their low intelligence in society.

Later research indicates that around 50% of IQ is individually inherited, the rest is influenced by conditions in the womb and the social and family environment. The way genes influence intelligence is still a mystery however. Genes associated with intelligence may directly affect aspects of cognitive ability such as processing speed or indirectly evoke environmental influences on IQ by creating characteristics such as ability to concentrate, motivation to learn etc. Alternatively perhaps the genes promote resistance to disease and the healthy development of the brain - lacking such genes might prevent the genius a fully healthy brain would give us all!

Understanding how genes influence intelligence may help us to adjust the environment to produce the most improvement in those who require it, without resorting to genetic manipulation.

Variables

WHAT DO PSYCHOLOGISTS INVESTIGATE?

VARIABLES
A variable is any object, quality or event that changes or varies in some way. Examples include: aggression, intelligence, time, height, amount of alcohol, driving ability, attraction.

OPERATIONALISATION
Many of the variables that psychologists are interested in are **abstract concepts,** such as aggression or intelligence. Operationalisation refers to the process of making variables physically measurable or testable. This is done in psychology by recording some aspect of **observable behaviour** that is assumed to be indicative of the variable under consideration. For example:
Aggression – a psychologist may record the number of punches thrown.
Intelligence – a psychologist may record the number of puzzles solved in an hour, or calculate the score on an IQ test.

Reification (regarding hypothetical variables like intelligence as having a real physical existence) is a danger, however.

INVESTIGATING VARIABLES

OBSERVATIONS, CASE STUDIES, SURVEYS, ETC.
In these methods variables are precisely measured in varying amounts of detail.

CORRELATIONS
Variables are measured and compared to see how they co-vary with each other (what relationship they have together).

EXPERIMENTS
One variable (the **independent variable**) is **altered** to see what **effect** it has on another variable (the **dependent variable**).
The independent variable is the variable that is manipulated in two or more conditions to see what effect it has on the dependent variable.
The dependent variable is the main measured outcome of the experiment, hopefully due to the manipulation of the independent variable.
For example, the independent variable (IV) of alcohol could be manipulated to see what effect it had on the dependent variable (DV) of driving ability by testing in two conditions, one with no alcohol and the other with four pints of lager.
However, many **extraneous variables** (other variables that could potentially influence the dependent variable apart from the independent variable), could spoil the experiment and so **controls** are employed to prevent extraneous variables from becoming confounding variables (those that actually affect the dependent variable strongly enough to distort the effect of the independent variable). Extraneous variables can be either **random** (unsystematic variables that can affect the dependent variable but should not affect one condition more than another) or **constant** (those that have a systematic effect on one condition more than another). While random errors will reduce the accuracy of the results, only constant errors usually truly confound the experimental results.

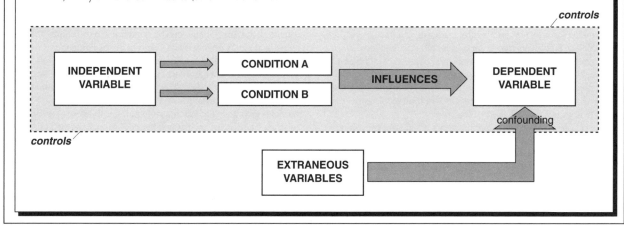

Hypotheses

HOW DO PSYCHOLOGISTS MAKE THEIR PREDICTIONS?

HYPOTHESES are *precise, testable statements*

THEY SHOULD BE

THEY CAN BE

BOLD

2-tailed hypotheses simply predict an effect, such as a difference or correlation.

1-tailed hypotheses predict a particular direction in the effect, e.g. that one condition will do better than another, or that a positive correlation will occur.

PRECISE

Precise hypotheses should contain fully **operationalised variables** and the words 'statistically significant' if inferential statistics are to be conducted on the results.

REFUTABLE

To be scientific every hypothesis should be capable of being **shown to be wrong**. For this reason a **null hypothesis** is proposed that states that there will be **no significant effect** (either difference or correlation). Sometimes, however, it is the null hypothesis which researchers wish to study.

EXPERIMENTAL HYPOTHESES

Predict significant differences in the dependent variable [DV] between the various conditions of the independent variable [IV].

2 - tailed
There will be a significant **difference in** [the DV] **between** [condition A of the IV] **and** [condition B of the IV].

1 - tailed
There will be a significant **increase in** [the DV] **in** [condition A of the IV] **compared to** [condition B of the IV].

or

There will be a significant **decrease in** [the DV] **in** [condition A of the IV] **compared to** [condition B of the IV].

2 - tailed example
There will be a **statistically significant** difference in **I.Q. scores** between **male subjects** and **female subjects**.

1 - tailed examples
There will be a **statistically significant** increase in **I.Q. scores** in **male subjects** compared to **female subjects**.

or

There will be a **statistically significant** decrease in **I.Q. scores** in **male subjects** compared to **female subjects**.

2 - tailed example
There will be **no** statistically significant difference in I.Q. scores between male subjects and female subjects.

1 - tailed examples
There will be **no** statistically significant increase in I.Q. scores in male subjects compared to female subjects.

or

There will be **no** statistically significant increase in I.Q. scores in female subjects compared to male subjects.

CORRELATIONAL HYPOTHESES

Predict significant patterns of relationship between two or more variables.

2 - tailed
There will be a significant **correlation between** [variable 1] and [variable 2].

1 - tailed
There will be a significant **positive correlation between** [variable 1] and [variable 2].

or

There will be a significant **negative correlation between** [variable 1] and [variable 2].

2 - tailed example
There will be a **statistically significant** correlation between **hours of psychology revision conducted** and **A level grade gained in psychology.**

1 - tailed example
There will be a **statistically significant** positive correlation between **hours of psychology revision conducted** and **A level grade gained in psychology.**

2 - tailed example
There will be **no** statistically significant correlation between hours of psychology revision conducted and A level grade gained in psychology.

1 - tailed example
There will be **no** statistically significant positive correlation between hours of psychology revision conducted and A level grade gained in psychology.

Experimental methods

HOW DO PSYCHOLOGISTS INVESTIGATE THEIR HYPOTHESES?

EXPERIMENTS

An experiment involves the **manipulation of the independent variable** to see what effect it has on the dependent variable, while attempting to **control** the influence of all other **extraneous variables.**

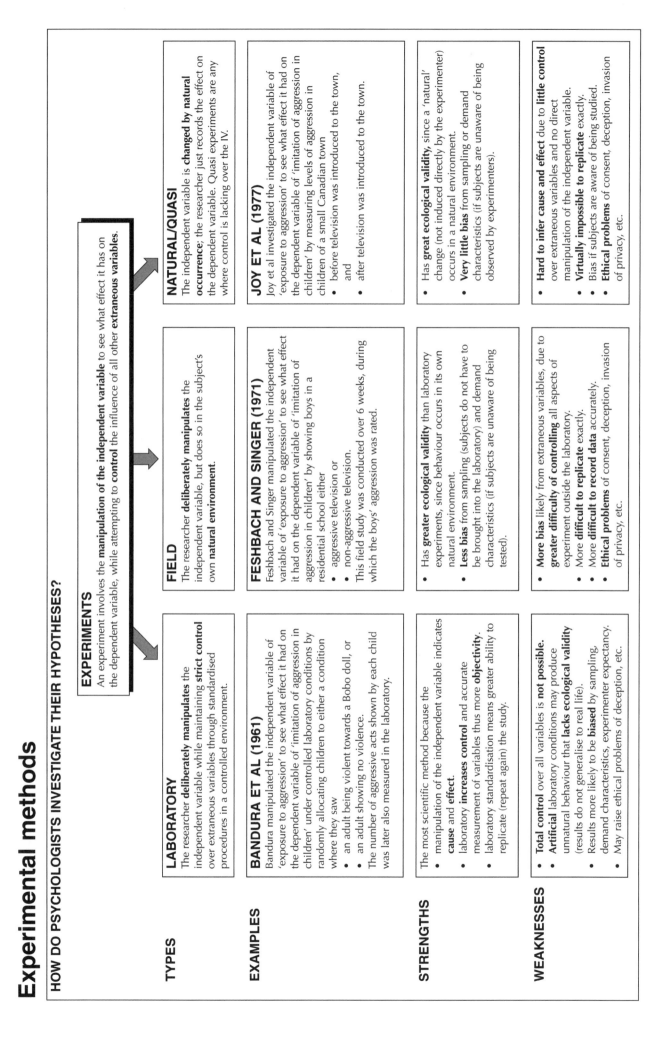

TYPES

LABORATORY

The researcher **deliberately manipulates** the independent variable while maintaining **strict control** over extraneous variables through standardised procedures in a controlled environment.

FIELD

The researcher **deliberately manipulates** the independent variable, but does so in the subject's own **natural environment.**

NATURAL/QUASI

The independent variable is **changed by natural occurrence;** the researcher just records the effect on the dependent variable. Quasi experiments are any where control is lacking over the IV.

EXAMPLES

BANDURA ET AL (1961)

Bandura manipulated the independent variable of 'exposure to aggression' to see what effect it had on the dependent variable of 'imitation of aggression in children' under controlled laboratory conditions by randomly allocating children to either a condition where they saw
- an adult being violent towards a Bobo doll, or
- an adult showing no violence.

The number of aggressive acts shown by each child was later also measured in the laboratory.

FESHBACH AND SINGER (1971)

Feshbach and Singer manipulated the independent variable of 'exposure to aggression' to see what effect it had on the dependent variable of 'imitation of aggression in children' by showing boys in a residential school either
- aggressive television or
- non-aggressive television.

This field study was conducted over 6 weeks, during which the boys' aggression was rated.

JOY ET AL (1977)

Joy et al investigated the independent variable of 'exposure to aggression' to see what effect it had on the dependent variable of 'imitation of aggression in children' by measuring levels of aggression in children of a small Canadian town
- before television was introduced to the town, and
- after television was introduced to the town.

STRENGTHS

- The most scientific method because the manipulation of the independent variable indicates **cause** and **effect.**
- laboratory **increases control** and accurate measurement of variables thus more **objectivity.**
- laboratory standardisation means greater ability to replicate (repeat again) the study.

- Has **greater ecological validity** than laboratory experiments, since behaviour occurs in its own natural environment.
- **Less bias** from sampling (subjects do not have to be brought into the laboratory) and demand characteristics (if subjects are unaware of being tested).

- Has **great ecological validity,** since a 'natural' change (not induced directly by the experimenter) occurs in a natural environment.
- **Very little bias** from sampling or demand characteristics (if subjects are unaware of being observed by experimenters).

WEAKNESSES

- **Total control** over all variables is **not possible.**
- **Artificial** laboratory conditions may produce unnatural behaviour that **lacks ecological validity** (results do not generalise to real life).
- Results more likely to be **biased** by sampling, demand characteristics, experimenter expectancy.
- May raise ethical problems of deception, etc.

- **More bias** likely from extraneous variables, due to **greater difficulty of controlling** all aspects of experiment outside the laboratory.
- More **difficult to replicate** exactly.
- More **difficult to record data** accurately.
- **Ethical problems** of consent, deception, invasion of privacy, etc.

- **Hard to infer cause and effect** due to **little control** over extraneous variables and no direct manipulation of the independent variable.
- **Virtually impossible to replicate** exactly.
- Bias if subjects are aware of being studied.
- **Ethical problems** of consent, deception, invasion of privacy, etc.

Non-experimental methods 1. Observation

HOW DO PSYCHOLOGISTS INVESTIGATE THEIR HYPOTHESES?

OBSERVATIONS
Observations involve the precise measurement of naturally occurring behaviour in an objective way.

	NATURALISTIC	**CONTROLLED**	**PARTICIPANT**
TYPES	Naturalistic observations involve the recording of spontaneously occurring behaviour in the subject's own natural environment.	Controlled observation involves the recording of spontaneously occurring behaviour, but under conditions contrived by the researcher (e.g. in the laboratory).	Participant observations involve the researcher becoming involved in the everyday life of the subjects, either with or without their knowledge.
EXAMPLES	• Fagot's (1973) naturalistic observation of parent-child interaction in gender socialisation in the home. • Sylva et al's (1980) naturalistic observation of types of play in children's playgroups. • Ethological observations of animal behaviour in the animal's natural habitat.	• Sleep studies – laboratory equipment is needed to record eye movements and changes in brain activity as subjects naturally fall to sleep. • Parent-child interaction - observed through one way mirrors. • Human sexual response, e.g. Masters and Johnson's work.	• Rosenhan (1973) used eight 'normal' undisclosed participant observers to gain admittance to psychiatric hospitals through faking symptoms and then record their experiences of being a psychiatric inpatient. • Whyte's (1955) participant observation of Italian gang behaviour in the USA.
STRENGTHS	• **High ecological validity** (realism) of observed behaviour if observer is hidden. • Can be used to **generate ideas** for or **validate findings** from experimental studies. • Sometimes the only ethical or practical method.	• **More control** over environment which leads to **more accurate** observations. • Greater control leads to **easier replication.** • Usually avoids ethical problems of consent, unless research purpose and observer are hidden.	• Very **high ecological validity** if participant undisclosed, less if disclosed depending upon level of integration with subjects. • Extremely **detailed** and **in depth knowledge** available, not gained from any other method.
WEAKNESSES	• **Cannot legitimately infer cause and effect** relationships between variables that are only observed but not manipulated. • **Lack of control** over conditions makes **replication more difficult.** • **Ethical problems** of invasion of privacy.	• **Participant reactivity** may distort the data if subject is aware of being observed, e.g. abnormal sleep patterns in unnatural laboratory conditions. • **Lower ecological validity** than naturalistic observations, can cause demand characteristics. • Cause and effect can not be inferred.	• **Difficult to record data promptly** and **objectively,** and impossible to **replicate** exactly. • Participant's behaviour may **influence subjects.** • **Ethical problems** of deception with undisclosed participants. • Cause and effect can not be inferred.

Non-experimental methods 2. Questioning

HOW DO PSYCHOLOGISTS INVESTIGATE THEIR HYPOTHESES?

QUESTIONING PEOPLE

There are many techniques for gathering **self report** data, which can be employed in varying detail – from the superficial survey of many people to the in-depth assessment of individuals.

TECHNIQUES	EXAMPLES	STRENGTHS	WEAKNESSES
INTERVIEWS All interviews involve direct verbal questioning of the subject by the researcher, but differ in how structured the questions are:		Generally, interviews generate a large amount of detailed data, especially about internal mental states/beliefs.	Generally interviews rely on self report data which may be untrue. Cause and effect can not be inferred.
• **Structured interviews** – contain fixed predetermined questions and ways of replying (e.g. yes/no).	Usually used in large scale interview-based surveys, e.g. market research.	Easy to quantify and analyse. Reliable, replicable and generalisable.	Less validity – distorts/ignores data due to restricted answers or insensitivity.
• **Semi-structured interviews** – contain guidelines for questions to be asked, but phrasing and timing are left up to the interviewer and answers may be open-ended.	Schedule for affective disorders and schizophrenia – a diagnostic interview. Most employment interviews.	Fairly flexible and sensitive. Fairly reliable and easy to analyse.	Flexibility of phrasing and timing could lead to lower reliability. Open-ended answers are more tricky to analyse.
• **Clinical interview** – semi-structured guidelines but further questioning to elaborate upon answers.	Piaget's interviewing of his children. Freud's interviewing of his patients.	Very flexible, sensitive and valid. Fairly reliable and easy to analyse.	Flexibility leads to more difficulty in replication and bias from interviewer.
• **Unstructured interview** – may contain a topic area for discussion but no fixed questions or ways of answering. Interviewer helps and clarifies interview.	Often used in humanistic based therapy interviews.	Highly detailed and valid data. Extremely flexible, natural and un-constrained.	Very unstandardised, therefore, not very replicable, reliable or generalisable. Difficult to quantify and analyse.
QUESTIONNAIRES Questionnaires are written methods of gaining data from subjects that do not necessarily require the presence of a researcher. They include:		Generally questionnaires collect large amounts of standardised data relatively quickly and conveniently.	Generally questionnaires lack flexibility, are based on self report data and are biased by motivation levels.
• **Opinion surveys,** e.g. attitude scales and opinion polls. Questions can be closed or open-ended and should be precise, understandable and easy to answer.	Likert attitude scales.	Highly replicable and easy to score (unless open-ended answers).	Biased by socially desirable answers, acquiescence (agreeing with items) and response set (replying in the same way).
• **Psychological tests,** e.g. personality and I.Q. tests. Items need to be standardised for a population and tested to show reliability, validity and discriminatory power.	Eysenck's personality inventory (to measure extroversion for example) or Bem's sex role inventory (to assess gender role identity).	Highly replicable and standardised between individuals. Easy to score.	Difficult to construct highly reliable and valid tests.

Non-experimental methods 3. Case study and correlation

HOW DO PSYCHOLOGISTS INVESTIGATE THEIR HYPOTHESES?

TECHNIQUES AND EXAMPLES

CASE STUDY
An idiographic method involving the **in-depth** and **detailed** study of an **individual** or particular group. The case study method is often applied to unusual or valuable examples of behaviour which may provide important insights into psychological function or refutation of psychological theory.
Examples of case studies include: Freud's studies of his patients and Piaget's studies of his children.

CORRELATIONS
A method of data analysis which measures the relationship between two or more variables to see if a trend or systematic pattern exists between them. Inferential statistics can be used to arrive at a correlation coefficient which indicates the strength and type of correlation, ranging from:

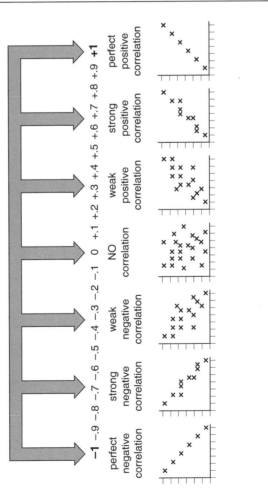

–1 –.9 –.8 –.7 –.6 –.5 –.4 –.3 –.2 –.1 0 +.1 +.2 +.3 +.4 +.5 +.6 +.7 +.8 +.9 **+1**

perfect negative correlation | strong negative correlation | weak negative correlation | NO correlation | weak positive correlation | strong positive correlation | perfect positive correlation

STRENGTHS

Highly detailed and in depth data is provided which superficial methods might miss or ignore.

High ecological validity of data obtained.

Often the only method suitable for studying some forms of behaviour, e.g. investigating the acquisition of human language in primates.

Often the only method possible due to rarity of behaviour, e.g. natural cases of human environmental deprivation, such as the case of Genie.

Precise information on the degree of relationship between variables is available in the form of the correlation coefficient. It can readily quantify observational data.

No manipulation of behaviour is required.

Strong significant correlations can suggest ideas for experimental studies to determine cause and effect relationships.

WEAKNESSES

No cause and effect can legitimately be inferred.

Lack of generalisability to the population due to single cases being too small and unrepresentative a sample.

Low reliability due to
• many case studies involving recall of past events, which may be open to memory distortion.
• subject reactivity
• lack of observer objectivity

Difficult or impossible to replicate.

Time consuming and expensive.

No cause and effect can be inferred.

Correlations should be plotted out on scattergrams to properly illustrate the relationship between variables – a zero correlation coefficient may not form a random pattern.
For example, both of these patterns would not yield a significant correlational result.

Sampling

HOW DO PSYCHOLOGISTS SELECT THEIR SUBJECTS?

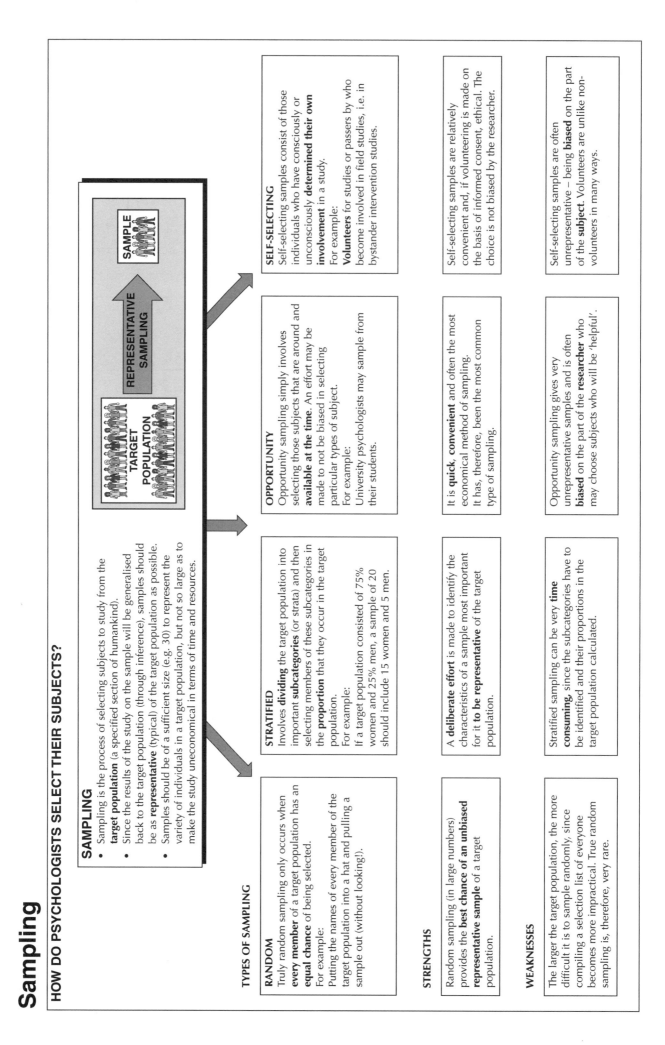

SAMPLING

- Sampling is the process of selecting subjects to study from the **target population** (a specified section of humankind).
- Since the results of the study on the sample will be generalised back to the target population (through inference), samples should be as **representative** (typical) of the target population as possible.
- Samples should be of a sufficient size (e.g. 30) to represent the variety of individuals in a target population, but not so large as to make the study uneconomical in terms of time and resources.

TARGET POPULATION

REPRESENTATIVE SAMPLING

SAMPLE

TYPES OF SAMPLING

RANDOM
Truly random sampling only occurs when **every member** of a target population has an **equal chance** of being selected.
For example:
Putting the names of every member of the target population into a hat and pulling a sample out (without looking!).

STRATIFIED
Involves **dividing** the target population into important **subcategories** (or strata) and then selecting members of these subcategories in the **proportion** that they occur in the target population.
For example:
If a target population consisted of 75% women and 25% men, a sample of 20 should include 15 women and 5 men.

OPPORTUNITY
Opportunity sampling simply involves selecting those subjects that are around and **available at the time**. An effort may be made to not be biased in selecting particular types of subject.
For example:
University psychologists may sample from their students.

SELF-SELECTING
Self-selecting samples consist of those individuals who have consciously or unconsciously **determined their own involvement** in a study.
For example:
Volunteers for studies or passers by who become involved in field studies, i.e. in bystander intervention studies.

STRENGTHS

Random sampling (in large numbers) provides the **best chance of an unbiased representative sample** of a target population.

A **deliberate effort** is made to identify the characteristics of a sample most important for it **to be representative** of the target population.

It is **quick, convenient** and often the most economical method of sampling.
It has, therefore, been the most common type of sampling.

Self-selecting samples are relatively convenient and, if volunteering is made on the basis of informed consent, ethical. The choice is not biased by the researcher.

WEAKNESSES

The larger the target population, the more difficult it is to sample randomly, since compiling a selection list of everyone becomes more impractical. True random sampling is, therefore, very rare.

Stratified sampling can be very **time consuming**, since the subcategories have to be identified and their proportions in the target population calculated.

Opportunity sampling gives very unrepresentative samples and is often **biased** on the part of the **researcher** who may choose subjects who will be 'helpful'.

Self-selecting samples are often unrepresentative – being **biased** on the part of the **subject**. Volunteers are unlike non-volunteers in many ways.

Experimental design

HOW DO PSYCHOLOGISTS USE THEIR SUBJECTS IN EXPERIMENTS?

REPEATED MEASURES

DESIGN

A repeated measures design involves using the **same subjects** in each condition of an experiment, e.g. giving a group of subjects a driving test with no alcohol, followed at a later time by the same test after a pint of lager.

Condition A = Condition B

STRENGTHS

- **Subject variables** (individual differences shown by every subject, e.g. intelligence, motivation, past experience, etc.) which could become extraneous variables are **kept constant** between conditions.
- **Better statistical tests** can be used because of less variation between conditions.
- **Fewer subjects** are required (because each is used more than once) therefore more economical.

WEAKNESSES

- **Order effects** such as learning, fatigue or boredom may become constant errors when one condition is done after another, e.g. a subject given the same test may do better due to practice.
- **Demand characteristics** may become a problem - as the subject does both conditions of the experiment, they may guess the aim of the study and act differently.
- **Different tests** may be needed.

INDEPENDENT MEASURES

DESIGN

An independent measures design involves using **different subjects** in each condition of the experiment, e.g. giving one group of subjects a driving test with no alcohol, and a different group of subjects the same test after a pint of lager.

Condition A ≠ Condition B

STRENGTHS

- **Order effects** such as learning, fatigue or boredom do not influence a second condition, since the subject only participates in one condition.
- **Demand characteristics** are less of a problem as the subject only participates in one condition, and is naive to the test, and is less likely to guess the aim of the study and act differently.
- The **same test** can be used.

WEAKNESSES

- **Subject variables differ,** which could become confounding variables unless controlled for.
- **Worse statistical tests** can be used because of more variation between conditions.
- **More subjects** are required (because each is used only once) and is, therefore, less economical.

MATCHED PAIRS

DESIGN

A matched pairs design involves using **different but similar subjects** in each condition of an experiment. An effort is made to match the subjects in each condition in any important characteristics that might affect performance,
e.g. in driving ability, alcohol tolerance, etc.

Condition A ≠ Condition B

STRENGTHS

- **Subject variables** are kept **more constant** between conditions.
- **Better statistical tests** can be used because of less variation between conditions.
- **Order effects** do not occur since the subject only participates in one condition.
- **Demand characteristics** are less of a problem as the subject only participates in one condition.
- The **same test** can be used.

WEAKNESSES

- **Subject variables** can never be perfectly matched in every respect.
- Matching subjects is very **time consuming** and **difficult.**
- **More subjects** are required (because each is used only once) and is, therefore, less economical.

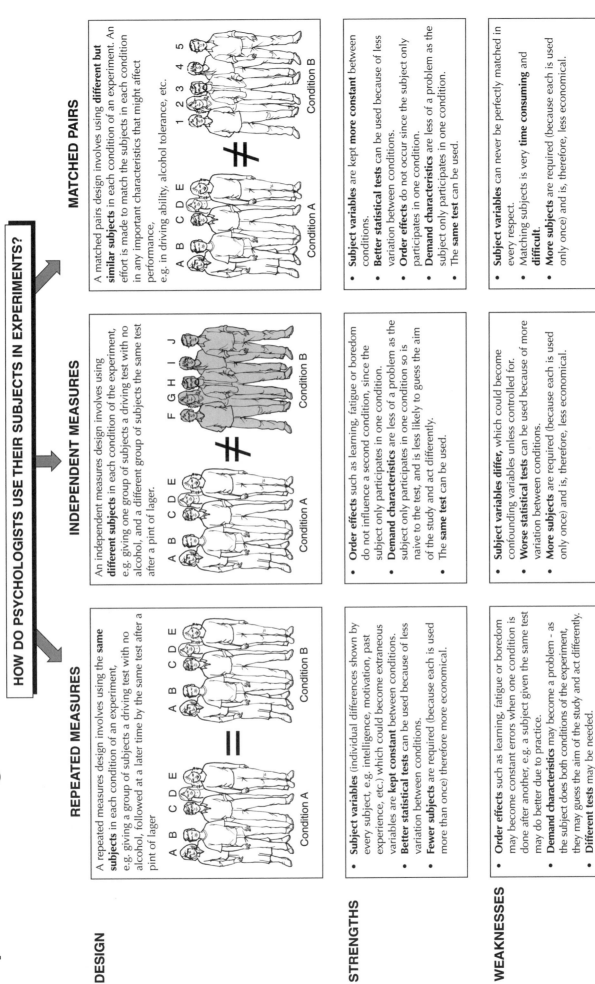

Controlling extraneous variables and bias

HOW DO PSYCHOLOGISTS CONTROL EXTRANEOUS VARIABLES AND BIAS IN THEIR STUDIES?

TYPE OF PROBLEM	PROBLEM	METHOD OF CONTROL
SUBJECTS	**INDIVIDUAL DIFFERENCES** Subject variables can become a problem especially in an independent measures design, creating random or even constant confounding effects.	**Sample large** and **randomly** to gain a representative sample. Use a repeated measures or matched pairs design. **Allocate** subjects **randomly** to each condition of an independent measures experiment to balance out subject variables.
METHOD	**ARTIFICIALITY** Laboratory environments and operationalised variables may lack ecological validity.	Use a **non**-laboratory environment instead, e.g. field study. Broaden or increase the number of definitions for the operationalised variable.
DESIGN	**ORDER EFFECTS** Where learning, boredom or fatigue can influence the second condition of an experiment using a repeated measures design.	Use independent measures design instead. Delay or change the second test. **Counterbalance** the conditions, by getting half the subjects to perform condition A before condition B, and the other half to perform condition B before condition A, thereby balancing the order effects equally between conditions.
	DEMAND CHARACTERISTICS Working out the aim of the study and behaving differently (e.g. trying to please the researcher or spoil the study).	Use independent measures design to stop exposure to both conditions of the experiment, therefore reducing chances of guessing the aim of the study. Use **deception** to hide research aim. However, there are ethical problems with this. Use **single blind method** – the subject does not know which condition of the experiment they are in, e.g. whether they have been given placebo or real pills.
	EXPERIMENTER EXPECTANCY Where the expectations of the researcher influence the results either by consciously or unconsciously revealing the desired outcome or through unconscious procedural or recording bias.	Use **double blind method** – neither the subject nor the researcher carrying out the procedure and recording the results knows the hypothesis or which condition the subjects are in. Use **inter-observer reliability** measures to overcome biased observation. An observer with no vested interest in the result, simultaneously, but separately, rates the same piece of behaviour with the researcher. When results are compared, a high positive correlation should be expected.
PROCEDURE	**DISTRACTION AND CONFUSION** Both sources of extraneous variables which could confound studies unless controlled for.	Standardised instructions should be given in a clear and simple form and the subject should be asked if they have questions, so each participant receives equal information. Standardised procedures should be employed so each subject is tested under equal conditions with no distractions.

Reliability and validity of studies

HOW DO PSYCHOLOGISTS TEST THE QUALITY OF STUDIES?

RELIABILITY
The reliability of a method of measurement (whether it be an experimental test, questionnaire or observational procedure) refers to how **consistently** it measures.

INTERNAL RELIABILITY
Internal reliability refers to **how consistently a method measures within itself**. If methods of measurement were not **standardised** they would give distorted final scores.
For example, internal reliability would be lacking if
- a ruler consisted of variable centimetres,
- an I.Q. test was made up of half ridiculously easy questions and half ridiculously difficult questions (virtually everyone would score half marks and be equally intelligent!) or
- different observers using the same observational definitions simultaneously scored the same individual differently.

Internal reliability could be checked for test items by the **split half method** – correlating the results of half the items with the other half (e.g. the odd numbers with the even numbers of the test) and gaining a high positive correlation coefficient.

EXTERNAL RELIABILITY
External reliability refers to **how consistently a method measures over time when repeated**. Methods of measurement should give similar scores when repeated on the same people under similar conditions.
For example external reliability would be lacking if
- a ruler measured an unchanging object different lengths each time it was used,
- an I.Q. test scored the same person a genius one day but just average a week later.

External reliability could be checked for test items by the **test-, re-test method** – correlating the results of the test conducted on one occasion with the results of the test conducted on a later occasion (with the same subjects) and gaining a high positive correlation coefficient.

VALIDITY
The validity of a method of measurement (whether it be an experimental test, questionnaire or observational procedure) refers to whether it **measures what it is supposed to measure** - how realistically or truly variables have been operationalised.

INTERNAL VALIDITY – refers to whether the results of a study were really due to the variables the researchers suggest were tested by their methodology.

EXTERNAL VALIDITY – refers to whether the results can be generalised if conducted in different environments or using different participants.

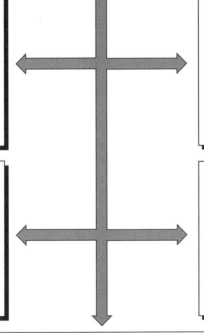

FACE/CONTENT VALIDITY
Face or content validity involves **examining** the content of the test to see if it **looks** like it measures what it is supposed to measure.
For example, examining the test items of an intelligence test to see if they seem to measure general intelligence, not just general knowledge or linguistic comprehension.

CONCURRENT VALIDITY
Concurrent validity involves **comparing** a **new** method or test **with** an already well **established** one that claims to measure the same variable(s). A high positive correlation should be gained between the results of the two tests.
For example, correlating the results from the same people tested by a new intelligence test and an older established one.

CONSTRUCT VALIDITY
Construct validity refers to whether the test or method can be used to **support** the **underlying theoretical constructs** concerning the variable that it is supposed to be measuring.
For example, if theory suggests the offspring of two highly intelligent parents raised in a stimulating environment should be intelligent, an IQ test should confirm this.

PREDICTIVE VALIDITY
Predictive validity refers to whether the test will **predict future performance** indicated by its results.
For example, high scorers on an I.Q. test at a young age should be predicted to later perform better in studies or jobs requiring intelligence.

ECOLOGICAL VALIDITY
Ecological validity refers to whether a test or method measures behaviour that is representative of naturally occurring behaviour. Too specifically operationalised tests or those conducted under contrived conditions may not reflect spontaneously occurring, natural behaviour. For example, do the items on an intelligence test represent all the types of behaviour we would describe as intelligent in everyday life?
However, since there is difficulty in saying what conditions are 'natural' or 'normal' (laboratories are human social situations too, while some field studies may be conducted under very unusual circumstances) ecological validity is perhaps best measured by the extent to which research findings can be generalised to other research settings.

Timing and location of investigations

WHERE SHOULD PSYCHOLOGISTS INVESTIGATE?

CROSS-CULTURAL STUDIES
In cross-cultural studies subjects from **different cultures** are given the same test and their results are compared.

MEAD (1935)
Mead studied three different tribes in New Guinea and compared their gender role behaviours.
Cross-cultural studies have investigated whether variation occurs in different countries in conformity, obedience, intelligence, perception and attachment – to name just a few examples in psychology.

- Combats an ethnocentric culturally biased view of human psychology.
- Widens the generalisability of results.
- Provides data on cultural differences or similarities which may increase understanding of psychological development.

- More time consuming, difficult (due to language barriers etc.) and expensive.
- Open to ethnocentric misinterpretation when researchers from one culture investigate another culture.
- Subject reactivity may increase with a cross-cultural observer, producing untypical behaviour.

WHEN SHOULD PSYCHOLOGISTS INVESTIGATE?

LONGITUDINAL STUDIES
In longitudinal studies the **same** subjects are investigated **over a long period of time**. It is a form of repeated measures design.

KOHLBERG (1971)
Kohlberg conducted a twenty year longitudinal study of moral reasoning.
Developmental psychologists concentrate on how abilities and behaviour may vary over time, from infancy to adulthood, and so may find that studying the same subjects over a long period of time is the most accurate way of discovering the principles and processes of development.

- Less bias from subject variables.
- In some areas of psychology, such as mental illness, a longitudinal study may be the only way of determining how a disorder progresses.

- Time consuming, expensive and high likelihood of losing subjects between conditions.
- Extremely difficult or impossible to replicate exactly.
- Longitudinal studies can be carried out retrospectively by examining the history of subjects, but this has many disadvantages, such as memory distortion and lack of objectivity.

CROSS-SECTIONAL STUDIES
In cross-sectional studies subjects of **different** ages are investigated **at one particular point in time**. It is a form of independent measures design.

EXAMPLES

ASCH (1951)
Asch's findings on conformity were not replicated by some later researchers, indicating that his findings may have been influenced by factors present in his society *at that particular time*.
Kohlberg (1981) compared the moral development of three groups of boys aged 10, 13 and 16.

STRENGTHS

- Immediate results can be gained, therefore, they are convenient.
- Cheaper and less time consuming than longitudinal studies.
- Less likelihood of losing subjects between conditions.

WEAKNESSES

- Cross-sectional studies may be overly influenced by the social environment of the time, and therefore need to be regularly replicated.
- All disadvantages of independent measures design, e.g. subject confounding variables, greater number of subjects needed, etc.
- Cohort effect may bias data.

Data recording techniques

TECHNIQUE	ADVANTAGES	DISADVANTAGES
BEHAVIOUR SAMPLING METHODS		
• **Event sampling.** Key behavioural events are recorded every time they occur.	Limits the behaviours observed, thus reducing the chance that the behaviour of interest will be missed.	It is difficult to observe all incidents of key behaviour over large areas. Other important behaviour may be ignored.
• **Time sampling.** Behaviour is observed for discrete periods of time.	Reduces the amount of time spent in observation and thus may increase accuracy.	Behaviour may be missed if random time samples are not taken across the day.
• **Point sampling.** The behaviour of just one individual in a group at a time is recorded.	Increases the accuracy of observation and number of behaviours that can be recorded.	May miss behaviour in others that is important for an understanding of the individual.
DATA RECORDING TECHNIQUES		
• **Frequency grids.** Nominal data is scored as a tally chart for a variety of behaviours.	Quick and easy to use and can record a larger number of behaviours at a time.	Nominal data provides little information, e.g. it cannot say how long or intensely a behaviour was shown.
• **Rating scales.** Scores ordinal level data for a behaviour, indicating the degree to which it is shown.	Provides more information on the behaviour.	Rating using opinion rather than fixed scales, such as timing, introduces subjectivity.
• **Timing behaviour.**	High accuracy of data.	Loss of descriptive detail of behaviour.
DATA RECORDING EQUIPMENT		
• **Hand-written** notes or coding systems.	Less intimidating than more mechanical methods of recording.	Data may be missed or subjectively recorded.
• **Audio-tape** recording.	Accurately records all spoken data for later leisurely and accurate analysis.	Omits important gestures and non-verbal communication accompanying speech.
• **Video**.	Accurately records all data in view for later analysis – increases objectivity.	May produce participant reactivity and unnatural behaviour due to intimidation.
• **One way mirrors** in laboratories.	Reduces participant reactivity.	Unethical if subjects are not informed.
CONTENT ANALYSIS A **quantitative** method for analysing the **communication** of people and organisations, e.g. in their conversations, or media records. The researcher first decides what media they are going to sample and then devises the **coding units** they are interested in measuring, e.g. the frequency of, or amount of time and space devoted to, certain words or themes.	Content analysis is a useful tool for gathering data on a variety of topics, from rhetorical devices used in political speeches to the stereotyping or aggressive content of books and films. It can be used to assess what is omitted from speech, not just what is included. The data gained is usually of high ecological validity.	It is sometimes difficult to arrive at objectively operationalised coding units and the technique can be time consuming. Content analysis can be used to examine the function that a person's or organisation's communication serves, e.g. justifying or criticising, but the analyst's interpretations are also open to interpretation!
QUALITATIVE DATA ANALYSIS The analysis of qualitative data in its own right, without reducing it to quantitative numbers, can be very useful. Qualitative data can be gained from a variety of methods, such as observations, interviews, case studies and even experiments - for example in terms of **how** the subject **behaved** during testing and what they **said**.	Qualitative data is useful to describe information lost in the quantified and narrowed analysis of figures. Interviews with subjects after experiments can often reveal the causes of their behaviour and provide ideas for future research. However, qualitative analysis can be a useful research tool in its own right – arriving at an in-depth analysis and discussion of behaviour.	Qualitative analysis is often attacked for its lack of objectivity. However, • techniques exist to check its reliability and validity, e.g. triangulation (using more than one method of investigation) and repetition of the research cycle (to check previous data). • subjective opinion and participant consultation is regarded as a strength by many researchers, e.g. feminists.

Numerical descriptive statistics

HOW DO PSYCHOLOGISTS SUMMARIZE THEIR DATA NUMERICALLY?

LEVELS OF DATA

NOMINAL
Nominal data is a simple **frequency headcount** (the number of times something occurred) found in **discrete categories** (something can only belong to one category).

For example, the number of people who helped or did not help in an emergency.

Nominal data is the simplest data.

ORDINAL
Ordinal data is measurements that can be put in an **order**, **rank** or **position.**

For example, scores on unstandardised psychological scales (such as attractiveness out of 10) or who came 1st, 2nd, 3rd, etc. in a race.

The **intervals** between each rank, however, are **unknown,** i.e. how far ahead 1st was from 2nd.

INTERVAL AND RATIO
Both are measurements on a **scale**, the **intervals** of which are **known and equal**. **Ratio** data has a **true zero** point, whereas **interval** data can go into **negative** values.

For example, **temperature** for interval data (degrees centigrade can be minus) **length** or **time** for ratio data (no seconds is no time at all).

The most **precise** types of data.

MEASURES OF CENTRAL TENDENCY

MODE
The value or event that occurs the most frequently.
The most suitable measure of central tendency for nominal data.
Not influenced by extreme scores; useful to show most popular value.
Crude measure of central tendency; not useful if many equal modes.

MEDIAN
The middle value when all scores are placed in rank order.
The most suitable measure of central tendency for ordinal data.
Not distorted by extreme freak values, e.g. 2, 3, 3, 4, 4, 4, 4, 5, 5, 6, 42.
However, it can be distorted by small samples and is less sensitive.

MEAN
The average value of all scores.
The most suitable measure of central tendency for interval or ratio data.
The most sensitive measure of central tendency for all data.
However, can be distorted by extreme freak values.

MEASURES OF DISPERSION

RANGE the difference between the smallest and largest value, plus 1. For example, 3, 4, 7, 7, 8, 9, 12, 4, 17, 17, 18 **(18 – 3) +1 = Range of 16**	ADVANTAGE	DISADVANTAGE
	• Quick and easy to calculate.	• Distorted by extreme 'freak' values, an extra value of 43 would give a range of 41.

SEMI-INTERQUARTILE RANGE
When data is put in order, find the first quartile (Q1) and third quartile (Q3) of the sample, subtract the Q1 value from the Q3 value and divide the result by two.
For example,
3, 4, 7, 7 8, 9, 12, 14, 17, 17, 18
    ↑   ↑   ↑
   Q1   Q2   Q3
   7   17
17 - 7 = 10 10 ÷ 2 = **Semi-interquartile range of 5**

- Less distorted by any extreme 'freak' values.
- Ignores extreme values.

STANDARD DEVIATION
The average amount all scores deviate from the mean.
The difference (deviation) between each score and the mean of those scores is calculated and then squared (to remove minus values). These squared deviations are then added up and their mean calculated to give a value known as the variance.
The square root of the variance gives the standard deviation of the scores.

score	mean	d	d squared
6 –	10 =	–4	16
8 –	10 =	–2	4
10 –	10 =	0	0
12 –	10 =	+2	4
14 –	10 =	+4	16
			40

mean of 40 = 8 = variance
square root of variance
= standard deviation = 2.8

- The most sensitive measure of dispersion, using all the data available.
- Can be used to relate the sample to the population's parameters.

- A little more time consuming to calculate but no important disadvantages.

Graphical descriptive statistics

HOW DO PSYCHOLOGISTS SUMMARIZE THEIR DATA PICTORIALLY?

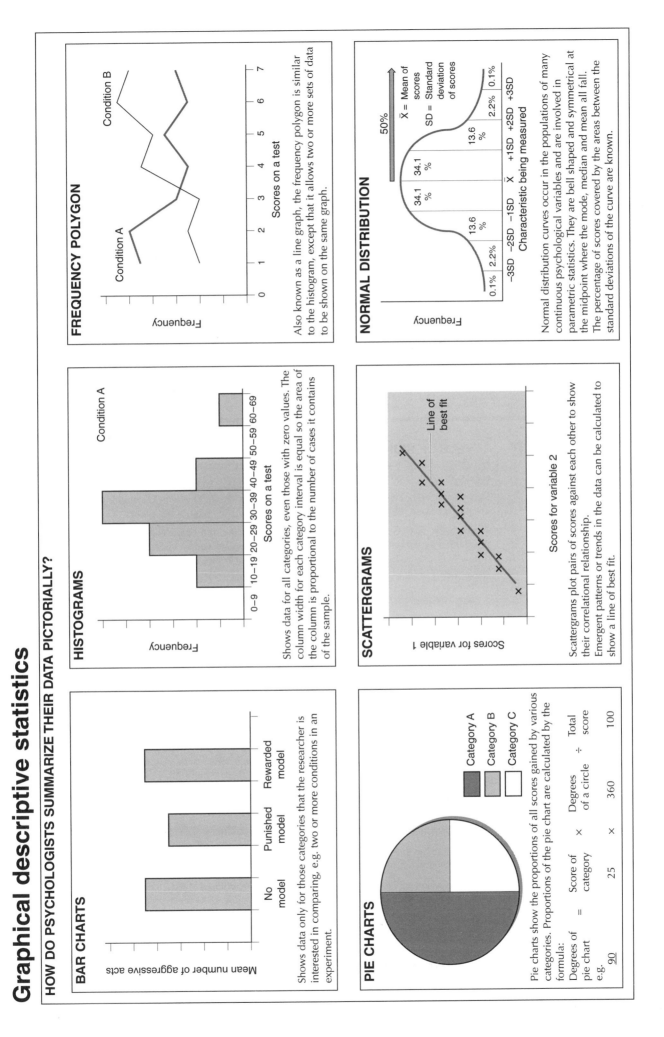

FREQUENCY POLYGON

Also known as a line graph, the frequency polygon is similar to the histogram, except that it allows two or more sets of data to be shown on the same graph.

NORMAL DISTRIBUTION

Normal distribution curves occur in the populations of many continuous psychological variables and are involved in parametric statistics. They are bell shaped and symmetrical at the midpoint where the mode, median and mean all fall. The percentage of scores covered by the areas between the standard deviations of the curve are known.

HISTOGRAMS

Shows data for all categories, even those with zero values. The column width for each category interval is equal so the area of the column is proportional to the number of cases it contains of the sample.

SCATTERGRAMS

Scattergrams plot pairs of scores against each other to show their correlational relationship.
Emergent patterns or trends in the data can be calculated to show a line of best fit.

BAR CHARTS

Shows data only for those categories that the researcher is interested in comparing, e.g. two or more conditions in an experiment.

PIE CHARTS

Pie charts show the proportions of all scores gained by various categories. Proportions of the pie chart are calculated by the formula:

Degrees of pie chart = Score of category × Degrees of a circle ÷ Total score

e.g. 90 = 25 × 360 100

Inferential statistics

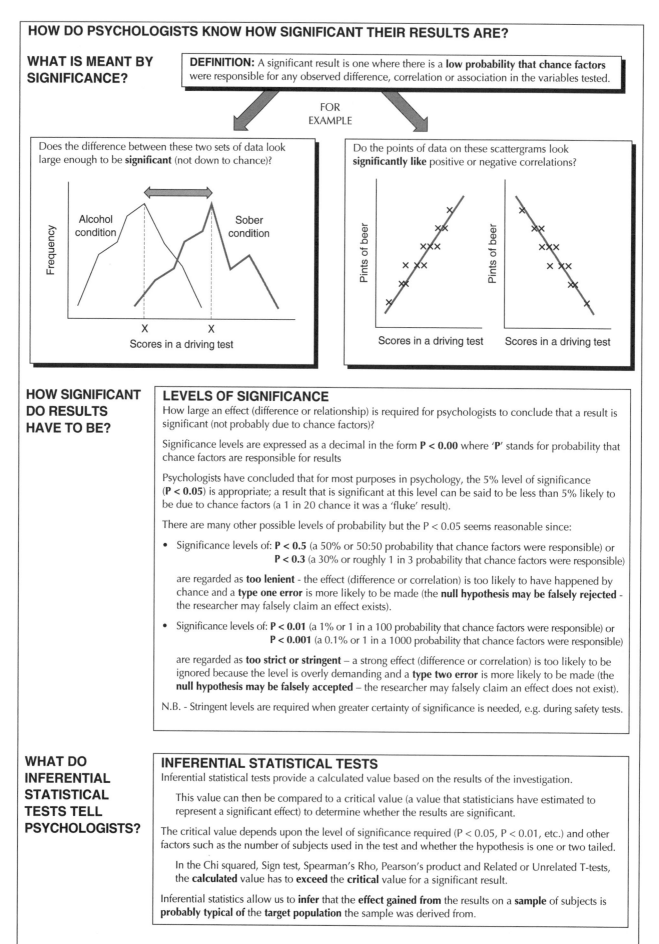

HOW DO PSYCHOLOGISTS KNOW HOW SIGNIFICANT THEIR RESULTS ARE?

WHAT IS MEANT BY SIGNIFICANCE?

DEFINITION: A significant result is one where there is a **low probability that chance factors** were responsible for any observed difference, correlation or association in the variables tested.

FOR EXAMPLE

Does the difference between these two sets of data look large enough to be **significant** (not down to chance)?

Alcohol condition
Sober condition
Frequency
X   X
Scores in a driving test

Do the points of data on these scattergrams look **significantly like** positive or negative correlations?

Pints of beer
Scores in a driving test

Pints of beer
Scores in a driving test

HOW SIGNIFICANT DO RESULTS HAVE TO BE?

LEVELS OF SIGNIFICANCE

How large an effect (difference or relationship) is required for psychologists to conclude that a result is significant (not probably due to chance factors)?

Significance levels are expressed as a decimal in the form **P < 0.00** where 'P' stands for probability that chance factors are responsible for results

Psychologists have concluded that for most purposes in psychology, the 5% level of significance (**P < 0.05**) is appropriate; a result that is significant at this level can be said to be less than 5% likely to be due to chance factors (a 1 in 20 chance it was a 'fluke' result).

There are many other possible levels of probability but the P < 0.05 seems reasonable since:

- Significance levels of: **P < 0.5** (a 50% or 50:50 probability that chance factors were responsible) or **P < 0.3** (a 30% or roughly 1 in 3 probability that chance factors were responsible)

  are regarded as **too lenient** - the effect (difference or correlation) is too likely to have happened by chance and a **type one error** is more likely to be made (the **null hypothesis may be falsely rejected** - the researcher may falsely claim an effect exists).

- Significance levels of: **P < 0.01** (a 1% or 1 in a 100 probability that chance factors were responsible) or **P < 0.001** (a 0.1% or 1 in a 1000 probability that chance factors were responsible)

  are regarded as **too strict or stringent** – a strong effect (difference or correlation) is too likely to be ignored because the level is overly demanding and a **type two error** is more likely to be made (the **null hypothesis may be falsely accepted** – the researcher may falsely claim an effect does not exist).

N.B. - Stringent levels are required when greater certainty of significance is needed, e.g. during safety tests.

WHAT DO INFERENTIAL STATISTICAL TESTS TELL PSYCHOLOGISTS?

INFERENTIAL STATISTICAL TESTS

Inferential statistical tests provide a calculated value based on the results of the investigation.

This value can then be compared to a critical value (a value that statisticians have estimated to represent a significant effect) to determine whether the results are significant.

The critical value depends upon the level of significance required (P < 0.05, P < 0.01, etc.) and other factors such as the number of subjects used in the test and whether the hypothesis is one or two tailed.

In the Chi squared, Sign test, Spearman's Rho, Pearson's product and Related or Unrelated T-tests, the **calculated** value has to **exceed** the **critical** value for a significant result.

Inferential statistics allow us to **infer** that the **effect gained from** the results on a **sample** of subjects is **probably typical of** the **target population** the sample was derived from.

Choosing inferential statistical tests

HOW DO PSYCHOLOGISTS CHOOSE AN APPROPRIATE STATISTICAL TEST?

1 TEST OF DIFFERENCE OR RELATIONSHIP REQUIRED?
2 WHAT EXPERIMENTAL DESIGN HAS BEEN USED?
3 WHAT LEVEL OF DATA IS BEING USED?
4 ARE ALL THREE PARAMETRIC CONDITIONS MET?
  a Interval or ratio data
  b Both sets of data normally
    distributed or from normally
    distributed populations
  c Both sets of data have
    similar variance.

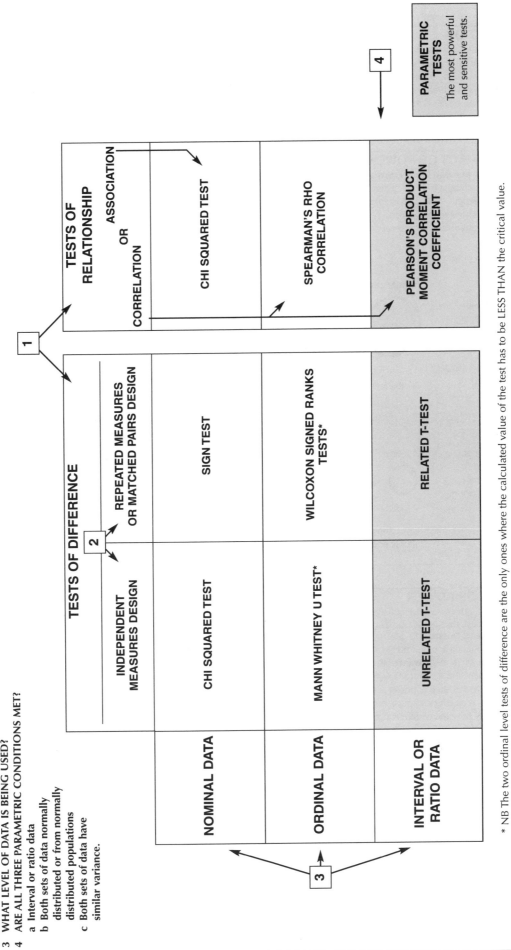

* NB The two ordinal level tests of difference are the only ones where the calculated value of the test has to be LESS THAN the critical value.

Social power

DEFINITION
Social power refers to the influence a person has to change another's thoughts, feelings, or behaviour. There are many sources of power, many ways in which it can work and many effects it can have on those who have it and those who yield to it.

NORMS OF POWER
Power relations are embedded in the hierarchical nature of society. Zimbardo et al's (1973) prison simulation experiment showed how the role of prison guard and the power that went with it could be readily assumed by subjects selected on the basis of their normality. Clearly, the norms of guard power (operating from coercive and legitimate power bases) can be readily understood (although exaggerated by media portrayal) and conformed to by anyone.

THE IMPACT OF POWER.
According to **social impact theory** (Latane, 1981), the strength of influence felt by a target is determined by three factors:
- The **strength** (or importance) of the influencer,
- The **number** of influencers,
- The **immediacy** (or closeness) of the influencer/s.

Increases in each of the above factors will cause the power of influence to increase, while decreases in these factors (or an increase in the target's strength or number) will have the opposite effect. For example, you are more likely to be influenced by several very important people standing in front of you, than by one unimportant person talking over the telephone.

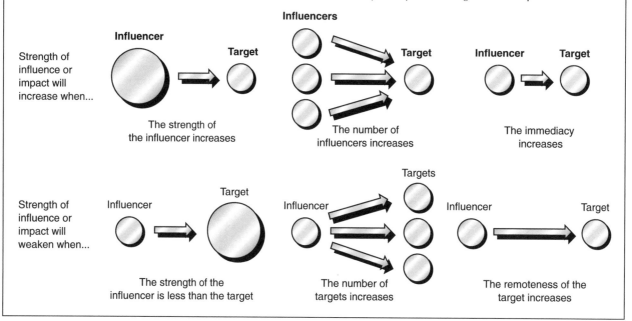

TYPES OF POWER
Raven and others have identified six different (although they can operate simultaneously) sources or *bases of power.*

1 Reward power
This influence is based on the ability to provide what others **want** or to remove what they do not want. Many people possess this source of power (e.g. parents, employers, friends), but note that they offer many different types of reward (e.g. love, money, approval). This power only works as long as the rewards can be given by the influencer and are wanted by the receiver.

2 Coercive power
This involves the ability to **punish**, by inflicting some form of negative stimulus (e.g. disapproval, ridicule, pain) or by removing pleasant stimuli (e.g. affection, wages). This power base requires constant supervision, since it produces negative feelings and attitudes in its victims who only tend to comply behaviourally to demands rather than really accepting them.

3 Referent power
This is the influence a person has because they are **respected** or admired. The target wishes to identify with (be like) the influencer and is more likely to follow their wishes. Role models and idols have this power, but only maintain it as long as they are liked or respected.

4 Legitimate power
This is where the target accepts the **norms** (probably internalised) that the influencer should have (has the right to) influence over them. The legitimacy of the power obviously depends on the situation – we accept that a referee can tell us what to do in a football match, but not outside of that situation.

5 Expert power
The power an influencer has because the target believes they possess **superior knowledge** in a desired area. We are thus at the mercy of our doctor's advice in matters of health, and at the mercy of garage mechanics when our cars need servicing.

6 Informational power
One person or a group of people, expert or otherwise, can have power if they provide socially accepted **information**. This ties in with the social reality hypothesis and Festinger's social comparison theory (we look to others to know how to react in certain situations).

'A study of prisoners and guards in a simulated prison' Haney, Banks, and Zimbardo (1973)

AIM
To demonstrate the situational rather than the dispositional causes of negative behaviour and thought patterns found in prison settings by conducting a prison simulation with 'normal' subjects playing the roles of guard and prisoner.

METHOD
Subjects: 22 male subjects selected (through personality assessment) from an initial pool of 75 volunteers based on their stability, maturity and lack of involvement in anti-social behaviour. They were mostly Caucasian, middle class, college students, who were strangers to each other and were randomly allocated to either prisoner or guard roles. Prisoners signed a consent document which specified that some of their human rights would be suspended and all subjects were to receive $15 a day for up to 2 weeks.

Apparatus: Prison – a basement corridor in Stanford University Psychology department converted into a set of 2 x 3 metre prison cells with a solitary confinement room (a tiny unlit closet), a 'yard' room and an observation screen (through which covert video and audiotape data recording could take place).
Uniforms – to facilitate role identification, guards were given khaki shirts and trousers, batons and reflecting sunglasses. Prisoners wore loose fitting smocks with identification numbers,

no underwear, a lock and chain around one ankle, and a nylon stocking cap to cover their hair.

Procedure: The procedure, as with the apparatus, was designed to establish 'functional equivalents' for the experience of prison life.
- Prisoners were arrested by real police outside their houses by surprise, taken to a real police station for finger-printing and processing, and were then driven blindfolded to the mock prison (where they were stripped naked, 'deloused', and dressed in prisoner's uniform). Prisoners remained in the 'prison' 24 hours a day and followed a schedule of work assignments, rest periods, and meal/toilet visits.
- Guards worked only 8 hour shifts, and were given no specific instructions apart from to 'maintain a reasonable degree of order within the prison necessary for its effective functioning' and a prohibition against the use of physical violence.

RESULTS
The effects of imprisonment were assessed by video and audio tape observation of behaviour and dialogue, self-report questionnaires, and interviews. The experiment had to be terminated after 6 days, instead of the intended 14, because of the pathological (abnormal) reactions shown by both prisoners and guards.

- **Effects on prisoners** – subjects showed what was termed the 'Pathological Prisoner Syndrome' – disbelief was followed by rebellion which, after failure, was followed by a range of negative emotions and behaviours. All showed passivity (some becoming excessively obedient) and dependence (initiating very little activity without instruction). Half the prisoners showed signs of depression, crying, fits of rage, and acute anxiety, and had to be released early. All but two of those who remained said they would forfeit the money if they could be released early.

The experimenters proposed that these reactions were caused by a loss of personal identity, emasculation, dependency, and learned helplessness brought about by the arbitrary and unpredictable control, and the norms and structures of the prison system.

- **Effects on guards** – subjects showed what was termed the 'Pathology of Power' – huge enjoyment of the power at their disposal (some worked extra time for no pay, and were disappointed when the study was over) led to the guards abusing it and dehumanising the prisoners. All prisoners' rights were redefined as privileges (going to the toilet, eating, and wearing eye-glasses became rewards), and punishment with little or no justification was applied with verbal insults. Although not all guards initiated aggressive action, none contradicted its use in others.
The experimenters proposed that these reactions were caused by a sense of empowerment legitimised by the role of 'guard' in the prison system.

EVALUATION
Methodological: Lack of ecological validity – A role play simulation lacks 'mundane realism' and may produce artificial results. The experimenters admit factors, such as the lack of physical violence and minimum duration of the sentence, limit the generalisability of the simulation, but point out that most of the functional equivalents of the prison system were implemented and that most of the subjects' excessive reactions went beyond the demands of the role play (prisoners called each other by their ID numbers in private, and guards showed aggression even when they thought they were not being observed).

Data analysis – Was mostly qualitative rather than quantitative.

Ethical problems – 1 The study was ethically approved beforehand – perhaps the dramatic and disturbing results cause the ethical objections, but these came from the subjects not the experimenters.

2 The subjects had signed an informed consent document, but were unaware that they would be arrested in public and of exactly how realistic their imprisonment would be.

3 The experiment was terminated early and debriefing and assessment of the subjects took place weeks, months and years afterwards.

Theoretical: The research provides support for social psychological explanations of behaviour, has wide ranging implications for the usefulness and ethics of existing penal systems, and has been used to facilitate our understanding of the psychological effects of imprisonment.

Links: Social influence – particularly power, leadership, obedience (see Milgram) and conformity.

Studies of conformity

CONFORMITY DEFINITIONS AND TYPES

Definition: 'Yielding to group pressure' Crutchfield (1962). According to Aronson (1976) the pressure can be real (involving the physical presence of others) or imagined (involving the pressure of social norms/expectations). Kelman (1958) suggests that the yielding can take the form of

- compliance – A change in behaviour without a change in opinion (just going along with the group),
- internalisation – A change in both behaviour and opinion (the group's and your own opinions coincide), or
- identification – The individual changes their behaviour and opinions to identify with the influencing group.

CONFORMITY STUDIES

JENNESS (1932)

Asked subjects to estimate the number of beans in a bottle, first individually and then as a group. When asked individually again, the subjects showed a shift towards the group's estimate rather than their own. This was rather a simple experiment, however.

SHERIF (1935)

Asked subjects to estimate how far a spot of light in a completely dark room moved. Sherif kept the point of light stable, but due to the autokinetic effect illusion (caused by small eye movements) each individual reported fairly consistent estimates that often differed from other subjects.

However, when subjects were put in groups, their estimates converged towards a central mean, despite not being told to arrive at a group estimate and despite denying that they had been influenced by the others in post experimental interviews.

ASCH (1951, 1952, 1956)

Asch wanted to test conformity under non ambiguous conditions and, therefore, devised a very simple perceptual task of matching the length of a line to one of three other comparison lines. The task was so easy that control subjects made almost no errors. In the experimental condition only one real (naive) subject was tested at a time, but was surrounded by seven confederates of the experimenter, who were also supposed to be subjects but had been told beforehand to all give the same wrong estimate on 12 out of the 18 trials. The only real subject was second to last to give their estimate, and was, therefore, faced with either giving their own opinion or conforming to the group opinion on the critical trials.

The average rate of conformity was 32%. 74% conformed at least once and 26% never conformed.
Asch conducted variations to identify factors influencing conformity, such as:

- increasing the group size – Asch found little increase above 3 or 4, although other studies have found that larger groups will increase conformity but at a decreasing rate.
- providing support for the subject – when Asch provided an ally that agreed with the naive subject's estimates, conformity dropped to 5.5%. It seems that the unanimity of the group is important. If the ally changed to the group's estimates, then the naive subject would often follow suit.
- increasing the difficulty of the task – when the comparison lines were made closer in length, the rate of conformity increased.
- when the naive subject could write down their response, conformity dropped.

Even subjects that did not conform, felt strong social pressure to do so. One was heard to exclaim 'I always disagree – darn it!', and on being debriefed, commented 'I do not deny that at times I had the feeling "to heck with it, I'll go along with the rest"'.

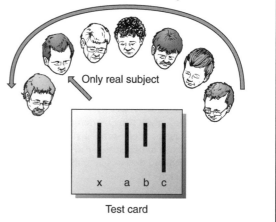

Direction that answers were given in

Only real subject

Test card

CRUTCHFIELD (1954)

Crutchfield tested for conformity without physical presence by placing subjects in individual cubicles with electronic display boards which supposedly let each subject know what the others had answered. In fact, he allowed each subject to believe they were the last to answer and presented them with uniformly wrong group answers on half the tasks.

With this more efficient and standardised procedure Crutchfield tested over 600 subjects using a variety of stimuli such as Asch's line comparison tests, obviously incorrect factual statements, and personal opinions. He found 30% conformity in Asch's line test, 46% conformity to the suggestion that a picture of a star had a larger surface area than a circle (when it was a third smaller), and 37% agreement to the statement 'I doubt that I would make a good leader' (which none agreed to when asked on their own).

CRITICISMS OF CONFORMITY STUDIES

- Artificiality – the above studies used well controlled and standardised procedures but mostly reflect conformity under laboratory conditions, with meaningless stimuli.
- The high conformity found may only reflect the norms prevalent in the USA in the 1950s. Replications have found widely varying rates of conformity in more recent times and when the studies have been conducted cross culturally.
- Ethics – subjects were deceived.

Theories of conformity

CRUTCHFIELD'S CONFORMING PERSONALITY THEORY (1955)

After Crutchfield had tested his subjects for conformity, he also gave them a number of personality and I.Q. type tests, and found, for example, that those subjects who conformed the most typically

- were less intellectually competent – perhaps they were more open to the expert power of others
- had less ego strength – perhaps making them less confident in their own opinion
- had less leadership ability – perhaps making them less able to assert their own opinion
- were more narrow minded / authoritarian – perhaps inclining them to stick to the majority answer

However, if conforming personalities exist, then they should conform in a variety of situations, but McGuire (1968a) has found inconsistency of conformity across different situations.

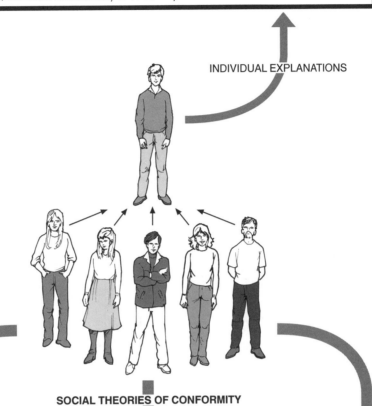

INDIVIDUAL EXPLANATIONS

SOCIAL THEORIES OF CONFORMITY

INFORMATIONAL SOCIAL INFLUENCE

Deutsch and Gerard (1955) have suggested that one motive for conformity is based on the **need** that everyone has **for certainty**.

When individuals are placed in ambiguous/**uncertain conditions**, they are more likely to refer to others to know how to react (Festinger called this **social comparison**).

Under these conditions, other people possess informational or **expert power** and individuals may show **internalisation** conformity – both their behaviour and opinions coincide with the group's.

Informational influence explains the conformity found in Sherif's study and much of the conformity in Asch's tasks – especially when the difficulty of the task was increased. A few of Asch's subjects seemingly experienced perceptual distortion, but the majority believed that the group's judgement was superior.

NORMATIVE SOCIAL INFLUENCE

Deutsch and Gerard (1955) have proposed that another motive for conformity is based upon the **need** for **social acceptance** and **approval**.

When individuals are put into a potentially **embarrassing situation**, such as disagreeing with the majority, they are faced with a **conflict** between their own and others' opinions.

Under these conditions other people have **reward** or **coercive power** which may lead individuals into **compliance** – publicly agreeing with the group, but privately maintaining their own opinions.

Normative influence explains some of Asch's conformity results, especially in the private answer variation. Some of his subjects reported private disagreement with the group's answers, commenting 'If I'd been the first I probably would have responded differently'.

REFERENT SOCIAL INFLUENCE

Turner (1991) suggests that people have a tendency to categorise themselves as members of different groups (Social Identity Theory) and argues that we are most likely to conform to the norms of those groups that we feel we are members of.

This occurs because people expect to agree with the members of such groups, but do not necessarily expect their views to coincide with those of other groups and are therefore less likely to conform to out-group than in-group pressure.

Under these conditions, members of the in-group possess **informational**, and perhaps also **reward** and **referent power**, which may lead the individual to **identification** conformity – their behaviour and beliefs coinciding with the group's, while they feel they are members of that group.

Milgram's (1963) study of obedience

AIM
To investigate how far people will go in obeying an authority figure .

PROCEDURE
Subjects were led to believe that the experiment was investigating the effects of punishment on learning. The subjects were tested one at a time and were always given the role of teacher (through a fixed lottery). The subject saw his apparent co-subject (in reality an actor) strapped into a chair with electrodes attached to him, since he was to be the 'learner'. The subject ('teacher') was told the shocks would cause no permanent tissue damage and was given a trial shock of 45 volts.

The subject then started the experiment in the shock generator room next door by testing the learner over an intercom, and was told by the experimenter (the authority figure) to administer increasing levels of electric shock for each wrong answer (which the actor gave often). In the basic set-up of the experiment the subject received feedback reactions from the learner he was 'electrocuting' only by a thump on the wall at 300 volts followed by no further reply. The experiment finished when either the subject refused to continue (disobeyed the experimenter's request), or had reached the maximum shock on the scale (450 volts). The subject was then fully debriefed as to the real nature of the experiment, re-introduced to the learner in a friendly way and reassured that no damage had been done since the learner had not really received any shocks at all!

SUBJECTS
They were 40 males between the ages of 20 and 50 from a range of occupations and were drawn from the New Haven area. They were obtained by newspaper ad's for participation in a study of learning at Yale University and were paid $4.50 just for turning up.

THE LEARNER
An actor was required to play the role of the learner – an Irish-American, 47-year-old accountant who appeared mild-mannered and likeable.

APPARATUS
Two rooms in the Yale Interaction Laboratory were used – one for the learner containing an 'electric chair' and an answering device, the other for the teacher and experimenter with an electric shock generator. The generator did not actually give shocks to the learner, and was used to measure the dependent variable of obedience. It was a convincing machine with a row of 30 switches ranging from 15 to 450 volts in increments of 15 volts, and was marked with descriptive terms of the shock effects – ranging from 'slight shock' through to 'Danger: severe shock' and 'XXX'.

THE EXPERIMENTER
He was 31 years old, dressed in a grey laboratory coat, and appeared somewhat stern and impassive through the experiment. If at any point the subject showed reluctance to administer the shock, he would command them to continue with standardised prompts ranging from "please continue" to "You have no other choice, you *must* go on".

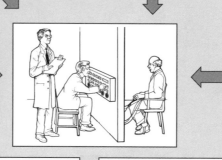

RESULTS
Levels of obedience expected
Psychology students and professional colleagues were asked what percentage of subjects would administer the highest degree of shock (450 volts) – the answers ranged from 1 to 3, with a mean of 1.2.

Levels of obedience obtained
65% of subjects continued to the maximum shock level of 450 volts. No subject stopped before 300 volts.

Subjects' realisation of shock effects
In the post-experimental interview the subjects were asked "How painful to the learner were the last few shocks that you administered to him?". The mean response was 13.42 out of 14 – 'extremely painful' on the scale.

Behavioural reactions to the study
"In a large number of cases the degree of tension reached extremes that are rarely seen in sociopsychological laboratory studies. Subjects were observed to sweat, tremble, stutter, bite their lips, groan and dig their fingers into their flesh. These were characteristic rather than exceptional responses to the experiment.... One sign of tension was the regular occurrence of nervous laughing fits.... Full-blown, uncontrollable seizures were observed for 3 subjects. On one occasion we observed a fit so violently convulsive that it was necessary to call a halt to the experiment. In the post experimental interviews subjects took pains to point out that they were not sadistic types, and that the laughter did not mean they enjoyed shocking the victim". Milgram (1963).

EVALUATION OF METHODOLOGY
Experimental validity
The procedure was well standardised and obedience was accurately operationalised as the amount of voltage given. Orne and Holland (1968) however, have argued that the subjects did not really think that the learner would come to harm. They suggested that the subjects were involved in a *'pact of ignorance'* with the experimenter and obeyed in much the same way as a member of a magician's audience will comply and put their head under a guillotine which has just split a cabbage head in two! The genuine distress of the subjects, their ratings of the shock pain and their comments during debriefing count against this criticism, as does the study by Sheridan and King (1972).

Ecological validity
Some psychologists have suggested that the experiment is an artificial test of obedience and therefore **lacks 'mundane realism'** or ecological validity. Milgram argues that while there are important differences between experimental and real life obedience, there is a fundamental similarity in the psychological processes at work – especially the process of agency.

The subjects were also American, male and volunteers – an unrepresentative sample that may have already been more obedient and helpful, but later studies have found similarly high rates of obedience using other samples and more everyday tasks and contexts (see replications and field studies of obedience). The methodology also caused numerous ethical problems (see ethics and obedience studies).

Studies of obedience

MILGRAM'S VARIATIONS ON THE BASIC STUDY

Milgram decided to conduct many **variations** of the study to determine the key factors that were responsible for the obedience (overall 636 subjects were tested during the 18 different variation studies). In the basic set-up of the experiment the subject received feedback reactions from the learner he was 'electrocuting' only by a thump on the wall at 300 volts followed by no further reply, but in a later condition vocal feedback was given (this was standardised by the use of a tape recording).
The table below shows some of the different variables that were carefully manipulated to see the effect on obedience (measured by the percentage that gave the maximum 450 volt shock).

Vocal feedback condition	
At **75 volts**	moans / groans.
At **150 volts**	requests to be excused from the experiment.
At **195 volts**	yelled "Let me out! My heart's bothering me."
At **285 volts**	agonised scream
At **300 volt**	kicked the wall and begged to be released.
At **315 volts**	no further responses.

65%	Remote – victim condition.	The victim in a separate room and no feedback until a bang on the wall at 300 volts. No subject stopped before 300 volts.
62.5%	Vocal – feedback condition.	With the verbal protestations, screams, wall pounding and ominous silence after 300 volts. Only a few stopped before 300 volts.
92.5%	Two teacher condition.	The subject was paired with another teacher (a confederate) who actually delivered the shocks while the subject only read out the words.
47.5%	Shift of setting condition.	The experiment was moved to a set of run down offices rather than the impressive Yale University.
40%	Proximity condition.	Learner moved into the same room so the teacher could see his agonised reactions .
30%	Touch proximity condition.	The teacher had to force the learner's hand down onto a shock plate when he refused to participate after 150 volts.
20%	Absent experimenter condition.	The experimenter has to leave and give instructions over the telephone. Many subjects cheated and missed out shocks or gave less voltage than ordered to.
10%	Social support condition.	Two other subjects (confederates) were also teachers but soon refused to obey. Most subjects stopped very soon after the others.

REPLICATIONS OF MILGRAM'S STUDY

Varying the subjects	**Gender** – women were found to show similar levels of obedience by Milgram, but other studies have found both lower levels (when asked to electrocute another woman) and higher levels (when asked to electrocute a puppy). **Nationality** – cross-cultural studies have found varying obedience levels - higher in Holland, Austria and Germany, but lower in Britain and Australia. The different procedures used in these studies make proper comparison difficult.
Varying the victim	**Gender** – a female victim has occasionally reduced obedience **Species** – Sheridan and King (1972) found 75% obedience when real electric shocks were used on puppies.
Varying the setting	See field experiments…

FIELD EXPERIMENTS ON OBEDIENCE

High levels of obedience have been shown many times under real life conditions.

Hofling et al (1966) investigated obedience in American hospitals. They found that 95.5% (21 out of 22) of the nurses tested obeyed an unknown doctor's telephone instructions to administer twice the maximum allowed dose of a drug (in fact a harmless placebo) that was clearly labelled with warnings against such an action and that was not on the ward stock list for the day. This was in contrast to 21 out of 22 nurses who replied that they would not have obeyed the doctor and broken the hospital regulations for medication when asked how they would have reacted in the same situation. This study was conducted under slightly unusual conditions however (although in a natural environment it still lacked ecological validity), and the results have not been replicated when the procedure was changed to make it more realistic, i.e. a drug known to the nurses, and with others around to consult.

Bickman (1974) investigated obedience on the streets of New York. He revealed that when an experimenter was dressed in a guard's uniform and told passers-by to pick up paper bags or give a coin to a stranger there was 80% obedience, compared to 40% when the experimenter was dressed more 'normally'. A milkman's uniform, however, did not have the same effect as the guard's on obedience.

Meeus and Raaijmakers (1986) investigated obedience in a business setting in Holland. They had an experimenter ask subjects to act as interviewers, supposedly in order to test the effects of stress on job applicants by delivering 15 increasingly distressing and insulting remarks to applicants (in fact confederates) at a time of high unemployment. 91.5% of their subjects obeyed the experimenter and made all 15 remarks despite the psychological distress shown by the applicants.

Explanations and ethics of obedience studies

EXPLANATIONS OF OBEDIENCE STUDIES

SOCIAL POWER EXPLANATIONS

THE IMPACT OF POWER - *Social impact theory* (Latane and Wolf) explains factors that affected obedience in Milgram's studies

1 The impact of the *experimenter's power on the subject* – The experimenter was close (immediacy of influence was high) and important (strength of influence was high) to the subject. When the experimenter gave instructions over the telephone obedience decreased (as immediacy decreased). When there were a number of (confederate) teachers who disobeyed in the social support condition, the subjects' obedience decreased as the experimenter's power and authority was spread amongst many teachers, having less impact on each one (diffusion of impact).

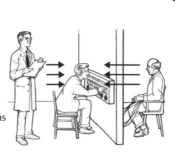

2 The impact of the *learner's distress on the subject* – The subject was not in close proximity to the learner (low immediacy of influence). When the consequences of the shocks were made more immediate (when the learner was brought into the same room) the impact of the learner's distress increased and obedience decreased. When there were two teachers, and the naive subject only had to read out the questions, he felt even less individually responsible for his actions (diffusion of impact) and obedience increased.

TYPES OF POWER USED

- The location of respectable Yale university added *legitimate power* to the situation (obedience decreased when the location changed).
- The experimenter represented scientific authority and possessed expert and legitimate power (obedience decreased when he was absent), especially with his grey laboratory coat which represents the power that uniform has in our society – see studies by Haney, Banks and Zimbardo (1973) and Bickman (1974).

MILGRAM'S AGENCY THEORY

- Milgram (1974) suggests that when faced with commands from legitimate authority figures we lose our sense of responsibility for our own actions and become the agents of others' wishes (the state of agency). Thus the high levels of obedience found in Milgram's studies resulted from the experimenter as the authority figure *taking responsibility* for the consequences of the obedience.
- According to Milgram (1974) agency involves a *cognitive shift in viewpoint* that results in people switching from their normal *autonomous state* (where they feel in control of, and responsible for, their actions) to the *agentic state* (where they regard themselves as "the instrument for carrying out another person's wishes").
- The purpose of the agentic state is to allow human hierarchical social systems to function properly – if people did not automatically yield to those of higher status then society would be disorganised and unable to achieve its collective goals efficiently (or at all) and disobedient, lower ranking individuals would constantly risk punishment from those above them in the hierarchy.
- Milgram proposed the agentic state was a product of evolution and pointed out that we grow up in a society where we constantly submit to those in authority from the moment we are born, e.g. to parents, teachers and employers.
- The agentic state can account for the horrific acts committed in the name of obedience – for example soldiers who have committed atrocities arguing they were only following orders and were not responsible for their actions.

EVALUATION OF THE ETHICS OF OBEDIENCE STUDIES

MILGRAM
Against the study
Baumrind (1964) criticised the study as being unethical since:
a It caused distress to the subjects. One had a violent seizure and all of the subjects could have suffered psychological damage, e.g. guilt or loss of self-esteem.
b Milgram deceived the subjects as to the true nature of the experiment, and therefore did not receive their informed consent.
c Milgram's study abused the right of subjects to withdraw from a psychology study – those wishing to leave were told to continue.

For the study
Milgram defended himself on ethical grounds by pointing out:
a The methodology was not unethical since the results obtained were completely unexpected, and although the subjects appeared uncomfortable with their obedience, Milgram concluded "momentary excitement is not the same as harm".
b Subjects could have left, they were not physically restrained. Indeed Milgram designed many variations to increase refusal/disobedience.
c All subjects were fully debriefed and reassured. They were shown that the learner was completely unharmed and had not received any shocks. A follow up opinion survey conducted a year later found that 84% were "glad to have been in the experiment", 15% were neutral, and only 1.3% were "sorry or very sorry to have been in the experiment". Around 80% of the respondents said there should be more experiments like Milgram's conducted, and about 75% said they had learnt something of personal value from their experience. The subjects were also examined by a psychiatrist one year after the study who found no signs of harm.

OTHER OBEDIENCE STUDIES
In a similar way to Milgram's studies virtually every later study of obedience has broken some ethical guidelines, ranging from deception and lack of fully informed consent over the true nature of the experiment to causing psychological distress, embarrassment and even physical harm to animals (the real electric shocks given to Sheridan and King's puppy).

Resisting influence

EXAMPLES OF RESISTING SOCIAL INFLUENCE

- **Independence in conformity and obedience experiments** – Although disobedience in Milgram's (1963) experiment was low (35% refused to give the maximum shock), Asch's (1951) conformity experiment showed higher rates of resistance (26% did not conform at all and all 50 were resistant at least once in the original test). Resistance was significantly increased by having social support – just one ally in Asch's study lowered conformity from an average of 32% to 5%, two other teachers disobeying in Milgram's study lowered obedience to 10%.
- **Rebellion** – Gamson et al (1982) found 97% of groups showed dissent and 50% completely rebelled to unfair requests from authority figures – probably because groups provide a greater opportunity for dissent to be expressed and discussed, and social support to justify and implement rebellion. However, although resisting authority, many participants were just *conforming* to others in the group who were rebelling.

TYPES OF RESISTANCE

Independent behaviour – involves the true rejection of social influence to behave in accord with one's own internal attitudes, regardless of whether they coincide with the influencer's.

Anti-conformity – involves resisting social influence by deliberately opposing the majority and refusing to behave like them. This behaviour is still affected by society however.

REASONS FOR RESISTING SOCIAL INFLUENCE

- **Group identity** – Different social groups have different goals and so may not want to follow other group norms.
- **Psychological reactance** – Brehm (1966) argued that perceived constraints on freedom lead some to resist in order to assert their freedom - telling people they are not allowed to do something is often a good way of getting them to do it!
- **Socialisation** – Individual experience and the society that one is raised in can affect the level of independence. Berry (1966, 1967) discovered that Eskimos, who live in an individualistic hunting society where self reliance is highly valued, showed more independent behaviour than members of the Temmi of Africa whose collectivist agricultural society is more dependent upon co-operation, agreement and conformity.

MINORITY INFLUENCE

At times minority groups may not only resist, but actually influence majority groups in society. Throughout history minorities (often defined in terms of political power rather than just number) such as scientific, religious, women's and black rights groups have changed the majority viewpoint (Kuhn called this a 'paradigm shift'). In fact, without minorities to introduce change and innovation, conformity to the majority status quo would stagnate progress in society.

STUDIES OF MINORITY INFLUENCE

Moscovici et al (1969) tested subjects in groups of 6 on their ability to judge the colour of 36 blue slides of varying brightness. Unknown to the rest of the subjects, 2 in each group were confederates who acted as a minority group. They found that when the minority:
1 *Consistently* judged the slides to be green rather than blue, the majority followed them on 8.42% of trials
2 *Inconsistently* judged the slides to be green rather than blue (on 2 in every 3 trials), the majority followed them on only 1.25% of trials
Furthermore, in later individual tests the subjects exposed to the minority were more likely (than control groups with no minority) to report ambiguous green/blue slides as green, *especially* if they had previously resisted the minority view, indicating a longer term influence.

- Nemeth et al (1974) replicated Moscovici et al's study but had their 2 confederates:
1 Randomly say green on half the trials and green/blue on the other half. This caused no minority influence because of the inconsistency.
2 Consistently say green or green/blue depending on the brightness of the slides. This consistency led to 21% minority influence.
3 Say green on every trial. This consistency caused no minority influence, perhaps because it was seen as being rigid and unrealistic.

- Maass and Clark (1983) studied majority and minority influence on attitudes to gay rights. Regardless of whether the majority view was for or against gay rights they found that their subjects' publicly expressed views followed the majority but their privately expressed views shifted towards the minority viewpoint. This indicates minorities cause a change in private opinions / attitudes *before* a change in public behaviour.

THEORIES OF MINORITY INFLUENCE

Dual Process theory – Moscovici (1980) argued that since minorities do not have the informational and normative influence of the majority (in fact they are often ridiculed by them), they must exert their influence through their *behavioural style – how* they express their views. *Consistency* of viewpoint, both over time and between members of the minority group, is the most important aspect of this style since this not only draws attention to the minority view and gives the impression of certainty and coherence, but also causes doubt about majority norms. Other important features of behavioural style are *investment* (the minority has made sacrifices for the view), *autonomy* (the view is made on principle without ulterior motives) and *flexibility* (the consistent viewpoint must not be seen as too rigid and dogmatic).
This behavioural style means that minorities and majorities exert their influence through 2 different processes (thus *dual* process theory)
- Majorities influence minorities quickly through *compliance* (the minority often changes their public behaviour but not private opinions)
- Minorities influence majorities more slowly through *conversion* (the majority gradually change their private opinions before their public behaviour). This conversion will hopefully lead to majority internalisation (both public and private acceptance of the minority view).
Moscovici argues that conversion occurs because minority views encourage *cognitive conflict* and therefore greater processing in the long term which may cause the restructuring of the majority group's attitudes.
Attribution theory – e.g. Kelley (1967) suggests consistency encourages the attribution of minority behaviour to internal causes (i.e. real belief) rather than situational ones (i.e. just a social fad).
Social Identity Theory - suggests opinion change is more likely if in-group rather than out-group members express the minority views.
Social impact theory – suggests minority views have increasing impact when high profile (greater immediacy) and when advanced by many people (increasing number of influencers) of higher status (increasing strength of influence).

Contemporary issue – Is hypnosis just role-playing?

WHAT IS THE TRADITIONAL VIEW OF HYPNOSIS?

Hypnosis has long fascinated both psychologists and the general public because of the dramatic changes in behaviour it produces. Hypnotised subjects can apparently experience the world in a different way - showing distortions of perception like tasting an onion as an apple or smelling ammonia as water and even hallucinations, such as seeing things that are not there or not seeing things that are. In addition they seem able to perform behaviours that they would not normally be willing or able to do – such as controlling severe pain, showing increased strength, retrieving forgotten memories or acting like a chicken.

The traditional view of hypnosis is known as the altered state or special process approach to hypnosis, which proposes that:

1 Hypnosis represents an altered state of consciousness, distinct from both waking and sleep states. Hilgard proposes the neo-dissociation theory, which suggests that hypnosis divides consciousness into separate channels of awareness.
2 Hypnosis is a special state since phenomena can be produced during it (like pain resistance) that cannot be shown under normal conditions.

SOCIAL INFLUENCE AND HYPNOSIS

In contrast to the traditional altered state view of hypnosis, some social psychologists support the non-state or social psychological approach to hypnosis, which argues that:

1 Hypnosis is really only a form of social influence, **not** an altered state.
2 All phenomena produced under hypnosis can be produced without it (by people motivated to simulate hypnosis).

It has therefore been suggested that the following social psychological concepts and research can account for the behaviour and experiences produced under hypnosis, without the need for a special state or division of consciousness:

CONFORMITY AND ROLE PLAYING

- Social psychologists suggest that people play a variety of *roles* in society (e.g. son, brother, student, football supporter, shop assistant etc.) and each role has a different set of *norms* (expected ways of behaving) that are *conformed* to in each role. We readily shift from one role to the next depending upon the social context and may thus behave very differently in various situations (we may not behave the same way at home as at work or at a football match). People are very aware of how those who are 'hypnotised' behave and may therefore, deliberately or not, conform to the norms of the role of 'hypnotised subject' in situations where it is expected. One could compare such behaviour to *demand characteristics* in research situations. Pressure to conform to the hypnotic role and its norms is often increased by the presence of people other than the hypnotist, such as audiences at hypnosis stage shows – where especially dramatic behaviour may be expected.
- Conformity could occur for two main reasons which might produce different kinds of role playing:
1 **Normative social influence** – not following suggestions in hypnotic situations is potentially very embarrassing, which may lead people to behave as expected but not believe they are really hypnotised (a kind of conformity known as compliance).
2 **Informational social influence** – people being hypnotised want to understand or justify what happens to them when hypnotised but may be uncertain as to how else to do so other than accept the traditional and socially accepted view that being in an altered state enables you to perform in extraordinary ways without being able to refuse. This may lead them to behave as expected, even if they do not want to, and really believe they are hypnotised (a kind of conformity known as internalisation).

OBEDIENCE TO AUTHORITY

- Studies of obedience such as Milgram's have consistently shown that we should not underestimate the ability of (non-hypnotised) people to follow the commands of an authority figure, even if reluctant to do, especially if close in proximity to them. It can be argued that the hypnotist is essentially an authority figure whose suggestions are obeyed and whose influence works at close proximity.
- Hypnotists who are perceived as legitimate and credible authority figures can thus produce extreme behaviour in their subjects through mere obedience since, by the very nature of the hypnotic situation, they take all responsibility for the actions produced. According to Milgram this causes a state of 'agency' which reduces the 'hypnotised' person's inhibitions. At the same time an increase in motivation may result from a fear of embarrassment or punishment if they disobey commands.

EVALUATION – Social psychologists who argue that social influence can account for hypnotic phenomena provide support for their view by either criticising altered state research or showing that motivated people can simulate (pretend) the same phenomena without hypnosis.

- *'Lie' detecting* – Coe and Yashinski (1985) found that people with post hypnotic amnesia increase their recall if led to believe that a lie detector test will find out if they are lying. Pattie (1937) showed that hypnotised subjects given the suggestion that they could not feel anything in one hand reported sensations administered to the fingers of both their hands if they were inter-linked (making it difficult to tell which was which). Subjects under the hypnotic suggestion of deafness have failed delayed auditory feedback tests that real deaf people pass. This suggests that the subjects were merely behaving *as if* they were hypnotised.
- *Physiological evidence* – Altered state researchers have found differences in brain activity levels between low and highly susceptible subjects when hypnosis is attempted. However critics suggest this finding may just reflect a state of relaxation rather than hypnotic trance.
- *Task performance* – Motivated simulators have performed many tasks in the same way as hypnotised subjects, e.g. eating onions while pretending they are apples or following an instruction to throw 'acid' at another person. Barber and Hahn showed that motivated subjects could reduce their experience of cold pressor pain (caused by immersing the hand in icy water) to a similar degree to hypnotised subjects. However, Orne et al (1968) found that hypnotised subjects responded to a suggestion to touch their forehead (when they heard the word 'experiment' mentioned throughout a 2 day period) more often than simulators. Colman (1987) argues that the fact that simulators can imitate many aspects of the hypnotic state does not mean that the state does not exist.
- *Trance logic* – Trance logic refers to the ability of hypnotised subjects to tolerate logical inconsistency. Orne showed hypnotised subjects can hallucinate a transparent image of a person sitting in a chair, even if that person was also seen standing next to them, without being perturbed by the inconsistency. Simulators asked to fake this hypnotic situation often do not behave in the same way.

Theories of attribution

WHAT IS ATTRIBUTION?
Social psychologists who have investigated social cognition (how we understand and think about people and social situations) have pointed out that people do not just passively observe their own and others' actions, but try to work out or explain what caused them. Attribution refers to the process of deciding what caused behaviour – whether:

1 the person performing the actions was responsible (an **internal / dispositional attribution** where the cause seems due to some aspect of the individual, i.e. their personality, ability, mood, etc.) or
2 the social situation and circumstances they were experiencing were responsible (an **external / situational attribution** where the cause seems due to some external influence, i.e. environmental factors, other people, chance, etc.).

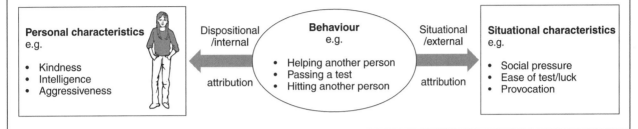

Personal characteristics e.g.
- Kindness
- Intelligence
- Aggressiveness

Dispositional /internal attribution

Behaviour e.g.
- Helping another person
- Passing a test
- Hitting another person

Situational /external attribution

Situational characteristics e.g.
- Social pressure
- Ease of test/luck
- Provocation

THEORIES OF HOW ATTRIBUTIONS ARE MADE

CORRESPONDENT INFERENCE THEORY
Jones and Davis (1965), Jones and McGillis (1976)

Correspondent inference theory **explains dispositional attributions** by suggesting that people attempt to find a *match* (correspondence) *between* the *behaviour* they observe and *underlying stable qualities in the person* that produced it. Internal, dispositional inferences are made in two main stages:

1 **Attributing intention** – did the person/actor deliberately mean to perform the behaviour or was it an accident? This is decided by whether the actor:
- *knew the effects* their actions would have
- *had the ability* to perform those actions.
2 **Attributing disposition** – this is achieved by assessing, for example, the:
- *non-common effects* of the behaviour – actions that have non-common (unusual) effects are seen as more likely to reflect individual dispositions than behaviour that produces common effects.
- *social desirability* of the behaviour – the more socially *undesirable* a behaviour is perceived as being, the more likely it is to be attributed to dispositional causes.

Evaluation
- Jones, Davis and Gergen (1961) found participants rated taped applicants' statements for the job of an astronaut or submariner more dispositionally (greater correspondent inference) when they were inconsistent with expectations (i.e. claiming they were 'inner-directed' when required to relate well to others in the enclosed confines of a submarine).
- Jones and Harris (1967) found more dispositional inferences were made in the USA for students who freely chose to deliver unpopular speeches (e.g. supporting Fidel Castro).
- Correspondent inference theory emphasised the idea that attribution may be *biased* towards dispositional causes (due to factors like hedonic relevance). This was supported by later research on attributional bias.
- The theory focuses on the *social comparison* of the individual's behaviour with that of others, looking for *unexpected* variations. It ignores, however, comparison with the individual's own *past behaviour* and the fact that behaviour that *fulfils expectations* or stereotypes is also useful in the attribution of causes. *Unintentional* behaviour is important for dispositional attribution too, e.g. clumsy actions.

KELLEY'S CO-VARIATION MODEL
Kelley (1967, 1972)

The co-variation model explains how **dispositional** or **situational attributions** are made of *people we know*, based upon our past knowledge of their behaviour and that of others. Attributions are made based on how the following sources of information co-vary with each other:

1 **Consensus** – concerns variation across people and refers to the extent to which *other people* behave in the same way to the same stimuli as the known person.
2 **Consistency** – concerns variation across time and refers to the extent to which the known person has behaved in the same way to the same stimuli on *past occasions*.
3 **Distinctiveness** – concerns variation across stimuli and refers to the extent to which the known person behaves in the same way to *different* (but perhaps similar) *stimuli*.

	Type of attribution		
	Dispositional	**Situational**	
Consensus	*LOW*	*HIGH*	*LOW*
Consistency	*HIGH*	*HIGH*	*LOW*
Distinctiveness	*LOW*	*HIGH*	*HIGH*

Evaluation
- McArthur (1972) gave participants descriptions like 'John laughed at the comedian' with different combinations of consensus, consistency and distinctiveness information, and found they generally attributed as the model predicted (apart from a tendency to prefer dispositional attributions and use less consensus information).
- Alloy and Tabachnik (1984) concluded that people find working out the co-variations difficult. Given that humans are usually cognitive misers (preferring to use the least mental effort possible), researchers like Hilton and Slugoski (1986) with their Abnormal Conditions Focus Model suggest mental 'shortcuts' are taken – only certain types of information are preferred for certain attributions (e.g. using just low consensus for internal attributions).
- People may often lack knowledge about others' behaviour and thus consensus, consistency and distinctiveness information. Under these conditions Kelley (1972) suggests we use causal schemata such as multiple sufficient causes, discounting and augmentation principles.

Bias in attribution

WHAT IS ATTRIBUTION BIAS?

Social psychologists have found that attributional decisions about one's own and others' behaviour are not always made in a logical and objective manner (as some 'normative' theories of attribution suggest) but may become distorted or biased since:

1 People are 'cognitive misers' – we do not wish to spend more mental effort than necessary and so may not examine all the attributional evidence available or may simply take mental short cuts to reach quick conclusions.
2 The information available may be insufficient or be received in ways that highlight some aspects more than others, e.g. due to viewpoint, salience or importance.
3 The information may be used in ways that maximise its use to us, e.g. for predicting future behaviour or maintaining our self-esteem.

FUNDAMENTAL ATTRIBUTION ERROR

What is it?

The fundamental attribution error (Ross, 1977) is the general *tendency* people have *to make internal, dispositional attributions* for *others' behaviour* rather than external, situational ones, when there may be equally convincing evidence for both types of cause. The fundamental attribution error (FAE) tendency to attribute dispositionally and hold the person and their characteristics responsible for behaviour increases with the *seriousness of the consequences* of the behaviour and its *personal (hedonic) relevance* to us.

Why does it occur?

Focus of attention – observers are more likely to notice the actor and their behaviour than the situation and more diffuse circumstances influencing behaviour.

Predictability of behaviour – attributions to personal, stable characteristics rather than changeable situational ones fulfil the observer's need to be able to predict and control the world.

Linguistic ease – the English language makes it easier to describe actors and their actions in the same way (e.g. we talk of 'aggressive' behaviour resulting from an 'aggressive' *person* rather than *situation*), thus facilitating the attributional link between them (Nisbett and Ross, 1980).

Evaluation

- Ross et al (1977) randomly assigned college students to be either 'questioners' (to invent and ask challenging questions based on their own expertise) or 'answerers' in a quiz. They found that the 'questioners' were rated as having better general knowledge ability (despite not actually answering any questions themselves!) than the 'answerers', by both the 'answerers' and observers of the quiz (but not themselves). This dispositional attribution ignored the 'questioners' situation of being able to create the questions and supports the FAE since later tests given by the researchers found no difference in general knowledge between the 'questioners' and 'answerers'.
- The FAE explains attributions in other studies, e.g. the tendency of observers of the Milgram experiment to attribute the potentially serious consequences of the participants' obedience to personal characteristics rather than social pressure (Bierbrauer, 1979).
- However, the FAE may not be as fundamental a tendency as first thought, Miller (1984) found cross-cultural variations in attributional tendencies with Indian-Hindus tending to prefer situational attributions to a greater degree than Americans.
- The FAE ignores attributions made by the actor about their own behaviour.

ACTOR-OBSERVER EFFECT

The actor-observer effect (Jones and Nisbett, 1972) refers to the tendency of people to attribute internal / dispositional causes when observing others' behaviour (as in the fundamental attribution error), but *attribute external / situational causes to their own behaviour* (when they are the actors).

Why does it occur?

Focus of attention – observers are more likely to notice the actor and their behaviour, while actors look out at, and therefore focus more on, factors in the environment.

Access to information – actors have more knowledge of intention and past behaviour (consistency information) than observers who therefore rely more on the FAE.

Evaluation

- Nisbett et al (1973) found that male college students were more likely to *attribute* their *own choice* of girlfriend and major study subject *to external factors* (e.g. she is a relaxing person, chemistry is a high paying field), but their *best friend's choices* to *dispositional factors* (e.g. needing someone to relax with, wanting to make a lot of money).
- Storms (1973) got actors to make more dispositional attributions by showing them videotapes of their behaviour, thus refocusing their attention as observers on to themselves.
- The actor–observer effect tends to focus on cognitive rather than motivational factors and so does not take into account whether the behaviour to be attributed was successful or not.

SELF-SERVING BIAS

The self-serving bias effect (Miller and Ross, 1975) refers to the tendency of *actors* to *attribute successful behaviour to dispositional causes*, but *unsuccessful behaviour to situational ones*, thus qualifying the actor–observer effect. The self-serving bias can lead to self-handicapping behaviour.

Why does it occur?

Motivational factors – Miller (1978) suggested that attribution is used to maintain self-esteem and for impression management of esteem in the eyes of others. Dispositional attributions of successful behaviour provide self-enhancement, situational attributions of unsuccessful behaviour provide self-protection.

Cognitive factors – since people usually expect to succeed based on their own abilities, unexpected/unintended failure is perceived as due to external factors.

Evaluation

- Kingdon (1967) interviewed successful and unsuccessful politicians and found that they tended to attribute their successes to dispositional factors, e.g. hard work and their reputation, and their defeats to external factors, e.g. national trends and lack of campaign money.
- Johnson et al (1964) found that students asked to teach other pupils attributed responsibility for increased performance to their teaching, but decreased performance to the student. However, this effect has not always been found with experienced teachers (e.g. Ross et al, 1974).
- Cross-cultural differences have been found, with more self-effacing and modest participants from China and Japan showing less self-serving bias than American participants.

Social perception

WHAT ARE THE SOCIAL AND CULTURAL INFLUENCES UPON THE PERCEPTION OF THE SOCIAL WORLD?
The influences come from *social and cultural knowledge and beliefs* that form the *content* of, for example, stereotypes and social representations.

STEREOTYPES

Stereotypes reflect *fairly precise categories* of social or cultural 'knowledge' and refer to mental representations of *particular shared beliefs* about the characteristics (e.g. personality traits and behaviour) of a group and its members.
The contents of these shared beliefs are:
- over-simplified and over-generalised
- variable across cultures – different cultures may possess different stereotypes
- fairly slow to change within a culture – as shown by the studies of Katz and Braly (1933) and Karlins et al (1969).

The contents may be based on:
- a grain of truth (based on limited experience)
- *illusory correlation* (a false impression due to an unusual and thus distinctive association between group members and a characteristic)
- false propaganda (due to political or inter-group motives and justifications).

SOCIAL REPRESENTATIONS

Social representations reflect *many different kinds* of social and cultural knowledge, and refer to *general shared beliefs* relating, for example, to ideas, objects, attitudes and people. Moscovici (1981) defines social representations as:
'a set of concepts, statements and explanations originating in life in the course of inter-individual communications. They are the equivalent, in our society, of the myths and belief systems in traditional societies; they might even be said to be the contemporary version of common sense.'
They are *consensual* (agreed upon) *understandings shared by group members* that:
- constantly change with the introduction of new ideas
- differ across different cultures and sub-cultures (who may develop their own shared representations).

HOW IS THE PERCEPTION OF THE SOCIAL WORLD INFLUENCED?
This refers to the *processes* involved in *using* social and cultural knowledge and the *consequent effects* of doing so.

THE PROCESS AND EFFECTS OF STEREOTYPING

Stereotyping involves the:
- allocation or categorisation of an individual to a group based on some observable cue (e.g. skin colour, clothing, accent, etc.).
- assumption that all members of the group share the same characteristics.
- assumption that the allocated individual also possesses those characteristics.

Stereotyping may influence the perception of the social world by causing:
- unfair *prejudgement* and allocation of characteristics to individuals that may not be true of them.
- *confirmatory bias* – the selective allocation of attention towards, and memory of, information that confirms the stereotype.
- *exaggeration* of perceived similarities within groups and differences between groups.
- *justification* of discriminatory behaviour towards stereotyped groups, based on the assessment of their supposed characteristics.

THE PROCESS AND EFFECTS OF FORMING SOCIAL REPRESENTATIONS

Social representations are formed by:
- the introduction of new and often complicated theories or concepts by specialists (through the mass media)
- everyday *informal communication* and discussion that popularises, simplifies and often distorts the ideas.
- the *anchoring* of new ideas by relating them to pre-existing social representational ideas.
- *objectifying* (simplifying the representation of ideas by making them more concrete) through *personification* – using the inventor to stand for the invention, e.g. 'Thatcherism', and *figuration* – using images to illustrate concepts, e.g. the 'world-wide-web'.

Social representations may influence the perception of the social world by:
- helping the individual *make sense of the world* by making the unfamiliar familiar.
- *shaping* an individual's *perception* of, and *reaction* towards, events and stimuli. Since people's beliefs are socially constructed, their attitudes will often reflect those of others in their culture.

Social theories of prejudice - social group explanations

STEREOTYPING

- As Pennington (1986) notes, stereotyping involves
  - a **categorising** people into groups based on visible **cues**, such as gender, nationality, race, religion, bodily appearance, etc.
  - b assuming **all** members of a group share the **same characteristics**.
  - c **assigning individuals to these groups** and presuming they possess the same characteristics based on little information other than their possession of the noticeable trait or cue.
- While stereotyping is an **in-built cognitive process**, it is important to realise that the **cues** seen as important to categorise (e.g. gender, skin colour, religion, etc.) and the **content** of the stereotype itself (e.g. personality traits) are not fixed, but historically determined and **changeable** over time.
- Stereotypes serve to **exaggerate** the **similarities within groups** ('those people are all the same') and exaggerate the **differences between groups** ('they are not like us').
- Stereotyping, therefore, literally involves **pre-judging** an individual, and, although it serves the important **functions** of categorising and generalising knowledge, it can lead to **unrealistic perceptions**, and **inter-group hostility**.

Evidence
- Karlins et al (1969) showed how the content of stereotypes concerning 'Americans' and 'Jews' changed over a 40 year period – the former seeming to become more 'materialistic' and the latter appearing to be less 'mercenary', for example.
- Many studies have shown how stereotyping can lead to prejudice, e.g. Buckhout (1974) and Duncan (1976).

Evaluation
- McCauley & Stitt (1978) propose that stereotypes are now best regarded as **probabilistic beliefs**. People are asked to estimate what percentage of a group would possess certain characteristics, and this is compared to the estimate for people in general, to arrive at a diagnostic ratio.
- Although the contents of stereotypes are usually derogatory, and stereotyping accounts for the **thinking** in prejudice, it does **not** explain the **strong negative emotions** nor all the discriminatory **behaviour** shown in society.

INTERGROUP CONFLICT THEORY

- According to Sherif, the prejudice in society is caused by:
  - a The existence of groups
  - b **Competition** between those groups
- Conflict exists between groups because each group will struggle to obtain limited resources. Sherif argued that competition will always provoke prejudice, and conducted a field study to investigate this idea.

Evidence
- Sherif et al (1961) conducted a field study in Robbers' Cave State Park in America. Two groups of 11 boys were created and a tournament was set up between them that was sufficient to produce fighting and name calling.
- The basis of many wars has been resource competition.

Evaluation
- Tyerman and Spencer's (1983) study on groups of boy scouts showed that competition is not always sufficient to cause conflict and discrimination.
- Sherif's study was ethically dubious given that its goal was to deliberately create prejudice and fighting over penknives was involved.

THE PROCESS OF STEREOTYPING

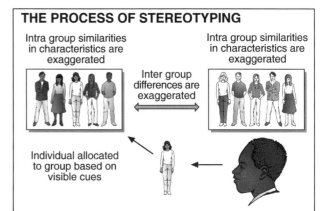

Intra group similarities in characteristics are exaggerated

Intra group similarities in characteristics are exaggerated

Inter group differences are exaggerated

Individual allocated to group based on visible cues

MINIMAL GROUP THEORY

- Minimal group theory suggests that merely dividing people into groups is sufficient to cause prejudice to occur between them. Tajfel and Turner (1979) explain this phenomena in terms of their social identity theory (SIT), which proposes that
  - a people allocate themselves to groups and gain their identity from those groups
  - b people need to feel good about themselves and, therefore, seek positive self-esteem
  - c people will want to feel they are in the best group and will, therefore, act to make it so, even if that means putting other groups down

Evidence
- Tajfel et al (1971) conducted a study on Bristol schoolboys, who they assigned to meaningless groups, in some cases completely randomly by the toss of a coin. Tajfel found that the individual members would not only allocate more points to their own group members but would often maximise the difference between the groups - even if it meant their own group receiving fewer points overall.

Evaluation
- Tajfel's results have received cross-cultural confirmation, but his experiments have been accused of artificiality and demand characteristics. The study may only reflect the norms of competition found in many societies – co-operative societies may not show the minimal group effect (Wetherall, 1982).

SCAPEGOATING THEORY

- Scapegoating theory has its roots in Dollard et al's frustration-aggression theory, which argues that socially **frustrating conditions** such as economic depression and unemployment **leads to aggression**.
- According to the theory, this aggression needs to be **displaced** and **blame** allocated, so a **scapegoat** is found – usually a **minority** 'out-group' which is in a less powerful position to defend itself.

Evidence
- Weatherley (1961) found that anti-Semitic subjects (those prejudiced against Jews), who were frustrated by being insulted, were later more aggressive in their descriptions of people with Jewish sounding names. However, it should be noted that verbal prejudice does not always show itself in discriminatory behaviour as LaPiere (1934) found.
- The scapegoating of minorities in times of economic hardship has been historically documented world-wide.

Evaluation
- This theory links well with intergroup conflict theory by elaborating on another effect of competition, the frustration it can provoke.
- The theory accounts for the fluctuations of prejudice and discrimination over time, reflecting changing economic conditions.

'Experiments in intergroup discrimination' Tajfel (1970)

AIM

To illustrate a fundamental cause of intergroup discrimination – the mere categorisation of people into groups. Tajfel proposed that because of the frequent competitive behaviour shown by groups in our society, individuals do **not** just learn to conform to **specific** prejudices, but learn a **general** tendency (a '**generic norm**') to categorise people into ingroups and outgroups ('us' versus 'them') and to act in favour of their own ingroups. This generic norm of discriminating against the outgroup soon comes to operate automatically in any group situation, **without**

- any individual interest reasons for the discrimination
- any previous attitudes of hostility or dislike towards the outgroup
- any need for negative attitudes to develop before the discrimination occurs

Tajfel aimed to support the above theory that people will automatically discriminate without any prior prejudice merely by being put into groups, by testing the effect of categorisation on children's behaviour without the effect of any pre-existing attitudes or self interest.

EXPERIMENT ONE
METHOD

Subjects: sixty-four, 14 and 15 year old schoolboys, previously acquainted with each other, tested in groups of eight at a time.

Procedure: All subjects took part in a study that they were told tested visual judgement, involving estimating the number of dots on a screen. The boys were then informed that they would be divided into groups such as 'over-estimators' or 'under-estimators' (supposedly based on their performance, but in fact at random) and were asked to participate in a task where they had to allocate reward and penalty points (that would later be translated into real money at a rate of 1 tenth of a penny per point) to other boys.

Each boy was then individually told which group they were in and tested in isolation from the others. Each received a booklet of matrices that showed how they could allocate different combinations of rewards and penalties to boys from the groups, but it was made clear that

- they would **not know** the **identities** of the boys they were allocating points to, **only** whether they were members of the **same group** as themselves (ingroup) or of the **other group** (outgroup)
- they would **never** be **allocating** points **to themselves** – their points would be determined by the actions of every other boy in the same way

Each matrix consisted of 14 combinations of rewards or penalties, with the top and bottom row points always going to the member of one of the groups. Six types of matrix, with differing combinations of rewards and penalties, were each presented with three different group choices, e.g.

1 Between **two ingroup** members:

Rewards for member 36 of 'overestimators'	1	2	3	4	5	6	7	8	9	10	11	12	13	14	Choice	8
Rewards for member 23 of 'overestimators'	14	13	12	11	10	9	8	7	6	5	4	3	2	1	example	7

2 Between **two outgroup** members:

Rewards for member 42 of 'underestimators'	1	2	3	4	5	6	7	8	9	10	11	12	13	14	Choice	7
Rewards for member 15 of 'underestimators'	14	13	12	11	10	9	8	7	6	5	4	3	2	1	example	8

3 Between an **ingroup** and an **outgroup** member:

Rewards for member 36 of 'overestimators'	1	2	3	4	5	6	7	8	9	10	11	12	13	14	Choice	14
Rewards for member 42 of 'underestimators'	14	13	12	11	10	9	8	7	6	5	4	3	2	1	example	1

In each matrix, subjects had to choose just one of the two point combinations for the group members (typical example choices are shown above).

RESULTS

Subjects could adopt one of three strategies: maximum ingroup profit, maximum fairness, or maximum generosity to outgroup. It was found that

- in choices between two ingroup members, or two outgroup members, the strategy of maximum fairness was usually adopted, but
- in choices between a member of the ingroup and outgroup a strategy nearer maximum ingroup profit was significantly shown.

EXPERIMENT TWO
METHOD

Subjects: forty-eight, 14 and 15 year old schoolboys, previously acquainted with each other, tested in three groups of sixteen at a time.

Procedure: Subjects were again randomly divided into two groups, supposedly based upon their preferences for the paintings of Klee and Kandinsky, and were given new matrices consisting of 13 combinations of rewards or penalties to further test ingroup favouritism choices.

Between an **ingroup** and **outgroup** member:

Rewards for member 17 of 'Klee group'	7	8	9	10	11	12	13	14	15	16	17	18	19	Choice	19	19	7
Rewards for member 25 of 'Kandinsky group'	1	3	5	7	9	11	13	15	17	19	21	23	25	example	25	25	1

RESULTS

Subjects could adopt one of three intergroup strategies: maximum ingroup profit, maximum joint profit, or maximum difference in favour of the ingroup. Subjects significantly tended to adopt the strategy of **maximum difference in favour of the ingroup** e.g. 7 / 1 at the expense of maximum ingroup profit, e.g. 19 / 25

EVALUATION

Methodological:
Artificiality – Groups are rarely meaningless.

Theoretical: The research opposes previous beliefs that competition was necessary and sufficient to produce prejudice.

Links: Prejudice. Self identity and self-esteem

Key application – The reduction of prejudice

METHOD OF REDUCTION	EXAMPLES	EVALUATION

EDUCATION

Educating children with notions of tolerance and providing them with an insight into the causes and effects of prejudice can help reduce prejudice and discrimination according to a number of theories. **Conformity to norms theory** would argue that education is necessary to prevent a 'non-conscious ideology' forming in communities where prejudice is so accepted it becomes an unquestioned norm.

Social learning theory suggests prejudice should be seen to be punished and tolerance rewarded if imitation in children is to be produced.

EXAMPLES

Jane Elliot conducted the 'blue eyes-brown eyes' study on her classes to teach them what it felt like to be the victim of prejudice (just based on eye colour). Interviews with the children as adults revealed that the study had inoculated them against discriminatory behaviour.

Public campaigns by minority groups, such as the 'Black is Beautiful' movement, had lasting effects on public awareness of racial issues in the USA.

EVALUATION

Education can reduce prejudice if it is carried out at a social level and is seen to be unacceptable by the majority in society.

Education has its greatest effect on the young. If adults 'are compelled to listen to information uncongenial to their deep-seated attitudes, they will reject it, distort it, or ignore it' (Aronson, 1992).

EQUAL STATUS CONTACT

Meeting members of other social groups can reduce prejudice by reducing **the effect of stereotypes**. This occurs as
- intergroup similarities are perceived (they are like us)
- outgroup differences are noted (they are not all the same)

Contact only changes group stereotypes if
- it is between individuals of equal status
- individuals are seen as representative of their group

EXAMPLES

Racial de-segregation studies have had some success.

Deutsch and Collins (1951) – found desegregated public housing increased inter-racial 'neighbourly activities' which were shown by 39% and 72% of the white housewives in the two desegregated housing projects but by only 1% and 4% of those in the two segregated projects. There was evidence that racial group perceptions changed dramatically for some, as one white housewife commented 'I started to cry when my husband told me we were coming to live here. I cried for three weeks... Well all that's changed... I see that they're just as human as we are... I've come to like them a great deal'.

Star et al (in Stouffer et al, 1949) found that 93% of white officers and 60% of enlisted men reported getting along 'very well' with the black troops they were fighting with in World War Two (everyone else said 'fairly well').

EVALUATION

Sherif, in the Robber's Cave study, found inter-group contact alone was insufficient to reduce prejudice between competing groups.

Equal status contact only acts to reduce prejudice at an interpersonal level and does not counter the prejudice of group stereotypes (individuals are seen as 'exceptions to the rule'), if inequality at a social level makes true equal status contact impossible.

Stephan (1978) reviewed desegregation studies and found no significant reduction in prejudice or increase in black children's self esteem (but see Hraba and Grant, 1970).

Star et al's study revealed that improved racial relationships in desegregated troops were not always generalised to interactions outside of fighting conditions, for example one white soldier commented 'they fought and I think more of them for it, but I still don't want to soldier with them in garrison'.

SUPER-ORDINATE GOALS

Star et al concluded that 'efforts at integration of white and coloured troops into the same units may well be more successful when attention is focused on concrete tasks or goals requiring common effort'. Making groups work together to achieve 'super-ordinate goals' (goals that cannot be achieved by groups working separately) is likely to reduce prejudice according to
- **intergroup conflict theory** – super-ordinate goals reduce the competition that causes prejudice.
- **social identity theory** – working together may merge 'in' and 'out' groups to one whole in-group identity.

EXAMPLES

Sherif et al (1961) significantly reduced intergroup hostility between two groups of children, the 'Eagles' and the 'Rattlers', by providing 'super-ordinate goals' in the last phase of their 'Robber's Cave' experiment.

Aronson et al (1978) used the 'jigsaw technique' with mixed race classroom groups. Each child received a part of the whole assignment and was dependent on the other children in the group to perform well in it. Inter-racial liking and the performance of ethnic minorities was increased.

EVALUATION

Inter-personal liking in these studies is not always generalised to social groups as a whole. When children leave their jigsaw classrooms they may return to a prejudiced family or society. Superordinate goals cannot always be set up between all groups and failure to achieve them may result in worse prejudice.

SOCIAL POLICY

Political and social measures can act to reduce institutionalised discrimination through
- ensuring political power sharing
- providing equal opportunities legislation
- affecting the media (which maintains and perpetuates unequal **stereotypes**)
- encouraging 'one-nation' in-group perception (**social identity theory**)
- targeting areas of economic frustration

EXAMPLES

The Supreme Court case of Brown vs. Board of Education in 1954 started the desegregation of public schools in the USA. Power sharing in South Africa ended Apartheid policies there.

Bogatz & Ball (1971) found that white children in the USA who watched mixed race TV programs like 'Sesame Street' developed more positive attitudes towards blacks and Hispanics.

EVALUATION

Policies like desegregation must be equally applied and regarded as inevitable and socially supported – half-hearted measures often cause more disruption.

There is a danger that discrimination will just shift to more subtle forms.

'Black is Beautiful: A Re-examination of Racial Preference and Identification' Hraba & Grant (1970)

AIM
A study by Clark and Clark (1947) conducted in 1939 reported that black children preferred white dolls and rejected black dolls when asked to choose which were nice, which looked bad, which they would like to play with, and which were a nice colour. This implied that they thought black is not beautiful and was interpreted as meaning they would rather be white. Later research tended to support the idea that for black children inter-racial contact with white children resulted in white preference, although some research indicated the opposite or no effect. Conclusions are difficult to draw, however, because the studies were not only conducted at different times, but also used different techniques, samples and settings. Hraba and Grant aimed to closely replicate the original Clark and Clark study to test their findings.

METHOD
Subjects: The sample was drawn from 5 public schools in Lincoln, Nebraska in May 1969 (where 1.4% of the population were black) that between them accounted for 73% of the black population of the correct age group of 4-8 year olds. The sample was 160 children, 89 were black (of whom 70% had white friends) and 71 were white (drawn randomly from the same classrooms).

Apparatus: 4 dolls – 2 black, 2 white that were identical in all other respects.

Procedure: Clark and Clark's procedure was followed as closely as possible. Children were individually interviewed with the dolls as part of a natural experiment (lack of experimenter control over the independent variables). The main independent variables were:
Race – operationalised by skin colour in 2 main conditions – black (later divided into light, medium and dark black) and white.
Time – the 1969 Hraba & Grant results were compared with the 1939 Clark & Clark results for black children.
The effect of the children's *age* was also investigated and the race of the interviewer was controlled for.
The dependent variables were **racial preference** and **racial identification** (operationalised by the children's answers to Clark and Clark's original 8 questions – see below) plus the **behavioural consequences** of racial preference and identification (operationalised by an additional question on the race of the children's best friend given to the children and their teachers).

RESULTS
Hraba & Grant found many differences in the doll choices of the black and white children in their study and many significant differences at P< .02 level or better between their results and those of Clark & Clark. Children mostly preferred same-race dolls.

DEPENDENT VARIABLES	INDEPENDENT VARIABLES		
	Clark & Clark (1939) *Black children*	*Hraba & Grant (1969)* *Black children*	*Hraba & Grant (1969)* *White children*
Racial preference Give me the doll that....	**white doll / black doll**	**white doll / black doll**	**white doll / black doll**
1 you want to play with	67% 32%	30% 70%	83% 16%
2 is a nice doll	59% 38%	46% 54%	70% 30%
3 looks bad	17% 59%	61% 36%	34% 63%
4 is a nice colour	60% 38%	31% 69%	48% 49%
Where percentages do not add up to 100% children failed to make a choice.	The black children's preference for the white doll occurred at all ages, and this **increased** with their **skin lightness** and **decreased** with **age**.	Black children preferred the black doll at all ages (**regardless** of **skin lightness** this tendency **increased** with **age**) and were more ethnocentric on question 4 than white children.	White children preferred the white doll and this trend also **increased** with **age** (except on question 4). They were more ethnocentric on questions 1& 2 than black children.
Racial identification Give me the doll that.... 5 looks like a white child 6 looks like a coloured child 7 looks like a Negro child **Racial self-identification** Give me the doll that.... 8 Looks like you	Correct identification for white dolls was 94%, coloured dolls 93% and Negro dolls 72%. Misidentification was more likely with younger and lighter skinned black children (80% of whom misidentified themselves as white)	Correct identification for white dolls was similar to Clark and Clark's - 90% for white dolls, 94% for coloured dolls and 86% for Negro dolls. Younger children misidentified themselves more but only 15% of lighter skinned children did.	White children were also more likely to misidentify themselves at younger ages.
Behavioural consequences What race is your best friend?		There was no relationship between doll preference and race of best friend by black or white children, even in those who always preferred same race dolls.	

DISCUSSION
Doll preference – 4 possible interpretations are proposed for the black children not being white-orientated in their interracial setting:
1 'Negroes are becoming Blacks proud of their race' – times may be changing, although not at the same rate across the country.
2 Black children in Lincoln, unlike in other cities, would have chosen black dolls 30 years ago. This cannot be tested now.
3 The black pride campaign organised by the 'Black Movement' in Lincoln may have modelled positive attitudes towards being black. 4 Interracial contact and acceptance may increase black pride – 70% of black and 59% of white children had opposite colour friends.
Doll preference and friendship – 3 reasons are given for why doll preference did not always reflect the children's friendship choices:
1 If 'Black is beautiful' means rejection of white, the black children should all have had black friends, but despite their preferences this may have been impractical because they were in predominately white schools.
2 The 'Black is beautiful' pride that caused the black children to choose black dolls may have been caused by contact with white friends; more black children who had friends of both races preferred black dolls on all questions (except question 4).
3 Doll choice may not be a valid measure of friendship choice since factors other than colour may be more important when making friends.

EVALUATION OF STUDY
Methodological – A forced 2-doll choice ignores the intensity of preference and may **lack validity** as a measure of race and self-liking.
Theoretical – Social Identity Theory is supported (the perception of groups we identify with affects our self perception).
Links – Social Identity Theory. Reduction of discrimination through contact and changing norms. Ethnocentrism.

Factors influencing the formation of attraction

SITUATIONAL FACTORS

PROXIMITY

This factor refers to the physical or functional distance between individuals, what Kerckoff (1974) called our 'field of availables', and suggests that the smaller the distance separating individuals, the greater the chance of attraction taking place. This factor is necessary for other influences, for example

- those who live near us are more likely to share our beliefs, social class, education etc. (see similarity)
- we have to be close to somebody in order to reward them (see learning theory)
- proximity allows increased exposure, which leads to familiarity (see familiarity)

Evidence

Festinger et al (1950) studied student friendship patterns in university campus housing and found that the students were most friendly with those living next door, less friendly with those living two doors away and least friendly with those living at the end of the corridor. Bossard (1931) found that couples in Chicago who lived within one block of each other were more likely to get married than those who lived two blocks apart, whereas Clarke (1952) found that more than 50% of people marrying in Colombus Ohio lived within walking distance of each other.

Evaluation

Proximity provides the minimum conditions necessary for attraction to start and maintain itself, but note that too close a proximity can invade our personal space and make us feel uncomfortable until our relationship has developed – the better we know someone the closer we allow them!

EXPOSURE AND FAMILIARITY

Zajonc investigated the 'mere exposure effect', which suggests that, all other things being equal, people prefer stimuli that they have seen more often. Close proximity clearly increases the chance of repeated exposure, which may lead to *familiarity* and a sense of trust.

Evidence

Zajonc et al (1971) asked subjects to evaluate photos of strangers and found that those strangers who appeared more often than others were rated more positively. This effect has also been found for repeated exposure of music, paintings, and political candidates. Segal (1974) studied police cadets who were assigned to their rooms and classroom seats alphabetically, and found that they were more likely to rate someone as a friend who was close in the alphabet to them. Newcomb (1961) conducted a two year study of liking patterns in rented accommodation. The best predictor of liking in the second year was familiarity.

Evaluation

Repeated exposure may give a greater chance that negative characteristics will be found in other people or that boredom or stimulus satiation may occur, in which case the proverb 'familiarity breeds contempt' may be supported. Most research however has supported the link between familiarity and attraction.

PERSONAL FACTORS

PHYSICAL ATTRACTIVENESS

A strong research finding is that people are not only drawn towards those who are *physically* attractive, but see these people as *psychologically* attractive as well - having a whole host of other positive traits (such as popularity, warmth, generosity etc.).

Evidence

Dion (1972) using photographs of 7-year-old children found that attractive children were less likely to be thought of as anti-social than unattractive children. Walster et al (1966), using the 'computer dance' procedure, found the most important factor in determining whether a woman would be asked for a second date was her physical attractiveness, regardless of the man's.

Evaluation

Physical attractiveness is not absolute or objective ('beauty is in the eye of the beholder'), and can be influenced by a number of characteristics, such as

- culture – Garfield (1982) found that different cultures have different conceptions of beauty, and even in the same culture norms of attractiveness will vary
- gender – in 'western cultures' men seem to be more attracted by physical beauty, whereas women's preferences are not predominantly physical – Sigall and Landy (1973) found that the physical attractiveness of the male's partner increased his status in the eyes of other males, whereas the reverse was not true for women
- context – The perception of a person's beauty can change with circumstances – those who disagree with us may lose their physical appeal. Efran (1974) found good looking criminals received more lenient sentences *unless* their looks were involved in the crime.

SIMILARITY

Although, ideally, we would want the most attractive person possible, in reality we tend to be attracted by similarity – not just of looks, but also of beliefs, attitudes and values ('birds of a feather flock together'). Rubin (1973) suggested similarity is rewarding because we are more likely to *agree* with similar people, which leads to more joint activities and confidence in ourselves and our opinions, and facilitates communication.

Evidence

Griffit and Veitch (1974) studied 13 males who spent 10 days in a nuclear fall-out shelter, and concluded that those who were the most similar liked each other the best by the end. Cann et al (1995) found attraction was greater towards a stranger who had similar attitudes. However, agreement that the same joke was funny had the strongest effect on attraction.

Evaluation

Winch (1955) has argued that in some cases **complementarity** is more important than similarity in determining the formation of attraction (i.e. 'opposites attract'). Snyder and Fromkin (1980) suggest that we dislike people who are too like us, as we like to see ourselves as unique. Rosenbaum (1986) proposed that although similar attitudes do not have much effect on liking, we are repulsed by dissimilar attitudes. This idea is not well supported.

RECIPROCAL LIKING

A more subtle form of similarity is that we like people who like us. Aronson proposed the reward-cost principle, which states that we will be attracted to those who like us and consistently make positive comments about us, as opposed to those who do not (presumably because it increases our self esteem). Aronson and Linder's (1965) 'gain-loss' theory is somewhat less obvious – we like people *more* who start off by disliking us and then change their mind, than we do those who liked us all along, and the same theory applies for those who start off by liking us and then change to dislike.

Evidence

Aronson and Linder (1965) found experimental support for the 'gain-loss' theory by letting subjects overhear (a confederate's) opinions of them. When the confederate started off by stating negative things about the subject and then switched to positive things, the subject rated the confederate more positively.

Evaluation

In general our liking depends upon how much we respect the opinions and motivations of the people who praise us. If the praise is seen as false flattery, then dislike occurs.

Theories of relationships

ECONOMIC THEORIES

- Researchers such as Homans and Blau explain relationships in terms of economic transactions – an assessment of the costs and rewards involved in interacting with others.
- **Exchange theory** – suggests that the attraction of others depends upon the profit they provide for us – the rewards of interacting with them (e.g. stimulation, money, love) minus the costs (e.g. effort, time, money) – relative to the profits of other relationships.
- **Equity theory** – proposes that participants in a relationship seek a fair (equitable) return of rewards in proportion to their initial investment in the relationship (the rewards that they bring to it).

Relationship formation and maintenance
Exchange and equity theories predict that relationships will be maintained when
- a both partners are satisfied with their 'comparison levels' of rewards (the agreed ratio of costs and rewards) in their current relationship (Thibaut & Kelley, 1959)
- b the comparison level for alternative relationships is low
- c the costs of leaving the relationship are high
- d partners are similar in their ability to reward each other

Relationship breakdown
The theories predict relationship breakdown when
- a one or both partners are dissatisfied with their comparison levels of rewards
- b the comparison level for alternative relationships is high (there are better relationships elsewhere)
- c the costs of leaving the relationship are low (one or both partners are able to leave the relationship with little loss)
- d partners are not similar in the ability to reward each other

Evaluation of theories
- It is difficult to quantify all psychological costs and rewards in a relationship to test the theories.
- However, just using the variable of physical attraction, Murstein (1972) found couples in intimate relationships were more likely to be equally attractive.
- The theory is rather 'mercenary', not dealing with emotions which can over-ride the calculation of profit in relationships.
- The theory is derived from the values of capitalistic societies.
- The theory may not apply to certain relationships, e.g. family.

LEARNING THEORY

- Byrne and Clore (1970) use the learning theory principles of classical and operant conditioning to explain attraction in terms of
  - a a conditioned emotional responses
  - b the consequences of interpersonal behaviour
- The reinforcement an individual provides depends upon what basic human needs they can satisfy for the other person, such as the need for resources (e.g. food), love, sex, etc.

Relationship formation and maintenance
- Learning theory predicts relationships will be maintained if
  - a partners are associated (by classical conditioning) with pleasant stimuli and life experiences such as successful careers or happy domestic environments
  - b partners positively reinforce each other with pleasant stimuli such as interaction, sex, presents, etc.

Relationship breakdown
- Learning theory predicts relationship breakdown when
  - a partners are associated with unpleasant life experiences, such as unemployment, poverty, etc. (classical conditioning)
  - b partners do not reinforce each other with pleasant stimuli (boredom) or inflict more negative than positive stimuli on each other (operant conditioning)

Evaluation of theory
- The theory links well with the economic theory notions of cost and rewards.
- Veitch & Griffith (1976) found the attraction shown towards a stranger depended upon whether he was associated with good or bad news.
- Some relationships exist despite very few rewards and the giving, not just receiving, of reinforcement (due to the norm of reciprocity) is regarded as important.

COGNITIVE THEORY

- Heider (1958) proposed balance theory, which argues that people strive for 'cognitive consistency' in their liking and disliking of others, and are motivated to achieve balanced relationships.

Relationship formation and maintenance
- A cognitive triad is a pattern of relationships involving three people. The triad will be balanced, and consistent relationships maintained, if the multiplication of the signs leads to a '+'.

A balanced triad where relationships are consistent.

Ex-boyfriend

− −

Boyfriend **+** Girlfriend

− = negative feeling
+ = positive feeling

Relationship breakdown
- Unbalanced liking patterns are due to inconsistent attitudes in relationships and produce unpleasant 'cognitive dissonance' that people are motivated to reduce by changing their attitudes.

An unbalanced triad where the relationships are causing cognitive dissonance

Ex-boyfriend

− +

Boyfriend **+** Girlfriend

Evaluation of theory
- Aronson & Cope (1968) found subjects liked a professor more when he showed hostility towards a graduate who had previously upset the subject.
- The theory realises that relationships are influenced by more than two people.
- The triad models only involve three people and ignore the strength of liking.

EVOLUTIONARY THEORIES

- Sociobiological theorists, such as Dawkins (1989), aim to account for attraction and relationships by looking at the evolutionary survival functions of it.

Relationship formation and maintenance
- Friendship and affiliation has probably evolved due to the advantages of increased protection and hunting efficiency that groups provide.
- Male-female bonds may have evolved to help care for helpless human infants. As the brain and head size of babies increased, they had to be born at earlier and less developed stages. The extra care required would involve both parents and attachment bonds that kept them together would be selected by evolution because of the increased survival rate of their offspring.

Relationship breakdown
- Unfaithfulness may be genetically advantageous for both sexes:
  - a **The male** optimal method of passing on genes is to mate with many females, since they cannot guarantee the offspring are their own and produce many gametes.
  - b **Females** produce and invest in a limited number of eggs, and so mating with a male of better genetic quality without discovery, will make their offspring fitter as well as receiving care from the current partner.

Evaluation of theories
- The theories propose that there are conflicting evolutionary tendencies to bond yet cheat, which perhaps explains the difficulty of maintaining intimate relationships.
- These ideas have ethical implications – what is natural is not necessarily moral.
- Pair bonding in humans may only have evolved to last long enough to provide care for helpless human infants.

The breakdown of attraction

- In addition to providing theories that explain the breakdown of relationships, social psychologists have identified the important factors and processes that are involved.

FACTORS LEADING TO BREAKDOWN OF RELATIONSHIPS

ENVIRONMENTAL FACTORS

PHYSICAL ENVIRONMENT
- **Distance** – Relationships involving a lack of proximity are difficult to maintain due to the lack of reinforcement, ability to share activities and intimacy, plus the inevitable extra costs involved (links with learning and exchange theories).
- **Hardship** – Lack of resources may cause frustration and aggression which may be directed at the partner (links with frustration-aggression theory). Negative emotions produced by hardship may become associated with the partner (by classical conditioning).

SOCIAL ENVIRONMENT
- **'Field of availables'** – The greater the number and quality of alternative partners in a social environment, the greater the comparison level for alternatives (this links with exchange theory).
- **Family and friends** – Competition for intimacy and attention or dissimilarity of attitudes and beliefs between one partner and the friends and/or family of the other partner (this links with cognitive balance theory) can cause problems.

INTER-PERSONAL FACTORS

BOREDOM
- **Lack of stimulation** – Unhappiness due to lack of stimulation and reinforcement (this links with learning theory) can lead to break-up in itself or by facilitating unfaithfulness by increasing the appeal of alternative relationships (this links with exchange theory).
- **Reduction in stimulation** – Sex is one of the most powerful reinforcers, but its frequency rapidly declines during the first four years of a relationship (Udry, 1980). However, 41% of married couples still have sex twice a week compared to 23% of single people.

CONFLICT
Only 1.2% of married couples report never having disagreements (McGonagle et al, 1992). Important factors in conflict are:
- **Rule-breaking** – Argyle and Henderson (1984) found the breaking of implicit rules of trust and intimacy were major factors in relationship break-down.
- **Compromise difficulties** – the discovery of differences over time reduces similarity, and the time-commitment of relationships reduces an individual's ability to achieve goals and indulge hobbies.
- **Conflict maintenance** – The tendency to respond in equally negative and destructive ways perpetuates conflict.

INDIVIDUAL FACTORS

BACKGROUND
According to Duck (1988) relationships are more likely to breakdown between individuals who:
- **Differ in demographic background** – perhaps due to dissimilarity of cultural attitudes and expectations.
- **Marry very early** – either in their relationship (due to lack of time for compatibility assessment) or in terms of age (due to lack of coping skills).
- **Have experienced a lack of relationship commitment** – either in their family or personal life.
- **Come from lower socio-economic or education levels.**

SOCIAL SKILLS
Baron & Byrne (1997) suggest lack of social skills can influence breakdown:
- **Coping strategies** – couples who differ in the way they cope with stress are less satisfied with their relationship (Ptacek & Dodge, 1995).
- **Conflict avoidance** – more men than women believe that avoiding conflict is a legitimate way of dealing with it. This can lead to a perpetuation of conflict and a lack of resolution.
- **Emotional expressiveness** – those unable to express emotions are less happy in relationships (King, 1993).

PROCESSES INVOLVING THE BREAKDOWN OF RELATIONSHIPS

DUCK'S STAGES IN PERSONAL RELATIONSHIP BREAKDOWN

INTRA-PSYCHIC PHASE
personal assessment of costs and rewards

DYADIC PHASE
confrontation and negotiation with partner

SOCIAL PHASE
involvement and use of social network

GRAVE DRESSING PHASE
retrospective analysis and public distribution of break-up story

CONFLICT
Rusbult and Zembrodt (1983) categorised four methods of dealing with relationship dissatisfaction.

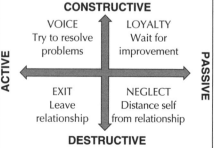

CONSTRUCTIVE

ACTIVE		PASSIVE
VOICE Try to resolve problems		LOYALTY Wait for improvement
EXIT Leave relationship		NEGLECT Distance self from relationship

DESTRUCTIVE

Love

WHAT IS LOVE?

Love is an abstract concept that is difficult to define. Rubin (1973) distinguished the respect and affection of 'liking' from the attachment, caring and intimacy of 'loving' by using rating scales. Other researchers have divided love into different types, such as:

- **Passionate or romantic love** – involving intense feelings of 'tenderness, sexuality, elation and pain, anxiety and relief, altruism and jealousy', and **companionate love** – involving 'a less intense emotion, combining feelings of friendly affection and deep attachment. It is characterised by friendship, understanding and a concern for the welfare of the other' (Hatfield, 1987).
- **Love styles** – such as *Ludus* (game-playing), *Mania* (possessive love), *Pragma* (logical love), *Agape* (altruistic love), *Storge* (companionate love) and *Eros* (romantic love), (Lee, 1973).

Sternberg (1988) focused on how different types of love were produced by different combinations of three components:

- **Passion** – refers to the degree of intense emotion and sexual attraction felt towards another.
- **Intimacy** – refers to the degree of emotional closeness, confiding and sharing with another
- **Commitment** – refers to the degree of intention to maintain a relationship with another.

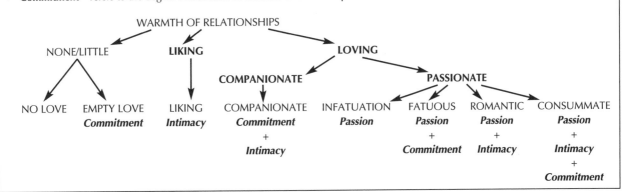

EXPLANATIONS OF LOVE

LEARNING THEORIES
Suggest that different kinds of liking and loving form as a result of positive conditioned emotional responses and mutual positive reinforcement by association with pleasant stimuli. The type of pleasant social, physical or sexual stimuli associated with an individual determine the degree of passion, intimacy and commitment experienced.

EVOLUTIONARY THEORIES
Suggest that:
1 'liking' evolved to promote social co-operation and grouping for collective defence and hunting
2 romantic/passionate love evolved to ensure mate selection, protection and copulation
3 companionate love evolved to maintain the pair bonds necessary to look after the helpless offspring produced.

SOCIAL THEORIES
Suggest that love, according to social construct theory, is a socially created and defined concept that varies according to the needs and values of different cultures. The popularity of different conceptions of love has been shown to change historically and culturally.

COGNITIVE THEORIES
Suggest that love is an emotional label attributed to explain physiological arousal in the light of culturally available concepts. Cognitive processes link the physiological and social aspects of relationships and may be involved in their formation and maintenance through a mental appraisal of their costs and rewards (exchange and equity theory).

PHYSIOLOGICAL THEORIES
Suggest that different types of love are the result of hormonally / neurochemically produced pleasant and unpleasant physiological arousal that motivates behaviour in response to the presence or absence of certain people, i.e. relatives, friends or potential mates.

SOCIAL / ENVIRONMENTAL THEORIES

INNATE / BIOLOGICAL THEORIES

THEORIES OF LOVE

Cultural differences in relationships

WHY STUDY CROSS-CULTURAL DIFFERENCES IN RELATIONSHIPS?

Moghaddam et al (1993) point out many differences between western and non-western cultures that can profoundly affect the nature of relationships. Hui and Triandis's (1986) 'individualistic' and 'collectivistic' dichotomy, as well as Hsu's (1983) distinction between 'continuous' and 'discontinuous' societies, illustrate some of these differences and their effects.

WESTERN CULTURES

Western cultures tend to be more:

Individualistic – emphasising the individual, their goals, rights, attitudes and needs. As a consequence there is:

- A focus on first acquaintances, close friendships and intimate partnerships between *two individuals*.
- A strong social norm of *monogamous* relationships and marriages (reflected in the society's laws).
- An emphasis on *voluntary choice* in relationships due to:
  a The western lifestyle of high mobility and easy long-distance communication, giving *greater availability* of relationships.
  b The notion of *romantic love* – that choosing a perfect match whom you love deeply is necessary to fulfil one's own needs.
- A tendency for relationship interactions to be more governed by individual, economic-based resource allocation and voluntary reciprocity (the returning of favours based on individual responsibility).

Discontinuous – youth and progress are emphasised and change is regarded as both important and inevitable. Consequently:

- There may be an increase in the preference for temporary relationships and increased rates of divorce.
- Rules in relationships may be less important, since if they are broken the relationships can be left and others found.

NON-WESTERN CULTURES

Non-Western cultures tend to be more:

Collectivistic – emphasising the group, its decisions, attitudes, needs and one's duties towards it. As a consequence there is:

- More emphasis on *long-term kinship* and *social group relationships*, often involving more than two people.
- A higher frequency of *polygamous* relationships and marriages (reflected in the society's laws).
- A lack of *voluntary choice* in relationships due to:
  a More stationary lifestyles, with less long-distance communication, leading to *less availability*.
  b Obligations to *family and social norms*. *Marriage* is supposed to take into account the wishes of others and is frequently *arranged*.
- A tendency for relationship interactions to be more governed by group need or equality-based resource sharing and obligatory reciprocity (the returning of favours as an important social responsibility).

Continous – showing a concern for heritage, customs, tradition and respect for the wishes of one's elders. Consequently:

- Change is viewed with suspicion, perhaps leading to greater stability in relationships.
- Rules in relationships are strictly and formally adhered to because of the need to maintain long-term, stable relationships.

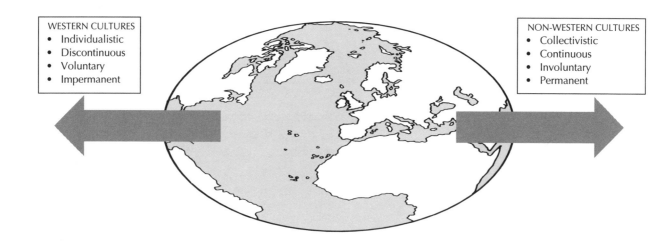

WESTERN CULTURES
- Individualistic
- Discontinuous
- Voluntary
- Impermanent

NON-WESTERN CULTURES
- Collectivistic
- Continuous
- Involuntary
- Permanent

Evaluation

- The research on Western relationships has seriously restricted implications for non-Western societies and has neglected certain kinds of relationship in its own society, e.g. the more collectivisitic relationships of rural communities and relationships with family members. However, due to the greater worldwide media control of Western nations, their cultural values are increasingly affecting non-Western values.
- There is a Western (ethnocentric) tendency to assume that Western relationships are superior due to ideological dogma. However, cross-cultural study of relationships points out reasons for their frequent failure in western societies – the individualistic values of independence, satisfaction of personal needs and personal control inherently conflict with the intimacy, sharing and compromise demanded by relationships, making them more difficult to maintain. In collectivistic societies the norms of dependency, sharing and lack of personal control aid the maintenance of relationships. Gupta and Singh (1982), for example, found that newly-weds in India who married out of love reported more intense feelings of love than those from arranged marriages. However, this pattern had reversed after five years and became more exaggerated after ten years.
- Studies have revealed similarities across cultures, however, for example in terms of feelings of sexual jealousy (although it may be triggered and expressed in different ways) and the notion of romantic love (although it may vary in commonness).

Sub-cultural differences in ('understudied') relationships

HOMOSEXUAL RELATIONSHIPS

HOW DOES SOCIETY REACT TO HOMOSEXUAL RELATIONSHIPS?

Reactions to homosexuality have varied over history and across cultures in terms of its social acceptance. Although reactions are showing some signs of change at the turn of the millennium, in recent history homosexual relationships in many Western cultures have been:

- **Pathologised** – regarded as a product of mental disorder (homosexuality or self-concern about being homosexual have been included in the DSM and ICD classification manuals).
- **Discriminated against** – both socially (in terms of family and peer rejection as well as verbal and physical attacks) and legally (homosexual relationships have been regarded as illegal or subject to different laws, e.g. concerning age of consent and economic allowances for partners).
- **Stereotyped** – over-generalised, oversimplified and distorted characteristics are attributed to all homosexuals and differences between straights and homosexuals are exaggerated.

WHAT EFFECTS DO THESE REACTIONS HAVE?

Such adverse social reactions can have **negative effects** upon:

- **The relationship** – homosexual partners face the problem of either concealing their relationship from society (affecting their work, domestic and leisure arrangements, and causing a constant fear of discovery and resentment that they are made to feel they have 'something to hide') or revealing it (and suffering from the stereotypes and discrimination).
- **The individual** – discrimination can lead to physical, financial, and mental harm (especially in terms of isolation and lack of support – which may in turn pressure the relationship). Stereotyping may cause homosexuality to become the central organising principle in governing interpersonal interactions and self-perception/identity, leading to a neglect of individual characteristics.

HOW DO HOMOSEXUAL AND HETEROSEXUAL RELATIONSHIPS COMPARE?

Some psychologists, e.g. Bee (1994), suggest that homosexual and heterosexual relationships are more alike than different.

- **Similarities** – both types of sexual orientation may share similar values, goals, experiences and factors influencing the formation, maintenance and breakdown of relationships.
- **Differences** – different social pressures and sex role interactions may result in a rejection of the 'heterosexual model' in homosexual relationships, leading to greater equality between partners, but less cohabitation and sexual exclusivity.

Evaluation – research is often based on qualitative, self-report measures from interviews and questionnaires, conducted on opportunity and self-selecting samples of homosexuals who have revealed their orientation. These methods have both strengths and weaknesses for results.

'ELECTRONIC' RELATIONSHIPS

WHAT ARE 'ELECTRONIC' RELATIONSHIPS?

- Electronic relationships are those that result solely from computer-mediated rather than face-to-face communication. Such communication happens over the Internet via electronic mail (e-mail), virtual posting boards or different versions of on-line chatrooms.
- Electronic relationships may differ from others formed through distance communication because they provide faster or more real-time interaction and responsiveness than letters, and greater anonymity than telephone conversation.

EVALUATION

- Still a relatively new area of research.
- Effects may change as technology advances, involving a greater number and variety of users, and an increased use of visual and even tactile modes of communication, e.g. video-conferencing and virtual reality devices.

SIMILARITIES WITH OTHER RELATIONSHIPS

- Similar influences in the formation and maintenance of other relationships are involved, e.g.
  1 exposure and familiarity ('intersection frequency' according to Wallace, 1999) effects.
  2 similarity of belief effects (aided by common interest Internet posting boards and chatrooms).
- Electronic relationships are reported to be just as deep and satisfying as other relationships (sometimes more so).

DIFFERENCES TO OTHER RELATIONSHIPS

Positive effects

- **Discovery** – greater access (especially for those with access problems) to a greater number and variety of people increases the relationship 'field of availables'.
- **Disinhibition** – the anonymity and ease of terminating communication increases confidence in communicating for those who find it difficult interacting through other means due to ability or stereotypes (e.g. relating to attractiveness, ethnicity and sexual orientation).
- **Disclosure** – the facilitating effects of disinhibition may allow greater self-disclosure and confiding that may aid friendship formation and emotional support.

Negative effects

- **Deception** – greater anonymity and ease of terminating communication also allows conscious or unconscious self-misrepresentation and the abuse of disclosure to occur with greater ease of escape.
- **Dependency** – 'net obsession' may reduce skills and opportunities relating to other relationships.

Social learning theory and aggression

SUPPORTING EVIDENCE

Bandura et al (1963) allowed one group of children to watch an adult model perform certain aggressive acts with an inflatable 'Bobo doll' which were unlikely to occur normally, such as throwing the doll up in the air, hitting it with a hammer and punching it while saying things like 'pow' and 'boom'. When these children were left in a playroom with the inflatable doll, they frequently imitated the same acts of aggression, compared to a control group who had not seen the model and showed none of the behaviours.

Bandura (1965) used a similar experimental set-up, but showed different consequences for the model's aggression to three groups of children. One group saw the model's aggression being rewarded, one group saw the model being punished for the aggression, and another group saw no specific consequences.

When allowed to enter the playroom, the children who had seen the model punished showed less imitative aggression than the other two groups. However, if all the children were offered rewards for doing what the model had done, all groups showed high levels of imitation. The children in the model punished group had clearly learnt the aggression by observation, but had not shown their potential to imitate it because they expected negative consequences.

SOCIAL LEARNING THEORY AND AGGRESSION

Social learning theory was developed mainly by Bandura and Walters, and suggests that much behaviour, including aggression, is **learnt** from the environment (rather than being instinctual) through reinforcement and the process of **modelling**. Modelling involves learning through the **observation** of other people (models), which may lead to **imitation** if the behaviour to be imitated **leads to desirable consequences**.

Bandura distinguished between the learning of behaviour and the performance of it. Behaviour may be learnt from models through observation, but the likelihood of it being imitated depends on the perceived consequences of the model's actions - if a child sees a model's behaviour being rewarded, this acts as vicarious (indirect) reinforcement for the child who will proceed to imitate it. If the child sees others punished for their actions then, although the behaviour is learnt, it is less likely to be imitated. The social learning theory can easily be applied to explain the learning and performance of aggressive behaviour. Models can be parents, peers or media characters (thus this theory has implications for the portrayal of behaviour like violence on television).

EVALUATION
Methodological

Bandura's social learning theory laboratory experiments have been accused of being overly **artificial** (hitting a Bobo doll is not the same as inflicting aggression on a real person) and of inducing **demand characteristics** (the children may have believed that they were meant to behave aggressively).
However, other experimental studies have demonstrated that children are more likely to hurt other children after viewing violent behaviour (Liebert and Baron, 1972).

Theoretical

The theory neglects the role of innate factors in behaviour like aggression. However, social learning theory does provide a more credible explanation of the transmission of behaviour like violence than the traditional behaviourist view of learning, and has investigated the types of models and behaviours that are most likely to be imitated. Social learning theory provides a more complete approach to explaining learning and has attempted to integrate cognitive and even psychoanalytic concepts with traditional behaviourist learning theory.

IMPLICATIONS FOR REDUCING/CONTROLLING AGGRESSION

The implication of social learning theory is that if aggressive behaviour is not observed or reinforced in a society, then it will not naturally occur.

However many examples of aggression already frequently occur in the great majority of societies, and so the theory would be more realistically applied to reducing aggression.

This could be achieved by ensuring that aggression is not reinforced, or that negative consequences are seen to follow it. The direct punishment of aggression raises problems though, since it may itself be perceived as an aggressive act that is socially approved of – indeed research consistently demonstrates that 'aggression breeds aggression'. Munroe and Munroe (1975) found cross-culturally that childhood aggression is highest in societies whose families highly punish their children for showing aggression.

Social learning theory would suggest that media violence should be dramatically reduced.

'Transmission of aggression through imitation of aggressive models' Bandura, Ross, and Ross (1961)

AIM

To demonstrate that learning can occur through mere observation of a model and that imitation can occur in the absence of that model. More specifically:

- Children shown aggressive models will show significantly more imitative aggressive behaviour than those shown non-aggressive or no models.
- Children shown non-aggressive, subdued models will show significantly less aggressive behaviour than those shown aggressive or no models.
- Boys should show significantly more imitative aggression than girls, especially with the male rather than female aggressive model.

METHOD

Subjects: 72 children, 36 boys and 36 girls, aged 37-69 months (with a mean age of 52 months) were used.

Design: Laboratory experiment, in which the independent variable (type of model) was manipulated in three conditions:

- Aggressive model shown
- Non-aggressive model shown
- Control condition, no model shown

The dependent variable was the amount of imitative behaviour and aggression shown by the children.

A matched pairs design was used with 24 children (12 boys and 12 girls) assigned to each condition, with an effort made to match subjects according to pre-existing levels of aggression. In addition to the above manipulations, in the experimental conditions:

- Half the subjects observed a same sex model.
- The other half observed opposite sex models.

Procedure: In the experimental conditions children were individually shown into a room containing toys and played with some potato prints and pictures in a corner for 10 minutes while either:

- The non-aggressive adult model (either male or female) played in a quiet and subdued manner for 10 minutes, or
- The aggressive model distinctively aggressed against a 5 foot inflated Bobo doll by **a** sitting on it and repeatedly punching it on the nose, **b** striking it on the head with a mallet, and **c** throwing it up in the air and kicking it around the room. The aggressive model also uttered verbally aggressive statements such as 'sock him in the nose', 'throw him in the air' and 'pow', as well as two non-aggressive statements – 'he keeps coming back for more' and 'he sure is a tough fella'.

All children (including the control group) were then individually taken to a different experimental location and subjected to mild aggression arousal by being stopped from playing with some very attractive toys. This arousal took place in order to give all groups an equal chance of showing aggression and also to allow the group shown the non-aggressive model to demonstrate an inhibition of aggressive behaviour.

All children were then shown into another room which contained both aggressive toys (e.g. a 3 foot high Bobo doll, a mallet, dartguns, and a tether ball) and non-aggressive toys (e.g. a tea set, dolls, and colouring paper), and were observed through a one-way mirror for 20 minutes.

Observers recorded (with inter-scorer reliabilities of .90 correlation coefficient) behaviour in the following categories:

- **Imitation behaviour of aggressive model**:
  a physical aggression, e.g. sitting on the doll and repeatedly punching it on the nose.
  b Verbal aggression, e.g. 'sock him' or 'pow'.
  c Non-aggressive speech, e.g. 'he sure is a tough fella'.
- **Partial imitation behaviour of aggressive model**, e.g. mallet aggression against other objects or sitting on the Bobo doll without punching it.
- **Non-imitative physical and verbal aggression**, e.g. just punching the Bobo doll, physical aggression with other objects and verbal non-imitative remarks 'shoot the Bobo' or 'horses fighting, biting'.
- **Non-aggressive behaviour**, e.g. non aggressive play or sitting quietly.

RESULTS

1. Children in the aggressive model condition showed significantly more imitation of the model's physical and verbal aggression and non-aggressive verbal responses than children who saw the non-aggressive model or no model at all in the control condition.
2. Children in the aggressive model condition usually showed more partial imitation and non-imitative physical and verbal aggression than those who saw the non-aggressive model or no model at all, but not always to a significant degree.
3. Children in the non-aggressive model condition showed very little aggression, although not always significantly less than the no model group.
4. Children who saw the same sex model were only likely to imitate the behaviour significantly more in some of the categories. For example, boys would imitate male models significantly more than girls for physical and verbal imitative aggression, non-imitative aggression and gun play; girls would imitate female models more than boys for verbal imitative aggression and non-imitative aggression only, but not significantly.

EVALUATION

Methodological:

Procedure – Not completely standardised presentation of model's behaviour (later experiments used videotape presentation)

Artificiality – Bizarre acts of aggression were shown and imitated against a Bobo doll, not a real person.

Ethical problems – Aggression was induced in, and taught to, children. Exposure to an adult stranger's aggression may have been frightening for the children.

Theoretical: The research provides reasonable support for the social learning theory idea that behaviour can be acquired through observation rather than direct personal experience, and that reinforcement is not required for learning to occur. This study has important implications for the effects of media violence on children.

Links: Social learning theory, aggression, socialisation, gender differences.

Frustration-aggression theory of aggression

SUPPORTING EVIDENCE
Experimental evidence
Barker et al (1941) found that children frustrated by being kept waiting a long time before they were allowed to play in a room full of attractive toys were more aggressive and destructive (throwing the toys against the wall and stamping on them) than a second control group of children who were not frustrated.

Correlational evidence
Hovland and Sears (1940) found a significant correlation between economic frustration (measured in terms of the price of cotton) and displaced aggression on scapegoats (measured in terms of the number of lynchings of blacks) in the southern states of America between 1882 and 1930.

REFINEMENTS OF THE THEORY
Studies have demonstrated that the greater the degree of frustration, the greater the likelihood of aggression. Frustration is increased by being **thwarted**

- **close to achieving the goal**
  Harris (1974) manipulated the variable of frustration by having confederates push into bus stop, cinema, and supermarket checkout queues either in front of **a** the second person in line (high frustration) or **b** the twelfth person (lower frustration). Verbal aggression was greater in the high frustration condition.

- **unexpectedly**
  Kulick and Brown (1979) led subjects involved in telephoning for charity donations to believe that they could expect either a high or low degree of success. When they actually gained no donations at all, those subjects with the greatest expectations were more frustrated and showed more aggression – slamming the phone down harder and speaking more harshly.

- **without good reason**
  In the same study, those subjects who were given legitimate reasons for donation refusal were less aggressive than those who were not.

FRUSTRATION-AGGRESSION THEORY
In proposing their frustration-aggression theory, Dollard et al (1939) suggested that:
**'...aggression is always a consequence of frustration and, contrariwise...
the existence of frustration always leads to some form of aggression.'**

Dollard et al's theory was an attempt to link the Freudian notion of aggressive drives to the behaviourist's ideas of stimulus-response interactions. According to the frustration-aggression theory, aggression is an **innate drive response** to frustrating external **stimuli** from the environment.
The frustrating stimuli can be any **social** conditions that thwart our satisfaction, such as poor housing, unemployment, etc.
The aggressive response can take many forms – such as overt aggressive behaviour against the cause of frustration, or indirect release through **displacement** of aggression onto scapegoats or even aggressive fantasy.

EVALUATION
Dollard et al's extreme version of the frustration-aggression hypothesis has now been rejected by research showing that

- **aggression is not always caused by frustration**
  There are many other social factors and theories that can explain the occurrence of aggression without frustration. Social learning theory argues that aggression may be caused by imitating other's – especially if their aggressive behaviour was positively reinforced; while conformity theory would suggest that aggression is caused by following the norms or expectations of the group.

- **frustration does not always lead to aggression**
  Frustration can lead to a range of responses, not just aggression, for example despair or depression (Seligman). **Berkowitz (1968)** suggested that frustration causes anger or a 'readiness' to aggress, but argues that aggression will only result if there are aggressive cues or provocative stimuli in the environment. Berkowitz and Le Page (1967) found, for example, that frustrated individuals showed greater aggression if they were in the presence of guns than neutral objects (the weapons effect).

IMPLICATIONS FOR REDUCING/CONTROLLING AGGRESSION
According to the original theory, since aggression is regarded as a drive response, the energy associated with it can not be destroyed and must be released in some form. There are, therefore, two implications:

- **Prevent or reduce frustration** in the first place, e.g. by improving economic conditions, but of course there will always be frustrations of some sort as long as resources are limited.

- **Control the expression of aggression** by finding harmless ways of displacing it, such as through vigorous exercise, sport or even through watching violent T.V. (emotional **catharsis**). The concepts of drive reduction and displacement have fallen into disrepute, however, through lack of experimental support.
  According to Berkowitz's modification of the original model, one major implication for the reduction of aggression is through the control of aggressive stimuli such as guns. As Berkowitz comments, weapons not only allow violence but can stimulate it as well: 'The finger pulls the trigger, but the trigger may also be pulling the finger'.

Pro-social behaviour

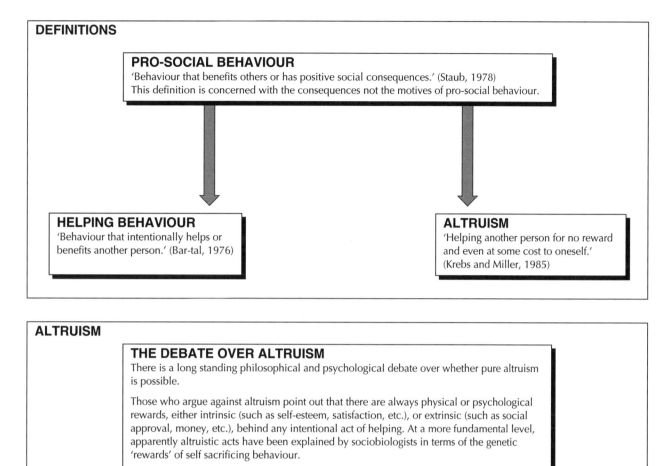

DEFINITIONS

PRO-SOCIAL BEHAVIOUR
'Behaviour that benefits others or has positive social consequences.' (Staub, 1978)
This definition is concerned with the consequences not the motives of pro-social behaviour.

HELPING BEHAVIOUR
'Behaviour that intentionally helps or benefits another person.' (Bar-tal, 1976)

ALTRUISM
'Helping another person for no reward and even at some cost to oneself.' (Krebs and Miller, 1985)

ALTRUISM

THE DEBATE OVER ALTRUISM
There is a long standing philosophical and psychological debate over whether pure altruism is possible.

Those who argue against altruism point out that there are always physical or psychological rewards, either intrinsic (such as self-esteem, satisfaction, etc.), or extrinsic (such as social approval, money, etc.), behind any intentional act of helping. At a more fundamental level, apparently altruistic acts have been explained by sociobiologists in terms of the genetic 'rewards' of self sacrificing behaviour.

This position of 'universal egoism' is almost irrefutable, however, for one can always think of rewards for an act of help but cannot guarantee that these rewards were the basis of the helper's intentions.

Those who think humans are capable of true altruistic behaviour, suggest that it is governed more by impulsive, *emotional* factors rather than cool, rational thought processes. Research into altruism in humans has therefore mainly focused on the role of emotional arousal and empathy.

EMOTIONAL AROUSAL
Piliavin et al (1981) suggest that the plight of others, especially in emergency conditions, can cause such emotional arousal in the bystander that it could lead to an impulsive, non-rational desire to give help.

However, the emotional arousal triggered in the bystander that provokes this urge is experienced as unpleasant, and thus helping serves to reduce it.

For this reason, the helping can be seen as selfishly motivated – reducing the unpleasant arousal and avoiding the guilt of not helping is seen as rewarding – and so arousal can become just another factor in the analysis of costs and rewards for helping.

EMPATHY
Empathy involves the desire to reduce another person's distress (rather than your own distress as a watching bystander). Coke et al (1978) have experimentally demonstrated that the emotion of empathy will increase helping behaviour, but its altruistic status is less clear.

Empathy involves the bystander taking on the perspective of the victim and, therefore, vicariously experiencing the distress of others. However, this interpretation could still involve selfishness, since the motive is based on thinking 'what if this happened to **me**?'.

Alternatively, people who feel empathy for others may feel saddened by the victim's plight and help in order to raise their own mood (Cialdini et al, 1987).

Batson, however, suggests that empathy involves a genuine desire to reduce other people's distress rather than our own. In a cleverly designed study, Batson et al (1981) found that empathetic observers would volunteer to receive electric shocks in the place of another, even if they could easily reduce their own distress at seeing the other person given shocks by leaving the experiment or putting less effort into a test that required a high score in order to let the observer swap places with the victim.

Factors affecting the decision to help

INFORMATION PROCESSING OF EMERGENCIES

Latane and Darley (1970) proposed an information processing explanation of helping behaviour that identifies several stages involved in the decision making process of whether to help another.

Is the situation needing help **NOTICED**?

Is the situation **DEFINED** as an emergency?

Does the potential helper **TAKE RESPONSIBILITY**?

Does the potential helper decide **HOW** to help?

Does the potential helper **ACT** upon the chosen way to help?

NO → **HELP NOT GIVEN**

YES → HELP GIVEN

NATURE OF BYSTANDER

Personal factors affecting the decision to help include
- the past reinforcement history of the individual for helping behaviour plus internalised norms
- the level of moral development reached
- the personality of the individual (those who are emotionally empathetic may help more)
- similarity to the victim (the greater the similarity, the greater the help given)
- the individual's relationship to the victim (greater helping if genetically related or friend)
- the mood of the bystander (good moods lead to more help)

COSTS AND REWARDS OF HELPING

Exchange theory - Proposes that the decision to help is made on rational grounds, by calculating the profits of intervening. If the costs of helping (e.g. loss of time, money, health) outweigh the rewards (e.g. praise) then help is unlikely. Experiments support this theory, but it may be over-rationalistic, ignoring the emotions aroused by the distress of victims.

		Costs of helping victim	
		LOW	**HIGH**
Costs of not helping victim	**HIGH**	Direct help	Indirect or no help
	LOW	Help depends on norms	No help

Arousal: cost-reward model - Piliavin et al (1981) suggested different kinds of helping situation may cause different motives for helping; 'one kind is triggered by quick, non-rational emotional arousal in response to emergencies, the other kind is influenced more by the potential helper's analysis of the costs and benefits of helping'

THE COSTS OF HELPING IN DIFFERENT SITUATIONS

THE COST OF TIME

Darley and Batson's (1973) 'Good Samaritan' study operationalised the cost of time for subjects by telling them that they were either on time, behind schedule or ahead of schedule to deliver a talk in the next building on the 'Good Samaritan'. Of those who had plenty of time to reach the building 63% helped a man in the corridor on the way who was slumped in a doorway, compared to 45% of those who were on schedule and 10% who thought they were late.

THE COST OF HELPING DIFFERENT VICTIMS

Piliavin et al tested helping behaviour for different victims by having confederates collapse in subway trains under different conditions. When the confederate
- had a walking cane, help occurred quickly and frequently
- had a bottle and smelt of alcohol, help occurred slowly and less frequently
- had (fake) blood dribbling from their mouth, help occurred frequently but indirectly

The costs of helping and not helping were different in each condition.

The situational determinants of helping behaviour

THE REACTIONS OF OTHERS

Pluralistic ignorance - if several people are present and nobody shows signs of concern or action, then the situation may be socially defined as 'in need of no action'. This is a form of informational social influence, bystanders look to each other to know how to react.

Latane and Rodin (1969)

Subjects sitting in a waiting room went to help a female experimenter (they had heard fall over next door) more often and more quickly when alone than when in the company of a confederate of the experimenter who did nothing.

Latane and Darley (1968)

Subjects completing a questionnaire in a waiting room that began to fill with smoke were more likely to report the smoke when alone than when in a group of three (despite being unable to see clearly after 6 minutes!).

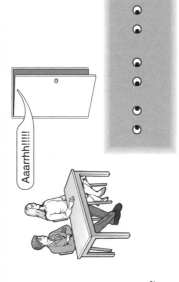

THE NUMBER OF BYSTANDERS

Social impact theory (Latane, 1981) suggests that a diffusion of responsibility occurs when many witnesses are present – the impact of a victim's plight is felt less strongly for each subject and so more witnesses can actually mean less helping.

Darley and Latane (1968)

Individual subjects, who were meant to be discussing social problems with other participants in separate cubicles over an intercom system (to prevent embarrassment), heard one of the group (in fact a tape recording of a confederate – there were no other real participants) explain that he was prone to have seizures when under stress – and later proceeded to have one!

The experimenters measured the percentage who helped within 4 minutes.

When the subject thought there were:

a 2 in the group, 85% intervened.
b 3 in the group, 62% intervened.
c 5 other subjects, 31% intervened.

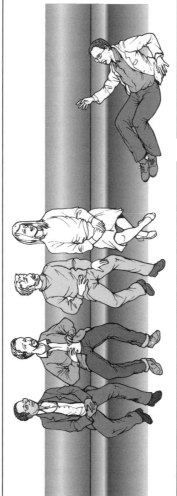

THE NORMS OF SOCIETY

Different social norms or expectations to help in certain situations may influence helping behaviour. Most societies conform to norms of reciprocity (help is given to those who are likely to return the favour); social responsibility (helping dependent others, e.g. beggars); and neighbourliness (helping those who live locally). However, norm theory does not predict which norms will be conformed to when there is a conflict between them, e.g. helping a beggar who is dependent but not likely to reciprocate the favour.

ENVIRONMENTAL LOCATION

Help is less likely to be given in built up urban areas than more rural areas, perhaps because of stimulus overload (Milgram, 1970), greater risks due to crime levels or the more impersonal environment of largely populated areas.

AMBIGUITY

Help is more likely to be given in clear-cut and emergency situations.

THE PROXIMITY OF BYSTANDERS

Social impact theory (Latane, 1981) suggests that as the remoteness between the bystander and victim increases (the greater the distance between them), the less directly responsible the bystander will feel. Someone requesting donations in front of you is more likely to be helped than someone asking by telephone.

Piliavin et al's (1969) subway studies revealed that help was offered just as frequently on crowded subways as uncrowded ones, suggesting that it is more difficult to refuse help in an immediate, face-to-face, non-remote situation, such as the enclosed space of a subway.

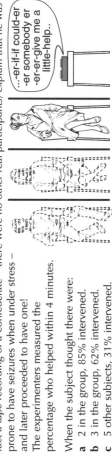

'Good Samaritanism: an underground phenomenon?' Piliavin, Rodin, and Piliavin (1969)

BACKGROUND

Social psychologists were prompted into investigating helping behaviour by the case of Kitty Genovese (a woman stabbed to death over a period of 30 minutes in front of 38 unresponsive witnesses). Most studies were conducted under strict laboratory conditions, using non-visual emergency situations. The main theories of helping behaviour involved diffusion of responsibility and the economic analysis of costs and rewards for helping.

AIM

To investigate, under real life conditions, the effect on the speed and frequency of helping, and the race of the helper, of

- the type of victim (drunk or ill)
- the race of the victim (black or white)
- the presence of helping models (present or absent)
- the size of the witnessing group

METHOD

Design
Field experiment

Independent variables (4):
- Type of victim (drunk or ill)
- Race of victim (black or white)
- Presence of helping models (present or absent)
- Size of the witnessing group

Dependent variables recorded:
- Frequency of help
- Speed of help
- Race of helper
- Sex of helper
- Movement out of area
- Verbal comments

Subjects
New York subway travellers between 11am and 3 pm, approximately 45% black, 55% white, mean of 8.5 bystanders in critical area, opportunity sample.

Situation
Non stop 7.5 minute journey in subway carriage

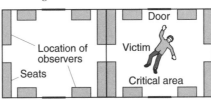

Location of observers / Seats / Door / Victim / Critical area

Procedure
4 teams of 4 researchers
- 2 female who recorded reactions
- 2 male, one acting victim, one model

Victims – 3 white, 1 black, all aged between 26–35, dressed and acted identically. Instructed to collapse after 70 seconds and remain on floor until helped.
Model instructed to help 70 seconds after collapse until end if no other help.

103 trials conducted in total, of which: 38 involved drunk victim (smelt of alcohol and carried a bottle in paper bag). 65 involved sober victim carrying a cane.

RESULTS | DISCUSSION OF RESULTS

RESULTS	DISCUSSION OF RESULTS
1 Frequency of help was impressive – overall 93% helped spontaneously (before the model), 60% of which involved more than one helper. Help was so spontaneous that the model's effect could not be properly studied.	Unlike earlier studies of helping behaviour, bystanders were continuously and visually presented with the emergency situation, making it difficult to ignore.
2 No diffusion of responsibility was found with group size.	Immediate situations decrease diffusion of impact.
3 A victim who appeared ill was more likely to receive help than one who appeared drunk. There was 100% help for the cane victim (of which 63 out of 65 trials involved spontaneous help) but 81% help for the drunk victim (of which 19 out of 38 trials involved spontaneous help). Help was also offered more quickly for the cane victim (a median of 5 seconds compared to 109 second delay with the drunk victim).	The Arousal: Cost-Reward Model proposes that the decision to help depends upon the costs and rewards of helping versus not helping. Therefore, less help for drunk victim since costs of helping are high (perhaps dangerous), costs of not helping are low (no blame), and rewards are low (probably less gratitude).
4 There was a tendency for same race helping to be more frequent, especially in the drunk condition.	Less costs of helping same race in terms of public censure, more witness arousal empathy with victim.
5 Men were significantly more likely to help the victim than women.	Less cost for men in terms of ability to physically help.
6 The longer the emergency continued without help being given: a The less impact the model had on the other bystanders. b The more likely bystanders were to leave the area. c The more likely it was that observers would discuss their behaviour.	Arousal: Cost-Reward Model argues that bystander arousal produced by the plight of others can be reduced by leaving the area or rationalising the decision not to help (e.g. by regarding the victim as undeserving) if help is not given.

STRENGTHS OF STUDY

- High ecological validity – study took place under naturally occurring conditions.
- Highly standardised procedure
- Yielded a lot of detailed data.
- Proposed a theoretical explanation to account for levels of helping in all conditions of the experiment.

WEAKNESSES OF STUDY

- Methodological weaknesses – conditions are under less strict control in field experiments than laboratory experiments. Insufficient trials conducted in some conditions of the experiment to yield reliable data, e.g. there were fewer drunk victims, only 8 black cane carriers.
- Ethical weaknesses – deception, lack of consent, no debriefing, and the production of anxiety and/or inconvenience for the bystanders are all ethically problematic.

Cultural differences in pro-social behaviour

EXAMPLES OF CROSS-CULTURAL DIFFERENCES IN PRO-SOCIAL BEHAVIOUR

Cultures show wide differences in pro-social behaviour in terms of:

1 frequency – how common helping behaviour is in the culture.
2 type – who is helped and in what form helping behaviour is shown.

- The Arapesh of New Guinea were described by Margaret Mead (1935) as gentle, kind, co-operative and generous.
- Children from traditional Maori, aboriginal and Blackfoot American Indian cultures have all scored high on pro-social behaviour.
- Children on Israeli Kibbutzim continue to co-operate on joint tasks even when individual achievement is rewarded (Moghaddam et al, 1993).

On the negative side, however:

- Mead (1935) described another New Guinea tribe, the Mundugumor, who were ruthless, uncaring and selfish.
- Chagnon (1974) studied the Yanomano of the Upper Amazon, an extremely fierce people whose society is in an almost constant state of warfare and where up to a third of males die violent deaths. Pro-social behaviour was uncommon.

Cross-cultural attitudes to helping illustrate differences too:

- Hindu Indians tend to see helping as a universal obligation.
- Americans consider the giving of help as more dependent upon factors like the nature of the help needed and the economic costs and benefits of helping.

WHAT CAUSES CROSS-CULTURAL DIFFERENCES IN PRO-SOCIAL BEHAVIOUR?

CULTURAL NORMS FOR PRO-SOCIAL BEHAVIOUR

Differences in helping across cultures are most likely to be due to their different cultural norms and values. For example:

- **Collectivistic cultures** – tend to emphasise the group, its decisions, attitudes and needs, and one's duties towards it. As a consequence there is a tendency for helping behaviour interactions to be more governed by **group need** or **equality-based** (everyone in the group receives equal proportions, regardless of what they give) **resource sharing** and **obligatory reciprocity** (the returning of favours as an important social responsibility).
- **Individualistic cultures** – tend to emphasise the individual and their goals, rights, attitudes and needs. As a consequence there is a tendency for helping interactions to be more governed by **individual needs**, economic, **equity-based** (you receive in proportion to what you give) **resource allocation** and **voluntary reciprocity** (the returning of favours based on individual responsibility).

WHAT CREATES THE CULTURAL NORMS FOR PRO-SOCIAL BEHAVIOUR?

LIFESTYLE

- The helping produced by collectivistic societies may result from the greater **long-term stability** and **inter-dependence of social groups** in these cultures that fosters reciprocal altruism. Individuals have *greater recognition* of those they help and are *more likely to be related* to them or have a *high chance of their favours being returned*.
- The helping produced by individualistic societies, however, may result from the **emphasis on individuality** and the **more transient, short-term stability of social groups** in these cultures. Individuals encounter more strangers and therefore have *less recognition* of those they help, are *less likely to be related* to them and have a *low chance of their favours being returned.*

BELIEF SYSTEMS

- **Religious belief systems** – helping behaviour is prescribed by many religions, e.g. Christianity and Hinduism, although its performance may depend upon people's commitment to their religious beliefs.
- **Political belief systems** – democratic, socialist and communist political systems all emphasise social helping in different ways. Bronfenbrenner (1970) found Russian children were raised to contribute more in domestic matters and show greater social responsibility than American children.

ECONOMIC FACTORS

- **Competition for resources** – Turnbull (1972) found that the Ik mountain people of Uganda, who lived in extreme poverty due to very scarce environmental resources, were extremely selfish, cruel and uncharitable. However, individual levels of helping can be higher in relatively poor countries, e.g. India, than relatively rich ones, e.g. the USA (although the same may not apply to national help).
- **Economic system** – capitalistic economies may be associated with more individualistic helping, based on an analysis of costs, rewards and profits. More traditional, agricultural or hunter-gatherer societies may be associated with more collectivistic, sharing norms.

HOW ARE THE CULTURAL NORMS TRANSMITTED IN THE CULTURE?

Conformity to cultural norms – Cultures that show greater expectation and encouragement of co-operation and helping behaviour produce more of it, even if surrounded by cultural neighbours that show less, e.g. the Amish society in America. Similar findings occur with Israeli children from Kibbutzim (collectivist communities) who show more helping behaviour than Israeli children from nearby cities.

Child-raising techniques – Sroufe (1978) concluded that empathy and altruism in children is fostered by a loving and caring relationship with a primary caregiver. Whiting and Whiting (1975) found greater childhood helping behaviour in cultures whose children are involved in family responsibilities, chores and sibling raising (e.g. Kenya and Mexico) than cultures whose children are paid for contributions to family life (e.g. USA).

Individual learning through reinforcement – rewards and praise have been shown to increase helping behaviour in children.

Contemporary issue – How does the media affect behaviour?

LABORATORY EXPERIMENTS ON MEDIA VIOLENCE

Bandura's experiments showed that aggression could be learnt and imitated from live, filmed or cartoon models.
Liebert and Baron (1972) found that children who had watched a violent programme were more likely to hurt another child. However laboratory studies may produce artificial results.

CORRELATIONS ON MEDIA VIOLENCE

Eron (1987) found a significant positive correlation between the amount of aggression viewed at age 8 and later aggression at age 30.
Phillips (1986) has found correlations between highly publicised incidents of aggression, such as murder cases or boxing matches, and the number of corresponding incidents in society at large. Correlation is not causation however.

NATURAL EXPERIMENTS ON MEDIA VIOLENCE

Joy et al (1986) measured children's levels of aggression in a Canadian town one year before and after television was introduced, and found a significant increase compared to the non significant increases in towns that already had television.

FIELD EXPERIMENTS ON MEDIA VIOLENCE

Parke et al (1977) showed juvenile delinquents in the USA and Belgium either violent or non-violent television for a week in their homes. Aggression was greater for the violent TV group especially in those who had previously shown higher levels. Field studies are hard to control and replicate however.

OBSERVATIONAL LEARNING

Violent behaviour could be learnt by observation and imitated if rewarding.

DISINHIBITION

Watching aggression could reduce inhibitions about behaving aggressively as it is seen as socially legitimate.

AROUSAL

Aggressive emotional arousal or excitement from watching aggression may lead to real violence.

DESENSITISATION

Watching aggression may lead to an increased acceptance or tolerance of it in society.

NEGATIVE EFFECTS (OF MEDIA VIOLENCE)

MEDIATING FACTORS

- The personality of the viewer. The effects of TV violence often depend on what the child brings to the screen.
- The amount of exposure to media violence.

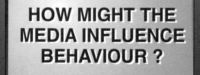

HOW MIGHT THE MEDIA INFLUENCE BEHAVIOUR ?

NO EFFECT

Howitt and Cumberbatch (1974) analysed 300 studies concluding that TV violence has no direct effect on children's behaviour. Freedman (1984, 1986) argues that although there is a small correlation between levels of viewing and behaving aggressively, the causal connection is very weak.

POSITIVE EFFECTS OF MEDIA VIOLENCE

INOCULATION

Watching antisocial violence could provide the opportunity to discuss its immorality or to see it come to no good (the 'baddie' loses).

CATHARSIS

According to Freud's ideas, watching violence could provide a relief from pent up aggression, as it is released through emotional sympathy.

STUDIES ON THE CATHARTIC EFFECT OF TV VIOLENCE

Feshbach and Singer (1971) claimed that children shown aggressive programs over a 6 week period showed *less* aggressive behaviour than those who saw non-violent TV. However, this study has been accused of methodological flaws, and more recent studies have not replicated or have found the opposite findings.

POSITIVE EFFECTS OF PRO-SOCIAL MEDIA

POSITIVE ROLE MODELS

Just as aggression could be learnt from aggressive media models, so pro-social role models could also provide a basis for observational learning and imitation – especially if their behaviour produces rewards such as public praise, social respect etc. (the 'goodie' always wins in the end).

STUDIES ON THE EFFECTS OF PRO-SOCIAL TV

Sprafkin et al (1975) found over 90% of children chose to help a puppy instead of personal gain after watching a program that involved helping ('Lassie'), while Baron et al (1979) found children were more co-operative after watching the 'The Waltons'.
Hearold (1986) analysed approximately 200 studies and concluded that pro-social television has around twice the effect on children's behaviour than anti-social television.

Methods of investigating brain function – measurement

MEASURING/OBSERVATIONAL TECHNIQUES

DIRECT RECORDING OF NEURONAL ACTIVITY
Microelectrodes are inserted into single neuronal cells and record their electrochemical activity, e.g.

Hubel and Wiesel measured the activity of single neuronal cells in the visual cortex of monkeys. By keeping the head still, various visual stimuli could be presented to different areas of the retina to discover both the area the cell represented and the stimuli it most responded to.

EVALUATION
Advantages
- Extremely precise – a very accurate way of studying the living function of neurones.

Disadvantages
- Very time-consuming – thousands of neurones occupy even a tiny area of brain.
- Too focused – it neglects the interactions between nerve cells that are responsible for brain functions.
- Invasive method – it, thus, has ethical problems, especially if applied to humans.

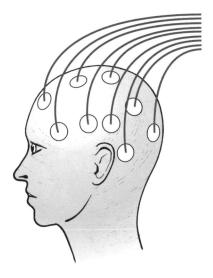

EXTERNAL RECORDING OF BRAIN ACTIVITY
Aims to detect brain activity from measurements made at the surface of the skull, e.g.
- electroencephalograms (EEG) – electrodes are attached to areas of the scalp, and the electrical activity of the brain beneath that they detect is amplified to reveal the frequency of the 'brain wave'. The frequency is the number of oscillations the wave makes in a second and ranges from 1–3 hertz (delta waves) to 13 hertz or over (beta waves).
- evoked potentials – record the change in the electrical activity of an area of brain when an environmental stimuli is presented or a psychological task is undertaken.

Electrooculargrams (EOG) measure electrical activity of eye movements, whereas Electromyograms (EMG) record activity from muscles to measure tension or relaxation.

EVALUATION
Advantages
- Non-invasive techniques – no alteration or intervention makes these methods of measuring brain activity more natural and ecologically valid.
- Practically useful – these methods can distinguish between levels of sleep and different types of subject, e.g. brain damaged, epileptic, those with Alzheimer's disease, etc.

Disadvantages
- Crude measure – the activity of millions of neurones is measured and averaged. EEGs indicate the activity level but not the precise function of the neurones involved.

SCANNING TECHNIQUES
1 **STILL PICTURES** – detailed three dimensional or cross-sectional images of the brain can be gained by the following non-invasive techniques:
   a **Computerised Axial Tomography** (CAT scan) – is produced by X-ray rotation.
   b **Magnetic Resonance Imaging** (MRI scan) – where magnetic fields are rotated around the head to produce an extremely detailed picture.

2 **DYNAMIC PICTURES** – moving coloured images of brain activity levels in different parts of the brain over time can be gained by techniques such as:
   a **Positron Emission Tomography** (PET scan) – which detects the metabolism level of injected substances (e.g. glucose) made mildly radioactive to show which parts of the brain are most active (using up energy) over a period of minutes.
   b **Functional Magnetic Resonance Imaging** (F-MRI scan) – shows metabolic activity second by second without injected tracers.
   c **Magnetoencephalography** (MEG scan) – detects actual nerve cell firing over thousandths of a second.

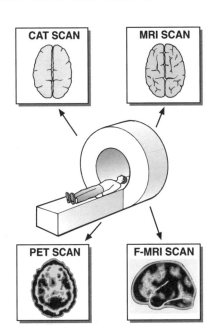

EVALUATION
Advantages
- Detailed knowledge – scans can gain information about the brain structure and function of conscious patients, some while they are performing psychological tasks.

Disadvantages
- Scanning techniques – are expensive and scans can be difficult to interpret and are sensitive to disruption, e.g. by small movements.

'Brain abnormalities in murderers indicated by positron emission tomography' Raine et al (1997)

INTRODUCTION
Previous research using a variety of techniques (e.g. brain damage effects and EEG measurements) on both humans and other animals has indicated that dysfunction in certain localised brain areas may predispose individuals to violent behaviour. Such brain structures include the prefrontal cortex, corpus callosum, left angular gyrus, amygdala, hippocampus and thalamus.

AIM
By using recent brain imaging techniques on a large group of violent offenders who have committed murder and a control group of non-murderers, this study hypothesises that dysfunction in the above brain structures should be found more often in the murderers than
1 dysfunction of the same areas in non-murderers
2 dysfunction in other areas of the murderers' brains that have been implicated in *non*-violent psychiatric disorders (e.g. the caudate, putamen, globus pallidus, midbrain and cerebellum)

METHOD
Subjects –The 'murderers' were 41 prisoners (39 male, 2 female) with a mean age of 34.3 years (standard deviation of 10.1), charged with murder or manslaughter in California. They were referred for brain imaging scans to obtain evidence or information relating to a defence of not guilty by reason of insanity, incompetence to stand trial or diminished capacity to reduce sentencing having been found guilty. The reasons for scanning referral were very diverse, ranging from schizophrenia (6 cases) to head injury or organic brain damage (23 cases). No murderer had psychoactive medication for 2 weeks before scanning (each was urine screened).

Controls – Each murderer was matched with a 'normal' subject for age, sex and schizophrenia where necessary. Each was screened to exclude physical and mental illness, drug taking and, of course, a history of murder.

Procedure – After practice trials, all participants were injected with a tracer substance (fluorodeoxyglucose) that was taken up by the brain to show the location of brain metabolism (activity) while they conducted a continuous performance task (CPT) requiring them to detect target signals for 32 minutes. A positron emission tomography (PET) scan was then immediately given to show the relative brain activity (glucose metabolised) for 6 main cortical areas (the outside of the brain) and 8 subcortical areas (inside the brain).

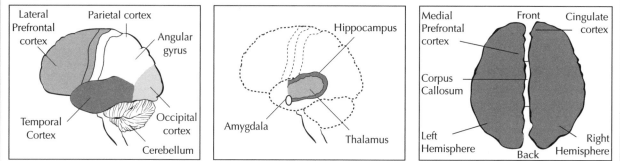

RESULTS

	Brain structure	Murderers' metabolic activity level	Interpretation
Cortex	Prefrontal cortex	Lower activity than controls	Linked to loss of self control and altered emotion.
	Parietal cortex	Lower activity than controls especially in the left angular and bilateral superior gyrus	Lower left angular gyrus activity linked to lower verbal ability, educational failure and thus crime.
	Temporal cortex	No difference compared to controls	No difference was expected.
	Occipital cortex	Higher activity than controls (unexpected)	May compensate on CPT for lower frontal activity.
Subcortex	Corpus callosum	Lower activity than controls	May stop left brain inhibiting the right's violence.
	Amygdala	Lower activity in left than right side of the brain in murderers than controls	These structures form part of the limbic system (thought to control emotional expression).
	Medial (inner) temporal including hippocampus	Lower activity in left than right side of the brain in murderers than controls	Problems with these structures may cause a lack of inhibition for violent behaviour, fearlessness and
	Thalamus	Higher activity on right side in murderers	a failure to learn the negative effects of violence.
	Cingulate, caudate, putamen Globus pallidus, midbrain and cerebellum	No significant differences were found in these structures between murderers and controls.	No differences were expected in these structures (which are involved in other disorders), supporting the specificity of brain areas involved in violence.

No significant differences were found for performance on the CPT, handedness (except left-handed murderers had significantly less abnormal amygdala asymmetry than right handed murderers), head injury or ethnicity.

DISCUSSION
Strengths – a large sample was used with many controls to rule out alternative effects on brain activity.

Limitations – the PET scan method can lack precision, the findings apply only to a subgroup of violent offenders (not to other types of violence or crime) and caution in the interpretation of the findings is needed, which need to be replicated.

The findings do not mean violence is caused by biology alone (other social, psychological and situational factors are involved), do not demonstrate that the murderers are not responsible for their actions, do not mean PET scans can diagnose murderers and do not say whether the brain abnormalities are a cause or effect of behaviour.

EVALUATION
Methodological	No control over the level of violence used in the murder. Brain scans can be difficult to interpret.
Theoretical	Previous findings on brain structures involved in violence are supported and new findings revealed.
Links	Brain scanning. Cortical functions. Freewill. Ethical implications of socially sensitive research.

Methods of investigating brain function – alteration

ALTERATION/EXPERIMENTAL TECHNIQUES

ACCIDENTAL DAMAGE

Researchers use these natural experiments to compare the alteration in psychological functioning with the location of damage (by scan, surgery or autopsy). Damage may be caused by

- **strokes/tumours** – e.g. blood clot damage has revealed much about the location of motor, sensory, and linguistic functioning in the brain.
- **head trauma** – e.g. a railroad construction accident blew a 3 foot long metal rod through Phineas Gage's left frontal lobe in 1848, changing his personality to make him impulsive and irritable.
- **virus** – e.g. the virus herpes simplex damaged the temporal lobe and hippocampus of Clive Wearing causing anterograde amnesia.

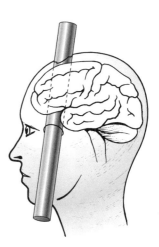

EVALUATION
Advantages
- The altering damage occurs 'naturally' so there are less ethical problems compared to other methods.

Disadvantages
- Lack of precision – the exact extent of damage is not controllable and may be difficult to assess.
- Comparison problems – comparison of the functioning in the individual before and after the damage is less objective, since it is often based on retrospective accounts of previous behaviour and abilities.
- Confounding variables – other non-physical effects of the damage may be responsible for behavioural differences. Social reactions to Phineas Gage's physical deformity may have affected his personality.

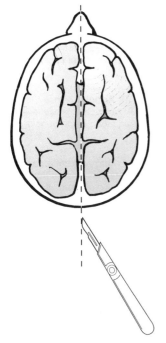

DELIBERATE DAMAGE
ABLATION/LESION STUDIES – aim to investigate function by removing areas of the brain or destroying links between areas. Some of the psychological functions investigated have included

- **Motivation** – ablation studies on the hypothalamus of rats have caused disrupted eating behaviour.
- **Aggression** – removing the amygdala of some animals has reduced their aggression.
- **Memory** – Lashley removed large portions of rat brains to find the location of memory.
- **Consciousness** – Sperry cut the corpus callosum of epileptic patients, producing a 'split mind'.
- **Psychopathology** – prefrontal lobotomy was performed on mental inmates to control behaviour.

EXPERIMENTAL EXPOSURE EFFECTS – aim to influence brain physiology by using environmental distortion or deprivation. Common examples are found in perceptual studies, e.g. Blakemore and Cooper's study of the visual cortex of cats exposed to an environment of vertical lines.

EVALUATION
Advantages
- Greater control – greater precision in the location of damage and the ability to compare behaviour before and after alteration leads to higher certainty over the effects of the damage.

Disadvantages
- Ethical problems of intervention – the deliberate change of behaviour is radical and irreversible.
- Non-human findings – may not be legitimately generalised to humans due to qualitative differences.
- Plasticity – the brain is a very flexible system which can compensate for damage. Removing one part of it will only show the performance of the rest of the system, not necessarily the missing part.

STIMULATION OF THE BRAIN
ELECTRICAL STIMULATION – aims to stimulate brain areas with microelectrodes to reveal their function through behavioural change. Examples include

- animal studies – Delgado stimulated areas of the limbic system to provoke aggression in monkeys and inhibit aggression in a charging bull (while standing in front of it!) by remote control.
- human studies – Penfield stimulated areas of the cortex in patients undergoing brain surgery and found locations that would produce body movement (primary motor cortex), body sensations (primary sensory cortex), memories of sound (temporal lobe) and visual sensations (visual cortex).

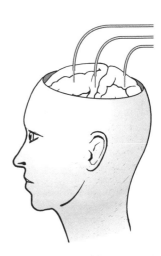

EVALUATION
Advantages
- Less harmful – the aim is to stimulate the brain rather than damage it (therefore more ethical).
- More valid – stimulation seems a better way of investigating the 'living' function of brain areas.

Disadvantages
- Invasive technique – the techniques still involve surgical operation, which can be risky.
- Interconnectedness – it is not easy to know exactly how far the stimulation has spread to other areas and the behaviour produced may not be natural, indeed it is often more stereotyped.

Localisation of brain function - exterior structure

LEFT SIDE VIEW OF BRAIN

FRONTAL LOBE OF CORTEX
- Involved in planning, initiative, and voluntary motor control. The frontal cortex is a very highly developed area in humans compared to other animals.
- Micro-electrode stimulation of the primary motor cortex produces twitches of movement in body parts.
- Damage causes lack of insight, loss of primitive reflex suppression, behavioural inertia (lack of spontaneity and initiative), and an inability to adjust behaviour to make it appropriate to the situation.

PARIETAL LOBE OF CORTEX
- Involved in sensing and monitoring of body parts.
- Micro-electrode stimulation to the primary sensory cortex produces sensations in various parts of the body.
- Contains many sensory association areas, such as the visual association area necessary for object recognition (damage does not cause blindness but visual agnosia - the inability to recognise the identity of whole objects by sight). Also integrates information from different sensory areas to enable cross-modal matching (e.g, pairing up the sight and sound of an object).

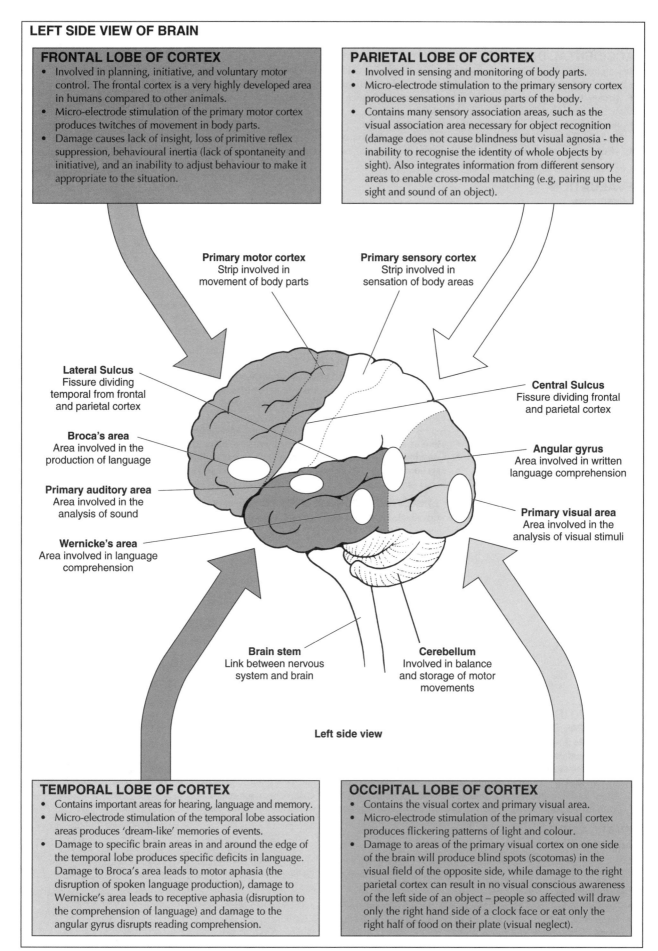

Primary motor cortex
Strip involved in movement of body parts

Primary sensory cortex
Strip involved in sensation of body areas

Lateral Sulcus
Fissure dividing temporal from frontal and parietal cortex

Broca's area
Area involved in the production of language

Primary auditory area
Area involved in the analysis of sound

Wernicke's area
Area involved in language comprehension

Central Sulcus
Fissure dividing frontal and parietal cortex

Angular gyrus
Area involved in written language comprehension

Primary visual area
Area involved in the analysis of visual stimuli

Brain stem
Link between nervous system and brain

Cerebellum
Involved in balance and storage of motor movements

Left side view

TEMPORAL LOBE OF CORTEX
- Contains important areas for hearing, language and memory.
- Micro-electrode stimulation of the temporal lobe association areas produces 'dream-like' memories of events.
- Damage to specific brain areas in and around the edge of the temporal lobe produces specific deficits in language. Damage to Broca's area leads to motor aphasia (the disruption of spoken language production), damage to Wernicke's area leads to receptive aphasia (disruption to the comprehension of language) and damage to the angular gyrus disrupts reading comprehension.

OCCIPITAL LOBE OF CORTEX
- Contains the visual cortex and primary visual area.
- Micro-electrode stimulation of the primary visual cortex produces flickering patterns of light and colour.
- Damage to areas of the primary visual cortex on one side of the brain will produce blind spots (scotomas) in the visual field of the opposite side, while damage to the right parietal cortex can result in no visual conscious awareness of the left side of an object – people so affected will draw only the right hand side of a clock face or eat only the right half of food on their plate (visual neglect).

Evaluation of neurophysiological findings

THE LIMITATIONS OF NEUROPHYSIOLOGICAL FINDINGS

- Neurophysiology often explains the hardware and function of different parts of the brain but often **ignores** the effect of **environmental experience** upon it. Some studies have looked at this issue, however, such as Blakemore & Cooper's (1970) exposure of animals to environments of vertical lines, and the effect of this on the striate visual cortex.

- Physiological explanations have not dealt with the **'mind body' problem** – they do not say how the physical structure and activity of the brain gives rise to the apparently non-physical conscious sensations and experience of mental life.

- There are many **limitations** of some of the **methods** used to identify brain activity, e.g. electrical stimulation of the brain may have a spreading activation effect to other areas (see methods of investigating brain function).

- The idea that neurophysiological explanations are sufficient to explain psychological functioning is dubious. In the case of visual perception, for example, Marr (1982) pointed out that the **aims** and **cognitive processes** of vision had to be considered rather than just the hardware. Indeed, once the processes by which perception occurs have been identified, the psychologist could change the hardware from the brain to a computer's circuits. There is, however, the possibility that vision could only be achieved by the complex biological hardware of the brain, but on the other hand, this biological complexity may also make a clear and useful explanation of perception impossible if the functions are spread in a parallel way over millions of neurones.

- Focusing just on the physiology of the brain may lead researchers to ignore the important implications that **psychological** research and theory has for the functions of brain areas. Hubel and Wiesel's 'bottom-up' description of feature detection in the cells of the visual cortex only focused on the 'input' from the retina, and thus ignored the 'top-down' influences of past experience and expectation that many psychologists such as Gregory (1970) have long pointed out. Recent investigations of the neural activity of cells that respond to the input of visual stimuli are now stressing the importance of the brain's background state of activity - 'It seems that the output of an individual neurone also depends on what the brain happens to be thinking about at the time' (McCrone, cited from *New Scientist*, December 1997). Maunsell and Treue (1996), for example, found the visual movement detection cells of monkeys would show increased activity to moving dots that they had been trained to pay attention to, compared to dots they could see but were not 'interested' in.

Integration of cortical areas devoted to speaking a written passage

Retinal information sent to the primary visual cortex is analysed to detect the lines and curves of letters in the text. Words are distinguished in the angular gyrus and transformed into a form that can be recognised and interpreted for meaning by Wernicke's area. Once the written passage has been understood and held in memory, Broca's area is involved in the formation of spoken words and the motor cortex initiates the physical production of them.

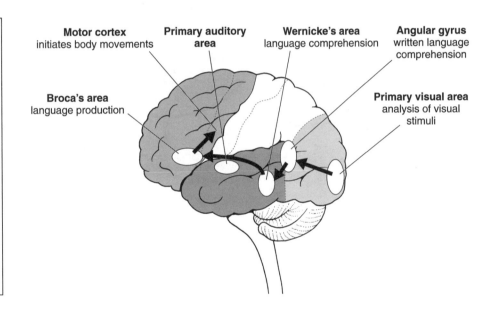

Motor cortex initiates body movements

Primary auditory area

Wernicke's area language comprehension

Angular gyrus written language comprehension

Broca's area language production

Primary visual area analysis of visual stimuli

ARGUMENTS AGAINST LOCALISATION OF FUNCTION

- **Localisation is not always clear cut.** In the case of brain asymmetry, for example, there are many variations in the location of function in the two cerebral hemispheres between male and female subjects and left and right handed subjects. The findings usually reported on the location of cerebral functioning are most representative of right-handed, male subjects.

- **The brain shows 'plasticity'.** According to some researchers, the brain is very flexible and can physically adjust the location of function if brain damage occurs (e.g. the recovery of language in children with left cerebral hemisphere damage), or specialisation to environmental conditions is required (e.g. blind Braille readers show an increase in the sensory cortex surface area devoted to the right forefinger, compared to non-Braille readers and their own left forefingers).

- **The brain is hugely integrated.** There are many different brain areas involved in abilities such as vision (Maunsell and Newsome, 1987, proposed there were at least 19 visual areas in macaque monkeys) and research needs to focus on how these areas **interact** together to produce function. The diagram above shows how just some of the areas involved in language interact in a simple task. Researchers such as Lashley believe in holism – that many functions are distributed across the whole brain. Lashley (1929) destroyed virtually all parts of rat brains in varying amounts to find the location of memory, and concluded that the 'law of mass action' applied -memory loss is related to the amount of damage inflicted upon a rat brain, not the location of it. Neuroscientists are currently accepting the view that the brain is a very dynamic system and that activity in one area of the brain is influenced by the background activity of the rest of the brain. We must 'stop thinking of neurones as if they are exchanging messages… most of the 5000 input lines to the average brain cell are actually parts of feedback loops returning via neighbouring neurones, or those higher up the hierarchy. Barely a tenth of the connections come from sense organs or mapping levels lower in the hierarchy. Every neurone is plumbed into a sea of feedback' (McCrone, cited in *New Scientist*, December, 1997)

Localisation of function – the cerebral hemispheres

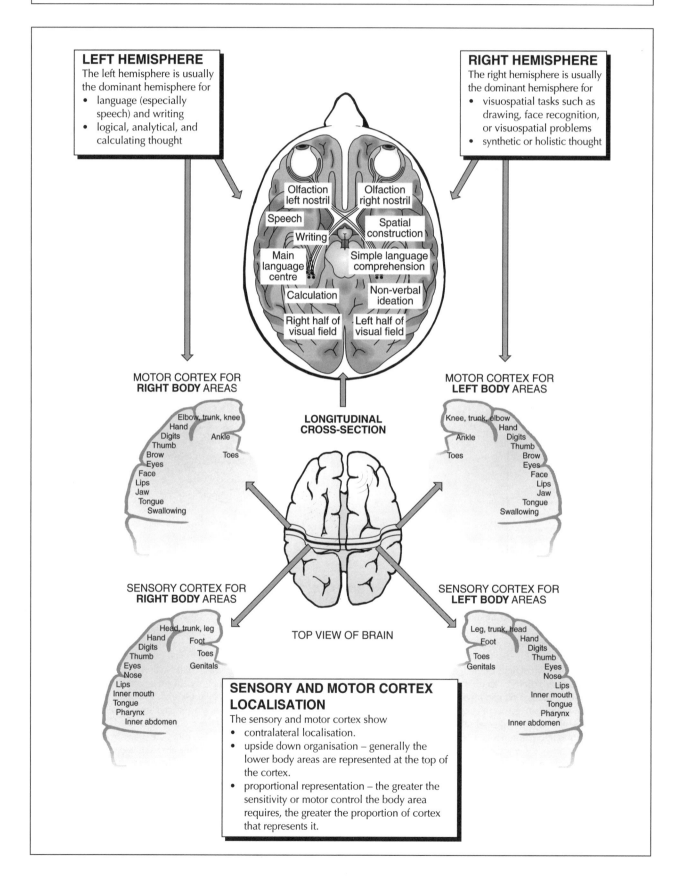

LEFT HEMISPHERE
The left hemisphere is usually the dominant hemisphere for
- language (especially speech) and writing
- logical, analytical, and calculating thought

RIGHT HEMISPHERE
The right hemisphere is usually the dominant hemisphere for
- visuospatial tasks such as drawing, face recognition, or visuospatial problems
- synthetic or holistic thought

Olfaction left nostril
Olfaction right nostril
Speech
Spatial construction
Writing
Main language centre
Simple language comprehension
Calculation
Non-verbal ideation
Right half of visual field
Left half of visual field

MOTOR CORTEX FOR **RIGHT BODY** AREAS

MOTOR CORTEX FOR **LEFT BODY** AREAS

LONGITUDINAL CROSS-SECTION

Elbow, trunk, knee
Hand
Digits
Thumb
Ankle
Brow
Toes
Eyes
Face
Lips
Jaw
Tongue
Swallowing

Knee, trunk, elbow
Hand
Ankle
Digits
Thumb
Toes
Brow
Eyes
Face
Lips
Jaw
Tongue
Swallowing

SENSORY CORTEX FOR **RIGHT BODY** AREAS

TOP VIEW OF BRAIN

SENSORY CORTEX FOR **LEFT BODY** AREAS

Head, trunk, leg
Hand
Foot
Digits
Toes
Thumb
Eyes
Genitals
Nose
Lips
Inner mouth
Tongue
Pharynx
Inner abdomen

Leg, trunk, head
Foot
Hand
Toes
Digits
Genitals
Thumb
Eyes
Nose
Lips
Inner mouth
Tongue
Pharynx
Inner abdomen

SENSORY AND MOTOR CORTEX LOCALISATION
The sensory and motor cortex show
- contralateral localisation.
- upside down organisation – generally the lower body areas are represented at the top of the cortex.
- proportional representation – the greater the sensitivity or motor control the body area requires, the greater the proportion of cortex that represents it.

'Hemisphere deconnection and unity in conscious awareness' Sperry (1968)

AIM
To present studies investigating the behavioural, neurological and psychological consequences of surgery in which the two cerebral hemispheres are deconnected from each other by severing the corpus callosum. Sperry uses these studies to argue that the 'split brain' shows characteristics during testing that suggest each hemisphere
- has slightly different functions
- possesses an independent stream of conscious awareness and
- has its own set of memories which are inaccessible to the other

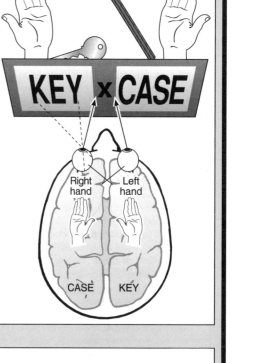

METHOD
Subjects: A handful of patients who underwent hemispheric deconnection to reduce crippling epilepsy.

Design: A natural experiment. Severing the corpus callosum prevents communication between the left and right hemispheres.

Procedure: Since each hemisphere receives information from, and controls the functioning of, the opposite side of the body, the capabilities of each can be tested by
- presenting visual information to either the left or right visual field when the subject is focusing straight ahead. If this is done at fast speeds (about 1 tenth of a second) the eye does not have time to move and re-focus. Thus information presented to the left visual field, will be received by the right hemisphere of the brain
- presenting tactile information to either the left or right hand behind a screen (to remove visual identification). Thus tactile information from objects felt by the right hand will be received by the left hemisphere.

RESULTS
Visual stimuli presented in one visual field at a time
- Objects shown once to a visual field are only recognised if presented again in the same visual field, not the other – implying different visual perception and memory storage for each hemisphere.
- Objects presented in the right visual field, and therefore received in the left hemisphere, can be named verbally and in writing, indicating the presence of speech comprehension and production as well as writing ability.
- Objects presented in the left visual field, and therefore received in the right hemisphere, can <u>not</u> be named verbally or in writing, but can be identified through pointing, indicating that the right hemisphere has language comprehension but not speech or writing.
  These tests imply that the two hemispheres of the brain have different abilities and functions.

Different visual stimuli presented simultaneously to different visual fields
- If different visual stimuli are presented simultaneously to different visual fields, e.g. a dollar sign to the left, a question mark to the right, and the subject is asked to draw with the left hand (out of sight) what was seen, the subject draws the stimuli from the left visual field (the dollar sign). If asked what the *left hand has just drawn*, the subject's verbal, left hemisphere replies with what was seen in the right visual field (the question mark).

- If two related words are simultaneously presented to the different visual fields, e.g. 'key' to the left and 'case' to the right, the left hand will select a key from amongst a variety of objects, whereas the right hand will write what it saw in the right visual field (a case) without being influenced by the meaning of the word in the left visual field.

Tactile stimuli presented to different hands
- If an object has been felt by the left hand only, it can be recognised by the left hand again but cannot be named by the subject or recognised by the right hand from amongst other objects.
  These tests imply that one side of the brain does not know what the other side has seen or felt.

Tests of the non-dominant right hemisphere
- The left hand can pick out semantically similar objects in a search for an object presented to the left visual field but not present in the search array of objects, e.g. a watch will be selected in response to a picture of a wall clock. The left hand can sort objects into meaningful categories.
- The right brain can solve simple arithmetical problems (pointing out the correct answer) and is superior in drawing spatial relationships.
- The right brain appears to experience its own emotional reactions (giggling and blushing in embarrassment at a nude pin up presented to the left visual field) and can show frustration at the actions of the left hemisphere.

EVALUATION
Methodological: *Validity* – Being a natural experiment there is a lack of control over variables – in particular the subjects' mental abilities may have been atypical before the operation.

Theoretical: There do seem to be functional asymmetries between the hemispheres. However, research has revealed many individual differences – the above findings appear most typical of right-handed men. It should not be forgotten that the left and right hemispheres share many functions and are highly integrated.

Applications: The research has implications for helping patients with brain damage.

Links: Cortical functions, consciousness, psychosurgery.

Body rhythms 1

CIRCADIAN RHYTHMS

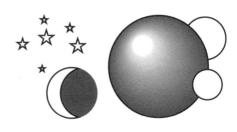

- Circadian rhythms cycle over 24 hours ('circa' = approximately, 'diem' = day). Humans show physiological changes over a 24 hour cycle in hormone levels, body temperature and heart, respiration and metabolic rate. Of most interest to psychologists however, has been the circadian sleep-waking cycle because of the dramatic changes in behaviour it produces.

THE SLEEP-WAKING CYCLE
The circadian sleep-waking rhythm determines our alertness and activity levels during the day and night. In humans it is regulated by:
- **The endogenous pacemakers or internal body clock** of the ***suprachiasmatic nucleus*** (SCN) and the ***pineal gland***. The SCN is part of the hypothalamus that regulates sleep-waking patterns by sending messages to the pineal gland to release melatonin – which is thought to stimulate the production of serotonin in the raphe nucleus to initiate sleep. Removal of the SCN in hamsters randomises their sleep – waking patterns. The sleep-waking body clock seems to be the product of evolution and is largely inherited, SCN cells will fire in a rhythmic way even if removed and placed in culture. In humans it seems to naturally run on a slightly longer cycle than a day (around 25 hours) but there seem to be inherited individual differences between people. If the SCN of mutant hamsters which causes different sleep-waking patterns is transplanted into normal hamsters who have had their SCN removed, they adopt the mutant's circadian patterns. The sleep-waking circadian rhythm can be adjusted to a certain degree by zeigebers, but seems mostly regulated by the internal body clock.
- The major **external re-setter (zeitgeber)** of the circadian body clock in humans is light, which is detected at the retina and can influence (via interconnecting nerve fibres) the SCN to synchronise our rhythms to the 24 hour cycle of the day. This has been demonstrated by studies that have removed the zeitgeber of light such as ***Siffre's cave study***. However, while the cycle/rhythm can slowly adjust to new starting points (as happens when zetigebers change due to human activities such as shift work or travel over time zones) and can be resisted with a struggle (e.g. in sleep deprivation studies) the basic pattern or ratio of sleep-waking activity is remarkably consistent due to its biological basis. Similar sleep-waking patterns are found cross-culturally, despite cultural zeitgebers such as siestas and environmental zeitgebers in countries who experience whole summers or winters of lightness and darkness (such as those in the arctic circle). The inflexibility of the rhythm has also been demonstrated under controlled laboratory conditions, where exposure to different ratios of light and dark hours do not affect the sleeping patterns of subjects beyond certain limits.

PSYCHOLOGICAL AND PHYSIOLOGICAL CHANGES OF THE CIRCADIAN RHYTHM

	PSYCHOLOGICAL EXPERIENCE	PHYSIOLOGICAL CORRELATES		
		EEG	EOG	EMG
WAKING STATES (Approx. 16 hours)	**Alertness** – involves open-eyed active consciousness with the full ability to concentrate on a task. **Relaxation** – involves a passive but awake conscious experience although the eyes may be shut.	Beta waves (13 hertz or above) Alpha waves (8 to 12 hertz)	Eye movements reflect task Eye movements reflect cognition	Muscle activity reflects task Muscle activity reflects relaxation
SLEEP STATES (Approx. 8 hours – around 80% NREM 20% REM in adults)	**NON-REM SLEEP** – involves a series of stages. **Stage 1:** Lightest stage of sleep. Easily awakened.	Theta waves (4–7 hertz)	Slow rolling eye movements	Muscles relaxed but active
	Stage 2: Light sleep. Fairly easily awakened. Some responsiveness to external and internal stimuli - name calling produces K-complex activity.	Theta waves sleep spindles, K-complexes	Minimal eye movement	Little muscle movement
	Stage 3: Deep sleep. Difficult to awaken. Very unresponsive to external stimuli.	Delta waves (1–3 Hz) 20-50% of the time	Virtually no eye movement	Virtually no muscle movement
	Stage 4: Very deep sleep. Very difficult to awaken. Very unresponsive to external stimuli.	Delta waves over 50% of the time	Virtually no eye movement	Virtually no muscle movement
	REM SLEEP It is difficult to awaken people from rapid eye-movement (REM) sleep. If woken, individuals report vivid dreaming far more often than if woken from non-REM sleep (Dement and Kleitman, 1957).	High levels of mixed wave brain activity	Eye movement – may reflect dream content	Muscles in a state of virtual paralysis

Key application – of physiological concepts to shift work and jet lag

WHAT PHYSIOLOGICAL CONCEPTS ARE RELEVANT?
- Physiological research into body rhythms such as the human sleep-waking circadian rhythm has revealed that both inner biological factors (*endogenous pacemakers* or body clocks) and external environmental factors (*zeitgebers*) can influence our pattern of sleeping and waking activity.
- However, research has also shown that the sleep-waking body clock is fairly consistent and slow to adjust, while zeitgebers such as work patterns and travel across time zones can change very quickly. Such a *mismatch between our natural body rhythms and activity patterns* can produce negative effects, which have been investigated by physiologically orientated psychologists.
- The *pattern of adjustment* is also important. Siffre, a French cave explorer, spent 6 months in a cave underground which effectively removed the external zeitgebers of the world above such as light levels and human activity patterns. No time cues were given via his telephone contact with the outside world and artificial lights were switched on when he woke up and off when he fell asleep. Under these conditions his natural body rhythms lengthened to around 25 hours so by the time he left the cave he had experienced fewer 'days' than everyone else. This means that adjustment to new zeitgebers is easier if they involve a *lengthening* of the day, since the *circadian cycle* itself seems to have a natural tendency to lengthen.

SHIFT WORK
Much shift work has involved three 8-hour working periods rotating anti-clockwise, e.g. from night shift to evening shift to day shift (a 'phase advance' rather than 'phase delay' schedule), frequently on a weekly basis or less. Physiological research on body rhythms informs us this can produce long-term disorientation, stress, insomnia, exhaustion and negative effects on reaction speed, co-ordination skill, attention and problem solving, since such work schedules:

1 Create a mismatch or desynchronisation between the body rhythms of arousal and the zeitgebers of activity levels.
2 Do not allow enough adjustment time for body rhythms to catch up with (become 'entrained' by) new activity levels.
3 Delay the catching up (entrainment) of body rhythms by shortening rather than lengthening the day.

This increases the chances of accidents occurring due to human error, even when other factors such as reduced hours of sleep, night-time supervision levels etc. are taken into account.

Czeisler et al (1982) studied a group of industrial workers who were following such a shift pattern and their suggestion that they moved clockwise in shifts (a phase delay schedule) on a three week rather than one week basis led to better worker health and morale, as well as higher productivity levels.

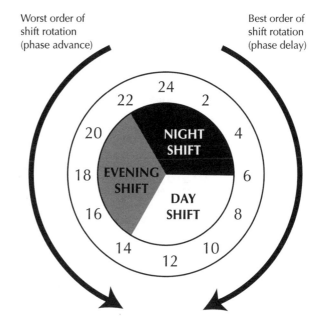

Worst order of shift rotation (phase advance)

Best order of shift rotation (phase delay)

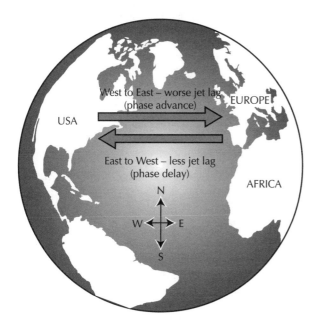

West to East – worse jet lag (phase advance)

East to West – less jet lag (phase delay)

USA
EUROPE
AFRICA

N
W E
S

JET LAG
Rapid air travel across time zones can produce jet lag - general disorientation and symptoms similar to those described for shift work, though not always as severe. This also:

1 Results from a mismatch or desynchronisation between the body rhythms of the old time zone, stored in the body clock you take with you, and the zeitgebers of the new time zone, such as human activity levels (e.g. mealtimes) and light levels.
2 Is harder to adjust to if the zeitgebers shorten the day and the circadian cycle – causing a phase advance. This explains why rapid travel from the west to the east across many time zones tends to produce worse jet lag than travelling from east to west (which lengthens the day and causes phase delay).

The influence of zeitgebers and endogenous pacemakers on jet lag are harder to identify since many other variables involved in travelling could cause the symptoms, such as stress, excitement, unfamiliarity and restricted posture.

Slower travel over fewer time zones as well as taking drugs that affect melatonin activity at appropriate times may reduce the severity of jet lag symptoms.

Body rhythms 2

	PSYCHOLOGICAL AND PHYSIOLOGICAL CHANGES	THE ROLE OF ENDOGENOUS PACEMAKERS AND ZEITGEBERS
CIRCANNUAL RHYTHMS (Rhythms lasting about a year)	• Much behaviour in animals varies over a yearly cycle, such as hibernation, mating and migration. • Some humans show Seasonal Affective Disorder (SAD) – a strong variation in mood over the year, usually involving depression during the winter months.	• A key external zeitgeber that regulates physiology and behaviour in yearly cycles is light levels. Greater winter darkness stimulates the pineal gland to produce melatonin – a hormone involved in controlling energy levels and mood. • However, many environmental and psychological factors can lead to winter depression, e.g. the colder weather.
INFRADIAN RHYTHMS (Rhythms lasting longer than 24 hours)	• The infradian rhythm of menstruation in women occurs over a 28-day cycle and is associated with physiological changes and discomfort relating to the shedding of the lining of the uterus wall and the behavioural changes of pre-menstrual syndrome (PMS). • The psychological effects that are suggested to occur begin around five days before menstruation in some women and can include mood change, irritability, dizziness and changes in energy levels and eating habits. The severity of the physiological symptoms varies among women and the extent of psychological changes associated with PMS has been the subject of some debate between psychologists.	• The endogenous pacemaker of the pituitary gland and its triggering of hormones such as prostaglandin internally regulate the menstrual cycle. The endogenous regulation of PMS via cycles in the endocrine system is supported by the finding of PMS cross-culturally. • The menstrual cycle can be quite variable at first and is open to modification by external stimuli – zeitgebers such as light levels (indicating a role for melatonin) and the presence of other women (studies show frequent interaction with particular women can cause synchronisation of menstruation, possibly due to pheromones – released chemically active scents). Since not all women experience it, PMS may result from psychological factors too.
ULTRADIAN RHYTHMS (Rhythms lasting less than 24 hours)	**DIURNAL (day) RHYTHMS** • Individuals seem to vary in their activity levels, some being more alert and receptive to information in the morning, others in the evening. • Horne and Osterberg (1976) used their 'Morningness-Eveningness' questionnaire to confirm this distinction, although research findings on the effect of time of day upon performance have been mixed. **NOCTURNAL (night) RHYTHMS** • The stages of sleep are cycled through around 5 times per night in the following way: **Relaxation to first cycle** – may involve hypnagogic experiences e.g. dream images or falling sensations. **First cycle** – Descent to deep stage 4 sleep (which lasts approx. 40 minutes), ends with a short REM period. **Second cycle** – Gradual descent to deep stage 4 sleep (approx. 30 minutes), ends with a short REM period. **Third cycle** – Mostly stage 2 sleep followed by up to 40 minutes of REM sleep. **Fourth cycle** – Around an hour of stage 2 sleep followed by around an hour of REM sleep. **Fifth cycle** – Stage 2 sleep followed by a shorter REM period or waking (possibly with hypnagogic experiences). • The level of dreaming and alertness is determined by when during the cycles a person is awoken. The deepest NREM sleep usually occurs in the first half of a night, while the most vivid dreaming REM sleep usually occurs in the second half.	• Morning types seem to reach their physiological peak (as measured by body temperature, metabolic rate etc.) earlier than evening types, indicating perhaps a 'phase advance' in their endogenously regulated circadian rhythms (Marks and Folkhard, 1985). • However, these variations could be the result (rather than the cause) of zeitgebers such as the subject's lifestyle and activity levels during the day. • The ultradian rhythm of alternating NREM and REM sleep results from the alternating activity of the endogenous pacemakers of the: 1 raphe nuclei (which releases inhibiting, NREM sleep-producing serotonin) and 2 locus coeruleus (which releases activating, REM sleep inducing acetylcholine and noradrenaline). • Destruction of the locus coeruleus stops REM sleep • Destruction of the raphe nuclei causes sleeplessness • Zeitgebers like alcohol can disrupt the cycle. 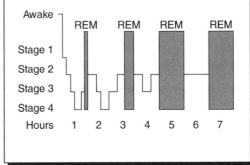

'The relation of eye movements during sleep to dream activity: an objective method for the study of dreams' Dement and Kleitman (1957)

AIM

Aserinsky and Kleitman found a relationship between rapid eye movement (REM) during sleep and reports of dreaming. Dement and Kleitman aimed to provide a **more detailed** investigation of how objective, physiological aspects of rapid eye movement relate to the subjective, psychological experience of dreaming reported by subjects, by testing whether

- significantly **more dreaming** occurs **during REM sleep** than non-REM sleep under controlled conditions.
- there is a **significant positive correlation** between the objective length of **time** spent **in REM** and the subjective **duration of dreaming** reported upon waking.
- there is a significant **relationship** between the **pattern of rapid eye movements** observed during sleep and the **content of the dream** reported upon waking.

METHOD

Subjects: 7 adult males and 2 adult females – 5 of which were intensively studied, 4 of which were used to confirm results.

Design: Laboratory experimentation and observation.

Procedure: Subjects slept individually in a quiet dark laboratory room after a normal day's activity (except that alcohol and caffeine were avoided during the days before testing). Electrodes were connected near the eyes to register eye movement and on the scalp to measure brain waves during sleep - these were the objective measures of REM sleep. Subjects were awoken at various times during the night (fairly evenly distributed across the average sleeping time of the subjects) by a loud doorbell noise, and immediately reported into a recording device whether they had been dreaming and the content of the dream *before* any contact with the experimenter (to avoid bias). Subjects were never usually told whether their eyes had been moving before being awoken. Dreaming was only counted if a fairly detailed and coherent dream was reported - vague impressions or assertions of dreaming without recall of content were not counted.

STUDY ONE

Subjects were awoken in one of four different ways during either REM or non-REM sleep, and were compared to see if they had been dreaming.
- 2 subjects were awoken randomly
- 1 subject was awoken during 3 REM sleep periods followed by 3 non-REM periods, and so on.
- 1 subject was awoken randomly, but was told he would only be awoken during periods of REM sleep
- 1 subject was awoken at the whim of the experimenter

STUDY TWO

Subjects were awoken either 5 or 15 minutes after REM sleep began and were asked to decide whether the duration of their dream was closer to 5 or 15 minutes.
The length of the dream (measured in terms of the number of words in their dream narratives) was also correlated to the duration of REM sleep before awakening.

STUDY THREE

Subjects were awoken as soon as one of four patterns of eye movement had occurred for 1 minute, and were asked exactly what they had just dreamt.
- Mainly vertical eye movements
- Mainly horizontal eye movements
- Both vertical and horizontal eye movements.
- Very little or no eye movement

RESULTS

Generally, REM periods were clearly observed in all subjects and distinguished from non-REM sleep periods. REM sleep periods occurred at regular intervals specific to each subject (although on average occurring every 92 minutes) and tended to last longer later in the night.

STUDY ONE

Regardless of how subjects were awoken, significantly more dreams were reported in REM than non-REM sleep.
When subjects failed to recall dreams from REM sleep, this was usually early in the night.
When subjects recalled dreams from non-REM sleep it was most often within 8 minutes after the end of a REM period.

STUDY TWO

Subjects were significantly correct in matching the duration of their dream to length of time they had shown REM sleep for both the 5-minute periods (45 out of 51 estimates correct) and 15-minute periods (47 out of 60 estimates correct).
All subjects showed a significant positive correlation at the $P < 0.05$ level or better between the length of their dream narratives and duration of REM sleep before awakening.

STUDY THREE

There was a very strong association between the pattern of REMs and the content of dream reports.
- The 3 vertical REM periods were associated with dreams of looking up and down at cliff faces, ladders, and basketball nets.
- A dream of two people throwing tomatoes at each other occurred in the only mainly horizontal REM period.
- 21 periods of vertical and horizontal REMs were associated with dreams of looking at close objects.
- 10 periods of very little or no REMs were associated with dreams of looking at fixed or distant objects.

EVALUATION

Methodological: Dreams may be recalled easier in REM than non-REM sleep because the latter is a deeper stage of sleep - perhaps dreams occur in deeper sleep, but are more difficult to recall from it.

The study used a limited sample, mostly men, therefore showed a lack of generalisability.

Theoretical: The research provides support for the idea that dreams can be studied in an objective way. This then opens up areas of research for the effect of environmental stimuli on dreaming.

Links: Sleep and dream research. Laboratory studies.

Theories of the function of sleep

SLEEP DEPRIVATION – IS SLEEP NEEDED?

ANIMAL STUDIES:
- Jouvet (1967) deprived cats of sleep by putting them on a floating island in a pool of water so that when they fell asleep they fell in and woke up. The cats developed abnormal behaviours and eventually died.
- Rechtschaffen et al deprived rats of sleep. They had all died after 33 days.

HUMAN STUDIES:
- Psychological effects – increased desire to sleep, difficulty sustaining attention (however, problem solving is less impaired), delusions, and depersonalisation.
- Physiological effects – minor changes, such as problems with eye focusing, but no significant major adverse effects. Sleep after deprivation is not cumulative (not much longer than usual), although more time is spent in REM sleep (a REM rebound effect). However, sleep deprivation studies are not indefinite.

THEORIES OF SLEEP FUNCTION

RESTORATION THEORY
Oswald (1966) suggests that the function of sleep, especially REM sleep, is simply to restore bodily energy reserves, repair the condition of muscles and cells and to allow growth to occur. Sleep could also allow brain neurotransmitters to replenish and aid psychological recovery.

Evaluation
For:
- Longer sleep (particularly stage 4) occurs after large amounts of physical exercise, and in growing children (REM occupies 50% of sleep in babies, 20% in adults).
- Growth hormones are released during stage 4 sleep, deprivation of which causes physical problems such as fibrositis.
- Sleep is greater after periods of stress and improves mood.

Against:
- Sleep duration is not reduced with lack of exercise.
- Deprivation of REM sleep does not produce significantly adverse effects.
- REM sleep involves an increase in energy expenditure and blood flow which *inhibits* protein synthesis.

MEMORY CONSOLIDATION THEORY
Empson and Clarke (1970) propose that sleep, especially REM sleep, facilitates the reinforcement of information in memory.

Evaluation
For:
- Subjects exposed to information before sleep remember less in the morning if deprived of REM sleep rather than non REM sleep.
- Perhaps more REM sleep occurs in younger humans because they have more to learn.

Against:
- There is little evidence against the theory, but memory consolidation can occur without sleep.

SLEEPING TO DREAM
Sleep may occur because the dreams that take place in it have important functions (see dream theories).

EVOLUTIONARY THEORY
All mammals sleep (the porpoise even shuts down one side of its brain at a time to do so), although the length of time varies according to the species. Given its universal nature and the fact that this unconscious and defenceless state seems a dangerous behaviour to show, sleep probably has an important evolutionary survival function, possibly to
- conserve energy when food gathering has been completed or is more difficult (e.g. at night), and/or
- avoid damage from nocturnal predators or accidents by remaining motionless.

Meddis (1975) suggests the duration of sleep a species shows depends upon its food requirements and predator avoidance needs.

Evaluation
For:
- Lions (which have few predators and meet their food needs in short bursts) and squirrels (who have safe burrows) sleep longer.
- Cattle (which have many natural predators) and shrews (which have high metabolic rates) sleep very little.

Against:
- Some evolutionary arguments suggest that animals who are highly preyed upon need to sleep little to keep constant vigilance for predators, however others suggest the opposite – that they need to sleep longer to keep them away from harm by remaining motionless.

Theories of the function of dreaming

THEORIES OF DREAM FUNCTION

CRICK AND MITCHISON'S REVERSE LEARNING THEORY

Crick and Mitchison (1983) argue that dreaming can be regarded as the **random** and **meaningless by-product** of the bombardment of the cortex with random stimulation from the brain stem during REM sleep, to serve the biological function of **clearing the brain** of useless or maladaptive information.

Evaluation
For:
- The two mammals that do not show REM sleep (the dolphin and spiny anteater) have abnormally large cortexes, perhaps to contain the useless memories they are not able to unlearn.

Against:
- The theory lacks detail over exactly how 'useless' information is identified and 'unlearned', and also neglects the apparent meaningfulness of many dreams.

REPROGRAMMING THEORY

Evans (1984) suggests that REM sleep is required by the brain to update itself in the light of new information received **during the day**, and that dreams are the interpretation of this assimilation.

Foulkes (1985), however, proposes that dreams reflect the way our cognitive systems organise and reprogram the stimuli received from random brain activity **during REM sleep**.

Evaluation
For:
- Subjects given unusual tasks before sleep, spend longer in REM sleep.

Against:
- If dreams interpreted the processed information so logically, why would dreams be so strange and incoherent?

WISH FULFILMENT

Freud suggested that dreams were the disguised expressions of unconscious desires and impulses. The recalled manifest content of the dream has been disguised by the dream censor through methods like symbolism to protect our conscious self from the anxiety provoking latent (hidden) meaning of the dream.

Evaluation
For:
- Many researchers have agreed that dreams are meaningful.

Against:
- There is little empirical evidence for Freud's theory in general and little reason for dream meanings to always be disguised.

HOBSON AND McCARLEY'S ACTIVATION SYNTHESIS THEORY

Hobson and McCarley (1977) propose a biological theory which regards dreams as the **meaningless** result of **random brain activity**. The activation part of the theory involves the random firing of giant cells in the reticular activating system (triggered by the presence of acetylcholine) which activates the sensory and motor areas of the brain during REM sleep. The synthesis part of the theory involves the attempt of higher parts of the brain to organise and make sense of the random activity – producing the semi-coherent dreams we experience.

Evaluation
For:
- The theory has biological support and explains how the content of dreams could be influenced by particular areas of brain activation (balance areas may produce dreams of flying) or external stimulation while asleep (water splashed on a sleeper's face can be incorporated into their dreams).

Against:
- Foulkes (1985) proposes that dreams are **meaningful** interpretations of REM random brain activity in the light of our cognitive systems' organisational abilities. Dreams reflect the way we interpret information, relate it to past experience and help us prepare for situations not yet encountered. Hobson and McCarley have come to agree with this view that dreams can be meaningful.

PROBLEM SOLVING

Cartwright proposes that dreams are a meaningful way of considering worries or problems from conscious everyday life. Dreams may use metaphors (but are not deliberately disguised as Freud thought) and may provide solutions for problems.

Evaluation
For:
- Subjects given problems before sleep are more likely to solve them realistically if REM sleep is uninterrupted.

Against:
- There is little other evidence for the theory and most problems can be more quickly solved while awake.

Physiological theories of motivation

HOMEOSTATIC DRIVE THEORY OF MOTIVATION

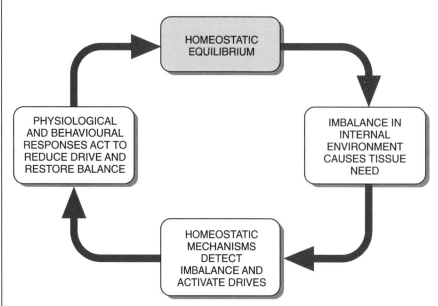

Homeostatic drive theory suggests that behaviour is motivated by biological needs.

Homeostasis refers to the process by which an organism maintains a fairly constant internal body environment (e.g. constant body temperature or blood sugar level). Body temperature homeostasis is maintained fairly automatically through sweating, vasoconstriction, etc. With imbalances in the body's **need** for food and water, however, the animal has to actively do something to restore balance and so **drives** are activated to **motivate** food and water seeking **behaviour**. **Drives** are only **reduced** when these motivated behaviours are effective in restoring homeostatic balance and satisfying the body's needs.

EVALUATION
Behaviour is not always motivated by homeostatic needs and drives
Homeostatic drive theory ignores higher psychological and social needs (e.g. self-esteem and achievement). It only seems to explain a handful of motivated behaviours for basic physiological survival needs and, even with these, it does not provide a complete explanation. A number of social, developmental and psychological factors are involved in all the basic drives, from hunger and thirst to sleep and sex. In the case of the hunger drive, for example, the homeostatic level for food intake required to satisfy tissue needs may well be dictated by a biological set point (different people may naturally require different amounts of food). However, research has indicated that even this homeostatic set point may be influenced by early environmental factors, e.g. over or under feeding as a child. Furthermore, eating behaviour is not governed strictly by the hunger drive – we can refuse to eat when hungry or can over eat when already full.

Drive reduction is not always necessary to motivate behaviour
Studies have found that animals will still perform many behaviours when physiological drives have been reduced and will even actively seek stimulation rather than reduce arousal. Optimal arousal theory suggests that drive reduction only applies if the organism is over stimulated and that many behaviours indicate that a certain level of drive **arousal** is desired. This has been termed sensation seeking behaviour.

BRAIN PHYSIOLOGY AND MOTIVATION
Physiologists have identified many areas of the brain involved in motivating a variety of behaviours:
- **The medial forebrain bundle** – Olds and Miller found that electrical stimulation of this 'pleasure area' in rats massively reinforced behaviour. Male rats that could administer self stimulation by pressing a lever pressed it thousands of times a day, even in preference to food or sexually receptive female rats.
- **The hypothalamus** – a small area of the brain involved in homeostasis and the motivation of a vast variety of behaviours, from feeding and drinking to aggressive and sexual behaviour.
- **The reticular activating system** – controls general arousal and activity levels.
- **The cerebral cortex** – probably the location of the more rational, cognitive sources of motivation.

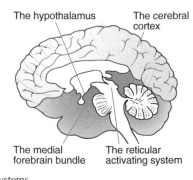

The hypothalamus   The cerebral cortex

The medial forebrain bundle   The reticular activating system

Evaluation
Even the most simple of motivated actions involve very complex interactions of many brain systems. Seeing brain centres as sources of motivation ignores the triggering influence of environmental stimuli. The most precise scientific studies have been conducted on rat brains due to the ethical objections of experimenting on human brains, raising the problem of generalising from animal studies to humans.

GENETICS, EVOLUTIONARY THEORY AND MOTIVATION
Evolutionary sociobiological theorists argue that ultimately all behaviour is motivated by evolutionary survival needs. Behaviours evolve to better adapt an organism to their environment to promote survival, therefore sexual behaviour is motivated by the genetic requirement to reproduce, aggression is motivated by the need to compete or defend against others, social behaviour is motivated by the survival benefits bestowed upon a socially integrated individual, etc.

Evaluation
Evolutionary theory is rather reductionist and often ignores contemporary social and cultural motives for behaviour.

Physiological mechanisms for the hunger drive

Much research has focused on the hunger drive as the best example of homeostasis affecting motivation. Many studies have sought to find both the short term mechanisms of feeding behaviour (the mouth, stomach, and duodenum) and the longer term mechanisms (the hypothalamus and blood glucose levels of the body).

THE HYPOTHALAMUS

Different areas of the hypothalamus are thought to be involved in different aspects of feeding behaviour:

The ventromedial nucleus of the hypothalamus (VMH) may act as a satiety centre – stopping eating once the animal has consumed the required intake.

The lateral nucleus of the hypothalamus (LH) may act as a feeding centre – initiating eating behaviour when intake is required.

Evidence

- Teitelbaum et al (1954) ablated the LH of rats which caused a loss of eating behaviour. Hess (1954) stimulated it with microelectrodes causing compulsive eating.
- Hetherington and Ranson (1942) damaged the VMH of rats, which caused dramatic over-eating (hyperphagia), whereas Olds (1958) found stimulation decreased eating.

Evaluation

Damage to the VMH may work not by just increasing appetite but by reducing the sensitivity to the internal cues of hunger and increasing sensitivity to external cues. The hyperphagic rats whose VMH had been removed became very fussy and sensitive about their food and would not eat it if quinine was added to give it a bitter taste. Schachter (1971) found that overweight people also seem to pay little attention to internal cues (hunger pangs) and base their eating habits more on external cues (the availability and taste of food). Overweight people respond less to the internal cues of stomach distension (Schachter et al, 1968) and are more likely to continue to eat food that is available but are less likely to search for it if it is not.

Although hypothalamic tumours have been associated with obesity in humans, it is more likely that the hypothalamus works differently in fat and thin eaters through the operation of a biological set point – a natural body weight determined by the balance between the VMH and LH. The set point may be affected by genetics, the number of fats cells in the body or damage to the LH or VMH to alter the balance between them.

BLOOD GLUCOSE LEVELS

Blood glucose levels are monitored by glucoreceptors in the hypothalamus, liver and blood system. When glucose levels drop, they may motivate eating behaviour to restore the loss.

Evidence

- Injections of glucose decrease appetite.
- Injections of insulin (which lowers glucose levels by converting it into fat) increases appetite.

Evaluation

Glucose levels remain very balanced and seem to be homeostatically controlled themselves, and so are unlikely to show the variation needed to respond to and activate eating behaviour.

THE MOUTH

Operations on rats, whereby the oesophagus was redirected out of the rat's body instead of connecting with the stomach, showed that the mouth and throat are only short term sensory receptors for hunger and satiety. The rats with the above operation stopped feeding after chewing and swallowing larger than normal meals, but soon began eating again.

THE STOMACH

Cannon believed that stomach contraction was the mechanism involved in monitoring and triggering the hunger drive.

Evidence

In an experiment by Cannon and Washburn (1912), Washburn swallowed a balloon so that stomach contractions could be measured and a correlation was found between contractions and self reports of hunger.

Evaluation

However, people whose stomachs have been surgically removed still get hungry, and hunger persists even if the neural pathways from the stomach to the brain are cut.

THE DUODENUM

A further short term mechanism of satiety is the release of cholecystokinin (CCK) by the duodenum in response to fatty acids in the intestine.

Evidence

Injections of this hormone into hungry rats or obese humans decreases their appetite.

...ological theories of motivation 1

...chological approaches incorporate biological
...on in some way, e.g. Hull or Freud's drive theories, or
...s lowest hierarchical levels. Other approaches reject it.

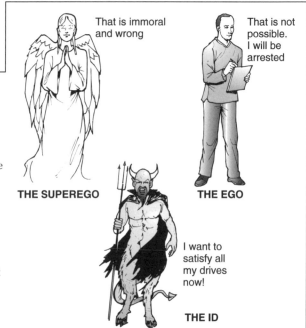

That is immoral and wrong

THE SUPEREGO

That is not possible. I will be arrested

THE EGO

I want to satisfy all my drives now!

THE ID

PSYCHOANALYTIC DRIVE THEORY OF MOTIVATION

Freud's ideas on motivation are based upon unconscious instinctual drives seeking expression in a society that imposes constraints upon them. Motivation stems from a dynamic struggle between the three aspects of the unconscious mind:

- **The id** – which seeks to release the two drives of sex (from Eros the life instinct) and aggression (from Thanatos the death instinct) regardless of time or place. The unconscious mind resembles a hydraulic closed energy system (like a steam engine) in that psychic energy from the drives builds up and, if not released, causes inner pressure or anxiety. Thus sex and aggression are the biological, instinctual motivating influences upon behaviour.
- **The ego** – which seeks to control the id in line with reality. The ego is motivated to defend the conscious mind and society against forbidden id impulses.
- **The superego** – which is motivated to control the id in line with moral principles.

Evaluation
Freud's ideas on motivation suffer from all the usual criticisms of drive theories, plus those of psychoanalytic theory in general, e.g. the lack of experimental evidence.

COGNITIVE THEORIES OF MOTIVATION

Cognitive theories emphasise the importance of psychological level motivational influences upon behaviour. Many of these influences go beyond biological needs and drives in that they
- may actually involve sensation-seeking behaviours – **increasing** arousal or drive levels rather than reducing them, and
- can combine with **social** motivational needs or desires to behave in socially appropriate ways – thus behaviour can be said to be **elicited** from without as well as motivated from within.

Examples of these cognitive and psychosocial motivational factors include:
- **Curiosity** – both animals and humans are motivated to explore and seek information, even when biological needs have been met.
- **Cognitive consistency** – humans are motivated to think and act in consistent ways to avoid unpleasant cognitive dissonance.
- **Need for control** – humans are motivated to assert control over their lives – perceived constraints upon freedom can produce resistance and a lack of control can lead to learned helplessness and depression.
- **Need for achievement** – the motive to achieve high standards of performance or success.

Evaluation
Many studies have supported cognitive motivational theories.
Harlow – found rhesus monkeys showed curiosity, since they would perform a task to be reinforced merely with **seeing something new**.
Festinger and Carlsmith – found humans would change their behaviour and opinions to make them consistent with their past actions.
McClelland – found evidence for the need for achievement with the Thematic Apperception Test (a rather subjective projective test).

HUMANISTIC THEORIES OF MOTIVATION

Maslow believes humans are motivated by needs beyond those of basic biological survival. Fundamental to human nature is the desire to grow and develop to achieve our full potential – referred to as 'self actualisation'.

Maslow proposed a hierarchy of needs ranging from lower level basic needs to higher level psychological and actualisation ones. Only when the bottom levels have been reasonably satisfied can the person move on to the higher ones.

Other researchers have proposed humanistic motivational influences upon behaviour – Rogers, for example, points out that individuals strive to achieve their ideal selves because they are motivated towards self-improvement.

Evaluation
Humanistic ideas on motivation gain strength from emphasising uniquely human motivational factors, rather than generalising from reductionist, biologically based theory and evidence gained from animal studies. Maslow's hierarchy integrates virtually all the other theoretical approaches to motivation. However humanistic concepts are difficult to test experimentally – how can self-actualisation be measured and how do we know when we have reached full potential?

MASLOW'S HIERARCHY OF NEEDS

NEED FOR SELF ACTUALISATION

NEED FOR ESTEEM

NEED FOR BELONGINGNESS AND LOVE

NEED FOR SAFETY AND SECURITY

PHYSIOLOGICAL NEEDS

Psychological theories of motivation 2

HULL'S DRIVE REDUCTION THEORY

Clark Hull (1943) was a behaviourist who integrated the idea of homeostatic drives into an influential theory of learning to explain the motivation of all animal behaviour.
Hull believed that drives could be combined with other motivational factors, such as **incentive** and **habit** (past experience), in a **mathematical formula** that would be able to predict the likelihood of a behaviour being produced.

Hull argued that the organism's **level of drive** was important, since **drive reduction** was the basis of reinforcement. Hull proposed
- reinforcement is linked to **biological needs**, e.g. for food
- when needs are thwarted and the animal is **deprived**, physiological **drives** (states of tension) are **energised** to make the organism seek for ways to fulfil its needs
- by **trial and error**, some responses **satisfy the need** and, therefore, **reduce the drive** (drive reduction is experienced as pleasurable)
- the responses are thus **reinforced** and are more likely to occur again

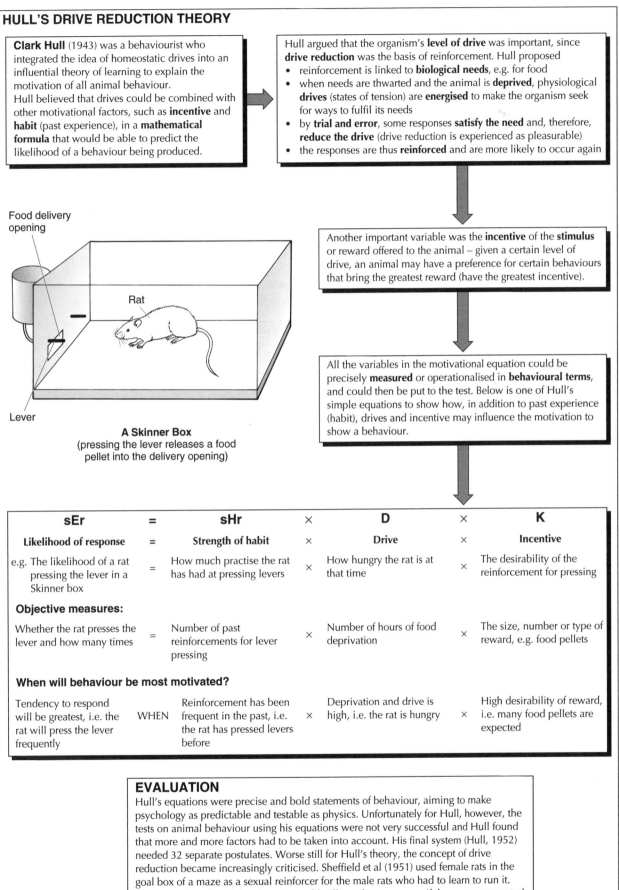

Food delivery opening

Rat

Lever

A Skinner Box
(pressing the lever releases a food pellet into the delivery opening)

Another important variable was the **incentive** of the **stimulus** or reward offered to the animal – given a certain level of drive, an animal may have a preference for certain behaviours that bring the greatest reward (have the greatest incentive).

All the variables in the motivational equation could be precisely **measured** or operationalised in **behavioural terms**, and could then be put to the test. Below is one of Hull's simple equations to show how, in addition to past experience (habit), drives and incentive may influence the motivation to show a behaviour.

sEr	=	sHr	×	D	×	K
Likelihood of response	=	**Strength of habit**	×	**Drive**	×	**Incentive**
e.g. The likelihood of a rat pressing the lever in a Skinner box	=	How much practise the rat has had at pressing levers	×	How hungry the rat is at that time	×	The desirability of the reinforcement for pressing

Objective measures:

Whether the rat presses the lever and how many times	=	Number of past reinforcements for lever pressing	×	Number of hours of food deprivation	×	The size, number or type of reward, e.g. food pellets

When will behaviour be most motivated?

Tendency to respond will be greatest, i.e. the rat will press the lever frequently	WHEN	Reinforcement has been frequent in the past, i.e. the rat has pressed levers before	×	Deprivation and drive is high, i.e. the rat is hungry	×	High desirability of reward, i.e. many food pellets are expected

EVALUATION
Hull's equations were precise and bold statements of behaviour, aiming to make psychology as predictable and testable as physics. Unfortunately for Hull, however, the tests on animal behaviour using his equations were not very successful and Hull found that more and more factors had to be taken into account. His final system (Hull, 1952) needed 32 separate postulates. Worse still for Hull's theory, the concept of drive reduction became increasingly criticised. Sheffield et al (1951) used female rats in the goal box of a maze as a sexual reinforcer for the male rats who had to learn to run it. The researchers found that the rats would still run the maze even if they were prevented from completing copulation with the females (certainly no drive reduction!).

Theories of emotion

Theories of emotion have mainly focused on the relationship between the physiological and psychological aspects of emotion.

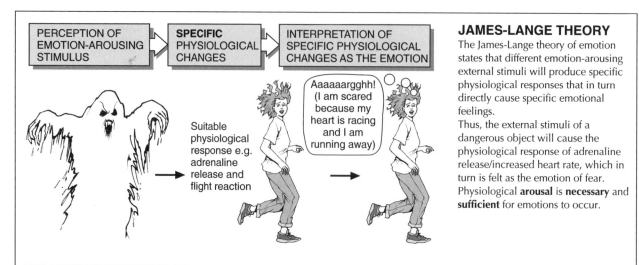

JAMES-LANGE THEORY

The James-Lange theory of emotion states that different emotion-arousing external stimuli will produce specific physiological responses that in turn directly cause specific emotional feelings.

Thus, the external stimuli of a dangerous object will cause the physiological response of adrenaline release/increased heart rate, which in turn is felt as the emotion of fear. Physiological **arousal** is **necessary** and **sufficient** for emotions to occur.

SUPPORT

Ax (1953) found different physiological changes associated with particular emotions, e.g. fear seemed associated with the physiological effects of adrenaline, anger with the effects of noradrenaline. Schwartz et al (1981) have also found distinct physiological reactions for anger, fear, happiness, and sadness. Laird (1974) found that facial feedback (e.g. making subjects adopt the muscular facial expression of a smile) affected mood (made them feel happier).

CRITICISMS

Specific physiological changes have not been found for every emotion, only the strongest and most basic ones.
Maranon (1924) found that physiological arousal is not sufficient to cause emotion, by injecting subjects with adrenaline. Over two thirds of them reported only physical symptoms – the rest merely reported 'as if' they were feeling an emotion.
Some researchers claim that physiological changes are not even necessary for emotion (see Cannon-Bard theory).

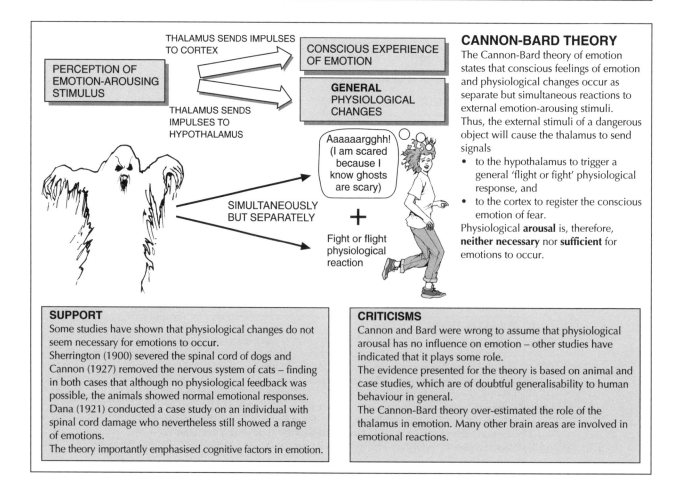

CANNON-BARD THEORY

The Cannon-Bard theory of emotion states that conscious feelings of emotion and physiological changes occur as separate but simultaneous reactions to external emotion-arousing stimuli.

Thus, the external stimuli of a dangerous object will cause the thalamus to send signals

- to the hypothalamus to trigger a general 'flight or fight' physiological response, and
- to the cortex to register the conscious emotion of fear.

Physiological **arousal** is, therefore, **neither necessary** nor **sufficient** for emotions to occur.

SUPPORT

Some studies have shown that physiological changes do not seem necessary for emotions to occur.
Sherrington (1900) severed the spinal cord of dogs and Cannon (1927) removed the nervous system of cats – finding in both cases that although no physiological feedback was possible, the animals showed normal emotional responses.
Dana (1921) conducted a case study on an individual with spinal cord damage who nevertheless still showed a range of emotions.
The theory importantly emphasised cognitive factors in emotion.

CRITICISMS

Cannon and Bard were wrong to assume that physiological arousal has no influence on emotion – other studies have indicated that it plays some role.
The evidence presented for the theory is based on animal and case studies, which are of doubtful generalisability to human behaviour in general.
The Cannon-Bard theory over-estimated the role of the thalamus in emotion. Many other brain areas are involved in emotional reactions.

Schachter and Singer's cognitive labelling theory

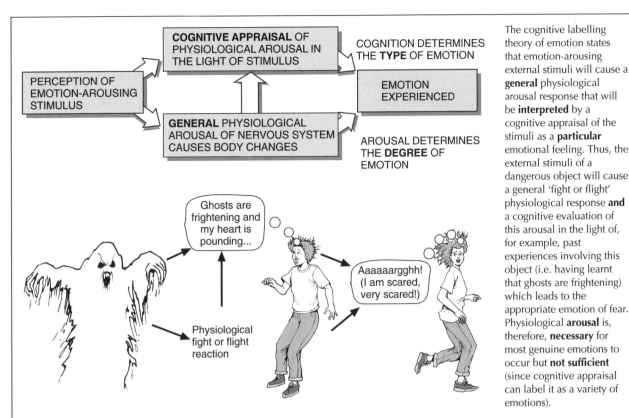

The cognitive labelling theory of emotion states that emotion-arousing external stimuli will cause a **general** physiological arousal response that will be **interpreted** by a cognitive appraisal of the stimuli as a **particular** emotional feeling. Thus, the external stimuli of a dangerous object will cause a general 'fight or flight' physiological response **and** a cognitive evaluation of this arousal in the light of, for example, past experiences involving this object (i.e. having learnt that ghosts are frightening) which leads to the appropriate emotion of fear. Physiological **arousal** is, therefore, **necessary** for most genuine emotions to occur but **not sufficient** (since cognitive appraisal can label it as a variety of emotions).

SUPPORT

Schachter and Singer (1962) told subjects that they were going to test the effects of a vitamin injection on their vision, but instead injected them with adrenaline. Subjects were then either:

A informed of the real effects (e.g. increased heart/respiration rate)

B misinformed of the effects – told false symptoms, e.g. itching

C given no information on the effects

A fourth group (**D**) were injected with a placebo of saline solution in place of adrenaline to provide a control group.

All subjects were then left in a waiting room with another subject (really a confederate of the experimenter) who began to act either

1 angrily, e.g. complaining about and then ripping up a questionnaire, or

2 Euphorically, e.g. laughing and throwing paper around.

The subjects were then rated by external observers who found groups **B** and **C** were more likely to follow the confederate's behaviour. The results showed some support for cognitive labelling theory in that

- those who did not have an accurate explanation for their physiological arousal (groups **B** and **C**) used the cues of the confederate's behaviour to identify and label their own emotion.
- those who already had an accurate explanation (group **A**) for the effects did not need other cues, so did not follow the confederate.
- those who changed their behaviour (groups **B** and **C**) did so according to cognitive appraisal of their emotions, rather than specific physiological arousal, indicating that only general arousal is required.

Dutton and Aron (1974) found further evidence for cognitive labelling of emotions. Male subjects approached by an attractive female experimenter on a high suspension bridge were shown to mislabel their fear as sexual attraction.

Hohmann's (1966) study appears to support the necessity of physiological arousal for genuine emotional feelings. He studied 25 males with spinal cord injury, and found the greater the damage to their nervous system feedback, the less intense were their emotional experiences. Subjects still reported emotions but when angry, for example, would describe it as 'a mental kind of anger'.

CRITICISMS

Schachter and Singer's (1962) experiment has been criticised in a number of ways:

- There was no assessment of the subjects' emotional state before the experiment began, or the emotional effect of receiving an injection.
- The emotional states produced by artificial injections under laboratory conditions are probably not typical of normal emotional reactions.
- Significant results were only found for the behavioural changes rated by the observers – no significant differences were found in the subjects' self report of their emotions.
- The results were not highly significant and other researchers such as Marshall and Zimbardo (1979) have not replicated Schachter and Singer's findings.

While the misattribution of emotions (the most typical experimental support for cognitive labelling theory) is perhaps an unusual occurrence in everyday life, it does indicate an important role for cognitive appraisal. Researchers such as Lazarus (1991) argue that cognitive processes can initiate both physiological arousal and emotion feelings, and that a cognitive appraisal of environmental stimuli at some level (conscious or unconscious) is a basic requirement for the elicitation of any emotion.

Although the majority of current theories on emotion involve cognitive appraisal, there is still some debate over its importance. Psychologists such as Zajonc (1984) still argue that cognition and emotion involve relatively separate systems, and that emotion can occur without any cognitive appraisal. Recent research indicates that emotional centres in the brain can receive information directly from the sensory areas.

'Cognitive, social, and physiological determinants of emotional state' Schachter and Singer (1962)

AIM

To describe an experiment that provides support for Schachter's (1959) theory of the interaction between physiology, cognition, and behaviour in emotional experience. Schachter believes that cognitive factors (thought processes) are very important in determining which emotion is felt. He argues that emotion-provoking stimuli, such as a gun being pointed at you, will automatically cause a general physiological level of arousal (the activation of the sympathetic nervous system), which is interpreted (cognitively) as fear (the emotion) in the light of our knowledge about the dangerous nature of guns. Schachter and Singer, therefore, propose the 3 following predictions from this theory:

A Given an **unexplained** state of general **physiological arousal**, the individual experiencing it will attempt to describe or **label it as a particular emotion** in terms of his **cognitive explanations** of its causes. Thus, the same state of arousal could be described or labelled as joy or fury, depending upon the situation he is in.

B Given a state of general **physiological arousal** for which an individual already has an **appropriate explanation** (e.g. I feel this way because I have been injected with adrenaline) there will be **no need** to use external situational cues **to label** his arousal as an emotion.

C Given **no** state of general **physiological arousal, despite situational cues** to label emotions with, an individual will experience **no emotion**.

METHOD

Subjects: 184 male college students, 90% of whom volunteered to get extra points on their exams.

Design: Laboratory experiment. Based on the above predictions, three independent variables were manipulated in an independent measures design to affect the dependent variable of experienced emotional state (measured by behavioural observation and self-report).

Independent variable	Conditions manipulated
1 Physiological arousal	**a** *Injection of epinephrine* (adrenaline) **b** *Injection of a placebo* (saline solution)
2 Explanation of arousal	**a** *Informed* (told correct symptoms) **b** *Misinformed* (told wrong symptoms) **c** *Ignorant* (told no symptoms)
3 Situational emotion cues	**a** *Euphoric stooge* **b** *Angry stooge*

Procedure: Subjects were told the experiment was a study of the effect of Suproxin – supposedly a vitamin supplement - upon vision. Subjects were tested individually and asked whether they would mind receiving a Suproxin injection (in fact either epinephrine or a placebo) and were assigned to one of the following conditions:

1 **Epinephrine informed** – given a Suproxin injection that was *really epinephrine* and told of its *real side effects* (general physiological arousal of the sympathetic nervous system causing accelerated heartbeat/breathing, palpitations etc.).
2 **Epinephrine misinformed** – given a Suproxin injection that was *really epinephrine* and told *false side effects* (e.g. itching, numbness, etc.)
3 **Epinephrine ignorant** – given a Suproxin injection that was *really epinephrine* and told there would be *no side effects* at all
4 **Control ignorant** – given a Suproxin injection that was *really a placebo* (a saline solution which has no direct effect on arousal of the sympathetic nervous system) and told there would be *no side effects* at all.

All subjects (with the exception of the epinephrine misinformed group, who were not exposed to the angry stooge) were then left alone with either
• **the euphoric stooge** (subjects saw a confederate behaving happily - throwing paper and playing with a hula hoop) or
• **the angry stooge** (subjects saw a confederate complain and behave in a outraged way, ripping up a questionnaire)
and then observed through a one-way mirror to rate their behaviour for how similar it was to the stooge's behaviour (implying that they were in the same emotional state). Self-report scales were also used to assess how good or angry they felt.

RESULTS

For subjects observing euphoric stooges:
• Self-reports of emotions and behaviour were mostly significantly happier in epinephrine ignorant and misinformed subjects (who did not have a relevant explanation for their arousal) than the epinephrine informed group (who did not need to use the external cues to explain their arousal). This supports predictions **A** and **B** above.
• There was no significant difference in mood between the epinephrine ignorant or misinformed subjects, and the placebo control subjects.
This indicates that prediction **C** above is not supported.

For subjects observing angry stooges:
Only behavioural observations were used, since subjects feared self-reports of anger at the experimenter would endanger their extra exam points.
• Epinephrine ignorant subjects behaved significantly more angrily than epinephrine informed or placebo subjects.
This supports predictions **A**, **B**, and **C**. However, placebo subjects still followed the angry behaviour more than the epinephrine informed subjects. The results support the predictions more strongly if adrenaline misinformed and ignorant subjects who attributed arousal to their injection and the placebo subjects who showed physiological arousal in response to just having an injection, are removed from the data.

EVALUATION

Methodological: *Artificiality* – Injection is an artificial way of generating physiological arousal and can cause (fear) arousal in itself. The laboratory lacks ecological validity and the situation of experiencing unexplained physiological arousal is rare.
Validity – Only male subjects and two-tailed tests were used and the results have not always been replicated.
Ethics – Deception over purpose of study and content of injection. Injection (although by permission) hurt.

Theoretical: Supports the importance of cognitive factors in emotional experience. Provides some support for Schachter's theory that physiological arousal and cognitive interpretation are **both necessary** but **not sufficient on their own** to cause emotions.

Links: Emotion.

The physiology of emotion

CEREBRAL CORTEX
Frontal cortex
The frontal cortex has been implicated in the mediation and expression of aggression. Bard removed the cortex of cats, causing attack behaviour that lacked appropriateness and co-ordination. Prefrontal lobotomies were used to pacify violent schizophrenics, although the precise reason for the effect is not known. Delgado stimulated the aggression centres of monkey brains but found that the aggression produced was usually directed towards weaker targets – indicating the modifying role of the frontal cortex. Unexplained arousal of the sympathetic nervous system can be labelled as a particular emotion by the more cognitive parts of the frontal cortex.

Hemispheric specialisation in emotion
Brain damage and brain scan research has indicated differences in emotional localisation between the hemispheres. The right hemisphere seems more involved in the perception and expression of emotional behaviour (particularly negative emotions) than the left hemisphere.

CROSS-SECTION OF THE BRAIN
(showing areas involved in emotion)

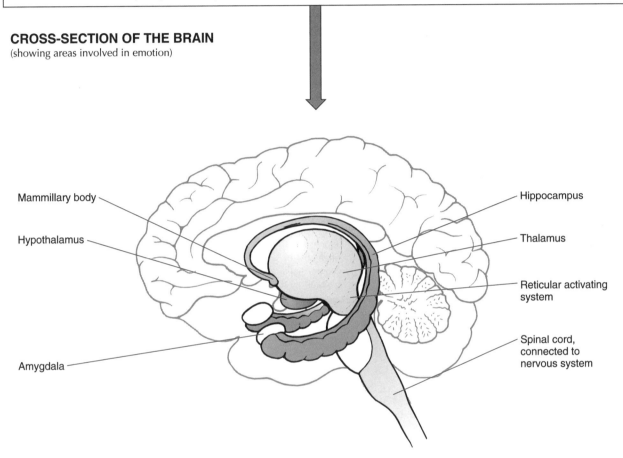

Mammillary body

Hypothalamus

Amygdala

Hippocampus

Thalamus

Reticular activating system

Spinal cord, connected to nervous system

LIMBIC SYSTEM
The limbic system is thought to play an important role in emotional experience and behaviour. It contains many brain structures, including the hypothalamus, septum, cingulate gyrus, hippocampus, and amygdala.
Papez (1937) proposed a model of how these structures were interlinked to regulate emotional behaviour, which became known as the Papez circuit. This model was modified by MacLean and is still regarded as an important contribution today, despite the acceptance that many other areas of the brain are involved in emotion.
One particular area of the limbic system that seems to be especially involved in strong emotions, such as aggression and fear, is the amygdala. Research has found that removing the amygdala from monkeys, rats, and humans has dramatically reduced aggressive behaviour, while stimulation has provoked it.

BRAIN STEM
The brain stem contains the reticular activating system and other structures responsible for releasing brain neurotransmitters, including:
- Norepinephrine – released by the locus coeruleus, it seems involved in pleasurable sensations while deficits are thought to be involved in depression.
- Dopamine – released by the substantia nigra and seems involved in the emotional disturbances of schizophrenia, as well as the positive feelings caused by drugs like cocaine.
- Endorphins – released by many neurones throughout the nervous system. They play a vital role in moderating the experience of pain, fear, and anxiety.

THE NERVOUS SYSTEM
The sympathetic branch of the autonomic nervous system, when activated, is responsible for the body's 'fight or flight' sensations.

HORMONES
Many hormones are involved in emotional behaviour.
Androgens released by the sex glands are implicated in feelings of aggression, for example.

Types of memory

ENCODING TYPES OF MEMORY

The human sensory systems, such as our eyes and ears, receive many different forms of stimulation, ranging from sound waves to photons of light. Obviously the information reaching our senses is transformed in nature when it is represented in our brains, and encoding refers to the process of representing knowledge in different forms.

IMAGERY MEMORY

- Some memory representations appear to closely resemble the raw, unabstracted data containing original material from our senses, such as the extremely brief iconic (visual) and echoic (auditory) after images that rapidly fade from our eyes and ears. Yet even after these have gone, we retain the ability to recall fairly vivid visual images of what we have seen and to hear again tunes we have experienced.
- Baddeley and Hitch (1974) have investigated this sort of short term imagery ability by suggesting that we have a 'visuospatial scratchpad' for summoning up and examining our visual imagery.
- Photographic (eidetic) memory is an extremely rare ultra enhanced form of imagery memory, shown in a weak form by perhaps 5% of young children (Haber, 1979).

PROCEDURAL MEMORY

- Also known as implicit memory, this is the memory for **knowing how** to do things such as talk, walk, juggle, etc. Although we retain these skills and abilities, we are often completely **unable to consciously introspect upon or describe** how we do them. Procedural memory is similar to Bruner's enactive mode.
- Procedural knowledge is very resistant to forgetting (we never forget how to ride a bicycle) and is also resistant to brain damage that eradicates other forms of memory – anterograde amnesiac patients, who forget simple events or verbal instructions after a few moments, are often able to learn new procedural skills such as playing table-tennis.

DECLARATIVE MEMORY

- Sometimes termed explicit memory, this type concerns all the information that we can **describe or report**, and as such has been the focus of the *majority* of research on memory. Declarative memory includes:
a **semantic memory** – this concerns memory for meaning, the storage of abstract, general facts regardless of when those facts were acquired e.g. *knowing what* a word means.
b **episodic** - this is 'knowing when' memory based upon personal experience and linked to a particular time and place in our lives. Episodic memory can be quite precise – Lindsay and Norman (1977) asked students "what were you doing on a Monday afternoon in the 3rd week of September, 2 years ago?", and found many actually knew. Very vivid episodic memories have been termed 'flashbulb' memories (Brown and Kulik, 1977) which involve recalling exactly what you were doing and where you were when a particularly important, exciting or emotional event happened.

DURATION TYPES OF MEMORY

Ever since William James (1890) distinguished between *primary* memory which feels like our present conscious experience, and *secondary* memory which seems like we are 'fishing out' information from the past, cognitive psychologists have been very interested in the possibility of different types of memory store based on the duration of time memories last for. Cognitive psychologists have proposed **three types** of time based store, each with differences in duration, capacity, coding and function.

SENSORY MEMORY

(sometimes called the short term sensory store or sensory register)

- The sense organs have a limited ability to store information about the world in a fairly unprocessed way for less than a second, rather like an afterimage. The visual system possesses **iconic** memory for visual stimuli such as shape, size, colour and location (but not meaning), whereas the hearing system has **echoic** memory for auditory stimuli.
- Coltheart et al (1974) have argued that the momentary freezing of visual input allows us to select which aspects of the input should go on for further memory processing. The existence of sensory memory has been experimentally demonstrated by Sperling (1960) using a tachistoscope.

SHORT-TERM MEMORY

- Information selected by attention from sensory memory, may pass into short-term memory (STM).
- STM allows us to retain information long enough to **use** it, e.g. looking up a telephone number and remembering it long enough to dial it. Peterson and Peterson (1959) have demonstrated that STM lasts approximately **between 15 and 30 seconds,** unless people rehearse the material, while Miller (1956) has found that STM has a **limited capacity** of around **7 'chunks'** of information.
- STM also appears to mostly **encode** memory **acoustically** (in terms of sound) as Conrad (1964) has demonstrated, but can also retain visuospatial images.

LONG-TERM MEMORY

- Long-term memory provides the lasting retention of information and skills, from **minutes** to a **lifetime**.
- Long-term memory appears to have an almost **limitless capacity** to retain information, but of course its capacity could never be measured – it would take too long!
- Long-term information seems to be encoded mainly in terms of **meaning** (semantic memory), as Baddeley has shown, but also retains procedural skills and imagery.

Research on sensory memory, short-term and long-term memory

SENSORY MEMORY

- Since sensory memory lasts less than a second, most of the material in it will have been forgotten before it can be reported! *Sperling* studied the sensory memory for vision (the iconic store) by using a **tachistoscope** – a device that can flash pictoral stimuli onto a blank screen for very brief instances. Using this device, Sperling was able to ask subjects to remember as many letters as they could from a **grid of 12 symbols** that he was going to display for just **one twentieth of a second**, and found that while they could only recall around **four** of the symbols before the grid faded from their sensory memory, they typically reported seeing a lot more than they had time to report.
- **Capacity** – Sperling presented the 12 symbol grid for 1/20th of a second, followed immediately by a **high, medium** or **low tone,** which indicated which of the three rows of four symbols the subject had to attend to from their iconic memory of the grid. In this partial report condition, recall was on average just over 3 out of the 4 symbols from any row they attended to, suggesting that the iconic store can retain **approximately 76**% of all the data received.

Step 1 Show grid	Step 2 Ring tone	Step 3 Recall letters
7 1 V F		? ? ? ?
X L 5 3	Medium tone	X L 5 3
B 4 W 7		? ? ? ?

- **Duration** – If there was a delay between the presentation of the grid and the sounding of the tone, Sperling found that more and more information was lost (only 50% was available after a 0.3 second delay and only 33% was available after a 1 second delay).

SHORT-TERM MEMORY

- **Duration** – Peterson and Peterson (1959) investigated the duration of short-term memory with their **trigram experiment**. They achieved this by
  1. asking subjects to remember a single nonsense syllable of three consonants (a *trigram* of letters such as FJT or KPD).
  2. giving them an *interpolated task* to stop them rehearsing the trigram (such as counting backwards in threes from one hundred).
  3. testing their *recall after 3, 6, 9, 12, 15 or 18 seconds* (recall had to be perfect and in the correct order to count). While average recall was very good (about 80%) after 3 seconds, this average dropped dramatically to around 10% after 18 seconds.

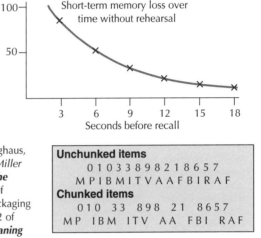

- **Capacity** – Many early researchers in the area of memory, including Ebbinghaus, noted that short term memory appears to have a limited storage capacity. *Miller* (1956) investigated this limited capacity experimentally, refering to it as '**The magical number seven, plus or minus two'**. Miller found that the amount of information retained could be increased by **chunking** the information – packaging it into larger items or units, although the STM can still only retain 7 + or – 2 of these chunks. Chunking is greatly improved if the chunks already have **meaning** from LTM.

Unchunked items
0 1 0 3 3 8 9 8 2 1 8 6 5 7
M P I B M I T V A A F B I R A F
Chunked items
010   33   898   21   8657
M P   I B M   I T V   A A   F B I   R A F

- **Encoding** – It has been argued that the main way information is encoded or retained in STM is through sound – an **acoustic code**. Regardless of whether we see or hear material, we tend to find ourselves repeating the information verbally to ourselves to keep it in mind (STM), and hopefully pass it on to long term storage. Conrad (1964) demonstrated acoustic STM encoding, finding that rhyming letters were significantly harder to recall properly than non rhyming letters, mostly due to acoustic confusion errors, e.g. recalling 'B' instead of 'P'. Baddeley found similar effects for rhyming vs. non-rhyming words.
Den Heyer and Barrett (1971) showed that STM stores visual information too.

1) B T C P G E D
2) F T Z Q W R N
3) MAT, CAT, SAT, BAT, HAT, RAT, FAT
4) PIE, SIX, TRY, BIG, GUN, HEN, MAN

Acoustic confusion errors are made when recalling lists 1 & 3, even though the letters are visually presented. This shows the material is retained acoustically in STM.

LONG-TERM MEMORY

- **Duration** – Ebbinghaus tested his memory using nonsense syllables after delays ranging from 20 minutes to 31 days later and found that a large proportion of information in LTM was lost comparatively quickly (within the first hour) and thereafter stabilised to a much slower rate of loss.
Linton used a diary to record at least 2 'every day' events from her life each day over 6 years, and randomly tested her later recall of them. She found a much more even and gradual loss of data over time (approx. 6 % per year).
- **Capacity** – Enormous but impossible to measure.
- **Encoding** – Baddeley (1966) showed that LTM stores information in terms of meaning (semantic memory), by giving subjects four lists to remember.
If recall was given immediately, list A was recalled worse than list B, but there was little difference between the recall of lists C and D, indicating acoustic STM encoding.
After 20 minutes, however, it was list C that was recalled worse than D since words with similar meanings were confused, indicating semantic LTM encoding.

Baddeley's (1966) lists:

List A – Similar sounding words
e.g. man, map, can, cap.

List B – Non similar sounding words
e.g. try, pig, hut, pen.

List C – Similar meaning words
e.g. great, big, huge, wide.

List D – Non similar meaning words
e.g. run, easy, bright.

Multi-store model of memory

- Much research was devoted to identifying the properties of sensory, short-term, and long-term memory, and cognitive psychologists such as Atkinson and Shiffrin (1968) began to regard them as **stores** – hypothetical holding structures.
- Atkinson and Shiffrin proposed the two-process model of memory, which showed how information flowed through the two stores of short-term and long-term memory, but like many of the models, they assumed the existence of a sensory memory that precedes the short-term memory, and so it is sometimes termed the multi-store model.

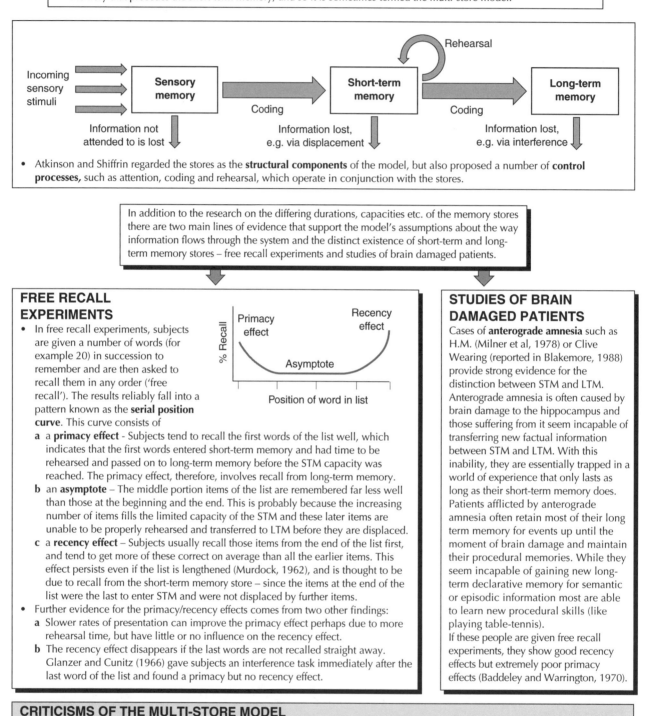

- Atkinson and Shiffrin regarded the stores as the **structural components** of the model, but also proposed a number of **control processes,** such as attention, coding and rehearsal, which operate in conjunction with the stores.

In addition to the research on the differing durations, capacities etc. of the memory stores there are two main lines of evidence that support the model's assumptions about the way information flows through the system and the distinct existence of short-term and long-term memory stores – free recall experiments and studies of brain damaged patients.

FREE RECALL EXPERIMENTS

- In free recall experiments, subjects are given a number of words (for example 20) in succession to remember and are then asked to recall them in any order ('free recall'). The results reliably fall into a pattern known as the **serial position curve**. This curve consists of

  a a **primacy effect** - Subjects tend to recall the first words of the list well, which indicates that the first words entered short-term memory and had time to be rehearsed and passed on to long-term memory before the STM capacity was reached. The primacy effect, therefore, involves recall from long-term memory.

  b an **asymptote** – The middle portion items of the list are remembered far less well than those at the beginning and the end. This is probably because the increasing number of items fills the limited capacity of the STM and these later items are unable to be properly rehearsed and transferred to LTM before they are displaced.

  c a **recency effect** – Subjects usually recall those items from the end of the list first, and tend to get more of these correct on average than all the earlier items. This effect persists even if the list is lengthened (Murdock, 1962), and is thought to be due to recall from the short-term memory store – since the items at the end of the list were the last to enter STM and were not displaced by further items.

- Further evidence for the primacy/recency effects comes from two other findings:

  a Slower rates of presentation can improve the primacy effect perhaps due to more rehearsal time, but have little or no influence on the recency effect.

  b The recency effect disappears if the last words are not recalled straight away. Glanzer and Cunitz (1966) gave subjects an interference task immediately after the last word of the list and found a primacy but no recency effect.

STUDIES OF BRAIN DAMAGED PATIENTS

Cases of **anterograde amnesia** such as H.M. (Milner et al, 1978) or Clive Wearing (reported in Blakemore, 1988) provide strong evidence for the distinction between STM and LTM. Anterograde amnesia is often caused by brain damage to the hippocampus and those suffering from it seem incapable of transferring new factual information between STM and LTM. With this inability, they are essentially trapped in a world of experience that only lasts as long as their short-term memory does. Patients afflicted by anterograde amnesia often retain most of their long term memory for events up until the moment of brain damage and maintain their procedural memories. While they seem incapable of gaining new long-term declarative memory for semantic or episodic information most are able to learn new procedural skills (like playing table-tennis).

If these people are given free recall experiments, they show good recency effects but extremely poor primacy effects (Baddeley and Warrington, 1970).

CRITICISMS OF THE MULTI-STORE MODEL

It is too simplistic, in that:

a It under-emphasises interaction between the stores, for example the way information from LTM influences what is regarded as important and relevant to show attention to in sensory memory and helps the meaningful chunking of information in STM.

b STM and LTM are more complex and less unitary than the model assumes. This criticism is dealt with by the Working Memory model of STM by Baddeley and Hitch (1974) and by research into the semantic, episodic, imagery and procedural encoding of LTM.

c Mere rehearsal is too simple a process to account for the transfer of information from STM to LTM – the model ignores factors such as the effort and strategy subjects may use when learning (**elaborative** rehearsal leads to better recall than just maintenance rehearsal) and the model does not account for the type of information taken into memory (some items, e.g. distinctive ones, seem to flow into LTM far more readily than others). These criticisms are dealt with by the Levels of Processing approach of Craik and Lockhart (1972)

Levels of processing and working memory

LEVELS OF PROCESSING APPROACH TO MEMORY – CRAIK AND LOCKHART (1972)

THE APPROACH
- Craik and Lockhart's important article countered the predominant view of fixed memory **stores**, arguing that it is what the person **does** with information when it is received, i.e. how much attention is paid to it or how deeply it is considered, that determines how long the memory lasts.
- They suggested that information is more readily transferred to LTM if it is *considered, understood* and related to past memories to gain *meaning* than if it is merely *repeated* (maintenance rehearsal). This degree of consideration was termed the '**depth of processing**' - the deeper information was processed, the longer the *memory trace* would last.
- Craik and Lockhart gave three examples of **levels** at which verbal information could be processed:
  1 **Structural** level – e.g. merely paying attention to what the words *look* like (very shallow processing).
  2 **Phonetic** level – processing the *sound* of the words.
  3 **Semantic** level – considering the **meaning** of words (deep processing).

EVIDENCE
- Craik and Tulving (1975) tested the effect of depth of processing on memory by giving subjects words with questions that required different levels of processing, e.g.
  'table'
  Structural – 'Is the word in capital letters?'
  Phonetic – 'Does it rhyme with "able"?'
  Semantic – 'Does it fit in the sentence "the man sat at the _____"?'
- Subjects thought that they were just being tested on reaction speed to answer yes or no to each question, but when they were given an unexpected test of recognition words processed at the semantic level were recognised more often than those processed phonetically and structurally.

MODIFICATIONS
Many researchers became interested in exactly what produced **deep** processing:
- **Elaboration** – Craik and Tulving (1975) found complex semantic processing (e.g. 'The great bird swooped down and carried off the struggling __') produced better cued recall than simple semantic processing (e.g. 'She cooked the __').
- **Distinctiveness** – Eysenck and Eysenck (1980) found even words processed phonetically were better recalled if they were distinctive or unusual.
- **Effort** – Tyler et al (1979) found better recall for words presented as difficult anagrams (e.g. 'OCDTRO') than simple anagrams (e.g. 'DOCTRO').
- **Personal relevance** – Rogers et al (1977) found better recall for personal relevance questions (e.g. 'Describes you?') than general semantic ones (e.g. 'Means?').

EVALUATION
- **Strengths** – good contribution to understanding the processes that take place at the time of learning.
- **Weaknesses** – There are many problems with defining 'deep' processing and why it is effective.
- Semantic processing does not always lead to better retrieval (Morris et al, 1977).
- It describes rather than explains.

THE WORKING MEMORY MODEL – BADDELEY AND HITCH (1974)

THE MODEL (AS OF 1990)
The working memory model challenged the unitary and passive view of the multi-store model's short-term memory store.
Working memory is an **active** store to hold and manipulate information that is currently being consciously thought about. It consists of 3 separate **components:**
- **The central executive** – a modality-free controlling attentional mechanism with a limited capacity, which monitors and co-ordinates the operation of the other two components or slave systems.
- **The phonological loop** – which itself consists of two subsystems,
  a The *articulatory control system* or 'inner voice' which is a verbal rehearsal system with a time-based capacity. It holds information by articulating sub-vocally material we want to maintain or are preparing to speak.
  b The *phonological store* or 'inner ear' which holds speech in a phonological memory trace that lasts 1.5 to 2 seconds if it does not refresh itself via the articulatory control system. It can also receive information directly from the sensory register (echoic) or from long-term memory.
- **The visuospatial sketchpad** – or 'inner eye' which holds visual and spatial information from either the sensory register (iconic) or from long-term memory.

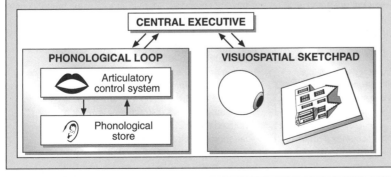

EVIDENCE
- The existence of separate systems in working memory has been shown experimentally by using concurrent tasks (performing two tasks at the same time) – if one task interferes with the other, then they are probably using the same component.
- Thus, if articulatory suppression (continually repeating a word) uses up the phonological loop, another task involving reading and checking a difficult text would be interfered with, but not a spatial task.

EVALUATION
- Working memory provides a more thorough explanation of storage and processing than the multi-store model's STM.
- It can be applied to reading, mental arithmetic and verbal reasoning.
- It explains many STM deficits shown by brain-damaged patients.
- However, the nature and role of the central executive is still unclear.

Reconstructive memory

WHAT IS THE RECONSTRUCTIVE APPROACH TO MEMORY?

- In contrast to much cognitive research on memory, which focuses on quantitative tests of how many randomly selected digits, words or nonsense syllables can be remembered under strictly controlled conditions, the reconstructive memory approach has tended to concentrate more on *qualitative changes* in what is remembered, often of more *everyday material* such as stories, pictures or witnessed events under more *natural conditions*.
- The pioneer of reconstructive memory research was **Bartlett** (1932) who argued that people do not passively record memories as exact copies of new information they receive, but *actively* try and *make sense* of it *in terms of what they already know* – a process he called *'effort after meaning'*. Bartlett therefore proposed that information may be remembered in a distorted way since memories are essentially 'imaginative reconstructions' of the original information in the light of each individual's past experiences and expectations; rather than remembering what actually happened we may remember what we think should or could have occurred. Bartlett termed the mental structures, that held past experiences and expectations and could influence memory so much, **schemas**.

SCHEMA THEORY

More recent research by cognitive psychologists in the 1970's aimed to specify in more detail the properties of schemas and how they affect memory. Rumelhart and Norman (1983), for example, described how schemas:

1. *represent* both simple and complex *knowledge of all kinds* (e.g. semantic, procedural etc.)
2. *link together* to form larger systems of related schemas (e.g. a restaurant schema links to other 'eating location' schemas) or smaller systems of sub-schemas (e.g. a restaurant schema consists of sub-schemas of ordering, eating and paying schemas)
3. have slots with *fixed values* (defining, unchangeable characteristics), *optional values* (characteristics that may vary according to the specific memory the schema is storing) and *default values* (the most typical or probable characteristic a schema is likely to encounter)
4. acquire their content through generalised personal *experience* or the taught beliefs and stereotypes of a group or society.
5. operate as *active recognition devices* – all schemas constantly try to make sense of new information by making the best fit with it.

An example of a picnic schema is given by Cohen (1993) below. Notice that if the food eaten at a particular picnic was forgotten, then it may be assumed that sandwiches were eaten by default. Cohen also points out five ways in which schemas may influence memory – by providing or aiding selection and storage, abstraction, integration and interpretation, normalisation and retrieval. These properties mean that there are both advantages and disadvantages of schemas for memory:

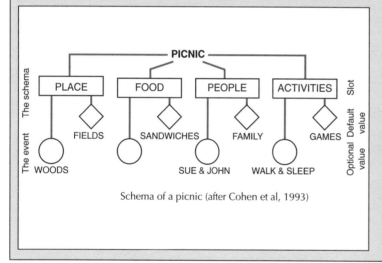

Schema of a picnic (after Cohen et al, 1993)

Advantages – schemas enable us to store the central meaning or gist of new information without necessarily remembering the precise details (abstraction, selection and storage), unless perhaps the details were particularly unusual. This saves memory resources. Schemas also help us understand new information more readily (integration and interpretation, normalisation) and fill in or guess missing aspects of it through the default values (retrieval). This makes the world more coherent and predictable.

Disadvantages – information that does not quite fit our schemas, especially the minor details, may be ignored and forgotten (selection and storage) or distorted (normalisation) so as to make better sense to us, while the guesses/filling-in of memory by the default values (integration and interpretation, retrieval) may be completely inaccurate. This may cause inaccurate, stereotyped and prejudiced remembering.

EVIDENCE FOR SCHEMAS RECONSTRUCTING MEMORY

- Bartlett (1932) found strong evidence for reconstructive memory by asking people to reproduce stories and pictures either serially (by remembering another person's reproduction) or by testing the same person on a number of occasions. When testing English subjects with an unfamiliar North American folk story, 'The War of the Ghosts', Bartlett found their recall became shorter (indicating the gist of the story had been removed) and also distorted by their culture (they omitted unfamiliar details and 'rationalised' the story to make it more coherent and familiar, e.g. recalling the ghosts in 'boats' not 'canoes').
- Brewer and Treyens (1981) tested memory for objects in an office that 30 subjects had waited in individually for 35 seconds. Their 'office schema' seemed to strongly affect their recall. *Expected* objects (e.g. a desk) that were in the room were recalled well but *unexpected* objects (e.g. a pair of pliers) were usually not. Some subjects *falsely* recalled *expected* objects that were not actually in the room (e.g. books and pens).
- Bransford and Johnson (1972, 1973) showed how schemas help to encode and store difficult to understand or ambiguous information.

EVALUATION OF RECONSTRUCTIVE MEMORY

- Bartlett's original research was more ecologically valid than most, but was criticised for its informal nature and lack of experimental controls. However, many recent and well-controlled experiments have consistently shown the reconstructive effect of schemas on memory.
- Bartlett and other reconstructive memory researchers have been accused of over-emphasising the inaccuracy of memory and using unfamiliar material to support the reconstructive effect of schemas on memory. Even quite complex real life material can often be accurately recalled.
- Often unusual information that cannot be easily incorporated into existing schemas (like a skull in the office of the Brewer and Treyens study) is well remembered. This distinctiveness effect has long been noticed and can be accounted for by the schema-plus-tag model of Graesser and Nakamure (1982).
- The concept of a schema and its action is still a little vague.

Retrieval and forgetting

TYPES OF RETRIEVAL

There are many ways that information may be either retrieved from long-term storage or demonstrate its existence in storage in a less direct manner. Some types are more powerful and accurate than others:

Recall – This involves the active searching of our memory with very few external memory cues, e.g. recalling a list of previously memorised digits or the timed essay situation (we have the question but have to search for the answer).

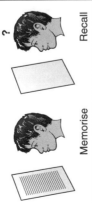

Memorise Recall

Re-learning – This involves not necessarily being able to recall or even recognise previously presented material, but being better able to re-learn it on later occasions. Ebbinghaus investigated this type of retrieval and found that there were re-learning savings (it took less time to re-learn material perfectly the more times the list was re-learnt). An everyday example could be re-learning a language that you have not studied for years – you may be unable to recall or even recognise some of the words you had previously learnt, but it would take you less time to re-learn them compared to other, unexperienced words.

Recognition – This involves a sense of familiarity with external material whether we can name/identify it or not, for example recognising a face or the correct answer in a multiple choice. In recognition, the material to be retrieved is matched to its external likeness. Recognition is an extremely powerful form of retrieval compared to recall – Standing (1973) showed that subjects in a memory test could correctly identify 10,000 previously presented photographs in recognition tests with very low error rates and little sign of an upper boundary for its capacity.

Subject   Later has to correctly
shown picture   identify original

Reconstruction – This involves retrieval that has **distorted** the original information due to our interpretation of it – based upon our past experiences, beliefs, schemas and stereotypes. Bartlett's subjects not only remembered less of the 'War of the Ghosts' story he presented them, but distorted the story when retelling it by making it more coherent and westernised.

Confabulation – This involves the usually unintentional **manufacture** or invention of material to fill in missing details during retrieval. The material added often serves the purpose of making the story more coherent and is likely to occur under conditions of high motivation or emotion.

Redintergration – This is where patchy details of an experience will pop into consciousness regardless of what is currently thought about and gradually become more coherent.

PROBLEMS WITH RETRIEVAL (FORGETTING)

When considering theories of forgetting it is useful to distinguish between the concepts of availability and accessibility.

Availability of memory refers to whether the material is actually there to be retrieved – it is not possible to retrieve what has not reached/lasted in long-term storage.

Accessibility of memory refers to the problems involved in retrieving available information – the tip of the tongue phenomena illustrates this type of difficulty.

There is however a **'grey area'** of ambiguity between these two concepts since we can never be 100% sure that what we have forgotten is unavailable – we may not have found the correct memory cue to 'jog our memory', and what cannot be directly recalled or recognised may still exist as a memory trace to aid re-learning.

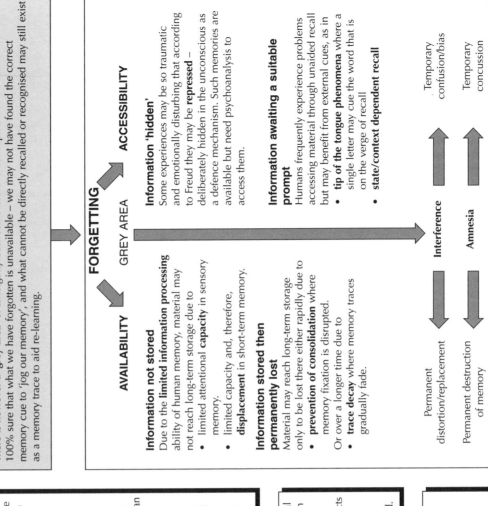

FORGETTING

AVAILABILITY

Information not stored
Due to the **limited information processing** ability of human memory, material may not reach long-term storage due to
- limited attentional **capacity** in sensory memory.
- limited capacity and, therefore, **displacement** in short-term memory.

Information stored then permanently lost
Material may reach long-term storage only to be lost there either rapidly due to
- **prevention of consolidation** where memory fixation is disrupted.
Or over a longer time due to
- **trace decay** where memory traces gradually fade.

Interference

Permanent distortion/replacement

Amnesia

Permanent destruction of memory

GREY AREA   **ACCESSIBILITY**

Information 'hidden'
Some experiences may be so traumatic and emotionally disturbing that according to Freud they may be **repressed** – deliberately hidden in the unconscious as a defence mechanism. Such memories are available but need psychoanalysis to access them.

Information awaiting a suitable prompt
Humans frequently experience problems accessing material through unaided recall but may benefit from external cues, as in
- **tip of the tongue phenomena** where a single letter may cue the word that is on the verge of recall
- **state/context dependent recall**

Temporary confusion/bias

Temporary concussion

Forgetting in short-term memory

Short-term memory contains information that is present in our minds and is currently being thought about at any one time, but which soon slips into the past – hopefully to long-term memory so that we can access it again.

Peterson and Peterson (1959) found 90% of STM information was forgotten after just 18 seconds without rehearsal, while memory span studies reveal that forgetting starts once more than 7+/- 2 items enter STM.

We have all been caught out by STM forgetting, e.g. when we forget some of the names of a large group of people we have only just been introduced to, or forget what we were about to say or do next. Cognitive psychologists have provided theoretical explanations of STM's limited duration and capacity.

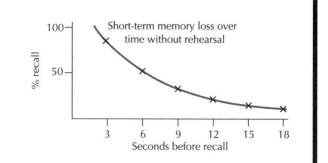

TRACE DECAY THEORY

- Trace decay theory seems to focus on explaining STM forgetting in terms of its limited duration.
- Donald Hebb (1949) suggested that information in STM created an active trace or engram in the form of a brief excitation of nerve cells that, unless refreshed by rehearsal, would spontaneously fade away or decay over time.
- Peterson and Peterson originally argued that the forgetting they found over their 3 to 18 second time delays occurred through trace decay.

Evaluation

- Pure trace decay is very difficult to test. Ideally no new information should be presented in the time between when the trace is acquired and when it is recalled to prevent confounding variables like displacement, yet Peterson and Peterson asked subjects to count backwards to stop them rehearsing.
- Reitman (1974) asked subjects to detect tones between presenting and recalling information, thinking this would hopefully prevent rehearsal without providing any new displacing material. Only about a quarter of information was forgotten after a 15 second delay which was more likely to be due to spontaneous trace decay than the Petersons' result.
- Baddeley and Scott (1971) concluded that 'something like trace decay occurs in the Peterson task, but is complete within five seconds, and is certainly not sufficiently large to explain the substantial forgetting that occurs in the standard paradigm' (quoted from Baddeley, 1997).

DISPLACEMENT THEORY

- Displacement theory seems to focus on explaining STM forgetting in terms of its limited capacity.
- Miller (1956) argued that the capacity of STM is approximately 7+/- 2 items of information. Despite the fact that these items can be chunked to increase their capacity, displacement theory suggests that there are only a fixed number of 'slots' for such information and that once they are full (capacity is reached) new information will push out or displace old material (which may be lost unless it was processed sufficiently to pass into LTM).
- In Peterson and Peterson's experiment, therefore, the increase of forgetting over time may have been a result of the counting backwards task increasingly displacing the original trigrams.

Evaluation

- Waugh and Norman (1965) used the ***serial probe technique*** where 16 digits are rapidly presented to subjects who are then given one of those digits (the probe) and have to report the digit which followed it. It was found that the nearer the end of the 16 digit sequence the probe was presented, the better was the recall of the following digit. This seems to support displacement theory since digits nearer the end of the sequence have fewer following digits to displace them.

> Order of Sequence presented **3 7 2 9 0 4 5 6 3 1 9 0 7 8 2 6**
>
> If probe = 8 then recall of digit (2) is good (little displacement)
> If probe = 4 then recall of digit (5) is poor (greater displacement)

- The poorer recall (asymptote) shown in the middle of the serial position curve that results from free recall studies could similarly be attributed to displacement.

EVALUATION OF STM THEORIES OF FORGETTING

- In some of the research it is unclear what the relative influences of displacement and trace decay are on STM forgetting. Researchers such as Shallice (1967) have found that presenting digits at faster speeds in serial probe tests increases the ability to recall the digits presented earlier in the sequence. Thus trace decay may be responsible for some of the STM forgetting, since the faster presentation means the digits nearer the beginning of the sequence have less time to decay before being tested.
- It is also unclear how distinct the concepts of displacement and trace decay really are. For example displacement in STM works on the assumption that it has a limited capacity, which is measured in terms of memory span (usually 7+/-2 items or chunks). However Baddeley et al (1975) have shown that fewer words can be retained in STM if they take *longer* to pronounce. It seems STM capacity for words depends on the *duration* of pronunciation (how long it takes to say them) rather than the *number* of meaningfully chunked items – in this case words.
- Finally it is also unclear what is actually happening in trace decay and displacement to cause the forgetting. Is the trace really fading or, because it is so fragile, is it being degraded by other incoming information? Similarly with displacement, is the new material nudging aside, overwriting or distracting attention from the old material (or just making it harder to discriminate)? While ***interference theory*** has some of the same kinds of questions to answer, it has been more successful in explaining STM forgetting by showing how the ***similarity*** of competing information from the interpolated task used (as well as from previous trials) can affect the recall of the Petersons' trigrams (see interference theory).

Forgetting in long-term memory

INTERFERENCE THEORY
- One explanation of LTM forgetting is that over time more and more material will be stored and become confused together.
- Interference is most likely to occur between similar material.
- **Proactive interference** is where material learnt first interferes with material learnt later.
- **Retroactive interference** is where material learnt at a later time interferes with material learnt earlier.

```
                    PROACTIVE INTERFERENCE
OLD                 ────────────────────────▶    NEW
MATERIAL            ◀────────────────────────    MATERIAL
                    RETROACTIVE INTERFERENCE
```

RESEARCH ON INTERFERENCE EFFECTS
- *Proactive interference* – Underwood (1957) found that the more nonsense syllable lists his students had previously learned, the greater their forgetting of new nonsense syllables was after a 24 hour delay. This was because the new nonsense syllables became increasingly confused with those from the old lists. Wickens et al (1963) found subjects could be released from proactive interference effects by changing the nature (and thus reducing the similarity) of the new items to be learned, e.g. from nonsense syllables to numbers.
- *Retroactive interference* – McGeoch and Macdonald (1931) presented subjects who had learnt a list of words with various types of interference list to learn for ten minutes afterwards. Recall of the original words was then tested and those students given an interference list of *similar meaning* words recalled on average far less (12.5%) than those given unrelated words (21.7%) or nonsense syllables (25.8%). Best recall (45%) was gained for subjects who were given no interference test at all.

EVALUATION
1. **Artificiality** – Some of the research has been conducted using nonsense syllables often learned under artificially compressed laboratory conditions (rather than the more everyday distributed learning over time) and so interference theory has declined in popularity as an explanation of forgetting. However, many interference studies have been conducted with greater ecological validity, e.g. Baddeley and Hitch (1977) found rugby players' forgetting of the names of teams they had played depended more on interference from the number of rugby matches played since than on the passage of time.
2. **Applications** – Release from proactive interference has been applied by Gunter et al (1981) to increase recall of news items by ensuring dissimilar items followed each other. Retroactive interference has been applied, e.g. by Loftus, to understand the effect of post-event information such as leading questions on the recall of eyewitness testimony.
3. **Reason for interference** – Some believe interference occurs when information is unlearned (Underwood, 1957) or over-written (Loftus, 1979) by other information. Tulving however, argues that interference of retrieval cues rather than stored material is responsible. Tulving and Pstoka (1971) found that the retroactive interference effect on a word list disappeared if cues (e.g. category headings of the words) were given for it.

CUE DEPENDENT RETRIEVAL FAILURE
Information may be *available* to recall but *temporarily inaccessible*, for example:
- Tulving (1968) found that different items from a list might be recalled if people are tested on it on three separate occasions, probably because of the different cues present in each test.
- The tip of the tongue phenomenon. Brown and McNeill (1966) induced this "state in which one cannot quite recall a familiar word" by reading definitions of infrequently encountered words and found the first letter and number of syllables could be identified before complete recall.

Memory **cues** or **prompts** may therefore be necessary to access information.

WHAT CUES AID RETRIEVAL?
Much research has investigated the type of cues that, depending upon their presence or absence, will determine retrieval failure.
- Tulving and Pearlstone (1966) studied intrinsic cues (those meaningfully related to the material to be remembered) by asking subjects to memorise lists of words from different categories. Subjects given the category headings as retrieval cues recalled more of the words than those who were not. Tulving proposed the *encoding specificity principle* to account for this - items committed to memory are encoded with the precise semantic context present at the time of learning.

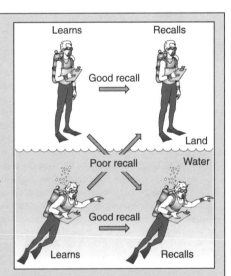

Evaluation – Thomson and Tulving (1970) confirmed this, but later research found cues not around at the time of learning can help too.
- **Context-dependent forgetting** is caused by the absence of *external* environmental cues that were present at the time of learning. Godden and Baddeley (1975) asked divers to learn word lists either on land or under water and found they recalled about 40% less in the opposite environmental context than in the same one. However, no effect was seen if a recognition test was used.
  Smith (1979) found more forgetting occurred a day later if subjects who had learnt 80 words in a distinctive basement room were then asked to recall them in a very differently furnished 5th floor room (12 words) compared to the original room (18 words). Interestingly, almost as many words were recalled (17.2) by a third group who sat in the 5th floor room but were asked to remember as much as they could about the basement room before recall.
Evaluation – Differences in environmental contexts have to be quite large before they significantly affect memory. However, imaginative context recreation can be applied to improve recall in eye-witness testimony.
- **State-dependent forgetting** is caused by the absence of *internal* bodily cues that were experienced at the time of learning.
  Bower (1981) found that his subjects recalled more memories learnt when sad if he tested them when hypnotised to be in a sad mood than a happy one. State-dependent effects have been found for alcohol (Goodwin et al, 1969) and other state-altering substances.
Evaluation – However, true state-dependent memory involving mood has not always been found for emotionally neutral information.

The role of emotion in forgetting

What effect do emotions have on forgetting?
Cognitive psychologists have sometimes neglected emotions in their models of memory, perhaps because of their focus on the information processing comparison with computers – who do not have them (yet!). However two concepts, repression and flashbulb memory, have created interest in the effect of emotion on memory – the first suggesting it could increase forgetting, the second that it could prevent it. Cognitive psychologists have tried to use their theories (e.g. of rehearsal, interference and cue dependency) to explain such emotional effects.

REPRESSION

- Repression is a concept from ***psychodynamic*** psychology which focuses heavily on emotion. Freud proposed that forgetting is ***motivated*** by the desire to ***avoid displeasure***, so embarrassing, unpleasant or anxiety-producing experiences are repressed – pushed down into the ***unconscious***.
- Repression is a protective ***defence mechanism*** that involves the ego actively blocking the conscious recall of memories – which become ***inaccessible***. Direct recall attempts will either fail, lead to distorted recall or digression from the topic. Psychoanalytic techniques, such as dream interpretation, free association etc., are necessary to access repressed memories.
- Freud argued that repression was the most important of defence mechanisms and that it not only accounted for his patients' anxiety disorders (the result of repressing more traumatic experiences) but was a common cause of everyday forgetting.

Evaluation

- Theoretically, forgetting more unpleasant than pleasant memories could just mean that people rehearse upsetting material less because they do not want to think, or talk to others, about it. It is also difficult to tell to what extent the repressor chooses not to search their memory or is unable to.
- Experimental evidence is difficult to gather due to the ethical problems of probing for traumatic memories or creating them by exposing subjects to unpleasant, anxiety-provoking experiences.
- Those studies that have been conducted show mixed results and, where negative emotions have been found to increase forgetting, there has been debate over the cause – emotion can affect memory without the need for an ego.
- Mild anxiety has been produced in the laboratory by giving false 'failure feedback', which does impair memory. However rather than causing repression, Holmes (1990) argues that it causes people to think about the failure which distracts attention away from the memory test (***interference theory***), since giving 'success feedback' also impairs recall.
- Higher anxiety was produced by Loftus and Burns (1982) who showed two groups a film of a bank robbery, but exposed one of the groups to a far more violent version where a young boy was shot in the face. The group that saw this version later showed far poorer recall of detail than the control group. Freud might have suggested repression, but Loftus (1987) could explain the forgetting with the ***weapons focus*** effect, where fearful or stressful aspects of a scene (e.g. the gun) channel attention towards the source of distress and away from other details. Alternatively people may need to be in the same state (i.e. anxious) to recall properly – this is a ***cue-dependent*** explanation.

FLASHBULB MEMORY

- Brown and Kulik (1977) suggested some events can be remembered in almost photographic detail – as if they are imprinted upon the mind. They called this type of recall 'flashbulb memory' and found it was most likely to occur when the event was not only surprising to the person but also had consequences for their own life.
- Thus they found around 90% of people reported flashbulb memories associated with personal shocking events, but whether they had such memories for public shocking events like assassinations depended upon how personally relevant the event was for them – 75% of black participants in their research had a flashbulb memory for the assassination of black-rights activist Martin Luther King, compared to 33% of white participants.
- Brown and Kulik (1977) argued that flashbulb memory was a ***special*** and ***distinct*** form of memory since:
1. The emotionally important event triggers a neural mechanism which causes it to be especially well imprinted into memory.
2. The memories were more detailed and accurate than most.
3. The structural form of the memory was very similar - people nearly always tended to recall where they were, what they were doing, who gave them the information, what they and others felt about it and what the immediate aftermath was, when they first knew of the event.

Evaluation

- Neisser (1982) however, disagrees that flashbulb memories are distinct from other episodic memories, since:
1. The long-lasting nature of the memory is probably due to it being frequently ***rehearsed*** (thought about and discussed afterwards) rather than being due to any special neural activity at the time. Existing memory theory, e.g. levels of processing, would explain meaningful and distinctive events lasting longer.
2. The accuracy of such memories has often been shown to be no different from most other events, e.g. McCloskey et al's (1988) study of memory after the Challenger space shuttle explosion and Wright's (1993) of the Hillsborough football tragedy.
3. The similar form of 'flashbulb memories' may just reflect the normal way people relate information about events to others.
Despite such criticisms some research still supports the notion of flashbulb memory. Conway et al (1994) argue that studies that use events that are really relevant to peoples' lives (e.g. their own on Margaret Thatcher's resignation) find more accurate flashbulb memories over time. Cahill and McGaugh (1998) think that because it is adaptive to remember emotionally important events animals have evolved arousing hormones that help respond in the short term and aid storage of the event in the long term.

SO ARE THE EFFECTS OF EMOTION POSITIVE OR NEGATIVE ON MEMORY?

- Research findings are mixed, e.g. Levinger and Clark (1961) found free associations to emotional words (e.g. 'quarrel' and 'angry') harder to immediately recall. However, other researchers found that after a longer delay the effect reversed and the emotional words were recalled better. Generally positive long-term effects on memory are found for slightly above average levels of arousal (perhaps supporting flashbulb memory), but negative effects for very high levels of arousal. Typical laboratory studies only produce lower arousal levels and have not provided much support for everyday repression, whereas profound amnesia might result from very traumatic or long-term negative emotional arousal which cannot be laboratory-generated.

Focused visual attention

- Definition – The focusing and concentration of mental effort that usually results in conscious awareness of certain aspects of external sensory stimuli or mental experiences (although most study has focused on the former).
- The vast amount of sensory information from all our senses has to be cut down to manageable proportions – while reading this you are probably not aware of the smells around you or the pressure on whatever part of your body you are resting on.

- Some studies have looked at **focused** or **selective** attention – how certain stimuli are selected over others through allocating attention.
- Other studies have looked at **divided** attention – how, within a limited capacity, attention can be allocated to more than one task at a time.
- The two senses most investigated by psychologists researching attention are vision and hearing.

FOCUSED VISUAL ATTENTION

- Even with just one sense, such as vision, there is too much information to precisely process at any one time – we cannot read all the words on this page at the same time. Since the two eyes work in unison, providing one input channel of visual information, attention serves to focus on different areas of the visual field, and thus physically limits the flow of information.
- There are many theories that aim to explain how attention focuses on and selects particular information from its background visual field.

THEORY		EVIDENCE FOR & AGAINST
Zoom lens • Visual attention is like the beam of a spotlight, which can be adjusted to cover a large area in little detail or a small focused area in greater detail.	+	• LaBerge (1983) presented 5 letter words with the task of either 1 identifying the middle letter – requiring a narrow attentional beam, or 2 identifying the whole word – requiring a broad attentional beam. A stimulus probe was randomly presented in the position of one of the five letters and it was located more quickly in the word than the letter identification task (unless it occurred in the position of the middle letter).
	–	• Juola et al (1991) found attention could be just as quickly and accurately focused at the periphery of the 'beam' as at the centre. • Neisser & Becklen (1975) displayed two films at once in the same area and found that attention could be paid to either one of the superimposed images at the expense of the other.
Feature detection • Neisser suggested basic features of a scene are automatically processed in a pre-attentive (not requiring conscious attention) and parallel (all at the same time) way, allowing several basic but separate features to be analysed at once. • Subjects aiming to locate a particular item do not have to be aware of the identification of all non-relevant items.	+	• Neisser showed that subjects could spot any one of up to ten possible target items equally quickly, indicating that the search had to be conducted in a parallel simultaneous way for all possible target items. In further visual search studies, Neisser found that subjects could locate a target letter from amongst many other letters if they were non-similar rather than similar.
	–	• Neisser's subjects did, however, make more mistakes searching for one of ten possible target items, than one of two or three possible items.
Feature integration • Treisman proposed that all basic features of a scene are processed rapidly in a parallel, automatic and pre-attentive way. • Integrated features (involving more than one basic feature at a time) are processed more slowly in a serial (one at a time), automatic way requiring concious attention.	+	• Treisman & Gelade (1980) asked subjects to visually search from an increasing number of surrounding distracter items for either 1 a single feature target item, e.g. a particular colour or letter, or 2 a conjunction target item – composed of two features integrated, e.g. an item consisting of a particular colour and shape. Single feature items were spotted equally well regardless of the number of distracter items indicating parallel processing. Conjunction items were more difficult to detect with increasing distracter items, indicating serial processing.
	–	The experiments were artificial using meaningless conjunctions of features, whereas most 'real-life' objects have meaningful combinations of features that may be pre-attentively recognised, e.g. the shape of a lemon and its colour.
Attentional engagement • Duncan & Humphreys proposed that all integrated items are analysed in terms of their features and segregated from each other. Any item searched for is then matched to its likeness in visual short term memory, the speed of this being determined by the amount of desegregation required and the similarity present in the non-target items.	+	• Studies have shown that searching for a target item takes longer when: 1 More segregation is required, e.g. when there is greater dissimilarity between non-target items. 2 More matching problems are encountered due to greater similarity between the target and non-target items.
	–	• There is much disagreement between researchers over the concepts of desegregation and conjunction of features.

Focused auditory attention 1

- Unlike visual attention, auditory attention involves many possible '**channels**' of information from the environment, since the ears can not be directed to provide one channel like the eyes can.
- Auditory attention serves to direct perception towards one of these channels, for example to pick out one conversation from amongst many surrounding us, as Cherry noticed with the 'cocktail party effect'.
- Psychologists have proposed that for auditory attention to work, the many channels must be **filtered** and one selected for further action. They differ, however, in whether they think this filtering (or '**bottleneck**' in the system) occurs early or late in the processing of information.

BROADBENT'S FILTER THEORY

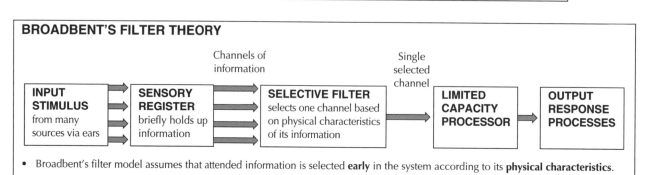

- Broadbent's filter model assumes that attended information is selected **early** in the system according to its **physical characteristics**.

EVIDENCE FOR

Cherry – binaural tests
Cherry presented **two** different messages simultaneously to **both** ears.
Result – Differences in the **physical aspects** of the messages, such as voice intensity and gender of the speaker, affected how easily they were attended to. If there were no physical differences (e.g. same voice and intensity) it was very difficult to distinguish between the two messages in terms of meaning.

Cherry – dichotic tests
Cherry presented **one** different message simultaneously to **each** ear with instructions to shadow (repeat out loud) one of the messages.
Result – Subjects could only notice the physical aspects of the **non-attended** (non-shadowed) message such as the gender of the speaker but could **not** discern any aspects of its **meaning** (even after numerous repetitions or if it was played backwards or changed to another language).

Broadbent – Split-span tests
Broadbent used a dichotic test where, for example, three different items of information are simultaneously presented to each ear in pairs.
Result – Subjects preferred, and were better at, recalling the information **by the ear of presentation** rather than by the order of presentation (one pair at a time). This implied to Broadbent that the ears functioned as separate channels and that it is difficult to change between channels.

EVIDENCE AGAINST

- Broadbent's theory assumes that non-attended information is not processed for meaning. However, at 'cocktail' parties, for example, people are capable of detecting their name being mentioned in other conversations that they thought they were not paying attention to.
- **Many studies** have shown that non-attended information can be processed for **meaning,** e.g. Moray (1959) found that a subject would detect their own name in the non-attended message of a dichotic shadowing test on around a third of occasions. See the evidence for Treisman's theory for more studies against Broadbent's idea that only physical features are selected early.
- Studies have shown that **attention can be switched** between channels far more easily and quickly than Broadbent thought possible, e.g. Gray and Wedderburn (1960). See evidence for Treisman's theory for more details.
- The early dichotic listening experiments used subjects unpractised in shadowing, who had to concentrate more on the task. Underwood (1974) found subjects highly experienced in shadowing could detect 67% of non-shadowed digits, compared to non-experienced subjects who only detected 8%.

Focused auditory attention 2

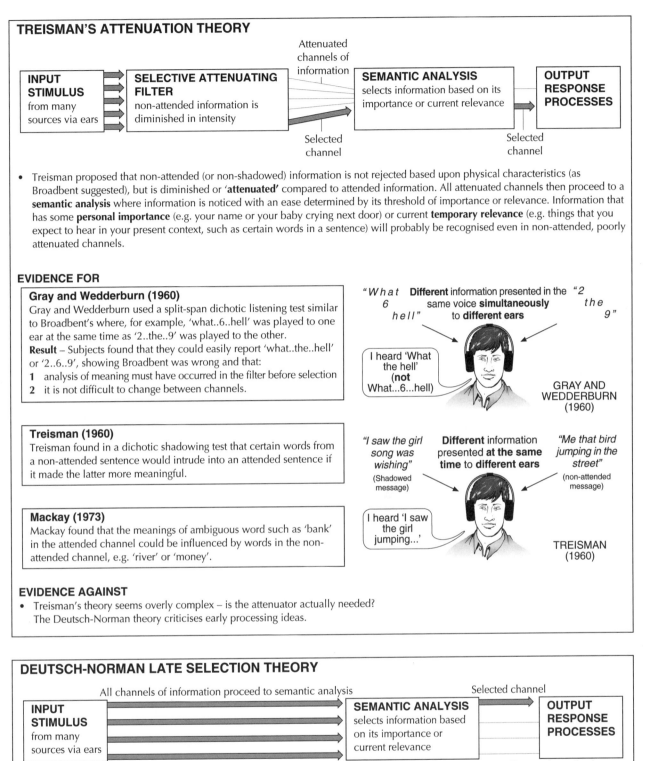

TREISMAN'S ATTENUATION THEORY

INPUT STIMULUS from many sources via ears → **SELECTIVE ATTENUATING FILTER** non-attended information is diminished in intensity → Attenuated channels of information / Selected channel → **SEMANTIC ANALYSIS** selects information based on its importance or current relevance → Selected channel → **OUTPUT RESPONSE PROCESSES**

- Treisman proposed that non-attended (or non-shadowed) information is not rejected based upon physical characteristics (as Broadbent suggested), but is diminished or '**attenuated**' compared to attended information. All attenuated channels then proceed to a **semantic analysis** where information is noticed with an ease determined by its threshold of importance or relevance. Information that has some **personal importance** (e.g. your name or your baby crying next door) or current **temporary relevance** (e.g. things that you expect to hear in your present context, such as certain words in a sentence) will probably be recognised even in non-attended, poorly attenuated channels.

EVIDENCE FOR

Gray and Wedderburn (1960)
Gray and Wedderburn used a split-span dichotic listening test similar to Broadbent's where, for example, 'what..6..hell' was played to one ear at the same time as '2..the..9' was played to the other.
Result – Subjects found that they could easily report 'what..the..hell' or '2..6..9', showing Broadbent was wrong and that:
1 analysis of meaning must have occurred in the filter before selection
2 it is not difficult to change between channels.

"What 6 hell" **Different** information presented in the same voice **simultaneously** to **different ears** *"2 the 9"*

I heard 'What the hell' (**not** What...6...hell)

GRAY AND WEDDERBURN (1960)

Treisman (1960)
Treisman found in a dichotic shadowing test that certain words from a non-attended sentence would intrude into an attended sentence if it made the latter more meaningful.

"I saw the girl song was wishing" (Shadowed message) **Different** information presented **at the same time** to **different ears** *"Me that bird jumping in the street"* (non-attended message)

I heard 'I saw the girl jumping...'

TREISMAN (1960)

Mackay (1973)
Mackay found that the meanings of ambiguous word such as 'bank' in the attended channel could be influenced by words in the non-attended channel, e.g. 'river' or 'money'.

EVIDENCE AGAINST
- Treisman's theory seems overly complex – is the attenuator actually needed? The Deutsch-Norman theory criticises early processing ideas.

DEUTSCH-NORMAN LATE SELECTION THEORY

All channels of information proceed to semantic analysis / Selected channel

INPUT STIMULUS from many sources via ears → **SEMANTIC ANALYSIS** selects information based on its importance or current relevance → **OUTPUT RESPONSE PROCESSES**

- The Deutsch-Norman Theory argues that **all** channels of information are analysed for **meaning** equally and the filter is a **late selection** one.

EVIDENCE FOR
- Norman (1969) found the last few words of non-attended messages could be remembered if the subject stopped halfway through shadowing.
- Their theory also accounts for the studies supporting Treisman's theory, but is more parsimonious (explains the same in a more simple way).

EVIDENCE AGAINST
- Treisman & Riley (1969) found target words were better detected in shadowed than non-shadowed messages. Why would this occur if all channels are processed semantically to the same degree as the Deutsch-Norman theory predicts?
- Filter theories generally lack flexibility. Johnston and Wilson (1980) found that selection can be made early or late depending upon the demands of the situation.

Divided auditory attention 1

- Divided attention concerns the ability to perform two tasks simultaneously.
- Eysenck and Keane (1995) identify three factors which affect the performance of dual tasks:

1 TASK DIFFICULTY

Task difficulty is not easy to define, but tasks become harder to perform at the same time, the more difficult they are (Sullivan, 1976).

2 TASK PRACTICE

Tasks can be performed more easily together if one or both are well practised. Allport et al (1972) found skilled pianists were able to sight read music and shadow speech at the same time. Practice may have its effects by

a using attentional resources more economically, thus freeing them up for other tasks

b developing new strategies to minimise interference between tasks (see 3).

3 TASK SIMILARITY

Non-similar tasks interfere with each other less and can be more readily performed at the same time. Allport et al (1972) found subjects could shadow speech and learn pictorial information at the same time, since the tasks used different modalities. Shaffer (1975) found skilled typists could type from sight and shadow speech, but could not type from speech and shadow speech, at the same time. Tasks disrupt each other if they require the use of

a the same modality, e.g. sight or hearing

b the same processing stage, e.g. word analysis or problem solving

c the same response mechanism, e.g. speech or manual response.

- Many types of theory have been proposed, including limited capacity, modular and synthesis theories.

KAHNEMAN'S LIMITED CENTRAL CAPACITY THEORY

- Kahneman (1973) views attention as a **skill,** rather than a process, and argues that there is just **one central processor** which **allocates** a central pool of attentional **resources** in a **flexible** manner across a variety of different tasks.
- Despite its flexibility, the central processor has a **limited capacity** or pool of attentional resources that it can allocate at any one time.
  1 Tasks requiring little capacity need **little mental effort** or attentional resources and so leave more **room** for performing **additional** tasks. Attention can be divided as long as the capacity is there – a task requiring a large amount of mental effort will leave no room for other tasks.
  2 The amount of capacity or mental effort tasks need, depends upon their **difficulty** and the individual's **past experience** (practice) of them.

3 The amount of total **capacity available** depends on **arousal levels** – the more alert someone is, the more attentional capacity they have.

4 The limited **capacity** available is **allocated** amongst tasks depending on

  a an evaluation of attentional demands – if the degree of mental **effort** required **exceeds capacity**, the central processor has to decide upon an **allocation policy**

  b momentary intentions – attentional resources are likely to be directed towards tasks related to **current goals**

  c enduring dispositions – some stimuli will **override** the **attention** paid to current goals because of their **importance,** e.g. new, startling or personally relevant (like the calling of your name) stimuli. This usually occurs naturally and without voluntary control.

Evidence for

- The model is far more flexible in processing than the filter theories.
- It can explain many of the findings of previous models, plus studies they found difficult to account for, e.g. the problems novice, compared to experienced, subjects had in attending to non-shadowed messages (Underwood, 1974) or the flexibility of processing (Johnston and Wilson, 1980).
- The theory has practical implications. It could explain Gopher and Kahneman's (1971) evidence that the efficiency of a pilot's attention-switching ability (presumably a reflection of the skill of the central processor) is positively correlated (r = .36 for 100 flight cadets) to their success in flight training.

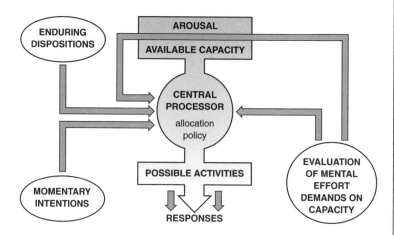

Evidence against

- The theory is not specific enough about how much capacity there is. Spelke et al (1976) trained two students to simultaneously perform two fairly complex tasks requiring the same processes (reading short stories while writing down auditory dictation), perhaps implying a much larger overall capacity than previously assumed, since they could eventually process both sources of information for meaning.
- The theory assumes that processing resources are general and undifferentiated rather than specialised. Module theories disagree with this.

- Norman and Bobrow's (1975) central capacity interference theory suggests that Kahneman neglected the importance of interference. They point out that **resource limitations** can be solved by allocating more attentional resources, but **data limitations** (where two tasks require the same type of resource, e.g. word usage) cannot be solved this way. Task similarity interference tests, e.g. Shaffer (1975) support this idea, and although the theory is descriptive rather than explanatory, it did lead to the idea of specialised resource modules.

Divided auditory attention 2

ALLPORT'S MODULE RESOURCE THEORY

- Allport proposes that attention consists of several **specialised** information processing **modules** for information, each with its **own resources** and **capacity**, rather than one central capacity processor.
- Tasks that are similar use the **same module's resources** and **interfere** with one another if they are attempted at the same time, preventing dual task performance.
- Tasks that are **not similar** use different modules and can be processed in **parallel,** without interfering with each other in any way.
- Wickens (1984) further suggests that resources are specialised to different aspects of a task, e.g. the input mode, processing mechanism, and output modality.

Evidence for

- Module theories can account for the way that dual tasks can be performed and attention divided if the tasks are non-similar. They, therefore, explain studies such as Allport et al's (1972) where the experienced piano players could sight read music and shadow spoken messages.
- Module theories have practical applications to everyday issues, such as whether the use of car phones interferes with driving. Despite the fact that car phones have been devised to make them 'hands free', so that manual responses are not interfered with, there is some evidence that calls demanding decision making can interfere with the perceptual and decision making skills made under difficult driving conditions. Brown et al (1969) got drivers to negotiate a set of obstacles while simultaneously verbally solving problems presented through headphones. Although the drivers usually drove more slowly, and the automatic, basic aspects of driving were unaffected by the auditory task, the demanding logical reasoning did interfere with the more difficult driving decisions - the drivers attempted to get through gaps between obstacles that were far too small. The quality of problem solving also decreased.
- Brain modularity has received support from brain damage studies which have found very specific skill deficits from specific damage.

DUAL TASKS	POSSIBLE MODULES INVOLVED		
	Input mode	Processing mechanism	Output mode
Sight reading music	Vision	Music recognition	Manual
Shadowing speech	Auditory	Speech recognition ⇧	Vocal
	No interference-good performance		
Demanding driving conditions	Vision	Decision making	Manual
Hands free demanding car phone call	Auditory	Problem solving ⇧	Vocal
	Interference-poor performance		

Evidence against

- Module theories do not specify
  1 how many modules there are – making the theory irrefutable, since another module can always be proposed to account for new findings.
  2 what types of module exist – Spelke et al's (1976) students were trained to accomplish two tasks that should have demanded similar modules. Shallice et al (1985), however, have provided some evidence that speech perception and production systems are functionally separate, perhaps accounting for the ability of some translators to listen, translate and speak their languages simultaneously.
  3 how the modules interact so smoothly with each other.

BADDELEY'S SYNTHESIS THEORY

- Baddeley proposed the working memory model, which combines a modality free, central, limited capacity processor (the central executive) plus specific modality processing systems (the phonological loop and visuospatial sketchpad).
- There is much experimental support for the model through the use of concurrent tasks and brain imaging techniques that verify different areas of the brain are active when different modules are active.
- Aspects of the model, such as the role of the central executive, need more investigation.
- See material on memory for more detail on working memory.

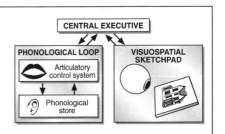

EVALUATION OF DIVIDED ATTENTION THEORIES

- Filter processing theorists still point out that central, modular and synthesis theories **cannot explain** the 'bottleneck' in information processing that is reflected by the **psychological refractory period effect**. This occurs when two stimuli requiring responses are presented rapidly one after the other and the response to the second stimulus is slower than the response to the first, even when the two tasks are not competing for modules (and, therefore, should be processed in parallel) and the subject is highly practised (so resources should not have to be allocated). This refractory period, estimated at around **one tenth of a second**, is possibly due to the time it takes to **switch attention** from one serial channel to another. Although small, as Barber (1988) points out, the consequences for a record breaking 100 metre sprinter of not attending to the starter's gun would be a lost metre on an attending rival.
- Studies and theories of divided attention have practical importance. Trainee pilots often fail, and bus drivers partly have accidents, 'because of a failure to divide attention among concurrent activities or among concurrent signals, or else because they are slow to recognise the significance of crucial signals which arrive on unattended channels' Gopher and Kahneman (1971), quoted in Barber (1988).

Automatic processing

Research has shown that if tasks are practised enough, they become automatic, need less attention, and can be successfully performed with other tasks, e.g. Allport et al's (1972) skilled pianists who were able to sight read music and shadow speech at the same time.

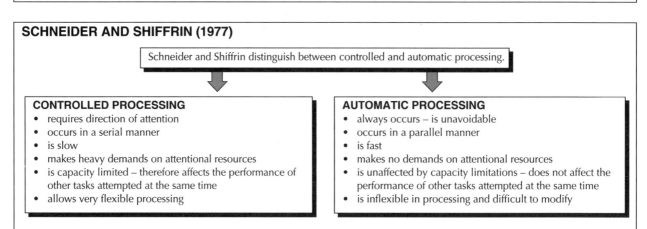

SCHNEIDER AND SHIFFRIN (1977)

Schneider and Shiffrin distinguish between controlled and automatic processing.

CONTROLLED PROCESSING
- requires direction of attention
- occurs in a serial manner
- is slow
- makes heavy demands on attentional resources
- is capacity limited – therefore affects the performance of other tasks attempted at the same time
- allows very flexible processing

AUTOMATIC PROCESSING
- always occurs – is unavoidable
- occurs in a parallel manner
- is fast
- makes no demands on attentional resources
- is unaffected by capacity limitations – does not affect the performance of other tasks attempted at the same time
- is inflexible in processing and difficult to modify

Evidence for
- Treisman's studies of the feature integration approach to focused visual attention support the above distinction – some aspects of a task (e.g. the detection of basic features) can be processed automatically in parallel, whereas others (e.g. those involving the detection of feature combinations) need a more complex analysis using conscious attention and have to be processed serially.
- Schneider and Shiffrin (1977) demonstrated using visual detection tests that
  1 automatic processing occurs rapidly and in parallel when a subject is searching for numbers among letters
  2 controlled attention processing occurs slowly and in a serial manner when a subject is searching for letters among other letters.
- Shiffrin and Schneider (1977), however, found that the search for letters among other letters could become automatic with extensive practice. After over 2000 trials, the letter detection times decreased until they were as fast as the automatic detection shown in the first study.
- Shiffrin and Schneider (1977) also demonstrated that once acquired, automatic processes become unavoidable and difficult to modify. When the target letters or their location in the detection area were changed, subjects found it difficult not to automatically search for the letters they had practised before, in areas they were used to looking. It took subjects around a 1000 trials of the new letters to even start showing automatic detection with them.
- The distinction between controlled and automatic processing has been useful in explaining other psychological phenomenon, such as social facilitation or inhibition. For example, subjects attempting a new or difficult task will show worse performance in front of an audience than on their own. The individual's lack of automatic processes means the distraction of conscious attention by other people will have dire consequences on performance.

Evidence against
- The idea that automatic tasks do not use up attentional resources, are unaffected by capacity limitations, and so do not affect the performance of other tasks attempted at the same time, is not strictly correct. Automatic tasks can interfere with simultaneously performed consciously controlled processing, as in the Stroop effect, where subjects asked to identify **the colour that words are written in** cannot ignore the content of the word if it describes a different colour, e.g. subjects will often report the colour of the word 'green' written in red ink as green rather than red. This occurs as reading skills are automatically triggered and intrude upon the attentional resources of the consciously processed colour detection task.
- How automatic processing occurs is not specified - does the speed of processing increase with practice or is there a change in the type of processing involving more efficient, economical techniques? Logan (1990) argues that automaticity develops through practice because the **retrieval of appropriate responses** becomes more rapid and does not require any intervening conscious thoughts or effort - just the accessing of 'past solutions'. Children, for example, will first have to continuously and laboriously work out addition sums such as '9 + 7 =' but each time they do that sum they leave a memory trace of the answer until eventually they can access that answer directly, without having to 'work it out'. Logan's ideas indicate that there are probably different degrees of task automaticity depending on the amount of past experience with them, a notion that Norman and Shallice (1986) have taken a little further.

NORMAN AND SHALLICE (1986)
Norman and Shallice propose different levels of automaticity:

- Fully automatic processing –   which involves no conscious awareness and is controlled by schemata.

- Partially automatic processing – involves slightly more conscious awareness and is not deliberately controlled but governed by a contention scheduling control system, which resolves conflicts amongst schema so they do not interfere with each other.

- Deliberate control –   involves conscious awareness governed by a supervisory attentional system, which allows decision making and flexibility of response in new situations.

Action slips

REASON'S (1992) THEORY

- Reason (1992) regards action slips - actions performed but not intended – as important contributions to our understanding of attention and automatic processing.
- Reason asked 35 subjects to keep a diary record of action slips over a 2 week period and found that, out of the 433 slips recorded between the subjects, the majority could be categorised into one of the following five types:

1 Storage failures
40% of slips involved forgetting or recalling inaccurately intentions and actions, which leads to the same action being repeated,
e.g. sugaring a cup of tea twice without remembering the first time.

2 Test failures
20% of slips involved forgetting or switching a goal because of a failure to monitor a planned sequence sufficiently,
e.g. going to make a cup of coffee but making tea instead.

3 Sub-routine failures
18% of slips involved omitting or re-ordering stages in an action sequence,
e.g. pouring cold water into a teapot or hot water into a teapot without tea in.

4 Discrimination failures
11% of slips involved failing to discriminate between two objects involved in different actions,
e.g. mistaking drinking yoghurt for milk, or shaving cream for toothpaste.

5 Programme assembly failures
5% of slips involved incorrectly combining the action sequences of different goals,
e.g. putting the tea bags in the refrigerator and the milk in the cupboard.

- Reason (1992) suggests that actions are under two types of control, either:
  1 'open loop' (automatic and non-conscious) control – which is fast but error prone, or
  2 'closed loop' (deliberate and conscious) control – which is slower but less prone to error.

Evidence for
Reason found that action slips happen with tasks that are highly practised and are, therefore, under open loop, automatic control. Since such tasks are performed without monitoring by conscious attention, automatic routines can occur inappropriately. For example,
a actions carried out by non-attended automatic channels are likely to be forgotten – leading to storage failures.
b automatic actions common to many situations may get confused if not monitored at crucial points in a sequence – leading to test failures.

Evidence against
- The data gained using the diary method may be unreliable since it is not known how many slips went unnoticed or on how many occasions slips could have occurred.
- Laboratory attempts to set up action slips (which could control for the faults of the diary method) lack ecological validity. They do not provide the same conditions under which natural 'absent-mindedness' occurs, and so may not produce slips caused by the same factors.
- The precise mechanisms underlying action slips are not specified - Sellen and Norman (1992) aimed to provide more detail on these.

SELLEN AND NORMAN'S (1992) THEORY

- Sellen and Norman suggest that action slips are the result of schemata – cognitive structures that enable us to deal with the world. They propose that there are two main types of schema:
  1 parent schemata – which are concerned with overall intentions such as making a cup of tea, and
  2 child schemata – which consist of the actions required to accomplish the parent schema's intention, such as filling the kettle with water, plugging it in, putting a tea bag in the cup, pouring the water in, etc.

- Each schema has a particular activation level for producing its behaviour which depends upon current intentions or triggering environmental conditions.
- An action slip will, therefore, occur if, for example, an error was made in forming a parent schema intention (so a whole set of inappropriate child schemata are activated) or incorrect child schemata are triggered (while making tea you walk past the coffee jar and unconsciously trigger the child schema for putting coffee in the cup rather than tea).

EVALUATION OF ACTION SLIP THEORIES

- The type of action slips investigated above usually occur when conscious attention is not being paid to a task, usually it is already 'pre-occupied' with a heavy workload of information. However, the theories do not take into account automatic errors made in tasks that subjects are paying close attention to. Healy (1976) found that subjects asked to circle all the letter 't's in a passage, missed out the 't' in 'the', one of the most common words in the English language. Although the task required conscious effort, since the word 'the' tends to be processed automatically as a whole unit, performance was disrupted. The stroop effect also involves automatic action slips despite conscious effort.
- Action slips are of practical importance. Langan-Fox and Empson (1985) found that air-traffic controllers made more action slips as workload (measured in terms of the number of aircraft in radio contact at any one time) increased.

Pattern recognition

SELFRIDGE'S PANDEMONIUM MODEL OF FEATURE DETECTION

- Selfridge's pandemonium model is a feature detection approach that can be used to explain how the perception of objects can be built up from the detection of their elementary features.
- Selfridge suggested the metaphor of a **hierarchy** of 'demons' to explain how the processing of features could occur in **parallel**. **Image demons** represent an external object as an image. **Feature demons** then 'shout' with a loudness that reflects how similar their feature speciality is to those features in the image. **Cognitive demons** represent combinations of features that form whole, meaningful patterns and scream with a loudness that reflects the number of features present in their pattern. **Decision demons** 'listen' to the various cognitive demons to find which has the 'loudest' combination of matching features.
- Lindsay and Norman (1972) applied the model to letter recognition, showing how letters can be analysed in terms of line, angle, pattern, and decision 'demons' to be correctly identified.

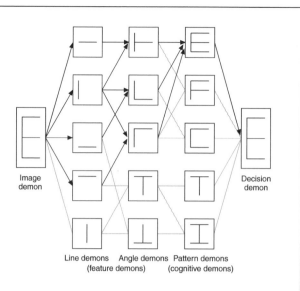

Image demon   Decision demon

Line demons Angle demons Pattern demons
(feature demons) (cognitive demons)

Evaluation

- Experimental support - Neisser (1964) found that it was easier to detect a target letter (e.g. a 'Z') when its features were different from other letters (e.g. 'B's and 'D's) it was embedded amongst, perhaps because there were less competing feature demons.
- Biological mechanisms support – the model has conceptual links to neurological findings (e.g. Hubel and Wiesel's) relating to retinal cells (image demons?) and simple, complex and hypercomplex cells (feature demons?) in the visual cortex that increase their firing rate (shouting?) in response to lines of different orientations and also seem to work in a bottom-up manner. Neuronal cells have also been found that respond selectively to whole, complex objects, such as hands or faces (cognitive demons?). The model's use of parallel processing also seems to reflect the way the brain's huge network of neurones interconnect with each other.
- Real-life conditions – the model does not explain how objects (especially 3D ones) are recognised when viewed from angles that distort line orientations or obscure parts of the pattern, nor how the features are arranged in the correct spatial configurations.
- Context and expectation (perceptual set) – the model does not deal with how top-down factors can influence feature analysis. A more dynamic, 'two-way' flow in the model (as in connectionist networks) would allow expected cognitive demons to 'shout back' down the system to bias the weighting of analysed features. Many studies show that context can bias the perception of features (see Gregory's theory of perception). Neurological findings also indicate that conscious attention and expectation can influence the firing rates of basic feature-detection cells in the primary visual cortex, increasing or decreasing their responsiveness.

BIEDERMAN'S (1987) RECOGNITION-BY-COMPONENTS or GEON THEORY

- Biederman suggested that objects are recognised in terms of the combination and spatial arrangement of the 'geons' they contain. Geons are basic shape components, such as cylinders, spheres, blocks, cones, wedges and arcs. There are approximately 36 basic geons.
- The geons are recognised by their combination of the five invariant properties of the edges that outline them, e.g. straight, converging, parallel, symmetrical and curving edges. Invariant properties refer to the fact that the characteristics of the edge can be detected from a variety of viewpoints and are likely to reflect actual or 'non-accidental' properties of objects in the real world.
- The geons are distinguished from each other by analysing the concave parts of an object's contour, since this is usually where one geon joins another.
- The combination and arrangement of geons in the object is then matched to stored representations of objects in memory (although identification can still occur if some geons are missing).

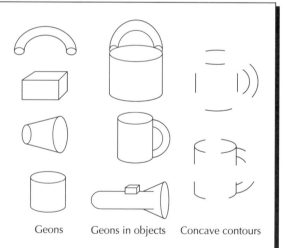

Geons   Geons in objects   Concave contours

Evaluation

- Experimental support – Biederman (1987) empirically demonstrated that object recognition was harder if the concave parts of contours were missing and that recognition could occur with less than a complete set of geons for an object.
- Biological mechanisms support – the theory links to neurological findings on visual agnosia (where brain damage causes problems identifying whole objects even though component parts can be perceived and distinguished), e.g. *The Man who Mistook his Wife for a Hat* (Sachs, 1985) described a 'continuous surface, infolded on itself' with 'five outpouchings', without recognising it as a glove.
- Real life conditions – the model does explain how objects (especially 3D ones) are recognised when viewed from angles that distort line orientations or obscure parts of the pattern, but does not seem to allow fine discrimination between very similar objects, e.g. faces.
- Context and expectation (perceptual set) – the theory also neglects the role of top-down factors in pattern recognition. Palmer (1975), for instance, found that presenting general context pictures, e.g. of a kitchen, biased the recognition of objects with similar features (arrangements of geons), e.g. a loaf of bread or an American mailbox.

Face recognition

BRUCE AND YOUNG'S (1986) MODEL

EXPRESSION ANALYSIS
Used to infer information relating to emotional state.

FACIAL SPEECH ANALYSIS
Used to gain facial (e.g. lip) movement information in speech perception.

DIRECTED VISUAL PROCESSING
To search for specific facial information, e.g. beards, that may aid recognition.

UNFAMILIAR FACES

STRUCTURAL ENCODING
Faces are represented.

VIEW-CENTRED DESCRIPTIONS

EXPRESSION-INDEPENDENT DESCRIPTIONS

FAMILIAR FACES

COGNITIVE SYSTEM

Holds additional information relevant to face recognition regarding features that certain types of people are likely to possess, e.g. face/hair colour, attractiveness, youth, etc., or contexts they are likely to be found in.

FACE RECOGNITION UNITS (FRUs)
Each unit contains structural information specific to known faces.

PERSON IDENTITY NODES (PINs)
Each node contains semantic information specific to people, e.g. job, interests, etc.

NAME GENERATION
Names are stored separately.

Research studies

- Cognitive neurological studies – have confirmed that familiar and unfamiliar faces are recognised through different processes. Studies of brain damaged individuals reveal that some have problems in recognition tests of familiar faces but not unfamiliar ones, whereas others show the opposite tendency. Brain scans of individuals without brain damage show slightly different areas are used when recognising familiar and unfamiliar faces.
- Experimental studies – regarding familiar face recognition, Young et al (1986a, 1986b – cited in Eysenck and Keane, 1995) confirmed that face recognition is achieved first, personal identity second and name generation last as the model predicted. They presented pictures of well known faces and found that decisions relating to the familiarity of a face were made faster than decisions relating to the occupation associated with the face, which in turn were made faster than decisions regarding the name.
- Diary/self-report studies – Young et al (1985) found that incidents of everyday face recognition problems recorded by their participants in diaries seemed to confirm the model's predictions. Sensing familiarity (activation of FRUs) before being able to remember anything else about the person (activation of PINs) occurred more often than remembering personal details (activation of PINs) but not the name (activation of name generation). Recalling the name without being able to recall anything else about the person was never reported.
- However, studies of brain damaged individuals who can match faces with names but not recall any personal information or those who show covert recognition (access to information about a person without necessarily consciously recognising them) cannot be explained by this model.

INTERACTIVE ACTIVATION AND COMPETITION (IAC) MODEL OF FACE RECOGNITION

- Burton et al (1990) developed the Interactive Activation and Competition (IAC) model of face recognition to overcome the problems with the Bruce and Young model (e.g. its lack of precision in areas) and explain all the research studies above.
- The IAC is a connectionist model that can be computer simulated. Informational excitation flows forwards and backwards between the units of three pools of information (face-recognition units, person identity nodes and semantic information units), while the units within each pool inhibit each other, until a *threshold is exceeded in a single person identity node* and an individual *person* becomes recognised.
- Names are regarded as just another aspect of semantic information that are usually retrieved last because they tend to be unique (we know many politicians, but usually only one Margaret Thatcher) and often meaningless – thus poorly integrated with other information.

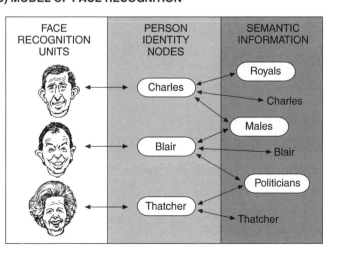

Neurophysiology of visual perception

LIGHT ENTERING THE EYE

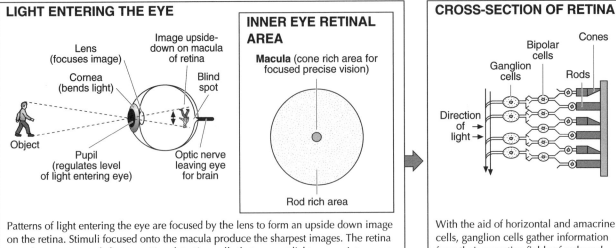

Lens (focuses image)
Image upside-down on macula of retina
Cornea (bends light)
Blind spot
Object
Pupil (regulates level of light entering eye)
Optic nerve leaving eye for brain

INNER EYE RETINAL AREA

Macula (cone rich area for focused precise vision)

Rod rich area

Patterns of light entering the eye are focused by the lens to form an upside down image on the retina. Stimuli focused onto the macula produce the sharpest images. The retina contains two types of photosensitive detection cells that convert light energy into nerve impulses:
- Cones – are fewer in number than rods, are sensitive to colour, and are mostly densely packed at the macula (providing greater sharpness or acuity of vision).
- Rods – respond to brightness only and are far more sensitive to weak illumination.

CROSS-SECTION OF RETINA

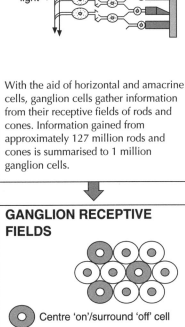

Cones
Bipolar cells
Ganglion cells
Rods
Direction of light

With the aid of horizontal and amacrine cells, ganglion cells gather information from their receptive fields of rods and cones. Information gained from approximately 127 million rods and cones is summarised to 1 million ganglion cells.

VISUAL PATHWAYS THROUGH THE BRAIN

Stimuli from the left visual field is detected by the right hand side retinal surfaces, the optic nerves of which travel to the right hand side of the brain. The opposite occurs for stimuli from the right visual field

Optic chiasm
Optic nerve fibres cross at this point.

Thalamus
Located at the top of the brain stem.

UNDERSIDE VIEW OF THE BRAIN

Optic nerves
Relay sensory stimuli from retinal surfaces to areas of the brain responsible for vision

Lateral geniculate nucleus
A relay centre for visual information. Sends information on to the primary visual cortex from each eye. Some is also sent to the superior colliculus.

Superior colliculus
This is involved in perceiving 'where' objects are by locating stimuli in the visual fields and orienting the head to focus on them.

Primary visual cortex (V1)
Often termed the striate visual cortex, Hubel and Wiesel (1962) found it consisted of hypercolumns of cells that respond to lines of the same orientation. Simple cells only respond to lines in a particular part of the visual field, complex cells respond to lines wherever they occur. Other visual areas may contain hyper-complex cells that respond to even more precise visual stimuli.

STRIATE VISUAL CORTEX

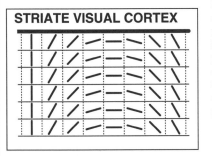

GANGLION RECEPTIVE FIELDS

Centre 'on'/surround 'off' cell

Centre 'off'/surround 'on' cell

There are different types of ganglion cells. Some are activated by stimulation to the centre of their receptive field, but are inhibited by stimulation to the surrounding area, others show the opposite pattern of activation. These patterns of activation allow edges to be more easily detected at higher levels of the visual system.

VISUAL ASSOCIATION AREAS

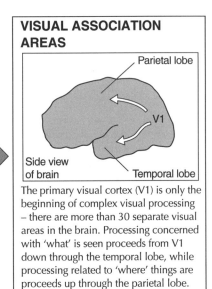

Parietal lobe
V1
Side view of brain
Temporal lobe

The primary visual cortex (V1) is only the beginning of complex visual processing – there are more than 30 separate visual areas in the brain. Processing concerned with 'what' is seen proceeds from V1 down through the temporal lobe, while processing related to 'where' things are proceeds up through the parietal lobe.

Research into visual information processing

SENSORY ADAPTATION

Sensory adaptation refers to the process of adapting to different levels of illumination. This allows us to see under a variety of light conditions, from bright daylight to dusk or moonlight. There are two types of adaptation:

Light adaptation – refers to the adjustment from dark to light conditions, which takes 5-10 minutes if the transition is very sudden.

Dark adaptation – refers to the adjustment from light to dark conditions, which takes 20-25 minutes if the transition is very sudden. Colours become increasingly hard to distinguish at low illumination levels.

Physiological explanations and evidence

Physiological research has shown that:

Light adaptation involves a constriction of pupils (to allow less light to enter) and the bleaching of the rhodopsin in the light-sensitive rods until they can no longer respond. Vision switches to the colour-sensitive cones whose photopigments require more energy to bleach and thus are still able to function.

Dark adaptation involves a dilation of pupils (to allow more light to enter) and the regeneration of the photopigment rhodopsin in the light-sensitive rods, which allows them to increase our sensitivity to light a millionfold. However, insufficient light energy results in reduced responsiveness from the colour-sensitive cones.

CONTRAST PROCESSING

Contrast processing refers to the ability of the visual system to detect contrasting light levels in the environment and thus distinguish the edges and contours of objects. This is necessary to distinguish the outlines of objects and to separate them from their background and each other – a pre-condition of actually recognising and identifying what those objects are.

Physiological explanation and evidence

Contrast processing is achieved by lateral inhibition from neighbouring cells in 'centre-on, surround-off' or 'centre-off, surround-on' ganglion receptive fields. This exaggerates the light contrasts at borders, making edges clearer.

How a 'centre-off, surround-on' ganglion receptive field responds in terms of firing rate to different light and dark stimulation, is illustrated below:

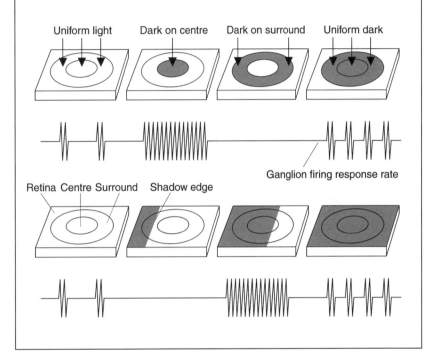

COLOUR PROCESSING

Theories of colour processing

Trichromatic theory - Young and Helmholtz suggested that human eyes contain 3 types of receptor for colour/hue – blue, green and red – and that combinations of these 3 could produce the perception of any other colour, e.g. green and red produce yellow. However, this theory could not account for red and green colour-blind people being able to see yellow.

Opponent-process theory – Hering proposed that human colour receptors must be organised in two opponent pairs; red-green and blue-yellow, and that activation of one colour inhibited perception of its opposite. This accounts for why opposite colour after-images occur and why we never see reddish-green or bluish-yellow colours.

Physiological explanations and evidence

Physiological research has shown that:

Three types of cone with photopigments sensitive to blue, green and yellow/green (still usually termed 'red' though!) wavelengths of light have been found in the retina.

P-type ganglion cells have been found that respond in a colour opponent way (red-green and blue-yellow, as Hering suggested). Light of one wavelength falling on the centre of a receptive field will increase ganglion cell response, but this can be cancelled by its opposite colour falling on the surround.

FEATURE PROCESSING

Feature processing begins from the retina but essentially the primary visual cortex (V1) is the place where a basic picture of a perceived object is represented. From V1, areas concerned with processing **what** the feature is run down through the temporal lobe, starting with basic shape analysis and colour detection (in V4) and later involving object recognition and memory associations (in the inferotemporal cortex). Areas involving **where** the object is run up through the parietal lobe, and process depth, movement (V5) and spatial location.

Physiological explanations and evidence

Physiological research has shown that:

Single cell recording (with fine micro-electrodes) has found simple and complex cells in V1 that increase their firing rate when lines of certain orientations are presented on the retina (Hubel and Wiesel), hypercomplex cells that respond to angles and corners (DeValois and DeValois, 1980, Shapley and Lennie, 1985) and even cells that respond to whole objects like hands (Gross et al, 1972).

Studies of brain damage (either accidental or deliberately caused) have shown that disruption to V1 may produce blindsight – the ability to locate visual stimuli with no conscious experience of seeing them (Weiskrantz, 1986), while damage to V4 and V5 has caused disturbed or loss of colour and movement perception respectively.

Brain scanning studies, e.g. PET scans, have revealed different areas of brain activity occur when different feature processing tasks are attempted. For example, tasks that require global or spatial analysis often produce increased activity in the right hemisphere while the analysis of detail is often reflected in left hemisphere activity.

Bottom-up theories of perception

WHAT DOES PERCEPTION INVOLVE?

Perception is the process of interpreting and organising the environmental information received by the senses. For visual perception, this involves taking the constantly fluctuating patterns of light, which arrive from all over the environment, up-side-down, on to our two-dimensional retinas and achieving:

1 **Feature or object detection** – detecting the shape of objects in the environment, e.g. distinguishing features from each other and their background.
2 **Depth perception** – establishing location in three-dimensional space, e.g. interpreting a two-dimensional retinal image as a three-dimensional object at a specific distance in three-dimensional space.
3 **Pattern or object recognition** – recognising an object in terms of its shape, size, brightness and colour, despite its:

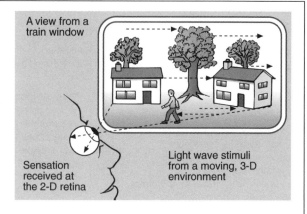

A view from a train window

Sensation received at the 2-D retina

Light wave stimuli from a moving, 3-D environment

- Viewpoint – an object seen from different angles will cast images of different shapes upon the retina, yet will be recognised as the same object (a phenomenon known as **shape constancy**).
- Distance – the same object at longer distances will cast smaller images on the retina but will be identified as the same size (a phenomenon known as **size constancy**).
- Luminescence – an object will be perceived as the same brightness despite changes in the overall level of luminosity (a phenomenon known as **brightness constancy**).

BOTTOM-UP THEORIES

- These theories emphasise the richness of the information entering the eye and the way that perception can occur from using all the information available.
- Gibson believes perception occurs directly from sensation, feature detection theories examine the processes involved in assembling perception from sensations.

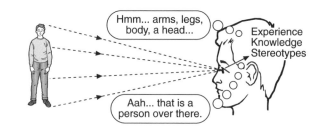

Hmm... arms, legs, body, a head...

Experience Knowledge Stereotypes

Aah... that is a person over there.

GIBSON'S THEORY OF DIRECT PERCEPTION

Gibson proposed that the optical array contains all the information needed to directly perceive a three dimensional world with little or no information processing needed. Light reaching the eye contains invariant information about the depth, location and even function of objects. 'Sensation is perception'.

1 DEPTH

Monocular depth cues
(capable of perception by one eye)

- **Texture gradients** – closer objects can be seen in greater detail than distant ones.
- **Overlap and motion parallax** – closer objects obscure more distant ones.
- **Linear perspective** – lines known to be parallel converge in the distance.

Binocular depth cues

- **Retinal disparity** – each eye sees a slightly different view, which gives us a three dimensional impression.
- **Ocular convergence** – our eyes converge the closer an object is to us.

2 LOCATION

Optic flow patterns
The point to which we are moving remains stationary while the rest of the view rushes away from it, giving information on speed and direction of movement.

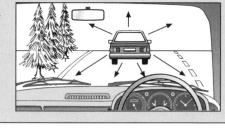

3 FUNCTION

Affordances
Gibson even argued that the perceptual system has evolved to inform us directly of the function of a perceived object, i.e. chairs are for sitting on.

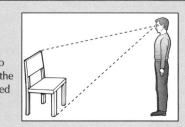

For: Gibson put perception back into the real world, stressing the importance of movement for perception and the richness of information available at the retina.

Against: Affordances are debatable and the theory neglects much of the processing that must take place in perception. Direct perception may apply more to innate reflexes where environmental stimuli directly affect behaviour, but much of human behaviour is governed by higher-order intervening processes between stimulus and response.

Top-down theories of perception

TOP-DOWN THEORIES

- Sometimes referred to as constructivist theories, these theories stress the factors in the construction of reality that go beyond the information received from the senses.
- Gregory's theory and perceptual set theory regard perception as a very active process, whereby the individual's past knowledge, expectations and stereotypes seek out sensory data to 'complete the picture'.

Hmm, there should be people around here.

Past experience
Expectations
Stereotypes

Aah, that looks like one over there.

GREGORY'S PERCEPTUAL INFERENCE THEORY

Gregory suggests that we go beyond the available sensory information in perception, 'a perceived object is a hypothesis, suggested and tested by sensory data'. Gregory points out that sensory information alone cannot account for perception –often all the information required is not present or we need to select information to prevent sensory overload - and he uses illusions and perceptual constancy to support his suggestion.

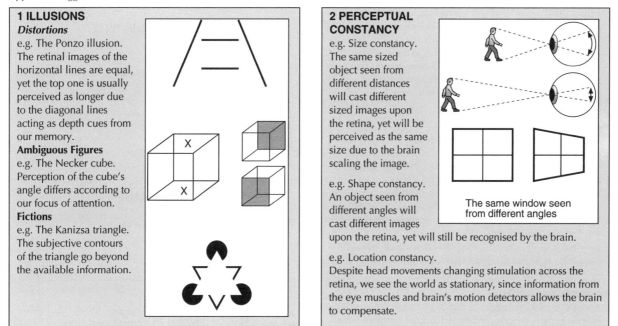

1 ILLUSIONS
Distortions
e.g. The Ponzo illusion. The retinal images of the horizontal lines are equal, yet the top one is usually perceived as longer due to the diagonal lines acting as depth cues from our memory.
Ambiguous Figures
e.g. The Necker cube. Perception of the cube's angle differs according to our focus of attention.
Fictions
e.g. The Kanizsa triangle. The subjective contours of the triangle go beyond the available information.

2 PERCEPTUAL CONSTANCY
e.g. Size constancy. The same sized object seen from different distances will cast different sized images upon the retina, yet will be perceived as the same size due to the brain scaling the image.

e.g. Shape constancy. An object seen from different angles will cast different images upon the retina, yet will still be recognised by the brain.

The same window seen from different angles

e.g. Location constancy. Despite head movements changing stimulation across the retina, we see the world as stationary, since information from the eye muscles and brain's motion detectors allows the brain to compensate.

For: Illusions and constancy show how the brain uses memory, expectation and unconscious processing to interpret environmental stimuli.
Against: Illusions are artificial stimuli and do not contain the rich amount of detail and information naturally received by the retina.

PERCEPTUAL SET THEORY

Perceptual set theory stresses the idea of perception as an active process involving selection, inference and interpretation. Perceptual set is a bias or readiness to perceive certain aspects of available sensory data and to ignore others. Set can be influenced by many factors such as:

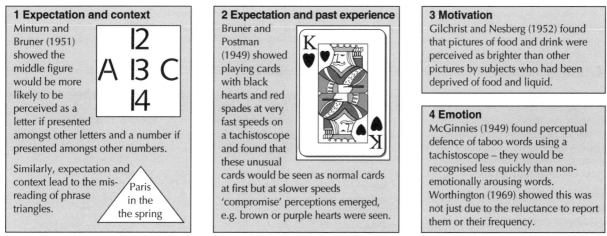

1 Expectation and context
Minturn and Bruner (1951) showed the middle figure would be more likely to be perceived as a letter if presented amongst other letters and a number if presented amongst other numbers.

Similarly, expectation and context lead to the mis-reading of phrase triangles.

Paris in the the spring

2 Expectation and past experience
Bruner and Postman (1949) showed playing cards with black hearts and red spades at very fast speeds on a tachistoscope and found that these unusual cards would be seen as normal cards at first but at slower speeds 'compromise' perceptions emerged, e.g. brown or purple hearts were seen.

3 Motivation
Gilchrist and Nesberg (1952) found that pictures of food and drink were perceived as brighter than other pictures by subjects who had been deprived of food and liquid.

4 Emotion
McGinnies (1949) found perceptual defence of taboo words using a tachistoscope – they would be recognised less quickly than non-emotionally arousing words. Worthington (1969) showed this was not just due to the reluctance to report them or their frequency.

For: Set theory links with many other areas in psychology, such as schemata and stereotypes, and has been supported by many studies.
Against: The experimental findings concerning perceptual defence and the validity of tachistoscope presentation have been much debated.

The development of perception 1

THE NATURE-NURTURE DEBATE IN THE DEVELOPMENT OF PERCEPTION

The research in this area aims to determine what particular aspects of perception are present at birth and what aspects are developed through experience with the environment. The physiology of the eye and brain can only tell us so much about this debate, so many different approaches have been taken to investigate it. All the approaches have their own strengths and weaknesses, however, and there is evidence for both nativist and empiricist views – suggesting an interaction of innate and environmental factors in the development of perception.

HUMAN INFANT STUDIES

Neonates (new born babies) are born with most of the features, such as rods and cones, of the adult eye and quickly demonstrate many perceptual abilities as their eyes and brain systems mature.

EVIDENCE SUPPORTING THE ROLE OF NATURE IN PERCEPTUAL DEVELOPMENT

Pattern and shape perception
- Fantz (1961) argued that very young babies are able to distinguish between patterns, and by 2–3 months prefer looking at complex stimuli if given a choice.
- Bower (1966) conditioned 2 month olds to respond to a triangle with a bar across it and found the response was generalised to a complete triangle (more than other possibilities), indicating the presence of the gestalt law of continuity and closure.

Depth perception
- Gibson and Walk (1960) argued that depth perception was innate using the visual cliff apparatus. Six month old babies would not crawl over the cliff edge onto the deep side, neither would newly born chicks or lambs.
- Campos et al (1970) placed two month old babies (who cannot crawl) onto the deep side of the visual cliff and found a decrease in heart rate compared to the shallow side, reflecting interest and a recognition of the difference.
- Bower et al (1970) found 20 day old babies would show an avoidance response to a large approaching box, but not if it was filmed and projected on a screen.

Constancy perception
- Bower (1966) found evidence that 2 month old babies possess size constancy. Having conditioned them to turn their head whenever they saw a 30 cm cube at a distance of 1 metre (using an adult playing 'peek-a-boo' as a reinforcer), Bower found they would respond more to the same 30 cm cube at a distance of 3 metres than they would to a 90 cm cube at 3 metres (which would cast the same size retinal image as the original 30 cm cube).
- Bower (1966) also showed shape constancy develops in the first few months by conditioning babies to respond to a shape and then rotating it.

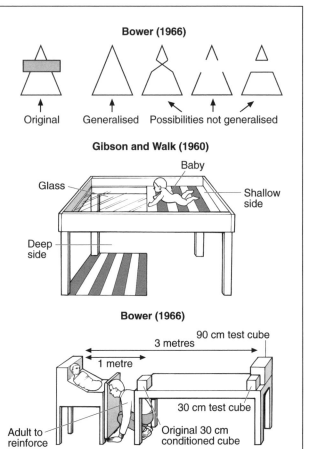

Bower (1966)

Original   Generalised   Possibilities not generalised

Gibson and Walk (1960)

Baby

Glass

Shallow side

Deep side

Bower (1966)

90 cm test cube

3 metres

1 metre

30 cm test cube

Adult to reinforce responses

Original 30 cm conditioned cube

Evaluation:
- Obviously it is impossible to rule out any environmental experience since birth.
- If neonates lack a perceptual ability, it may be due to a lack of biological maturation rather than lack of experience.
- The certainty of perception in babies is less reliable because of their lack of verbal report. Therefore, non-verbal methods of perceptual response have to be used, such as preferential looking, conditioned body movement or sucking, heart and brain activity changes.

PERCEPTUAL ADAPTATION & READJUSTMENT STUDIES

These studies assume that if perception can be adjusted to cope with artificial perceptual distortions, then perceptual abilities are more flexible and open to environmental influences – lending support to the nurture side of the nature-nurture debate in this area.

Evidence supporting the role of nature in perceptual development
- Studies on animals, e.g. Sperry's (1943) rotation of salamander eyes through 180 degrees, found they could not adjust their perception.

Evidence supporting the role of nurture in perceptual development
Using devices which invert or distort visual stimuli many researchers have found that human perception can readjust itself, e.g.
- Stratton (1896) wore an inverting telescope and had adjusted completely after 8 days, with only a location constancy after image afterwards.
- Ewart (1930) found inverting binoculars only produced motor

adaptation (vision-body co-ordination) not true perceptual adaptation.
- Snyder and Pronko (1952) used inverting and reversing goggles and found that the adaptation gained after 30 days lasted for years.

Evaluation:
- What is learnt is not necessarily a new way of perceiving but a new set of body movements.
- Showing that adults can learn to perceive does not mean that babies learn to perceive.

The development of perception 2

ANIMAL EXPERIMENTS

Animal studies into the development of perception usually involve the deprivation or distortion of the animal's normal visual experience from birth and noting the consequences for later perceptual abilities. Much of the evidence appears to emphasise the need for environmental stimulation for normal perception to develop. However, whether this involves learning to perceive, is less certain.

Evidence supporting the role of nurture in perceptual development

These studies imply that there are no innate abilities in perception and show that **active environmental stimulation** of **normal patterned light** is necessary for normal perceptual development in animals, e.g.

Blakemore and Cooper (1970)

- Riesen deprived animals such as chimpanzees and kittens of either:
  a All light – for the first 16 months of life and found no visual perception because retinal cells failed to develop properly. When then allowed light, normal object recognition was shown at 21 months, although if light was denied until 33 months, the subsequent development of perceptual abilities was poorer.
  b Just patterned light – the animals wore translucent goggles, which only allowed unpatterned light to be seen, and found that only general aspects of brightness, colour and size could be responded to. No object or pattern recognition was immediately evident.
- Blakemore and Cooper (1970) exposed kittens to an environment consisting of either only vertical or only horizontal lines and found that they would only respond to a pointer presented in the same orientation. Furthermore, the cells of each cat's primary visual cortex would only fire in response to lines presented in the orientation they had been raised in and not to lines of the opposite orientation.
- Held and Hein (1963) claimed active interaction with the environment is needed for the development of perception. Their 'kitten carousel' enabled two kittens to experience exactly the same kind and amount of environmental stimulation, but one did so actively, the other passively (it could not move itself). When tested, only the active kittens were able to visually guide their paws or respond to approaching objects.

Evaluation:

- There are major ethical problems with these studies. In one study Riesen tested the blindness of a light deprived chimpanzee by seeing if it would avoid a visually presented object that was associated with a painful electric shock.
- These studies aim to prevent or distort environmental experience or learning to **stop perceptual abilities being acquired** from the environment and thus may imply that there are no innate abilities in perception. However,
  a deprivation may physically **damage** or **prevent** the **maturation of innate abilities** rather than prevent learning – chicks kept in the dark from birth to 10 weeks cannot recognise and peck at grain, whereas normal chicks can do this immediately on hatching without learning (Govier and Govier, cited in Radford and Govier, 1991).
  b distortion of normal visual experience may merely **distort** the **development of innate abilities** – in Blakemore and Cooper's study, the stimulated visual cortex cells may have grown to dominate cells of other orientations that would otherwise have naturally responded.
- Animals cannot report their subjective experience and their perception can only be inferred from behaviour – Held and Hein's passive kitten probably lacked the ability to co-ordinate motor actions with perception rather than perception itself.
- Animal perception and development may be qualitatively different to human perceptual development.

HUMAN CATARACT PATIENTS

- Patients who have undergone cataract operations are provided with sight for the first time as adults and may shed light upon whether perceptual abilities are innate, i.e. shown immediately after the cataracts are removed, or are dependent upon experience and learning.
- Hebb (1949) studied the reports of 65 cases of cataract removal by von Senden and concluded that some aspects of vision were innate (figural unity) while others were learned (figural identity).
- Gregory and Wallace (1963) studied a 52 year old patient, S.B., who had undergone a corneal graft to restore his sight after being blind since he was 6 months old. Some aspects of vision were very quickly shown, others were not – implying a mixture of nature and nurture.

Evidence supporting the role of nature in perceptual development

- Hebb found that figural unity – the ability to fixate upon, scan, follow and detect shapes from their background (figure-ground perception), was shown by those patients whose sight had been restored, indicating these abilities were innate.
- Gregory and Wallace found that S.B. could quickly detect objects, walk around the hospital guided by sight alone and identify objects by sight that he had experienced through touch (showing good cross-modal matching). These abilities may have been aided by his experience of vision in his first 6 months of life.

Evidence supporting the role of nurture in perceptual development

- Hebb found that the cataract patients had great problems with figural identity – recognising objects. The patients could detect and scan a shape such as a triangle but would not be able to identify it by sight unless they counted the angles. They also lacked perceptual constancy.
- Gregory and Wallace found that S.B. had problems with identifying objects by sight that he had not experienced through touch before, detecting mood by visual facial expressions and depth perception (thinking a 40 foot drop from a window was manageable).

Evaluation:

- The adult patients' sensory systems would not be the same as those of babies due to adaptation to the loss of vision. Visual systems present at birth may have deteriorated through disuse or other sensory systems have over-developed to compensate, so interfering with vision.
- Methodologically these studies can be regarded as natural experiments, and so there is a lack of control over variables such as the degree of visual experience before the cataract developed, the age when the cataract was removed, and the emotional trauma of cataract removal.

Culture and perception

WHY STUDY CROSS-CULTURAL DIFFERENCES IN PERCEPTION?

A major assumption of cross-cultural research is that differences between cultures are more likely to be caused by the differing physical and social environments experienced by the members of those cultures, whereas similarities across cultures are more likely to reflect biological, inherited abilities common to the whole species. Cross-cultural differences in perception might therefore be caused by differing experiences influencing perceptual set.

Many studies have shown individual experience can affect perceptual set and thus perception. Bugeleski and Alampay for example (1961) discovered that subjects presented with pictures of animals and then the ambiguous 'rat-man' figure were more likely to see the rat than a control group who were more likely to see the man. The culture a person is raised in may therefore affect not only object recognition but also the more basic perceptual processes such as size constancy and depth perception.

Rat-man illusion

CROSS-CULTURAL DIFFERENCES

ILLUSION STUDIES

*   Rivers (1901) in a very early study discovered that Murray Islanders, both adults and children, were more susceptible to the vertical – horizontal illusion but less susceptible to the Muller-Lyer illusion than English subjects.
*   Allport and Pettigrew (1957) found that a rotating trapezoid was more likely to be seen as a swaying rectangle by western cultures and urban Zulus who are used to seeing rectangular windows but more likely to be seen for what it was by non-urban Zulus.
*   Segall et al (1963) conducted a very large scale study, testing around 1,900 subjects over a six year period, and argued that Africans and Filipinos were less susceptible than European subjects to the Muller-Lyer illusion because they did not live in such a 'carpentered world' where right angles are so frequently encountered that they are readily learnt as depth cues.
    However the 'carpentered world hypothesis' cannot account for findings that some groups of subjects living in rectangular constructed environments also fail to show susceptibility to the Muller-Lyer illusion (Mundy-Castle and Nelson, 1962) or that no difference has been found in its perception between urbanised and non-urbanised aborigines (Gregor and McPherson, 1965).

SIZE CONSTANCY

*   Turnbull (1961) suggested that size constancy may be lacking in pygmies living in dense rain forests without the open space required to develop the ability. When taken to an open plain to see a herd of buffalo in the distance one pygmy reported being unable to identify such 'strange insects' and was amazed at what happened as they drove closer to the herd and the insects appeared to grow into buffalo. This was not a rigorously controlled experiment however.

OBJECT RECOGNITION IN PICTURES

*   Western missionaries and anthropologists have often reported that the non-western cultures they made contact with had difficulty in recognising western pictures of objects. However, differences in the materials and artistic styles used in the pictures may have influenced their recognition ability.

DEPTH PERCEPTION IN PICTURES

*   Hudson (1960) discovered that people from African cultures have difficulty perceiving two-dimensional pictures as 3 dimensional objects. However, the unnatural materials and lack of natural depth cues such as texture gradient may have influenced the African subjects' perception.

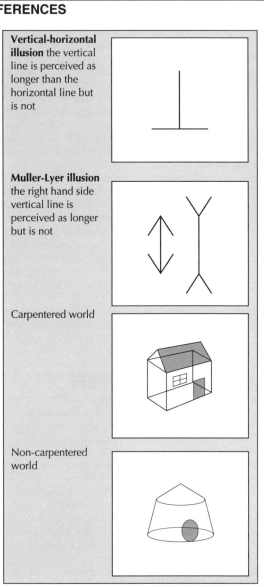

Vertical-horizontal illusion the vertical line is perceived as longer than the horizontal line but is not

Muller-Lyer illusion the right hand side vertical line is perceived as longer but is not

Carpentered world

Non-carpentered world

EVALUATION

Cross-cultural differences in perception are often regarded as evidence for the idea that perception is flexible and so influenced by learning. However, the evidence:
*   is not always conclusive and does not always show very large differences,
*   ignores the vast similarity in perceptual ability across cultures,
*   may only reflect the artificial methodologies and un-ecological materials used
*   may even be due to biological factors since, for example, there is evidence that physiological differences in the eye can account for differences in susceptibility to the Muller-Lyer illusion in different subjects.

'Pictorial perception and culture' Deregowski (1972)

AIM

To present studies to show that different cultures perceive pictures in different ways. Cross-cultural studies of picture perception:
1 provide an insight into how perception works (indicating the role played by learning in perception) and
2 investigate the possibility of a universal cross-cultural means of communication (a 'lingua franca').

EVIDENCE

Pictorial object recognition studies

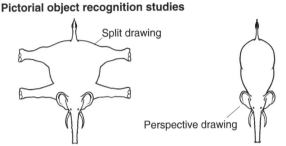

Split drawing

Perspective drawing

Pictorial depth recognition studies

What is the man doing?

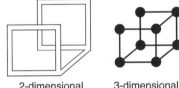

2-dimensional picture

3-dimensional model

2-dimensional model

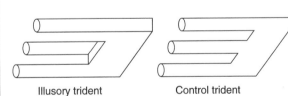

Illusory trident

Control trident

- Anecdotal reports from missionaries and anthropologists living among remote cultures have shown these cultures to have difficulties recognising objects from pictures, especially from accurate perspective drawings which do not represent all aspects of an object. Some studies have shown that African subjects from remote villages can pick out the correct toy from pictures of familiar animals (e.g. lions) though not unfamiliar ones (e.g. kangaroos).
- Hudson showed that African children and adults prefer split drawings to correct perspective drawings.

Hudson tested South African Bantu workers to see whether they could interpret a combination of three pictorial depth cues as a three dimensional representation:
- Familiar size – where the larger of two objects is drawn further away,
- Overlap – where nearer parts of a picture obscure farther away parts, and
- Perspective – where lines known to be parallel converge at the horizon.

The subjects were asked questions about the relationship between objects in the picture to see whether they had two- or three-dimensional vision. For example in the picture opposite, a three-dimensional viewer would say that the man is about to throw his spear at the antelope, a two-dimensional perceiver would say that the man is about to throw his spear at the elephant.

Hudson found two-dimensional perception in African tribal subjects across all ages, educational and social levels, and this finding was confirmed by pictorial depth measuring apparatus developed by Gregory.

Hudson showed Zambian subjects a drawing of two squares (arranged so that western subjects perceive them as a three-dimensional cube) and asked them to build a model of it out of modelling clay and sticks. Most of the Zambians built two-dimensional models, whereas the few who showed three-dimensional perception built a three-dimensional cube.

A group of Zambian school children, having been divided into two- and three-dimensional perceivers, were shown a picture illusion which three-dimensional western perceivers become confused by (since they attempt to see it as a three-dimensional picture of a trident). Three-dimensional perceivers spent longer looking at the illusory trident than a normal control trident, compared to the two-dimensional perceivers who showed no significant difference in viewing the two, when asked to copy the tridents.

EVALUATION

Methodological:

Design - A wide range of methods used in the subject's own environment. However, most involve natural experiments, with a consequent lack of experimenter control over the independent variable (culture) and extraneous variables during testing.

Apparatus - Pictures lacked important depth cues, such as texture gradient, and were presented on paper rather than on ecologically natural materials.

Theoretical: Three explanatory theories are given, but little evidence is used to support or decide between them. There is an ethnocentric assumption that western methods of pictorially representing objects especially involving depth cues are more correct than others and should be universally recognised.

Links: Nature-nurture debate in perception. Cross-cultural psychology.

Language and thought 1

> **WHAT IS THE RELATIONSHIP BETWEEN LANGUAGE AND THOUGHT?**
> Does language shape thought, reflect thought, describe thought or is it the same as thought?

SAPIR AND WHORF'S LINGUISTIC RELATIVITY HYPOTHESIS

Sapir and Whorf's linguistic relativity hypothesis (LRH) suggests that **language shapes thought**. It has links with the ideas of certain social psychologists (e.g. social constructionists) and cognitive psychologists (e.g. Bruner and Vygotsky).

In its strong version the hypothesis proposed that language **determines** thought processes so that:
- the vocabulary and grammar acquired from a culture provide the concepts for thinking.
- the individual can only think and perceive the world using the concepts provided by language.
- cultures with different languages may have variations in their vocabulary and grammar that will produce different concepts and ways of thinking and perceiving the world.

The strong version has little evidence in its favour. A weaker version of the linguistic relativity hypotheses suggests that language merely influences thought and perception but does not determine them, for example it may serve to:
- direct attention towards certain perceptions, concepts and attributions.
- make some ways of thinking easier than others.
- facilitate or bias memory towards the retrieval of some concepts or perceptions rather than others.

EVIDENCE RELATING TO THE STRONG VERSION OF THE LRH

For

Whorf's evidence for the strong version was based upon his analysis of vocabulary and grammatical differences across languages, particularly comparisons of Native North American languages with English. Whorf described a number of linguistic differences that he thought must affect the way the people who spoke them could think, e.g.:
- Apache grammar expresses concepts in a manner 'utterly unlike our way of thinking', e.g. 'it is a dripping spring' is expressed in Apache as 'as water, or springs, whiteness moves downwards'.
- Hopi language has 'no words, grammatical forms, constructions or expressions that refer directly to what we call 'time', or to past, or future'.
- Eskimos have more words for snow in their language compared to English.
- Colour vocabulary differs across languages – the Navaho use one word for green and blue, while the Dani of New Guinea only have two colour words: for dark or bright hues.

Against

Researchers, such as Brown (1958) and Pinker (1994) have criticised Whorf's evidence and theory as follows:
- Whorf's translations were clumsy, thus making the thinking behind them appear different. Pinker (1994) suggests that 'it is a dripping spring' could be equally translated as 'clear stuff – water – is falling'. By turning the tables he points out that 'he walks' could be clumsily expressed in English 'as solitary masculinity, leggedness proceeds'.
- Whorf made mistakes since he did not study the people, only limited samples of their language – Malotki (1983) showed the Hopi have many words and tenses relating to time.
- Martin (1986) reported how the number of words Eskimos have for snow became an exaggerated cultural myth – they only have 12 at the most, about the same as in English.
- Words and word order differ across and within many languages, these are choices of expression rather than constraints on thought, e.g. differences in colour words does not mean that different colours cannot be perceived.

EVIDENCE RELATING TO THE WEAK VERSION OF THE LRH

- Nisbett and Ross (1980) suggest that the English language makes it easier to describe actors and their actions in the same way (e.g. we talk of 'aggressive' behaviour resulting from an 'aggressive' *person* rather than *situation*), thus facilitating the attributional link between them and the likelihood of making the fundamental attribution error.
- However, research has revealed cross-cultural differences in the use of the fundamental attribution error but this has not reliably been linked to language rather than other cultural differences.
- Bloom (1981) found that because English language has the subjunctive (*if* this had happened, then they *would have*...) but the Chinese language does not, English speakers were more able to show counter-factual reasoning (98% accuracy) than Chinese speakers (7% accuracy).
- However, Au (1983) found that the counter-factual stories Bloom used were presented in stilted Chinese and were more ambiguous to the Chinese who had better knowledge on the subject of the story (science). Liu (1985) argued that Chinese speakers can show counter-factual reasoning but it might take them a little longer to express it.
- Carmichael et al (1932) found that verbal labels attached to ambiguous pictures would later distort the recall of those pictures in line with the labels, e.g.

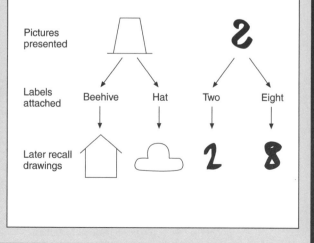

Pictures presented

Labels attached: Beehive — Hat — Two — Eight

Later recall drawings

Language and thought 2

OTHER VIEWS ON THE RELATIONSHIP BETWEEN LANGUAGE AND THOUGHT

WATSON'S BEHAVIOURIST VIEW

Watson suggested that in physical terms spoken language *is* thought (an even stronger deterministic relationship between language and thought than the linguistic relativity hypothesis!). Watson believed that tiny movements in the vocal apparatus represented an inaudible (to others) form of private speech, which was the same as thought.

For

Tiny movements in the voice box of humans were detected.

Against

Smith et al (1947) showed that these movements were not responsible for thought by reporting the thoughts he had while paralysed with curare.

VYGOTSKY'S CONVERGENCE VIEW

Vygotsky proposed (in contrast to the linguistic relativity hypothesis) that language and thought start off as separate processes but gradually converged to influence each other.

To begin with, thought is non-linguistic (occurring mostly in images) and speech is used as a social tool (to interact with others).

From the age of two language and thought begin to converge such that language becomes rational (more understood/meaningful) and thought becomes verbal. Language can then be used to publicly communicate thoughts to others and to privately direct or monitor thinking (although initially the child may do this out loud – egocentric speech).

For

Modern linguistic theorists like Pinker (1994) would agree that language and thought are separate processes with different origins.

Against

Vygotsky did not provide sufficient research studies to support his ideas.

PIAGET'S COGNITIVE VIEW

Piaget believed (in opposition to the linguistic relativity hypothesis) that language only describes thought and that certain concepts had to develop *before* language could meaningfully describe them. Linguistic terms for ideas could be taught but not understood until cognitive development created the underlying concepts, e.g. infants may apply the word 'dog' to cats because they lack a proper concept of a 'dog'. Object permanence may thus explain the vocabulary explosion at 18 months.

For

Studies of babies, animals and older humans who lack language indicate that thinking can occur without language.

Against

Bruner would suggest that language does not just describe thought but allows a new way of representing information and can hasten cognitive development.

SOCIAL AND CULTURAL ASPECTS OF LANGUAGE USE

CULTURAL ASPECTS OF LANGUAGE USE

Cross-cultural aspects of language use have been thoroughly studied in relation to the Linguistic Relativity Hypothesis and its evaluation. However, sub-cultural linguistic differences within a society may also affect thinking and/or have important social consequences.

SOCIAL / SUB-CULTURAL ASPECTS OF LANGUAGE USE

- Sub-cultural differences in the *same language* that occur within a society are referred to as dialects.
- A dialect results from dialogue between members of a particular group that creates a shared set of distortions to vocabulary and/or grammatical rules compared to those of other groups using the same language.
- Social groups that commonly create dialects through frequent communication include those relating to social class, geographical area, ethnic origin and age.
- The degree of distortion can vary (profound distortion may create a new 'language') and when distortions are high problems can arise in inter-group communication and discrimination, e.g. when one group's dialect is used as a standard to judge another's.

BERNSTEIN'S RESEARCH

Bernstein (1971) suggested that:

- Working-class children's language uses a 'restricted code' compared to the 'elaborated code' shown in the speech of middle-class children.
- Compared to an elaborated code, a restricted code is more context bound and limited in vocabulary, grammatical complexity, and the ability to allow abstract thought.
- The codes have cognitive consequences – with a more restricted language, working class children are at an educational disadvantage in fulfilling their intellectual potential, especially when faced with middle-class teachers who use an elaborated code they find hard to understand.

Evaluation – Bernstein's research had certain methodological faults, e.g. only using middle-class researchers to gather data and failing to distinguish between the effects of language versus other factors associated with social class. The distinction between, and origin of, the codes is also debatable.

LABOV'S RESEARCH

Labov (1970) studied the 'Black English Vernacular' (BEV) dialect which Bernstein regarded as a restricted code and concluded:

- BEV is not a restricted code but is just as grammatically regulated and expressive as Standard English. The main difference lies in the more direct way of expressing ideas without convoluted language in BEV.
- BEV is perceived as ungrammatical and inferior because of ethnocentrism, prejudice and because it is not understood by standard speakers.
- BEV can put those who speak it at an educational disadvantage if their teachers do not use it or if it forms the basis of ability discrimination.

Evaluation – Labov has shown BEV grammatical construction to be logical by pointing out its similarities with other (non-English!) languages. He also found working-class speakers followed their grammatical rules more consistently than middle-class speakers and academics (Pinker, 1994).

Language acquisition - Skinner's learning theory approach

The Behaviourist learning theorist Skinner, in his book 'Verbal Behaviour' (1957), argued that language was acquired through the principles of **operant conditioning** – trial-and-error learning, selective reinforcement and behaviour shaping.
It is important to remember that words, according to Skinner, are merely behavioural responses emitted because they have been reinforced by the environment. In the case of language, reinforcement is provided by the parents whose smiles, attention and approval are pleasant to the child (parents are secondary reinforcers because they are associated with the primary rewards of food, warmth etc.). Any verbal response that leads to pleasant consequences is more likely to be repeated again (the Law of Effect)

The acquisition of language behaviour

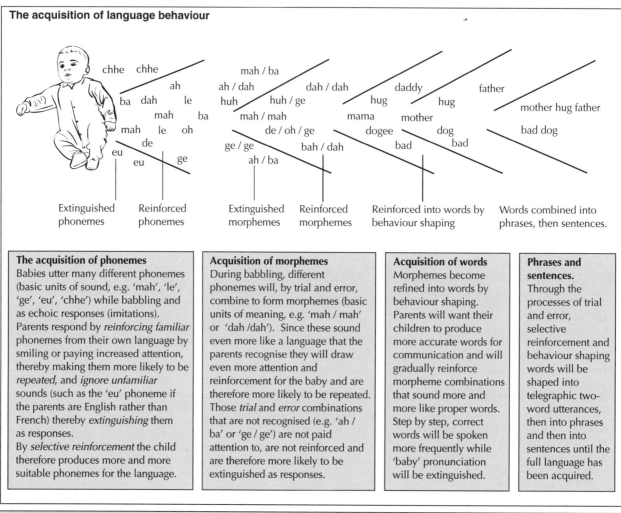

The acquisition of phonemes
Babies utter many different phonemes (basic units of sound, e.g. 'mah', 'le', 'ge', 'eu', 'chhe') while babbling and as echoic responses (imitations). Parents respond by *reinforcing familiar* phonemes from their own language by smiling or paying increased attention, thereby making them more likely to be *repeated*, and *ignore unfamiliar* sounds (such as the 'eu' phoneme if the parents are English rather than French) thereby *extinguishing* them as responses.
By *selective reinforcement* the child therefore produces more and more suitable phonemes for the language.

Acquisition of morphemes
During babbling, different phonemes will, by trial and error, combine to form morphemes (basic units of meaning, e.g. 'mah / mah' or 'dah /dah'). Since these sound even more like a language that the parents recognise they will draw even more attention and reinforcement for the baby and are therefore more likely to be repeated. Those *trial* and *error* combinations that are not recognised (e.g. 'ah / ba' or 'ge / ge') are not paid attention to, are not reinforced and are therefore more likely to be extinguished as responses.

Acquisition of words
Morphemes become refined into words by behaviour shaping. Parents will want their children to produce more accurate words for communication and will gradually reinforce morpheme combinations that sound more and more like proper words. Step by step, correct words will be spoken more frequently while 'baby' pronunciation will be extinguished.

Phrases and sentences.
Through the processes of trial and error, selective reinforcement and behaviour shaping words will be shaped into telegraphic two-word utterances, then into phrases and then into sentences until the full language has been acquired.

The acquisition of the 'meaning' of words.
Producing words in the right context is also reinforced , as words gain their 'meaning' (not a word favoured by the behaviourists) through their associations, either classical or operant, with objects, events or activities. The word 'more' for example will be produced to gain additional food, cuddles etc. because it has previously been associated with increases in these pleasurable stimuli. Skinner distinguished between two different types of verbal behaviour that parents will reinforce in different ways:

1 A **'mand'** is verbal behaviour that is reinforced by the child receiving something it wants. For example the word 'chocolate' is reinforced by receiving some.

2 A **'tact'** is verbal behaviour caused by imitating others, e.g. parents in the correct context, and is reinforced by approval. For example the word 'tree' is caused by imitating the parent's speech and is reinforced by a smile and / or approval.

Language acquisition – Skinner's learning theory evaluated

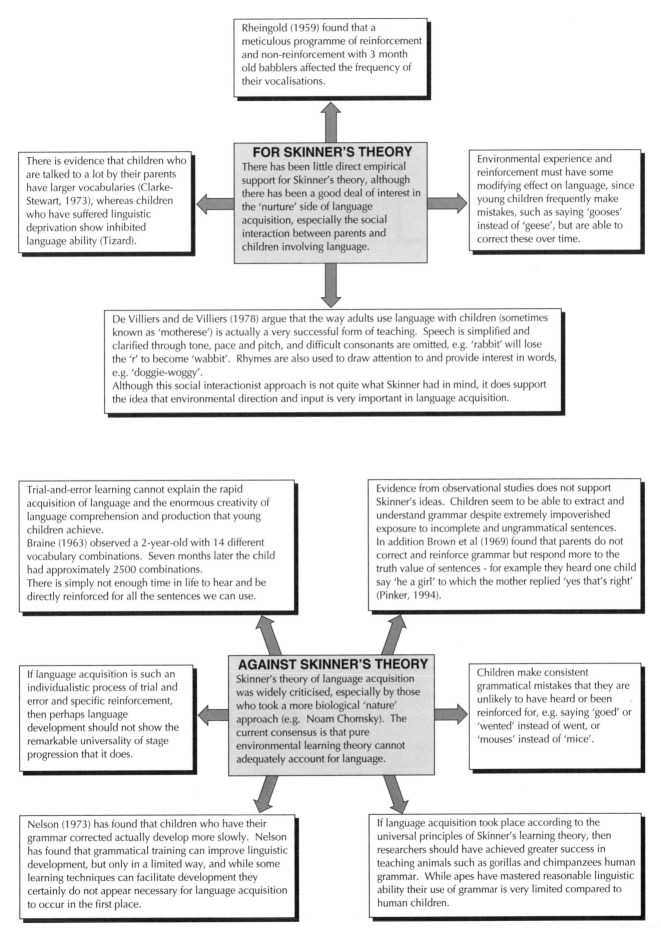

Rheingold (1959) found that a meticulous programme of reinforcement and non-reinforcement with 3 month old babblers affected the frequency of their vocalisations.

FOR SKINNER'S THEORY
There has been little direct empirical support for Skinner's theory, although there has been a good deal of interest in the 'nurture' side of language acquisition, especially the social interaction between parents and children involving language.

There is evidence that children who are talked to a lot by their parents have larger vocabularies (Clarke-Stewart, 1973), whereas children who have suffered linguistic deprivation show inhibited language ability (Tizard).

Environmental experience and reinforcement must have some modifying effect on language, since young children frequently make mistakes, such as saying 'gooses' instead of 'geese', but are able to correct these over time.

De Villiers and de Villiers (1978) argue that the way adults use language with children (sometimes known as 'motherese') is actually a very successful form of teaching. Speech is simplified and clarified through tone, pace and pitch, and difficult consonants are omitted, e.g. 'rabbit' will lose the 'r' to become 'wabbit'. Rhymes are also used to draw attention to and provide interest in words, e.g. 'doggie-woggy'.
Although this social interactionist approach is not quite what Skinner had in mind, it does support the idea that environmental direction and input is very important in language acquisition.

Trial-and-error learning cannot explain the rapid acquisition of language and the enormous creativity of language comprehension and production that young children achieve.
Braine (1963) observed a 2-year-old with 14 different vocabulary combinations. Seven months later the child had approximately 2500 combinations.
There is simply not enough time in life to hear and be directly reinforced for all the sentences we can use.

Evidence from observational studies does not support Skinner's ideas. Children seem to be able to extract and understand grammar despite extremely impoverished exposure to incomplete and ungrammatical sentences.
In addition Brown et al (1969) found that parents do not correct and reinforce grammar but respond more to the truth value of sentences - for example they heard one child say 'he a girl' to which the mother replied 'yes that's right' (Pinker, 1994).

AGAINST SKINNER'S THEORY
Skinner's theory of language acquisition was widely criticised, especially by those who took a more biological 'nature' approach (e.g. Noam Chomsky). The current consensus is that pure environmental learning theory cannot adequately account for language.

If language acquisition is such an individualistic process of trial and error and specific reinforcement, then perhaps language development should not show the remarkable universality of stage progression that it does.

Children make consistent grammatical mistakes that they are unlikely to have heard or been reinforced for, e.g. saying 'goed' or 'wented' instead of went, or 'mouses' instead of 'mice'.

Nelson (1973) has found that children who have their grammar corrected actually develop more slowly. Nelson has found that grammatical training can improve linguistic development, but only in a limited way, and while some learning techniques can facilitate development they certainly do not appear necessary for language acquisition to occur in the first place.

If language acquisition took place according to the universal principles of Skinner's learning theory, then researchers should have achieved greater success in teaching animals such as gorillas and chimpanzees human grammar. While apes have mastered reasonable linguistic ability their use of grammar is very limited compared to human children.

Language acquisition – Chomsky's innate approach

- Noam Chomsky (1957) was a linguist who took a **biological** approach to language acquisition by suggesting the ability is innate (inborn) in humans. Chomsky therefore falls on the nature side of the nature–nurture debate in language.
- According to Chomsky children will **automatically** acquire language merely by being exposed to it – *no* external reinforcement or operant conditioning is required.

- Chomsky proposed that human children have an **innate language acquisition device** (LAD), an in-built mechanism which automatically allows a child to *decode* any spoken language it hears around it, to reveal the basic rules and principles.
- The child is therefore pre-disposed to recognise and use the **linguistic universals** (e.g. nouns, adjectives, verbs) that every language contains.

- Chomsky suggests that languages differ only in their **surface structure** but all share a similar underlying **deep structure** (the fundamental meanings and actions that the words convey). For example the sentences:
  'Mary ate the apple' and
  'The apple was eaten by Mary'
  have different surface structures but the same deep structure.

- The language acquisition device provides humans with the **transformational grammar** that gives us the rules to extract deep structure from the surface structure.
- Children use these rules to understand and create language in an infinity of new situations, although sometimes they will over-use the rules, e.g. saying 'goed', 'knowed', 'mouses' etc. instead of 'went', 'knew' and 'mice'.
- Chomsky calls these errors in **performance**, not errors in **competence**.

- Braine (1963) aimed to support Chomsky's ideas by investigating the **syntactic** rules that children will show and use at the two-word utterance stage.
- Braine studied his son and found that even in early two-word utterances children will employ simple word ordering rules, which he termed **pivot/open grammar**.
- Some words (which Braine called '*pivot* words') were always used in a *fixed* position, either first (e.g. 'allgone' or 'big') or last (e.g. 'pretty'), while other words (termed 'open words') could be used in *any* position, first or second (e.g. 'mummy' or 'sock'). Greene (1990)

- Bloom (1970) argued that Braine's pivot/open grammar only looked at syntactic word ordering regardless of the meaning of the utterance. For example, one child she studied used the utterance 'mummy sock' in different contexts – when having a sock put on and when picking up her mother's sock (Greene, 1990). Bloom therefore investigated **semantic** grammatical rules of the different types of **meanings** a child may want to convey.

Lenneberg (1967), a biologist, agreed with this nativist view of language, but also argued that language development had to occur within a critical time period before puberty because:

1 Adults never seem to learn a second language as well or as quickly as they learn their first. Newport (1993) agrees with this, concluding from her studies on people learning English both as a first and second language that 'Language learners who begin acquiring language at an early maturational state end up performing significantly better in that language than those who begin at a later maturational state'.
2 There are significant correlations between motor milestones such as crawling and walking and language milestones such as babbling and one-word utterances, suggesting maturation in language development.
3 Brain damage to the language centres in the left side of the brain often causes permanent interference with ability in adults, whereas if the same damage occurs before puberty language functioning is usually recoverable.

Language acquisition – Chomsky's theory evaluated

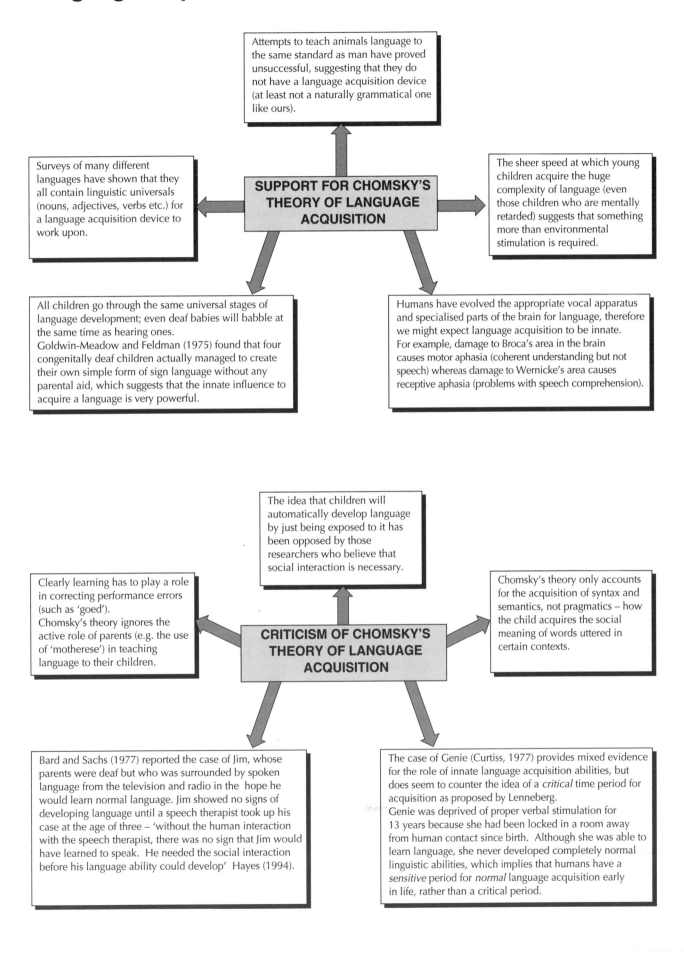

Attempts to teach animals language to the same standard as man have proved unsuccessful, suggesting that they do not have a language acquisition device (at least not a naturally grammatical one like ours).

Surveys of many different languages have shown that they all contain linguistic universals (nouns, adjectives, verbs etc.) for a language acquisition device to work upon.

SUPPORT FOR CHOMSKY'S THEORY OF LANGUAGE ACQUISITION

The sheer speed at which young children acquire the huge complexity of language (even those children who are mentally retarded) suggests that something more than environmental stimulation is required.

All children go through the same universal stages of language development; even deaf babies will babble at the same time as hearing ones.
Goldwin-Meadow and Feldman (1975) found that four congenitally deaf children actually managed to create their own simple form of sign language without any parental aid, which suggests that the innate influence to acquire a language is very powerful.

Humans have evolved the appropriate vocal apparatus and specialised parts of the brain for language, therefore we might expect language acquisition to be innate.
For example, damage to Broca's area in the brain causes motor aphasia (coherent understanding but not speech) whereas damage to Wernicke's area causes receptive aphasia (problems with speech comprehension).

The idea that children will automatically develop language by just being exposed to it has been opposed by those researchers who believe that social interaction is necessary.

Clearly learning has to play a role in correcting performance errors (such as 'goed').
Chomsky's theory ignores the active role of parents (e.g. the use of 'motherese') in teaching language to their children.

CRITICISM OF CHOMSKY'S THEORY OF LANGUAGE ACQUISITION

Chomsky's theory only accounts for the acquisition of syntax and semantics, not pragmatics – how the child acquires the social meaning of words uttered in certain contexts.

Bard and Sachs (1977) reported the case of Jim, whose parents were deaf but who was surrounded by spoken language from the television and radio in the hope he would learn normal language. Jim showed no signs of developing language until a speech therapist took up his case at the age of three – 'without the human interaction with the speech therapist, there was no sign that Jim would have learned to speak. He needed the social interaction before his language ability could develop' Hayes (1994).

The case of Genie (Curtiss, 1977) provides mixed evidence for the role of innate language acquisition abilities, but does seem to counter the idea of a *critical* time period for acquisition as proposed by Lenneberg.
Genie was deprived of proper verbal stimulation for 13 years because she had been locked in a room away from human contact since birth. Although she was able to learn language, she never developed completely normal linguistic abilities, which implies that humans have a *sensitive* period for *normal* language acquisition early in life, rather than a critical period.

Problem-solving

WHAT IS PROBLEM-SOLVING?
Problem-solving as a mental concept refers to the cognitive processing that allows a desired goal to be reached from a current situation where there appears to be no immediately obvious means of doing so. Problems can be well-defined or ill-defined depending upon the clarity of the current situation, the goal, and the possible means of achieving the goal. Behaviourists assumed that problems were solved by trial and error eventually leading to the correct behaviour (the solution) being reinforced by achieving the goal. This behaviour was assumed to require no mental processing, yet Gestalt and information processing psychologists began to suspect that cognitive processes must be involved in the more sophisticated problem-solving shown by humans.

THE GESTALT APPROACH

GESTALT PROBLEM-SOLVING
- Takes a **holistic** approach to problem-solving.
- Problems are solved when a cognitive re-arrangement or **reorganisation** of the different aspects of the problem (the situation, the means and the end goal) results in a new **structural understanding of the relationship** between them.
- **Insight** occurs as a sudden revelation or 'aha' experience as pieces of the solution slot into place.
- **Productive thinking** involves finding new solutions to problems, while **reproductive thinking** applies past solutions and experiences to new problems.
- Reproductive thinking may **inhibit progress** in problem-solving because it leads to:
  Mental set (using previously successful strategies out of habit to solve new problems when better strategies may exist).
  Functional fixedness (failure to see that an object can have other uses from its normal one).
  Confirmation bias (failure to look for disconfirming evidence that would eliminate useless strategies).

EVALUATION OF GESTALT PROBLEM-SOLVING IDEAS
For
- Kohler argued that his chimpanzee Sultan solved problems through productive thinking and insight rather than trial and error. However, perhaps the chimp applied past experience of which Kohler was unaware (reproductive thinking).
- Metcalfe (1986) found people could accurately predict whether they could solve memory problems before they did so, but not insight problems, implying the later involves a new productive use of information.
- Maier's (1931) 'pliers and hanging rope', and Dunker's (1935) 'candle and box of pins' studies support functional fixedness.
- Luchins' (1942) 'water jar study' supports the effect of mental set.

Against
- Gestalt theory overemphasises the negative effects of reproductive learning, which can be very useful for most everyday problems.
- Some Gestalt concepts are too vague, e.g. how does reorganisation work to produce insight? Information-processing theorists have tried to make these concepts more precise, e.g. by specifying the conditions that lead to reorganisation (adding, elaborating and re-categorising information, relaxing constraints on acceptable solutions, etc.).

THE INFORMATION-PROCESSING APPROACH

INFORMATION-PROCESSING AND PROBLEM-SOLVING
- Takes a **reductionist** approach to problem-solving.
- Newell et al (1958) **divide** problem-solving into a **set of stages**, involving **representing** the problem, selecting appropriate **strategies** to tackle it and then **evaluating progress** achieved.
- **Algorithmic strategies** involve a systematic search through all possible solutions. This guarantees a solution but becomes increasingly impractical and time-consuming the greater the number of possible solutions.
- **Heuristic strategies** involve rules of thumb for approaching and solving problems, including:
  Means-ends analysis – breaking a problem down into a set of sub-problems, by working backwards from the goal state to the present state, and solving each in turn to reduce the distance (mental problem space) between the two situations. The analysis proceeds by identifying the goal state, the obstacles that stand in the way, and the operators (resources or methods) available to overcome the obstacles.
  The analogy heuristic strategy – Novick and Holyoak (1991) suggest this involves applying past knowledge to a current problem by identifying a similar past problem through matching similar elements in both and adapting strategies that were successful in dealing with the past problem for the new one.

EVALUATION OF INFORMATION-PROCESSING PROBLEM-SOLVING IDEAS
- The approach can be applied to well-defined problems (algorithmic or means-ends analysis are most efficient) and ill-defined problems (the analogy heuristic is most appropriate).
- Means-ends analysis has been investigated using the Tower of Hanoi and Missionaries and Cannibals (orcs and hobbits) problems. Thomas (1974) found that problem-solvers experienced the most problems with, and took longer analysing, steps in these problems that involved an *increase* in current-goal state difference (mental space), as means-end analysis predicts.
- Newell and Simon (1972) were able to scientifically model information-processing strategies on a computer called the General Problem Solver (GPS) that they programmed to work using human parameters, i.e. with a limited short-term memory, serial processing and access to long-term memory storage.
- Unfortunately the GPS showed differences in the type of difficulty it encountered in solving Missionaries and Cannibals problems compared to human problem-solvers.

Decision-making

DECISION-MAKING, RISK-TAKING AND PROBABILITY ASSESSMENT

Decision-making refers to *making choices* between alternative courses of action. This involves a comparative *assessment of the costs and benefits* of the different courses of action, however the future value of a choice is not always fixed or known before it is made. **Risk-taking** refers to decision-making when the *outcomes* of particular choices *are not guaranteed* and the consequent uncertainty means that an *assessment of* the *probability* (chance) of a positive or negative outcome has to occur. Given that human thinking about probability is prone to many errors and biases, there are many important *practical implications* for risk-taking behaviour.

ERRORS IN THINKING ABOUT PROBABILITY

THE REPRESENTATIVENESS (SIMILARITY) HEURISTIC

- The representativeness heuristic refers to estimating the probability of a particular sample of events based on their *similarity* to characteristics we feel are typical of the whole category population of those events.
- This may lead to the impression that some events are more likely than others and that certain trends can be predicted.
- However, if people do not follow the true principles of representativeness, i.e. if they ignore information on probability base-rates or forget that small samples are less likely to be representative, then the similarity of the sample to population characteristics can lead to false estimates (as in stereotypes).
- Thus if people believe events are drawn from a random population, like head (H) or tail (T) coin tosses, a small sample of events that 'looks' random, e.g. H T T H T H, will be thought of as more probable than events that appear orderly, e.g. H H H H H H, even if they are equally likely.

Evidence
Kahneman and Tversky (1972) found people incorrectly judged the birth order B B B G G G as less likely than G B B G B G (B=boy, G=girl), because the latter appeared more characteristic of the general randomness of birth order. They also found people tended to see small and large samples of births from different sized hospitals as being equally representative.
Kahneman and Tversky (1973) found people would ignore base-rate probability information (the base-rate fallacy) on the frequency of different professions if a description of a person's characteristics were similar to those thought to be stereotypical of a rarer profession.

Practical implications
The representativeness heuristic explains the gambler's fallacy, e.g. thinking that some random outcomes are more likely than others and small runs of bad luck must be followed by runs of good luck. Lottery players may therefore select 'random-looking' number combinations, e.g. irregular patterns with roughly equal odd and even numbers, or those that have appeared less often, and to continue playing despite 'a run of bad luck'.

Evaluation
People do not always ignore base-rate information in favour of similarity stereotypes.

1	11	21	31	41
2	12	22	32	42
3	13	23	33	43
4	14	24	34	44
5	15	25	35	45
6	16	26	36	46
7	17	27	37	47
8	18	28	38	48
9	19	29	39	49
10	20	30	40	

THE AVAILABILITY HEURISTIC

- The availability heuristic involves estimating the probability of an event based on how easy it is to remember past examples of it.
- This may lead to familiar and recent events being more available to memory and thus seen as more probable.
- However, if experience of the world's events is not typical or if the events themselves are random, familiarity and recency will not be useful predictors of probability.
- Thus a recent freak accident or biased reporting of accidents in the media can increase estimates of accident probability.

Evidence
Tversky and Kahneman (1973) presented people with lists of 39 names consisting of 19 women and 20 men (or vice versa). When the minority group of men or women consisted of famous names, 80% later estimated that they had occurred more frequently.
Weber et al (1993, cited by Willson, 2000) found doctors were more likely to make a certain diagnosis if they had recently made a similar diagnosis.

Practical implications
High media publicity of lottery winners and a recent win will tend to increase people's probability estimates of winning.
Recent examples of highly publicised murders or plane crashes in a country may dissuade people from travelling there by increasing their perception of the probability of the same thing happening to them.

Evaluation
People do not always use their own experience when making judgements about probability. If they lack knowledge in the relevant area, they may use the anchoring and adjustment heuristic. This involves using an initial guess or externally provided information (an 'anchor') to adjust final estimates of probability towards.
There are many other influences on decision-making, such as the framing of probability (the way probabilities are phrased, e.g. in terms of the possibility of loss or gain), that can also affect the willingness to take risks. If people recall that they heard something has a 50% chance of failing, they may be more likely to think it will fail than if they heard it has a 50% chance of success. However, these heuristics do not always lead to inaccurate decision-making.

The cognitive developmental approach to psychology

ORIGINS AND HISTORY

- Researchers can be said to adopt a cognitive developmental approach when they not only focus their research on the *inner mental processes of thinking and reasoning* (as do cognitive psychologists in general) but are also interested in how these *change over time* and *can account for behaviour* shown at different ages.
- The study of the development of knowledge and understanding (epistemology) has long interested philosophers and a variety of psychologists have also attempted to explain cognitive development, but have differed in their views on *why* cognitive abilities change over time – whether it is more due to nature (e.g. biology, genetics) or nurture (e.g. environment, social instruction). There has also been some debate as to *how* the changes occur over time – whether qualitatively (in discrete stages) as most suggest or quantitatively (gradually in degree rather than type).
- Piaget is probably the best known cognitive developmental researcher who suggested thinking progressed through qualitative changes (in stages) due to the increasing biological maturity of mental structures with age and environmental interaction. He applied his stage theory to explain a wide variety of children's comments, judgements and actions, for example how their morality developed over time.
- Other researchers have disagreed with Piaget, for example over the cause of cognitive development (e.g. Vygotsky and Bruner believe society plays a more important role) or over the cognitive structures that are changing (e.g. information-processing theorists).
- Most cognitive developmental research has focused on the changes of mental abilities in childhood, however the approach has been applied throughout the life span, for example to the changes of old age.

Jean Piaget
'What makes their [cognitive] theories 'developmental' is the belief that the ways in which we process experience – be it physical, mathematical, or moral experience – normally change in an orderly, increasingly adaptive, species-specific fashion.' Flanagan (1984)

ASSUMPTIONS

Cognitive developmental psychologists assume that:

1. It is necessary to refer to *inner mental concepts* such as thoughts, beliefs and cognitive structures in order to understand behaviour.
2. These mental concepts *change in important ways* over time, particularly in childhood, and these changes have a major influence on people's behaviour, judgement and attitudes at different ages.

METHODS OF INVESTIGATION

Cognitive developmental psychologists have used methods such as:

- Observation – e.g. Piaget's naturalistic observations of children's everyday statements and play.
- Longitudinal study – e.g. Piaget's study of changes in his own children over the course of their childhood or Kohlberg's study of moral reasoning in the same adults over many years.
- Experimentation – e.g. cross-sectional experiments comparing the ability of two different age groups to pass conservation tests.

CONTRIBUTION TO PSYCHOLOGY

Cognitive developmental psychologists have sought to explain:

- *Cognitive changes* – e.g. in the intellectual abilities of children and older adults.
- *Social cognition* – e.g. moral behaviour and reasoning about moral situations at different ages.
- *Social behaviour* – e.g. play and helping behaviour.
- *Socialisation* – e.g. gender and self-development.

CONTRIBUTION TO SOCIETY

The cognitive developmental approach has had a fairly specialised range of applications, for example to:

- *Education* – e.g. the application of cognitive developmental theory to improve classroom practice and aid student progression.
- *Child care* – e.g. to facilitate care in play and peer relations.
- *Criminology* – e.g. children's ability to understand and be held responsible for their crimes, or the link between moral development and criminal behaviour in adolescence and adulthood.

STRENGTHS

The cognitive developmental approach has:

- Overcome the rather static view of mental processes that has dominated traditional cognitive psychology, and has tried to account for the origin of such processes.
- Shown that a straightforward link between age and behaviour cannot be fully made or understood without considering the changing nature of underlying mental structures.
- Had useful practical applications and implications for society.
- Usually conducted scientific and objective research to support its theories.

WEAKNESSES

Unfortunately the cognitive developmental approach has:

- Had a fairly specialised and thus limited contribution to psychology and society.
- Tended at times to underestimate the discrepancies between cognition and behaviour, e.g. between what people say and do about moral situations, and between the ability a child possesses and shows (e.g. due to demand characteristics).
- Not always justified whether cognitive changes are best viewed as occurring in qualitatively different stages rather than in a more gradual quantitative manner.
- Neglected individual differences in cognitive development.

Piaget's theory of cognitive development

BACKGROUND

- Jean Piaget, although a zoologist by training, was involved in the early development of intelligence tests. He became dissatisfied with the idea that intelligence was a fixed trait, and came to regard it as a process which developed over time due to biological maturation and interactive experience with the world, which adapted the child to its environment.
- Piaget was interested in the kind of mistakes that children make at different ages, thinking that these would reflect the cognitive progress they had made, and so spent many years studying children (especially his own) via the clinical interview method, informal experiments, and naturalistic observation.

Jean Piaget

Intellectual development occurs through <u>active interaction</u> with the world
Increased understanding only happens as the child actively interacts with and *discovers* the world, children do not passively receive their knowledge, they are *curious* and *self-motivated*.

Intellectual development occurs as a <u>process</u>
Piaget thought that children think in *qualitatively* different ways from the adult, we are not born with all our knowledge and understanding 'ready-made', but have to develop our intelligence in **stages**.

Individuals <u>construct</u> their understanding of the world
Through interaction, each individual has to **build** their own mental framework for understanding and interacting with their environment.

WHAT DOES THE CHILD BUILD?

HOW DOES THE CHILD BUILD?

SCHEMATA
A schema is an internal representation of a specific physical or mental action. It is a basic building block or unit of intelligent behaviour which enables the individual to interact with and understand the world. The infant is born with certain reflexive action schemata, such as sucking or gripping, and later acquires symbolic mental schemata. The schemata continue to develop and increase in their complexity and ability to let their owners function well in the world.

ASSIMILATION
This is the process whereby new objects, situations or ideas are understood in terms of the schemata the child already possesses. The world is 'fitted in' to what the child already knows.

ACCOMMODATION
This is the process whereby the existing schemata have to be modified to fit new situations, objects or information. The existing schemata are expanded or new ones are created.

OPERATIONS
In middle childhood, **operations** are acquired – these are higher order mental structures which enable the child to understand more complex rules about how the environment works. Operations are logical manipulations dealing with the relationships between schemata.

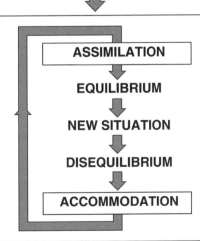

ASSIMILATION

↓

EQUILIBRIUM

↓

NEW SITUATION

↓

DISEQUILIBRIUM

↓

ACCOMMODATION

A baby uses its innate feeding schema to suck on all nipples (mother's or baby bottle's).

The child can deal with the world.

The baby encounters a drinking beaker for the first time.

The baby's sucking schema is not appropriate – a big mess is made!

The baby has to modify its feeding schema so it can use all beakers (ie return to assimilation).

(Adapted from Gross, 1996)

Piaget's stages of cognitive development 1

Piaget proposed four stages of cognitive development which reflect the increasing sophistication of children's thought. Every child moves through the stages in a sequence dictated by biological maturation and interaction with the environment.

1 THE SENSORIMOTOR STAGE
(0 to 2 Years)

The infant at first only knows the world via its immediate senses and the actions it performs. The infant's lack of internal mental schemata is illustrated by;

- profound *egocentrism* – the infant cannot at first distinguish between itself and its environment.
- lack of *object permanence* – when the infant cannot see or act on objects, they cease to exist for the child.

Throughout this stage internal representations are gradually acquired until the *general symbolic function* allows both object permanence and language to occur.

Evidence for
Piaget investigated his children's lack of object permanence during this stage by hiding an object from them under a cover. At 0 to 5 months, an object visibly hidden will not be searched for, even if the child was reaching for it. At 8 months the child will search for a completely hidden object.

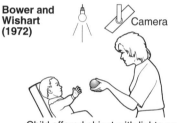

Bower and Wishart (1972) Camera

Child offered object with lights on. Child begins to reach for object.

Evidence against
Bower and Wishart (1972) offered an object to babies aged between 1 to 4 months, and then turned off the lights as they were about to reach for it. When observed by infra-red camera, the babies were seen to continue reaching for the object despite not seeing it.

Bower (1977) tested month-old babies who were shown a toy and then had a screen placed in front of it. The toy was secretly removed from behind the screen, and when the screen itself was taken away, Bower claimed that the babies showed surprise that the toy was not there.

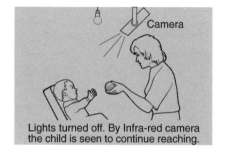

Camera

Lights turned off. By Infra-red camera the child is seen to continue reaching.

2 THE PRE-OPERATIONAL STAGE
(2 to 7 Years)

The child's internal mental world continues to develop, but

- is still **dominated by** the external world and the **appearance** of things.
- shows **centration** – the child only focuses on one aspect of an object or situation at a time.
- **lacks** the mental sophistication necessary to carry out logical **operations** on the world.

The pre-operational child, therefore, shows
- *class-inclusion problems* – difficulty in understanding the relationship between whole classes and sub-classes. The child focuses on the most visibly obvious classes and disregards less obvious ones.
- *egocentrism* – the difficulty of understanding that others do not see, think and feel things like you do.
- *lack of conservation* – the inability to realise that some things remain constant or unchanged despite changes in visible appearance. By only focusing on the most visible changes, the child fails to conserve a whole host of properties, such as number, liquid and substance.

Evidence for
Class-inclusion tests – if a child is shown a set of beads, most of which are brown but with a few white ones, and is asked 'are there more brown beads or more beads', the child will say more brown beads.

Piaget and Inhelder (1956) – demonstrated the egocentrism of pre-operational children with their 'Three-Mountain Experiment'. Four year olds, when shown a mountain scene and tested to see if they could correctly describe it from different view-points, failed and tended to choose their own view. Six year olds were more aware of other viewpoints but still tended to choose the wrong one.

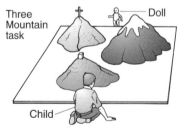

Three Mountain task — Doll

Child

Conservation experiments – Piaget tested for many different types of conservation. The child would fail in each case, since it lacked the necessary operations.

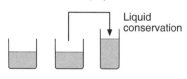

Liquid conservation

Evidence against
McGarrigle et al modified Piaget's class inclusion tasks to make them more understandable and appropriate. They first asked pre-operational children (with an average age of 6) a Piagetian type question – 'Are there more black cows or more cows?' They then turned all of the cows on their sides (as if asleep) and asked 'Are there more black cows or more sleeping cows?' The percentage of correct answers increased from 25% to 48%.

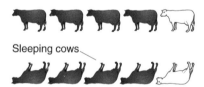

Sleeping cows

Hughes demonstrated that 3.5 – 5 year olds could de-centrate and overcome their egocentrism, if the task made more 'human sense' to them. When these children had to hide a boy doll from two policemen dolls (a task that required them to take into account the perspectives of others but had a good and understandable reason for doing so) they could do this successfully 90% of the time.

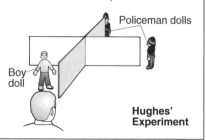

Policeman dolls

Boy doll

Hughes' Experiment

Piaget's stages of cognitive development 2

3 CONCRETE OPERATIONAL STAGE

(7 to 11 years)

At the concrete operational stage, the child's cognitive complexity allows it to

- carry out mental **operations** on the world – that is logical manipulations on the relationships between objects and situations. Two such operations are **compensation**, and **reversibility**.
- **de-centrate** – that is more than one aspect of an object or situation can now be taken into account at the same time.

An important limitation on the child's thought at this stage, however, is that the mental operations cannot be carried out purely in the child's head – the physical (concrete) presence of the objects being manipulated is needed. Thus, although the conservation tests can be successfully completed, the child needs to see the transformation taking place.

Evidence for
Liquid conservation

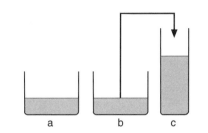

When liquid is poured from **b** to **c**, a concrete operational child can compensate for increasing height with decreasing width and can mentally reverse the pouring, therefore conserving liquid (realising that the amount of liquid remains the same).

Number conservation

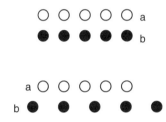

When row **b** is spread out, the concrete operational child can realise that the number remains unchanged, despite the alteration in appearance.

Piaget conducted many tests of conservation on concrete operational children and found that their mental operations allowed them to think about problems in new ways.

Evidence against

McGarrigle and Donaldson (1974) demonstrated that pre-operational children of between 4 to 6 years could successfully conserve if they were not misled by demand characteristics into giving the wrong answer. McGarrigle and Donaldson therefore added an 'accidental transformation' condition where a 'naughty teddy' arrives and disarranges one of the rows. Under this condition more children (63%) could conserve number since the transformation was not meant to have been deliberately intended.

Row 1 ○ ○ ○ ○ ○ Are there the same number?
Row 2 ● ● ● ● ● Answer = Yes

Naughty Teddy 'accidentally' disarranges row 2 to make it longer

○ ○ ○ ○ ○ Are there the same number?
● ● ● ● ● Answer = Yes

---

4 FORMAL OPERATIONAL STAGE

(11 onwards)

At the formal operational stage, the child's mental structures are so developed and internalised that

- ideas can be manipulated in the head and reasoning/deductions can be carried out on verbal statements, without the aid of concrete examples.
- the individual can think about hypothetical problems and abstract concepts that they have never encountered before.
- the individual will approach problems in a systematic and organised way.

Evidence for
Transitive inference tasks -

the child can follow the abstract form of arguments, e.g.

if A > B > C, then A > C.

They can solve problems, such as 'Edith is fairer than Susan. Edith is darker than Lily. Who is the darkest?', *without* needing to use dolls or pictures to help them.

Deductive reasoning tasks -

problems, such as the pendulum task, where the child is given string and a set of weights and is asked to find out what determines the swing, are carried out logically and systematically.

Evidence against

Gladwin (1970) is one of many investigators who have questioned the appropriateness of Piagetian experimental tasks for testing non-western cognitive development. Often detailed investigation has found that formal operational thought has been acquired, but in a culturally specific manner. For example, the Pulawat navigators of Polynesia show complex formal operational thought when guiding their canoes at sea, yet will tend to fail standard western tests of cognitive development.

Evaluating Piaget's theory of cognitive development

THEORETICAL CRITICISMS

AGES
- Much research has seemingly demonstrated that children possess many of the cognitive abilities that Piaget outlined at ages much *earlier* than he expected.
- Often improving upon, or altering, the method of testing/assessing the child reveals their cognitive abilities better (see Bower, Hughes, McGarrigle, etc. below).
- In addition, Piaget seemed to have over-estimated people's formal operational ability - some research has even suggested that only one third of the population actually reach this stage.

CONCEPTS
- While Piaget's theory provides us with a detailed description of development, some have said that it does not really provide us with an explanation of it.
- Some of the concepts are vague, and the stages often show so much overlap (decalage) that development is perhaps better regarded as a *continuous process.*
- By focusing on the child's mistakes, Piaget may have over-looked important abilities that children do possess, or may have wrongly deduced the reason for their failure.

NEGLECTS
- Piaget neglected many important **cognitive** factors that could have accounted for the *individual differences* in development that children show, such as *memory* span, motivation, impulsiveness, practice, etc.
- Overall, in many researchers' view (e.g. Bruner, Light, etc.), he severely underestimated *social influences* on development. By concentrating on individual maturation and *self* construction of mental life, Piaget neglected
  - **a** the role of society in facilitating and providing increased understanding,
  - **b** the child's understanding of social situations (especially in Piaget's experimental situations), and
  - **c** children's ability in and use of language at different ages.

METHODOLOGICAL CRITICISMS

INAPPROPRIATE TESTS
- A frequent criticism is that Piaget's experiments were *over-complicated* and *difficult to relate to.*
- By simplifying the tasks and ensuring that they made what Donaldson has termed 'human sense', researchers such as Bower and Wishart (1972) (with their object permanence experiment), and Hughes (1975) (with his 'Policeman Doll' experiment) have demonstrated cognitive abilities in children who would not be expected to show them.

DEMAND CHARACTERISTICS
- Even in fairly uncomplicated tasks, Piaget's experiments *ignored* the child's *social understanding* of the test, and may have led the child to give a socially desirable or expected answer instead of what the child really thought and understood.
- McGarrigle and Donaldson (1974) with their 'Naughty Teddy' Experiment, and Rose and Blank (1974) with their one question variation, both demonstrated significantly greater conservation rates in pre-operational children.

OVERALL METHODS
- Piaget's use of the clinical interview method, informal experimentation, and small sample sizes, *lacked scientific rigour.*
- Although these methods had their advantages, the generalised conclusions drawn from them may have been somewhat biased.

STRENGTHS

THEORETICAL IMPORTANCE
- Piaget`s theory has received a lot of longitudinal, cross-sectional and cross-cultural *support* over many years, and while the theory has been subject to modification and criticism, many fundamental aspects of his theory are still accepted as valid contributions today.
- Many psychologists have taken Piaget's ideas far more rigidly than they were intended. Piaget modified his theory to take into account certain criticisms and hoped that one day it could be integrated with other theories that dealt with aspects of children's internal life that he had ignored (for example Freud's theory of emotional and personality development).

PRODUCTIVITY
- Piaget's ideas *generated* a huge amount of critical *research* which has vastly increased our understanding of cognitive development.
- Bruner and more socially orientated theorists have used Piaget's views as a 'spring board' to develop their own and to answer many of the issues raised by Piaget's research.

APPLICATIONS
- Piaget's views have had an important impact on *educational* practice – changing the way children are taught today and hopefully making education more effective and enjoyable.
- Piaget has also contributed to psychological theories of children's play and moral development.

'Asking only one question in the conservation experiment' Samuel and Bryant (1984)

AIM

To support, using a more detailed procedure and a wider age range of subjects, Rose and Blank's experimental criticism of Piaget's conservation studies. Piaget and Szeminska (1952) found pre-operational children (below the age of seven) could not conserve (realise that some properties, such as number, volume, and mass, remain the same despite changes in their physical appearance) by conducting experiments, whereby:

1 They showed 2 rows of counters and asked a pre-transformation question 'are there the same number in each row?' The answer was usually '**yes**'.

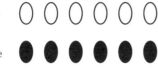

2 They then lengthened one of the rows and asked the (same) post-transformation question 'are there the same number in each row?' The answer given was then usually '**no**'.

Piaget took the 'no' answer to mean that the children thought there were now a greater number of counters in the lengthened row and that these children could not conserve. However, Rose and Blank (1974) disagreed with this conclusion. They argued that Piaget had made a methodological error by imposing **demand characteristics** – when an adult deliberately changes something and asks the same question twice, children think that a different answer is **expected**, even though they may well be able to conserve. Rose and Blank (1974) conducted a study where they only asked one question (the post transformation one) to reduce these misleading expectations, and found that more children were able to conserve when they only had to make one judgement than when they had to make two in the standard Piagetian presentation.

Samuel and Bryant (1984) wanted to replicate this study on a larger scale using
* four age groups (5, 6, 7 and 8 year olds),
* three types of conservation test (number, mass, and liquid volume), and
* three ways of presenting the tests (standard Piagetian way, one judgement/question way, and fixed array with no visible transformation).

METHOD

Subjects: Independent measures design was used. 252 boys and girls were divided into 4 age groups (of 5, 6, 7 and 8 year olds).
Procedure: In each age group every child was tested 4 times each for conservation of number, mass, and liquid volume in one of three ways:

* The standard Piagetian way: (asking the pre- and post-transformation questions)

* The one judgement way: (asking only the post-transformation question)

* The fixed array way: (asking only the post-transformation question, *without seeing* the transformation)

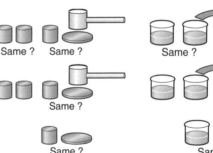

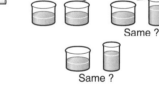

In all three methods of presentation, the 12 conservation tests each child experienced were systematically varied to prevent order effects. Two different versions of each type of conservation test were given to ensure the child could show a proper understanding of the concepts involved.

RESULTS

Mixed design analysis of variance and Newman-Kreuls tests showed that
* Children were significantly more able to conserve in the one judgement task.
  This supports Rose and Blank's (1974) experiment and criticism of Piaget's methods.
* Older children did significantly better than younger children in conservation.
  This supports Piaget's theory of cognitive development in general.
* The conservation of number task was significantly easier than the other tasks.
  Indicating support for Piaget's notion of decalage.

MEAN ERRORS OUT OF 12 CONSERVATION TESTS

Age	Standard	One judgement	Fixed Array
5	8.5	7.3	8.6
6	5.7	4.3	6.4
7	3.2	2.6	4.9
8	1.7	1.3	3.3

EVALUATION

Methodological: *Good methods* – The study used a control group, different tests of conservation, and different aged subjects.
Good data analysis – The data was extensively analysed to reveal its significance.

Theoretical: *Implications* – The study supports some of Piaget's notions and some of those of his critics.

Links: Child cognitive development. Research methods – demand characteristics.

Bruner's theory of cognitive development

BRUNER'S ASSUMPTIONS

Jerome Bruner was a cognitive scientist who agreed with Piaget that active interaction with the world could increase a child's underlying cognitive capacity to understand the world in more complex ways. Bruner differed from Piaget, however, in that he:

- Was more concerned with **how** knowledge was **represented** and organised as the child developed, and therefore proposed different **modes** of representation.
- Emphasised the importance of **social** factors in cognitive development, in particular the role of language, social interaction and experience, which could pull the child towards better understanding. Cognitive growth depends upon the mastery of 'skills transmitted with varying efficiency and success by the culture' and occurs 'from the outside in as well as from the inside out' Bruner (1971).

MODES OF REPRESENTATION

Bruner's theory is concerned with **ways** of **representing** or thinking about knowledge at different ages, not stages as such. Bruner proposed **three modes** of representation that develop in order and allow the child to think about the world in more sophisticated ways, but all exist in the adult (we do not lose these ways of thinking like in Piaget's stages). The modes are:

- The enactive mode (0 – 1 years) – this mode of representation is dominant in babies, who first represent or interact with the world through their actions. Knowledge is therefore stored in '**muscle memory**'.
- The iconic mode (1 – 6 years) – this mode represents knowledge through visual or auditory **likenesses** or **images**. Children dominated by their iconic mode have **difficulty** thinking beyond the images, to categorise the knowledge or understand relationships between objects.
- The symbolic mode (7 years onwards) – this mode enables children to encode the world in terms of information storing symbols such as the words of our language or the numbers of mathematics. This allows information to be **categorised** and summarised so that it can be more readily **manipulated** and considered. The symbolic mode allows children to think beyond the physical images of the iconic mode.

THE ROLE OF LANGUAGE AND EDUCATION

Like Vygotsky, Bruner stressed education and social interaction as major influences upon cognitive development, and in particular proposed that society provides our language which gives us symbolic thought. Unlike Piaget, who thought that language was merely a useful tool which reflects and describes the underlying symbolic cognitive structures such as operations,

Bruner believed that language is symbolic/logical/operational thought – the two are inseparable. According to Bruner therefore, **language training** can speed up cognitive development, a suggestion that Piaget's theory rejects (since he believed that cognitive structures could only be developed through the child's individual maturation and interaction with the world).

LANGUAGE ACCELERATING DEVELOPMENT

- Francoise Frank (reported by Bruner, 1964) showed how the ability of pre-operational children to give the correct answer in liquid conservation tasks could be improved if they were encouraged to use and rely upon their linguistic descriptions (i.e. their symbolic mode) of the task.
- Frank reduced the visual (iconic mode) effect of the conservation changes by screening most of the beakers during the experiment. Once the children were less dominated by their iconic mode, they could concentrate on their verbal (symbolic mode) descriptions of what was happening, and were more able to conserve.
- Once the 5 and 6 year olds had used their language to solve the conservation task, they showed an increased ability to pass other non-screened conservation tasks. 5 year olds showed an increase from 20 to 70%.
  6-7 year olds increased from 50 to 90%.

Step 1 Show standard beakers with equal water and a wider beaker of the same height.

Step 2 Screen the beakers so the water level is hidden, but mark the level of the water on screen.

Step 3 Pour water from the standard beaker into the screened wider beaker.

Step 4 Ask the child, without it seeing the water 'which has more to drink or do they have the same?'
Result - in comparison with an unscreened pre-test there is an increase in correct answers:
4 year olds – increase from 0% to 50%
5 year olds – increase from 20% to 90%
6 year olds – increase from 50% to 100%
Children justify their response linguistically by saying for example 'You only poured it'.

Step 5 The screen is removed and:
4 year olds – all revert to the pre-test answer of less water in the wider beaker, overwhelmed by the appearance of the water (iconic mode).
5-6 year olds – virtually all stick to the right answer, relying on their previous verbal justification (symbolic mode) 'You only poured it from there to there'.

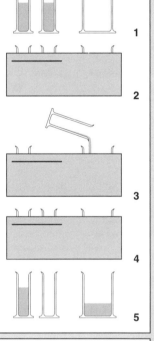

Sonstroem et al (1966) encouraged children who failed conservation of substance tests to use all of their modes of representation to increase their ability to conserve. The children who rolled the plasticine into a ball themselves (enactive mode) while watching their own actions (iconic mode) and verbally describing what was happening, e.g. 'it's getting longer but thinner' (symbolic mode) showed the greatest improvement in conservation.

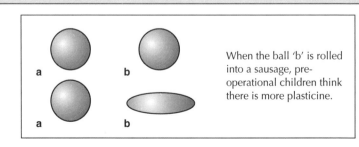

When the ball 'b' is rolled into a sausage, pre-operational children think there is more plasticine.

Vygotsky's theory of cognitive development

VYGOTSKY'S APPROACH
- Vygotsky was a Russian psychologist whose ideas on cognitive development were very similar to Bruner's. Vygotsky focused on the importance of *social interaction* and *language* as major influences on children's development of understanding.

SOCIAL INTERACTION
- Vygotsky sees the whole process of cognitive development as being social in nature – *'we become ourselves through others'*.
- At first the child responds to the world only through its actions, but society provides the *meaning* of those actions through social interaction.
- Vygotsky illustrates this with the example of pointing – the child may reach towards an object and fail to grasp it, but the parent will *interpret* this as a pointing gesture.
- 'The original meaning to this unsuccessful grasping movement is thus imparted by others. And only afterwards, on the basis of the fact that the child associates the unsuccessful grasping movement with the entire objective situation, does the child himself begin to treat the movement as a pointing gesture. Here the function of the movement itself changes: from a movement directed towards an object, it becomes a movement directed towards another person, a means of communication, the grasping is transformed into pointing.' Vygotsky (1978)

INTERNALISATION AND LANGUAGE
- Cognitive development, therefore, proceeds, according to Vygotsky, as the child gradually *internalises* the meanings provided by these social interactions. The child's thinking and reasoning abilities are at first primitive, crude and do not involve the use of language, and so the greatest advance comes when we internalise *language*.
- Speech starts off as communication behaviour that produces changes in others, but when language becomes internalised, it converges with thought – *'thought becomes verbal and speech rational'* Vygotsky (1962). Language allows us to 'turn around and reflect on our thoughts' – directing and *controlling* our thinking, as well as communicating our thoughts to others.
- Eventually, language splits between these two functions as we develop an abbreviated inner voice for thinking with, and a more articulate vocabulary for communicating with others. Internal language vastly increases our powers of problem solving.
- The use of language can be said to progress in three stages:
1 Pre-intellectual social speech (0–3 years), where thinking does not occur in language and speech is used to provoke social change.
2 Egocentric speech (3–7 years), where language helps the child control behaviour but is spoken out loud.
3 Inner speech (7 years +), where the child uses speech silently to control their own behaviour and publicly for social communication.

ZONE OF PROXIMAL DEVELOPMENT
- Because cognitive development is achieved by the *joint* construction of knowledge between the child and society, it follows that any one child's potential intellectual ability is greater if working in *conjunction* with a more expert person / other than alone. Vygotsky defines the *zone of proximal development* (ZPD) as

'the distance between the actual developmental level as determined by individual problem solving and the level of potential development as determined through problem solving under adult guidance or in collaboration with more capable peers. The zone of proximal development defines those functions that have not yet matured but are in the process of maturation, functions that will mature tomorrow but are currently in an embryonic state. These functions could be termed the "buds" or "flowers" of development rather than the "fruits" of development'.

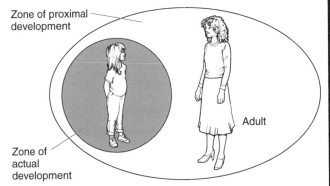

Zone of proximal development

Zone of actual development

Adult

EVALUATION OF VYGOTSKY'S THEORY
Vygotsky's ideas have:
- become increasingly popular as it became clear that Piaget had under emphasised the role of social factors in cognitive development.
- been developed by others such as Bruner who have conducted more research to provide evidence for them than Vygotsky himself did.
- been successfully applied to education.

The information-processing approach to cognitive development

ASSUMPTIONS

- The information-processing approach to cognitive development is a recent approach that aims to apply experimental cognitive psychological research from a number of areas, such as attention, perception and memory, to explain children's development of understanding.
- In the usual cognitive psychological style, children's minds can be regarded as computers that gradually develop in their ability to process information – to receive it, store it and use it appropriately. Just as the efficiency of a computer depends upon the speed of its processor, the amount of RAM it has to manipulate information at any one time and the sophistication of its software programs, so young children will, at first possess similar limited information-processing abilities.

PROCESSING SPEED

- Young children are actually physically slower at transmitting information along neurones – as the brain matures, nerve fibres become myelinised and can transmit their electrical messages faster, thereby increasing their processing speed.

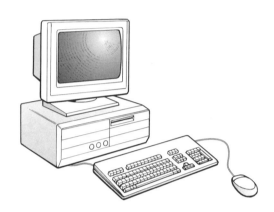

Siegler's (1978) balance beam tests show how children's ability to solve problems is directly related to the number of aspects of a problem they can recognise and combine at the same time. (Processing skill is needed to identify the aspects of the problem, processing capacity is needed to combine them at the same time).

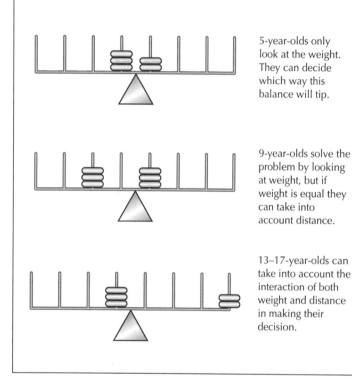

5-year-olds only look at the weight. They can decide which way this balance will tip.

9-year-olds solve the problem by looking at weight, but if weight is equal they can take into account distance.

13–17-year-olds can take into account the interaction of both weight and distance in making their decision.

PROCESSING CAPACITY

- Case (1992) proposes that young children have a limited 'mental space' or working/short-term memory with which to hold and think about information – thus making it difficult to take into account more than one aspect of a problem at a time (Piaget called this centration, and argued that it led to conservation errors). As the child grows older, 'mental space' increases as
  a neural processing speeds up and
  b strategies for processing information become more automatic with practice and, therefore, need less conscious attention – thus freeing up 'mental space' for other work (rather like experienced drivers being more able to concentrate on other tasks while driving when their driving skills become automatic through practice).

Evidence

- Tests on short-term memory capacity support the idea that processing capacity increases with age – people's ability to recall digits after hearing them just once improves with age (adults can recall around seven, plus or minus two).

PROCESSING SKILLS

- As the child grows and gains experience in the world, its skills for processing information (organising, categorising and problem-solving) develop, becoming faster, more complex and flexible. More efficient strategies can be used, such as chunking and organising information, to improve short- or long-term memory, and heuristics or 'rules of thumb' enable problems to be solved more quickly.
- Fischer (1980) has developed a theory that shows how skills develop and, like many other researchers in the area, argues that different children will develop particular skills or talents in different 'domains' of ability depending upon their environmental experience. Domain skills may not be entirely dependent on environmental stimulation, however, since Baron-Cohen (1990, 1995) proposes that autism, now widely held to be a congenital disorder, is due to a lack of 'theory of mind' – the domain of mental representation and social understanding.

Evidence

- Chi (1978) found that children skilled at chess could remember patterns of chess configurations better than adults who were inexperienced at chess, indicating that domain skill rather than general capability was most important. In computer terms a more efficient program on a less powerful machine was more efficient.

'Does the autistic child have a 'theory of mind'?' Baron-Cohen, Leslie and Frith (1985)

INTRODUCTION
- Baron-Cohen et al describe childhood autism as a severe developmental disorder affecting around 4 in 10,000 children and see the key symptom as being a ***profound problem in understanding and coping with the social environment*** – finding it unpredictable and confusing. This causes impaired verbal and non-verbal communication and a failure to develop normal social relationships – autistic children seem to treat people and objects in the same way and tend to be withdrawn or disruptive in their interactions with others.
- Autistic social problems could be partly caused by other symptoms that such children show – many for example are mentally retarded. However autistic children with normal IQs also lack social competence, while non-autistic retarded children such as those with Down's Syndrome are relatively socially competent. Baron-Cohen et al therefore suggest that autistic children ***lack a specific cognitive mechanism*** that is distinct from general IQ, namely a '**theory of mind**'.
- A theory of mind enables one to realise that '***other people know, want, feel, or believe things***' and as such is vital for social skills. It is a form of '***second –order' representation***' or metarepresentation (a representation of another person's representation of the world, or a belief about another's belief), which also gives the ability to pretend in play – something autistic children are very poor at.

AIM
If a theory of mind that enables one to attribute mental states to others:
1 is specifically lacking in autistic children and is not related to general intelligence
2 allows people to work out what others *believe* about certain situations and thus predict what they will do next
then it can be hypothesised that autistic children whose IQs are in the average range will perform significantly worse on a task that requires such belief based prediction than non-autistic but severely retarded children with Down's Syndrome.

METHOD
Design A natural or quasi experiment was used, employing an independent measures design.
The independent variable was the type of child, naturally manipulated in 3 conditions; autistic, Down's Syndrome, clinically 'normal'.
The dependent variable was the ability to correctly answer the belief question of the Sally-Anne test.
Subjects 20 autistic children aged around 6–16 years old (average approx. 12) of higher average intelligence than the other groups
14 Down's Syndrome children aged around 6–17 (average approx. 11).
27 clinically 'normal' pre-school children aged around 3–5 (average approx. $4\frac{1}{2}$).
Procedure The experimenter sits at a table opposite the child with two dolls, Sally and Anne. Sally puts a marble into her basket, then leaves the scene. Anne transfers the marble and hides it in her box. Sally returns and the experimenter asks the critical **Belief Question** – "Where will Sally look for her marble?". If the children point to the previous location of Sally's basket they pass the belief question since they can represent the doll's false belief. If they point to the current location of Anne's box then they fail the question since they cannot take into account Sally's false belief. The scenario was repeated, but this time the marble was transferred to the experimenter's pocket.
Controls –To ensure the validity of the belief question, 3 control questions were asked – the Naming Question asking which doll was which (to ensure knowledge of the dolls' identities), the Reality Question "Where is the marble really?" and the Memory Question "Where was the marble in the beginning?" (to ensure knowledge of the marble's location at each point in the scenario).

RESULTS

% failure on Questions	Autistic group	Down's Syndrome group	'Normal' pre-schoolers
Naming, Reality, Memory	0%	0%	0%
Belief Question	80% on both trials	14% on both trials	15% on both trials

Belief Question differences were significant at P<0.001. All 16 autistic children who failed pointed to the current marble location.

DISCUSSION
The controls rule out explanations of position preference, negativism, random pointing, misunderstanding/forgetting the task or general intellectual ability. The experimenters therefore conclude that the autistic children specifically lacked a theory of mind to enable them to attribute belief to the doll and thus distinguish their own belief from the doll's. The four autistic children who did not fail the Belief Question may have possessed a theory of mind and were predicted by Baron-Cohen et al to show differences from the other autistic children in their type of social impairment and pretend play deficiency (testing of this was not reported). The *conceptual* perspective-taking tested here is distinguished from the *perceptual* perspective-taking tested by Piaget and Inhelder's 'three-mountain' test.

EVALUATION
Methodological The scenario and use of dolls is rather artificial (dolls do not believe!). Realistic tests using people have confirmed the results.
Theoretical The study initiated a large amount of research into theory of mind and links with certain aspects of Piaget's egocentrism.
Links Child cognitive development. Natural or quasi experimentation.

The development of IQ test performance – nature approach

EVIDENCE FOR GENETIC CAUSES	EVALUATION

SELECTIVE BREEDING STUDIES

- Thompson (1952) selected rats that were 'maze-bright' or 'maze dull' by timing how long they took to negotiate a maze. By selectively breeding the two types of rats (only letting them breed with rats from their own group) Thompson found that the maze learning differences between the offspring of the maze-bright and maze-dull rats increased with the number of generations, until, by the sixth generation, the bright rats made approximately 80% fewer mistakes than the dull rats.
- Henderson (1970) found that the ability of rats to negotiate obstacles to find food would not always improve if their environmental conditions were enriched (as nurture orientated theorists would predict). However, the fact that some of the rats did show some improvement, indicates at least some interaction between genetic abilities and environmental experience.

- Cooper and Zubek (1958) found that there was no significant difference in the performance of selectively bred maze-bright and maze dull rats if they were both raised in either very deprived or enriching environmental conditions (which there should have been if maze learning was under genetic control). Studies of rats raised in enriched environments indicate that physiological changes in the synaptic connections of their brains occur as a result.
- In Thompson's (1952) experiment, it is important to note that only maze-learning was genetically transmitted, not the learning of other tasks.
- Studies on the selective breeding of rats are useful, since we can not selectively breed humans, but there are problems in generalising the results to humans.

GENETIC RELATEDNESS AND IQ

- Family resemblance studies on the heritability of IQ have been conducted on the assumption that the closer the genetic relationship between two people, the closer their IQs will be.
  However, it is equally likely that more closely related people will probably live together in very similar environments, and so the best evidence for genetic influences in this area is gained from studying the similarity of IQ between genetically identical subjects (monozygotic/identical twins) who have been raised in different environments, due to adoption for example (a high positive correlation between them would strongly support a large role for genetic factors in the development of IQ).
- Bouchard and McGue (1981) conducted a review of 111 world-wide studies on family IQ, ignoring studies which they claimed had methodological deficiencies, and came up with the following average correlations of IQ.

	Average correlation
Identical twins reared together	.86
Identical twins reared apart	.72
Non-identical twins reared together	.60
Siblings reared together	.47
Siblings reared apart	.24
Cousins	.15

Bouchard and McGue (1981)

The strongest evidence for genetic influences on IQ from these results is the finding that identical twins raised apart have more similar IQs than non-identical twins raised together.
- Bouchard et al (1990) have continued this line of investigation in their Minnesota Twin Study, but have focused more on studying the IQ similarity of identical twins reared apart. From their intensive studies of the twins so far, they estimate that 70% of the variance in IQ scores are due to genetic inheritance, a larger estimate than that made by Bouchard & McGue (1981) in their earlier review.

Methodologically, studies on genetic relatedness and IQ have been subject to many criticisms, e.g. by Kamin (1977):

1 It is very difficult to control for environmental influences to arrive at an accurate estimate of the genetic contribution to intelligence. Even studying adoption cases is problematic, since:
   - Different environments can not be guaranteed – in some cases an effort has even been made to place the adopted children in similar family environments.
   - The infants may not have been separated exactly from birth and share the same womb experience anyway.
   - The self-selecting sampling techniques employed in studies such as Bouchard et al's (1990) Minnesota Twin Study have been accused of leading to an exaggeration of the similarities between separated identical twins.
   - The different types of IQ test used in the different studies makes it hard to compare the results since they are standardised in different ways.

2 The experimenter bias sometimes exhibited in this controversial area has led to:
   - The questioning of the validity of some findings, e.g. Cyril Burt's data on separated identical twins, which was used to support the claim that 80% of the variance in intelligence is genetically determined, but was thoroughly rejected by Kamin (1977).
   - An overly genetic interpretation of the data in some studies and a neglect of environmental influences, e.g. the noticeable differences in Bouchard & McGue's (1981) correlations between:
   a Identical twins reared together and identical twins reared apart (a difference of .14).
   b Siblings reared together and siblings reared apart (a difference of .23).
   In both cases, the genetic relatedness is the same and the differences are more attributable to environmental experiences.

The development of IQ test performance – nurture approach

EVIDENCE FOR ENVIRONMENTAL CAUSES	EVALUATION

EFFECTS OF EARLY PRIVATION ON IQ

If measured intelligence can be significantly reduced by environmental privation, then support is provided for the nurture approach.
- Sameroff and Seifer (1983) identified ten environmental factors, such as the mental health and educational level of the mother, the presence of the father, etc., each of which could lead to a loss of approximately 5 IQ points.
- Vernon (1965) in a cross cultural study revealed that children from disadvantaged backgrounds with little education and a poor home life scored lower on IQ tests, even on the spatial and non-verbal items.
- Many studies, e.g. Koluchova (1972) have shown that measured intelligence can be drastically reduced by extreme early environmental privation, but can also be dramatically improved, even to normal levels, by later normal or enriched conditions.

The dramatic recovery of IQ after extreme privation does seem to indicate the strong motivating effects of genetic influences. Correlational studies often neglect the possibility that genetic influenced behaviour can elicit different reactions – children with lower IQ may be rejected or abused by their parents or just cause their parents to give up attempts to educate them.

ENVIRONMENTAL ENRICHMENT AND IQ

If measured intelligence can be significantly increased through environmental enrichment, then support is provided for the nurture approach.
- Caldwell and Bradley (1978) devised the Home Observation for Measurement of the Environment (HOME) checklist, which is capable of measuring the quality of the home environment for children and its implications for intellectual development. Using the HOME checklist it has been found that factors like the emotional responsiveness and stimulation of the child by the parents are of key importance.
- Operation Headstart was an attempt by the government of the USA in 1965 to provide extra learning experiences for pre-school children from disadvantaged backgrounds. It produced some short lasting gains in IQ, but a longer term 'sleeper effect' in improved academic grades and attitudes to academic work (Collins, 1983).
- Scarr and Weinberg (1976, 1983) found that black children adopted from poor backgrounds and raised in white families of higher income and educational level showed an average IQ of 106 (110 if adopted within 12 months of birth) compared to a control group from a similar background who had an average IQ of 90.
- Skeels (1966) reports the case of 13 infant orphans who, with an average IQ of 64 were transferred to a special institution and given enriching interaction with older girls. By the age of seven they had gained an average of 36 points compared to a control group of orphans who remained in the orphanage and whose IQ dropped by an average 21 points from an original average of 86.
- Lynn and Hampson (1986) have reported rises in the national average IQ of Britain (by 1.7), Japan (by 7.7) and the USA (by 3.0) over a 50 year period (1932-1982), which can not be accounted for in terms of genetic factors.
- Howe (1990) has argued that the degree of hard work and practice shown by children with exceptional abilities is often underestimated – even genius needs to be fuelled.

The nature approach would predict that if IQ is under largely genetic control then IQ scores should remain reasonably consistent over time. Jensen (1969) argued that projects like Headstart were a waste of time and resources since poor and minority children were genetically less able to take advantage of them. The strategies employed in projects like Headstart have been accused of
- not producing the long term effects they were designed for.
- being inappropriate for the children they were applied to.
- being overly focused on improving and measuring IQ.

However, Headstart did provide some long term gains and other intervention projects have been more successful.

Attempts at 'hothousing', or intensively educating children, can have negative effects on other areas of functioning and be stressful to the children.

EVALUATION OF NATURE-NURTURE DEBATE IN IQ DEVELOPMENT

All researchers in the area agree that both genetic and environmental influences interact in very complex ways – the genotype of an individual can only be expressed through a phenotype that is the product of genes building physical structures from environmental resources. The environmental influences on intelligence begin in the womb, indeed Denenberg et al have even shown that rats with inherited brain abnormalities which are transplanted into the wombs of healthy rats do better on learning tests than rats with the same abnormality raised in 'unhealthy' wombs. This indicates that the 'uterine environment can have long-term broad and beneficial behavioural effects' (Denenberg quoted in *New Scientist*, March 1998) and is important for the development of cognitive abilities.

The precise genes involved in intelligence have proven difficult to locate, perhaps due to the lack of funding provided for this socially sensitive area of research in the Human Genome Project. However, Plomin (1997) has claimed to have discovered a gene called IGF2R which can account for 2% of the variation in IQ test results.

Plomin's finding reflects another major problem – that not only are IQ tests often lacking in reliability as measures of intelligence, but intelligence may not be a unitary phenomenon – some aspects may be under more genetic control than others. IQ tests do take into account some different 'kinds of intelligence' and the Minnesota Twin Study has found that, whereas verbal ability correlations between separated identical twins are high, the correlations for memory are lower and spatial ability are variable.

Cognitive developmental theories of moral development 1

COGNITIVE DEVELOPMENTAL THEORIES

PIAGET'S THEORY

- Piaget proposed that the level of **moral reasoning** a child showed would change in a qualitative way over time. Piaget suggested two main types of moral thinking:

    1 **Heteronomous morality** – Shown mostly by 5–9 year old children who regard morality as **obeying other people's rules** and laws. The thinking of this stage is typical of **pre-operational** thought and shows **moral realism** – rules and laws are understood as almost real and **fixed** things that are to be strictly obeyed or automatic punishment will follow (**immanent justice**). Immoral acts are judged by their **observable consequences** rather than intentions – a large amount of *accidental* damage is seen as worse than a small amount of *deliberate* damage.

    2 **Autonomous morality** - Shown mostly by those above 10 years, who regard morality as **following their own set of rules**/laws. The thinking of this stage is typical of **concrete** and later **formal operational** thought and shows **moral relativism** – rules and laws are understood as social creations agreed by mutual consent and the **intentions** of actions can be taken into account.

- Piaget believed the moral thinking of 7–9 year olds and sometimes even adults can be a mixture of heteronomous and autonomous morality, but the main shift from the former to the latter occurs when the child no longer shows egocentrism and is less dependent on the authority of adults. This implies that both cognitive development and social experience are required.

KOHLBERG'S THEORY

- Kohlberg attempted to produce a more detailed theory of moral development by presenting individuals of all ages with moral dilemmas in the form of short stories to solve.
- The dilemmas involved ten universal moral issues, such as the ethics of punishment, liberty and truth; and the reasoning used to justify the answer indicated the level of moral development.
- Kohlberg proposed six universal stages, reflecting three major levels of morality, which everyone progresses through in order.

Level	Stage	Moral reasoning shown
Pre-conventional	1 Punishment & obedience orientation.	Rules are kept to avoid punishment.
	2 Instrumental – relativist orientation.	'Right' behaviour is that which ultimately brings rewards to oneself.
Conventional	3 Good boy – nice girl orientation.	'Good' behaviour is what pleases others – conformity to goodness.
	4 Law & order orientation.	Doing one's duty, obeying laws is important.
Post-conventional	5 Social contract orientation.	'Right' is what is demo-cratically agreed upon.
	6 Universal principles orientation.	Moral action is taken based on self chosen principles.

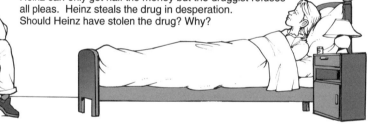

Heinz's wife is dying of cancer. Only one man has the drug to help her but is charging 10 times what it cost to make it. Heinz can only get half the money but the druggist refuses all pleas. Heinz steals the drug in desperation. Should Heinz have stolen the drug? Why?

EVALUATION OF COGNITIVE DEVELOPMENTAL THEORIES OF MORAL DEVELOPMENT

Piaget supported his theory of moral development by questioning children about their understanding of rules (in **games** like marbles) and by presenting them with **moral stories**, whereas Kohlberg presented people with **moral dilemmas**.

Piagets stories have been criticised for over-emphasising consequences. Kohlberg's dilemmas are criticised as
- **too difficult** for children to relate to,
- **too hypothetical**,
- **too culturally biased** and
- **too biased towards male** ideas of morality, such as justice, rather than female moral notions like caring, sympathy and responsibility (**Gilligan** 1982).

Piaget and Kohlberg **ignored** the **relationship** between a person's moral **thought** and **behaviour** – knowing what should be done does not always lead to doing it.
- **Bandura and McDonald** (1963) found children would imitate a model's immoral behaviour regardless of their level of moral development

Some of Kohlberg's ideas and studies have been successfully supported:
- **Longitudinally** – **Colby et al** (1983) studied 58 American males over 20 years and found they went through 4 of Kohlberg's stages.
- **Cross-culturally** – **Snarey** (1985) found evidence for Kohlberg's first 4 stages in many cultures. Cultures differ, however, in their moral priorities.
- **Cross-sectionally** – **Fodor** (1972) found that delinquents operated at lower levels of moral development than non-delinquents.

Some studies have found that stage six morality is rarely reached and that some people may actually **skip stages** or **revert** to earlier stages, which goes against Kohlberg's ideas. Eisenberg (1986) has found parallels with Kohlberg's stages in pro-social helping in dilemmas.

Cognitive developmental theories of moral development 2

EISENBERG'S THEORY OF PROSOCIAL MORAL REASONING

Eisenberg et al (1983) investigated the moral reasoning behind **prosocial** behaviour, typically concerning situations where another person required help that would inconvenience the potential helper in some way. **Dilemmas** were presented to children of different ages, such as the 'Mary dilemma' below, that involved deciding whether to help another person, but where the alternative was to just satisfy one's own needs rather than breaking any laws or moral rules (as was more the case with Kohlberg's dilemmas).

Eisenberg suggested that such prosocial moral reasoning would change over time as general cognitive development allowed individuals to take on the **perspective** of other people, **empathise** with others and gain some **insight** into their own motives for helping.

Eisenberg et al found that moral reasoning was **not** always **consistent**, but generally progressed through **five levels**.

EISENBERG'S FIVE LEVELS OF PROSOCIAL MORAL REASONING

Level	Helping behaviour based on...	Age range
1. **Hedonistic** (self-centred)	Concern for oneself – if help provides benefits for oneself.	Pre-school to early primary school.
2. **Needs-** (of others) **orientated**	The needs of others – but without much evidence of guilt or sympathy.	Pre-school to mostly primary school.
3. **Approval-orientated**	Doing what is perceived as good and approved of by others.	Primary school to secondary school.
4. **Empathetic or transitional**	Inner motives of sympathy and guilt – based on perspective role-taking. Some vague consideration of abstract principles and values.	Older primary school to secondary school.
5. **Strongly internalised**	Strongly internalised values, norms and principles – to maintain self-respect.	Very few at secondary school.

Source: based on Eisenberg, Lennon and Roth (1983)

Evaluation

- Despite some similarities to Kohlberg's research, Eisenberg's theory has drawn attention to a different aspect of, and has emphasised the role of **emotion** in, moral reasoning.
- Some of Eisenberg's findings have **contradicted** those of Kohlberg, e.g. the occasional *reverting* to lower levels of moral reasoning.
- Although Eisenberg et al found moral reasoning was not always consistent, they did find some evidence that the level of prosocial reasoning was linked to appropriate prosocial behaviour. Younger children who gave 'needs of others' responses to dilemmas were more likely to later show more spontaneous sharing with others than those who replied with 'hedonistic' reasoning, while more mature moral reasoners were more likely to help someone they disliked if they really needed it compared to less mature reasoners.

Mary will miss all the ice cream, cake and games at her friend's birthday party if she helps a girl who has fallen down and hurt her leg. What should Mary do? Why?

Adult interviewer

Help, or she will not be able to respect herself

Level 5 child

Level 1 child

Not help - she will miss all the cake!

GENDER AND MORAL REASONING

Gilligan (1982) argued that Kohlberg's theory was **biased** towards men because:

- It was developed based upon interviews with males.
- Men show a 'morality of justice' – that everyone should be treated the same, whereas women reason based upon a 'morality of care'– that no one should be hurt. Gilligan (1982) suggested that female morality progresses towards an ideal of nonviolence via 3 stages:

Stage 1 – Care for one's own survival.
Stage 2 – Care for others.
Stage 3 – Care for integrity (for self and others).

Women may therefore be rated as morally inferior (e.g. at Kohlberg's stage 3) using male moral standards, which are more likely to portray men as reaching stage 4.

Evaluation

- Although Gilligan found some evidence that women favour a morality of care over one of justice, most research shows men and women use both types of reasoning.
- Walker (1984) found that women are not rated differently using Kohlberg's dilemmas.

CULTURE AND MORAL REASONING

While research has found some cross-cultural support for moral progression through Kohlberg's first 4 stages, little evidence has been found of post-conventional moral reasoning in other cultures. This has led to the criticism that Kohlberg's theory is biased towards western, industrialised cultures because:

- It was developed based upon interviews with participants from Western, industrialised countries.
- Such countries possess different moral values and priorities compared to other countries – in particular the emphasis on stage 6 'universal' ethical principles such as equality may result from the individualistic, capitalist values of the culture rather than the collectivistic values of other cultures.

People from non- Western, industrialised cultures may therefore be rated as morally inferior using such moral standards.

Evaluation

- Shweder et al (e.g. 1987, 1990) found Indian participants reasoned about Kohlberg's dilemmas differently to western participants, saw different values as having 'universal' validity and rated different acts as morally offensive based upon their religion.

Attachment in infancy 1

WHAT IS MEANT BY ATTACHMENT?
- An attachment is a strong, long lasting and close emotional bond between two people, which causes distress on separation from the attached individual.
- Psychologists have been particularly interested in the development of first attachments in infancy since they appear to have important consequences for later healthy development, especially concerning later relationships.

HOW DOES ATTACHMENT DEVELOP?
Attachment in infancy occurs gradually over a sequence of phases:

• Pre-attachment phase	0 – 3 months	Infant preference for humans over other objects is shown by preferential looking and social smiling (before 6 weeks the infant is said to be asocial).
• Indiscriminate attachment phase	3 – 7 months	Infant can distinguish between people and allows strangers to handle it.
• Discriminate attachment phase	7 – 9 months	Infant develops specific attachments to certain people and shows distress on separation from them. Avoidance or fear of strangers may be shown.
• Multiple attachment phase	9 months onward	Infant becomes increasingly independent and forms other bonds despite the stronger prior attachments.

THEORIES OF ATTACHMENT

PSYCHOANALYTIC
- Freud believed that infants become attached to people who satisfy their need for food at the oral stage. Oral gratification causes drive reduction, which is experienced as pleasant.
- While Freud was right that attachment is important for later development, his drive theory and idea that attachment is due to food has not been supported.

COGNITIVE
Schaffer (1971) points out that infants usually form attachments:
- Once they can reliably distinguish one caregiver from another.
- With the caregivers that stimulate and interact with them the most intensely.

LEARNING THEORY
- Learning theory suggests that attachment should occur as parents become associated with pleasant stimuli such as food and comfort via classical conditioning.
- Harlow and Harlow (1969), however, showed that rhesus monkeys had an innate preference to form attachments to surrogate mothers that provide contact comfort rather than food.

BOWLBY'S ATTACHMENT THEORY
- Bowlby (1951), influenced by ethological studies on imprinting, suggested infants were genetically programmed to form attachments to a single carer (the mother in most cases), within a critical time period (approximately 2 and a half years). Bowlby argued that attachment between infant and caregiver has evolved because it is an adaptive behaviour that aids survival. In particular, attachment provides food, security, a safe base from which to explore the world, exposure to important survival skills shown by the parent and an internal working model of relationships with others. For the parent it ensures a greater likelihood of their offspring surviving (and thus passing on their own genes for attachment formation). Various innate social releasers have also evolved to elicit care giving, such as crying and smiling. If attachments have not been formed by the end of the critical time period then Bowlby suggested that a number of negative effects would result (see deprivation and privation).
- While Bowlby's ideas on attachment were important, research indicates that multiple attachments can be formed, within a sensitive time period (Rutter, 1981). Many researchers have disputed the idea that an internal working model of relationships formed during attachment always influences later relationships and behaviour (see deprivation and privation research).

Attachment in infancy 2

HOW DO WE KNOW AN ATTACHMENT HAS FORMED?

Attachment can be tested via the 'Strange Situation' method developed by Ainsworth et al (1971), where the mother and child are taken to an unfamiliar room and subjected to a range of timed, increasingly stressful (for an attached child) set of scenarios, such as:

1 A stranger is introduced to the child in the presence of the mother.
2 The mother leaves the infant with the stranger.
3 After the mother returns and re-settles the infant, it is left alone.
4 A stranger enters and interacts with the lone infant.
5 Mother returns again and picks up infant.

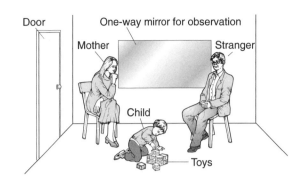

WHAT DIFFERENT KINDS OF ATTACHMENT ARE THERE?

Ainsworth et al (1978) discovered three main types of infant attachment using the Strange Situation, which occurred in various proportions:

Type A – Anxious-avoidant or **detached** (approx. 20% of sample)
The infant ignores the mother, is not affected by her parting or return and although distressed when alone is easily comforted by strangers.

Type B – Securely attached (approx. 70% of sample)
The infant plays contentedly while the mother is there, is distressed by her parting, is relieved on her return and although not adverse to stranger contact treats them differently from the mother.

Type C – Anxious-resistant or ambivalent (approx. 10% of sample)
The infant is discontented while with mother, playing less, is distressed by her parting, is not easily comforted on her return and may resist contact by mother and stranger.

Replicating studies have revealed slightly different proportions.

WHAT CAUSES DIFFERENCES IN ATTACHMENT?

Parental sensitivity – Ainsworth et al (1978) suggested that secure attachment is dependent upon emotionally close and responsive mothering, whereas insecure attachments result from insensitive mothers. Although other factors are involved the effects of maternal sensitivity have been supported.

Infant temperament – Researchers such as Kagan (1982) suggest innate differences in infant temperament and anxiety may cause certain kinds of parental reaction and attachment.

Family circumstances – Attachment type may vary over time and setting with social and cultural environmental conditions, e.g. if a family undergoes stress (Vaughn et al, 1979).

Reliability of classification – Strange Situation methodology has been criticised and other attachment types proposed, e.g. D, insecure-disorganised/disorientated.

CROSS-CULTURAL DIFFERENCES IN ATTACHMENT

Using the Strange Situation method (Ainsworth et al, 1978) cross-cultural studies of differences in attachment types have been conducted. Van Ijzendoorn and Kroonenberg (1988) compared the results of 32 cross-cultural studies and found that there was often more consistency across cultures than within them in terms of variation in attachment. However, while the majority of children in each culture seem to be securely attached, there do seem to be variations in the proportion of avoidant and resistant attachments in certain countries. German infants appear to have a slightly higher proportion of avoidant attachments which Grossman et al (1985) have suggested might result from a cultural tendency for German parents to maintain a large interpersonal distance and wean offspring early from close contact. Some studies of Israeli children raised on kibbutzim have revealed a higher proportion of resistant attachments, e.g. Sagi et al (1985), which may result from the fact that the children have contact with parents but are mainly raised communally in a large group. However, the Strange Situation may be based on American cultural assumptions and therefore be a flawed technique for making cross-cultural comparisons.

Country	Number of studies	Percentage of each type of attachment		
		Secure	Avoidant	Resistant
WEST GERMANY	3	57	35	8
GREAT BRITAIN	1	75	22	3
NETHERLANDS	4	67	26	7
SWEDEN	1	74	22	4
ISRAEL	2	64	7	29
JAPAN	2	68	5	27
CHINA	1	50	25	25
UNITED STATES	18	65	21	14
Overall average		65	21	14

Percentages to nearest whole number reported by Van Ijzendoorn and Kroonenberg (1988).

Deprivation of attachment in infancy

BOWLBY'S MATERNAL DEPRIVATION HYPOTHESIS

Bowlby (1951) proposed that if infants were deprived of their mother (whom he regarded as their major attachment figure), during the critical period of attachment of the first few years of life, then a range of serious and permanent consequences for later development would follow. These included mental subnormality, delinquency, depression, affectionless psychopathy and even dwarfism.

Evidence for:
- Goldfarb (1943) studied children raised in institutions for most of the first three years of their lives, and found they later showed reduced IQ compared to a fostered control group.
- Bowlby (1946) studied 44 juvenile thieves and argued that their affectionless psychopathy was the result of maternal deprivation.
- Spitz and Wolf (1946) investigated infants in South American orphanages and found evidence for severe anaclitic depression in them.
- Harlow and Harlow (1962) researched the effects of social deprivation on rhesus monkeys. Deprived of an attachment figure, they interacted abnormally with other monkeys when they were eventually allowed to mix with them and were unable to form attachments to their own offspring after being artificially inseminated.

Evidence against:
- All the above studies had their methodological flaws, from failing to take into account the amount of environmental stimulation available in institutions, to generalising from animal studies.
- Rutter (1981), in 'Maternal Deprivation Reassessed', a thorough review of research in the area, concluded that Bowlby:
  1 was not correct in his ideas about monotropy (attachment to one figure only) or strict critical periods for attachment.
  2 failed to distinguish between the effects of deprivation (losing an attachment figure) and privation (never having formed an attachment).

POSSIBLE EFFECTS OF DEPRIVATION

SHORT-TERM EFFECTS
- Symptoms of the 'Syndrome of Distress:
  1 Protest – the infant expresses their feelings of anger, fear, frustration, etc.
  2 Despair – the infant then shows apathy and signs of depression, avoiding others.
  3 Detachment – interaction with others resumes, but is superficial and shows no preferences between other people. Re-attachment is resisted.
- Temporary delay in intellectual development.

LONG-TERM EFFECTS
- Symptoms of 'Separation Anxiety':
  1 Increased aggression.
  2 Increased clinging behaviour, possibly developing to the point of refusal to go to school.
  3 Increased detachment.
  4 Psychosomatic disorders (e.g. skin and stomach reactions).
- Increased risk of depression as an adult (usually in reaction to death of an attachment figure).

Evidence

Robertson and Bowlby (1952) based their conclusions regarding the short-term effects of deprivation on observations of the behaviour of children aged between 1 and 4. These children were being hospitalised or placed in residential nurseries. However, the emotional and behavioural effects of the attachment separation may be difficult to distinguish from effects relating to their new environment and situation.

Cockett and Tripp (1994) found more long-term attachment deprivation effects in children from re-ordered families (where parents had divorced and the child now lived away from a parental attachment figure) than those children who lived in intact but discordant (arguing parent) families. However, factors relating, for example, to the disruption of moving house rather than attachment deprivation could also be responsible.

EVALUATION

According to Rutter (1981), there are many sources of individual differences in vulnerability to the short and long-term effects of deprivation, including:

- Characteristics of the child, e.g.
  1 Age – children are especially vulnerable between 7 months and 3 years (Maccoby, 1981).
  2 Gender – boys, on average, respond worse to separation than girls.
  3 Temperament – differences in temperament, like aggressiveness, may become exaggerated.

- Previous mother-child relationship – The infant's reaction to separation may depend upon the type of attachment, e.g. secure, anxious-resistant or anxious-avoidant (Ainsworth et al, 1978).

- Previous separation experience – Infants experienced in short-term stays with (for example) relatives are more resistant to the effects of deprivation (Stacey et al, 1970).

- Attachments to others – Since Schaffer and Emerson (1964) revealed that multiple attachments are possible (in opposition to Bowlby's (1951) ideas), infants who are not deprived of all attachment figures manage the effects better.

- Quality of care – Research has revealed that both the short- and long-term effects of deprivation can be dramatically reduced by high quality care in crèches and institutions respectively.

- Type of separation – Some research has indicated that long-term separation due to death or illness, if accompanied by harmonious social support, has less of a long-term effect than separation due to divorce.

Privation of attachment in infancy

- According to Rutter (1981), the most serious long-term consequences for healthy infant development appear to be due to privation - a lack of some kind - rather than to any type of deprivation/loss. However, in his review of the research, Rutter found that the many proposed adverse effects of privation were **not** always **directly** due to a lack of an emotional attachment bond, but often to a deficiency of other important things that an attachment figure may provide (e.g. food, stimulation or even family unity), but an orphanage or dysfunctional family may not. An extreme example of this is the case of Genie (Curtiss, 1977).

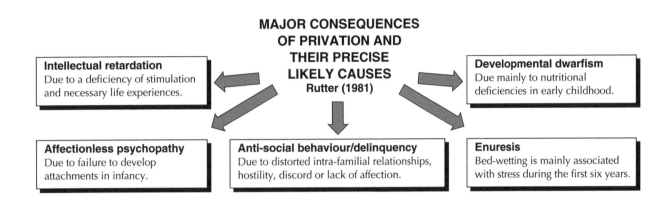

MAJOR CONSEQUENCES OF PRIVATION AND THEIR PRECISE LIKELY CAUSES
Rutter (1981)

Intellectual retardation
Due to a deficiency of stimulation and necessary life experiences.

Developmental dwarfism
Due mainly to nutritional deficiencies in early childhood.

Affectionless psychopathy
Due to failure to develop attachments in infancy.

Anti-social behaviour/delinquency
Due to distorted intra-familial relationships, hostility, discord or lack of affection.

Enuresis
Bed-wetting is mainly associated with stress during the first six years.

MEDIATING FACTORS
Factors likely to affect the severity of privation effects include:
- **Type of childcare available** - orphanages, for example, which provide a high standard of care may reduce the effects of lack of stimulation or stress, but may still have a high turnover of staff that prevents attachments forming with the orphans.
- **The duration of the privation** - the longer the time delay before making an attachment, the greater the chance of failure to form an attachment and thus developing affectionless psychopathy. Although research unequivocally says that experiences at all ages have an impact it seems likely that the first few years do have a special importance for bond formation and social development.
- **Temperament and resilience of the child** - perhaps most importantly, there has been the repeated finding that many children are not excessively damaged by early privation, and that the effects of it can be reversed.

EVIDENCE FOR THE REVERSIBILITY OF PRIVATION EFFECTS

CASE STUDIES OF EXTREME PRIVATION
Freud and Dann (1951) studied six 3-year-old orphans from a concentration camp who had not been able to form attachment to their parents. These children did not develop affectionless psychopathy, probably because they formed close attachments with each other (rather like the two twins raised in extreme privation studied by Koluchova, 1972), and despite developing a number of emotional problems, their intellectual recovery was unimpaired.

Such extreme case studies clearly involve many sources of privation, not just of attachment figures, but also indicate the strong resilience that children's development can show.

ISOLATED RHESUS MONKEYS
Novak and Harlow (1975) found that rhesus monkeys kept in social isolation from birth could develop reasonably normally if they were given 'therapy' by later being allowed to occasionally play with monkeys of their own age.

However, despite indicating the possibility of recovery from total social isolation, generalising the results from rhesus deprivation studies to human deprivation ignores the large differences between the two species.

ADOPTION STUDIES
Hodges and Tizard (1989) found that institutionalised children (who had not formed a stable attachment), adopted between the ages of two and seven, could form close attachments to their adoptive parents.

However, the children returned to their own families had more problems forming attachments and all the institutionalised children had problems with relationships outside their family.

Kadushin (1976) studied over 90 cases of late adoption, where the children were over five years old, and found highly successful outcomes, indicating that early privation does not necessarily prevent later attachment.

'Social and family relationships of ex-institutional adolescents' Hodges and Tizard (1989)

AIM

To investigate (longitudinally and with a matched comparison group of control children) whether experiencing early institutionalisation with ever-changing care-givers until at least two years of age will lead to long term problems in adolescence for adopted and restored children. Early studies by Bowlby (1951) and Goldfarb (1943a) found that there were many short and long term effects of the early institutionalisation of children, which were attributed to maternal deprivation or privation and were regarded as largely irreversible. However, later studies by Tizard and others on a group of adopted, fostered and restored children with early institutional experience showed that there were markedly less dramatic effects on intellectual and emotional development (probably due to improved conditions) but still difficulties in interpersonal relationships. The children were studied at age 4 and again at age 8, by which time the majority had formed close attachments to their parents, but showed, according to their teachers, more problems of attention seeking behaviour, disobedience, poor peer relationships and over-friendliness. The present study was conducted as a follow up study to see:

• If these children would continue to 'normalise' and lose further effects of early institutionalisation at age 16 or worsen with the stresses of adolescence.

• If adopted children would continue to do better than restored children by age 16, as earlier studies had indicated.

METHOD

Subjects:

All 51 children studied at age 8 were located, of which 42 were available to study at age 16. From these, 39 were interviewed: 23 adopted (17 boys, 6 girls), 11 restored (6 boys, 5 girls) and 5 in institutional care (3 boys, 2 girls). A comparison group of children who had not experienced institutionalisation was gathered for the **family** relationship study, matched, for example, in terms of age, gender, parental occupation and position in the family. Another comparison group of children who had not experienced institutionalisation was formed for the **school** relationship study from the classmate nearest in age of the same sex.

Procedure:

• The adolescents were interviewed on tape and completed the 'Questionnaire of Social Difficulty' (Lindsay and Lindsay, 1982).

• Mothers or careworkers were interviewed on tape and completed the 'A' scale questionnaire (Rutter et al, 1970).

• Teachers were asked to complete the 'B' scale questionnaire (Rutter et al, 1970) on the adolescent's behaviour.

RESULTS

• Institutionalised children differed in their degree of attachment to their parents in that
  a adopted children were **just as attached** to their parents as the comparison group
  b restored children were **less attached** to their parents than the comparison group and adopted children.

• Institutionalised children had **more problems** with siblings than the comparison group, especially the restored children.

• Adopted children were **more affectionate** with parents than restored children (who were less affectionate than the comparison group).

• No difference was found in confiding in, and support from, parents between institutionalised children and comparisons, although the former were less likely to turn to peers.

• Institutionalised children showed significantly worse peer relationships, were less likely to have a particular special friend, and were noted by teachers to be more quarrelsome and less liked by, and show more bullying of, other children.

EVALUATION

Methodological:

Longitudinal methods – Many advantages and disadvantages, e.g. loss of subjects using this method.

Design – Lack of control over this natural experiment, since children were obviously not randomly assigned to adoptive, restored and control groups, there always remains some doubt over the effect of the children's personality characteristics on the results.

Procedure – Problems of self-report questionnaires and interviews as far as socially desirable answers or deception is involved on the subject's part, and experimenter expectation on the interviewer's part.

Data analysis – A thorough statistical analysis was conducted on the results.

Ethical problems – Of asking children and their guardians questions that might disrupt their interpersonal relationships, e.g. asking mothers if they loved all their children equally.

Theoretical: Implies that while Bowlby was wrong about many of the more dramatic effects of early institutionalisation, some long lasting effects on interpersonal relations do persist into adolescence. Further follow up study needs to be conducted to see if adolescent behaviours and feelings persist into adulthood, however. There are some important practical implications for adoption practices from this study.

Links: Child attachment, longitudinal studies.

The effects of day care

WHAT IS DAY CARE AND WHY INVESTIGATE IT?

Day care refers to the minding of children by people other than the family they live with, either in their home or outside it, when the family is away during the day. Day care became an issue of concern as increasing levels of external female employment and the reduction of the extended home family in industrialised societies, led to a greater need for outside carers. These factors, combined with Bowlby's research on maternal deprivation and various social / political agendas, have created concern that day care will have:

1 Negative effects on children – although it is now clear that children can form multiple attachments and to carers other than the mother, the concern was that, once the mother went to work, there would be no consistent carer left to provide for the child's attachment and stimulation needs, and that outside carers would not meet these needs in the same way.

2 Negative effects on parents – in particular the sexist pressure of society on women to either stay at home to provide the care and feel frustrated (and possibly resent, and thus negatively affect, their child care) or go to work and feel guilty about the effects it may have.

Overall, research has tended to reveal no significant negative effects of high quality day care. Early studies were a little too simplistic in their approach and the current opinion is that the effects of day care depend upon an interaction of influences.

PARENTAL INFLUENCES

Parents can affect:
- The security of their children's attachment bond through their sensitivity / responsiveness
- The level of stimulation they provide outside of day care
- The quality of day care through their economic status and concern over choices available
- The amount of time away

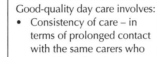

QUALITY OF DAY CARE

Good-quality day care involves:
- Consistency of care – in terms of prolonged contact with the same carers who are able to devote sufficient time
- Quality of stimulation – in terms of degree of verbal interaction, emotional responsiveness and activity resources.

CHILD INFLUENCES

There are individual differences in how children respond to day care based upon, for example:
- Their prior temperament and sociability, e.g. level of shyness
- Their prior security of attachment
- The age at which they experience day care

RESEARCH METHODOLOGY

Assessment of the emotional, social and cognitive effects of day care depends upon the validity of the tests used to measure them. The Strange Situation method may not be a valid test of emotional effects in some studies since the child could have other (or more important) attachment figures than the mother who are not involved in the test. Also, the reactions day care children show on their mother's return may reflect their increasing independence or enjoyment of day care rather than just their emotional reaction to her. Different studies may use different cognitive and IQ tests of varying reliability and validity.

SOCIAL-EMOTIONAL EFFECTS

- It has been suggested that day care could result in:
  1 The child being unable to form an attachment (causing privation effects) or disruption to the bond if attachment had been already made (causing deprivation effects).
  2 Increased sociability and social skills due to greater exposure to the outside world.
- Belsky and Rovine (1988) found infants were more likely to develop insecure attachments if they received day care for over 20 hours per week before they were a year old, while other research in America has linked greater child care with worse peer relationships and emotional health.
- However, these effects are not inevitable and may ignore the pre-existing attachments and quality of day care.
- Kagan et al (1980) set up their own nursery with consistent and high quality day care and compared 33 infants from a variety of backgrounds who attended it from 3.5 months of age with a matched home care control group. They found no significantly consistent differences between the two groups in attachment and sociability.
- Clarke-Stewart et al (1994) found peer relationships were more advanced in children who had experienced day care.
- Other research indicates that the length of time in day care in itself does not significantly affect attachment and that the individual differences children show to it is more related to the quality and consistency of the day care, maternal sensitivity and the child's pre-existing characteristics.

COGNITIVE EFFECTS

- It has also been suggested that day care could result in:
  1 Less verbal interaction, stimulation and exploration by the child due to a lack of a secure attachment figure as a base, if the day carers encourage quietness and passivity, do not want to form emotional attachments and are often changed.
  2 More stimulation, interaction and educational activities for children who would not otherwise receive them.
- Operation Headstart in the USA in the mid-1960s involved several hundred thousand socially disadvantaged pre-school children receiving intensive day care education. Initial short term gains in school and cognitive performance were found as well as longer term academic and social benefits.
- While the limited duration of the school performance gains in the Headstart programme and those studies that find worse cognitive development if day care takes place before one year of age should not be ignored, it should be noted that the cognitive effects depend upon the quality of day care *relative to that the child would otherwise have received*.
- Andersson (1992) conducted a longitudinal study on 100 Swedish children and found those who entered day care before the age of one had better school performance at age 8 and 13 than those who did not have any day care (who performed the worst). However, the former did have richer parents. Sweden has very high standards of day care and its greater parental leave allowance probably enables stronger attachments to be made before the child enters day care.

Freud's psychoanalytic theory of personality

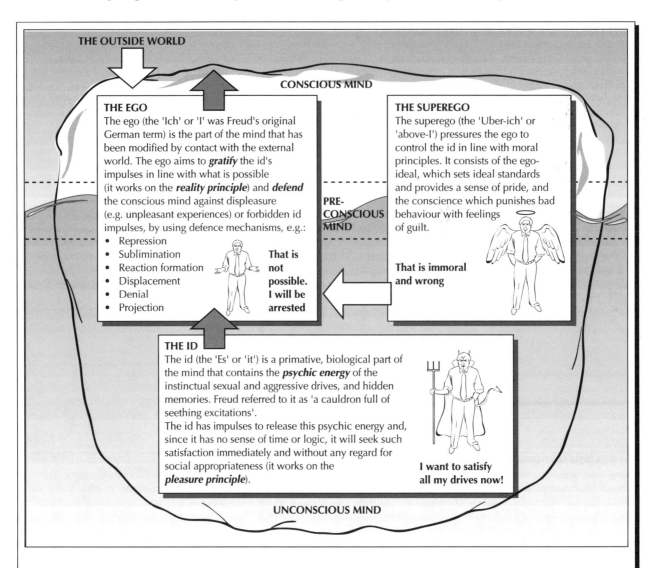

THE OUTSIDE WORLD

CONSCIOUS MIND

THE EGO
The ego (the 'Ich' or 'I' was Freud's original German term) is the part of the mind that has been modified by contact with the external world. The ego aims to *gratify* the id's impulses in line with what is possible (it works on the *reality principle*) and *defend* the conscious mind against displeasure (e.g. unpleasant experiences) or forbidden id impulses, by using defence mechanisms, e.g.:
- Repression
- Sublimation
- Reaction formation
- Displacement
- Denial
- Projection

That is not possible. I will be arrested

PRE-CONSCIOUS MIND

THE SUPEREGO
The superego (the 'Uber-ich' or 'above-I') pressures the ego to control the id in line with moral principles. It consists of the ego-ideal, which sets ideal standards and provides a sense of pride, and the conscience which punishes bad behaviour with feelings of guilt.

That is immoral and wrong

THE ID
The id (the 'Es' or 'it') is a primative, biological part of the mind that contains the *psychic energy* of the instinctual sexual and aggressive drives, and hidden memories. Freud referred to it as 'a cauldron full of seething excitations'.
The id has impulses to release this psychic energy and, since it has no sense of time or logic, it will seek such satisfaction immediately and without any regard for social appropriateness (it works on the *pleasure principle*).

I want to satisfy all my drives now!

UNCONSCIOUS MIND

FREUD'S TOPOGRAPHICAL MODEL
This divided the mind into three levels or layers of consciousness (these can be illustrated with the iceberg analogy above):
1 **The Conscious** –This contains all we are directly aware of, but only represents 'the tip of the iceberg' since although we may think we know why we do things, we often do not. According to Freud, unconscious causes are of great importance.
2 **The Pre-conscious** – This contains material that can become conscious.
3 **The Unconscious** – The part of the mind that is not accessible and contains our inner drives and repressed experiences. It is also where the unconscious struggles that affect our behaviour take place. The unconscious mind resembles a hydraulic closed energy system (like a steam engine) in that psychic energy from the drives builds up and, if not released, causes inner pressure or anxiety.

FREUD'S STRUCTURAL MODEL
Freud also suggested a model that involved dynamic struggle between three aspects of the mind – the **id**, **ego** and **superego** (illustrated above). The ego has the task of satisfying the demands of the id, superego and society, as well as attempting to keep unpleasant experiences out of consciousness. These *conflicting influences* have many important *consequences* for human behaviour, including *dreams, the development of personality traits* and *disordered behaviour*.

FREUD'S DREAM THEORY
- Freud suggested that dreams represent *unfulfilled wishes* from the id, which try to break into consciousness and seek satisfaction while we are 'off guard'. Dreams are the way these id wishes are *disguised* by the dream censor using defensive measures such as *symbolism* (using a dream image or event to stand for an id wish), condensation (the merging of many unconscious meanings into one dream image) and *displacement* (where emotions are separated from their true source and attached to trivial sources in the dream). Dreams still demonstrate many aspects of id 'thinking', being so disjointed, illogical, and generally showing little appreciation for time and reality, but can still act as the '*guardians of sleep*' to protect us from our own unconscious while asleep.
- Dreams are thus a very important source of unconscious information since, by undoing the 'dreamwork' of the *manifest content* of the dream (what is consciously remembered) the *latent content* (the hidden id impulses or meaning) can be discovered. This is achieved by free associating to each element of the manifest content to trace it back to the latent content, decoding the symbolism of the manifest content (some symbols are personal but many have universal meanings, e.g. phallic symbols such as guns and knives) and identifying the event (within the previous 24 hours according to Freud) that acted as the trigger for the dream.

Freud's stage theory and personality development

PSYCHOSEXUAL STAGES OF DEVELOPMENT

Drives and development – Freud proposed that we are driven or motivated by our *instinctual drives*, which come from two basic instincts. Thanatos, the death instinct, is responsible for aggressive drives, whereas Eros, the life instinct, is responsible for the sex drive or libido. Freud saw the life instinct and sex drive as exerting the most influence in the early years of life and thus childhood is a time of key importance in personality development.

Freud proposed a stage theory of infantile psychosexual development that suggested that children are polymorphously perverse – able to derive sexual pleasure from any part of their bodies, but as they grow older the sexual drive becomes focused upon (and seeks expression and satisfaction from) different parts of the body. The stages are governed by biological maturation.

The stages of psychosexual development

- **Oral stage** – where pleasure is gained first from passively and dependently sucking and swallowing (the oral receptive sub-stage) and later, as the teeth emerge, from biting and chewing (the oral aggressive sub-stage).
- **Anal stage** – gratification shifts to the anus where pleasure is gained first from expelling and playing with faeces (the expulsive sub-stage) and then, during toilet training, from holding on to and controlling bowel movements (the retentive sub-stage).
- **Phallic stage** – from around 3 to 5 or 6 years of age the libido becomes focused upon the genitals, and pleasure involving them becomes directed towards the opposite sex parent. Both boys and girls at this age unconsciously desire the opposite sex parent, but differ slightly in the way they deal with this situation, which Freud termed the Oedipus Complex.
  The Oedipus complex for boys involves sexual attraction towards the mother and wishing his rival for the mother's affection, his father, out of the way (ideally dead). However, the boy fears that the more powerful father will discover his illicit desires and will punish by depriving the boy of what he currently holds most dear – his phallus. This 'castration complex' is resolved when, out of fear of castration, the boy identifies with the father figure, introjecting all his values, attitudes and behaviour, so that in becoming like his father the boy can indirectly have the mother through his fantasies and later grow up to have mother-like figures in the same way as his father.
  The Oedipus complex for girls (sometimes referred to as the Electra Complex) involves the girl's desire for the father. The girl believes that she has already been castrated, and out of penis envy she turns to her father to provide her with a symbolic penis substitute – a baby. However, out of fear of losing her mother's love plus the symbolic gains of imitating a person the father is attached to, the girl identifies with her mother and by becoming like her she too can indirectly satisfy her sexual desires.
- **Latency stage** – after the turmoil of the phallic stage the child enters a stage where the child's desires diminish somewhat.
- **Genital stage** – occurs with the onset of puberty and involves the reawakening of the libido and its attachment to external love objects outside the family.

Id, ego and superego development – Freud suggested that by the end of the phallic stage, the three main aspects of the mind would have developed – the id, ego and superego. Babies begin life dominated by the unsocialised id, seeking immediate gratification (crying for food, sleeping and defecating) with no regard for time and place (as parents will testify!). The ego gradually develops through contact with the external world with all its restraints on behaviour, thus toilet training during the anal stage is a particularly important time for its development. The ego is free from moral constraint until the superego develops, mainly as a result of the internalisation of parental values in the Oedipus complex.

STAGES AND PERSONALITY DEVELOPMENT

Fixation and trauma - Freud therefore believed that the early years of development are of utmost importance, since the experiences of childhood shape the structure of the unconscious mind and the majority of human personality. Freud suggested that too much or too little pleasure at a stage might lead to *fixation* at it, causing the individual in later life to still want to indulge in its pleasures (stage *regression*). For example fixation at the oral receptive stage due to over-indulgence (the slightest whimper brought food and oral gratification) may lead to an optimistic personality or one that gains pleasure from being dependent and passive. Any traumatic events, especially of a sexual nature, in early life might also become hidden in the unconscious and influence later behaviour.

Defence mechanisms and stage fixations

The ego cannot allow many of the id's sexual and aggressive impulses to reach respectable, adult, conscious life and so uses defence mechanisms to control, alter, deny or redirect the impulses whenever they may occur. Ego defence mechanisms used to cope with fixations may thus affect personality, e.g.:

- **Sublimation** – usually the most successful defence, it allows the expression of id impulses through behaviour that is a socially acceptable symbolic alternative. For example fixation at the oral stage may later lead to seeking oral pleasure, not from sucking the mother's breast in public, but from sucking at one's thumb, pen or cigarette. Anal expulsive desires to handle faeces may lead to an enjoyment of pottery. A phallically fixated desire to expose one's penis may lead to a later sublimated career choice of a fireman, who can happily drive large hoses and extending ladders with much attention through the streets, after sliding down the fire station pole (Kline, 1984).
- **Repression** – not a very successful defence in the long term since it just involves forcing disturbing wishes, ideas or memories into the unconscious where, although hidden, they will create psychic pressure or anxiety and constantly seek expression. Thus someone may repress homosexual feelings and become a latent (hidden) homosexual who may consciously report attraction to the opposite sex, but has to use other defence mechanisms, such as denial or reaction formation, to control their unconscious urges.
- **Reaction formation** – if unconscious impulses become too powerful then the ego can only maintain control by forcing the individual to consciously feel and act in *exactly the opposite* way to that unconsciously desired. Thus latent homosexuals may feel and show an excessive hatred of overt homosexuals, while those with an 'anal character' (an exaggerated concern for orderliness, cleanliness, control and routine) may be reacting against their anal expulsive desires to mess. If while reading this you are getting a little *too* angry in your objection to some of Freud's ideas, then your ego is probably helping you react against your anxiety provoking unconscious recognition of their truth!

There are many other defence mechanisms, like *displacement* where feelings are expressed by redirecting them onto something or somebody powerless and convenient rather than the original cause (we do not slam a door because we hate it!). They make humans and their society the way they are. Without the restraints defence mechanisms impose, civilisation would not be possible.

Balance – Freud also argued that the overall balance between the id, ego and superego would affect personality. A strong superego, for example, might result in a very moral person while a very weak one may result in an emotional psychopath. An over influential id might lead to irresponsible and impulsive behaviour or even violence and crime.

Jung's analytical psychology

JUNG & ANALYTICAL PSYCHOLOGY ASSUMPTIONS

Carl Gustav Jung (1875–1961) was a Swiss psychiatrist who worked in a Zurich mental hospital before moving on to his own private practice. He was, at first, a favourite disciple of Freud's, and applied psychoanalytic concepts to his study of schizophrenics, but increasingly developed his own theories that differed from Freud's Psychoanalysis and the two men parted company on bad terms in 1913. Jung pursued his 'Analytical Psychology', and developed a range of theories on personality and mental disorder.

In contrast to Freud, Jung put greater emphasis on:

- Processes occurring *within* the individual rather than on the relationships between individuals and society. Jung regarded the goal or end point of development as *individuation* – the self-actualisation of the individual's potential and the achievement of psychic balance, the integration of opposites and self-realisation.
  Thoughts, emotions and behaviour result from a *self-regulating* psyche / mind that constantly tries to *seek balance* and integration between the conscious and unconscious, and between different aspects of personality. Imbalance will cause *compensations*. Compensations result in personality characteristics, dreams and symptoms of mental disorder.
- Spiritual and religious rather than physical aspects of human nature – people seek more than honour, power, wealth, fame, and the love of women as Freud put it. Jung believed everyone needs a myth or set of beliefs to live by to give their life some meaning and purpose. These myths do not necessarily have to be objectively 'true' to have this positive function. If people become alienated from their beliefs, as indeed Jung himself felt alienated from Orthodox Christianity, anxiety and a sense of incompleteness results.

METHODS

Jung employed similar methods to Freud, but often used and interpreted them in different ways.

- **Analysis and interpretation of symbolism** – Jung spent more time on the cross-cultural study of symbolism in mythology. He frequently found important similarities in the myths and symbols of cultures that did not seem to have any contact with each other, especially mystical 'mandala' symbols, such as circular shapes, crosses or other divisions of four, that represent psychic balance and harmony. He interpreted this as evidence for a collective unconscious.
- **Word association tests** - like free association, a person has to reply with the first word that comes to mind that is associated with other words. Jung carried this out in a more scientific way, not just recording the associated word but also measuring the exact time it took for an association to be made to each word in his list as well as the physiological response to it (recorded by skin conductance using a polygraph or 'lie-detector' apparatus). Collections of words that produced variations from normal responses would indicate a common emotional link or 'complex'.
- **Dream interpretation** – Jung disagreed with Freud that dreams are always disguised wish fulfilment resulting from past circumstances. Jung suggested that dreams reflect current preoccupations and may be compensations for conscious attitudes and behaviour that are causing imbalance. Dreams are a symbolic language, difficult to always understand in linguistic terms, but not deliberately disguised. Dreams come from everyday emotional problems in the personal unconscious (and may suggest ways of solving such problems in the future) or from images/symbols from the deeper collective unconscious.

THEORY OF THE UNCONSCIOUS

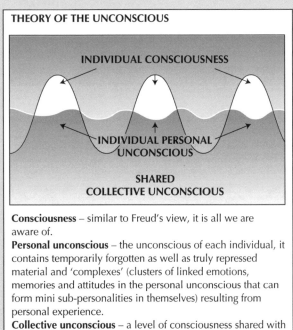

Consciousness – similar to Freud's view, it is all we are aware of.

Personal unconscious – the unconscious of each individual, it contains temporarily forgotten as well as truly repressed material and 'complexes' (clusters of linked emotions, memories and attitudes in the personal unconscious that can form mini sub-personalities in themselves) resulting from personal experience.

Collective unconscious – a level of consciousness shared with other members of our species that contains common archetypes. Archetypes are inherited predispositions to feel, act and experience the world in certain ways, thus people may behave in similar ways as their ancestors and people in other cultures they have never met. Important archetypes include The Persona (our social mask), The Shadow (our animal urges, similar to the id but more positive in its influence) and The Anima/Animus (our female or male sides).

THEORY OF PERSONALITY

Jung's analytical psychology suggests the psyche has many aspects and that personality can be influenced unconsciously by complexes and archetypes. In addition, however, Jung suggested that personality is also shaped by how we consciously react towards and experience the world.

Extraversion and introversion – These are two attitudes or ways of directing our libido (Jung saw this as more of a general life force rather than just sexual energy) towards the world. *Introverts* direct their libido inwards towards their mental world and so prefer to keeps themselves to themselves, avoid excessive social contact, and may be somewhat self-absorbed. *Extraverts* direct their libido outwards to the external world and so have an outgoing, confident and friendly nature that adapts easily to situations and seeks social stimulation.

The four functions – These are ways of experiencing the world:
Sensation (registering the existence of things)
Thinking (identifying and understanding things)
Feeling (judging the pleasantness or worth of things)
Intuition (anticipating or predicting things).

Jung suggested one function might predominate, and that sensation and intuition were opposed to each other, as were thinking and feeling. Thus those guided by emotion might not think logically through decisions, while those always anticipating the future might be blind to things happening under their very noses.

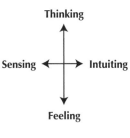

Evaluation of Freud's and Jung's theories

Freud's methods
- Freud used an unrepresentative sample and lacked objective data upon which to base his theory. He mostly studied himself, his disordered patients and only one child in detail. Freud thought this unimportant, believing in only a quantitative difference between people – we are all neurotic to some extent, including himself. Freud's case notes consisted of his memories of his clients' memories (often of early childhood), however since he regarded many childhood recollections as fantasies anyway he guessed at what had taken place in his patient's past.
- Freud may have shown researcher bias in his interpretations – since he originally wanted a general theory of sexual causation that would "open all secrets with a single key" he may have tended to interpret all symbols as sexual, only pay attention to or remember information that supported his theories and ignore information or other explanations that did not fit them. E.g. Little Hans' horse phobia may have resulted from his fright on seeing a horse collapse rather than an unconscious fear of castration from the father (Hans had actually been threatened with castration, but by his mother).

Psychoanalytic Theory
- Freud over-emphasised sexual causes – Breuer even said Freud was prone to "excessive generalisation".
- Freud's theory was biased by a cultural, sexist male viewpoint, e.g. on female inferiority and penis envy.
- The unconscious is difficult to test objectively.
- The theory is very good at explaining but not predicting behaviour. Symbolism is so vague and subjective, and defence mechanisms are so flexible, that they can be used to support any theory of the unconscious, indeed they seem to make Freudian theory unrefutable (incapable of being shown wrong) and thus unscientific e.g. any research finding the exact opposite of what Freudian theory would predict could be explained through the defence of reaction formation. Kline (1972) argued that psychoanalytic theory can be broken down into testable hypotheses if they are made *two-tailed* to predict either outcome and refutable by finding no significant effect.

Freud's contribution
- Freud developed his theory throughout his life and proposed explanations for a huge variety of phenomena, from humour and forgetting to crowd behaviour, customs and warfare. Many psychologists and psychoanalysts, although often disagreeing with some of his ideas, have been inspired by his theories to develop their own. Psychoanalytic terms and concepts have become ingrained into western psychology and society, and Psychoanalysis is still practised today.
- Philosophers and writers had long considered the importance the unconscious, dream interpretation, defence mechanisms etc. whereas Freud's more original ideas concerning them have been criticised, leading psychologists, e.g. Eysenck (1985), to agree with Ebbinghaus that "what is new in these theories is not true, and what is true is not new".
- More negatively, Freud's Oedipus complex may have led to genuine cases of child abuse being dismissed as childhood sexual fantasies.

EVALUATION OF FREUD'S PSYCHODYNAMIC THEORIES

Subsequent research
- Reviews of research attempting to scientifically validate Freudian concepts are largely negative in their conclusions, because it is difficult to show that the unconscious mechanisms Freud proposed are responsible.
- Freud emphasised the importance of the Oedipus complex, calling it the `kernel of neurosis` yet while Social Learning Theory research has found imitation of same sex parents does occur, there has been no conclusive evidence that unconscious motives like castration fear are responsible.
- Freud regarded repression as `the cornerstone on which the whole of psychoanalysis rests`, yet although research has linked trauma to amnesia, the degree to which repressed events are truly unconscious has been questioned and other causes have been suggested as more likely.
- While *Kline and Storey* (1977) found evidence for oral and anal personality traits by using personality questionnaires, it has not been demonstrated that these traits have been caused by Freudian fixation at a stage.

- Freud suggested that a woman's desire for a baby was a symbolic substitute for their desire to gain the penis they envy in men and feel they have been deprived of. Harris and Campbell (1999) investigated whether unconscious motivations might be involved in pregnancy. They thought pregnancy might involve other symbolic gains. Harris gave semi-structured interviews to 128 North London women designed to measure the quality of their lives and sexual partnerships and their degree of *secondary gain* from becoming pregnant (e.g. an improvement in their circumstances or relationships). Women with unplanned pregnancies were found to be significantly more likely to have been in a situation of secondary gain, especially relating to their partnerships, than women with planned pregnancies or no pregnancy. This was particularly the case for those women with unplanned pregnancies who were shocked when they found out they were pregnant. Unfortunately the study cannot conclusively demonstrate that the motivations were truly unconscious – the women were not asked to rate the secondary gain themselves and there are problems relying on retrospective data (based on their memory of events before they were pregnant) gained from interview and self report methods (the secondary gain scale only had an inter-rater reliability of .69)

- **Developmental theory** – Jung focuses very much on the development of the *individual* and their inner life, and tends to ignore human relationships, the past and childhood experiences.
- **The collective unconscious and archetypes** – While evolutionary theory also argues for inherited species-specific characteristics and tendencies, the cross-cultural similarities in myth and symbolism Jung found could just have resulted from similar *experiences* shared by different cultures rather than a shared unconscious.

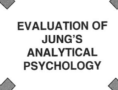

EVALUATION OF JUNG'S ANALYTICAL PSYCHOLOGY

- **Therapy** – Jung's therapy became increasingly focused on middle-aged clients with high levels of insight, time and money, and with relatively minor problems or just those seeking more meaning in their lives. Lacking objective therapeutic outcomes, it is unclear when full individuation is reached.
- **Contribution to psychology and society** – Jung's ideas have not been as popular as Freud's, perhaps because they were a little more mystical and obscure, and less clearly explained. However, some of Jung's ideas influenced humanist psychology and Eysenck used introversion and extraversion as the basis for his personality dimensions.

Social learning theory and personality development

- Social Learning Theory (later re-named Social Cognitive Theory by Bandura) was developed to create a learning theory that went beyond the behaviourist learning theories (e.g. of operant conditioning) to incorporate the important *cognitive processes* that humans seem to possess between the environmental stimuli they receive and the behavioural responses they make.
- Personality refers to relatively permanent characteristics possessed by individuals that may distinguish them from others and influence their behaviour in different situations. **Bandura and Walters** (1963) in their book '*Social Learning and Personality Development*' suggested that such characteristics would be acquired over time from **environmental experience** through **observational learning**. The 'development' of personality according to this theory would result from a continuous accumulation of experiences with age from every different environment encountered, which would rule out any fixed stages of development and would seem to imply an inconsistent 'personality', lacking permanent characteristics, that changed with every new experience.
- However, unlike behaviourist learning theorists who saw people as being passively programmed by their environment, Bandura saw humans as *actively influencing their environment* through their *cognitive abilities*, *acquired beliefs* and the *effects of their behaviour*, which may lead to some characteristics persisting longer than might otherwise be expected in a changing environment.

THE ENVIRONMENT

Includes the physical and social environment. **Models** provide information about *behaviour* (actions, statements, skills etc.) and its *consequences* (whether it leads to positive or negative outcomes). Important sources of models are:

| The media | The family | The peer group |

THE PERSON

Bandura perceives the person as actively influencing the world as well as being influenced by it. Every person possesses:

- **Observation learning ability** – being able to automatically learn behaviour from just being exposed to models, without the need for reinforcement.
- **Cognitive processes** – such as *attention* and *memory* abilities that may change with age and allow the person to:
  1 focus on relevant models and behaviour, e.g. based on past memories of who and what is most useful and appropriate to imitate in a given environment.
  2 store a memory representation of how to reproduce what was said or done.
  3 remember information concerning the past consequences of the behaviour, e.g. whether they saw it rewarded in others, whether they were rewarded for it themselves or if they felt good about it last time (self-reinforcement).
- **Cognitive beliefs** – such as *self-efficacy* (the person's belief in their ability to effectively achieve their goals) or the morality of behaviour (conscience).
- **Physical characteristics** – which also affect interactions with the environment and the ability to imitate certain behaviour.

BEHAVIOUR

Behaviour is imitated if:

- proper attention is paid to the model that produced it.
- the behaviour is effectively stored.
- desirable consequences are expected for the behaviour (or at least unfavourable ones are not expected).
- the person believes they are able to successfully imitate the model (self-efficacy).
- the person is physically capable of imitating the model.

A person's behaviour influences other people and the environment, which in turn will influence the person's future behaviour. This interaction of influences is known as **reciprocal determinism**.

EVALUATION OF SOCIAL LEARNING THEORY OF PERSONALITY

- The theory incorporates many important social, cognitive and learning influences upon the development of personality.
- It is questionable just how much Social Learning Theory can tell us about the *development* of personality and how enduring and consistent learnt personality characteristics really are.
- The theory neglects the role of innate, biological factors upon the development of personality, e.g. the genetic inheritance of traits.

Gender development – terms and issues

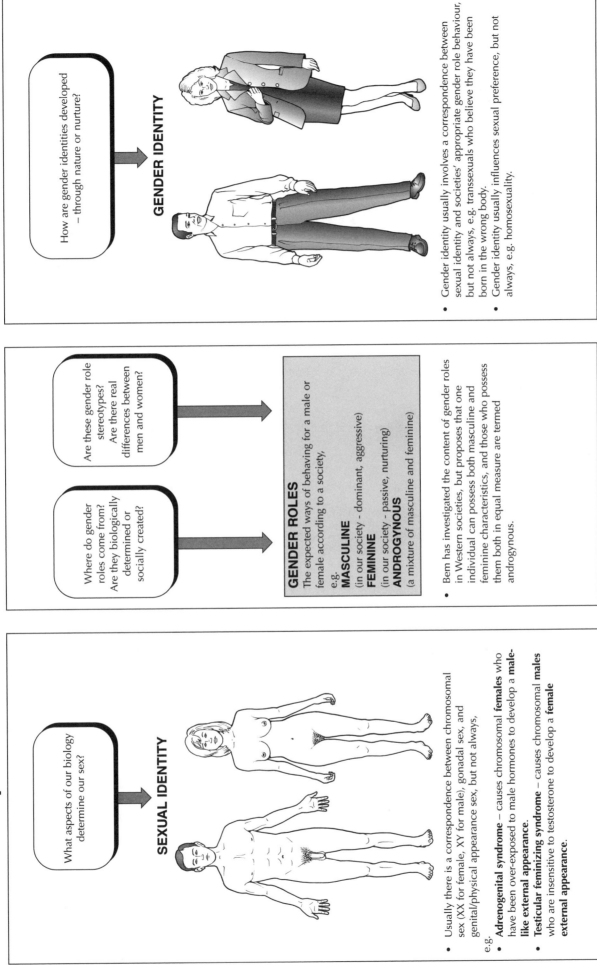

GENDER IDENTITY

How are gender identities developed – through nature or nurture?

- Gender identity usually involves a correspondence between sexual identity and societies' appropriate gender role behaviour, but not always, e.g. transsexuals who believe they have been born in the wrong body.
- Gender identity usually influences sexual preference, but not always, e.g. homosexuality.

GENDER ROLES

Where do gender roles come from? Are they biologically determined or socially created?

Are these gender role stereotypes? Are there real differences between men and women?

GENDER ROLES
The expected ways of behaving for a male or female according to a society,
e.g.
MASCULINE
(in our society - dominant, aggressive)
FEMININE
(in our society - passive, nurturing)
ANDROGYNOUS
(a mixture of masculine and feminine)

- Bem has investigated the content of gender roles in Western societies, but proposes that one individual can possess both masculine and feminine characteristics, and those who possess them both in equal measure are termed androgynous.

SEXUAL IDENTITY

What aspects of our biology determine our sex?

- Usually there is a correspondence between chromosomal sex (XX for female, XY for male), gonadal sex, and genital/physical appearance sex, but not always,
e.g.
- **Adrenogenital syndrome** – causes chromosomal **females** who have been over-exposed to male hormones to develop a **male-like external appearance.**
- **Testicular feminizing syndrome** – causes chromosomal **males** who are insensitive to testosterone to develop a **female external appearance.**

Gender development – biologically based theories

THE BIOLOGICAL APPROACH

- The biological approach proposes that the development of gender is dictated by **physiological processes** within the individual and occurs as **biological maturation** takes place.

- From an **evolutionary** point of view, the human male appears to have been equipped with greater physical strength, aggression and visuospatial ability, but lower sensitivity to pain (perhaps adapting them better for hunting/competition), whereas women seem to have evolved more regular activity levels and greater social sensitivity and verbal ability (perhaps adapting them better for more passive/nurturing behaviour).

- These supposedly natural behavioural tendencies are regulated by **hormone** levels – just as hormones trigger the physical changes of puberty, so they also affect the thoughts and behaviour of males and females. The hormone **testosterone** seems especially active in triggering the increased amounts of aggression and 'rough and tumble' play that males show even at young ages.

EVIDENCE FOR THE BIOLOGICAL APPROACH

- **Money** (1972) studied 25 girls with **adrenogenital syndrome** due to an overdose of male hormones while in the womb, and found that 20 of them showed **'tomboyish' behaviour** – showing greater interest in outdoor activity and less in dolls, childcare and self adornment.

- **Imperato-McGinley et al** (1974) studied members of the **Batista family** who, due to a mutant gene, were born with the external features of (and grew up as) young girls, but **physically changed into men** at puberty. The large increase in testosterone at puberty activated a process that should have occurred during embryonic development and their vaginas healed over, their testicles descended, they grew full sized penises and became men – showing **masculine behaviour** (including marrying women).

- **Animal studies** have shown that female monkeys **given testosterone** show male monkey behaviours, such as increased aggressiveness, dominance and even sexual behaviour.

CRITICISMS OF THE BIOLOGICAL APPROACH

- Girls with adrenogenital syndrome may show more masculine behaviour because they look like males, and therefore may be **treated like males**, rather than because of the testosterone.

- The Batistas may have been able to adopt masculine behaviour more readily, despite being raised as girls, because of their **supportive environment**, rather than biological changes.

- The evidence of the link between testosterone levels and aggression is often correlational. Studies have shown that testosterone levels can increase **after** successful dominant behaviour.

- It is not legitimate to generalise from animal gender studies to human gender behaviour.

THE BIOSOCIAL APPROACH

- The biosocial approach moves **away from** the **direct** influence of **physiological** factors on gender behaviour and identity, and focuses on the **interaction** of biological and social factors:

  a **Biological predispositions** for male babies to be more irritable and harder to pacify than female babies may lead to different **social reactions** from the caregivers around them. Male babies may, therefore, be treated as more independent and aggressive than female babies, and may become so.

  b The **anatomy** (physical appearance) of males and females may serve as a **cue** for the **social labels** and expectations that society possesses for masculine and feminine behaviours.

  c **Social factors** have a **greater influence** upon gender identity and behaviour than biological ones, but there may be a **critical** or **sensitive time period** to acquire gender identity.

EVIDENCE FOR THE BIOSOCIAL APPROACH

- **Money and Ehrhardt** (1972) studied girls with adrenogenital syndrome who were raised and treated as boys because of their male looking genitalia. If the mistaken classification was discovered and **corrected before the age of three**, then adjustment to the new gender usually proceeded without many problems. However, this was not the case after three years.

- **Money and Ehrhardt** (1972) also studied chromosomal males with testicular feminizing syndrome, which caused them to be raised as females due to their female external appearance. In the majority of all cases these individuals identified fully with their (female) role of upbringing regardless of their underlying biology.

- Cases of **sexual reassignment** for penis amputation and hermaphrodites have also supported the notion that social and psychological factors outweigh the influence of biological factors in the development of gender identities.

CRITICISMS OF THE BIOSOCIAL APPROACH

- There have been some cases which have **contradicted** the **critical age** of reassignment idea, such as the Batistas.

- Most of the studies supporting the biosocial approach involve individuals with **unusual biological conditions**, and so may **not** be **representative** of gender role development in the majority of the population.

Gender development – psychological theories

PSYCHOANALYTIC THEORY

- Freud suggested that the **Oedipus complex** could adequately account for the development of gender role behaviour (although he was less certain about the so called electra complex for girls).
- The successful **internalisation** of the **same sex parent's** behaviour at the end of the Oedipus complex is crucial to the development of gender identity and sexual orientation. **Both** parents need to be present for this to occur.
- Freud would argue that gender identity is virtually **complete** by the age of **five or six.**

EVIDENCE FOR THE APPROACH

Freud's ideas have not received much experimental support, although Hetherington (1966) reports that the absence of the father before the age of four tends to make boys less masculine and females more awkward in their later interactions with men.

CRITICISMS

- Freud's theory has been criticised on many grounds, but especially for the electra complex and the notion of penis envy, even by other psychoanalysts such as Horney (1924).
- Many studies of children brought up by 'untypical' Freudian families, for example composed of single parents or homosexual/lesbian parents, have found that 'normal' gender role development occurs in virtually all cases.
- Freud's theory ignores the many other influences, both biological and social, that will affect a child's gender development.

SOCIAL LEARNING THEORY

- Proposes that gender identity/behaviour is **learnt** through **observation, imitation** and **behaviour shaping.**
- Gender role behaviour for both sexes is learnt automatically through observation of male and female social models (such as parents, peers, media characters, etc.) but the **performance** of the appropriate gender behaviour depends upon the reinforcement received (or expected) for it from society. Imitation causes gender identity.

EVIDENCE FOR THE APPROACH

There is evidence that society treats boys and girls in different ways:

- **Fagot** (1978) conducted **naturalistic observations** of parent/child interactions and found that boys were **encouraged** to be independent and active, girls to be dependent and passive.
- **Condry and Condry** (1976) **experimentally** showed that adult **perceptions** of, and reactions to, babies' behaviour change depending upon whether they think they are seeing a baby boy or girl.
- **Mead** (1935) proposed **cultural relativism** – gender roles depend upon the society, which supports the nurture rather than nature approach. Mead's study of New Guinea tribes found that men and women of the

    a Arapesh – both showed stereotypically western 'feminine' characteristics,
    b Mundugumour – both showed stereotypical 'masculine' characteristics,
    c Tchambuli – showed the reverse of western stereotypical gender roles.

CRITICISMS OF THE APPROACH

- **Maccoby and Jacklin** (1974) reviewed a large number of studies on gender acquisition and concluded the **evidence for imitation** is very **mixed** — especially for young children, who often imitate **both** parents.

COGNITIVE DEVELOPMENTAL THEORY

- Kohlberg (1966) argued that a child's **understanding** of its gender **develops** over time.
- The child classifies itself at around the age of three as male or female, and this **gender identity causes imitation** of appropriate masculine or feminine behaviour.
- Understanding of gender is complete at about 7, when the child realises that it remains **stable** over time and **constant** across situations.
- Bem proposes the idea of gender **schemas.**

EVIDENCE FOR THE APPROACH

Kohlberg (1966) questioned children aged around two or three about their understanding of gender. These children often **lacked**

- gender stability – thinking, for example, that they could become a mother **or** a father when they grew up, and
- gender constancy – illustrated, for example, by boys thinking that their gender could change if their hair grew long or they wore a dress.

CRITICISMS

- Many studies have shown that **gender** typical **behaviours** are shown by boys and girls at the age of **2 or less** (e.g. toy preference, Kuhn et al, 1978).
- Kohlberg's claim that gender constancy and stability only **start** at the age of **three** is contradicted by Money and Erhardt's finding that **gender reassignment** is **problematic after** this age.

Social development in adolescence 1

Adolescence is the transitional time between childhood and adulthood, associated with:
- Physiological changes – of puberty
- Social changes – in terms of new roles and responsibilities
- Cognitive changes – according to Piaget, formal operational thought allows the consideration of new possibilities, beliefs and self-conceptions.

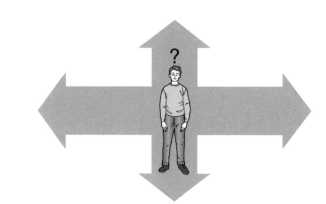

IDENTITY FORMATION IN ADOLESCENCE

TRADITIONAL/CLASSICAL VIEW
Identity crisis, storm and stress
The traditional view of identity formation in adolescence is that it involves a *fairly long period* of *identity crisis*, which may be experienced as *highly stressful* for the adolescent.

ALTERNATIVE VIEW
of adolescent identity development
The alternative view of identity formation in adolescence is that it does not always involve a long period of transition, that there may be little confusion over identity, and that it may not be experienced as highly stressful for the adolescent.

ERIKSON'S PSYCHOSOCIAL THEORY
Erikson, a psychodynamic theorist, suggested that all humans pass through 8, genetically determined **psychosocial crises** in their lives, each of which could have a **positive or negative outcome** for healthy personality development. The 5th stage occurred during adolescence (around 12–18 years) and concerned **identity versus role confusion**.

During a socially created **moratorium** (delay in becoming an adult) adolescents can try out different roles, attitudes, beliefs and even occupations to achieve a stable identity. Failure to do so, or choosing an identity too early (premature foreclosure of the moratorium), can result in identity/role confusion. This could lead to adopting an extreme **negative identity** (e.g. delinquent) rather than have no identity at all, problems with **intimacy** in close relationships, problems with **time perspective** in making plans for the future or problems with the level of **industry** (e.g. being unable to concentrate or concentrating too much on one task).

Evaluation
Marcia (1980) divided Erikson's 5th crisis into **4 identity statuses** (diffusion/confusion, foreclosure, moratorium and achievement) and used interviews to empirically test them. Marcia found evidence for increasing identity achievement with age, but the process may take longer than Erikson thought and may vary with gender and parental style of upbringing and across historical time periods and cultures. There could also be many aspects of identity, not all of which may be achieved at the same time (or ever).

CROSS-CULTURAL RESEARCH
Cross-cultural researchers, e.g. Mead (1928), have suggested that in many cultures there is no extended moratorium between childhood and adulthood but a swift transition – usually marked by some kind of initiation ritual (which may or may not be highly stressful). The western moratorium probably results from the educational, legal and career systems of industrialised, individualistic cultures, which are likely to create 'crises' with their emphasis upon freedom of choice and the complex set of opportunities and identities they provide. In collectivistic cultures, with traditional group identities, lifestyles and occupations these choices and pressures are less likely to exist and 'adolescents' will often unquestioningly accept parental occupations and identities (Marcia would see this as foreclosure, but no identity crisis necessarily results). In addition, rituals or rites of passage actually provide guidance and clarity about adult identity.

COLEMAN'S FOCAL THEORY
Coleman (1974) suggests that identity formation in adolescence does not always involve crisis and 'storm and stress'. Most issues and worries that adolescents have to deal with seem to peak (or come into focus) at different ages and only when several coincide at once will stress occur.

Evaluation
Coleman's theory has received a good deal of support from research studies. The objectivity of Mead's research has been questioned and problems with the interview method (she may have been misled by her participants) mean her conclusions may lack validity.

Social development in adolescence 2

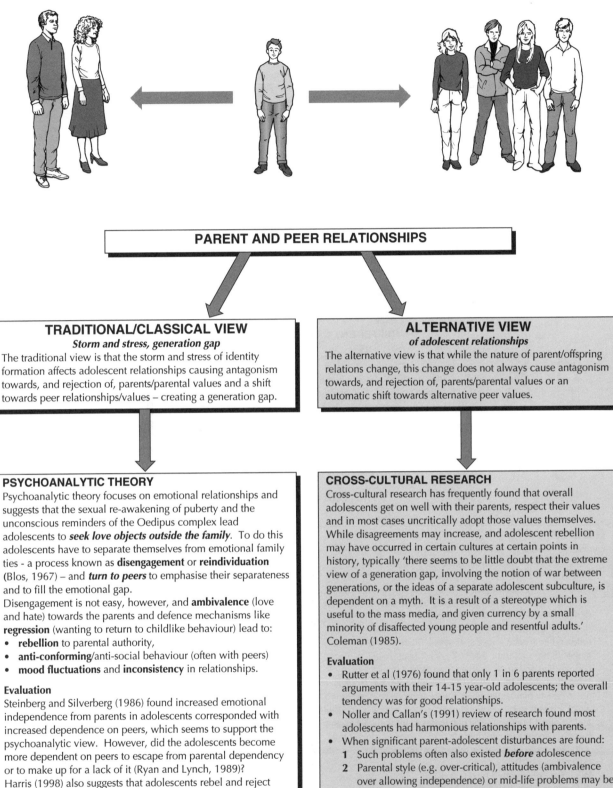

PARENT AND PEER RELATIONSHIPS

TRADITIONAL/CLASSICAL VIEW
Storm and stress, generation gap
The traditional view is that the storm and stress of identity formation affects adolescent relationships causing antagonism towards, and rejection of, parents/parental values and a shift towards peer relationships/values – creating a generation gap.

ALTERNATIVE VIEW
of adolescent relationships
The alternative view is that while the nature of parent/offspring relations change, this change does not always cause antagonism towards, and rejection of, parents/parental values or an automatic shift towards alternative peer values.

PSYCHOANALYTIC THEORY
Psychoanalytic theory focuses on emotional relationships and suggests that the sexual re-awakening of puberty and the unconscious reminders of the Oedipus complex lead adolescents to **seek love objects outside the family**. To do this adolescents have to separate themselves from emotional family ties - a process known as **disengagement** or **reindividuation** (Blos, 1967) – and **turn to peers** to emphasise their separateness and to fill the emotional gap.

Disengagement is not easy, however, and **ambivalence** (love and hate) towards the parents and defence mechanisms like **regression** (wanting to return to childlike behaviour) lead to:
- **rebellion** to parental authority,
- **anti-conforming**/anti-social behaviour (often with peers)
- **mood fluctuations** and **inconsistency** in relationships.

Evaluation
Steinberg and Silverberg (1986) found increased emotional independence from parents in adolescents corresponded with increased dependence on peers, which seems to support the psychoanalytic view. However, did the adolescents become more dependent on peers to escape from parental dependency or to make up for a lack of it (Ryan and Lynch, 1989)?

Harris (1998) also suggests that adolescents rebel and reject parental values in favour of peer values, often without conscious awareness of why they do it, but suggests an evolved tendency for peer group socialisation is responsible.

CROSS-CULTURAL RESEARCH
Cross-cultural research has frequently found that overall adolescents get on well with their parents, respect their values and in most cases uncritically adopt those values themselves. While disagreements may increase, and adolescent rebellion may have occurred in certain cultures at certain points in history, typically 'there seems to be little doubt that the extreme view of a generation gap, involving the notion of war between generations, or the ideas of a separate adolescent subculture, is dependent on a myth. It is a result of a stereotype which is useful to the mass media, and given currency by a small minority of disaffected young people and resentful adults.' Coleman (1985).

Evaluation
- Rutter et al (1976) found that only 1 in 6 parents reported arguments with their 14-15 year-old adolescents; the overall tendency was for good relationships.
- Noller and Callan's (1991) review of research found most adolescents had harmonious relationships with parents.
- When significant parent-adolescent disturbances are found:
  1. Such problems often also existed **before** adolescence
  2. Parental style (e.g. over-critical), attitudes (ambivalence over allowing independence) or mid-life problems may be just as (or more) responsible as adolescent behaviour.
- Attachment to peer/friendship groups does not necessarily involve disengagement from parental attachments.

Play – categories and factors

PARTEN'S (1932) CATEGORIES OF <u>SOCIAL</u> PLAY

Parten outlined 6 types of play based on her naturalistic observation of free play in nursery school children.

- **Unoccupied** – either doing nothing but looking around or showing random, purposeless actions.
- **Solitary** – absorbed in own individual activity and unconcerned with other children
- **Onlooker** – shows interest in other children's activities but does not join in.
- **Parallel** – playing side by side with others, even with the same kind of activity or toy, but independently without interaction.
- **Associative** – interaction and sharing of play activity or toys but without really shared goals or mutual gain.
- **Co-operative** – direct interaction, organisation and sharing of play goals, e.g. complementary role-playing like doctors and nurses or team games.

Despite much overlap, children seem to progress through these types of play with age, e.g. from solitary play (0–2 years), through parallel play (2–3 years) to co-operative play (3 years +).

PIAGET'S <u>COGNITIVE</u> CATEGORIES OF PLAY

Piaget distinguished between three different types of play based upon a child's level of cognitive development (the ages indicate when the type of play is most dominant).

- **Mastery** play (0–2 years) – practice play that helps master schemas and skills.
- **Symbolic** play (1½–7 years) – pretend or make-believe play where one object or person is made to stand for another.
- **Rule-governed** play (7+ years) – where play is organised and governed by regulations that all have to follow.

SYLVA'S <u>ACTIVITY</u> CATEGORIES OF PLAY

Sylva et al (1980), based upon an observational study of 120 3-5-year-old children (with 20-minute observations of each target child), distinguished between:

- **Simple play** – or ordinary play is performed just for pleasure or to release energy and 'merely keeps children occupied'.
- **Complex play** – or elaborated play contributes to educational development and involves high yield activities that challenge the child by requiring systematic and structured behaviour to reach a clear, self-reinforcing goal.

DIFFERENT CATEGORIES OF PLAY

PLAY

Play is difficult to define and can be categorised in different ways (see above) but generally involves behaviour that is voluntarily engaged in, experienced as pleasurable and does not seem to *directly* contribute to survival needs (as do work and rest). Play does, however, according to many theorists, have a range of possible functions.

FACTORS AFFECTING PLAY

GENDER

Gender influences the play of children in the following ways:

- **How they play** – Erikson suggested girls construct inner spaces while boys build towers and protrusions when they play, reflecting genital differences. More established findings are that boys show more boisterous, 'rough and tumble' play than girls (Maccoby, 1988) and that when pretend play develops role-playing, e.g. of mothers and fathers, is followed in gender appropriate ways. Piaget argued that the games of boys after the age of 7 are more complex, competitive and rule-governed than girls' games.
- **Who they play with** – As Shaffer (1996) notes, preferences for same-sex playmates develop very early, 2-year-old girls already prefer to play with other girls (La Freniere et al, 1984) and by age 3 boys seek boy playmates more than girl ones. By age 6 and a half, children spend 10 times as much time with playmates of the same rather than opposite sex (Maccoby, 1988).
- **What they play with** – Again, as Shaffer (1996) notes, sex differences in toy preference also develop very early. At 14–22 months boys usually prefer cars and trucks to other objects, while girls would rather play with dolls and soft toys (Smith and Daglish, 1977). Some children will refuse to play with cross-sex toys, even when there are no other objects available for them to play with (Caldera et al, 1989). Differences in toy choice persist throughout childhood although boys are more likely to play with 'sex-appropriate' toys than girls according to Richardson and Simpson's (1982) analysis of 750, 5-9-year-olds' letters to Father Christmas.

PARENTAL ENCOURAGEMENT

Parents can influence children's play in the following ways:

- **The quality of play** - Parents may influence, through their parental style, the security of their children's attachment bond. Securely attached children at 1–1½ years of age have been found to later show more creative and complex play (Pipp et al, 1992) and to initiate play in nursery school more often than children who had insecure attachments (Waters et al, 1979). Sylva et al's (1980) study recommended that parents set tasks and monitor play to increase its quality and educational value. Fein and Fryer (1995) found that young children play at a more advanced level with their mothers, but this does not continue when they go on to play alone or with others.
- **The type of play** – Parents (especially fathers) may encourage gender appropriate play through their play interactions, reactions and provision of sex-typed toys. Fagot et al (1992) found that parents who most clearly reinforced their sons and daughters in different ways were more likely to have children who showed a clearer understanding of gender differences and stronger sex-typed play and toy preferences. Snow et al (1983) found that fathers would not offer dolls to their baby sons but would offer their daughters a truck. Fathers also engage in more 'rough and tumble' play with sons than daughters.

Play – theories and therapy

THEORETICAL PERSPECTIVES ON PLAY

COGNITIVE DEVELOPMENTAL APPROACH TO PLAY

The cognitive developmental approach to play focuses on how play **reflects** and/or **contributes to** increasing **mental ability** over time.

Piaget (1951) regarded play as mostly *assimilation* – the child repeats already acquired behaviours for the joy of it or makes the world fit into their schemas and plans, e.g. when pretending one thing is something else they want it to be. Piaget contrasted play with strictly intellectual activity, which involves accommodation (as when the child learns new skills or imitates others). He said play *reflects* underlying changes in cognitive development.

- *Mastery play* reflects the repetition of increasingly sophisticated, already acquired physical and conceptual schemas during the sensorimotor stage. The child progresses from playing with its body to playing with objects (e.g. building blocks), first as things to be manipulated, sucked or banged, then later for the purpose they were intended (e.g. building).
- *Symbolic*, pretend play begins in a basic form once the general symbolic function is gained towards the end of the sensorimotor stage, but develops in complexity during the pre-operational stage.
- *Rule-governed* play reflects the increasingly logical and organised thinking of the concrete and formal operational stages. The shift from heteronomous to autonomous morality around the age of 9–10 occurs as the rules underlying games become more understood.

Evaluation

- Piaget based his theory of play upon extensive observations of, and clinical interviews with, children at play (including his own, longitudinally). The theory fits in well with his other ideas on general cognitive development, but lacks experimental investigation.
- Other cognitive developmental psychologists like Vygotsky and Bruner, put more emphasis on the ability of play to *improve* intellectual ability (rather than just reflect it) and its social influences. Vygotsky believed play created a zone of proximal development that allowed the child to show abilities above their current level. Bruner agreed, suggesting that play lets children work out new solutions to problems, and that the presence of another playmate and adult models contributes significantly to the quality of play. Fisher's (1992) meta-analysis of research concluded that children who show more pretend play perform better on tests of cognitive, language and creativity development.
- Cognitive developmental theorists neglect play *after* childhood.

PSYCHODYNAMIC APPROACH TO PLAY

Psychodynamic theorists focus on how play **reflects** and helps **cope** with emotions and feelings.

Freud believed that play helps reduce or control pent-up emotions and wishes/impulses by:

- *Catharsis* – repeating actions or events (in behaviour or imagination) that are associated with unconscious impulses or traumatic experiences is seen as cathartic – every repetition relieves the excitation and is thus pleasurable.
- *Mastery* – in pretend play the child can actively create and/or alter outcomes and events in a more pleasing way and thus provide more ego control over unconscious impulses or traumatic experiences.
- *Ego defence mechanisms* – aid catharsis and mastery in play, e.g. a child may attribute her own naughty behaviour to her doll (projection) or attack it when angry at being told off (displacement).

Evaluation

Freud based his theory of play upon his general psychoanalytic theory, which had been developed from studying adults but very few children.

Other psychodynamic theorists, such as Erikson, agree with Freud on many points but focus more on how play helps the *ego* deal with *current*, *external*, social problems or crises rather than inner id impulses and past issues.

Erikson based his ideas on case studies of children as well as adults and, unlike both Freud and Piaget, saw the importance of play as extending throughout the life span, e.g. adult creative problem-solving play.

THE THERAPEUTIC VALUE OF PLAY

Many theoretical approaches see play as therapeutic but play therapy seems to have been most influenced by psychodynamic principles. Sylva and Lunt (1982) summarise the psychoanalytic background to play therapy as follows:

- 'Play is the child's natural medium of expression' – since children lack the verbal ability to report their problems and free-associate.
- 'What a child does in free play may symbolise 'unconscious' wishes, fears or preoccupations that he is not aware of. (Some play therapists make interpretations to the child to increase his awareness.)' – play can thus be used for diagnosing problems.
- 'A child may 'play out' unconscious feelings and thus bring them out into the open or into his 'conscious' mind. By becoming aware of his feelings and expressing them he may learn to understand and deal with them, control them or otherwise come to terms with them.' – this links with Freud's aim of providing insight and greater ego control.
- 'The relationship between child and therapist is important. This relationship facilitates the child's spontaneous play and expression; it may also give him the opportunity to 'project' feelings (which he may have for his mother and father) onto an adult, thus expressing them 'safely'' – this links with Freud's notion of transference.

Evaluation

- Axline (1971) provided support for play therapy in her case study report 'Dibs: In Search of Self'. Dibs was a withdrawn, lonely and sometimes aggressive child who Axline allowed to express himself by playing freely, at his own pace and without judgement or direction. By playing with dolls and a doll's house Dibs revealed his family problems and was able to express, and gain more control of, his emotions in a 'safe' environment.
- The subjective nature of interpreting play symbolism and defence mechanisms makes the accuracy of diagnosis difficult to evaluate.
- Play therapists, even psychodynamic ones, can differ in:
  1 their approach, e.g. whether the play is free or structured, or whether the therapist is active or passive.
  2 the function they think play serves, e.g. as just a means of communication or a diagnostic/therapeutic tool.
  3 whether play reflects current or past problems.
- It is therefore uncertain which aspect or aspects of play therapy produce improvement.

Development of friendships

AGE	BEHAVIOURAL TRENDS IN PEER RELATIONSHIPS *e.g. who is interacted with and how*		COGNITIVE TRENDS IN PEER RELATIONSHIPS *e.g. the underlying basis of peer relationships or understanding of friendship*
1	0–6 months – peer interest shown by looking only. 6–12 months – infants smile, vocalise and gesture towards peers, but these actions are often not noticed or returned due to a lack of social skills. Parallel play is shown.		
	12–18 months – infants begin to look more at peers than parents and show reactions to each other's gestures. Peers are regarded as responsive toys. 18–24 months – infants show co-ordinated and reciprocal interactions with peers, e.g. imitating each other. Attachment may occur to **preferred playmates** and interactions with these 'friends' are qualitatively different to those with other peers.		18–24 months – infants are able to show self-recognition and can discriminate themselves from others.
2 **3**	2–4 years - **increased social skills and complexity of behavioural interactions** with peers. Increase in association and co-operative play. More sophisticated pretend play, affection and approval is shown with peers who are friends rather than acquaintances. Play occurs in small groups – usually of 2 – 3 friends.	2–3 years – children stay near adults but show more complex physical and cooperative social pretend play with peers, e.g. role-playing. 3–6 years - children are found to be 'generally willing to give up their own valuable play time to perform a dull task if their efforts would benefit a friend; yet this same kind of self-sacrifice was almost never made for a mere acquaintance. Young children also express more sympathy in response to the distress of a friend than to that of an acquaintance, and they are more inclined to try to relieve the friend's distress as well' (Kanfer et al, 1981, Costin and Jones, 1992 – reported in Shaffer, 1996). Children do this *before* they say such behaviour is important for friendship.	2–3 years – children increasingly use the general symbolic function and show motor co-ordination improvements (they stop 'toddling'). 3–4 years – ability to show metarepresentation (understanding others have beliefs) allows more sophisticated social pretend play and **planning** of play to occur.
4 **5**	4–5 years – **ethnic preference** in playmates and friends begins to emerge and may create ethnic groupings in the playground, although this is not inevitable. 5–6 years – play group size and **number of friends begins to increase**, especially with boys.		4–5 years – basic ethnic identity emerges. Selman (1980) suggested cognitive development in social perspective or role-taking skills increasingly allows children to understand the meaning of friendship. (The following ages are approximations.)
6 **7** **8** **9** **10**	6–10 years – true, stable and regular **friendship groups** emerge that have a shared identity and set of norms that regulate behaviour, as well as an organisational structure and/or hierarchy. Groups begin to segregate more strictly according to sex. Friendships are predominately of a same-sex nature. Receptivity to peer group pressure to commit anti-social behaviour steadily increases (reaching a peak by the age of 15). *Best* friendships remain stable.	6–14-year-old Scottish and Canadian children were asked by Bigelow and LaGaipa (1980) (cited by Smith in Bryant and Colman, 1995) to write an essay about their expectations of best friends. Based on a content analysis of these essays, they arrived at a 3-stage model of friendship expectations that suggested 'a shift towards more psychologically complex and mutually reciprocal ideas of friendship during middle school years, with intimacy and commitment becoming especially important in later adolescence'. Up to 8 years – 'Reward-cost' stage – based on common activities, living nearby and having similar expectations. 9–10 years – 'Normative' stage – emphasised shared values, rules and sanctions.	3–6 years – children are egocentric and are dominated by the appearance of situations. A friend is therefore anyone who the child has met and successfully played with. 6–8 years – children still base their friendships upon common activities and although they now realise that others may have different views and choose to be friends, relationships are still very much one-way. If a peer does not follow the child's views and desires, they are not a friend. 8–10 years – children can now better understand how their views and interests differ or coincide with those of their friends. Psychological similarity rather than common activities, and mutual or reciprocal fairness in the friendship become important.
11	10–11 years – the number of peers regarded as friends begins to drop as children approach adolescence, particularly with girls who tend to play in pairs more often and emphasise intimacy and exclusiveness in their friendships to a greater degree.	11–12 years – 'Empathetic' stage – showing a more mature conception of friendship based on understanding and self-disclosure as well as shared interests.	10 onwards – children increasingly develop expectations of how a good friend should behave – not necessarily always agreeing, but showing intimacy, loyalty and mutual understanding.

Popularity in childhood

MEASURING POPULARITY

Popularity in childhood is measured by two main sociometric methods:

- Observation – e.g. of play, to record the amount and kind (positive or negative) of interactions children have with their peer group.
- Self-report – e.g. using questionnaires or interviews to ask children to rate their classmates/peer group on a scale for popularity/degree of friendship, or simply nominate their three best friends (or peers they like least).

From these methods researchers can then construct:

- Sociometric status categories.
- Sociometric association networks.

Evaluation

- Observational studies of behavioural interactions may not reflect the children's opinions of popularity, while asking them relies upon their self-reports (which may be inaccurate or biased). Shaffer (1996), however, reports that "Even 3–5-year-olds can respond appropriately to sociometric surveys (Denham et al, 1990); and the choices (or ratings) that children provide correspond reasonably well to teacher ratings of peer popularity, thus suggesting that sociometric surveys provide valid assessments of children's social standing in their peer groups (Hymel, 1983)".
- According to Smith (in Bryant and Colman, 1995) there may be ethical problems with asking children to rate their peers positively or negatively. For example, such questions might bring about increased negative behaviour to disliked peers, 'but so far ill effects have not been found' (Hayvren and Hymel, 1984).

SOCIOMETRIC STATUS CATEGORIES

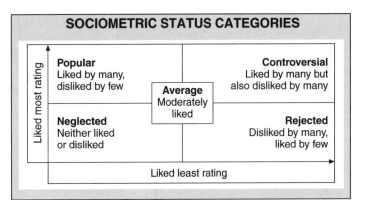

SOCIOMETRIC ASSOCIATION NETWORK

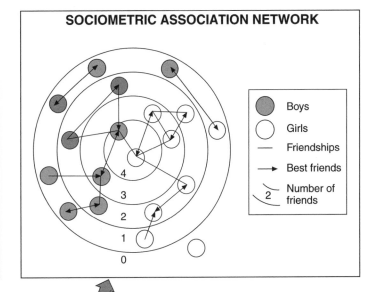

WHO IS POPULAR?

POPULARITY

WHY ARE THEY POPULAR?

PHYSICAL CHARACTERISTICS

Physical attractiveness – facially attractive children and those with athletic builds are more likely to be popular than unattractive children among their peers from an early age (Langlois, 1986). This could result from the positive reactions attractive children receive from adults and peers due to the 'beautiful-is-good' stereotype (Dion, 1972), which becomes a self-fulfilling prophecy. Negative reactions to unattractive children could lead to feelings of rejection and anger, which could create anti-social behaviour, which in turn would lead to further unpopularity.

Rate of maturity – among boys, those who mature early are often rated as more popular than those who mature late. This may result from increased physical competency and success in peer competition.

Similarity – children who appear different from the majority, e.g. in terms of ethnicity, become less popular. According to Social Identity Theory, those who appear different are more likely to be categorised as 'out-group' members and therefore discriminated against. Such categorisation processes exist at all ages but are particularly conspicuous in childhood.

PSYCHOLOGICAL CHARACTERISTICS

Many studies conducted on children of all ages have revealed that personality, behavioural style and social/cognitive skills are very important influences on popularity. These characteristics may result from different attachment bonds, parental styles, birth order (later born children may have more experience interacting with older siblings), innate temperaments and/or cognitive ability.

Popular children – are consistently found to be outgoing, co-operative and supportive. They are able to assess and show behaviour that is socially acceptable for the peer group. They contribute positively to peer group activities without becoming disruptive and resolve disputes peacefully.

Rejected children – show characteristics that annoy peers, for example by being aggressive and disruptive in joint activities or by showing behaviour that differs from the social norm.

Neglected children – do not show characteristics of rejected children and may possess some of the qualities of popular children, but tend not to initiate interactions or draw attention to themselves.

Controversial children – are often aggressive but use their aggression in socially skilled ways to gain peer group status.

Cultural differences in peer relationships

CULTURE AND PEER RELATIONSHIPS

Despite many similarities in peer relationships across cultures, for example in terms of playmates chosen (most cultures show gender segregation in friendships), activities undertaken (such as forms of play) and influences imposed (such as conformity to peer norms), there are also differences between cultures. Perhaps the most influential differences relate to those found between individualistic and collectivistic cultures.

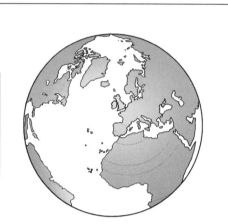

WHAT ARE INDIVIDUALISTIC CULTURES?

In individualistic cultures there is an emphasis on the individual, their goals, rights, attitudes, and needs. They are usually associated with Western, industrialised nations.

WHAT ARE COLLECTIVISTIC CULTURES?

In collectivistic cultures there is an emphasis on the group, its decisions, attitudes, needs and one's duties towards it. They are usually associated with non-Western, traditional nations.

INDIVIDUALISTIC CULTURES AND PEER RELATIONSHIPS

Most psychological research has been conducted in industrial, westernised, individualistic cultures, and has revealed that:

* Competition amongst siblings is a common occurrence, often despite parental intervention. This may actually be a result of parental interference in establishing peer dominance hierarchies or the presence of more toys and parental attention to compete over in these cultures (Harris, 1998).
* Sibling care during parental absence is rarer and usually undertaken by much older peers (often for payment).
* Friendships are often chosen from the same age group, based upon a more 'economic' assessment of costs and rewards, for example similarity of common rewarding interactions (Social Exchange Theory). Best friendships may be enduring, while other friendships / acquaintances may fluctuate over time.
* Popularity is often determined by sociability and dominance in individualistic cultures.
* The emphasis on independence and success means that peer competition is frequently shown, e.g. in academic performance.
* Peer, inter-group hostility is often easily established when competition is introduced, as demonstrated by Sherif et al's (1961) Robber's Cave study. Based on Tajfel's minimal group experiments on Bristol Schoolboys, Wetherell (1982) found that (individualistic) Europeans were more prone to compete and show discrimination when merely divided into groups than (collectivistic) Maori and Samoan participants.

COLLECTIVISTIC CULTURES AND PEER RELATIONSHIPS

Cross-cultural research has frequently found that in collectivistic cultures:

* Family peers are frequently involved in the care of younger siblings. For example, LeVine et al (1994) report that mothers of the Gusii people of Africa hand over care of their infants to an older child (often no more than 6 or 7) because they have to return to the fields to work as soon as possible (Schaffer, 1998, in *Psychology Review*).
* Domination by older children, especially siblings, is often considered natural (Whiting and Edwards, 1988) but seems to decrease rather than increase sibling rivalry and competition (Harris, 1998).
* Friendships are often chosen from extended family networks and a slightly wider range of age groups.
* Popularity may be determined by different norms, for example shy children are likely to be unpopular in Canada but popular in China where being quiet and reserved is a more socially desirable trait (Chen, Rubin and Sun, 1992, cited in Shaffer, 1996).
* Co-operation and support rather than competition is more likely to be shown in peer groups – 'in Asian countries – Japan, for instance... kids are criticised by their classmates for misbehaving and cheered for doing well. Misbehaviour by one child is seen as a blot upon the entire class; one child's improvement is seen as a triumph for everyone' (Harris, 1998).
* Peer, inter-group hostility is less frequently found when competition is introduced compared to individualistic cultures in replications of Sherif et al's (1961) study.

EVALUATION OF CULTURAL DIFFERENCES IN PEER RELATIONSHIPS

It is important to realise that cultural differences relating to individualism and collectivism refer to broad generalities. There are many individual and sub-cultural influences upon peer relationships and even within cultures regarded as collectivistic variations occur. This is especially true as western, individualistic values increasingly invade collectivistic cultures, most often through media representations and economic policy.

Early and middle adulthood

	ERIKSON'S THEORY	LEVINSON'S THEORY	GOULD'S THEORY
15	Erikson described **two psychosocial crises** relating to early and middle adulthood (the 6th and 7th of the 8 he outlined over the lifespan). As with all Erikson's stages the ego has to resolve the crisis society presents the individual for healthy psychological development.	Levinson et al (1978) described a **life structure** theory of adult development, based upon interviews with 40 men between the age of 35 and 45, which suggested that people experience a series of alternating **stable** (structure-building) and **transitional** (structure-changing) **phases**.	Gould (1978), based on psychiatric work and a questionnaire given to over 500, 16-50-year-old people, suggested the evolution of adult consciousness occurs as we **lose false childhood assumptions** and accept control over our own lives.
20	**Intimacy versus isolation** – according to Erikson the challenge of early adulthood is to achieve intimacy in relationships. Friendships become important and successful resolution of the crisis enables one to love and show commitment and compromise in relationships. A stable identity from the previous stage of development is required so as not to lose oneself in the relationship, otherwise fear of commitment and an inability to form loving relationships results in isolation.	**Early adult transition** (17–22 years) – involves achieving independence from pre-adulthood through emotional and physical separations from the family and the exploration of new lifestyles, relationships and occupations. **Entering the adult world** (22–28 years) – involves a stable, structure building phase where one lives with the initial choices and learns from the mistakes and successes experienced. The individual begins to make commitments, yet also wants to explore possibilities and keep options open. **Age 30 transition** (28–33 years) – a feeling of time pressure results in changing the first life structure where necessary, based upon the limitations of the first choices. **Settling down** (33–40 years) – involves consolidating one's life choices, establishing a niche in society and seeking advancement in one's life goals. The increasing sense of self-sufficiency and achievement in the later part of this phase is referred to as 'becoming one's own man' (BOOM).	**Assumption 1** (late teens, early 20s) – 'I will always belong to my parents and believe in their world'.
25			**Assumption 2** (the 20s) – 'Doing it their way with will power and perseverance will probably bring results. But when I become too frustrated, confused, or tired, or am simply unable to cope, they will step in and show me the way'.
30			**Assumption 3** (late 20s, early 30s) – 'Life is simple and controllable. There are no significant coexisting, contradictory forces within me.'
35	**Generativity versus stagnation** – generativity refers to concern over 'establishing and guiding the next generation' Erikson (1980). The individual may express generativity through parenthood or other creative or altruistic contributions to society. Caring only for oneself leads to self-centredness and stagnation		**Assumption 4** (35–50) – 'There is no evil in me or death in the world. The sinister has been expelled.' Like Erikson and Levinson, Gould regarded this period of life as one of 'midlife crisis', provoked by realising that we are no longer young, that our children are beginning to leave home, our parents are starting to depend on us instead of vice versa, and time for change is beginning to run out.
40		**Midlife transition** (40 – 45 years) – involves the assessment of whether one's life choices and achievements have been worthwhile. Dissatisfaction may result in a midlife crisis and a re-thinking of values and goals. **Entering middle adulthood** (45 – 50 years) – involves adjustment to new goals, choices and changes in relationships, career, domestic situation (e.g. the leaving of children from home), lifestyle, etc. **Age 50 transition** (50 – 55 years) – a further questioning of life choices is made and a midlife crisis may be experienced at this point if one was not had at the midlife transition. **Culmination of middle adulthood** (55 – 60 years) – Levinson et al have relatively little to say about development from this phase onwards since their interview sample was not old enough to provide sufficient information.	
45	According to Sugarman (1986) there is **much** disagreement amongst researchers over the age boundaries for Erikson's **adult** stages, for example some see the intimacy versus isolation stage ending at 40 (Havighurst, 1973), others at 34 (Turner and Helms, 1979) and still others at 25 (Bee and Mitchell, 1984).		
50			**Life after 50** – Once the four main false assumptions of childhood are overcome, Gould argues that we finally come to recognise that we own ourselves. This enables contact to be made with our inner core which provides greater strength to face life's problems.
55			
60			

Evidence for the existence of crises and transitions

- All the above theories suggest an identifiable structure involving crises and transitions in adulthood. However, despite certain common views (e.g. on the existence of midlife crisis), each theory differs in the number, type and timing of the transitions.
- The evidence for the theories comes mainly from qualitative, self-report data, collected through interviews and questionnaires, sometimes gathered from samples limited in terms of age and gender (Levinson's 35-45-year-old men) or social class and culture (Gould's white, middle-class adults). These methods have both strengths and weaknesses.
- Other researchers have pointed out that there may be considerable variation in the timing and nature of the transitions across individuals, genders, cultures and historical time periods (a better approach may be to focus on certain critical life events, regardless of when they occur). Although there are broad similarities in biological, psychological and social changes over time, not everyone shares the same social and cultural experiences / lifestyles, or indeed reacts to life changes in the same way.

Family and relationships in adulthood

Life Events	THE EFFECTS OF LIFE EVENTS UPON THE INDIVIDUAL *Effects may concern cognitive (e.g. attitudes), emotional (e.g. satisfaction) and behavioural changes*		
	GENERAL EFFECTS	**GENDER DIFFERENCES IN EFFECTS**	**CULTURAL DIFFERENCES IN EFFECTS**
MARRIAGE	In general, research conducted in western, industrialised countries, has revealed that, on average: • *Married people* are *happier* and *healthier* than the *unmarried, divorced* and *widowed* in the long term. • Married couples who are *both* externally *employed* report *more dissatisfaction* than single-earner couples. **Why?** Marriage may provide more emotional support and financial security, however if the latter takes priority (i.e. both work), the former might suffer (i.e. less time and attention may be devoted to providing emotional support). However, the research is often correlational and may neglect marriages that do not last (healthier and happier couples may stay married longer).	Some research, mostly conducted in western, industrialised countries, has revealed marked differences in the effects of marriage upon men and women. On average: • *Married men* are physically and mentally *healthier* than *unmarried men.* • *Married women* are *less* physically and mentally *healthy* than *unmarried women* and *married men* (Gove, 1972). • *Married women* report *less satisfaction* with their marriage than *married men.* **Why?** Married women in these countries are often more likely to: • Undertake more domestic chores than men, despite also having external employment. • Stay at home compared to men, and therefore feel more thwarted in their ambitions. • Provide a confiding, supportive relationship for their partners compared to men.	Cross-cultural research has revealed differences in the effects of marriage across societies. For example: • *Marital satisfaction* has been found to *decrease with age* in the USA, but *not* in Japan (Kamo, 1993), and the *reverse* is true in some cultures, e.g. India (Gupta and Singh, 1982) where marriages may be arranged. • The *reasons* for marital satisfaction may vary across cultures too. In Western, individualistic cultures marital happiness seems to depend more on *love*, whereas in collectivistic cultures, economic, social and family factors assume greater importance (Levine et al, 1995). • In some cultures women report greater satisfaction and experience increased status after marriage.
PARENTHOOD	In general, research conducted in a number of countries has revealed that, on average: • A decrease in quality of life and marital satisfaction is often experienced after the birth of the first child. • Parenthood is associated with cognitive changes in identity, attitudes and priorities, often along more traditional and sex-typed lines (this links with Erikson's crisis of generativity versus stagnation). **Why?** Young children redirect attention and resources from the self and partnership towards offspring. However, it is difficult to tell how much dissatisfaction and identity change are causes or effects of parenthood.	Research conducted in many countries has revealed that, on average: • More women than men feel pressure to be the primary caregiver of offspring and to sacrifice their careers for parenthood. • Women experience a greater decrease in quality of life and satisfaction during parenthood than men. • Men often feel excluded from the childcare and bonding experience. **Why?** Small et al (1994) reported that 10–20% of mothers are depressed in the first year of childbirth due to a lack of social and emotional support, illness and exhaustion, and a lack of time for themselves. Lamb et al (1985) found that mothers were more satisfied with parenthood when the fathers were more supportive.	Cross-cultural research has revealed differences in the effects of parenthood across societies. For example: • In cultures where there is a greater degree of family and social support in childcare, and where parenthood is highly valued, parental satisfaction and quality of life is greater (particularly for women). • There are wide differences in the degree to which fathers will assume traditional parental roles and thus contribute towards domestic chores and childcare. In Western countries, such as the USA, Sweden and Britain, there has been an increasing trend towards greater paternal contributions (e.g. Lewis, 1986). • There are wide cultural differences in parental attitudes towards offspring, ranging from pragmatic (i.e. extra sources of income) to sentimental.
DIVORCE	In general, research has revealed that divorce commonly leads to: • Emotional, social and economic disruption and disorganisation (often lasting around two years). • A decrease in physical and mental health. **Why?** Disrupted family and friendship networks, legal proceedings. However, for some it is an emotionally positive event.	Research indicates that after divorce: • Women may suffer more financially and in terms of identity changes. • Men, especially older men, find emotional adjustment difficult and suffer more mental health problems. **Why?** Because of traditional gender roles, female identities may be more family-related. Women who maintain employment suffer less from identity problems and financial losses after divorce. Men usually lose more emotional support than women.	There are wide cultural differences in: • The frequency of divorce – rates in some western countries, e.g. the USA, are far higher than elsewhere. • The social and economic disruption caused by divorce – which reflect the frequency of divorce, the legal procedures, social support networks and the religion of the culture. • The psychological consequences – the frequency and disruption of divorce in a society may affect its emotional consequences.

Late adulthood – retirement and adjustment

EFFECTS OF RETIREMENT

ATCHLEY'S FIVE PERIODS OF ADJUSTMENT

Atchley (1982, 1988) suggested traditional retirement typically involved 5 periods of adjustment.

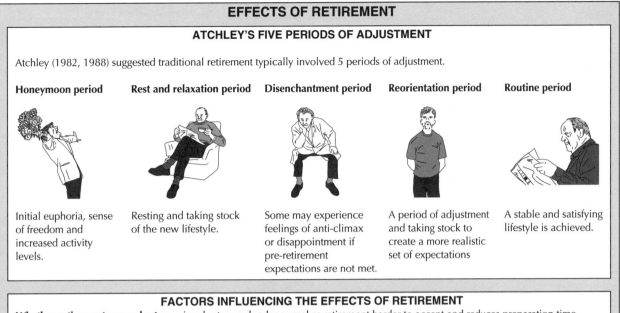

Honeymoon period	Rest and relaxation period	Disenchantment period	Reorientation period	Routine period
Initial euphoria, sense of freedom and increased activity levels.	Resting and taking stock of the new lifestyle.	Some may experience feelings of anti-climax or disappointment if pre-retirement expectations are not met.	A period of adjustment and taking stock to create a more realistic set of expectations	A stable and satisfying lifestyle is achieved.

FACTORS INFLUENCING THE EFFECTS OF RETIREMENT

Whether retirement was voluntary – involuntary redundancy makes retirement harder to accept and reduces preparation time.
Pre-retirement education – mental preparation and financial planning make the transition to retirement easier.
Interests outside employment – those whose identity and interests are highly work-related find retirement more difficult.
Good health and financial security – both enable retirement plans and activities to be fulfilled.

ADJUSTMENT TO OLD AGE

DISENGAGEMENT THEORY

Cumming and Henry (1961) suggest that adjustment to old age involves the elderly and society gradually **withdrawing from one another**. Society increasingly **frees** the elderly of their **responsibilities** and social roles through their attitudes or legal means (e.g. compulsory retirement), while along with decreasing activity levels the elderly are seen as **voluntarily** becoming more reflective and less concerned with other people and events. This process of **mutual separation** is seen as **natural**, **inevitable** and **positive**, and occurs in 3 phases:

1 Shrinkage of life space – i.e. fewer interactions and roles.
2 Increased individuality.
3 Acceptance of life changes.

Evaluation
It is based on a 5-year study of 275 50–90-year olds, however others suggest the process is not natural and inevitable, there are cross-cultural differences and not everyone disengages (for those who do, personality rather than age is probably the reason).

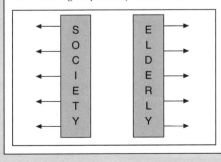

ACTIVITY THEORY

Havighurst et al (1968) argue that the elderly frequently prefer to remain active and productive, and actually resist disengagement, despite the ageist social attitudes and barriers they encounter.

Evaluation
Dolen and Bearison (1982) studied 122 healthy 65-89-year-olds in New York and found no significant decline in social participation. However, activity theory possibly over-estimates the control the elderly have to resist society's disengagement and neglects the idea that some actually prefer to disengage. Like disengagement theory, activity theory neglects individual and cultural differences, tarring all the elderly with the same brush.

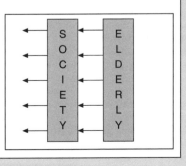

SELECTIVITY THEORY

Field and Minkler (1988) propose that the elderly, faced with reduced time, become more concerned with the quality of the relationships they maintain. For this reason they will select relationships that provide the emotional security and comfort they desire and disengage from unrewarding relationships.

Evaluation
Like activity theory, selectivity theory may over-estimate the control the elderly have over social interaction. Reduced activity, mobility and resources, as well as the death of peers, may restrict their choice.

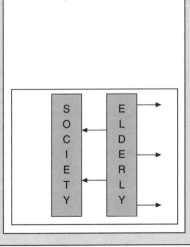

Contemporary issue – Do cognitive changes persist into old age?

The issue of whether cognitive changes, such as those relating to intelligence and memory, persist into old age is one that has important implications for the way that the elderly:

1 are treated by society, in terms of ageist discrimination for example
2 view themselves, and the effects such views may have on their behaviour and cognitive abilities

Cognitive developmental psychologists are interested in the issue since they investigate:

1 changes in cognitive abilities over time
2 whether such changes are qualitative in kind or quantitative in degree
3 whether such changes are more a result of biological maturation or social environment.

1. DO CHANGES IN COGNITIVE ABILITIES OCCUR IN OLDER PEOPLE?
The overall answer to this question is *yes, some genuine changes* in cognitive abilities do occur with old age, however:

- The degree of change is likely to be *exaggerated* by *negative stereotypes* in some cultures, such as older people becoming senile.
- There are *large individual differences* between older people in *how much change* occurs and *how late* in the life span it occurs.
- Some of the changes reflect the influence of *variables other than just age* on cognitive abilities, such as those resulting from the *cohort effect*. This is when different age groups in a society at any one time will differ in other characteristics, such as the level of education or nutrition they have experienced, which may influence cognitive abilities but be unrelated to the duration of their lives. This is supported by the finding that *longitudinal studies* of the same individuals over time *reveal less change* in cognitive abilities than *cross-sectional studies* that compare different people of different ages.

2. ARE COGNITIVE CHANGES IN OLD AGE QUALITATIVE OR QUANTITATIVE IN KIND?
- Both changes in degree and kind of memory and intellectual ability have been suggested.
- Intelligence – while research has shown that older people show decreases in the speed of their mental processing, a steady accumulation of life experience may provide the greater expert knowledge and insight into life associated with wisdom in old age. This may link with the finding that *crystallised intelligence* (which involves the use of knowledge that has already been acquired) appears to increase with age, while *fluid intelligence* (which concerns the ability to solve problems that have not been encountered before) seems to decrease with age. Some cognitive developmental researchers have even suggested a *fifth, post-formal stage* of intellectual ability in late adulthood, involving an acceptance of contradiction, ambiguity and complexity.
- Memory – Salthouse (1990) found evidence for a decline in the efficiency of *working memory* in elderly participants. Performance on tests of recall is worse in older than younger people, but there seems little or no difference in tests of recognition.

3. ARE COGNITIVE CHANGES IN OLD AGE A RESULT OF BIOLOGICAL OR SOCIAL FACTORS?
As with childhood cognitive development, changes in cognitive abilities in old age may be a result of both biological and social factors.
- Biological deterioration of mental abilities can be caused by the degeneration of neurones resulting from either natural cell death with age or diseases such as Alzheimer's. Studies have shown that *dramatic* cell loss, particularly in parts of the temporal lobe and hippocampus of the brain can occur in people with Alzheimer's disease, but is not an inevitable consequence of ageing.
- A number of social environmental changes that occur in old age can affect mental abilities. The elderly may experience decreasing activity levels and *less stimulating environments* which could adversely affect their cognitive abilities - especially in cultures where older people have less family and social contact or are put in care homes with poor facilities, repetitive routines and limited social variability. Such environments may not present sufficient opportunity to practice and apply fluid intelligence. Baltes and Willis (1982) found that training older adults on the aspects of IQ that usually decline over time significantly improved their performance, even in long term follow-up studies of those adults in their early 80s.
  In addition, negative cultural stereotypes about the forgetfulness of old age or positive stereotypes about the wisdom old age bestows, may affect memory abilities by becoming *self-fulfilling prophecies*. This was supported by Levy and Langer (1994) who found that older American participants exposed to negative stereotypes about the effect of age on memory performed worse on memory tests than younger Americans (for whom the negative stereotype did not yet apply), older deaf Americans (who would have been less exposed to the stereotype) and older Chinese participants (who are exposed to positive stereotypes about age bringing wisdom).
- There are a number of cognitive psychological explanations for mental deficits in old age that cannot always be clearly distinguished as either biological or social. Slower mental processing speed could result from either neuronal deterioration or older people having more ways of solving problems available to them. Retrieval of memory may decline with age because of trace decay, interference from a greater number of memories, or a lack of cues in their present life to prompt the access to memories of the past.

Late adulthood – bereavement

COPING WITH BEREAVEMENT

FACING BEREAVEMENT

KUBLER-ROSS (1969) STAGES OF DYING

These five stages were developed based on research with those facing their own death. Some have also applied them to those facing bereavement.

- **DENIAL** – resistance to the initial discovery by seeking other opinions or refusal to accept death will occur.
- **ANGER** – often directed at others out of resentment, frustration and feelings of injustice (why me?).
- **BARGAINING** – with God, fate or medical professionals to change the situation.
- **DEPRESSION** – when the inevitability of death is realised, preparatory grieving or depression may occur for all that will be lost.
- **ACCEPTANCE** – giving up to death, becoming more resolved, withdrawn and emotionally drained.

FULTON (1970) STAGES OF GRIEVING

These stages apply to a person facing bereavement.

- **DEPRESSION** – the emotional reaction of grief.
- **HEIGHTENED CONCERN** – the behavioural reaction of showing extra care and interaction to help support the dying, to achieve goals before it is too late and to prevent later guilt.
- **REHEARSAL FOR DEATH** – the cognitive reaction in terms of mental preparation of coping strategies.
- **ADJUSTMENT TO CONSEQUENCES** – further cognitive and emotional coping strategies are employed.

AFTER BEREAVEMENT

PARKES (1975) PHASES OF MOURNING

NUMBNESS – the initial reaction of shock normally produces emotional numbness. This may delay emotional distress but can become problematic if it persists.

PINING – the dead are intensely missed and intrusive thoughts occur. Stress is experienced and coped with depending upon the degree of attachment, personality of the bereaved and circumstances of the death. Grief is usually experienced in episodic pangs of anxiety, and restlessness may be caused by the desire to search for the person and objects or events associated with them.

MITIGATIONS – compensatory hallucinations, obsessive reviewing and depersonalisation may occur while cognitive restructuring and adjustment begins to take place.

RECOVERY – begins when the bereaved start to gain a new identity and habituate to the loss (Dodd, 1991).

RAMSAY AND de GROOT'S (1977) 9 COMPONENTS OF GRIEF

These apply to those who have just faced bereavement.

1. **SHOCK** – often the initial reaction.
2. **DISORGANISATION** – disturbed ability to plan.
3. **DENIAL** – behaving as if the deceased is still alive.
4. **DEPRESSION** – pining or despair
5. **GUILT** – for thoughts or behaviour towards the dead.
6. **ANXIETY** – about inability to cope with changes.
7. **AGGRESSION** – resulting from anger or frustration.
8. **RESOLUTION** – increasing acceptance of death.
9. **REINTEGRATION** – reorganisation and adjustment.

EVALUATION OF COPING THEORIES

- The evidence for the above stage and component theories comes mainly from numerous clinical observations.
- There are obviously ethical restrictions in the study of this area.
- The research has implications for death and bereavement counselling and the training of health care professionals.
- However, as the researchers themselves point out, large individual, social and cultural variations in reactions, means the stages and components cannot be regarded as universal or fixed, thus reducing their predictive power concerning what reactions will be shown and when.
- Some important factors that strongly affect coping with death, include:
  Degree of attachment – bereavement effects increase with stronger attachment bonds.
  Social support – family and friends can provide an emotional and practical support network.
  Religion – often provides a ritualised structure for grieving and a belief system for coming to terms with loss of life.
  Death expectancy – pre-warning or high death rates sometimes facilitate greater preparation, acceptance and coping strategies.
  Age – children's understanding of the concept of death will change and have consequences for coping at different ages. Older people may accept their deaths more than younger people, depending upon life satisfaction.

CULTURAL DIFFERENCES IN COPING WITH BEREAVEMENT

Cultural variations are found in the:

- **Expression of grief** – from Japanese stoicism to Muslim wailing.
- **Duration of grief** – from the four-day mourning period of Navajo and Mayan Indians to the one-year mourning period of Orthodox Jews.
- **Rituals of grief** – from the relatively unstructured process of mourning in Christianity to the highly ritualised process of Orthodox Judaism.
- **Attitudes towards the dead** – from the fear and dislike of the dead shown by Hopi Indians to the worshipping of ancestors by Japanese Shintoism and Buddhism.

Evaluation – such cultural differences are likely to result from a mixture of traditional, religious and practical factors and have psychological consequences for adjustment to bereavement.

Evolutionary explanations of animal behaviour

THE THEORY OF EVOLUTION

Charles Darwin's claim that humans evolved from other animals provided the starting point for comparative psychology. The basic principles of evolutionary theory are

- **genetic mutation and phenotype variation** – during reproduction genetic mutation and chromosome variation occurs, which affects the physiology and behaviour of the offspring
- **adaptation** – some genetic mutation and chromosome variation results in changes of physiology and behaviour that allows an organism to adapt itself better to its particular environment (ecological niche)
- **selective pressure** – those aspects of the environment that favour certain characteristics of animal physiology and behaviour over others
- **natural selection** – individuals with adaptive physiology and behaviour will be more likely to survive in their environment and compete successfully with other members of their species who do not have the same advantage
- **fitness** – increased survival chances and competitiveness means an increased likelihood of producing more offspring, who will also possess the favourable genetic mutations (survival of the fittest)
- **evolution** – species develop from other species, genetically and physically, over very long periods of time (though not necessarily in a smoothly continuous way). A species exists when the genetic variation of a group becomes different enough from the species it evolved from to prevent reproduction occurring with it

Charles Darwin

SOCIOBIOLOGY

- Sociobiology is the theoretical system applied to social ethology, and, unlike previous approaches, examines the evolution of social behaviour in terms of the survival consequences it has for the genes each animal possesses. Genes are regarded as the fundamental unit of evolution, their 'purpose' is merely to replicate copies of themselves. Behaviour evolves not for the good of the species or even the individual, but for the good of the genes. According to Dawkins (1976) all animals are merely 'survival machines' to carry our 'selfish genes' and the more adaptive their physiology and behaviour, the greater their fitness (ability to produce offspring that will themselves pass on copies of their genes).
- By focusing on genes, the idea of inclusive fitness and the social co-evolution of evolutionary stable strategies between and within species, sociobiologists such as Wilson, Hamilton, Trivers, and Dawkins have been able to explain many aspects of human and non-human social behaviour (including altruism, a topic that presented many problems to previous explanatory theories).
- Sociobiology has extended its theoretical basis to incorporate the idea of cultural evolution and the interaction it might have with genetic evolution. Here the concept of the 'meme' has been proposed – an **idea** or concept that forms the basic **unit** of cultural evolution, which replicates itself from one **mind** to another and is subject to the same evolutionary pressures and laws as genes.
- Sociobiological theory has proposed some powerful arguments for the origin of animal and human behaviour, but has been criticised theoretically and ethically, so its ideas should be applied with caution.

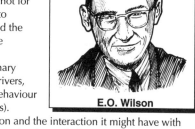

E.O. Wilson

EVALUATION OF EVOLUTIONARY EXPLANATIONS

ADVANTAGES

- The study of evolutionary processes places behaviour in an important environmental and historical **context**.
- Evolutionary findings tend to counterbalance the nurture approach – showing how learning can be subject to genetically evolved biases.
- Evolutionary theory is supported by comparative research of behavioural similarities between species and analysis of the function of behaviour in its environmental setting. Studies of mutation rates in DNA also support evolution's assumptions.

DISADVANTAGES

- It is wrong to assume that behaviour must always have evolved for a particular purpose, it may be just a by-product or left-over of evolution. To give a famous dinosaur example – Tyrannosaurus Rex arms did not evolve to be so small for a reason, they were left over from evolutionary ancestors that walked on all fours.
- It is wrong to assume adaptation is an optimal solution – evolutionary adaptation always builds on past adaptation, which may not be an ideal base.
- 'Armchair adaptionism' (Lea, 1984) – it is easy to think up theoretical speculations or stories to explain evolutionary function, rather than rely on empirical research. Evolutionary theory may produce contradictory theories for the same behaviour.
- Evolutionary theory is reductionist and may be seen as overly deterministic. Other levels of explanation are necessary, e.g. social/psychological.
- Evolutionary explanations of behaviour tend to underestimate or ignore the learning capabilities which influence behaviour and that may even over-ride the influence of genetic evolution on behaviour.
- Evolutionary explanations may overexaggerate similarities between species and show anthropomorphism – a tendency to project human traits on to animals, e.g. saying a cat that is rubbing itself against your legs (probably to mark its territory) 'loves' you.
- Sociobiological ideas may be misunderstood or misapplied, e.g. to justify eugenic or capitalist politics (the latter may even have influenced sociobiological theory).

Evolutionary explanations of apparent altruism

THE PROBLEM OF ALTRUISM

Apparent altruism refers to the way in which some animal behaviour seems unselfish – providing a service to another individual at a cost to the helper. Sociobiological evolutionary theory argues that true altruistic behaviour should not occur since those who help others at a cost to themselves are less likely to survive to pass on their altruistic genes, compared to selfish individuals.

Research shows that instances of 'true altruism' are only likely to occur on a non-voluntary or mistaken basis, due to deception or exploitation by a parasitic recipient, e.g. birds that are deceived into caring for cuckoo eggs. For this 'true altruistic' behaviour to continue, the costs must not be so great as to wipe out all those who possess the genes for it.

Where a species has evolved apparently altruistic behaviour that seems costly to the organism, research has indicated that there is either
- a **genetic reward** in terms of **survival for copies of genes possessed by the organism** (e.g. kin 'altruism') or
- a **long term reward** for the **organism** involved (e.g. delayed reciprocal 'altruism')

KIN 'ALTRUISM'

The most common instances of extremely self sacrificing behaviour occur towards genetically related individuals.

Examples:

Care of offspring – parental care involves many costs to the parent in terms of biological resources (e.g. egg investment, gestation, and lactation in mammals), time and effort (e.g. feeding) and danger (e.g. competition for resources and offspring defence). Parents are not the only kin altruistic providers of offspring care, however, since 'nest helpers' are found in some species where offspring stay with their parents to help raise further parental offspring. Mumme (1992) found that Florida scrub jays have sibling helpers who increase the chances of later offspring surviving to 60 days by five times.

Warning signals – are often altruistic, since they can attract the attention of predators to the caller while increasing the survival chances of those warned. Warning calls made by species that live in social groups containing many genetically related individuals will increase their genetic fitness. Caution must be used when ascribing kin altruistic motives, since some species, such as Belding ground squirrels, emit different kinds of warning call – one in response to goshawks which produces a confusing group dash for cover (selfishly disguising the caller), another in response to coyotes which immediately attracts the attack towards the caller (Sherman, 1985).

Eusocial insects – such as ants, termites, and some species of bee and wasp contain workers that help raise offspring and even sacrifice their lives to defend them, despite being unable to reproduce themselves.

Explanation

Since the 'aim' of evolution is to replicate copies of genes, organisms should be expected to be 'helpful' towards individuals who share partial copies of their genes – their relatives. Close relatives, like full brothers or sisters, who share half our genes can, therefore, be regarded as 'offspring equivalents' and so self-sacrificing behaviour that saves the lives or increases the fitness of many relatives may be phenotypically altruistic yet genotypically selfish (Barash, 1982).

If altruistic genes allow a sufficient number of relatives sharing copies of your genes to survive, then individual self-sacrificing behaviour will result as an evolutionary stable strategy – an individual will have made a genetic gain if the self sacrificing behaviour saves at least two brothers or eight cousins. Hamilton (1964) used the term 'inclusive fitness' to describe the overall genetic gain made by individuals who show kin altruistic behaviour towards those sharing part or whole copies of their genes.

DELAYED RECIPROCAL 'ALTRUISM'

Under certain conditions individuals of a species will help another **unrelated** individual at some **short term cost** if there is a high probability of a **long term return** of the favour.

Examples:

Baboon coalitions – Packer (1977) found that pairs of young male baboons without mates would co-operate together to gain access to the dominant male's partner. One distracts the dominant male (risking damage) while the other mates with the partner. The distracting baboon's seemingly altruistic behaviour exists since the favour may be returned by the other baboon in the future, providing at least some chance of reproductive success.

Vampire bat feeding – Wilkinson (1984) found that vampire bats living in groups would regurgitate blood to genetically unrelated individuals who had not managed to feed, since the favour was likely to be returned if the donors themselves were unsuccessful in feeding in the future.

Explanation

Delayed reciprocal 'altruism' only evolves as an evolutionary stable strategy if individuals can recognise each other and impose sanctions upon cheats who do not return favours. Axelrod and Hamilton (1981) used game theory analysis of the prisoner's dilemma to show that a long term 'tit-for-tat' strategy (starting co-operatively and then following the last person's behaviour of helping or cheating) would enable altruistic helping to emerge as an evolutionary stable strategy without constant abuse of reciprocation.

Classical conditioning

Classical conditioning is concerned with **learning by association**, and refers to the **conditioning of reflexes** – how animals learn to **associate new stimuli with innate bodily reflexes**. The principles of classical conditioning were first outlined by **Pavlov**, and were then adopted by behaviourists, such as Watson, who attempted to use them to explain how virtually all of human behaviour is acquired. Pavlov was a physiologist who, while studying the salivation reflex, found that the dogs he was using in his experiments would sometimes start salivating before the food had reached their mouths, often at the sight of the food bucket. Clearly the dogs had learnt to **associate new external stimuli** (such as sights and sounds), with the **original stimulus** (food) that caused the salivation reflex. In a series of thorough and well controlled experiments, Pavlov found many new stimuli could be associated with reflexes and went on to introduce special terms for, and investigated many aspects of, the conditioning process.

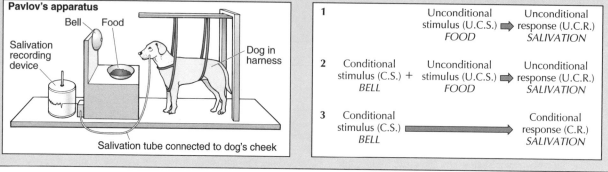

Pavlov's apparatus

Bell — Food — Salivation recording device — Dog in harness — Salivation tube connected to dog's cheek

1. Unconditional stimulus (U.C.S.) *FOOD* ➡ Unconditional response (U.C.R.) *SALIVATION*

2. Conditional stimulus (C.S.) *BELL* + Unconditional stimulus (U.C.S.) *FOOD* ➡ Unconditional response (U.C.R.) *SALIVATION*

3. Conditional stimulus (C.S.) *BELL* ➡ Conditional response (C.R.) *SALIVATION*

ASPECTS AND PROCESSES OF CLASSICAL CONDITIONING

TIMING

The law of temporal contiguity
Pavlov found that for associations to be made, the two stimuli had to be presented close together in time. If the time between the presentation of the C.S. (bell) and the presentation of the U.C.S. (food) is too great, then learning will not occur.

Variations in contiguity
There are different ways to present the C.S. and U.C.S. together.
• **Forward conditioning** – involves presenting the C.S. (bell) just before and during presentation of the U.C.S. (food), producing the strongest learning.
• **Backward conditioning** – is where the C.S. (bell) is presented after the U.C.S. (food), but produces very little learning.
• **Simultaneous conditioning** – is where the C.S. (bell) and U.C.S. (food) are presented at the same time.
• **Trace conditioning** – involves presenting and removing the C.S. (bell) before the U.C.S. (food).

DURATION

Reinforcement
The learning link will last as long as the U.C.S. (food) is occasionally re-presented with the C.S. (bell).
It is the reflex-based U.C.S. which acts as the reinforcer and strengthens the learning link.

Extinction
If the C.S. (bell) is continually presented without the U.C.S. (food), then the C.R. (salivation) will gradually die out or extinguish.

Spontaneous recovery
If a period of time is left after the C.R. has extinguished, then the C.R. will be exhibited again if the C.S. is presented.

Inhibition
The fact that the C.R. can show spontaneous recovery at a later date after extinction shows that the C.R. does not fade away, but has been actively inhibited by the non-presentation of the U.C.S.

FLEXIBILITY

Generalisation

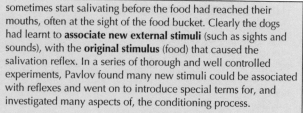

Amount of salivation — A B C D E Tones

Pavlov found that the C.R. could be triggered by stimuli which resembled the original C.S. – the closer the resemblance the greater the C.R., e.g. if the original C.S. bell had a tone of C, then the dogs would salivate to a lesser degree to tones of B and A.

Discrimination

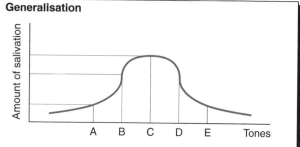

Amount of salivation — A B C D E Tones

By only presenting the U.C.S. with the original C.S., discrimination from the similar C.S.s occurs.

Higher order conditioning
Once the C.S. is reliably producing the C.R., the C.S. acquires some reinforcing properties itself – a new C.S. can be associated with the original C.S., until the new C.S. will also produce the C.R.

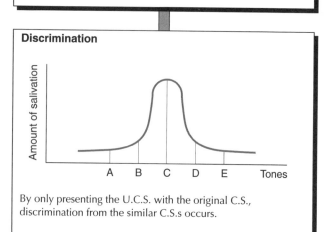

Operant conditioning

THE BASIC THEORY

Operant conditioning involves learning through the consequences of behavioural responses. The principles of operant conditioning were first investigated by **Thorndike**, and were then thoroughly developed by the famous behaviourist Skinner, who applied them to explain how many aspects of human behaviour are acquired.

Thorndike studied the way cats would learn to escape from his puzzle box by **trial and error**. Cats did not immediately acquire the desirable escape behaviour, but gradually increased in their ability to show it over time. Nevertheless, Thorndike found that any response that led to desirable consequences was more likely to occur again, whereas any response that led to undesirable consequences was less likely to be repeated – a principle which became known as the **Law of Effect**.

However, as with classical conditioning, the law of contiguity applies - associations between responses and consequences have to be made close together in time for learning to occur.

Thorndike's puzzle box

Cats had to emit the response of pulling the string inside the box to release the catch on the door to provide escape (a pleasant consequence). Time to escape decreased with each trial (the number of times the cat was put back in the box).

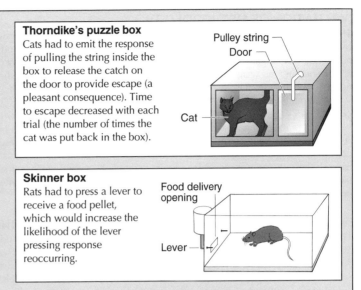

Skinner box

Rats had to press a lever to receive a food pellet, which would increase the likelihood of the lever pressing response reoccurring.

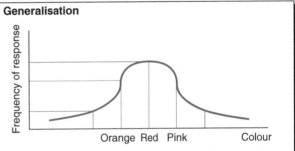

ASPECTS OF REINFORCEMENT

CONSEQUENCES

Positive reinforcement
This increases the likelihood of a response by providing pleasant consequences for it, e.g. food.

Negative reinforcement
This increases the likelihood of a response that removes or provides escape from unpleasant consequences, e.g. stopping an electric shock.

Punishment
This decreases the likelihood of a response being repeated if it is followed by inescapable negative/unpleasant consequences, e.g. an electric shock.

Secondary reinforcement
Secondary reinforcers are those that are associated with naturally occurring primary reinforcers (e.g. food, water, warmth, etc.), for example money, tokens, or parents.

FREQUENCY

Schedules of reinforcement
Continuous schedules – involve reinforcing every response made.
Partial schedules – involve reinforcing responses in varying frequencies to affect response and extinction rates, for example:
- *Fixed ratio schedule* – reinforcing a fixed number of responses (e.g. a food pellet for every ten lever presses in a Skinner box).
- *Variable ratio schedule* – reinforcing an average number of responses (e.g. a food pellet on average every ten lever presses, sometimes after 8 sometimes after 12 presses).
- *Fixed interval schedule* – reinforcing after a fixed amount of time (e.g. a food pellet for a lever press each minute in a Skinner box).
- *Variable interval schedule* – reinforcing after an average amount of time (e.g. a food pellet on average each minute, sometimes after 50 seconds sometimes after 70.

Extinction
If the response is not reinforced, it will gradually die out or extinguish.

FLEXIBILITY

Generalisation

Skinner found animals would make responses that resembled the originally reinforced response - a pigeon reinforced for pecking a red key, would also peck (although less frequently) at an orange or pink key.

Discrimination

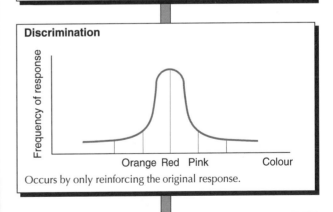

Occurs by only reinforcing the original response.

Behaviour shaping
By reinforcing responses that increasingly resemble a desired end behaviour in a step by step manner, very complex behaviour can be built up from simple units.
The first responses are reinforced until perfected and then reinforcement is withheld until the behaviour is refined to the next desired behaviour.

Evaluation of classical and operant conditioning

EVALUATION OF METHODOLOGY

STRENGTHS – The theories of classical and operant conditioning were the product of behaviourist psychology with its emphasis on observable behaviour and laboratory experimentation. With such objective and standardised methodology the principles of classical and operant conditioning could be reliably replicated while reducing the effect of possible confounding variables. Animals such as dogs, cats, pigeons and rats were frequently used as experimental subjects since the behaviourists believed the laws of learning were universal and they have the advantage of being practically and ethically easier to test (they can be tested under more controlled conditions, do not try to work out the nature of the test and are given less ethical rights etc.).

WEAKNESSES – Unfortunately the methods employed also had disadvantages. The experimental subjects often demonstrated learning of only a small range of unnatural responses, e.g. animals pressing levers or pushing buttons, under artificially controlled conditions, e.g. Albert B was not allowed to suck his thumb (he failed to show the same fear response when he did so). This may have led the behaviourists to ignore behaviour their subjects might have found difficult to learn and neglect other influences upon the learning process. This criticism was especially relevant to the study of non-human animal learning which may be qualitatively different to human learning in important ways. There were also serious ethical problems with some of the procedures used in classical and operant conditioning studies.

EVALUATION OF CLASSICAL AND OPERANT CONDITIONING THEORIES

STRENGTHS – The behaviourists used the theories of classical and operant conditioning to explain a wide variety of psychological phenomena, from the processes of learning to the products of it such as phobia and language acquisition. In addition many practical applications of the theory were developed, from animal training to human education and the treatment of disordered behaviour. In many cases such applications have been shown to be efficient in producing behavioural change.

WEAKNESSES – Unfortunately classical and operant conditioning did not take into account the role of inherited and cognitive factors in learning, and are thus incomplete explanations of the learning process in humans and other animals. By focusing on just a few species such as rats or pigeons and generalising the results to all animals, the behaviourists not only ignored the differing cognitive influences on learning that different species show (e.g. the ability of humans to learn by observation and imitation), but importantly neglected the innate abilities in learning that every species will have evolved to better adapt themselves to their environmental niche.

INNATE BIASES IN LEARNING ABILITY

Ethologists would argue that animals have `built-in` biases in natural learning ability that they have evolved to better adapt them to their environment. The laws of learning are therefore not the same for all species, for example:

- **Selectivity of associations and phobias** – Garcia and Koelling (1966) found that rats given a novel tasting solution and made to feel sick up to 3 *hours* afterwards would still learn to associate the two events and avoid that solution on future occasions, even after *only one* such trial in some cases. It therefore seems likely that rats have evolved a highly sensitive learning capability between taste and sickness, especially since this sensitivity makes `evolutionary sense` – it aids survival. Seligman (1970) proposed the concept of **biological preparedness** and argued that humans have also evolved selective associations for survival reasons, in the form of **phobias** for example. The most frequently occurring phobias, e.g. of heights, snakes, spiders etc., all share the evolutionary characteristic of being dangerous to us, and these sort of stimuli have been experimentally shown to be more easily classically conditioned with fear than non-dangerous stimuli such as flowers and grass, which are far more rarely found as phobias. Also of interest is the finding that modern day dangerous objects such as guns and cars are also rare phobias since evolution has not had time to *prepare* us for these stimuli.

- **Imprinting and language acquisition** – Lorenz (1935) showed an increased learning sensitivity to particular stimuli could occur at *certain times* in an animal's life when it is most important to acquire this learning. In his studies of imprinting he found that goslings would form strong attachments to moving, conspicuous objects in their environment during the first hours after hatching, and will follow and stay close to this object.
  In a similar way some researchers have argued that human *language acquisition* takes place during a sensitive time period early in life. A species-specific, evolved human potential for language (a Language Acquisition Device according to Chomsky) would account for the ease with which young children learn to speak and understand complex grammar as well as the failure to teach human language to apes to the same standard.

COGNITIVE FACTORS IN LEARNING

Classical and operant conditioning also ignore the cognitive factors between the stimulus and response that influence learning. In operant conditioning for example, a number of researchers have demonstrated that learning does not always happen by trial and error, reinforcement is not always necessary for learning to occur and learning can produce changes in mental representations rather than just behaviour.

- **Insight learning** – Kohler found primates often seem to solve problems in a flash of insight (involving a cognitive rearrangement of the elements of the problem) rather than by laborious trial and error.
- **Latent learning** – Tolman found rats will learn mazes without reinforcement and that they acquire mental maps of the mazes rather than a series of left and right turning behaviours.
- **Social Learning theory** – suggests:
1 Humans can learn *automatically* through *observation* rather than requiring reinforcement through personal experience.
2 Observed behaviour may be *imitated* if desirable consequences are expected (whole 'chunks' of behaviour can be copied without the need for gradual trial-and-error practice).

Social learning in non-human animals

EXPLANATIONS OF SOCIAL LEARNING

WHAT IS IT?
Social learning refers to behaviour that is acquired as a result of experience with others rather than that acquired alone (individual learning). Individual learning in animals has been shown to occur through classical and operant conditioning, but there is debate as to whether additional methods of learning are involved in social learning.

WHY DOES IT OCCUR?
There are many possible benefits of social learning, not least that useful survival behaviour relating to foraging and predator avoidance can be acquired faster and more safely by learning from others than by having to discover them individually by trial and error. The evolutionary importance of social learning is illustrated by the finding that in some species parents spend time and effort helping their offspring acquire important survival techniques.

HOW DOES IT OCCUR?
Heyes (1993) points out that other animals can provide useful information concerning both the environment and behaviour used in interacting with it, however, social learning of this information by observation may occur through different methods:

- **Stimulus enhancement** – involves learning about the **environment** through observing others. It is the tendency to **pay attention to**, and thus interact with, certain **places or objects** in the environment after observing others successfully interacting with them. The **behaviour** of the other animal is **not copied** directly, but it increases the chance that the observer will **learn by individual trial and error** to perform similar behaviour to gain the same **rewards**. Information about the stimulus not response is learned.
- **True imitation** – involves learning about the actual **form of behaviour** by observing others. In true imitation the observation of another's pattern of behaviour is causal to changing the observer's pattern of behaviour and allows **novel** (not previously shown) and **complex actions** to be **automatically learned** without the need for reinforcement. Performing the behaviour may or may not depend on reinforcement. True imitation, learning about responses rather than stimuli, is rarely shown in animals.

STUDIES OF SOCIAL LEARNING

BIRDS
Foraging – Fisher and Hinde (1949) suggested that the ability of blue tits and other birds to open the tops of milk bottles to gain the cream was due to imitation, given the rapid spread of the behaviour from town to town. However, since pecking and tearing objects are pre-existing foraging behaviours of these birds rather than novel actions, stimulus enhancement is a more likely explanation – the attention of birds was drawn to bottle tops opened by others, thus increasing the chance of pecking being directed at that particular stimulus. The birds already knew how to peck; they only learned what and where to peck. Similarly, birds may learn where to nest, migrate or not be afraid by following others to certain locations. The presence of other birds may also have a social facilitation effect – encouraging behaviour by increasing motivation or reducing fear (Sherry and Galef, 1990).

Bird song – is more likely to represent a limited form of true imitation in some species, e.g. chaffinches who imitate local dialects or parrots and mynahs who can mimic human speech.

MONKEYS
Foraging – Itani (1958) reported how, in one colony of Japanese macaques, a juvenile named 'Imo' discovered how to wash sweet potatoes and separate food from sand with water, and the behaviour spread to her playmates and their mothers. Rather than imitation, the behaviour (which took a long time to spread) was likely to be due to stimulus enhancement and individual learning (as Imo drew attention to potatoes and water) or inadvertent reinforcement by the researchers who provided the food. However, macaque mothers do guide stimulus enhancement by pulling away their infants from strange food or objects and modelling certain styles of potato washing (Kawai, 1963, 1965a).

PRIMATES
Foraging – Boesch (1991) reported that chimpanzee mothers actively 'teach' their young how to open nuts with stone tools. This involves elaborate stimulus enhancement through the provision of materials, demonstration and corrective intervention. Imitation cannot be ruled out, but is thought to be less likely if the 'simpler' and well-established processes of stimulus attention and trial-and-error learning can adequately explain the learning.

Problem solving – Many studies have shown that 'enculturated' primates seem to show complex forms of delayed imitation. However, Call and Tomasello (1995) found orang-utans do not readily use imitation to solve problems. This is in contrast to observations by Russon and Galdikas (1995) of orang-utans being rehabilitated in Indonesia who have been seen using complex sequences of imitated behaviours to attempt to re-light a fire (by using kerosene scooped out of a drum with a cup and fanning the embers with a cooking lid) or even to steal laundry (by emptying a canoe of water and using it to sneak past a guard) and wash it (using soap and scrubbing brush).

Intelligence in non-human animals

WHAT IS ANIMAL INTELLIGENCE?

The assessment of intelligence in non-human animals is hampered by the difficulty of defining what intelligence is. Intelligence is an abstract concept and attempts to define and test it may be biased by the values and conceptions of the definers and testers – this has already happened with human testing and becomes even more problematic when attempting to judge other animals by human criteria. In general terms, intelligence has been defined as the ability to learn from experience and to adapt to changes in the environment as a result – acquiring and using knowledge efficiently. The extent to which organisms can learn and adapt depends upon:

- The range of abilities they have – e.g. perceptual, learning, reasoning, memory, spatial, numerical, linguistic, meta-cognitive, etc.
- The complexity of those abilities – e.g. higher level types of learning and reasoning (more intelligent species may be able to use imitation and insight rather than trial-and-error learning, or use self-monitoring and social attribution to select the best strategies).
- The efficiency and speed of applying those abilities – e.g. based on physical ability and/or experience/practice (highly trained or enculturated animals show more complex and rapid adaptive behaviour).

Two particular examples of abilities that have been associated with intelligence in animals are self-recognition and theory of mind.

EVIDENCE FOR INTELLIGENCE IN ANIMALS

SELF-RECOGNITION

Self-recognition may be the physical sign of self-awareness in animals, which may be important in enabling animals to monitor their own thoughts, feelings and behaviour. Self-awareness may help animals to predict the outcome of behaviour, select appropriate strategies and understand other animals' motivations and behaviour (see theory of mind).

- Self-recognition has only been found (using the mirror self-recognition test) in humans and primates (chimpanzees, gorillas and orang-utans).
- Gallop (1970) found that chimps could learn to recognise themselves in mirrors since they:
  1 Gradually stopped reacting (e.g. threatening or calling) as if another animal was present.
  2 Learned to use the mirrors to explore parts of their body they could not normally see.
  3 Touched areas on their heads that had been coloured red more often when in front of a mirror than not.
- Criticisms have been made of Gallop's mirror recognition method since, for example, the red marks had to be applied under anaesthetic which may have affected body touching behaviour and the same results are not reliably found.
- However, Savage-Rumbaugh and Lewin (1994) report that chimpanzees will react to their own image on live-video monitors (e.g. making faces, bobbing up and down, or using it with a torch to look down their own throats) and can use such information to guide arm movements they cannot directly see (e.g. to retrieve food through a small arm hole), but will respond differently to previously taped images of themselves. Also the interest and use of mirrors differs across individual chimpanzees and within the same individual over time, which may account for the unreliability of the mirror test results.
- There is also doubt over whether self-recognition is a valid indicator of conscious self-awareness (rather than of just a body image).

THEORY OF MIND

Theory of mind refers to the ability to realise that others also have intentions, knowledge, beliefs and emotional states, but that these may differ from one's own. A theory of mind allows the possessor to attribute knowledge to others and, practically, to use differences in knowledge to deceive others.

Experimental studies

- Povinelli et al (1990) found chimpanzees could attribute knowledge to humans by selecting the correct hiding place for food (which they could then eat) when two researchers each pointed to a different possible location, but only one had been seen to have knowledge of the true location (the other was outside when the chimp had seen the researcher hide the food but behind a screen).
- Woodruff and Premack (1979) found chimps, who knew the location of hidden food that they could not reach, tended to indicate the correct location to an unaware researcher if that researcher had been cooperative (given the food to the chimp). However, if the researcher had been competitive (keeping the food if directed to the correct location) but the chimp had received the food if it had indicated the wrong location, then the chimps tended towards deception. This involved an attribution of intent to the humans by the chimps.
- However, in both of these laboratory experiments, the chimps may just have been responding to some other cue, such as learning to associate different researchers with different rewards through operant conditioning.

Naturalistic observations

- Byrne and Whiten (1987) gathered reports of examples of tactical deception (where the animal intends to deceive by using 'an 'honest act' from his normal repertoire in a different context, such that even familiar individuals are misled') from over a hundred researchers studying animal behaviour in the wild. By applying strict criteria they found relatively few examples, all of which were shown by apes, mostly chimpanzees (Savage-Rumbaugh and Lewin, 1994). These usually involved deceptions over food by, for example, pretending not to have seen food that others had failed to notice in order to avoid sharing or losing it.

Navigation/Homing behaviour

Homing involves learning to locate home sites/territories after absence
Homing can involve returning to home sites after short term forays for food, or the longer term and longer distance journeys involved in migratory behaviour. It seems that homing ability involves a range of innate and learnt abilities in interaction with each other.

INSTINCTUAL INFLUENCES

The initiation of migratory behaviour is largely under instinctual control. Migration evolved to cope with the differing environmental locations of food, warmth, and mating sites which would often be influenced by seasonal variation. Some species have, therefore, developed an instinctual behavioural tendency to migrate in a certain direction at a certain time, that seems to be triggered by environmental cues, such as temperature and day length, rather than experience or imitation. For example:

- European warblers appear to have internal genetic cues to migrate – some fly south to the Mediterranean, others to southern parts of Africa. When kept in a laboratory cage with constant daylength, these birds become restless in the spring and autumn. Those who migrate the furthest are restless the longest, and they even move towards the end of the cage nearest the direction of travel (Slater, 1985).

- Young European starlings will migrate in a fixed south-westerly compass direction to their normal wintering areas. Even if captured en route and displaced several hundred miles south, they will continue in an off-course Southwest direction, rather travelling Northwest to counteract the course change.
- Monarch butterflies travel northwards and southwards across North America with the changing seasonal temperatures.

However, although instinctual impulses can explain the initiation and general directional movement of migration, they do not account for the precise location of original home sites on the return journey – clearly learning is required for this.

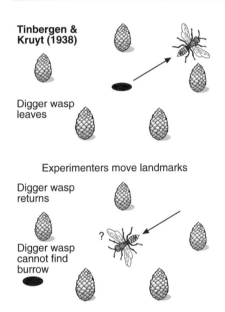

Tinbergen & Kruyt (1938)

Digger wasp leaves

Experimenters move landmarks

Digger wasp returns

?

Digger wasp cannot find burrow

LEARNING OF LANDMARKS

The precise location of home sites can be explained by experience – animals simply learn landmarks on the way out and 'reverse the order on the way back' (Ridley, 1995). For example:

- Tinbergen and Kruyt (1938) showed how digger wasps learn the environmental landmarks surrounding their burrow very fixedly before leaving. If these landmarks are moved in a systematic way, the wasp will search for the burrow in the wrong place. Watson found gulls show a similar fixedness of learning when approaching their nest sites.
- Most wild fowl are thought to learn their migratory route through following adults; while cuckoos, who migrate individually, apparently learn it themselves. Salmon learn the chemical traces of the river water they were born in, so they can later return to it to breed, sometimes after travelling vast distances.

Although learning can account well for the short range location of home sites, it is a less satisfactory explanation of the very long range homing behaviour seen in migration. Surely the amount of route information memorised over sometimes thousands of miles after just one such journey is enormous – and this all needs to be recognised in reverse on the return journey. Even if this does occur, it does not account for the ability of some animals to reach home after having been blown or moved 'off course'. This has led researchers to investigate whether true navigational ability is found in animals.

TRUE NAVIGATIONAL ABILITY

Perdeck (1958) found that although juvenile European starlings would migrate according to a general compass direction, adult starlings had developed navigational skills and could adjust their flight if their starting position was artificially moved to the south. True navigation, as opposed to route learning, should only be suspected, however, if animals are taken to completely unfamiliar locations and still manage to find their way home. Although the existence of true navigation has been debated by researchers such as Baker (1984), the following studies indicate it exists, in some birds at least:

- Kenyon and Rice (1958) sent albatrosses by air from Midway Island to various points in the North Pacific, such as Japan, the Philippines, and Hawaii, and found that 14 out of 18 homed successfully (the furthest albatross in the Philippines travelled 4,120 miles in 32 days).
- Walcott and Schmidt-Koeng (1973) showed that homing pigeons could successfully find their way home if released from a variety of unfamiliar sites, even when transported under anaesthesia or in rotating cages to prevent them from learning the route on the way out, or if fitted with translucent lenses that prevented them identifying visual landmarks from the air unless they were very close to them.

True navigation seems to be an innate ability that improves with practice. Matthews (1972) found that visual landmark learning ability in pigeons bore no relation to their success in homing, in fact there was a slight negative correlation between the two abilities. However, homing pigeons have long been recognised to improve their ability if allowed to practice and explore their home site from the air.

There is still confusion over how animals navigate - humans achieve it through possessing a compass and a map to tell them where they are. Researchers have identified a number of possible sources for the 'compass' in animals, for example pigeons use the position of the sun in the sky, plus an internal clock to make allowances for its change throughout the day, to give them their direction (Hoffman, 1953, altered this internal clock by artificially changing the pigeons' day/night light cycles and found predictable navigational errors occurred). Under cloudy conditions, pigeons seem to be able to detect magnetic direction (attaching magnets to their head will ruin their navigation if the sun is not visible) and many creatures including pigeons, bees, and migratory fish have been found to possess magnetite particles in their bodies.

Signalling systems – function and evolution

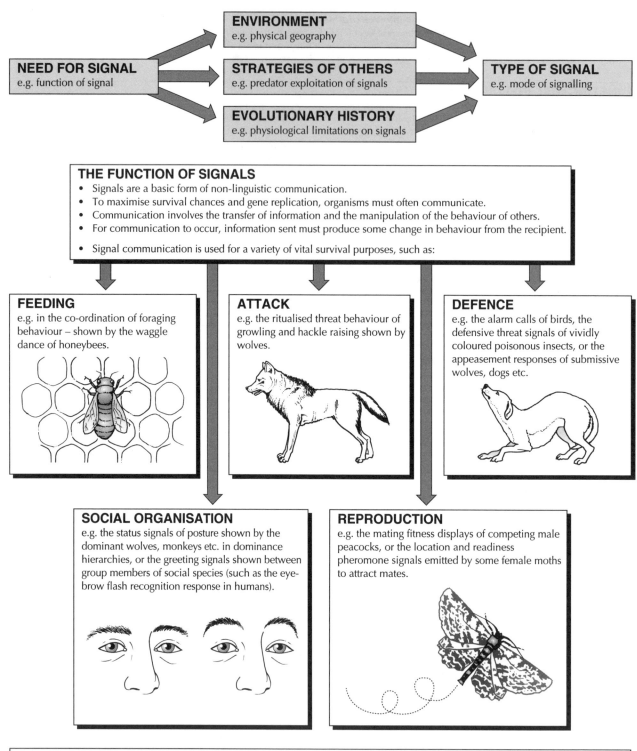

ENVIRONMENT
e.g. physical geography

NEED FOR SIGNAL
e.g. function of signal

STRATEGIES OF OTHERS
e.g. predator exploitation of signals

TYPE OF SIGNAL
e.g. mode of signalling

EVOLUTIONARY HISTORY
e.g. physiological limitations on signals

THE FUNCTION OF SIGNALS
- Signals are a basic form of non-linguistic communication.
- To maximise survival chances and gene replication, organisms must often communicate.
- Communication involves the transfer of information and the manipulation of the behaviour of others.
- For communication to occur, information sent must produce some change in behaviour from the recipient.

- Signal communication is used for a variety of vital survival purposes, such as:

FEEDING
e.g. in the co-ordination of foraging behaviour – shown by the waggle dance of honeybees.

ATTACK
e.g. the ritualised threat behaviour of growling and hackle raising shown by wolves.

DEFENCE
e.g. the alarm calls of birds, the defensive threat signals of vividly coloured poisonous insects, or the appeasement responses of submissive wolves, dogs etc.

SOCIAL ORGANISATION
e.g. the status signals of posture shown by the dominant wolves, monkeys etc. in dominance hierarchies, or the greeting signals shown between group members of social species (such as the eyebrow flash recognition response in humans).

REPRODUCTION
e.g. the mating fitness displays of competing male peacocks, or the location and readiness pheromone signals emitted by some female moths to attract mates.

THE EVOLUTION OF SIGNALS

Visual communication displays often evolve from behaviours shown in feeding, body maintenance or movement, and become increasingly stereotyped and divorced from their original function as they become used for communication, e.g. mallard duck courtship displays appear to have originally evolved from feather preening movements.

The use of behaviour for signalling often starts through approach-avoid conflicts between competing males, or in courtship when communication of intent becomes important for survival – a male may risk damage in a fight, but needs to compete; he risks an aggressive rejection from a female, but needs to mate to pass on his genes. Under these stressful conditions, hesitation in intention movements or displacement activity (behaviour unrelated to the present situation) may act as signals – which will become more effective if presented in clear stereotyped and ritualised ways. Thus the mallard duck, caught in a dilemma over whether to approach or avoid a female duck, may have started preening himself as a displacement activity in his anxious state of indecision. This would have acted as a signal for the female to know his intentions (and so stay or approach the male if interested or remove herself if not).

Communication can co-evolve between the sender and the receiver by acting directly on the nervous system, e.g. sign signals automatically triggering fixed action patterns of behaviour (see Tinbergen's (1952) study of the stickleback).

Signalling systems – modes of signalling

MODE OF SIGNAL	ADVANTAGES	DISADVANTAGES	EXAMPLES
TACTILE SIGNALS	1 High certainty that the message will be received due to intimacy of contact.	1 Extremely limited in range. 2 Fairly limited in the amount and complexity of information.	• Herring gull chicks peck at the beaks of their parents to stimulate feeding behaviour. • Bonobo chimpanzees signal conciliation through sexual touching behaviour.
SOUND SIGNALS	Allow communication to occur 1 over long distances 2 past physical obstacles 3 quickly 4 in the absence of light 5 in a detailed and complex way since much information can be sent in sound waves 6 multi-directionally – good for reaching many receivers	Sound waves, however 1 lack directional control, and are, unfortunately, easily detected by predators. Some calls seem designed to minimise the chances of location by predators 2 are costly in terms of energy to produce them and are short lasting (fade quickly) 3 may distort over distance	• Humpback whale song has an extremely long transmission range. • Bird warning calls are effective since they transmit the message very quickly and to many receivers simultaneously. • Bird mating songs are efficient signals since they convey enough detail to distinguish one species from another and can be received by others through obstacles such as thick foliage. • Dolphin clicks and whistles can transmit information through very murky water. • Human language – the most detailed form of communication, is capable of transmitting an infinite variety of messages.
CHEMICAL SIGNALS	1 Long-ranging 2 Long-lasting 3 Do not require the continued presence of the sender 4 Fairly discrete – some signals are only detectable by members of the same species 5 Transmits messages past physical objects and in the dark	1 Fairly slow in delivering information 2 Relatively limited in complexity of information sent 3 Difficult to control direction and duration, due to wind conditions, for example	• Moth pheromones can be detected and followed by the male from several kilometres away. • Cats, dogs, and rabbits mark their territory with chemicals in their urine or faeces, or even rub their scent glands against objects. The scents act as territory signals without the continual presence of the animal itself and are fairly long lasting. • Ants communicate primarily through chemical signals ranging from alarm to trail following signals.
VISUAL SIGNALS	1 Fast 2 Fairly large amounts of information can be sent 3 Directional 4 Can be long lasting and energy efficient, e.g. body markings	1 Limited range 2 Blocked by obstacles 3 Requires light 4 Visible to predators	• Birds use colourful mating displays that visually indicate the sexual fitness of the signaller. • Squid are capable of sending different visual messages in the form of colour patterns on different parts of their body, sometimes simultaneously in different directions to different receivers. • Wasp coloration sends a continuous warning to predators.

Natural animal language

WHAT IS LANGUAGE?

Language is a form of communication which is distinct from signalling in many ways. Hockett (1960) and Aitchison have proposed various design criteria to define language, which involve aspects of its particular function, structure, and delivery.

- **FUNCTION** – language should allow
  interchangeability – the ability of the possessor to send and receive messages
  semanticity – the use of symbols to stand for or refer to objects, situations, events, concepts, etc.
  displacement – communication about things not currently present
  productivity – the creation of an infinite variety of new messages/meanings
  prevarication – the creation of conversation about things that have not happened, e.g. fiction or lies
  learnability and transmission - the acquisition of language and transferral to the next generation
  reflexiveness – the ability to use language to talk about language

- **STRUCTURE** – the form of language should show
  arbitrariness – the symbols used do not have to resemble the objects they stand for
  specialisation – the linguistic behaviour has developed only for communication
  duality and organisation – the language should be divisible into subcomponents which can be combined
  structure dependence – the possession of grammatical rules for combining units of language

- **DELIVERY** – the language should enable messages to be transmitted in the following ways
  spontaneously – the sender can initiate language at will and does not have to wait for triggers
  turn taking – communicators alternate conversational turns
  feedback – the user can hear the message it sends

HONEY BEES

Research by von Frisch (1967) revealed that honey bees communicate information about the distance and direction of food sources from the hive through the form of dance on the honeycomb that they perform upon returning from a foraging expedition. Distance is indicated by the speed of the dance and waggling of the abdomen, direction by the angle of the dance relative to the sun and gravity. More recent research by Kirchner and Towne (1994) using robotic honeybees and laser analysis of sound vibrations has revealed that both sound and dance are needed to communicate information about the location of food.

The honey bee dance certainly fulfils many language criteria, such as interchangeability, semanticity, and displacement, but has limited productivity and no prevarication, structure dependence, etc.

BIRD SONG

Marler (1970) proposed that some bird song shows certain functional and physiological similarities to human language. The chaffinch, for example, has at least 15 distinct calls for different functions and transmits regional dialects to its offspring.

EXAMPLES OF NATURAL ANIMAL LANGUAGE?

Some animal communication may be sophisticated enough to fulfil some of the criteria for language.

VERVET MONKEYS

Seyfarth and Cheyney (1980) identified three alarm calls in vervet monkeys which stand for distinct types of predator:

- Eagle call – caused vervets to look skywards and run for bush cover.
- Leopard call – caused listening vervets to look around them and climb trees.
- Python call – caused vervets to scan the floor area around them.

These calls show interchangeability, semanticity, and a degree of learnability and transmission (young vervets modify their calls by watching adults). However, productivity is very limited.

DOLPHINS

Dolphins communicate through a variety of squeaks, whistles and clicks, often in the ultrasonic sound range. The meanings of these sounds seem fairly specialised within particular dolphin groups – Bright (1984) recorded the sounds made by a dolphin being captured and played them to other members of the captive's social group. They turned and fled, whereas the same sounds played to a different group of dolphins only produced curiosity (indicating learnability and semanticity, for example). Bastian (1965) claims that captive dolphins which were separated from, but able to hear, each other, were able to communicate complex information about training to each other by sound alone.

188 Animal cognition

Teaching human language to non-human animals 1

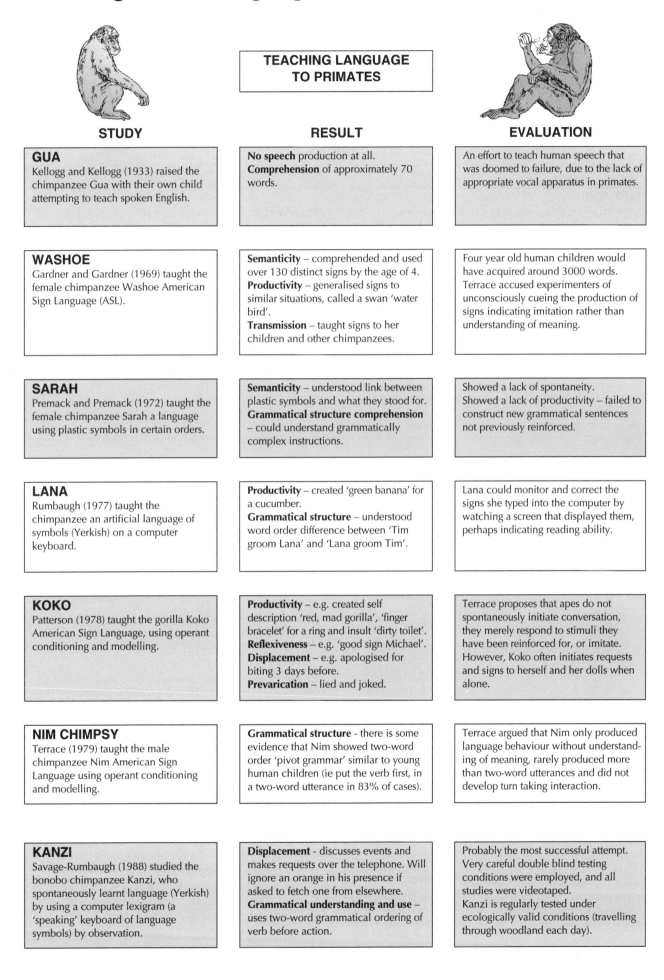

TEACHING LANGUAGE TO PRIMATES

STUDY	RESULT	EVALUATION
GUA Kellogg and Kellogg (1933) raised the chimpanzee Gua with their own child attempting to teach spoken English.	**No speech** production at all. **Comprehension** of approximately 70 words.	An effort to teach human speech that was doomed to failure, due to the lack of appropriate vocal apparatus in primates.
WASHOE Gardner and Gardner (1969) taught the female chimpanzee Washoe American Sign Language (ASL).	**Semanticity** – comprehended and used over 130 distinct signs by the age of 4. **Productivity** – generalised signs to similar situations, called a swan 'water bird'. **Transmission** – taught signs to her children and other chimpanzees.	Four year old human children would have acquired around 3000 words. Terrace accused experimenters of unconsciously cueing the production of signs indicating imitation rather than understanding of meaning.
SARAH Premack and Premack (1972) taught the female chimpanzee Sarah a language using plastic symbols in certain orders.	**Semanticity** – understood link between plastic symbols and what they stood for. **Grammatical structure comprehension** – could understand grammatically complex instructions.	Showed a lack of spontaneity. Showed a lack of productivity – failed to construct new grammatical sentences not previously reinforced.
LANA Rumbaugh (1977) taught the chimpanzee an artificial language of symbols (Yerkish) on a computer keyboard.	**Productivity** – created 'green banana' for a cucumber. **Grammatical structure** – understood word order difference between 'Tim groom Lana' and 'Lana groom Tim'.	Lana could monitor and correct the signs she typed into the computer by watching a screen that displayed them, perhaps indicating reading ability.
KOKO Patterson (1978) taught the gorilla Koko American Sign Language, using operant conditioning and modelling.	**Productivity** – e.g. created self description 'red, mad gorilla', 'finger bracelet' for a ring and insult 'dirty toilet'. **Reflexiveness** – e.g. 'good sign Michael'. **Displacement** – e.g. apologised for biting 3 days before. **Prevarication** – lied and joked.	Terrace proposes that apes do not spontaneously initiate conversation, they merely respond to stimuli they have been reinforced for, or imitate. However, Koko often initiates requests and signs to herself and her dolls when alone.
NIM CHIMPSY Terrace (1979) taught the male chimpanzee Nim American Sign Language using operant conditioning and modelling.	**Grammatical structure** - there is some evidence that Nim showed two-word order 'pivot grammar' similar to young human children (ie put the verb first, in a two-word utterance in 83% of cases).	Terrace argued that Nim only produced language behaviour without understanding of meaning, rarely produced more than two-word utterances and did not develop turn taking interaction.
KANZI Savage-Rumbaugh (1988) studied the bonobo chimpanzee Kanzi, who spontaneously learnt language (Yerkish) by using a computer lexigram (a 'speaking' keyboard of language symbols) by observation.	**Displacement** - discusses events and makes requests over the telephone. Will ignore an orange in his presence if asked to fetch one from elsewhere. **Grammatical understanding and use** – uses two-word grammatical ordering of verb before action.	Probably the most successful attempt. Very careful double blind testing conditions were employed, and all studies were videotaped. Kanzi is regularly tested under ecologically valid conditions (travelling through woodland each day).

'Teaching sign language to a chimpanzee' Gardner and Gardner (1969)

BACKGROUND

- One way to investigate whether another species might be able to learn human language is to try and teach it. Chimpanzees, being regarded as intelligent and sociable animals (although strong and occasionally difficult to handle), are regarded as good subjects for this kind of study.
- Past attempts at teaching chimps vocal language, e.g. Hayes and Hayes (1951) with the chimpanzee Vicky, failed because of the chimpanzee's inappropriate vocal apparatus. Since chimpanzees employ a variety of gestures in their natural environment, the aim of the study was to see if a chimpanzee could be taught American Sign Language.

METHOD

Design: a longitudinal case study of one chimpanzee.

Subject: Washoe (named after the county where the University of Nevada was situated) was a wild caught female chimpanzee aged between 8 and 14 months in June 1966 when the study began. Although Washoe was at first very young and dependent, it was decided to work with a chimpanzee so young in case there was a critical time period for language acquisition.

Equipment: trainers able to communicate in American Sign Language (ASL), a gestural language used by the deaf, were required. Although some ASL gestures are symbolically arbitrary, others are quite representational or iconic (they resemble what they stand for). Finger spelling was avoided as far as possible. Since ASL is currently used by humans, comparisons of young chimpanzee and human performance could be made. Washoe was always in the company of the researchers during her waking hours, all of whom used ASL in their games and activities with her.

Procedure: training methods made use of

imitation – past researchers noted that chimpanzees naturally imitated visual behaviour, so the researchers repeatedly signed in Washoe's presence. Washoe would readily imitate gestures but not always on command or in appropriate situations at first, so correct and exaggerated gestures were repeatedly made as prompts until Washoe emitted the correct sign. Routine activities, such as bathing, feeding, and tooth-brushing also helped produce (delayed) imitation.

babbling – Washoe's spontaneously emitted gestures were encouraged and shaped into signs by indulging in appropriate behaviour.

instrumental conditioning – tickling was used as a reinforcer to shape more accurate signs by withholding it until a clearer version of the sign was shown.

RESULTS

- **Measurement:** detailed records of daily signing behaviour were kept until 16 months, when their increasing frequency made such record keeping difficult. From 16 months, new signs were recorded on a checklist when three different observers noted a sign occurring in the correct situation without specific prompting. A sign was said to have been acquired when it was correctly used without prompting at least once a day for 15 consecutive days.

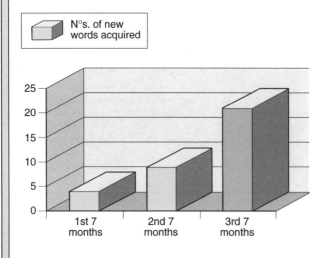

- **Vocabulary:** thirty signs met the above criteria by the end of the twenty-second month, plus four more which occurred on more than half the days of a 30 consecutive day period. Four new signs were shown in the first 7 months, nine signs during the next seven months and 21 during the following seven months.

- **Differentiation:** Washoe's signing became more context and object specific over time, even showing the ability to distinguish between the use of 'flower' (originally used for all smells) and 'smell'

- **Transfer:** Washoe spontaneously generalised signs acquired in one context to other contexts, e.g. 'picture' to all pictures, 'dog' to unknown dogs, etc.

- **Combinations:** Washoe used signs in combination once she had 8 to 10 signs at her disposal. Some combinations were shown spontaneously, before they had been used by the researchers, e.g. 'gimme tickle' or 'listen dog'.

EVALUATION

Methodological: The training and testing conditions were not ideal (although controlled tests were being developed) and there are many practical problems with trying to teach chimpanzees language (they get distracted and frustrated).

Theoretical: There are many problems involved in deciding whether Washoe was acquiring language. She seemed to be showing semanticity, displacement, and productivity (creativity) but did not show structure dependence (no grammatical word order – although this was not reinforced by the researchers).

Ethics: The research has implications for the rights of apes, if they can talk should they not be given human rights?

Links: The debate over animal language. The use of animals as subjects. The ethics of testing animals.

Teaching human language to non-human animals 2

TEACHING LANGUAGE TO CETACEANS

Herman et al (1984) taught dolphins a symbolic language in two forms:

- **Akeakamai** – was taught an artificial, visual language of signs based on gestures and movements of the trainers' arms.
- **Phoenix** – was taught an artificial acoustic language based on computer generated whistling noises.

Each dolphin was taught a specific set of rules for combining the symbols of the language.

Herman et al were only interested in testing the linguistic comprehension, not production, of the dolphins.

RESULTS

Semanticity – could obey instructions to manipulate certain objects if the instructions were phrased in linguistic sounds or signs used to represent those objects.

Productivity – responded appropriately to grammatically specific and completely new combinations of words.

Displacement – followed instructions to search for objects in places hidden from view, and could even signal that an object was not present if asked to search for something that had not been placed in the pool.

EVALUATION

The majority of all attempts to teach dolphins language focus on comprehension rather than production.

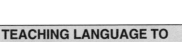

TEACHING LANGUAGE TO PARROTS

Pepperberg (1983) has taught the African Grey Parrot, Alex, English spoken language through observation of human models communicating in social situations.

Selective reinforcement is also used, whereby correct responses are rewarded by the object being discussed and by verbal praise.

RESULTS

Semanticity – Alex uses language to show understanding of whether one object is the same or different from another.

EVALUATION

The primary focus of Pepperberg's studies is to investigate the cognitive abilities of the parrot rather than just language.

CONCLUSIONS

- **Productivity vs. comprehension** – there is a large debate over how important the production of language is compared to its comprehension. Dolphin studies were geared towards comprehension, and Savage-Rumbaugh sees it as the most important aspect of language.
- **The importance of grammar** – as it became increasingly clear that apes could produce language, some researchers, e.g. Terrace, began to emphasise how they produced it. Apes have demonstrated comprehension of fairly complex grammatical sentences and show two word pivot grammar in their production, but have not progressed much further. However, word order is not always consistent in human language (e.g. Finnish) or language use (deaf people make word order errors).
- **Comparative abilities** – the speed and extent of language and grammar acquisition in other animals, however, is far slower than in humans. A human child at age four is more linguistically competent than any other older animal.
- **Comparative physiology** – for some researchers 'the big question has been: do chimpanzees have the architecture in the brain that supports language?' (Hopkins of the Yerkes Primate Centre, cited in *New Scientist*, January 1998). Many think not, especially for the grammatical aspects of language, however, recent research by Gannon et al has discovered that 17 out of 18 chimpanzee brains they examined, showed development of the planum temporale (PT) on the left side of the cortex. In humans the PT is in the middle of an area involved in language comprehension, and this asymmetry of the brain was previously thought to be unique to humans.
- **Objectivity of research** – many would argue that the attachments researchers in this area develop to their subject matter and their tendency to show anthropomorphism to animal behaviour, distorts the objectivity of their studies, leading to over-exaggerated findings. Ape researchers in particular, however, would argue that close interaction and support is necessary to teach a language to any animal.
- **Alternative explanations** – Terrace argues that language-like behaviour in apes merely reflects ever increasing sophistication of operant conditioning responses to gain reward, not understanding of the meaning of those responses. The case of 'Clever Hans', a horse that seemingly understood language and could perform mathematical equations, shows how easy it is to be misled about animal abilities. All the horse had learnt was to detect the unconscious facial cues given by the trainer (out of relief when the right answer had been reached) for the reward of food. The majority of animal language researchers disagree with Terrace's view of ape language, however.

Memory in non-human animals

EXAMPLES OF THE IMPORTANCE OF MEMORY IN ANIMALS

NAVIGATION
Navigation involves the orientation and movement towards different locations in the environment. Memory enables animals to move between locations associated with different activities such as sheltering, hiding, breeding, nesting and feeding.

Research studies

Tinbergen's (1952) field experiments on digger wasps illustrated the importance of memory for the spatial arrangement of landmarks in locating home sites after absence, by shifting and altering them around the digger wasp's burrow.

Tolman (1946) demonstrated spatial memory in rats navigating through mazes. Others have used submerged platforms.

FORAGING
Foraging is the seeking of food from the environment. Memory is important for foraging animals to remember where safe and productive food sites are located and where they may have previously hidden food (caching).

Research studies

Balda and Kamil (1992) found that captive Clark's nutcrackers, birds that each hide thousands of seeds in autumn, were able to remember their cache locations up to 40 weeks later.

Menzel (1973) found chimpanzees carried around an enclosure while a researcher hid food, could later remember where most of it had been buried and collect it using efficient shortcuts.

WHAT MEMORY IS REQUIRED?
Both navigation and foraging involve memory for locations (recognition of features), the associations of locations (what activity, e.g. feeding, nesting etc., is associated with each place), and the spatial arrangement of locations in relation to each other. Navigation and the location of food sites can therefore occur by route following and the serial recognition (matching visual images to stored memories) of locations and their associations. Some researchers, however, have proposed that cognitive maps are also formed in memory.

EXPLANATIONS OF NAVIGATION AND FORAGING MEMORY

PHYSIOLOGICAL THEORY – THE HIPPOCAMPUS
The hippocampus of animals has been suggested to be an important centre for spatial memory representation. The hippocampus seems to have '*place cells*' that respond to movement into specific '*place fields*' in the environment, and appears to regulate spatial memory through the use of the neurotransmitter *acetylcholine*.

Research studies

- *Case studies* of human patients with hippocampal damage reveal they have problems after the damage in finding their way around unfamiliar locations. However, the study of accidental cases means there is a lack of precision over the extent of the brain damage, meaning other areas may be affected.
- *Surgical removal* of the hippocampus or the *drug inhibition* of acetylcholine activity in rats, however, has been shown to affect their ability to learn new radial or Morris water mazes.
- *Microelectrode recording* of rats' hippocampal cells has found that particular (place) cells will repeatedly respond when the rat moves into particular parts (place fields) of a maze and/or carries out particular behavioural acts, e.g. feeding (O'Keefe and Nadel, 1978).

EVOLUTIONARY THEORY – ADAPTATION
Researchers such as Sherry et al (1992) have suggested that spatial memory *evolves* in species whose existing behaviour and *environment niche* requires this *adaptation*. Thus a species with a greater need to explore its environment for food, mates, nesting sites etc. will evolve greater memory abilities in order to survive.

However, it is uncertain whether animals will adapt by developing specific spatial memory abilities (as the '*spatial adaptation model*' proposes) or more general ones (as the '*pliancy model*' suggests).

Research studies

- Tests of spatial memory have shown that bird species that cache food perform better than closely related species that do not cache, while mammals (e.g. voles or gibbons) that explore larger territories are better at spatial memory tests (e.g. maze learning) than those that explore less or have smaller territories.
- However, not all studies have revealed similar results, indicating that the need to use memory for *other* purposes may lead to the evolution of *general* memory abilities.
- Comparisons of relative hippocampus size in species of bird and mammal indicate that those that cache food or have large home territories have a larger hippocampus for their size.
- However, judging relative brain sizes across species is difficult to achieve and may ignore the interconnectivity of the brain.

COGNITIVE THEORY – COGNITIVE MAPS
Researchers such as Tolman, O'Keefe and Nadel have argued that a cognitive map is a powerful memory of landmarks that does not just represent spatial arrangements but also allows **novel** (not previously experienced) **short cuts** to be made between locations.

Research studies

- Some tests on rats in mazes, chimpanzees in areas of hidden food and even bees moving between nectar patches have appeared to show that animals can take short cuts and arrange optimal routes between locations, thus indicating the use of a cognitive map.
- However, Bennett (1991, 1996) in his review of such studies has argued that none had yet conclusively ruled out all alternative simpler explanations of such behaviour, e.g. guaranteeing that the short cut had not actually been taken before or that the locations had not just been visually recognised from new angles.

Sexual selection and human reproductive behaviour 1

WHAT IS SEXUAL SELECTION?

EVOLUTION
Occurs due to **variations** in characteristics between individuals being **inherited** due to those features being better **adapted** (allowing survival and reproduction) to **selective pressures**.
These selective pressures come from two sources.

NATURAL SELECTION
Refers to selective pressures on individuals' characteristics from the physical environment, e.g. climate, predators, food scarcity, etc. Characteristics will therefore evolve that increase the ability to survive and thus have the ***opportunity*** to reproduce.

SEXUAL SELECTION
Refers to selective pressures on individuals' characteristics from the social environment, e.g.:
- **intersexual** competition (the **mate choice** and preference of the opposite sex)
- **intrasexual** competition (the **mate competition** between members of the same sex)

Characteristics will therefore evolve that increase the ***access*** to reproduction.

WHY DOES SEXUAL SELECTION OCCUR?

Sexual selection occurs as a result of the different levels of parental investment between males and females, as well as between different individual men or women, that encourages them to choose and compete over members of the opposite sex who appear to invest the most in reproduction and parenting. Overall, in humans, it is the female who biologically invests more than the male.

THE EVOLUTION OF SEX DIFFERENCES IN PARENTAL INVESTMENT

Why do human females invest more than males?
- Anisogamy – females invest in producing relatively few, large, long lasting and energy rich gametes (ovum), while men produce many, short lived and rapidly renewable gametes (sperm).
- Gestation and lactation – females provide more resources by developing the zygote internally for nine months (gestation) and producing milk for offspring nutrition (lactation).
- Parental certainty – because of anisogamy and internal conception, the female always knows the offspring are hers, whereas the male does not necessarily have this guarantee.
- Commitment to resources – because of the previous factors and the helpless nature of human infants, females are likely to continue caring for offspring after birth to ensure their survival and avoid wasting an already significant investment of time and effort.

Small gamete producers are male

Large gamete producers are female

Abandon care of offspring to mate more often

Care for fewer offspring to help them survive

Male investment after conception is more uncertain due to lack of paternal guarantee (caring for the offspring of other males will increase their reproductive success at the expense of one's own) and the ease of desertion to mate again (due to their lack of initial investment and the fact that females are left 'holding the baby'). Further male investment depends upon:
- The number and availability of other females – a low female-to-male ratio, a high degree of competition from other males (mate competition), and a low appeal of the male to other females (mate choice) will all increase the likelihood of investing in offspring care rather than attempting to mate again.
- The likelihood of infant survival – increased male care may occur when harsh climate, many predators or lack of food and other social support means helpless human infants are less likely to survive with only the mother's care.

WHAT ARE THE EFFECTS OF SEXUAL SELECTION ON HUMAN REPRODUCTIVE BEHAVIOUR?
SEXUAL SELECTION AND HUMAN MATING STRATEGIES/SYSTEMS

The sex differences in parental investment have implications for male and female mate choice and competition in terms of the **number** and **duration** of sexual relationships that they should prefer. The optimal evolutionary strategies are for females to prefer quality and commitment, but males to prefer quantity, quality and exclusive access without commitment. In practice environmental conditions and mate competition will combine with mate choice preferences to produce different types of mating strategies or systems.

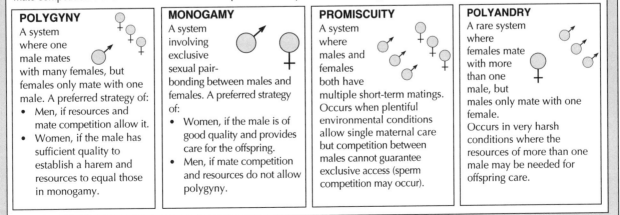

POLYGYNY
A system where one male mates with many females, but females only mate with one male. A preferred strategy of:
- Men, if resources and mate competition allow it.
- Women, if the male has sufficient quality to establish a harem and resources to equal those in monogamy.

MONOGAMY
A system involving exclusive sexual pair-bonding between males and females. A preferred strategy of:
- Women, if the male is of good quality and provides care for the offspring.
- Men, if mate competition and resources do not allow polygyny.

PROMISCUITY
A system where males and females both have multiple short-term matings. Occurs when plentiful environmental conditions allow single maternal care but competition between males cannot guarantee exclusive access (sperm competition may occur).

POLYANDRY
A rare system where females mate with more than one male, but males only mate with one female.
Occurs in very harsh conditions where the resources of more than one male may be needed for offspring care.

Sexual selection and human reproductive behaviour 2

WHAT ARE THE EFFECTS OF SEXUAL SELECTION ON HUMAN REPRODUCTIVE BEHAVIOUR?

SEXUAL SELECTION AND HUMAN MATE CHOICE, PREFERENCES AND BEHAVIOUR
The sex differences in parental investment also have implications for male and female mate choice and competition in terms of the **type of sexual partner** that they should prefer and the **kinds of reproductive behaviour** they should show. Inter-sexual competition (mate choice) and intra-sexual competition (mate competition) will have a number of effects on males and females:

FOR MALES
Males invest less biologically than females but will invest time and effort competing with males for access to females and seeking for resources.

If environmental conditions are favourable, the male optimal evolutionary strategy is to prefer quantity, quality and exclusive access with minimal commitment of resources to each partner, so as to father as many offspring as possible.

Preferred features in females
The features males have evolved to find attractive in females are those concerning signs of the following qualities:
- The ability to conceive, birth and raise children – signs of fertility are those associated with youth and reproductive physique. Men thus find women more attractive if they:
  Look younger – younger women are more likely to conceive and have a longer reproductive life ahead of them. Childlike facial features, such as big eyes, small noses and full lips will also be preferred as signs of 'beauty'.
  Possess an 'hour-glass' figure – wide hips may indicate ability to deliver children, a narrow waist indicates a lack of pregnancy. Larger breasts and buttocks also indicate nutritional health (suitable fat deposits) and the ability to nurture, and will therefore be found attractive.
- Physical/genetic health – physical signs of these that will be found attractive include clear skin, glossy hair, high energy levels and symmetrical facial and bodily features (indicating genetic and nutritional health).
- Chastity and sexual faithfulness – these are harder to assess after loss of virginity but will increase paternity likelihood.

Reproductive behaviour
Because of initial parental investment and mate preferences, males are likely to have evolved to:
- Be less choosy, which may lead to greater infidelity with females of variable quality.
- Be more attracted/aroused by physical characteristics.
- Exaggerate their resources and fake commitment.
- Be more jealous and disturbed by sexual infidelity in their female partners (since it reduces paternal certainty).
- Approve of marriage contracts to encourage sexual exclusivity with females.

FOR FEMALES
Females invest more biologically than males, only require one male to fertilise them, and cannot afford to waste their greater investment.

The optimal evolutionary strategy for females is therefore to prefer males with signs of quality, resources and commitment, so as to ensure as many of their own offspring survive as possible with this extra, and in some cases vital, investment.

Preferred features in males
The features females have evolved to find attractive in males are those concerning signs of the following qualities:
- The ability to provide resources – signs of this are the possession of resources or traits that help compete for them. Females therefore find males more attractive if they:
  Have status and dominance – usually shown by older males since they may have had more time to acquire resources and prove they are capable of competing successfully for them.
  Possess promising qualities – such as drive, ambition, intelligence, skill and/or strength to gain resources in the future. Such qualities will be also seem desirable because they may be inherited by the mother's sons (thus increasing the chance of grandchildren).
- Physical/genetic health – physical signs of these that will be found attractive include size, musculature, clear skin, glossy hair, high energy levels and symmetrical facial and bodily features (indicating genetic and nutritional health).
- Commitment of resources – through pre-mating signs of kindness, generosity and resource sharing.

Reproductive behaviour
Because of initial parental investment and mate preferences, females are likely to have evolved to:
- Be choosier, which may lead to infidelity occurring only with males of higher quality.
- Be more attracted/aroused by psychological characteristics.
- Emphasise or exaggerate their physical attributes.
- Be more jealous and disturbed by emotional infidelity in their male partners (since it indicates risk of abandonment and thus loss of resources).
- Approve of marriage contracts to encourage commitment of resources from males.

EVIDENCE AND EVALUATION
- A comparison of male-female body size differences and male testicle size between humans and species of primate indicates that humans seem biologically best adapted to polygyny in the form of serial monogamous relationships.
- Buss's (1989) questionnaire survey of over 10,000 people from 37 cultures found high levels of cross-cultural agreement (ranging from 92 to 100%) for the evolutionary predictions that women value earning potential in their partners more than men, while men value physical attributes and younger partners more than women. Questionnaires and physiological measures have also found that men are more distressed than women at the thought of sexual infidelity in their partners.
- The content analysis of Lonely Hearts personal advertisements in the USA, Britain, Holland and India has consistently revealed that men tend to seek attractiveness and offer resources, while women tend to offer attractiveness and seek resources as evolutionary theory predicts (Dunbar, 1995).
- Singh (1993) found men rating body shapes preferred a low waist-to-hip ratio of 0.7, regardless of exact body weight.
- Averaged composite faces of men and women containing more symmetry have been rated as more attractive than less symmetrical faces, while women with symmetrical breasts have been found to be more fertile and men with symmetrical bodies have greater mating success.
- However, in many studies the effects of socially created norms have not been completely excluded as explanations.

The evolution of mental disorders

EVOLUTIONARY EXPLANATIONS OF MENTAL DISORDERS

Researchers such as Nesse and Williams (1996) and Stevens and Price (1996) suggest that the existence and form of mental disorders can be explained using the same evolutionary principles that have been applied to account for the origin of other aspects of physiology and behaviour. The processes of *genetic inheritance*, *evolutionary adaptation* and the *survival function* of mentally disordered behaviour and emotion can be applied to explain:

- **Why they may have arisen in the first place** – evolutionary theory suggests that *aspects* of the behaviour or emotional reaction that appear disordered actually have *important evolutionary survival functions* and may in fact be shown to some degree by non-disordered members of the population. Mental disorders would therefore be *linked to genes that have an adaptive function*.
- **Why they seem maladaptive** – mental disorders may cause maladaptive behaviour and an increased risk of death since they may:
  - Represent *over-activity* or *excessive genetic expression of useful traits* (much as we have evolved a vital immune system that can become over-reactive).
  - *No longer be adaptive in the modern world* since they evolved in a *different environment of evolutionary adaptation* (the genome lag hypothesis); in other words, they may have been adaptive for our pre-civilisation evolutionary ancestors.
- **Why they still exist** – emotions and behaviours that are maladaptive should be '*selected out*' and decrease in frequency by reducing the fitness of those showing them. However the mental disorders will still persist if they:
  - Are strongly linked to genes for adaptive behaviour.
  - Do actually confer some benefit to genetic relatives (inclusive fitness).
  - Only result from genetic predisposition when triggered by environmental cues.
  - Have not had sufficient evolutionary time to disappear due to new environmental selection conditions and pressures.

THE EVOLUTION OF ANXIETY DISORDERS

It has been suggested that anxiety disorders evolved based upon *defensive evolutionary survival functions* relating to *vigilance*, *avoidance* and *readiness* to deal with *dangerous environmental stimuli*. Evolutionary theory predicts that humans should be *biologically prepared* by evolution to show, or be able to quickly learn, defensive anxiety reactions and emotions (e.g. worrying, hyper-alertness, dread, avoidance, apprehension and physiological fight or flight fear arousal) towards stimuli that could damage or kill them. The evolutionary functions of these reactions are illustrated by the most common phobic stimuli.

Phobic stimuli	Reaction and evolutionary rationale
Snakes, spiders	Withdrawing/fleeing avoids bites
Blood	Fainting reduces blood pressure and loss
Heights	Freezing prevents falling
The dark	Avoids unseen predators and pitfalls
Open spaces	Avoids separation from secure home base
Public behaviour	Shyness avoids inept status-losing behaviour

Phobias may be maladaptive because:
- They developed as exaggerations of normal fear reactions because the costs associated with them (time and energy) were outweighed by the costs of ignoring these stimuli (death).
- In many modern environments fear of the above stimuli is usually not in line with the reality of the danger.

Evaluation
- The most frequently occurring phobias are those associated with stimuli that were dangerous to our evolutionary ancestors.
- Studies on humans and other animals have illustrated that phobias of dangerous stimuli (e.g. snakes) can be learned more readily than non-dangerous objects (e.g. flowers).
- Humans show less fear than might be expected of modern-day dangerous objects (e.g. cars) since evolution has not had sufficient time to prepare fear reactions for them.

THE EVOLUTION OF DEPRESSION

It has been suggested that mood disorders, such as depression and mania, evolved based upon normal reactions and attitudes towards loss and gain, failure and success. The feelings of *sadness* triggered by a *failure* or *loss* may be adaptive since they would *discourage* the behaviour that led to them, preventing even greater losses. However behaviour (especially creative) that resulted in *gains* and *success* would be *motivated* by the feelings of self-confidence, optimism, high energy levels and euphoria that are associated with *happiness.*

Rank theory suggests that losses or gains in *dominance* resulting from competition with others would trigger these emotions. Depression would allow defeated individuals to display yielding behaviour and desist in further competition that might result in further loss, while mania would allow victors to take advantage of their success and possibly gain further.

Inclusive fitness theory suggests that depression and suicide may have evolved as a strategy of individuals who feel they are unsuccessful or a burden to others to promote the inclusive fitness of their relatives by not reproducing and passing on these traits (depression is associated with reduced reproductive ability) or removing themselves completely.

Clinical depression and mania may be maladaptive because:
- They developed as pathological exaggerations of normal, adaptive emotional reactions or became too easily triggered. Depressed feelings of worthlessness, hopelessness, lack of energy and lack of enjoyment that are triggered by *consistent* failure and *major* losses are maladaptive. They involve a general lack of motivation for all behaviours not just those associated with failure or loss, which could lead to even greater loss, which is not adaptive. Similarly the over-confident, over-optimistic, euphoria and risk taking that are associated with mania (rather than just happiness) leads to unrealistic goals which may actually cause future loss.
- In many modern environments increased media exposure to successful, wealthy and attractive competitors may make people feel failures and thus depressed to a greater extent.

Evaluation
- Happiness and sadness are found cross-culturally and genetic predispositions for mood disorders have been proposed indicating there may be a biological adaptive function.
- Higher rates of female defeat in competition with males due to the latter's greater dominance may explain the higher rates of female depression.
- Evolutionary theories of depression and mania remain rather speculative and there are many other explanations that do not assume these mood states are linked with adaptive features.

Evolutionary factors in the development of human intelligence

ECOLOGICAL FACTORS

Human intelligence and brain size could be associated with ecological factors, such as environmental complexity. This could involve the challenges encountered in foraging and the unpredictability of the environment, for example:

- The distribution food may require sophisticated search skills or cognitive maps of the environment.
- The capture of food may require co-ordinated planning and attack strategies, or the fabrication of tools and invention of food processing strategies.
- The unpredictability of food sources may require adapting or inventing new strategies.

Thus the development of hunting skills to provide more protein rich meat may have caused the increase in hominid brain size.

Evaluation

- Although environmental complexity and unpredictability may provide more cognitive challenge, many primates, mammals and even birds show co-ordinated hunting and foraging over large ranges with much smaller brains.
- Although specific brain structures may increase in size to match environmental demands, overall brain size does not correlate well with environmental complexity.
- Hunting for meat may have evolved to feed already large energy-demanding brains rather than vice-versa.
- Intelligence involves more than foraging and spatial ability.

SOCIAL FACTORS

Human 'Machiavellian' intelligence and thus brain size may have evolved to adapt humans to the social requirements of living in large social groups. Social group complexity and cognitive challenge may result from:

- The need to achieve the most individual gain while still co-operating to maintain the foraging and defensive benefits of living in a group. Intelligence may be required to keep track of co-operative alliances and enemies, manipulate others without detection, ensure that favours are repaid, etc.
- The need to predict the behaviour of others, which may require the development of a 'theory of mind'.
- Larger groups, which will inevitably involve more numerous and complex relationships.

Thus the development of social intelligence to cope with larger social groups may have caused increasing hominid brain size.

Evaluation

- A positive correlation has been found in many species between group size and ratio of brain neo-cortex.
- High social intelligence is not just shown by humans but by many mammals with smaller brains, e.g. vervet monkeys.
- Social intelligence is only one type of intelligence - vervets can be very unintelligent in non-social matters.
- Orang-utans have large brains and are thought to be intelligent but do not live in large social groups.

BRAIN SIZE AND INTELLIGENCE

Why is brain size associated with intelligence?

- The brain is regarded as the source of mental abilities such as intelligence.
- The human brain has trebled in size over the last 2.5 million years (compared to the australopithecines that marked the beginning of human evolution from that of the apes). This increase correlates with the development of behavioural signs of hominid intelligence, e.g. the fabrication of sophisticated stone tools, cave painting etc.
- The human brain is 3 times larger than expected for a primate of our body size. Apes in turn have higher encephalisation quotients than most other mammals. We regard ourselves as more intelligent than apes, and apes as more intelligent than many other mammals.
- The human brain is evolutionarily very costly to develop. It uses a fifth of our basic metabolic rate but is only 2% of our mass. Increased brain size has increased the risk of childbirth death and has resulted in premature and helpless infants who require more care.
- Human intellectual abilities increase with brain development through childhood.

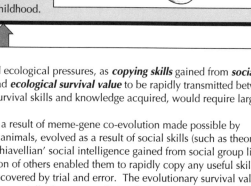

CULTURAL FACTORS

Human intelligence and brain size may actually result from both social and ecological pressures, as **copying skills** gained from **social interaction** in groups allowed new skills, discoveries and inventions that had **ecological survival value** to be rapidly transmitted between, and accumulate within, individuals. The copying skills, as well as all the survival skills and knowledge acquired, would require larger and more powerful brains.

Blackmore (1999) suggests this kind of selective cultural pressure occurs as a result of meme-gene co-evolution made possible by imitation. Blackmore proposes that true imitation, which is rarely found in animals, evolved as a result of social skills (such as theory of mind or reciprocal altruism) that themselves evolved as a result of the 'Machiavellian' social intelligence gained from social group living. Furthermore, she suggests that the ability humans have to show true imitation of others enabled them to rapidly copy any useful skills, ideas or behaviours (memes), such as stone tool making, that others had discovered by trial and error. The evolutionary survival value of such memes meant that there would be selective pressure to imitate others, especially the most proficient imitators, and mate with them. However, since cultural skills, ideas and behaviours readily combine and change very rapidly 'the genes have been forced into creating brains capable of spreading them – big brains' (Blackmore, 1999).

Evaluation

- Blackmore presents many persuasive arguments to support her theory and has suggested certain empirical tests of her ideas, e.g. that species who imitate the best should have larger brains for their size, and that brain scans should reveal that imitative tasks use more energy and produce more activity in the evolutionary newer areas of the brain.
- Because of its recency the theory has not been thoroughly evaluated and tested at present.

Defining abnormality

STATISTICAL INFREQUENCY

Abnormality can be defined as deviation from the average, where statistically common behaviour is defined as 'normal' while **statistically rare behaviour** is 'abnormal'. Thus autism is sufficiently statistically rare (it occurs in 2–4 children per 10,000) to be `abnormal`, as is multiple personality disorder. This does not necessarily mean the behaviour concerned is qualitatively different from 'normal' – many human characteristics are shown by everyone in the population to a certain degree, and if they can be measured every individual can be placed upon a dimensional scale or continuum that will reveal how common their score is in comparison to everybody else's. These comparisons can be standardised by the use of **normal distribution curves**. Many characteristics could be placed upon normal distribution curves as dimensions, such as intelligence. Most people fall somewhere in the middle of these continuums, but if an individual shows an extreme deviation from this average then they may be regarded as abnormal.

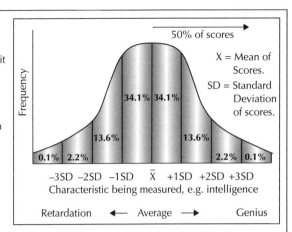

X = Mean of Scores.
SD = Standard Deviation of scores.

−3SD −2SD −1SD X̄ +1SD +2SD +3SD
Characteristic being measured, e.g. intelligence

Retardation ← Average → Genius

Evaluation

1. There are problems deciding how statistically rare (2 or 3 standard deviations?) behaviour has to be to be considered abnormal.
2. Some currently accepted mental disorders are probably not statistically rare enough to be defined as abnormal, e.g. phobias.
3. Statistical deviation from the average does not tell us about the desirability of the deviation – both mental retardation and genius are statistically rare but only the former is regarded as abnormal.
4. By this definition different subcultures may show behaviour that is statistically rare in the majority culture and be defined as abnormal.

DEVIATION FROM SOCIAL NORMS

Norms are expected ways of behaving in a society according to the majority and those members of a society who do not think and behave like everyone else break these norms and so are often defined as abnormal. The definition is based on the facts that:

1. Abnormal behaviour is seen as vivid and unpredictable, causes observer discomfort and violates moral or ideal standards (Rosenhan and Seligman, 1989) because it differs from most other people's behaviour and standards.
2. Abnormal thinking is delusional, irrational or incomprehensible because it differs from commonly accepted or usual beliefs and ways of thinking.

The deviation from social norm definition of abnormal behaviour is thus a **socially based definition** and is explained by social constructionism and social identity theories. Researchers such as Szasz (1960) have argued that 'abnormality', especially relating to certain mental disorders, is a socially constructed concept that allows people who show different, unusual or disturbing (to the rest of society) behaviour to be labelled and thus treated differently from others – often confined, controlled and persecuted. Social identity theory would argue that people who do not share similar behaviour and beliefs are not included in the 'in-group' (in this case the majority in a society) and are therefore categorised as 'other' (abnormal) and discriminated against.

Evaluation

Since deviation from social norms is a socially based definition, it implies that different societies with different norms will define different behaviours as abnormal and may even disagree over whether the same behaviour is abnormal. This means that an objective definition of abnormal behaviour that is fixed and stable across cultures and time is difficult if not impossible to achieve, and this may lead to unfair and discriminatory treatment of minorities by majorities. Indeed concepts of abnormal behaviour have been shown to differ cross-culturally (a belief in voodoo in one culture may be thought to be paranoia in another) and in the same culture over time (unmarried mothers in Britain and political dissidents in the Soviet Union have been confined to institutions for their 'abnormal' behaviour).

FAILURE TO FUNCTION ADEQUATELY

Maladaptive behaviour, which causes a failure to function adequately in the social and physical environment, seems a more objective way of defining abnormality. Everyone experiences difficulties coping with the world sometimes but if an individual's abnormal behaviour, mood or thinking adversely affects their well being (e.g. ability to maintain employment, a bearable quality of life, normal social relations etc.) then the definition will draw attention to the fact that help is needed. On a more extreme level, if an individual's abnormal behaviour becomes a danger to their own safety (e.g. neglecting self care, self mutilation, suicidal etc.) or the safety of others (e.g. dangerous behaviour) then they may be defined as abnormal and institutionalised ('sectioned' under the Mental Health Act, 1983, for example).

Evaluation

Failure to function adequately may not be recognised (e.g. by those who are in a psychotic state) or cared about (e.g. those with anti-social personality disorder), so the definition may have to be applied by others in society. However difficulties in functioning adequately may be the result of social rejection and 'adequate' functioning is, to some extent, a social judgement which may be based more on threats perceived by the majority in society than actual threats or a genuine concern to help.

DEVIATION FROM IDEAL MENTAL HEALTH

The idea that a single characteristic can be used as the basis of a general definition of abnormality has been rejected by some in favour of a set of criterion characteristics of abnormality or normality. Jahoda (1958) has described several characteristics that mentally healthy people should possess, such as the ability to introspect, integration and balance of personality, self-actualisation, autonomy, ability to cope with stress and see the world as it really is, and environmental mastery.

Evaluation

Unfortunately this criterion approach has also had its problems as a definition, since just how many of these characteristics do you have to lack or possess, and to what degree, to be regarded as normal or abnormal? Jahoda's characteristics of mental health have been regarded as too idealistic, in fact it is 'normal' to fall short of such perfect standards, and humanistic psychologists such as Maslow would argue that very few people actually reach self-actualisation. Not everyone agrees with the ideal characteristics or that all are necessary for mental health, for example other cultures may disagree with the ideals of autonomy and independence, and view other characteristics as more important.

The medical model of abnormality

MEDICAL MODEL

ASSUMPTIONS

Also known as the somatic, biological, or physiological approach.

NOTION OF NORMALITY

- Properly functioning physiology and nervous system and no genetic pre-dispositions to inherit mental disorder.

NOTION OF ABNORMALITY

- Like physical illness, **mental illness** has an **underlying physical/bodily cause.**
- **Genetic, organic, or chemical disorders** cause mental illness, which gives rise to behavioural and psychological **symptoms.**
- These symptoms can be classified to **diagnose** the **psychopathology,** which can then be treated through **therapy** in psychiatric **hospitals** to **cure the patient.**
- Note the use of medical terminology which this approach has borrowed.

ETHICAL IMPLICATIONS

There are both positive and negative ethical implications of the medical model definition of abnormality:

1 Positively for the abnormal individual, the idea that they are mentally 'ill' means that the individual is **not** to be held **responsible** for their predicament – they are more likely to be seen as a **victim** of a disorder that is **beyond their control** and, therefore, they are **in need of care** and **treatment.** The medical model is, therefore, intended to be a more caring and humane approach to abnormality - especially given the blame, stigmatisation, and lack of care for abnormality that had been the norm before the approach.

2 Negatively, the medical model's assumptions have produced many unfavourable ethical consequences.

   a The assumption that abnormal people are mentally ill and, therefore, **not responsible** for their actions can lead to
   - the **loss of rights**, such as the right to **consent** to treatment or institutionalisation, and even the right to vote if sectioned under the Mental Health Act.
   - the **loss of an internal locus of control,** loss of self-care, and an abdication of responsibility to others.
   - the assumption that **directive therapy** is needed for the benefit of the mentally ill individual. The concept of directive therapy may be less debatable with acute schizophrenia, where insight may be totally lacking, but becomes more controversial when we consider the rights of depressed patients to withdraw from electro-convulsive therapy which may prevent their suicide.

   b The assumption that there is always a **biological underlying cause** for mental disorder may be incorrect and, therefore, lead to the **wrong** diagnosis and/or treatment being given.
   - There is not always a clearly identifiable underlying biological cause for disorders.
   - Many disorders have a large psychological contribution to their cause, such as the learning theory explanations of phobia acquisition.
   - Heather (1976) suggests that the basis of defining abnormality is often governed by social and moral considerations rather than biological – thus the inclusion of psychosexual disorders such as paedophilia.

   c The assumption that mentally well people are **distinctly different** from those defined as abnormal under the medical model.

PRACTICAL IMPLICATIONS

The use of the medical model to define abnormality as mental illness can lead to:

1 **The use of sectioning** under the Mental Health Act (1983) – the compulsory detention and even treatment of those regarded as mentally ill, if they represent a danger to their own or others' safety. This is based on the medical model assumption that mental illness leads to a loss of self-control and responsibility; but note that a social worker is required to section somebody, in addition to a GP and a psychiatrist (implying that social as well as physical factors need to be taken into account).

Section 2 of the Act can be used to detain people for up to 28 days for observation and assessment of mental illness.
Section 3 of the Act involves the enforced application of treatment and loss of rights.

Power is firmly in the hands of society, since

   a Section 5 of the act can prevent the right of even the nearest relative to withdraw the sectioned individual from care.

   b Section 136 gives the police the right to arrest in a public place anybody deemed to show mental illness to maintain security.

   c Section 139 removes all responsibility for mistaken diagnosis from those involved in sectioning, providing the diagnosis was made in good faith and the legal procedures were carried out correctly.

2 **Institutionalisation** – which can have both positive and negative implications:
   - **Positively,** institutionalisation allows the removal to a controlled environment of individuals who may represent a danger to themselves or others. The controlled environment allows the close monitoring, support, and treatment of those suffering from mental illness.
   - **Negatively,** institutionalisation may worsen the condition of the patient, providing them with an abnormal environment and causing the internalisation of the passive and dependent role of 'mental inmate'. Rosenhan's study 'On Being Sane in Insane Places' revealed the often negative treatment received in mental institutions.

3 **Biological treatments** – which include the administering of drug treatment, electro-convulsive therapy, or even psychosurgery, all of which have their dangers and side effects as well as the possibility of beneficial effects.

Psychological models of abnormality

THE PSYCHOANALYTIC APPROACH

Notion of normality
Balance between id, ego, and superego. Sufficient ego control to allow the acceptable gratification of id impulses. No inconvenient fixations or repression of traumatic events.

Notion of abnormality
Emotional disturbance or neurosis is caused by thwarted id impulses, unresolved unconscious conflicts (e.g. Oedipus complex), or repressed traumatic events deriving from childhood. Psychological and physical symptoms are expressions of unconscious psychological causes. Conflict and neurosis is always present to some extent – the difference between the 'normal' and 'abnormal' is only quantitative.

ETHICAL IMPLICATIONS
- **Directive therapy** – due to the unconscious cause of psychological problems and the resistance patients put up to unconscious truths, the patient must trust the therapist's interpretation and instructions. However, psychoanalysis does occur under voluntary conditions.
- **Anxiety provoking** – psychoanalysis can reveal disturbing repressed experiences.
- **Humane** – psychoanalysts do not blame or judge the patient, who is not responsible for their problems.

PRACTICAL IMPLICATIONS
- **Expensive** – Freud argued you do not value what you do not pay for.
- **Long term** – several sessions a week for many months are usually required, although Mallan's Brief Focal Therapy is faster.
- **No institutionalisation** required.
- **Low success rates** – with many disorders, e.g. psychoses.

THE BEHAVIOURAL APPROACH
(Also known as the behaviourist or learning theory approach)

Notion of normality
A learning history that has provided an adequately large selection of adaptive responses.

Notion of abnormality
Maladaptive responses have been learnt or adaptive ones have not been learnt. Observable, behavioural disorder is all abnormality consists of. Abnormal behaviour is not a symptom of any underlying cause.

ETHICAL IMPLICATIONS
- **Directive therapy** – due to the environmental determinism of behavioural problems, patients need to be re-programmed with adaptive behaviour.
- **Stressful** – behaviour therapy can be painful and disturbing, e.g. flooding and aversion therapy.
- **Humane** – specific maladaptive behaviours are targeted, the whole person is not labelled.

PRACTICAL IMPLICATIONS
- **Relatively cheap** – due to the fairly quick nature of treatments.
- **High success rates** – with certain disorders.
- **Institutionalisation** – may be required to ensure environmental control with certain treatments, e.g. selective reinforcement for anorexia.

THE COGNITIVE APPROACH

Notion of normality
Properly functioning and rational cognitive thought processes that can be used to accurately perceive the world and control behaviour.

Notion of abnormality
Unrealistic, distorted, or irrational understanding and thoughts about the self, others, or the environment. Difficulty in controlling thought processes or using them to control actions.

ETHICAL IMPLICATIONS
- **Semi-directive therapy** – due to the client's problems controlling their thoughts, external aid has to be provided by the therapist, although this will vary in its directiveness depending on how forceful the persuasive techniques used by the therapist are.
- **Stressful** – rational emotive therapy can be disturbing although most cognitive therapy is humane.

PRACTICAL IMPLICATIONS
- **Relatively cheap** – depending on length of therapy.
- **Fairly high success rates** – with certain disorders and when combined with behavioural therapies.
- **No institutionalisation** is usually necessary.

THE HUMANISTIC APPROACH
(Also known as the phenomenological or existential approach)

Notion of normality
Positive self regard, ability to self actualise, healthy interpersonal relationships, and responsibility and control over life.

Notion of abnormality
It is wrong to talk of abnormality, since everyone is unique and experiences 'problems with living' occasionally. These problems stem from interpersonal relationships (which prevent healthy interpersonal relationships, and thwarting environmental circumstances (which prevent self actualisation). The client should not be labelled or directed.

ETHICAL IMPLICATIONS
- **Non-directive therapy** – clients have free will and, therefore, the responsibility and capability to change their thoughts and behaviour (with insightful help).
- **Humane** – the happiness of the client is of most importance. The client is given unconditional positive regard.
- **Non-labelling** – humanist therapists believe labelling is counter-productive and irrelevant, since each person is a unique individual.

PRACTICAL IMPLICATIONS
- **Fairly expensive** – based on length of therapy required.
- **No institutionalisation** – is necessary, since treatment is completely voluntary.
- **Low success rates** – with many disorders, e.g. psychoses. Better success with 'problems with living' in interpersonal areas.

Diagnostic classification systems

THE PURPOSE OF CLASSIFICATION

The classification of mental disorder involves the **identification of groups** or patterns of behavioural or mental **symptoms** that reliably occur together to form a **type** of disorder. This process of classification allows

- psychiatrists, doctors and psychologists to **identify** and talk more easily about **groups** of similar sufferers

- a **prognosis** (prediction about the future course of the disorder) to be made

- researchers to **investigate** these groups of people to determine what the **causes** (aetiology) of the disorder are

- a suitable **treatment** to be developed and administered to all those showing similar symptoms

Thus, classification fulfils important communicative and investigative functions, ultimately serving to benefit the individual who has been identified.

CLASSIFICATION SYSTEMS

Emil Kraepelin developed the first comprehensive classification system for mental disorders, believing that they could be diagnosed from observable symptoms, just like physical illness.

Two major western classifications systems exist today - the American Psychiatric Association's 'Diagnostic and Statistical Manual of Mental Disorder' (DSM IV), and the World Health Organisation's 'International Classification of Diseases' (ICD 10).

These systems have undergone many revisions, e.g. from the first, very unreliable DSM in 1952, to the DSM II in 1968, DSM III in 1980, the revision of this (DSM III-R) in 1987, and currently the DSM IV in 1994.

Compared to the DSM, the ICD lists the same disorders but some are given different names and are classified under different headings. The ICD has no separate axes and is more likely to indicate causes rather than purely symptoms

TECHNIQUES OF ASSESSMENT

Behavioural observation, e.g. behaviour coding systems and rating scales.

- **Advantages** – provides direct and detailed information.
- **Weaknesses** – problems with inter-observer reliability and subject reactivity. Some symptoms cannot be observed.

Clinical interview, e.g. open-ended questions or the more standardised and reliable structured interview (such as 'The Schedule for Affective Disorders and Schizophrenia').

- **Advantages** – a detailed, flexible, and sensitive method.
- **Weaknesses** – lacks objectivity. Self report responses are interpreted by the therapist, and subjects may be unable or unwilling (due to embarrassment) to give accurate data.

Psychological tests, e.g. IQ tests or personality inventories (such as The Minnesota Multiphasic Personality Inventory).

- **Advantages** – objectively rated, quick, and standardised.
- **Weaknesses** – personality tests rely on self report and literacy.

Physiological tests, e.g. static brain scans (magnetic resonance imaging) or dynamic scans (positron emission tomography).

- **Advantages** – gives precise data on brain structure or activity
- **Weaknesses** – expensive and cannot be used to diagnose disorders alone.

THE DSM IV CLASSIFICATION SYSTEM

The 'Diagnostic and Statistical Manual of Mental Disorder' defines a mental disorder as a clinically significant syndrome associated with distress, a loss of functioning, an increased risk of death/pain, or an important loss of freedom.

The manual emphasises that the problem should stem from within the individual, but does not specify whether it is biological, behavioural, or psychological in nature.

The manual describes over 200 specific diagnostic categories for mental disorder and lists the **specific diagnostic criteria** that have to be met for a diagnosis to be given.

Assessment is usually made on five axes to provide a more complete picture of the individual.

AXIS 4 PSYCHOSOCIAL STRESSORS

All potentially stressful events (e.g. loss of job) or enduring circumstances (e.g. poverty) that might be relevant to the disorder are rated for severity on a scale ranging from 1 (none) to 6 (catastrophic) for the past year.

AXIS 5 GLOBAL ASSESSMENT OF FUNCTIONING

Rates the highest level of social, occupational, and psychological functioning on a scale of 1 (persistent danger) to 90 (good in all areas) currently and during the past year.

AXIS 3 MEDICAL CONDITIONS

Physical problems relevant to the mental disorder.

AXIS 1 CLINICAL SYNDROMES

Axis 1 refers to the major diagnostic classification arrived at by the clinician, e.g. 'catatonic schizophrenia', 'major depressive disorder', 'generalised anxiety disorder', etc.

AXIS 2 DEVELOPMENTAL AND PERSONALITY DISORDERS

Additional diagnostic classifications that may contribute to an understanding of the Axis 1 syndrome.

The practical and ethical implications of diagnostic classification 1

PRACTICAL IMPLICATIONS – CAN CLASSIFICATION BE EFFECTIVELY MADE?

RELIABILITY

For classification systems to be reliable, different diagnosticians using the same system should arrive at the same diagnosis for the same individual. The reliability of the early systems, e.g. the DSM II was very poor:

Beck et al (1962)
Found that agreement on diagnosis for 153 patients (where each patient was assessed by two psychiatrists from a group of four), was only 54%. This was often due to vague criteria for diagnosis and inconsistencies in the techniques used to gather data.

Cooper et al (1972)
Found New York psychiatrists were twice as likely to diagnose schizophrenia than London psychiatrists, who were twice as likely to diagnose mania or depression, when shown the same video-taped clinical interviews.

Rosenhan (1973)
Found that 8 'normal' people could get themselves admitted to mental hospitals as schizophrenics merely by claiming to hear voices saying single words like 'hollow' and 'thud'. Rosenhan also found that the staff of a teaching hospital, when told to expect pseudo-patients, suspected 41 out of 193 genuine patients of being fakers.

Classification systems have improved in reliability due to a multi-axial approach, more standardised assessment techniques (e.g. the Schedule of Affective Disorders and Schizophrenia), and more specific diagnostic criteria, but are still far from perfect.

Di Nardo et al (1993)
Studied the reliability of the DSM III-R for anxiety disorders. Two clinicians separately diagnosed each of 267 people seeking treatment for anxiety and stress disorders, and used the Kappa statistic to test how similar diagnosis was (the nearer 1 the value is, the closer the agreement). They found high reliability for obsessive-compulsive disorder but lower reliability for generalised anxiety disorder, due to problems with interpreting how 'excessive' a person's worries had to be (see table on the right). The DSM IV corrected this fault.

Diagnostic category	Kappa
Obsessive-compulsive disorder	.80
Generalised anxiety disorder	.57
Panic disorder with agoraphobia	.72
Social phobia	.79
Major depression	.65

VALIDITY

For a classification system to be valid it should meaningfully classify a real pattern of symptoms, which result from a real underlying cause, which can, therefore, lead to a suitable treatment and prognosis (predictive validity). Very few underlying causes are known, however, and there are a wide range of treatments for the same disorder. Some classifications such as 'undifferentiated schizophrenia' (for those whose symptoms do not fit into any of the other sub-types of schizophrenia), are rather meaningless as diagnostic categories. Valid diagnosis for mental disorder is more difficult than physical disorder, due to the lack of objective physical signs of disorder like temperature, blood pressure, etc.

BIAS

Since diagnostic classification is not 100% objective and reliable, bias may result from the expectations or prejudices of the diagnostician. Diagnosticians are likely to expect that people seeking psychiatric help are disturbed and are more likely to make what social psychologists call the fundamental attribution error – over-emphasising personality rather than situational/environmental causes of behaviour.

Temerline (1970)
Found that clinically trained psychiatrists and clinical psychologists could be influenced in their diagnosis by hearing the opinion of a respected authority. After watching a video-taped interview of (a completely psychologically 'healthy') individual, some subjects heard the respected authority state that, although the person seemed neurotic, he was actually quite psychotic. These diagnosticians were highly influenced by the statement in their own diagnosis of the individual.

ETHICAL IMPLICATIONS – SHOULD DIAGNOSIS BE MADE CONSIDERING THE DIFFICULTIES OF CLASSIFICATION?

Szasz questions both the validity and purpose of classification, arguing that in many cases diagnosis is made on a political and social basis, rather than a psychological or biological one, and suggests that the majority in power in a society attach stigmatising labels to those who show different or frightening behaviour and so justify their control and treatment.

Szasz in his book *The Manufacture of Madness* goes so far as to say that mental illness is actually created by society, and adds that where the biological causes of mental disorders are known, they should be defined as 'diseases of the mind', but if there is not a supportable underlying cause of disorder, then the term 'problem with living' should be used. Scheff (1966) proposes a similar criticism of the basis of classification, suggesting that labelling people as abnormal helps society overcome its anxiety and establish clear norms of reality and appropriate behaviour. The major ethical implication here is that the classification systems serve the purposes of the majority in society only, and that it is wrong to assume they are helpful.

Some would argue that society has merely tried to 'medicalise' disruptive behaviour – to find a cause 'within' the person for bad behaviour, rather than looking to the environment for causes. Thus, classifications such as anti-social personality disorder, or kleptomania, are really only medical terms for evil or bad people. Originally the medical model of mental illness was just a useful metaphor, but the underlying assumption has developed that there are underlying biological causes for mental disorder.

A counter argument to Szasz's proposal that we are merely labelling eccentric people, is the fact that medical and behavioural treatments have helped people to overcome their disorders, and that many people (such as those suffering from anxiety and depression) volunteer for treatment.

Classification aims to help those with mental disorders, and, therefore, fulfils a potentially very useful function – medical diagnosis had, and still has, problems with classification, yet we would not think of rejecting it today. The classification systems have led to the development of many effective therapies and treatments that have helped to either cure, alleviate, or control a wide variety of disorders. Perhaps diagnosis should be made more idiographic, and focus on particular problems rather than grouping people together in a category that may not be helpful, especially where biological causes are not known. However many categories have demonstrated themselves to be useful.

Diagnostic classification has improved as the classification systems have developed. Rosenhan's pseudo-patients would probably not succeed in gaining admission to mental hospitals today (or would have to lie a lot more!).

The practical and ethical implications of diagnostic classification 2

PRACTICAL IMPLICATIONS – WHAT ARE THE CONSEQUENCES OF CLASSIFICATION?

TREATMENT

Since there are problems with the validity of diagnostic classification, unsuitable treatment may be administered, sometimes on an involuntary basis. There are many practical and ethical problems involved in choosing and applying different treatments and therapies.

INSTITUTIONALISATION

Institutionalisation can lead to loss of responsibility. Rosenhan's study found that institutionalisation can lead to depersonalisation, dependency, and a loss of self care skills, thereby worsening the disorder. Goffman (in *Asylums*) speaks of the 'career' of the mental inmate, where the identity of the patient is gradually lost to the institution.

Patients may actually be taught abnormal behaviour from those around them in the institution, and conditions do not help normal functioning since they are not treated as normal people would be.

CARE IN THE COMMUNITY

Rosenhan talked of the 'stickiness' of diagnostic labels – when an individual returns to society, their record of mental illness goes with them (the pseudo-patients left with a diagnosis of 'schizophrenia in remission'). This can lead to stigmatisation, stereotyping, and discrimination against those who have been mentally disordered, making reintegration back into the community difficult.

LABELLING

Scheff (1966) points out that diagnostic classification 'labels' the individual, and this can have many adverse effects, such as

*   **Self-fulfilling prophecy** – Patients may begin to act as they think they are expected to act – Goffman argues that they may internalise the role of 'mentally ill patient' and this could worsen their disorder rather than improve it. Doherty (1975) points out that those who reject the mental illness label tend to improve more quickly than those who accept it, although this is not always the case, since accepting the label of 'alcoholic' can help alcoholics recover.

*   **Distortion of behaviour** – Diagnosis of mental disorder tends to label the whole person – once the label of diagnosis is attached, then all the individual's actions become interpreted in the light of the label. Sometimes even normal behaviour is ignored or interpreted as a sign of the individual's mental disorder – in Rosenhan's study, the pseudo-patients' behaviours were regarded as symptoms of their psychopathology.

*   **Oversimplification** – Labelling can lead to reification – making the classification a real, physical disorder, rather than just a descriptive term to help diagnosticians talk about patients or a hypothesis about what is troubling the person. Labelling may have a major effect not just on an individual's identity, but also on their self-esteem.

LEGAL IMPLICATIONS

Sectioning under the Mental Health Act (although rare) can lead to loss of rights and enforced treatment. Legally, the insane can be found not guilty due to a lack of responsibility for their actions.

ETHICAL IMPLICATIONS – SHOULD DIAGNOSIS BE MADE CONSIDERING THE CONSEQUENCES OF CLASSIFICATION?

An ethical decision has to be made regarding the justification of classification, given the profound implications of being classified as mentally disordered.

*   Do the benefits of classification (care, treatment, safety) outweigh the costs (possible misdiagnosis, mistreatment, loss of rights/self responsibility, and prejudice due to labelling)?

    Gove (1970, 1990) has found that the stigmatising effects of labelling are only short-lived, while Major and Crocker (1993) have found that the effect of labelling on a person's self-esteem is difficult to predict.

    Prejudice from society clearly does occur, however, and is even shown by mental health professionals. Langer and Abelson (1974) showed a videotape of a younger man telling an older man about his job experience. If the viewers were told that the man was a job applicant, he was judged to be attractive and conventional looking, whereas if they were told that he was a 'patient', he was described as tight, defensive, dependent, and frightened of his own aggressive impulses.

*   Is society right to administer treatment when misclassification is quite likely and the underlying causes are not known?

    Some researchers have argued that, overall, there are too many criticisms of the basic assumptions of classification to justify its use and consequences.

    The assumption that mental disorder can be classified into types is ethically questionable. Classification ignores the fundamental uniqueness of human minds and goes against the right of every person to be treated as an individual.

    An idiographic, rather than a nomothetic, approach to mental disorder may be more appropriate, considering the huge individual variations in patients' symptom expression and individual circumstances. If nomothetic comparisons have to be made, then perhaps it is best to regard mental health and disorder as on a continuum, so that there is only a quantitative rather than qualitative difference between them. Classification only works if there are enough differences **and** similarities between patients.

*   Should individuals lose their rights of consent and self-responsibility?

    Humanists would argue that the classification systems are overinfluenced by the medical model's assumptions about lack of control and freewill. In some cases these assumptions have been used as a method of political control.

*   Why does society have double standards about responsibility and mental disorder?

    Legally, the insane can be found not guilty due to a lack of responsibility for their actions. However, 'insanity' is a decision made by the legal system and, due to society's need to blame people to make them account for their crimes, this verdict may not be given. Many criminals have been clearly mentally disordered, but have been found guilty of their crimes and sent to prison.

'On being sane in insane places' Rosenhan (1973)

AIM

To illustrate experimentally the problems involved in determining normality and abnormality, in particular
- the poor reliability of the diagnostic classification system for mental disorder at the time (as well as general doubts over its validity)
- the negative consequences of being diagnosed as abnormal and the effects of institutionalisation

METHOD

Subjects: Eight sane people (3 women and 5 men from a small variety of occupational backgrounds), using only fake names and occupations, sought admission to a range of twelve hospitals (varying in age, resources, staff-patient ratios, degree of research conducted, etc.).

Procedure: Each pseudo-patient arranged an appointment at the hospital and complained that he or she had been hearing voices. The voices were unclear, unfamiliar, of the same sex and said single words like 'empty', 'hollow', and 'thud'. Apart from the aforementioned falsifying of name and occupation and this single symptom, the pseudo-patients did not change any aspect of their behaviour, personal history or circumstances. On admission to the hospital ward, every pseudo-patient immediately stopped simulating any symptoms and responded normally to all instructions (except they did not swallow medication) and said they were fine and experiencing no more symptoms. Their tasks were then to
- seek release by convincing the staff that they were sane (all but one pseudo-patient were very motivated to do this)
- observe and record the experience of the institutionalised mentally disordered patient (done covertly at first, although this was unnecessary)

RESULTS

Admission: Pseudo-patients were admitted to every hospital, in all cases except one with a diagnosis of schizophrenia, and their sanity was never detected by staff – only by other patients (35 out of 118 of whom voiced their suspicions in the first three hospitalisations). To check the poor reliability of diagnosis, and to see if the insane could be distinguished from the sane, a later study was conducted where a teaching hospital (who had been informed of Rosenhan's study) was told to expect pseudo-patients over a three month period. During that time 193 patients were rated for how likely they were to be pseudo-patients – 41 patients were suspected of being fakes, 19 of which were suspected by both a psychiatrist and one other staff member, even though no pseudo-patients were sent during that time.

Release: Length of stay ranged from 7 to 52 days, with an average of 19 days. All except one were released with a diagnosis of 'schizophrenia in remission', supporting the view that they had never been detected as sane.

Observation results:
- **Lack of monitoring** – very little contact with doctors was experienced, and a strong sense of segregation between staff and patients was noted.
- **Distortion of behaviour** – all (normal) behaviour became interpreted in the light of the 'label' of 'schizophrenia', for example:
  a A normal case history – became distorted to emphasise the ambivalence and emotional instability thought to be shown by schizophrenics.
  b Note taking – pseudo-patients were never asked why they were taking notes, but it was recorded by nurses as 'patient engages in writing behaviour', implying that it was a symptom of their disorder.
  c Pacing the corridors out of boredom – was seen as nervousness, again implying that it was a symptom of their disorder.
  d Waiting outside the cafeteria before lunch time – was interpreted as showing the 'oral-acquisitive nature of the syndrome' by a psychiatrist.

- **Lack of normal interaction** – for example, pseudo-patients courteously asked a staff member 'Pardon me, Mr (or Dr or Mrs) X, could you tell me when I will be presented at the staff meeting?' or 'When am I likely to be discharged?'. They found mostly a brief, not always relevant, answer was given, on the move, without even a normal turn of the head or eye-contact (psychiatrists moved on with their head averted 71% of the time and only stopped and talked normally on 4% of occasions).
- **Powerlessness and depersonalisation** – was produced in the institution through the lack of rights, constructive activity, choice, and privacy, plus frequent verbal and even physical abuse from the attendants.

EVALUATION

Methodological:

Lack of control groups – Only the experimental condition was conducted.

Data analysis – Was mostly qualitative rather than quantitative.

Ethical problems – The study involved deception, but it might be argued that the hospitals had the power not to be deceived and were in fact being tested in their jobs. In addition, the study's ends (its valuable contribution) outweighed its slightly unethical means, and kept data confidentiality.

Theoretical: Despite the fact that 'schizophrenia in remission' is an unusual diagnosis according to Spitzer (1976), the study is widely held to have fulfilled its aim of showing the deficiencies of the classification system for mental disorder at the time (the DSM II) and the negative consequences of being labelled and institutionalised for mental disorder. Studies like these led to pressure to revise and improve the accuracy of the classification systems.

Links: Problems with the diagnosis and classification of mental disorders. Stereotyping.

Multiple personality disorder

WHAT IS MULTIPLE PERSONALITY DISORDER?

Multiple Personality Disorder (MPD) or Dissociative Personality Disorder (DPD) refers to a mental disorder involving:

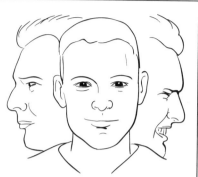

- **Dissociation of the self** – the self becomes divided into two or more distinct personalities, each with their separate thoughts, characteristics and memories.
- **Alternation of control by the personalities** – bodily control and access to consciousness switches between the personalities, although some may be more dominant than others and thus spend more time in control.
- **Amnesia and unconscious barriers between personalities** – there may be a mutual or one-way lack of conscious awareness and memory access between personalities. Some may experience 'blackouts' or lost time when others take control, some can be directly aware of other personalities' existence, thoughts and memories.

A case of MPD

A famous example is Sybil (Schreiber, 1973) who had 16 alternative personalities of varying genders (those named 'Mike' and 'Sid' were male) and ages ('Ruthie' was only 2 years old), possibly as a result of being beaten and tortured by her (probably) schizophrenic mother. Each personality had a name and was reported by her psychiatrist to have different vocabulary, handwriting, speech patterns, body images, attitudes to sex, jealousies (including those relating to each other's knowledge and memories), interests, religious attitudes, taste in books, painting ability and vocational ambitions. Sybil (the primary personality) was initially unaware of the existence of these other personalities until her psychiatrist diagnosed her condition. In common with other cases of MPD it was suggested that each personality emerged for a particular reason and fulfilled a particular psychological function (e.g. expressive or defensive) by representing certain people, emotional events or abilities. Hypnosis was used to try and integrate the personalities, apparently with some success.

IS MULTIPLE PERSONALITY DISORDER A SPONTANEOUS OR IATROGENIC PHENOMENON?

HAVE THERAPISTS JUST CLASSIFIED A MENTAL DISORDER OR CREATED ONE?

MPD AS A SPONTANEOUS PHENOMENON

MPD could represent a spontaneous, pre-existing mental disorder that therapists discovered and classified, and then were able to diagnose and treat. Many theories have been proposed to try and explain the origin of MPD, including psychodynamic, cognitive and behavioural learning ones. For example it has been suggested that MPD can spontaneously result from:

- Defensive amnesia or repression of traumatic childhood events.
- Self-hypnotic role playing escapism as a coping mechanism.
- Powerful state-dependent memory effects.
- Selective reinforcement for different behaviours in different social contexts.

Evaluation

- Evidence for MPD comes from numerous hours of interviews, observation and personality tests from many case studies.
- Evidence is occasionally provided from physiological methods, e.g. electroencephalograms, galvanic skin responses, and brain scans.
- The disorder is often developed in childhood and is associated with traumatic or disturbed family relationships (the causes far precede therapy).
- MPD is more common in women than men, which may reflect the higher level of childhood abuse suffered by girls than boys.
- Increased rates of MPD may reflect increased public awareness of the disorder, which could have enabled or encouraged therapists and sufferers to more readily recognise the symptoms and seek or provide treatment for it.
- Just because cases of MPD have been simulated and may have been faked to avoid responsibility for crimes, does not mean there are no genuine cases.

MPD AS AN IATROGENIC PHENOMENON

Alternatively, MPD may not be a spontaneous disorder but one created by therapists themselves through:

- **Treatment techniques that suggest the disorder** – the mistaken theoretical *expectation* that MPD can explain memory lapses or erratic behaviour may lead therapists to suggest its presence in the patient. Leading and suggestive interviews, selective attention and social reinforcement, and hypnotic suggestion and prompting may actually have created, maintained and legitimised MPD.
- **The construction of a mistaken diagnostic label** – this may have unconsciously led other people who heard about the disorder to think they have the problem, explain their memory lapses or troubled and poorly understood behaviour in terms of it, and thus seek treatment for it. Others may use the disorder to escape responsibility for their actions and consciously fake it.

Evaluation

- Self-report and non-experimental methods may have made it easier for therapists to have been duped or misled about the existence of MPD in the first place or to transmit their expectations to the patient.
- Physiological differences could just reflect the different demands of role-playing different personalities and, of course, the therapist could still have created the personalities.
- False memories of early abuse could be invented by fakers of MPD (although some cases have been independently verified) or created by therapeutic suggestion and hypnosis (false memory syndrome).
- If MPD is due to spontaneous repression of abuse, escapism, state-dependent memory and selective reinforcement, it might be expected to occur more frequently than it does.
- Cases of MPD have dramatically increased with media coverage and public awareness of it in recent times, and mostly in the USA rather than other countries (suggesting a culturally created disorder). The vast majority of MPD cases are reported by just a minority of therapists (are they specialised at diagnosing or creating MPD?).
- Simulators can convincingly fake MPD (any differences could just be due to lack of practice) and if fakers recall memories they should not be able to, they can easily switch identities or create a new one.

'A case of multiple personality' Thigpen and Cleckley (1954)

AIM

To describe the case study of a 25-year-old married woman referred to two psychiatrists for severe headaches and blackouts, but soon discovered to have a multiple personality. The article presents evidence for the existence of this previously rare condition in the subject, in a cautious but convinced manner.

SUMMARY OF THE CASE

The first few interviews with the woman, Eve White, only found her to have 'several important emotional difficulties' and a 'set of marital conflicts and personal frustrations'. The first indication of multiple personality was when the psychiatrists received a letter from Eve that she did not remember sending and which contained a note at the end written in a different and childish handwriting. On her next visit, after a period of unusual agitation, she reported that she occasionally had the impression that she heard a voice in her head – and then suddenly and spontaneously showed a dramatic change in her behaviour, revealing the character (and answering to the name) of Eve Black. Over a period of 14 months and around 100 hours of interview time, the two psychiatrists investigated the two Eves, first using hypnosis, but later without the need for it. Eve White was found not to have access to the awareness and memories of Eve Black (experiencing blackouts when Eve Black took over control) although the reverse was true for Eve Black (who often used the ability to disrupt Eve White's life by taking over and getting her into trouble or by giving her headaches).

Later during the course of therapy, a third personality emerged called Jane – again suddenly and with a different set of characteristics. Jane had access to the consciousness of both Eves, but incomplete access to their memories before her emergence, and could only emerge through Eve White.

The authors admit the possibility of fakery, although they think it highly unlikely, and argue for more research to answer some fundamental questions concerning the multiple personality phenomena.

EVIDENCE FOR THE EXISTENCE OF MULTIPLE PERSONALITY

Personality distinctions gained through interview:

- Character – Eve White – self-controlled, serious, matter of fact, and meticulously truthful.
  Eve Black – childish, carefree, shallow, mischievous, and a fluent liar.
- Attitudes – Eve White – distressed about failing marriage, warm love for daughter.
  Eve Black – thought Eve White's distress and love was silly, seemed 'immune to major affective events in human relationships'.
- Behaviour – Eve White – responsible and reserved.
  Eve Black – irresponsible, pleasure and excitement seeking, sought the company of strangers to avoid discovery.
- Mannerisms – 'A thousand minute alterations in manner, gesture, expression, posture, of nuances in reflex... of glance' between the two Eves.

Personality distinctions gained through independent psychological testing:

- Psychometric tests – IQ of Eve White was 110, IQ of Eve Black was 104, differences between the two were found in memory function.
- Projective testing – Rorschach revealed
  a Eve Black to show regression and hysterical tendencies, but to be far healthier than Eve White.
  b Eve White to show repression, anxiety, obsessive-compulsive traits, and an inability to deal with her hostility.

The psychologist was of the opinion that the tests revealed one personality at two stages of life – that Eve Black represented a regression to a carefree state, as a way of dealing with her dislike of marriage and maternal pressures.

Personality distinctions gained through physiological EEG testing:

Eve White and Jane were found to show similar Electroencephalograph readings, with Eve Black definitely distinguishable from the other two.

Evidence for multiple personality as a distinct and valid disorder:

- Clearly distinguishable from other disorders, such as schizophrenia, but with some similarities to disorders like dissociative fugue.
- Eve's behaviour showed such remarkable consistency within characters that two psychiatrists were persuaded she was not deliberately faking.
- Shows similarities of symptoms with other multiple personality cases such as patterns of amnesia between personalities and similar causal circumstances that provoke a denial of parts of the self.

EVALUATION

Methodological:

Case study method – Lack of objectivity when involved with the patient, especially when trying to help through therapy, rather than attempting rigorous experiments to test the possibility of fakery.

Unreliability of testing – Those tests that were conducted were of doubtful validity, because they could have been affected by deliberate attempts to fake (except perhaps the EEG test, although what the differences found represented is open to interpretation) and projective tests are also of doubtful reliability due to the subjective nature of their interpretation.

Theoretical: Doubts about the validity of this study are caused by Chris Sizeman (the real name of Eve) later revealing that she had other personalities before (and after) 1954, yet these were not detected or mentioned at the time. Doubts about the validity of multiple personality disorder in general are caused by the fact that they are often investigated through hypnosis and are becoming increasingly common in America but not other countries. There are ethical and legal implications involved in accepting multiple personality as a valid disorder, e.g. culpability.

Links: Abnormality (particularly problems in diagnosing), personality, freewill, case studies, hypnosis.

Research into cross-cultural differences in the determination of abnormality

CROSS-CULTURAL DIFFERENCES IN ABNORMALITY

There are many cross-cultural differences in the determination of abnormality, both in prevalence and type of disorder. However, there are also many cross-cultural similarities. Gross (1995) argues that disorders show enough recognisable core symptoms in every culture to be regarded as universal (for example all schizophrenics world-wide show incoherent thought patterns and speech, delusions, etc.) but show cultural variations in

- the precise **form** that the **symptoms** take
- the **reasons** for the onset of disorder
- the **prognosis** for recovery

However, it has been proposed that some disorders are **culturally relative** - that is unique to a particular culture. Western psychiatrists are likely to say that if a syndrome is distorted beyond a certain point, then a **culture-bound syndrome** is identified. Researchers (e.g. Fernando, 1991) suggest that anorexia nervosa and pre-menstrual syndrome may be western **culture-bound syndromes**, while 'Amok' (which involves short-lived outbursts of aggressive behaviour in males involving attempts to kill or injure) may be a Southeast Asian culture-bound syndrome, since it is identified as a disorder in Malaysia, Thailand, and Indonesia. The ICD10 recognises that some disorders seem to be particularly frequent in some cultures, and includes, in subsection F48.8 called 'Other specified neurotic disorders':

- **Dhat syndrome** – anxiety involving 'undue concern about the debilitating effects of the passage of semen'.
- **Koro** – a disorder involving 'anxiety and fear that the penis will withdraw into the abdomen and cause death'.
- **Latah** – involving 'imitative and automatic response behaviour'.

BIOLOGICAL EXPLANATIONS

Biological effects can account for the widespread **similarities** in abnormality across cultures, but probably have a more limited role in determining cross-cultural differences. The idea that disorders are **absolute** – that is 'culture free' (found in all cultures in exactly the same form) has received very **little support**. Even with disorders with strong biological influences, it seems that cultural factors can affect the prevalence, types of symptoms, and prognosis for recovery.

CULTURAL/ENVIRONMENTAL EXPLANATIONS

The idea that disorders are **universal** – they occur in all cultures but are subject to cultural modification due to **learning influences** in their causes or expression, has received the most support. Many of the cross-cultural differences can be attributed to environmental factors, such as the different levels of stress, different social learning effects, different norms, etc. found in those societies. According to Gross (1995),

- different cultures will learn different ways of expressing their symptoms, for example schizophrenics complaining of thought invasion by mysterious forces in western societies have kept pace with technological developments. In the 1920s they thought that voices were being transmitted directly into their heads via radio, in the 1960s it was accomplished by space satellites, and in the 1970s and 80s it was done through microwave ovens. In Nigeria, where the culture believes that others can curse or direct evil spirits at you, schizophrenics show a higher prevalence of paranoia and persecution symptoms.
- many disorders are thought to be provoked by stressful environments. However, different cultures may differ in the amount of environmental stress their members experience and what they find socially distressful. Unless these culturally determined influences are understood, the causes of the disorder may remain a mystery.
- Lin and Kleinman (1988) have found that schizophrenics are more likely to recover in a non-industrialised society than an industrialised society, despite more advanced medical resources in the latter. They argue that this is probably because non-industrialised cultures are less individualistic and competitive, providing more family and social support for the sufferer and more stable and predictable environments to aid recovery.

DIAGNOSTIC DIFFERENCE EXPLANATIONS

Different cultures vary in the way they perceive and identify abnormality, so the difference in disorders between cultures could be due to the **different notions** of normal and abnormal behaviour found in those cultures. Thus, it has been argued that in some cultures the symptoms of schizophrenia, such as strange visions, speech, and behaviour, might be regarded as special or sacred rather than abnormal and undesirable. However, research by Murphy (1976) on non western cultures (such as Inuit tribes) has indicated that linguistic distinctions are made between the 'shaman' and 'crazy people' in their society. Alternatively, other cultures may regard those defined as suffering from Anti-social Personality Disorder by western diagnostic systems as just plain evil or bad. Western societies have 'medicalised' disorder to a greater degree than non western societies in Africa and India for example, where mental well-being is far more tied up with religious and social well-being. Even in different western cultures, different diagnostic classification systems and expectations have been shown to influence the determination of abnormality, e.g. Cooper et al's (1972) study on New York and London psychiatrists.

Culture-bound syndromes

WHAT IS A CULTURE-BOUND SYNDROME?

A culture-bound syndrome (CBS) refers to a pattern of symptoms that:

1 Do *not easily fit into the categories* and classifications of supposedly universal disorders identified by the ICD-10 and DSM-IV diagnostic manuals.

2 Occur almost exclusively in *specific* geographical *locations* or cultural *populations*.

3 Are *indigenously regarded* to be illnesses or afflictions and thus have local names.

The above points raise the possibility that diagnostic classification manuals and systems may be culturally biased by the society that created them. Thus the ICD-10 and DSM-IV diagnostic manuals may only categorise disorders that are familiar, local and of concern to those living in Western cultures.

ARGUMENTS FOR THE EXISTENCE OF CBSs

According to researchers such as Pfeiffer (1982), some syndromes may truly be regarded as culture-bound since:

1 The pattern of *symptoms* shown in one culture *may not correspond* in important ways to those of disorders identified by other cultures. Attempting to fit CBSs into other ICD or DSM categories may distort or ignore the importance of some of the symptoms.

2 The symptoms may be *triggered* off and/or *expressed* differently due to specifically *different pressures* relating to environmental locations or cultural norms. The same pressures and norms may not exist to create the disorder elsewhere.

3 The symptoms may only be *understood* or classified as problems in the light of certain *cultural beliefs*. The same behaviours in other cultures may not be regarded as a disorder or source of affliction.

ARGUMENTS AGAINST THE EXISTENCE OF CBSs

According to researchers such as Yap (1974), some syndromes may only appear exotic and culturally bound but in fact may 'be local expressions of some universal disorders already known and classified' (Berry et al, 1992) since:

1 The symptoms of apparent CBSs can often be related to, or *only differ in degree* from, those of standard ICD and DSM categories. Only small adjustments may be needed to make the fit.

2 The *same pattern* of symptoms can sometimes be found in *many* different environmental locations and cultures (without any need for adjustment), thus questioning whether they are truly bound by culture.

3 The same *underlying processes* or *causes* may link culture-bound syndromes with each other and with standard ICD and DSM categories. The expression and name of the disorders may differ but the same kind of underlying mechanism can often be understood.

HOW CULTURE-BOUND ARE CULTURE-BOUND SYNDROMES?

A few examples of CBSs (at least 36 have been identified) that can be examined in the light of the above criteria and arguments are:

KORO

Thought to specifically occur in Chinese cultures, it involves:

- The belief that the penis is shrinking and will eventually withdraw into the abdomen and cause death.
- Physiological and emotional reactions to this belief associated with fear and anxiety.
- Behavioural countermeasures to prevent penis retraction, e.g. clasping the genitals or tying objects such as weights and chop-sticks to the penis.

Evaluation

Syndromes similar to Koro have been (rarely) identified in other cultures. However, they have often shown:

- Important variations in symptoms – e.g. lacking the belief that death will occur.
- Different provoking cultural causes – e.g. outbreaks of Koro in China and India have been triggered by different beliefs.
- Different underlying mechanisms and responses to treatment – Koro usually responds to reassurance whereas the Koro-like symptoms shown in other cultures have often disappeared when other mental disorders, e.g. schizophrenia, were treated.

Nevertheless, some Western psychiatrists still regard Koro as just a particular form of hypochondria or phobic anxiety disorder.

DHAT

Thought to specifically occur in Indian-Hindu cultures, it involves:

- The belief that semen is leaking out of the body and sapping the body of power.
- Excessive anxiety and concern in reaction to this belief.
- Feelings of exhaustion, weakness and lethargy.

Evaluation

- Syndromes similar to Dhat have been identified in other cultures, e.g. Sri Lankan, Chinese and (Victorian) British ones.
- Furthermore the symptoms shown and underlying beliefs that trigger the disorder across cultures are very similar in nature.
- It seems only culture-bound in terms of the prevalence of the underlying beliefs, which in turn depend on access to and belief in scientific medical knowledge.

OTHER CBSs

- **AMOK** – a sudden and short lasting outburst of violent or homicidal aggression – found most commonly in Malaysian cultures but also elsewhere. Amok may be caused by similar underlying factors, but have different norms of expression, across cultures.
- **KURU** – a progressive dementia and psychosis – found in cannibalistic tribes of New Guinea and probably due to the ingestion of proteins that provoke a variant of CJD (Creuzfeldt-Jacob Disease).
- **PIBLOKTOQ** – a sudden and short lasting period of frantic, dangerous and bizarre behaviour – found in Eskimo cultures in Greenland but also throughout the Arctic. Sometimes termed 'arctic hysteria'.

Schizophrenia – symptoms and diagnosis

BACKGROUND
Some studies indicate that there is approximately a 1% life time risk of developing schizophrenia. Kraepelin (1902) described the symptoms of 'dementia praecox' (senility of youth) as being delusions, attention deficits, and bizarre motor activity, due to a form of mental deterioration that began in youth. Bleuler (1911) observed that deterioration did not continue and often began after adolescence, and so introduced the term 'schizophrenia' (split mind) to describe how psychological functions had lost their unity.

DIAGNOSIS
The DSM IV diagnostic criteria are:
1 **Two** or more of the following symptoms present for a significant amount of time in a one month period:
   - **Hallucinations** (if there are extensive auditory hallucinations of voices, then no other symptoms have to be present)
   - **Delusions** (if these are very bizarre, then no other symptoms have to be present)
   - **Disorganised speech**, e.g. incoherent
   - **Catatonic or disorganised behaviour**, e.g. repetitive movements or gestures
   - **Negative symptoms**, e.g. emotional blunting

2 Disturbance must last for 6 months (including 1 month of the above symptoms).

3 The symptoms must have produced a marked deterioration in functioning at work, in social relations, and in self care (axis 5 of the DSM IV).

SYMPTOMS

EMOTIONAL
Emotions can be either
- flat, unresponsive and insensitive, or
- inappropriate to the situation and changeable

BEHAVIOURAL
Somatic disturbance, e.g.
- psychomotor agitation – fixed, repetitive gestures
- catatonic stupor – keeping the same position for long periods of time

PERCEPTUAL
- Auditory hallucinations, usually voices commenting upon behaviour and thoughts in the third person, are heard.
- Visual hallucinations, such as size, space, and colour distortions occur.

COGNITIVE
Disruption occurs to
- **thought processes** – schizophrenics show **cognitive distractibility** (they are unable to maintain a consistent train of thought); **attentional deficits** (focusing on irrelevant stimuli); and **thought passivity** (where they think that others block, insert or withdraw the thoughts in their head).
- **thought content** – includes delusions, e.g. of persecution, control, or grandeur.

SUBTYPES OF SCHIZOPHRENIA
The DSM IV lists five sub-categories of schizophrenia, because of the huge variety of symptoms shown.

DISORGANISED SCHIZOPHRENIA
Symptoms mostly involve
- **incoherent** thoughts and speech
- **bizarre** delusions and hallucinations
- **inappropriate** emotions and behaviour

UNDIFFERENTIATED SCHIZOPHRENIA
The classification for those whose symptoms are not classifiable under any of the other subtypes. This is the least useful of the diagnostic classifications.

CATATONIC SCHIZOPHRENIA
Involves alternating between
- catatonic **stupor** and **negativism**, and
- catatonic **excitement** – prolonged, frenzied, even violent behaviour

PARANOID SCHIZOPHRENIA
Involves organised and complex delusions (often of persecution), mostly auditory hallucinations, and relatively few other symptoms.

RESIDUAL SCHIZOPHRENIA
Involves the gradual development of many minor problems, e.g. unusual behaviour, social withdrawal, emotional blunting, and apathy.

ALTERNATIVE TYPOLOGIES
- **Type 1 schizophrenia** – is characterised by positive symptoms, e.g. hallucinations and delusions
- **Type 2 schizophrenia** – is characterised by negative symptoms, e.g. emotional blunting and avolition

Explanatory theories of schizophrenia

BIOLOGICAL THEORIES

GENETIC CAUSES

Family studies – Children of two schizophrenic biological parents are around 46% likely to develop the disorder. These studies do not rule out environmental learning though.

Twin studies – Studies from many countries have produced different estimates, but Gottesman (1991) suggests that monozygotic identical twins (who have the same genes) have significantly higher concordance rates (48%) for schizophrenia than dizygotic non-identical twins (17%). Concordance rates refer to whether **both** twins develop the disorder.
However, identical twins also share more similar environments.

Adoption studies – When adopted subjects' environments are matched, the rates of schizophrenia are higher for adoptive children with schizophrenic biological parents compared to adoptive children with non-schizophrenic biological parents (Kety et al, 1975). Ideally, identical twins with schizophrenia, raised apart in different adoptive environments, would be the best evidence for genetic causes, but obviously these cases are extremely rare.

Genetic factors do not account 100% for schizophrenia, however. People probably inherit a genetic predisposition for schizophrenia, which **may** be triggered by environmental factors.

BIOCHEMICAL CAUSES

A very popular theory of schizophrenia was the dopamine hypothesis – that over-activity of the neurotransmitter dopamine in the synapses of the brain caused type 1 positive symptoms of schizophrenia. Evidence for the hypothesis included the findings that
- large doses of amphetamines (which increase dopamine activity) can create amphetamine psychosis, which closely resembles acute paranoid schizophrenia. Small doses can trigger symptoms in schizophrenics.
- anti-schizophrenic drugs like chlorpromazine work by blocking the post synaptic receptor sites of dopamine, thereby reducing its activity. If schizophrenics are given too much of these drugs, they develop symptoms similar to Parkinson's disease (caused by too little dopamine).
- post-mortems and Positron Emission Tomography scans have found higher amounts of dopamine and dopamine synaptic receptor sites.

However, the dopamine hypothesis is an over simplistic explanation, since new anti-schizophrenic drugs (e.g. clozapine) work by affecting other neurotransmitters, especially serotonin.

BRAIN STRUCTURAL CAUSES

Enlarged ventricles – research has found that these fluid filled cavities in the brain are larger in schizophrenics due to brain cell loss. Cell loss in the temporal lobes of the brain (responsible for cognitive and emotional functions) has been associated with negative symptoms. However, the evidence is correlational – enlarged ventricles may be a symptom not a cause, and non-schizophrenics can also show them.

Brain area activity – schizophrenics' brain scans do not show the usual prefrontal activation of the cortex when given problem solving tasks. Brain scanning can not yet predict the presence of schizophrenia.

PSYCHOLOGICAL/ ENVIRONMENTAL THEORIES

PSYCHOLOGICAL CAUSES

A variety of theories have sought to explain schizophrenia at the psychological level, including:

Psychoanalytic theory – Freud suggested that regression to a state of 'narcissism' in the early oral stage could be responsible, where there is no developed ego to test reality. Psychotic thought resembles the id's primary process thinking, and is untreatable through psychoanalysis because the narcissistic person has given up any attachment to the outside world (preventing transference, for example).

Existential theory – Psychiatrists, such as Laing, have proposed that people withdraw from reality as a normal response to the pressures of a mad world. Schizophrenia is a social and interpersonal experience which can be regarded as a potentially beneficial journey of self discovery.

Labelling theory – Scheff (1966) has argued that schizophrenia may be largely a social role that, once assigned by diagnosis, is conformed to and becomes a self-fulfilling prophecy. The internalisation of the schizophrenic role is strengthened by the reactions of other people and hospitalisation. Szasz has taken these ideas further to argue that schizophrenia is a myth created by society to control those who are different.

Cognitive theory – Frith (1979) proposes that disruption to an attentional filter mechanism could result in the thought disturbance of schizophrenia, as the sufferer is overloaded with sensory information. Studies on continuous performance and eye-tracking tasks indicate that schizophrenics do show more attentional problems than non-schizophrenics. Perhaps reduced short-term memory capacity could account for some schizophrenics' cognitive distractibility.

SOCIAL/ENVIRONMENTAL CAUSES

Social or environmental factors could act to trigger schizophrenia in those with a genetic predisposition.

Family stresses – Faulty interpersonal relationships in the families of schizophrenics have been found by Fromm Reichmann (who proposed the idea of the 'schizophrenogenic mother'); Bateson (who discovered ambivalent 'double bind' communication between schizophrenic children and their parents); and Lidz and Fleck (who described 'schism' and 'skew' in the families of schizophrenics).
However, the evidence is correlational – perhaps schizophrenics cause stress and disturbance in their families.

Environmental stresses – Some studies have found schizophrenia is 8 times more common in the lower socio-economic groups. However, this could be a cause (providing greater stress) or a result (of downward social drift) of schizophrenia.

Viruses – Many viruses, e.g. influenza have been proposed to trigger genetic causes of schizophrenia.

Mood disorders - symptoms and diagnosis

BACKGROUND

Mood disorders are one of the most frequently occurring psychopathologies, the risk of developing one is around 9%. The DSM IV distinguishes between two main categories of mood disorder: unipolar depression and bipolar (manic) depression. Major unipolar depression occurs at least 5 times more frequently than bipolar depression (it has been called 'the common cold of mental illness'), and mania can occur on its own (although this is very rare). It is important to remember that we all have our emotional 'ups and downs' but these mood disorders differ in degree from 'normal', natural reactions, both in their severity, frequency and duration, and may lead to suicide attempts.

UNIPOLAR DEPRESSION

Diagnosis – Unipolar depression can present four types of symptoms. The DSM IV states that either depressed mood or loss of pleasure, plus at least another 4 symptoms (out of those listed opposite) must be shown during the same two-week period for the diagnosis to be made.

Prevalence – There is at least a 5% lifetime risk of developing unipolar depression. It appears cross-culturally, but is diagnosed twice as often for women.

EMOTIONAL SYMPTOMS
Intense feelings of sadness or guilt, along with a lack of enjoyment or pleasure in previous activities or company.

MOTIVATIONAL SYMPTOMS
Passivity and great difficulty in initiating action and making decisions.

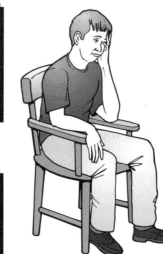

COGNITIVE SYMPTOMS
Frequent negative thoughts, faulty attribution of blame (blame themselves), low self-esteem, and irrational hopelessness.

SOMATIC SYMPTOMS
Loss of energy or restlessness. Disturbance of appetite, weight, and sleep.

BIPOLAR DEPRESSION

Diagnosis - Bipolar depression involves the symptoms of depression, followed by mania or hypomania (shorter, less severe mania). Mania involves 4 types of symptoms. The DSM IV states a manic episode must involve 'a distinct period of abnormally and persistently elevated, expansive or irritable mood, lasting at least a week', plus at least 3 additional symptoms (out of those opposite).

Prevalence – There is around a 1% lifetime risk of developing bipolar depression.

EMOTIONAL SYMPTOMS
Abnormally euphoric elevated or irritable mood, and increased pleasure in activities.

MOTIVATIONAL SYMPTOMS
Increase in goal-directed activity and increase in pleasurable activities that have a high risk of painful consequences.

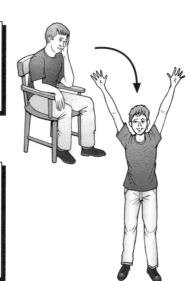

COGNITIVE SYMPTOMS
Inflated self-esteem or grandiosity, racing ideas and thoughts, distractibility of attention.

SOMATIC SYMPTOMS
Decreased need for sleep, psychomotor agitation, more talkative and rapid, pressured speech.

OTHER MOOD DISORDERS

The DSM IV and ICD 10 list many other varieties of mood disorder, including:

- **Dysthymia** – A classification given to those who suffer chronic mild depression over a period of not less than two years, where a depressed mood and other symptoms of mild depression are suffered **a** for most of the day, **b** on more days than not, and **c** without a break of more than two months in the two year period.
- **Cyclothymia** – The bipolar equivalent of dysthymia. It is a classification given to those who suffer from mild depression, interspersed with periods of hypomania, for more than two years.
- **Mania** – A classification given to those who suffer from full blown symptoms of mania without corresponding periods of depression. The symptoms must last for at least one week and must be sufficiently severe to interfere with social and/or occupational functioning.
- **Seasonal affective disorder** – A classification given to those who suffer a mood disorder that systematically varies with seasonal changes, often involving depression in winter months and sometimes also bipolar mania in the summer.

Explanatory theories of mood disorders

BIOLOGICAL THEORIES

PSYCHOLOGICAL THEORIES

ENVIRONMENTAL THEORIES

Genetics
There is moderate evidence for a genetic predisposition to suffer from unipolar depression, but much stronger evidence for the role of genes in bipolar depression. Monozygotic twin **concordance** studies and family studies have led Katz and McGuffin (1993) to suggest that genetic factors account for 52% of the variance in unipolar depression, but up to 80% of the variance in vulnerability in bipolar depression.

Learning theory
Looks at the role of **reinforcement** and **punishment**. Depressives may suffer from a lack of positive reinforcement that may lead to 'sad' behaviour which, when noticed, may itself be reinforced by the attention it draws. However, since depressed people tend to be avoided in the long run, this only leads to further lack of reinforcement and a vicious circle.
Seligman found that dogs repeatedly subjected to unavoidable punishment would no longer initiate any action to avoid electric shocks when it was made possible to do so. Seligman argued that the dogs had **learned helplessness** and showed behaviour similar to that showed by human depressives.

Life events
Depression occurs not only after major stressful life events (particularly the early loss of attachment figures), but is also reliably linked with continual levels of stress and 'hassles'.

Neurochemicals
One of the most popular theories is that a **lack** of the neurotransmitters **norepinephrine** (noradrenaline) and **serotonin** are responsible for depression. These biochemicals are involved in the areas of the brain involved in emotional behaviour, and evidence for their involvement in depression comes from studies into the action of anti-depressant drugs (which increase their activity) and the drug reserpine, which causes depression (because it decreases norepinephrine and serotonin levels).
The very successful effect of lithium carbonate in treating bipolar depression indicates a strong role for biological causes in this disorder.
Some studies have indicated that hormones, such as cortisol, have a role to play in unipolar depression.

Cognitive theory
Based on his experiments on **learned helplessness**, Seligman proposed a cognitive theory suggesting that people become depressed when they **believe** that nothing they do will improve their situation.
Learned helplessness makes the depressive see
- causes as internal (blaming themselves not the situation)
- situations as stable (showing extreme pessimism about the future)
- failure as global (not specific to one situation)
In other words the depressed person thinks 'its me, its going to last forever, and everything I do will go wrong'.

Aaron Beck came up with some similar ideas by proposing his **cognitive triad** of negative thoughts (about the self, present experience, and the future) and looked at the depressive's **errors in logic** (distortions of thought processes, such as false magnification or minimisation of events, over-generalisation, personalisation, etc.).
Cognitive psychologists emphasise faulty attributions.

Socio-economic background
Depression is proportionally more common in women, but especially in 'working class', house-bound women with three or more children. Clearly, stress and lack of environmental reinforcement is greater in these circumstances.

Seasonal variation
Seasonal affective disorder may be caused by the variations in daylight hours that occur as the seasons change. Less daylight in the winter months may account for the higher reports of depression at this time.

Psychoanalytic theory
Focuses on **unconscious** causes of depression. According to Freud, depressives turn their aggressive drive and anger that they feel towards other people or situations inwards and are, therefore, punishing themselves.

Evaluation
The role of the above neuro-transmitters and hormones in depression is extremely complex, and anti-depressant drugs have effects on many other neurochemicals, apart from norepinephrine and serotonin, so we cannot guarantee that these are the only substances involved.

Evaluation
Learning theory does not take into account the idea that different people sharing a similar set of environmental experiences will not always become equally depressed. Seligman's finding on animals can not be legitimately generalised to humans. The psychoanalytic theory of depression lacks scientific support.

Evaluation
These factors should perhaps be regarded as **triggers** of depression for people who are already predisposed to suffer from it, since not all people will react in the same way to these environmental stresses – some cope, others do not.

INTERACTION EXPLANATIONS
Researchers, such as Checkley (1992), have pointed out that stress causes the release of adrenal steroid hormones, such as cortisol, and these hormones are thought to play a role in regulating the effect of genetic influences.

Other researchers such as Weiss and Simson (1985) have found that rats exhibiting the behavioural symptoms of learned helplessness induced by unavoidable shock, often showed large decreases in the production of the neurotransmitter norepinephrine.

Eating disorders – symptoms and diagnosis

BACKGROUND
Eating disorders like anorexia and bulimia are fairly recent arrivals to the classification manuals – appearing for the first time in the DSM III in 1980. There is debate over whether these disorders have always existed, but what is certain is that they have increased in prevalence in recent years. This could be due to increasing media publicity drawing attention to the disorder and thus making referral and diagnosis more common, or due to the media actually influencing the increase in the frequency of the disorder (see theories). These disorders are ten times more common in women than men and often occur together in the same individual.

ANOREXIA NERVOSA
DIAGNOSIS: 'Anorexia' comes from the Greek term for 'loss of appetite' and involves problems maintaining a normal body weight. The DSM IV states that the four symptoms below must be shown for the classification to be made.
The DSM IV also suggests two sub-types:
The 'restricting type' maintains low body weight by refusing to eat and/or indulging in frequent exercise.
The 'binge-eating/purging type' maintains low body weight by refusing to eat in combination with bingeing and purging (like bulimia below but usually less frequently)
PREVALENCE – 0.5 – 1% of females in adolescence to early adulthood.

BEHAVIOURAL SYMPTOMS
1 A refusal to maintain a body weight normal for age and height (weight itself is less than 85% of that expected).

COGNITIVE SYMPTOMS
2 Distorted self-perception of body shape (over-estimation of body size) and over-emphasis of its importance for self-esteem. Denial of seriousness of weight loss.

EMOTIONAL SYMPTOMS
3 An intense fear of gaining weight even though obviously under-weight.

SOMATIC SYMPTOMS
4 Loss of body weight and absence of menstruation for 3 consecutive months.

BULIMIA NERVOSA
DIAGNOSIS: 'Bulimia' is derived from the Greek for 'ox appetite' and involves binge eating followed by compensatory behaviour to rid the body of what has just been consumed.
The DSM IV states that the symptoms opposite must be shown for the classification to be made, and includes a 'non-purging' subtype who binges but uses excessive physical exercise instead of purging to compensate.
PREVALENCE – Around 1 – 3% of females in adolescence to early adulthood.

BEHAVIOURAL SYMPTOMS
1 Recurring binge eating – excessive quantities consumed within a discrete period of time (e.g. 2 hours) without a sense of control over what or how much is consumed.
2 Recurring inappropriate compensatory behaviour to prevent weight gain – such as self-induced vomiting, misuse of laxatives or fasting.
3 Binge eating and compensatory behaviours occur on average at least twice a week for three months.

COGNITIVE SYMPTOMS
4 Self-image is overly influenced by body size and shape.

HOW SIMILAR ARE THE TWO DISORDERS?
- The main differences are that bulimia sufferers usually maintain their weight within the normal range (although bulimia causes much other damage to their bodies) and, despite some anorexia sufferers being obsessed with food and reporting hunger, bulimia involves an urge to overeat that often causes bingeing long before purging and other methods are used as compensations.
- However, some researchers think anorexia and bulimia should be thought of as two variants of the same disorder, since they have many features in common, are often both found in the same person (anorexia can progress to bulimia with age), and have similar theories provided to explain them.

Explanatory theories of eating disorders

BIOLOGICAL THEORIES

PSYCHOLOGICAL THEORIES

Genetics

Family studies have shown that there is a higher risk of developing anorexia or bulimia if a first-degree relative suffers from it, while monozygotic (MZ) twin concordance studies have suggested there may be a stronger genetic link with anorexia than bulimia.

Holland et al (1984) found the likelihood of one identical (*MZ*) twin also getting *anorexia* if the other developed it was *55%*, compared to *7%* for non-identical, dizygotic (*DZ*) twins.

Kendler et al (1991) reported concordance rates of *23%* for *MZ* twins and *8.7%* for *DZ* twins with bulimia however.

Physiology

Early research indicated that disruption to the ventromedial or lateral areas of the hypothalamus could severely affect eating behaviour – ablating the ventromedial hypothalamus in rats for example caused them to overeat until they became obese, while removal of the lateral hypothalamus caused them to refuse to eat. Set Point Theory suggests an imbalance in the relative influences of these areas of the hypothalamus may be involved in eating disorders.

Eating disorders have been linked to depression and some studies have found lower levels of the neurotransmitter serotonin in sufferers of bulimia. The neurotransmitter noradrenaline and the hormone CCK-8 may also be involved.

Evaluation

Some twin studies have not always controlled for the effect of similar shared environments (e.g. by using adoption studies) or have found more environmental than genetic influences in eating disorders. Since concordance rates are nowhere near 100% for MZ twins, environmental triggers do seem to be involved. It is also uncertain what is actually inherited to cause the eating disorder, some researchers suggest personality traits such as perfectionism, others a predisposition to inherit mental disorder in general.

The biological cause and effect of eating disorders is difficult to determine since the physical disorders found in anorexia and bulimia may be an effect of starvation and purging rather than a cause. Post mortem studies have not revealed damage in the hypothalamus of those with eating disorders, however anti-depressants that increase serotonin levels are also effective in treating bulimia.

Psychoanalytic theory

Psychoanalytic theory has produced various explanations for eating disorders.

The anorexic's refusal to eat has been interpreted as an unconscious denial of the adult role and wish to remain a child (in figure at least) provoked by the development of sexual characteristics in puberty. The timing of onset in anorexia and the loss of menstruation support this idea.

Another psychoanalytic interpretation is that anorexics are unconsciously rejecting their bodies as a reaction to sexual abuse in childhood.

Cognitive theory

Cognitive psychologists have suggested that irrational attitudes and beliefs, and distorted perception are involved in eating disorders. These beliefs may concern unrealistic ideals or perception of body shape, or irrational attitudes towards eating habits and dieting (e.g. the disinhibition hypothesis – once a diet has been broken, one might as well break it completely by bingeing).

Cognitive researchers have also proposed that sufferers of anorexia and bulimia may be seeking to assert control over their lives to an excessively idealistic extent - Dura and Bornstein (1989) found this drive for perfection in hospitalised anorexics extended to academic achievements which were at a much higher level than their IQ scores would predict.

Learning theory

Learning theory explains eating disorders in terms of reinforcement consequences for eating behaviour.

Social praise or respect from a society that places a high value on slim female appearance may reward weight loss or control. Alternatively, the attention and concern shown towards someone with an eating disorder may be reinforcing. Social learning theory would suggest that thin or dieting role models would be imitated, while some learning theorists have proposed that a weight gain phobia is involved in eating disorders.

Evaluation:

Psychological level theories gain more strength when integrated with the following, social, cultural and family research findings.

The idea that cultural exposure to socially desirable conceptions of body shape is responsible for eating disorders has received much support. For example, anorexia and bulimia occur most in:

- Cultures where thinness is socially desirable, e.g. North America, Western Europe and Japan. Indeed evidence suggests that immigrants to these countries show higher levels of eating disorder than their native countries.
- Western women – physical attractiveness is the best predictor of self-esteem in western girls.
- Groups where thinness is particularly valued, e.g. ballet dancers, models and gymnasts.

Many researchers have found that the families of children with eating disorders show the following characteristics:

- Less emotional and nurturing – this may lead to eating disorders developing as an attention-gaining tactic.
- Overly protective – restricting independence may force the child to assert its own control and autonomy through the eating disorder.
- Middle class, overachieving parents – whose high expectations of success may lead to overly idealistic notions of success in matters of weight control.

However, although anorexics may develop their symptoms at puberty and may have been sexually abused in some cases, the effects of these events are often more convincingly explained in non-psychoanalytic terms. While cultural and family experiences do seem correlated with eating disorders, it is difficult to always work out the cause and effect and not all people will react in the same way to these experiences – some under-eat, others over-eat.

Anxiety disorders – symptoms and diagnosis

PHOBIAS

Diagnosis
The symptoms are unambiguous and diagnosis is easy:
- Persistent fear of a specific situation out of proportion to the reality of the danger.
- Compelling desire to avoid and escape the situation.
- Recognition that the fear is unreasonably excessive.
- Symptoms not due to another disorder, e.g. schizophrenia.

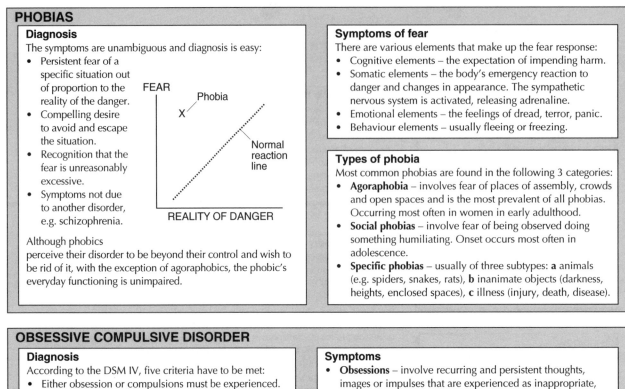

Although phobics perceive their disorder to be beyond their control and wish to be rid of it, with the exception of agoraphobics, the phobic's everyday functioning is unimpaired.

Symptoms of fear
There are various elements that make up the fear response:
- Cognitive elements – the expectation of impending harm.
- Somatic elements – the body's emergency reaction to danger and changes in appearance. The sympathetic nervous system is activated, releasing adrenaline.
- Emotional elements – the feelings of dread, terror, panic.
- Behaviour elements – usually fleeing or freezing.

Types of phobia
Most common phobias are found in the following 3 categories:
- **Agoraphobia** – involves fear of places of assembly, crowds and open spaces and is the most prevalent of all phobias. Occurring most often in women in early adulthood.
- **Social phobias** – involve fear of being observed doing something humiliating. Onset occurs most often in adolescence.
- **Specific phobias** – usually of three subtypes: **a** animals (e.g. spiders, snakes, rats), **b** inanimate objects (darkness, heights, enclosed spaces), **c** illness (injury, death, disease).

OBSESSIVE COMPULSIVE DISORDER

Diagnosis
According to the DSM IV, five criteria have to be met:
- Either obsession or compulsions must be experienced.
- The sufferer has to recognise that the obsessions or compulsions are excessive or unreasonable.
- The obsessions or compulsions are time consuming (taking over one hour a day), interfere with occupational or social functioning, and cause marked distress.
- The obsessions or compulsions are not confused with the preoccupations of other disorders, e.g. food with eating disorders, or drugs with substance abuse disorders.
- The obsessions or compulsions are not directly caused by medication or other known physical conditions.

Symptoms
- **Obsessions** – involve recurring and persistent thoughts, images or impulses that are experienced as inappropriate, intrusive and anxiety provoking, and are not just excessive worries about real life problems. The sufferer realises that these thoughts, etc. are the product of their own mind, and attempts to ignore or suppress them, often by thinking another thought or performing some action.
- **Compulsions** – involve repetitive and rule following behaviours (e.g. hand washing, checking) or mental acts (e.g. counting, praying) that the sufferer feels driven to perform (often in response to an obsession) to reduce distress or to avoid an imagined catastrophe. These acts are excessive and not realistically linked with what the sufferer is trying to avoid.

PANIC ATTACK

Diagnosis
According to the DSM IV a panic attack involves
- a discrete period of intense fear or discomfort, reaching a peak within 10 minutes.
- at least four (out of a list of 13) other symptoms occur very rapidly.

Symptoms
Somatic symptoms – such as sweating, trembling, palpitations, breathlessness, chest pain, nausea, dizziness, numbness, tingling or hot flushes.
Emotional symptoms – such as feelings of choking, smothering, derealization, depersonalisation, and fear of losing control, going mad or dying

GENERALISED ANXIETY DISORDER

Diagnosis
According to the DSM IV generalised anxiety disorder involves
- excessive, and difficult to control, worry and anxiety.
- significant distress and disruption to functioning.
- worry occurring more days than not for at least 6 months.
- worry not involving another disorder (e.g. depression).

Symptoms
Three additional symptoms must also be shown, e.g.
- restlessness and irritability,
- muscle tension, rapid physical fatigue, and sleep disturbance,
- concentration problems.

POST-TRAUMATIC STRESS DISORDER

Diagnosis
According to the DSM IV, post-traumatic stress disorder (PTSD) involves exposure to a traumatic event that was responded to with fear, helplessness or horror, plus the presence of the following symptoms for more than 1 month:
- The traumatic event is persistently re-experienced, e.g. as recurrent and intrusive recollections, flashbacks or dreams.
- Persistent avoidance of stimuli associated with the trauma and numbing of general responsiveness.
- Persistent symptoms of increased arousal, e.g. sleep difficulty, anger outbursts, exaggerated startle response, concentration difficulty.

Explanatory theories of anxiety disorders

BIOLOGICAL THEORIES

PSYCHOLOGICAL THEORIES

Genetics

The usual methods have been employed to assess the genetic causes of anxiety disorders:

- **Twin studies** – anxiety disorder concordance rates for monozygotic twins are fairly high, especially in comparison with dizygotic twin rates (Carey & Gottesman, 1981).
- **Relative studies** – some studies have shown that people with first degree relatives (e.g. mother, brother) who have experienced panic attacks are 10 times more likely than controls to also have them. Relatives of obsessive compulsives, however, are not more likely to develop obsessive compulsive disorder itself, but are more likely to suffer from some kind of anxiety disorder.

It appears that agoraphobia and panic disorder have the most **specific** genetic transmission, whereas other disorders seem to transmit a general tendency to inherit some kind of anxiety.

The genes for anxiety disorders have proven difficult to isolate however, and their method of action is unknown.

Evolutionary reasons for phobias

Seligman has talked of the 'biological preparedness' of phobias – that we are instinctively biased to acquire certain phobias because they have good evolutionary survival functions. Evidence for this comes from analysing the survival functions of the most common phobias (which usually involve dangerous stimuli, e.g. heights, snakes, the dark, etc.) and conditioning experiments, for example on monkeys which can be conditioned to fear snakes but not leaves or flowers. This also accounts for why modern dangerous objects, such as guns and cars, are rarely involved in human phobias - they have no evolutionary history.

Marks & Nesse argue that anxiety has evolved as 'a normal defence mechanism... People who are afraid of heights, for example, may "freeze" when confronted by a sudden drop, thereby reducing the chances of a fall'.

This does not explain why some people develop a particular phobic response compared to others.

Immediate biological causes

An excess of sodium lactate has been proposed as an explanation of panic attacks – infusions of this substance will provoke panic attacks in susceptible subjects significantly more than in controls. The same substance could be involved in phobias. Lactate may work by increasing blood carbon dioxide levels, thereby increasing respiration rates and provoking panic, or it may reduce serotonin, thereby reducing this neurotransmitter's calming effects. Evidence comes from the fact that anti-anxiety drugs block lactate effects.

PTSD may disrupt the locus coeruleus – the brain's alarm and arousal centre in the brain stem. This may be responsible for the PTSD symptoms of hyperalertness, difficulties in concentration and sleep, and exaggerated startle response.

Biological theories on their own can not provide a complete explanation – bodily effects still need to be cognitively interpreted, and an explanation of why certain people develop certain anxiety disorders needs to be provided.

Psychoanalytic theory

Freud proposed that phobias are caused by the displacement of unconscious anxiety onto harmless external objects. The anxiety stems from unconscious conflict, which has to be resolved before the phobia can be dealt with – even if one phobia goes, another will take its place until the underlying disorder is treated. The classic evidence that Freud provided was the case study of 'Little Hans' (1909), where Hans's unconscious fear of castration was displaced onto a fear of being bitten by white horses (which symbolised the father). Freud would have attributed PTSD to repressed traumatic events.

There are many criticisms of this approach and therapy.

Learning theory

Learning theorists propose that phobias come about as an originally neutral stimulus becomes associated with an unpleasant or traumatic experience and so becomes a fear-eliciting conditional stimulus. The classic example is the case of 'Little Albert' demonstrated by Watson & Rayner (1920).

Neutral Stimulus	+	Unconditional Stimulus	→	Unconditional Response
RAT	+	**SUDDEN LOUD NOISE**	→	**FEAR**
Conditional Stimulus				Conditional Response
RAT			→	**FEAR**

The persistence of phobias (i.e. why they do not extinguish easily) is explained by Mowrer's (1960) 'Two- factor' theory. It suggests that phobias are acquired through classical conditioning (as above) but are maintained through negative reinforcement – as the avoidance of unpleasant phobic situations is reinforced.

The degree of PTSD suffering is related to the severity of the trauma experienced, perhaps indicating a strong form of classical conditioning is involved.

Behaviourist views of phobia learning have to compromise with:
- biological preparedness (not all fears are equally easy to learn)
- vicarious learning of fear responses via social learning theory.

Cognitive theory

Clark (1986) proposes that faulty cognitive processes (thinking) are to blame for panic attacks. The sufferer tends to focus their attention internally, so are more aware of bodily sensations, and are more likely to misinterpret those sensations as catastrophic. This thinking can lead to a vicious circle as an increased heart rate is misinterpreted as a sign of impending harm – this leads to anxiety – which in turn leads to increased heart rate!

People suffering from generalised anxiety disorder show the attentional problem of over-vigilance – they are extremely sensitive to even minor danger cues.

Expectancies are important in determining whether traumatic events will cause PTSD. If people in the emergency services are not prepared for traumatic events, they are likely to suffer PTSD.

Obsessive compulsives appear to use their obsessive thoughts and compulsive actions as a way of **suppressing** or controlling some underlying anxiety or worry. These thoughts and actions may be negatively reinforced by providing momentary escape from the underlying anxiety.

'Analysis of a phobia in a five-year-old boy' Freud (1909)

AIM
To present the case study of Little Hans, a young boy who was seen as suffering from anxiety that led to a number of phobias. Freud uses this case study as strong support for his psychoanalytic ideas concerning:

- **Unconscious determinism** – Freud argues that people are not consciously aware of the causes of their behaviour. Little Hans was not consciously aware of the motivations for his behaviour, fantasies, and phobias.
- **Psychosexual development** – Psychoanalytic theory proposes that the sex drive seeks gratification through different erogenous zones at different ages, e.g. oral stage (0–1 years), anal (1–3 years), phallic stage (3–5 or 6 years). Little Hans was currently experiencing the phallic stage, according to Freud, gaining pleasure through masturbation and showing an interest in his own and other people's genitals.
- **The Oedipus complex** – Central to Freud's theory of personality, this occurs during the phallic stage as young boys direct their genital pleasure towards the mother and wish the father dead. However, young boys fear that their illicit desires will be found out by the father who will punish in the worse way possible – castration. Out of castration anxiety, the boy identifies with the father. Little Hans was regarded as a 'little Oedipus' wanting his father out of the way so he could be alone with his mother.
- **The cause of phobias** – Freud believed that phobias were the product of unconscious anxiety displaced onto harmless external objects. Little Hans's unconscious fear of castration by the father was symbolically displaced as a fear of being bitten by white horses.
- **Psychoanalytic therapy** – Aims to treat disturbed thoughts, feelings and behaviour by firstly identifying the unconscious causes of the disturbance, and secondly bringing them 'out into the open' to consciously discuss and resolve them. Thus Little Hans' behaviour was analysed, and its unconscious causes inferred and confronted.

SUMMARY OF THE CASE
Little Hans started showing a particularly lively interest in his 'widdler' and the presence or absence of this organ in others, and his tendency to masturbate brought threats from the mother to cut it off. When he was three and a half, he gained a baby sister, whom he resented, and consequently developed a fear of the bath. Later Hans developed a stronger fear of being bitten by white horses which seemed to be linked to two incidents – overhearing a father say to a child 'don't put your finger to the white horse or it will bite you' and seeing a horse that was pulling a carriage fall down and kick about with its legs. His fear went on to generalise to carts and buses. Little Hans, both before and after the beginning of the phobias, expressed anxiety that his mother would go away and was prone to frequent fantasies including imagining: **a** being the mother of his own children, whom he made to widdle, **b** that his mother had shown him her widdler, **c** that he had taken a smaller crumpled giraffe away from a taller one, **d** that a plumber had placed a borer into his stomach while in the bath on one occasion and had replaced his behind and widdler with larger versions on another occasion, and **e** that he was the father of his own children with his mother as their mother and his father as their grandfather. Having received 'help' from his father and Freud, his disorder and analysis came to an end after this last fantasy.

METHODS OF ANALYSIS
Little Hans was analysed and treated through his father (a firm believer of Freud's ideas) based on the latter's reports of Hans's behaviour and statements. Treatment was achieved by
- inferring the unconscious causes of Hans' behaviour through rich interpretation and decoding of psychoanalytic symbols
- confronting Hans with the unconscious causes by revealing to him his hidden motivations and consciously discussing them

RESULTS OF ANALYSIS

Event	Freudian Interpretation	Conclusion
Anxiety of mother's desertion	Sexual arousal of being taken into mother's bed for comfort	Oedipus complex love for the mother
Fear of bath	Death wish against sister due to jealousy over mother's attention	
Asking why mother did not powder his penis	Seduction attempt	
Taking smaller giraffe from the bigger one	Taking mother away from father	
Fear of heavily loaded carts and buses	Fear of another birth due to jealousy over mother's attention	
Fear of being bitten by white horses	Father (with spectacles and moustache) symbolic of white bus horse (with black blinkers and muzzle), bitten finger symbolic of castration	Fear of castration by father
Fantasy of plumber providing larger widdler	Wanting to be like (identifying with) his father	Resolution of Oedipus complex
Fantasy of being father with his mother	Fulfilment of growing up to have mother while making his father a grandfather instead of killing him	

EVALUATION
Methodological:
Case study method – Advantageous for therapeutic use but also many disadvantages, e.g. generalising results.
Lack of objectivity – Analysis was conducted second hand via the father and all data interpreted in the light of psychoanalytic theory. Freud was aware of objectivity problems and putting words in Little Hans' mouth, but argued 'a psychoanalysis is not an impartial scientific investigation but a therapeutic measure. Its essence is not to prove anything, but to alter something'.

Theoretical: There are many other explanations of Little Hans' behaviour that are more credible, e.g. those of Fromm (castration anxiety from the mother), Bowlby (attachment theory) and learning theory (classical conditioning of phobias).

Links: Freud's theory of socialisation, personality development and abnormality (its causes and treatment).
Links to case study of Thigpen and Cleckley in methodology.

Classical conditioning and phobias

PHOBIAS AS CONDITIONED EMOTIONAL RESPONSES

Behaviourist learning theorists such as Watson suggested that phobias were conditioned emotional responses. Certain stimuli, such as sudden loud noises, naturally cause fear reactions, and stimuli that become associated with them will acquire the same emotional response. In classical conditioning terms, if a rat does not originally produce fear, it can be made to do so by being associated with a loud noise, as follows.

First – test emotional response to rat	**RAT** (neutral stimulus)	⟶	**NO EMOTIONAL RESPONSE**
Second – test natural fear reaction to loud noise		**SUDDEN LOUD NOISE** (unconditional stimulus) ⟶	**FEAR** (unconditional response)
Third – associate rat and loud noise (more associations produce stronger learning)	**RAT** ＋	**SUDDEN LOUD NOISE** ⟹	**FEAR**
Fourth – test emotional response to rat *without* the loud noise	**RAT** (conditional stimulus)	⟶	**FEAR** (conditional response)

THE CASE OF LITTLE ALBERT – WATSON & RAYNER (1920)

Watson and Rayner aimed to provide experimental support for the conditioning of emotional responses such as phobias using a 'stolid and unemotional' young infant, Albert B, to test four questions:

1 ***Can a fear of an animal e.g. a white rat be conditioned by visually presenting it and simultaneously striking a steel bar to create fear?***
- At approx. 9 months Albert, who had been reared almost from birth in a hospital environment, was suddenly presented with stimuli such as a white rat, a rabbit, a dog, a monkey, masks (with and without hair), cotton wool and burning newspapers. Albert showed no fear reaction at any time – a typical response since he practically never cried and had never been seen to show either fear or rage before.
- Two stimuli were used to try and produce a fear response in Albert – the sudden removal of support (dropping and jerking the blanket he was lying on) and sharply striking a suspended steel bar with a hammer behind his head. The first stimuli was tried exhaustively but was not effective in producing a fear response, while the second stimuli caused Albert to start violently, catch his breath and raise his arms on the first blow, do the same but pucker and tremble his lips on the second blow, and burst into tears on the third blow.
- At 11 months and 3 days of age the bar was struck behind Albert's head as he began touching the white rat that had been suddenly presented to him. He jumped violently and fell forward, burying his face in the mattress. When he touched the rat with his other hand, the steel bar was struck a second time – having the same effect and causing him to whimper.
- At 11 months and 10 days of age, Albert was presented with the rat and appeared apprehensive about touching it. After five further joint presentations of the rat and the noise, the rat was again presented alone. The instant he saw it he began to cry, fell over, and then crawled away so fast that he was caught with difficulty before reaching the edge of the table.

2 ***Is there transfer (stimulus generalisation) of the conditioned emotional response to other objects?***
- At 11 months and 15 days of age, Albert was presented with a variety of stimuli. He reacted with most fear to the rat and rabbit, slightly less fear to the dog and a seal fur coat and showed avoidance towards cotton wool, Watson's hair and a Santa Claus mask. He played happily with his blocks (smiling and gurgling) and with the hair of other people however.
- At 11 months and 20 days the reactions to the rat and rabbit were not as violent so the bar was struck again with the rat, rabbit and dog to strengthen the response before Albert was moved to a different room. The fear did transfer to this new location, but with less intensity.

3 ***What is the effect of time upon conditioned emotional responses?***
Since Albert was due to leave the hospital, only a one-month delay could be left before further testing. At 1 year and 21 days of age Albert showed avoidance of the Santa Claus mask, fur coat, rat, rabbit and dog. He cried on contact with the coat, rabbit and dog, but not the rat (he just covered his eyes with both his hands).

4 ***Can conditioned emotional responses be removed?***
Albert was removed from the hospital on the day the above tests were made and so the authors stated 'the opportunity to build up an experimental technique by means of which we could remove the conditioned emotional responses was denied us'. They suggested they might have tried continually presenting the fearful stimuli to encourage fatigue of the fear response, associating the fearful stimuli with pleasant stimuli, e.g. stimulation of the erogenous zones or food, and encouraging imitation of non-fearful responses.

EVALUATION

Methodological The study has serious ethical problems. Watson and Rayner reported that they hesitated about proceeding with the experiment but comforted themselves that Albert would encounter such traumatic associations when he left the sheltered environment of the nursery anyway. This is not a very good ethical defence, especially since they believed such associations might persist indefinitely and did not leave sufficient time to remove them afterwards, despite knowing Albert was due to leave.

Theoretical The authors claim the study supports the conditioning of emotional responses and point out that their ideas contradict Freudian theories on the primacy of the emotion of love/sex and the origin of phobias. Nevertheless Albert did show a good deal of resistance to the conditioning process and did not show a fear reaction if he was allowed to suck his thumb.

Somatic/biomedical treatments 1

AIM OF THERAPIES

To cure the underlying physical causes of mental illness or to alleviate the symptoms of these causes.

Physically based treatments for mental disorder have a long and horrific history – ranging from bleeding, vomiting, and high speed rotation, to cold baths, and insulin coma therapy.

Biological treatments have been applied to a range of disorders and have the highest success rates with serious psychoses. However, they involve powerful techniques that can cause many side effects.

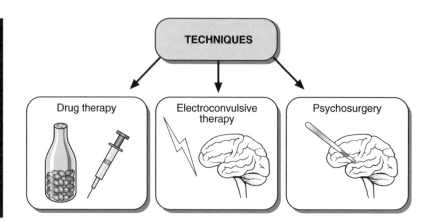

TECHNIQUES

Drug therapy

Electroconvulsive therapy

Psychosurgery

PSYCHOSURGERY

TECHNIQUE

Neolithic skulls with trepanned holes in were perhaps the first attempts at physically rectifying mental problems. When Moniz introduced psychosurgery in the form of prefrontal lobotomy in 1935, some might argue that the scientific justification and techniques were not much more advanced. Prefrontal lobotomy involved severing the connection between the frontal lobes of the brain and the deeper underlying structures (often by hammering a rod through the eye socket and rotating it around) in the hope of producing calm and rational behaviour. Today only very precise bundles of nerve fibres are destroyed, but it should still be noted that the effects are irreversible.

APPLICATION

Psychosurgery was originally performed on tens of thousands for a wide variety of mood, anxiety and personality disorders, but was especially employed for schizophrenia because of its dramatic symptoms and resistance to treatment (before drug therapy). Today it is usually used mainly as a last resort for severe depression or obsessive compulsive disorder, but virtually never for schizophrenia.

EFFECTIVENESS

Psychosurgery was initially hailed as a 'wonder cure' for psychoses, probably due to the need for a cheap, effective, and 'scientific' treatment to give the mental health profession respectability (Valenstein, 1986). However, long term follow up studies of prefrontal lobotomy patients found it to be ineffective at combating the precise symptoms of disorders. A National Commission review of psychosurgery in the USA in 1976, concluded that psychosurgery could be effective for certain disorders, such as severe depression.

APPROPRIATENESS

The indiscriminate use of psychosurgery between 1935 and 1955 led to it virtually becoming a method of social control. The development of drug therapy replaced it. Many undesirable psychological side effects were produced in most patients with prefrontal lobotomies, such as profound changes in personality, motivation, and cognitive abilities (Barahal, 1958). Patients also suffered seizures and a 1–4% likelihood of death.

ELECTROCONVULSIVE THERAPY

TECHNIQUE

ECT involves applying an electric shock of approximately 100 volts to one side of the brain (unilateral ECT) or both sides (bilateral ECT) to induce a seizure. When the patient recovers, they remember nothing of the treatment, but report a relief of symptoms.

The treatment is usually repeated at least six times over a period of around 3 or 4 weeks. Unilateral shocks are usually administered to the non-dominant hemisphere and muscle relaxants and anaesthetic are given to reduce physical damage.

APPLICATION

ECT was originally applied to schizophrenics under the mistaken assumption that they did not suffer epilepsy (which involves disruptive electrical activity in the brain). Today ECT is rarely applied to schizophrenics but is used to treat severe cases of depression, usually if drug treatment has failed and the risk of suicide is high.

EFFECTIVENESS

ECT is considered a very effective treatment for depression, producing symptom relief in 60-80% of cases. However, its mode of action is unknown. Possible explanations are that the shock

- destroys neurones in brain areas responsible for emotion
- affects the balance of neurotransmitters involved in emotion
- acts as a form of punishment for depressive behaviour or negative reinforcement for recovery behaviour (feeling better to avoid shocks)
- produces memory loss that allows thoughts to be restructured

APPROPRIATENESS

ECT replaced insulin coma therapy, being a more controllable and less risky procedure. However, ECT has been over-used and abused in the opinion of many and does cause side effects such as memory loss and around a 3 in 10,000 mortality risk.

Ethical problems arise with using a treatment whose mode of action is unknown and also with consent (should ECT be forcibly applied to depressed patients with a high risk of suicide?). ECT can save lives.

Somatic/biomedical treatments 2

DRUG THERAPY

Many drugs are used to treat a wide variety of disorders. Neuroleptic drugs are thought to have their effect by controlling the activity of brain neurotransmitters at the synapse.

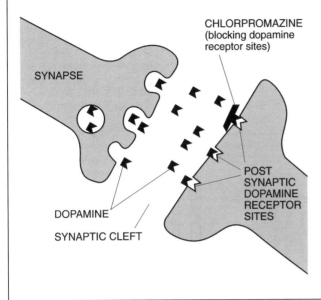

APPLICATIONS

Anti-psychotic drugs

Drugs such as the phenothiazine chlorpromazine are used to reduce the activity of the neurotransmitter dopamine by blocking its post synaptic receptor sites, while a more recent anti-psychotic drug, clozapine, blocks serotonin receptors.

Anti-depressant drugs

Each group of anti-depressant drugs work in a different way:

*   Tricyclic anti-depressants, such as imipramine, work by blocking the re-uptake of neurotransmitters like norepinephrine, making more of it available.
*   Monoamine oxidase (MAO) inhibitors, increase the amount of norepinephrine available by inhibiting the enzyme (monoamine oxidase) which breaks it down.
*   Selective serotonin reuptake inhibitors (SSRIs), such as Prozac, specifically increase the amount of serotonin available in the synaptic cleft.
*   Lithium carbonate effectively reduces both the effects of mania and depression in manic depressives.

Anti-anxiety drugs

Often termed minor tranquillisers, drugs like valium have been administered to reduce anxiety disorders and panic attacks.

EFFECTIVENESS OF DRUG TREATMENT

*   Anti-psychotic drugs have massively reduced the need for institutionalisation, enabling many schizophrenics to be cared for in the community. However, around 25% of schizophrenics do not improve on traditional neuroleptics and a further 30–40% do not show full remission of symptoms. More recent anti-psychotic drugs, such as Clozapine have been found to improve both positive and negative symptoms in around 50% of those who resisted previous drugs, perhaps because they affect the neurotransmitter serotonin.
*   The tricyclic anti-depressants have a delayed effect, providing relief in up to 75% of all cases after 2 to 3 weeks. Although not all patients respond to them, they are generally more effective than MAO inhibitors. SSRIs, like Prozac, have been shown to be of equal effectiveness to prior anti-depressants, are easier to administer, and have less unpleasant side-effects. Lithium carbonate has proven very successful at countering bipolar depression – up to 80% show full or partial recovery, and its use can decrease the risk of relapse.
*   Typically, anti-anxiety drugs, such as valium, have been shown to be beneficial for those suffering from generalised anxiety disorder, but not those suffering from panic attacks or obsessive compulsive disorder. Anti-depressant drugs are usually used in these latter cases, and some studies have shown them to be effective for obsessive compulsive disorder in up to 50% of cases.
*   The effectiveness of drugs is best tested by using longitudinal studies with placebo (fake pill) control groups and double blind assessment techniques (where neither the patient nor the doctor assessing improvement knows who is receiving the real drug).

APPROPRIATENESS OF DRUG TREATMENT

Side effects:

*   Phenothiazines can produce many unpleasant minor side-effects for schizophrenics, such as dryness of the mouth and throat, drowsiness, and weight gain or loss; and two major side-effects – symptoms similar to Parkinson's disease (body stiffness or body spasms), and tardive dyskinesia (involuntary movements of the tongue and mouth).
*   Clozapine does not appear to produce the above side-effects in schizophrenics, but does produce a lethal blood condition in about 1% of patients. Weekly white blood cell monitoring is required.
*   MAO inhibitors can be lethal if combined with certain foods such as cheese, and tricyclics can produce weight gain, drowsiness, and constipation. SSRIs appear relatively free of side-effects. Lithium carbonate requires close medical supervision.
*   Anti-anxiety drugs can produce physiological and psychological dependence or addiction in approximately 40% of cases after 6 months.

Not a complete cure:

*   Anti-schizophrenic drugs have been called pharmacological strait-jackets – they only alleviate or contain symptoms rather than providing a complete 'cure'. While they have enabled care in the community, hospital re-admission rates are very high – the relapse rate is around 70% in the first year after discharge if the patient discontinues medication (which is likely given the side effects). Anti-anxiety and depression drugs do not 'cure' either.
*   No drug has provided a specific, 100% cure for any mental disorder, and the neurochemical reasons for their effectiveness are still a subject of much debate.
*   The biological approach may neglect many important psychological or social factors that contribute to the development of the disorder or its treatment. Social skills training for schizophrenics and their families, for example, will help them readjust to living in society, while cognitive and behavioural therapy may be necessary to overcome anxiety disorders and depression completely.

Behaviour treatments – behaviour therapy (treatments using classical conditioning techniques)

SYSTEMATIC DESENSITISATION

TECHNIQUE

Aims to **extinguish** the fear response of a phobia, and **substitute** a relaxation response to the conditional stimulus **gradually**, step by step. This is done by

- forming a hierarchy of fear, a list of fearful situations, real or imagined, involving the CS that are ranked by the subject from least fearful to most fearful.
- giving training in deep muscle relaxation techniques.
- getting the subject to relax at each stage of the hierarchy, starting with the least fearful situation, and only progressing to the next stage when the subject feels sufficiently relaxed to do so.

APPLICATION

This therapy was developed mainly by Wolpe (1958). Mary Cover Jones applied systematic desensitisation to infants with phobias, such as the case of 'Little Peter'. Little Peter was a three-year-old child who had a strong phobia of rats and rabbits, and initially 'fell flat on his back in a paroxysm of fear when a white rat was dropped into his playpen', (Walker, 1984). Peter's treatment began by being presented with a rabbit in a cage at the same time as he ate his lunch, and ended 40 sessions later with him stroking the rabbit on his lap with one hand and eating his lunch with the other!

EFFECTIVENESS

This method of treatment has a very high success rate with specific phobias, e.g. of **particular** animals rather than a **general** fear of being in open spaces), and is thought to work because it seems impossible for two opposite emotions (like fear and relaxation) to exist together at the same time.

APPROPRIATENESS

This conclusion is questioned by studies that claim to have found that neither relaxation or hierarchies are actually **necessary**, and that the essential factor is just **exposure** to the feared object or situation.

Systematic desensitisation is considered more ethical and less directive because the patient has more control over the treatment - progression only occurs when they feel suitably relaxed.

IMPLOSION/FLOODING

TECHNIQUE

Both methods of forced reality testing aim to produce the **extinction** of a phobic's fear by the **continual** and **dramatic** presentation of the phobic object or situation.

In implosion therapy, the phobic individual is, therefore, asked to continually **imagine** the worst possible situation involving the worst possible situation is in flooding therapy the worst possible situation is actually **physically** and continuously presented.

APPLICATION

Wolpe (1960) forced a girl with a fear of cars into the back of a car and drove her around for 4 hours until her hysterical fear completely disappeared, while Marks et al (1981) used flooding on agoraphobics. Prolonged exposure and compulsive response prevention is used for obsessive compulsives.

EFFECTIVENESS

Marks et al (1981) found continued improvement for up to nine years after the treatment. The key to the therapy is that the dramatic presentation is continuous and **cannot be escaped from or avoided**. Therefore, the patient's anxiety is maintained at such a high level that eventually some process of stimulus 'exhaustion' takes place (you can not scream forever!) and the conditioned fear response extinguishes.

APPROPRIATENESS

These methods are considered to be

- the most successful at treating phobias, especially flooding, which Marks et al, 1971, found to be consistently more successful than systematic desensitisation, suggesting that **in vivo exposure** is crucial.
- quick and cheap but involve ethical problems of suffering and withdrawal from therapy (which could worsen the phobia).

AVERSION THERAPY

TECHNIQUE

Aims to **remove undesirable responses** to certain stimuli **by associating** them with other **aversive** stimuli, in the hope that the undesirable responses will be avoided in the future. In essence, this therapy actually tries to condition some kind of 'phobia' of the undesirable behaviour, although it is important to note that fear is not always the conditioned response.

APPLICATION

Aversion therapy has been used to treat alcoholism.

Alcohol   Emetic drug   →   Nausea
Alcohol   +   Emetic drug   →   Nausea
Alcohol   →   Nausea

More controversially, aversion therapy has been used to prevent a number of sexual behaviours, ranging from homosexuality to fetishism. Shocks have been paired with self damaging behaviours to stop them.

EFFECTIVENESS

Some studies have claimed limited success using aversion therapy to treat alcoholism – Meyer and Chesser (1970) found that about half their alcoholic patients abstained for at least one year following their treatment, although O'Leary and Wilson (1987) have reported mixed results. Marks et al (1970) claimed aversion therapy was effective on sexual behaviours for up to 2 years, although Marshall et al (1991) found no effectiveness.

APPROPRIATENESS

However, relapse rates are very high – the success of the therapy depends upon whether the patient can avoid the stimuli they have been conditioned against, to maintain the aversion. If the alcoholic continues to go to bars then the nausea response to alcohol may extinguish under repeated exposure.

There are ethical problems involved in deliberately conditioning aversions.

Behavioural treatments – behaviour modification (treatments using operant conditioning techniques)

BEHAVIOUR SHAPING

TECHNIQUE

This technique works by positively **reinforcing successive approximations to the desired behaviour** step by step.
Very complex behaviours can, therefore, be acquired from the more simple ones that make them up.

APPLICATION

Lovaas et al (1967) used behaviour shaping to improve the social interaction and speech of autistic children by

- associating food with verbal approval whenever the child made eye-contact with, or paid attention to, the therapist
- reinforcing any speech sound the child made with food and approval
- gradually withholding reinforcement until the child made the correct sounds, syllables, words then sentences.

EFFECTIVENESS

Lovaas et al (1976) reported long lasting gains in social and verbal behaviour that were maintained if the children were returned to a supportive home environment and parents who had also been trained in shaping techniques.

APPROPRIATENESS

Many serious psychoses, like schizophrenia, **cannot** fundamentally be 'cured' by learning treatments – when these treatments have been applied to them, they often show superficial short term effects unless continually reinforced.

SELECTIVE POSITIVE REINFORCEMENT

TECHNIQUE

This works by **reinforcing desirable behaviour** with a stimulus the individual finds rewarding, but **withholding** it if the desirable behaviour is not emitted.
The first task of the therapist is to find what is rewarding to the patient, so the therapist will look for a behaviour that the patient shows more frequently than others, presumably because they find it pleasant.

APPLICATION

Stunkard (1976) has successfully used selective positive reinforcement with anorexics to encourage them to eat normally. Once their rewarding behaviours have been identified, i.e. watching television or talking with other patients, then the therapist will **deprive** the patient of them until they first eat a required amount of food. If this is done, then the eating behaviour is positively reinforced with a certain amount of the rewarding behaviour (e.g. each mouthful of a whole meal might be rewarded with five minutes of television) making the eating behaviour more likely to occur again; if not, the reward is withheld.

EFFECTIVENESS

Selective positive reinforcement has been used very successfully for a long time on a number of different behaviours ranging from behaviour problems in educational situations to the eradication of self-mutilating behaviour.

APPROPRIATENESS

Reinforcement needs to be kept consistent and behaviour needs to be monitored closely for selective reinforcement to work efficiently.
Reinforcement for desirable behaviour appears to work better than aversion therapy for undesirable behaviour.

TOKEN ECONOMY PROGRAMMES

TECHNIQUE

Tokens act as **secondary reinforcers**, and many studies have shown that both animals and humans will emit behaviours for tokens that are exchangeable for primary reinforcers at a later time.

APPLICATION

Allyon and Azrin (1968) have used the principle of secondary reinforcement to reward the socially desirable behaviour of long term inmates in psychiatric institutions by giving **tokens** that can later be exchanged for certain primary reinforcers. Each time an appropriate behaviour is demonstrated by the inmate, such as making their bed or brushing their teeth, then a token will be issued - and the more desirable the behaviour, the greater the number of tokens (e.g. 6 tokens for washing up for ten minutes). These tokens can then be used to **buy** desired rewards (e.g. 3 tokens for a favourite TV show).

EFFECTIVENESS

Token economies have produced improvements in self care and pro-social behaviour, even in chronic, institutionalised schizophrenics. Paul and Lentz (1977) found token economies more effective than other hospital management methods.

APPROPRIATENESS

Token economies can make the individuals involved dependent on the tokens. Some patients may become quite mercenary, **only** producing desirable behaviour if they are going to get a token for it, and there may be serious problems in transferring improved behaviour and skills to the outside world. In addition, the beneficial effects of token economy schemes may be, in part, a result of the improved attitude of the staff towards the patients – if the staff are more optimistic about improvements in patients' behaviour, then they may start treating them more positively, and this may become more reinforcing than the tokens.

Key application – of psychodynamic concepts to mental health

FREUD AND THE CAUSES OF MENTAL HEALTH PROBLEMS

A number of Freudian psychoanalytic concepts have been applied to explain the origin of mental disorders:

- **Repression of traumatic events** – traumatic experiences, especially in childhood, may be repressed and become a later source of unconscious anxiety. Freud concluded that neurotics suffer from reminiscences (memories).
  Evidence – research on traumatic events leading to dissociative states like fugue (where people forget their previous life and start a new one) or multiple personality disorder (where a person may have different personalities that are unaware of each other's existence due to amnesic barriers) supports the possibility of repression and its effects.
- **Sublimation into somatic symptoms** – underlying anxiety may be symbolically expressed in physical symptoms as in hysteria. Hysteria, as it was understood in Freud's time was a medical term applied to patients who seemed to be suffering symptoms of disorder to the nervous system (e.g. pain or temporary paralysis or blindness), for which no *physical* neurological cause could be found.
  Evidence – Freud presents numerous case study examples of his patients' hysterical disorders as evidence, e.g. Anna O.
- **Regression** – the disorganised and delusional thinking of schizophrenia may result from a regression to a self absorbed state of 'narcissism' in the early oral stage where the irrational id dominates and there is no well developed ego to make contact with reality. Depression may also result from regression to an early state of dependency due to a loss in later life triggering the emotional effects of a more serious childhood loss.
  Evidence – many studies have supported the idea that early parental loss and childhood trauma are correlated with later mental disorder, but are not able to tell whether repression and regression are the causes.
- **Displacement** – unconscious anxiety may be displaced onto external symbolic objects and situations, resulting in phobias.
  Evidence – Freud regarded the case of Little Hans as good supporting evidence for this.

FREUD AND THE TREATMENT OF MENTAL HEALTH PROBLEMS

Traditional psychoanalytic therapy involves first identifying the unconscious source of disorder (such as the blockage of id impulses or the repression of traumatic experiences) and then trying to relieve the blockage by making the unconscious causes conscious. This is not easy since the patient is not only unaware of what is causing their problems, but will show resistance to the therapist's attempts to interpret them as the ego tries to maintain its defences.

1 **Identifying the problem** – Freud used three methods for un-rooting the unconscious causes of disorder:
- **Free association** – thought associations expressed from the client to the analyst without inhibition could contain clues regarding the source of unconscious anxiety. Pauses in, or drying up of, associations meant unconscious resistance was being met.
- **Dream analysis** – which Freud regarded as the 'royal road' to the unconscious. By unravelling the disguised symbolism of the manifest content of the dream (what was remembered), the latent content (what the dream actually meant) could be revealed.
- **Behaviour interpretation** – Freud believed that both normal (e.g. slips of the tongue) and abnormal behaviour were due to unconscious causes which could be carefully deduced from what people said and did – "He that has eyes to see and ears to hear may convince himself that no mortal can keep a secret. If the lips are silent, he chatters with his finger-tips; betrayal oozes out of him at every pore" (Freud 1901).

2 **Producing improvement** - this is achieved by:
- **Catharsis** – Freud originally thought that discharging the emotion (psychic energy) associated with repressed impulses or traumatic memories brought about improvement, but what seemed more important was that the unconscious conflict was brought out into the open for discussion. This is where transference is important.
- **Transference** – the process whereby unconscious feelings of love and hate are projected onto the analyst. These feelings provide a basis for identifying, accepting and discussing the analyst's interpretation of the problem.
- **Insight** – Freud regarded this as the crucial therapeutic element since it increases ego control over revealed unconscious causes.

JUNG AND THE CAUSES OF MENTAL HEALTH PROBLEMS

Jung generally agreed with Freud's interpretations of hysterical neuroses, but thought his theory of schizophrenia too incomplete. A number of Jung's analytical psychological concepts have also been applied to explain the origin of mental disorders:

- **Individuation and growth** – If a person is not able to proceed in their growth then neurosis will develop. Unlike Freud, Jung believed neurosis was caused by *present rather than past problems*, which only trigger memories of similar troubles from childhood as a result. Neuroses were even sometimes a result of the spirit of the times.
- **Balance** – Mental and behavioural disorder, like dreams and personality traits, are the result of *imbalance* in the psyche. Jung believed excessive introversion might lead to complete withdrawal from reality and schizophrenia, while excessive extraversion may lead to hysteria.
- **Compensation** – Since symptoms are the result of compensation, they can often be regarded as serving a *positive function*, indicating deficiencies and ways in which a more healthy and balanced set of behaviour or attitudes could be achieved in the future. Jung believed that even schizophrenic delusions were attempts of the mind to create new explanations of, or ways of seeing, the world.
- **Archetypes and complexes** – Since the self is not one personality but many, Jung saw the fragmentation of schizophrenic and dissociative disorders such as multiple personality as differing only in extreme (quantitatively not qualitatively) from 'normality' (a term Jung disliked). Problems may result from the imposition of complexes and archetypes, e.g. infatuation with a member of the opposite sex usually involves the projection of the archetypical anima or animus upon them, leading to an exaggerated view of their perfection.

JUNG AND THE TREATMENT OF MENTAL HEALTH PROBLEMS

Jung's therapy was more of a face-to-face (Freud sat out of his client's view, Jung sat opposite them), co-operative and joint process between therapist and client, both seeking answers to the problems. Analysis was less frequent, partly to ensure patients did not lose touch with their everyday lives, and aimed to restore balance and meaning to the client's life. Balance could be restored by bridging the gap between the conscious and unconscious through creative and imaginative activities (such as painting and play) or imaginary dialogues with archetypal figures, and by engaging in activities *opposite* to a dominant attitude (introversion/extraversion) or function (thinking, feeling, intuiting etc.).

Contemporary issue – Should people undergo traditional psychoanalysis?

The debate over the effectiveness and appropriateness of psychodynamic therapies was first sparked off by criticisms of Freudian Psychoanalysis. Many attacks were made on Freud's underlying psychoanalytic theory and methodology, and this naturally led people to question whether a therapy based on such disputed foundations could be worthwhile. Since Freud developed his therapeutic techniques, many other psychodynamic therapists have developed their own variations of the therapy that often differ in important respects from traditional psychoanalysis, and all should not be tarred with the same brush. It is instructive, however, to look at some of the issues surrounding the debate over just how effective and appropriate Freud's therapy is, since the debate is more complicated than it appears.

WHAT ARE THE AIMS OF PSYCHOANALYSIS?

Aims – The notion of a cure, according to Freud, involves not merely eradicating symptoms but identifying the deeper, underlying unconscious mental causes of disorder and dealing with them as best as possible. However, since Freud regarded all humans as neurotic to some extent his notion of a cure was very modest, to "turn neurotic misery into common unhappiness" by providing the client with more self-control – "where id was, there shall ego be" (Freud, 1933). Freud discovered the unconscious causes of disorder by interpreting the symbolism of his clients' behaviour, dream reports and free associations. The process (cathartic and transference) of revealing the hidden causes of their behaviour and above all the insights Freud provided regarding them provided the relief of anxiety and ego control required to improve their condition.

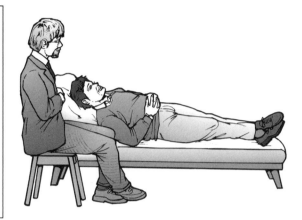

EFFECTIVENESS

Freud's own patients – It has been suggested (e.g. by Webster, 1995) that Breuer and Freud may have misdiagnosed their patients and that many who were supposedly cured through psychoanalysis, including Anna O, continued to show their symptoms after treatment by it. Some patients would have probably been classified as suffering from organic, physical disorders today, such as forms of epilepsy (Anna O), Tourette's Syndrome (Emmy von N, Freud's first hysterical patient treated by psychoanalysis) or even tumours (M-l, who died from a tumour of the stomach, had her stomach pains diagnosed as hysterical by Freud).

Criteria of success and the causes of psychoanalytic effectiveness

This is difficult to assess since psychoanalysis aims to change the unconscious processes that cause disturbed behaviour. However
1 unconscious progress may not always produce immediate observable changes (this affects the criteria and measurement of success)
2 unconscious changes can not be measured and may not be responsible for changes in behaviour.
Lacking an objective goal for therapeutic success, Freud's therapy essentially involved retrieving information about the patient until a cause could be found, but the only way the problem memories could be identified was when talking about them coincided with improvement in the patients symptoms. Freud stated "I accustomed myself to regarding as incomplete any story that brought about no therapeutic improvement". Since psychoanalysis took so long, the symptoms may have spontaneously recovered (disappeared on their own) and the 'story' being recalled at the time could just have been coincidental.

Effectiveness studies

Eysenck (1952) found that psychoanalytic therapy had lower success rates (44%) than alternative psychotherapies (64%) or spontaneous remission (72%). This finding has been hotly disputed, because of its very high spontaneous remission rate (some research suggests 30%) and criteria for success. When the criteria are changed, psychoanalytic success rates improve. A meta-analysis of general therapeutic success rates by Smith and Glass (1977) shows that psychoanalysis is more effective than no therapy at all for most people, but has slightly lower success rates than other therapies. Sloane et al (1975) found psychoanalysis was most effective for clients with less severe problems.

APPROPRIATENESS

Who can benefit? – Rather than asking 'should people undergo psychoanalysis?' a better question might be '*who* should undergo psychoanalysis?' Freud applied psychoanalysis to a range of disorders such as hysteria, phobias and obsessive compulsive disorder (e.g. the 'Rat Man'), yet it seems more appropriate for minor neuroses and anxiety disorders, with more intelligent and articulate clients. Freud himself argued psychotic disorders could not be treated because they lacked insight and the ability to form transference attachments to the therapist (although psychoanalysis with schizophrenics has been attempted in combination with drug therapy). In addition free-association may be inappropriate for obsessive-compulsive patients and transference may encourage further dependency in depressed patients.
What are the costs and benefits? – Psychoanalysis offers a therapy distinct from most other therapies and, using certain criteria, can produce progress and self-reports of improvement (although the latter, as with all therapies, may just reflect the patients' and therapists' justification of the time and effort they have committed). In terms of costs, the need for long-term analysis makes psychoanalysis very expensive and time consuming, although shorter versions have been developed, e.g. Malan's Brief Focal Therapy. Ethically speaking psychoanalytic therapy can be distressing for the patient (some say it can be counter-productive for schizophrenics because of its emotional stress) although it is not the only therapy with negative side effects. In terms of therapist-patient power and control the therapy involves complete trust in the interpretations of the analyst. Because of the concept of unconscious resistance, the therapist may directly or indirectly discourage the patient's right to withdraw from therapy since refusing or leaving therapy could indicate ego defence to progress in uncovering hidden truths.

Psychotherapy – cognitive therapies

AIMS OF THERAPIES
To cure or alleviate the underlying mental causes of disorder by restructuring the maladaptive thought processes that are causing it. Cognitive therapies aim to alter the way people think about themselves and their environment, to prevent illogical or irrational thoughts and to enable thought to control behaviour and emotion. Cognitive therapists concentrate on current thinking.

TECHNIQUES

There are a variety of cognitive behavioural therapies that differ in technique and directiveness. All, however, aim to alter thought processes (the cognitive part) and monitor the effectiveness of this on everyday behaviour or in role play situations (the behaviour part).

Beck's cognitive restructuring therapy

Beck's therapy (Beck et al, 1979) involves the identification and restructuring of faulty thinking as a collaborative process between the client and therapist. The therapist challenges the client's assumptions by gently pointing out errors in logic and contradictory evidence in their life and letting the client decide for themselves whether their thinking is accurate.

Ellis's rational emotive behaviour therapy

Ellis's therapy (Ellis, 1962) involves identifying generalised irrational and false beliefs (such as 'I must be successful at everything I do' or 'I must be liked by everyone') and forcibly persuading the client to change them, often through reality testing, to more rational beliefs.

Meichenbaum's self-instructional training

Meichenbaum (1975) assumes many problems are caused by negative, irrational and self-defeating inner dialogues – individuals may talk themselves into maladaptive behaviours with internal thoughts such as 'I can't do this' or 'something is going to go wrong'. The therapy identifies these maladaptive inner dialogues and gets the client to substitute them for better inner statements such as 'I can do this' by verbally repeating them until they become internalised, natural, and self guiding.

Kelly's personal construct therapy

Kelly's (1955) therapy is based upon his theory of personality. The client's personal constructs (ways of seeing the world) are identified through the use of the Repertory Grid technique and then altered or 'loosened' so they become more accurate or functional.

APPLICATION

Cognitive therapies have been applied to treat a variety of mental disorders including:

- **Depression** – Beck's therapy aims to correct the cognitive triad of negative thoughts about the self, the environment, and the future.
- **Anxiety disorders** – Beck's therapy and attribution training have been used to counter panic attacks and phobias.
- **Impulsive children** – Meichenbaum's self instructional training has been used to internalise dialogues of self-control.
- **Stress** - Meichenbaum has also applied his ideas to stress management in industry.
- **Schizophrenia** – Cognitive therapists, such as Beck, have even tried to help schizophrenics cope with, if not remove, their delusions and hallucinations.

EFFECTIVENESS

With depression, cognitive therapies have been shown to be just as effective as drug therapy – some studies have even reported higher success rates. Perhaps more importantly, lower relapse rates are gained if cognitive therapy is used in conjunction with medication.

Anxiety disorders also respond well to cognitive behavioural therapy although some research indicates that they are not superior to pure behavioural techniques, such as systematic desensitisation in some cases.

APPROPRIATENESS

Ellis's therapy is more forceful and directive than the others, but generally cognitive therapies aim to empower the patient with self-control strategies. Although cognitive behavioural therapies emphasise thought processes, they do tackle all aspects of a problem and are thus more complete in their approach. As Ellis's (1993) 'ABC' principle illustrates, many therapists assume that an activating event (A), such as being rejected for a job, directly causes an emotional consequence (C), low self-esteem. However, in reality it is often the intervening belief (B), such as 'I am suitable for all jobs', that is responsible for the emotional effect.

Psychotherapy - humanistic therapies

AIM OF THERAPIES

To help the client achieve positive self-regard, acceptance of the self, and self-actualisation in order to overcome any problems with living. This is achieved through focusing on the client's unique conscious experience of the world as well as his or her aims and goals, and by providing them with insight into their lives so that they can make positive freewill choices to improve their condition.

TECHNIQUES

There are a variety of humanistic therapies that differ in technique and directiveness. All, however, regard the client's conscious experiences and aims in life as important, and are insight based.

Rogers' client-centred therapy

Rogers' therapy aims to provide the client with positive self regard and set them on the path to self actualisation in a non-directive way. Through providing unconditional positive regard (warmth), empathetic understanding, and accurate insight into the client's life, the therapist encourages the client to exert their free-will to make choices that will bring them closer to the person that they want to be. Rogers' therapy focuses on current behaviour and events rather than delving into the past like psychoanalytic therapy.

Fritz Perls' gestalt therapy

Fritz Perl's therapy aims to enable the client to recognise and accept all aspects of themselves to become a whole (gestalt) person. The therapist may be quite directive in forcing the client to avoid phoney or non-genuine behaviours and statements, and may employ the empty chair technique (where role play conversations with various aspects of the self or important others can be imagined) to make decisions or solve interpersonal problems.

Other humanistically orientated therapies include:

- **Existential analysis** – developed by therapists such as Rollo May to help clients find meaning in their lives.
- **Encounter groups** – developed by therapists like Rogers, the participants provide group therapy for each other by discussing members' problems aided by a therapist who acts as a facilitator.
- **Transactional analysis** – pioneered by Eric Berne, clients identify and explore the child, adult, and parent aspects of their character in role play situations.

APPLICATION

- Counselling for stressful life events or interpersonal problems, e.g. marriage, divorce, bereavement, etc.
- Advice for improving quality of life – some people go into therapy with no major problems, but to enrich or seek meaning in their lives.
- Milieu therapy – a humanistic based therapeutic community that acts as a 'half-way house' for chronic institutionalised patients where they can develop a sense of self-worth and control over their lives by participating in the running of the community.

EFFECTIVENESS

Smith et al's (1980) meta-analysis showed that humanistic therapies were the most successful for promoting self-esteem, but were the least successful for treating anxiety disorders when compared to other approaches.

Many researchers including Rogers have argued that the basic element for the success of any therapy is the supportive therapeutic relationship between therapist and client (involving genuiness, empathy, etc.), regardless of what is done in the therapy. While it is true that receiving any therapy is better than receiving none, some research indicates that genuineness and empathy are neither necessary nor sufficient for recovery – the expectations of improvement on the part of the client seem more important.

APPROPRIATENESS

Humanistic therapies cannot directly tackle the causes of serious disorders such as psychoses – where insight based therapy is not very effective.

As a supportive therapy, however, humanist based counselling has much to offer and is now extensively used in a wide variety of problems – including family therapy for the relations of schizophrenic patients.

Difficulties assessing the appropriateness of intervention (should treatment be given, and if so which treatment?)

DIFFICULTIES ASSESSING EFFECTIVENESS

WHAT DO WE MEAN BY AN EFFECTIVE TREATMENT?

To consider how effective a treatment is, one must first define what its aim is. Some treatments aim to 'cure' the individual (e.g. flooding for phobias) while others seek only to alleviate or control the disorder (e.g. drugs for schizophrenia).

One major problem, however, is that different therapeutic approaches have different ideas about what constitutes a 'cure' – for behavioural therapists the removal of maladaptive responses may be sufficient, but for psychoanalysts an underlying unconscious solution must be found, regardless of current behaviour. Indeed, given Freud's quantitative views on abnormality, we may all be neurotic to some extent and so a cure may only involve 'reducing neurotic misery to common unhappiness'.

Relapse rates must also be considered when assessing effectiveness – how long should a cure last?

HOW DO WE KNOW WHEN WE HAVE CURED?

There are several difficulties involved in assessing when a treatment has been effective:

- Generalisability – an individual may appear cured in the controlled conditions of the clinician's place of work, but sometimes relapse will occur when the individual returns to the real world. For example, people exposed to token economy systems often do not generalise their improved behaviour, and alcoholics treated with aversion therapy often relapse when returned to public life.
- Monitoring effectiveness – who decides when a treatment has been effective - the therapist or the client? Both the therapist and the patient want to see success and may therefore make type one errors in assessment. The patient may show the 'hello-goodbye' effect, exaggerating their disorder at the beginning to ensure they are taken seriously, and exaggerating their recovery at the end of therapy out of gratitude. Psychometric tests used to monitor improvement may be unreliable.

HOW DO WE KNOW WHAT MADE THE INTERVENTION EFFECTIVE?

There are many factors, other than those the therapy intends, that could affect recovery, such as

- spontaneous remission – many disorders disappear themselves, without any treatment and, in some cases, without reappearing again. Estimates of spontaneous recovery vary according to the disorder but overall it is generally thought to occur in around a third of all cases.
- mere attention – it has been suggested that just the increased attention and support from another can lead to improvement (the Hawthorne effect). In addition the expectation of recovery can cause self-fulfilling prophecy.

For the above reasons control groups are needed to test therapy effectiveness, e.g. using placebos in drug testing.

ETHICAL ISSUES OF INTERVENTION

TREATMENT VS. NO TREATMENT

The first ethical decision that has to be made, concerns whether treatment should be administered, given that

- there is a chance that spontaneous remission will deal with around a third of all cases anyway.
- there are potentially many costs involved in intervention, such as money, time, and side-effects.
- some therapies, such as psychoanalysis, have been accused of being less successful than spontaneous remission.

POWER AND CONSENT

One of the most difficult ethical problems involves the issue of power in the therapist-patient relationship.

- Treatment may be enforced if the patient is sectioned under the Mental Health Act (1983).
- The choice of goals in some therapies is determined by the therapist or the norms of society, not the patient. This is especially relevant in psychoanalytic therapy where the patient has to accept the therapist's interpretation.
- The therapist may deem it necessary to discourage the patient from exercising their right to withdraw – for example when close to the unconscious 'truth' in psychoanalytic therapy, during flooding, or when forcibly restructuring thoughts and perceptions in rational emotive therapy.

SUFFERING VS. SUCCESS

Many therapies involve making decisions between success and suffering. Drugs and electroconvulsive therapies can cause many unpleasant side-effects or even death. However, their use could be potentially very beneficial – preventing greater suffering from the disorder or suicide (especially in cases of depression).

TESTING ON HUMANS

Many therapies have to be tested on humans rather than animals for validity. However,

- should patients be given new treatments whose mode of action is unknown? Even in the case of ECT, which has been used for many years, its reason for effectiveness is unknown.
- should patients be allocated to control groups with no treatment? Should not every patient have the right to the best treatment available?

CONFIDENTIALITY

Should the patient's disorder be made publicly known, given the stigmatising effects of labelling in our society?

Recent developments in social approaches to therapy

CARE IN THE COMMUNITY
WHAT IS IT?

Care in the community involves providing treatment and support for those suffering from mental disorder under **more socially integrated**, naturalistic and less controlling conditions, rather than in long-term institutions, wherever possible.

While those with very serious disorders or those who represent a danger to themselves and others (see 'sectioning' under the Mental Health Act, 1983) may require round the clock care, support and control, others may benefit from varying degrees of these factors. Care in the community can therefore take the form of:

- **Short-term inpatient care** in local hospitals or **residential treatment programs** – these involve high degrees of support, control and/or therapy, but for shorter periods than in long-stay institutions.
- **Half-way houses**, '**family group' homes**, **night-care** or **sheltered housing** – these involve higher degrees of support and less official therapeutic measures, but are still tied to less socially integrated residential arrangements. Individuals can indulge in productive and everyday activities during the day, e.g. employment, but still live with others with mental health difficulties and access to support is usually on hand from health care staff.
- **Home care** (ideally with respite care arrangements), **day-care**, **outpatient therapy** at local hospitals or **drop-in centres** – these involve socially integrated independent residence or home residence with relatives, with some access to therapy.

THE ORIGIN AND DEVELOPMENT OF COMMUNITY CARE

Community care in Britain and the USA developed as a response to:
- the many problems of long-term institutionalisation for the mentally ill (see Rosenhan's 'On Being Sane in Insane Places' study)
- a humanistic questioning of the motives behind institutionalisation (e.g. who does it benefit – society or the mentally disordered?)
- financial pressures to find a more efficient use of tax-payers' money (institutions are supposedly more expensive to run, but of course this depends on the quality of community care provided).

In the USA the Joint Commission on Mental Illness and Health began an examination of state hospitals in 1955 and advised in 1961 that no more large institutions be built for the mentally disordered since their function seemed largely custodial rather than therapeutic. In 1963 President Kennedy advanced the Community Mental Health Centres Act that began to implement the Commission's recommendations.

In Britain the trend towards community care and deinstitutionalisation began later, with the first serious changes beginning in 1980 when long-stay institutions for the mentally disordered were phased out. In 1990, The Community Care Act put into legislation the idea that local authorities should be responsible for community care provision and should encourage private and voluntary agencies to provide domestic, day-care and respite care (for relatives looking after those with mental health problems) services.

EVALUATION OF COMMUNITY CARE
Advantages

- The therapeutic rationale for community care is that more normal living conditions and social integration will encourage greater independence, self-care skills, social skills, self-esteem, and 'normal' and productive interactions, activities, relationships and behaviour, compared to care in institutions.
- The various methods of community care can more flexibly meet individual needs and abilities since mental health problems differ in severity between individuals and over time. Work, friend and family relationships can be more readily maintained.

Disadvantages

- Problems are encountered in assessing, monitoring and financing individuals' mental health needs.
- The difficulties of diagnosing and treating mental disorders as well as insufficient government funding and local authority provision means some individuals may not receive all the support, control or therapy they need without the necessary contact with health professionals.
- Practically, stigmatisation and prejudice against the mentally disordered may make social integration difficult. This is not helped by media publicity of the comparatively rare cases where released mentally disturbed individuals have attacked or murdered others.
- Home care may become unbearably stressful for both relatives and the mentally disordered.
- The above problems may lead to patients dropping out of care/not taking medication and becoming homeless.

THE GROWTH OF COUNSELLING
WHAT IS IT?

According to Nelson-Jones (1982), counselling can be viewed as:
- **A helping relationship** – provided by a counsellor who creates 'core conditions' for therapy through certain skills and attitudes.
- **A set of activities or methods** – based on therapeutic principles derived from psychological theories.
- **An area of special therapeutic focus** – catering for the needs of the less seriously disturbed.

'Counselling psychology is an applied area of psychology which has the objective of helping people to live more effective and fulfilled lives. Its clientele tend to be not very seriously disturbed people in non-medical settings. Its concerns are those of the whole person in all areas of human psychological functioning, such as feeling and thinking, personal, marital and sexual relations, and work and recreational activity' (Nelson-Jones 1982).

THE ORIGIN AND DEVELOPMENT OF COUNSELLING

Counselling developed from *psychological approaches* (humanistic, psychodynamic and behavioural learning) that were strongly concerned with how the individual is influenced by, and adjusted to, their *social environment* (e.g. family, friends, partner and work relations). Counselling became more distinguished from clinical psychology and psychiatry in the USA and Britain with the establishment in 1947 of the American Psychological Association's 'Division of Counselling and Guidance' and the creation of the British Association of Counselling in 1977. It has become ever more prevalent and has been applied to marital, family, accident, bereavement and educational problems.

EVALUATION OF COUNSELLING
Advantages

Compared with clinical psychology, counselling psychology:
- Focuses more on *social contexts* and relationships rather than problems within individuals. Thus counselling may involve relatives and partners not just the individual with problems.
- Emphasises well-being and fulfilment rather than sickness and maladjustment – looking for what is right and how to use it, rather than what is wrong and how to treat it (Super, 1977).
- Is more proactive – it can be applied to prevent or limit the development of problems, e.g. trauma counselling, rather than just responding to already developed problems.

Limitations

- Not always suitable on its own for more severe mental disturbance.

Key application – of memory research to eyewitness testimony

THE NATURE OF THE WITNESS AFFECTING EYEWITNESS TESTIMONY

RECONSTRUCTIVE MEMORY e.g. Bartlett's work on how schemas, expectations and stereotypes change memory has been applied to explain the effects of:

- **Prejudice** – Allport and Postman (1947) found that prejudice influenced the recall of whether a black or white person was holding a cut throat razor in a picture.
- **Inferences** – Harris (1978) found that over 60% of subjects would infer information not present in testimony based on their expectations, even when trained not to. For example if given the testimony 'I ran up to the burglar alarm in the hall' many would later assert that the burglar alarm had been rung.
- **Expectations** – List (1986) found subjects who had watched videos of shop-lifting incidents a week earlier recalled more of the actions that had a high probability of occurring during shoplifting than a low probability. They even falsely remembered high probability actions they had not witnessed on the video.
- **Stereotypes and face recognition** – Bull (1982) revealed people were willing to identify strangers as criminals just by their appearance. Yarmey (1982, 1993) found people readily stereotype faces as 'good guys' and 'bad guys' and discovered that the elderly were more likely to misidentify innocents as criminals based on their stereotypes of what they thought a criminal looked like. Racial stereotypes may also influence eyewitness testimony since Shepherd et al (1974) found cross-racial face recognition is poor.

THE NATURE OF THE EVENT AFFECTING EYEWITNESS TESTIMONY

CUE-DEPENDENT MEMORY e.g. state- and context-dependent retrieval have been applied to explain the effects of:

- **Stress** – Clark et al (1987) suggest that recall of violent crime may be more difficult because it occurs in a less aroused state.
- **Face recognition and context** – Shapiro and Penrod (1986) suggest matching witnessed faces to mug shots, photo-fits or line-ups may be difficult because of the different contexts on witnessing and recall; mug-shots and photos-fits being 2-dimensional and without expressive movement may provide insufficient cues, while line-ups involve different locations and clothing. Crime re-enactments may help by recreating context.

MEMORY PROCESSING MODELS e.g. rehearsal and depth of processing have been applied to explain the effects of:

- **Timing** – Clifford and Richards (1977) found better recall of details for a person who had approached police officers for 30 rather than 15 seconds. Potential jurors rated crime duration, and thus time to get a good look at the suspect, the 4th most important influence on eyewitness accuracy out of 25 variables (Lindsay, 1994). Greater exposure may allow more processing.
- **Processing and face recognition** – Shapiro and Penrod (1986) found subjects asked to make judgements about a face rather than just look at it showed more accurate later recall. Research shows that more familiar and distinctive faces are remembered better after long delays, as processing models would predict.

HOW ACCURATE IS EYEWITNESS TESTIMONY?

Cognitive research has been applied to answer this question...

EYEWITNESS TESTIMONY

POST EVENT INFORMATION AFFECTING EYEWITNESS TESTIMONY

INTERFERENCE THEORY and *RECONSTRUCTIVE MEMORY THEORY* have been applied to the following:

- Loftus has shown how information received after a witnessed event (especially in the form of leading questions) can have a retroactive interference effect on the memory of that event. Information can be:

1 **Added to an account** – Loftus and Zanni (1975) showed subjects a film of a car accident, and got more subjects to incorrectly recall seeing a broken headlight by asking "did you see *the* broken headlight?" than asking "did you see *a* broken headlight?". Loftus (1975) even got subjects to recall seeing a non-existent barn in a picture by using a similar technique of adding post-event information.

2 **Distorted** – Loftus and Palmer (1974) received higher estimates of speed when asking "how fast were the cars going when they *smashed* into each other?" than when the verb '*hit*' was used.

3 **Substituted** – Loftus et al (1978) changed the recognition of a 'stop' sign to a 'yield' sign with misleading questions.

However there are many debatable issues involved in this area:

1 **Artificiality** – Yuille and Cutshall (1986) found the eyewitness testimony of a **real life** and quite traumatic event was very accurate and resistant to leading questions. This was only a single case study however.

2 **Demand characteristics** – McCloskey and Zaragoza (1985) suggest that subjects may just be following the expectations to recall the (misleading) information that was last given to them. However warnings that incorrect post event information has been given does not appear to stop incorrect information being recalled (Lindsay, 1990).

3 **Degree of interference possible** – Loftus (1979) has shown that *obviously* incorrect post event information has little or no effect on accurate recall. Interference is most likely to occur with minor details and if post event information is given after a long time delay.

4 **Nature of interference** – Loftus (1979) is convinced that post event information replaces the original information – which cannot be recalled even if money is offered for accurate information. McCloskey and Zaragoza (1985) disagree – they showed that if subjects are given misleading information and are later offered a choice of the original or a neutral alternative, they tend to choose the original, indicating that the original material is not 'overwritten' or permanently distorted.

- **Interference and face recognition** – Davis and Jenkins (1985) found the accuracy of face recognition is significantly reduced if subjects are shown composite photo-fit pictures of other faces beforehand. Gorenstein and Ellsworth (1980) found witnesses are more likely to identify (correctly or otherwise) a person from a line-up if they had appeared in mug shots the witness had searched beforehand.

'Reconstruction of automobile destruction' Loftus and Palmer (1974)

BACKGROUND

There is much support for the idea that most people, when they are witnesses to a complex event, such as a traffic accident, are very inaccurate when reporting numerical details like time, distance, and especially speed, even when they know that they will be questioned on them (e.g. Marshall, 1969). As a consequence, there can sometimes be large variations in estimates between witnesses and so it seems likely that such inaccurate testimony could easily be influenced by variables such as the phrasing of questions or 'leading' questions.

AIM

Loftus and Palmer, therefore, aimed to investigate the effect of leading questions on the accuracy of speed estimates in, and perceived consequences of, a car crash.

EXPERIMENT ONE

Subjects: 45 students, tested in groups of different sizes.

Design: Laboratory experiment.

Procedure:

7 films of traffic accidents, ranging in duration from 5 to 30 seconds, were presented in a random order to each group.

After each film, the subjects had to give a general account of what they had just seen and then answer more specific questions about the accident. The critical question, 'About how fast were the cars going when they hit each other?' acted as the independent variable, since it was manipulated in five conditions. Nine subjects heard the sentence with the verb 'hit' in it, and then an equal number of the remaining subjects were asked the same question but with the verb 'smashed', 'collided', 'bumped' or 'contacted' instead of 'hit'. The estimated speed was the dependent variable.

Results

Speed estimates for the verbs of experiment one		Significance of result	Accuracy of subjects' speed estimates		
Verb	Mean speed estimate	Results were significant at the P < .005 level, according to analysis of variance of the data.	In 4 of the 7 films the speed of the cars was known.		
				Actual speed of collision	Mean speed estimate
Smashed	40.8		Film 1	20 mph	37.7 mph
Collided	39.3		Film 2	30 mph	36.2 mph
Bumped	38.1		Film 3	40 mph	39.7 mph
Hit	34.0		Film 4	40 mph	36.1 mph
Contacted	31.8				

Discussion

The results indicate that not only are people poor judges of speed, but they are systematically and significantly affected by the wording of a question. However, this finding could be attributed to either response-bias (the subject remembers accurately but is pressured by the word to increase or decrease the estimate) or a genuine change in the subject's memory of the event (the word makes the subject recall the event as worse than it was). If the latter explanation is true, then the subject might be led into recalling details that did not occur. The second experiment was designed to determine which explanation of different speed estimates was correct.

EXPERIMENT TWO

Subjects: 150 students, tested in groups of different sizes.

Design: Laboratory experiment.

Procedure:

A film lasting just less than a minute was presented to each group which featured four seconds of a multiple traffic accident. After the film, the subjects had to give a general account of what they had just seen and then answer more specific questions about the accident. The critical question concerning the speed of the cars was the independent variable, and it was manipulated by asking 50 subjects 'About how fast were the cars going when they hit each other?', another 50 'About how fast were the cars going when they smashed into each other?' and another 50 acted as a control group who were not asked the question at all. One week later the dependent variable was measured - without seeing the film again they answered ten questions, one of which was a critical one randomly positioned in amongst the ten questions, asking 'Did you see any broken glass? Yes or no?'. Although there was no broken glass it was expected that some might be falsely remembered if the leading question of a week ago had changed the memory of the event to seem worse than it was.

Results

Verb	Mean estimate	Response	Smashed	Hit	Control	Probability of seeing broken glass with speed estimate			
						Verb	1–5 mph	6–10 mph	11–15 mph	16–20 mph
Smashed	10.46 mph	Saw broken glass	16	7	6	Smashed	.09	.27	.41	.62
Hit	8.00 mph	Did not see glass	34	43	44	Hit	.06	.09	.25	.50

Discussion

The authors conclude that the results show that the verb 'smashed' not only increases the estimates of speed, but also the likelihood of seeing broken glass that was not present. This indicates that information from the original memory is merged with information after the fact, producing one distorted memory. This shift in memory representations in line with verbal cues has received support from other research.

EVALUATION

Methodological: A well operationalised and controlled experiment, but lacked the ecological validity of having real life events and involved witnesses.

Theoretical: The research supports the idea that memory is easily distorted and has implications for eyewitness testimony in court.

Links: Interference and forgetting in memory, practical applications of memory, laboratory experimentation.

Contemporary issue – does hypnosis recover accurate memories?

WHAT IS HYPNOSIS?

The word 'hypnotism' is derived from the Greek for sleep – 'hypnos', however there are distinct differences between the two phenomena. Hypnosis is characterised by:

1 **Relaxation and suspension of planning** – hypnotised subjects sit quietly and do not seem to plan or initiate activity. Control is given over to the hypnotist.
2 **Suggestibility** – hypnotised subjects will respond to suggestions and obey instructions with little sign of inhibition, even if the request is unusual or seemingly impossible to do.
3 **Atypical behaviour** – hypnotised subjects can apparently perform behaviours that they would not normally be willing or able to do, such as controlling severe pain, experiencing hallucinations and, of course, retrieving forgotten memories.

Depth of hypnosis can be measured, e.g. by the Stanford Hypnotic Susceptibility Scale – a list of 12 hypnotic suggestions that are increasingly difficult to follow. About 15% of people are highly hypnotisable, 15% are very resistant to it, and the rest are somewhere in between.

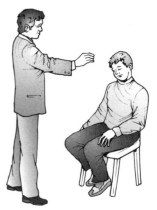

Cognitive psychological research on repression, interference, reconstructive memory and cue dependent memory can be used to help understand the accuracy of memories retrieved through hypnosis in two main situations - during therapy and police investigation. The former tends to focus on the victim's memory, while the latter has been applied to both victim and eyewitness recall.

CLINICAL HYPNOSIS AND MEMORY

Much debate has been generated over the accuracy of memories of childhood abuse, satanic abuse and even alien abduction retrieved using hypnosis during therapy that had not been remembered up until that point. It is often assumed that such ***recovered memories*** are due to the ***repression*** of these traumatic events and that ***hypnotic regression*** was required to retrieve them. Victims frequently find that the recovered memories help them make sense of disturbances in their behaviour, beliefs or emotions.

Evaluation of hypnosis for recovering repressed memory

For – there may be many genuine cases, since:
- child abuse is disturbingly common and amnesia for such traumatic events does occur – Herman and Schatzow (1987) found 28% of female incest victims reported severe childhood memory losses, especially the more violent the abuse.
- hypnotic age regression is an established technique (it is item 7 on the Stanford Hypnotic Susceptibility Scale) and may work through reducing recall inhibitions, overcoming memory blocks through accessing a different level of consciousness or even aiding context recreation of the time (***cue-dependent memory***).

Against – given the sensitivity and implications of such claims, many researchers think hypnotically recovered memories should not be relied upon without objective corroborative evidence, since:
- The concept of psychoanalytic repression and the extent of the unavailability it claims to produce has been criticised.
- Hypnosis may lead to ***false memory syndrome***. Therapists may give ***leading suggestions*** before or during hypnosis which may distort original memories by acting as ***retroactive interference*** or encourage confabulation of fictitious memories by aiding ***imaginative reconstruction***. Support for this is that:

1 Hypnosis increases the ability to imagine and even hallucinate.
2 Very hypnotisable people may be even more imaginative and/or have a 'fantasy-prone personality' (Wilson and Barber, 1983)
3 Hypnosis can produce experiences of future or even past lives.
4 Certain therapists tend to retrieve certain types of recovered memory – some frequently find abuse, others alien abduction (a more recent culture-bound and less credible phenomena).
5 Clients want to find causes for their problems and, being unaware of them, may readily believe they forgot others were to blame.
6 Independent corroboration has refuted many recovered memories.

POLICE HYPNOSIS AND MEMORY

In contrast to the clinical use of hypnosis to recover memories the client did not know they had, forensic or investigative hypnosis is usually employed in criminal investigations to try and access consciously forgotten information that victims or witnesses think they do, or might, possess.

The information gained can be used as forensic evidence or for investigative purposes to create leads that can be corroborated. Far more objection is raised to the former use than the latter.

Evaluation of hypnosis for victim and witness testimony

For - Police officials hope that the relaxed and focused state of hypnosis, as well as the more specific hypnotic techniques such as context recreation (based on ***cue-dependent memory*** theory) and the 'freeze-framing' of mental scenes to focus on detail, will greatly increase the amount and accuracy of previously inaccessible material recalled (a property termed hypermnesia).

- Geiselman and Machlowitz (1987) reviewed 38 experimental studies on hypnosis; 21 found significantly more correct information recalled, 4 significantly less and 13 no difference. However 8 experiments found an increase in errors while 10 showed no effect on error rate. Hypnosis was most effective in the studies using interactive interviews (not fixed questions), on more realistic material, after longer time delays.

Against – Gudjonsson (1992) suggests the highly suggestible, compliant and imaginative state of hypnosis may lead witnesses to greater ***confabulation*** and vulnerability to ***leading questions***, as well as overconfidence in the accuracy of their recall.

- Putnam (1979) revealed that hypnotised subjects made more errors and were more likely to follow misleading information when answering questions on a videotape of an accident.
- Sanders and Simmons (1983) discovered hypnotised subjects who had witnessed a pick-pocket on video were less accurate in their interview answers (although just as confident) and identity parade identification (which they were more likely to be misled on) compared to non-hypnotised subjects.
- Geiselman et al (1985) found American law enforcers using the Cognitive Interview technique (which involves context recreation and different recall perspectives) produced greater correct recall of a violent crime video (41.2 items) than a standard interview conducted under hypnosis (38 items).

Attribution bias and eyewitness testimony

WHAT IS ATTRIBUTION?

- Social psychologists who have investigated social cognition (how we understand social situations) have pointed out that people do not just passively observe their own and other people's actions, but try to work out or explain what caused them. Attribution refers to the decisions we make over what was responsible for witnessed behaviour – the personality of the individuals performing the actions (an internal / dispositional attribution) or the social situation / circumstances they were experiencing (an external / situational attribution).
- Social psychologists have revealed that these decisions are not always made in a logical and objective manner but are influenced by psychological biases (such as those discussed below). Attribution research therefore has much to say on how we allocate responsibility and blame for criminal behaviour, and how such attributions may bias our recall of witnessed events. As Pennington (1986) notes, the difference between murder and manslaughter depends upon the relative attribution of internal versus external causes.

FUNDAMENTAL ATTRIBUTION ERROR

- The FAE (fundamental attribution error, Ross, 1977) is the general **tendency** people have **to make internal, dispositional attributions** for others' behaviour rather than external, situational ones, when there may be equally convincing evidence for both types of cause.
- Due to the FAE witnesses may attribute a criminal's behaviour to a defective personality rather than social circumstances like unemployment and poverty, and thus be more predisposed to think of them as more blameworthy and deserving of greater punishment.
- For example, witnesses to car crashes may be more likely to attribute the cause to reckless driving than road conditions. This may bias recall towards incrimination. Barjonet (1980) reported that people tended to over-attribute road accidents to the driver rather than to the vehicle or the road conditions (Hogg and Vaughan, 1995).
- Pettigrew (1979) extended the fundamental attribution error to *inter-group* attributions with his ultimate attribution error – the prejudiced tendency to attribute negative out-group behaviour to internal factors, but positive out-group behaviour to external factors in order to preserve negative out-group stereotypes.
- Duncan (1976) found white participants who had watched a video of an argument tended to make negative internal attributions (e.g. a violent nature) when a black man pushed a white one, but were 5 times less likely to do so if a white man pushed a black one (interpreting the behaviour as 'playful').

FACTORS THAT INCREASE THE FAE

- **The amount of damage caused** – the greater the damage, the more likely an individual is to be blamed. Walster (1966) found that participants who heard a story about a parked car rolling down a hill were likely to attribute blame to the owner in proportion to the damage done.
- **Hedonic relevance** – refers to the **personal importance** witnessed actions and events have for the observer. If an event has high hedonic relevance for an individual, e.g. if a crime was committed against the witnesses themselves, their property or people they care about, they are **even more likely** to **make internal, dispositional attributions** for others' behaviour.
- **Locus of control** – those who themselves perceive they have control over their actions are more likely to think others do too. Phares and Wilson (1972) found that people with an internal locus of control regarded a driver of a car as more responsible for an accident than those with an external locus of control.

ACTOR-OBSERVER EFFECT

- The actor-observer effect (Jones and Nisbett, 1972) refers to the tendency of people to **attribute internal / dispositional** causes when **observing** others' behaviour (as in the fundamental attribution error), but **attribute external / situational** causes to their **own** behaviour when they are the actors.
- Thus criminals are more likely to attribute the causes of their behaviour to external factors (e.g. blaming society or their victims) while the victims or the police tend to attribute internal causes (personality defects). For example, rapists are likely to attribute blame externally by perceiving their victims as sexually provoking.
- Saulnier and Perlman (1981) found that offenders blamed the environment for their crimes, while prison staff made internal attributions (Brewer, 2000).

SELF-SERVING BIAS EFFECT

- The self-serving bias effect (Miller and Ross, 1975) refers to the tendency of **actors** to **attribute successful behaviour to dispositional causes**, but **unsuccessful behaviour to situational ones**, thus qualifying the actor-observer effect.
- On an inter-group level this may explain in-group favouritism and prejudice in recall – the self-serving bias results in positive or socially desirable behaviour being attributed internally to characteristics of one's own group, and negative behaviour to be attributed to external factors. This may lead people to think that those like them are less likely to commit criminal acts or have a good excuse for doing so (see Duncan, 1976 above).

Offender profiling

THE AIMS OF OFFENDER PROFILING

Offender profiling aims to aid the identification, apprehension and conviction of an unknown criminal by providing:
- Descriptions of the likely social (e.g. employment, marriage), physical (e.g. age, race) and mental (e.g. IQ, education, motivational) characteristics of the offender.
- Predictions about when, where and against whom they are likely to commit their next offences.
- Possible interview strategies to elicit confession of guilt or information relevant to their crimes (e.g. motivation or missing evidence).

DIFFERENCES IN TECHNIQUE

Boon and Davies (1992) drew a basic distinction between the original American and British approaches to offender profiling in terms of the way their profiles seem to be created and applied.

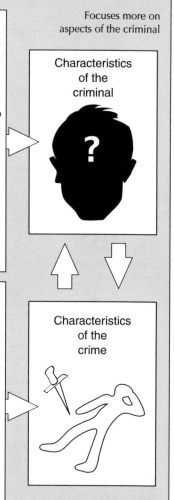

Focuses more on aspects of the criminal

Characteristics of the criminal

Characteristics of the crime

Focuses more on analysis of data provided by the crime

THE US 'TOP-DOWN' APPROACH TO PROFILING

Pioneered by members of the FBI such as Ressler, Burgess and Douglas. The approach seems to rely more on:
- The **creation** of general typologies of criminal behaviour and motivation based on **interviews with captured criminals** and **impressions of past crime scenes**.
- The **intuitive analysis** of data based on **personal experience** in law enforcement.
- Matching a particular **type** of criminal to the features of a **particular crime**.

FBI investigators initially interviewed 36 serial murderers to fill out a 57-page document relating to factors such as what led to the offending, what early warning signs there were, what encouraged or inhibited their offences etc. (Douglas and Olshaker, 1995). From the insights they gained and a thorough analysis of the crime details they distinguished between typologies such as *organised* and *disorganised* offenders. Organised offenders are often of above average intelligence, in a skilled occupation and socially/sexually competent, and their crimes typically appear planned, controlled in execution and involve the removal of evidence. Disorganised offenders, however, are often of below average intelligence, in unskilled work and live alone, and tend to commit crimes spontaneously, with little control and leave evidence at the crime scene.

Gaining data from interviews with volunteering, manipulative offenders has been criticised, although the interviewers suggest their thorough briefing on the facts of the case helped detect deception.

THE BRITISH 'BOTTOM-UP' APPROACH

Pioneered by psychologists, particularly David Canter and Paul Britton, working with the police. This approach seems to focus more on:
- The data-driven, building up of more individualistic profiles through the identification of specific associations between particular **characteristics of the offence** and the **offender**.
- The use of **scientific statistical analysis** and the **application of psychological principles**.
- Finding what kind of criminal behaviours were associated together and therefore might be the work of the same type of criminal.

Canter's initial profiles were based on an individualistic analysis of particular serial crimes, but he began to statistically analyse larger numbers of solved crimes (using techniques like *smallest space analysis*, which reveals clusters of events that commonly occur together) in order to derive typologies. In each case the *behaviour* of the criminal (e.g. their choice of, and interactions with, victims, the location and timing of their offences, content analysis of speech, etc.) was used as a data source rather than interviews with the actual offenders. Canter also used environmental psychological concepts such as mental maps to understand offender behaviour, e.g. finding that most British serial rapists lived within their 'offence circle' of rape locations.

Canter's approach seeks to make the process of profiling scientifically explicit rather than intuitive.

POINTS OF COMPARISON IN TECHNIQUE

The above distinctions between the US and British approaches mostly appear to concern their different emphasis on scientific methodology resulting from their originators' different backgrounds and access to data, and hide many common assumptions, for example:
- Use of typologies – Canter and Heritage (1990) have built up their own typologies, e.g. those based on the statistical analysis of rape acts that seem to involve the victim as a person, object or vehicle for the rapist's needs.
- The offender consistency hypothesis – both approaches assume that criminal behaviour (especially extreme behaviour) will reflect characteristics that are typical of that person and will remain relatively consistent across offences.
- Evolution of criminal careers – both approaches propose that criminals may well adjust their modus operandi as a result of experience, increased forensic awareness, etc., but also suggest that there are fundamental motivations or needs ('signatures' in Douglas's terms, 'central narrative themes' in Canter's) that will remain more static.
- Similar strengths and weaknesses – both approaches have had high-profile, spectacular successes that have drawn attention away from profiling failures. Studies actually reveal similarly low rates of success for each approach; Holmes (1989) reported that only 17% of FBI profiles contributed to arrests, while Copson and Holloway (1997) found British detectives believed UK profiles helped to solve 16% of cases they were used in (Harrower, 1998). Nevertheless, such figures still represent a significant contribution to police work, providing inaccurate profiles do not outweigh it by misdirecting cases and wasting valuable time and money.
- Range of application – both approaches have been applied to a range of crimes, e.g. burglary, arson, blackmail, hostage-taking, etc.

Jury decision-making 1

INDIVIDUAL / MINORITY INFLUENCES ON JURY DECISION-MAKING

WHAT JUROR CHARACTERISTICS MAY INFLUENCE JURY DECISION-MAKING?

If certain juror characteristics such as age, sex, race, socio-economic status, occupation, education or personality can be linked to a willingness to convict defendants generally, or for certain crimes, then efforts to scientifically select jury members could affect the outcome of court cases. The characteristics of jurors are of interest to the defence and prosecution since lawyers and attorneys in Britain and the USA have the right of 'peremptory challenges' or 'voir dire' (to object to a limited number of potential jurors) and so may try to select jurors more sympathetic to their case.

SUPPORT FOR SELECTION OF JURORS

Some studies have found that:

- Jurors with previous jury experience are more likely to convict (see foreperson election).
- Younger jurors are less likely to convict.
- Female jurors are more likely to convict rapists and child abusers (although longer deliberation may modify this effect).
- Jurors with authoritarian personalities are more likely to convict (perhaps because of their support of convention, police authority and their tendency to be dogmatic in sticking to one possible view).
- The race of the juror may affect their willingness to convict defendants of different races (see characteristics of the defendant).
- Those who do not oppose the death penalty are more likely to convict such cases (disturbing, since those who do object are excluded from such trials).

EVIDENCE AGAINST SELECTION OF JURORS

Overall, the research seems to find a lack of empirical support for scientific juror selection, e.g.:

- Baldwin and McConville (1979) concluded that British research, and Hastie et al (1983) concluded that American research, indicates that no single social / demographic factor leads to significantly consistent effects on verdicts.
- Zeisel and Diamond (1978) found that jurors rejected by attorneys but still asked to attend the trial (forming a shadow jury) would have influenced the verdict in 3 out of 12 cases.
- Olczak et al (1991) found that lawyers were not accurate at predicting the verdicts of jurors and were no better than students at doing so.
- Acre (1995) suggests that studies on the effects of juror characteristics on verdicts have tended to neglect the type of case (some personality variables only respond to certain kinds of crime or victim) and factors such as the strength of the evidence or persuasiveness of the lawyers.

HOW MIGHT JUROR CHARACTERISTICS INFLUENCE VERDICTS?

JUROR'S CHARACTERISTICS INFLUENCING OWN VERDICT

Pennington and Hastie (1990) suggest that jurors make their decisions by creating hypothetical reconstructive stories that could explain the evidence and then match the story to a verdict.

However, people may differ in:

- The kinds of stories they tend to construct or believe based upon their personality, attitudes and experience.
- The complexity and number of alternative stories they are willing and able to consider.
- How early they form their stories and how selective they are in attending to evidence that supports or refutes them.

MINORITY INFLUENCE UPON OTHERS' VERDICTS

Moscovici (1976) suggests that one or a small minority of like-minded individuals may influence the majority vote by conversion over a longer period of deliberation, if they:

- Are consistent and committed in their opinions and arguments.
- Seem to be acting on principle rather than out of self-gain and incur some cost (e.g. in terms of group acceptance and more time spent arguing).
- Are not overly rigid and unreasonable in their opinions and arguments.

FOREPERSON INFLUENCES UPON OTHERS' VERDICTS

The foreperson of the jury regulates the discussion in the jury room, may be perceived as a leader and thus may be able to influence the verdict. This could be important since studies show that elected forepersons are generally men, those of higher socio-economic status, those who first start discussion and those who have had previous jury experience. However, Baldwin and McConville (1980) found no relationship between the social characteristics of forepersons and jury verdicts, and McCabe and Purves (1974) found forepeople did not seem to overly influence jury deliberation.

Jury decision-making 2

SOCIAL / MAJORITY INFLUENCES ON JURY DECISION-MAKING

WHAT EFFECTS MAY SOCIAL PRESSURE HAVE ON JURY DECISION-MAKING?

An important assumption behind trial by jury is that group decisions should be of better quality than individual decisions since a greater range of life experiences and group deliberation should enable more alternative interpretations of the evidence to be expressed, more errors in reasoning to be spotted and individual biases to be countered. However, based on studies of real juries (before this was made illegal) Kalven and Zeisel (1966) proposed the 'liberation hypothesis' – that jurors have usually decided on a verdict before they retire to deliberate and jury deliberation consists of merely trying to persuade others to the same opinion. Social group pressure may thus lead to illogical, biased and ill-considered verdicts from juries, for a number of reasons:

GROUP POLARISATION

A group tends to make more extreme decisions (either riskier or more cautious) through a process of social comparison and increasing conformity to the group's initial majority decision, e.g. many studies find juries make more lenient decisions than individuals.

- Kalven and Zeisel (1966) found that out of 215 juries with an initial majority vote, 97.2% then went on to reach the same final verdict.
- Tanford and Penrod (1986) found the side with the majority verdict at the first ballot in mock jury studies were 95% likely to achieve the same final verdict. (Hastie et al, 1983, found around 75%).
- Nemeth (1977) found that juries are more likely to agree with a majority not guilty verdict than a majority guilty verdict.
- Baldwin and McConville (1980) found the chances of acquittal virtually doubled if juries deliberated for more than 3 hours.

CONFORMITY

Group pressure to agree with majority verdicts may result in a lack of consideration for alternative, minority opinions. Social pressure may result from uncertainty over the verdict and the need to refer to others for guidance (informational social influence) or from the need to behave in socially approved of ways (normative social influence). The pressure may increase with:

- **The severity of the crime/sentence** – more severe penalties may actually discourage conviction.
- **The need for a majority rather than unanimous verdict** – juries only required to make majority decisions, e.g. 10:2, spend less time discussing the case and put more pressure on the minority to agree (Hastie et al, 1983).
- **The size of the jury** – in 6-person juries a minority of 1 against 5 could be less able to resist majority pressure than a proportional minority of 2 against 10 (see Asch's ally effect). However, Vollrath and Davis's (1980) review suggests jury size does not significantly affect verdicts.

GROUPTHINK

Illogical decisions may be made under pressure by cohesive and isolated groups dominated by a directive leader. Groups of individuals with similar opinions are more likely to show groupthink through confirmatory bias – not equally considering evidence against their joint beliefs. Smaller, 6-person juries may be even less representative of the population and produce homogenous (similar) jurors.

- Acre et al (1992) found that homogenous groups were more likely to change their initial opinions to agree with each other.

SOCIAL LOAFING

Individuals in the jury may be inclined to deliberate less than they would alone and let others think for them.

DO THESE EFFECTS OCCUR?

The accuracy of jury decision-making

Whether juries make different decisions because of group pressure could be discovered by comparing their verdicts with those of others.

- Kalven and Zeisel's (1966) classic questionnaire survey of 3576 trials revealed that judges agreed with their jury's verdict in 75% of cases and concluded from this that juries were competent decision-makers. However, this is still a high degree of disagreement that on further analysis by Stephenson (1992) revealed a great deal more disagreement over not guilty compared to guilty verdicts.
- A number of questionnaire studies in Britain (e.g. Zander, 1974) have found around 6 – 12% of verdicts were reported as 'perverse acquittals' by judges and solicitors.
- Studies of shadow juries (where a mock jury sits in on the trial and their deliberations can be recorded and analysed), e.g. by McCabe and Puves (1974), reveal that decisions are made similar to those from real juries.

Problems assessing the accuracy of jury decision-making

- Comparing the verdicts of juries with other sources implies that one source is more likely to be accurate and objective than the other. It is significant that the rate of 'perverse acquittals' varies according to who one asks, e.g. the prosecution and police, judges or the defence.
- Questionnaire studies have their problems (the Kalven and Zeisel one has been heavily criticised for its unrepresentativeness – it only sampled 3% of all trials and only 15.8% of judges responded) and experimental jury simulations and shadow juries can never replicate the realism, pressures and responsibilities with 100% accuracy.

The effects of defendant characteristics on the jury

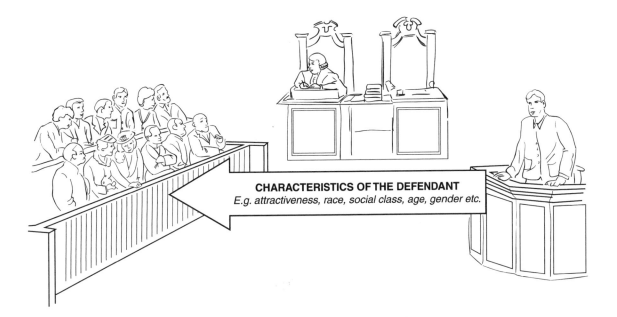

CHARACTERISTICS OF THE DEFENDANT
E.g. attractiveness, race, social class, age, gender etc.

PHYSICAL ATTRACTIVENESS

As Baron and Byrne (1997) note 'One of the more consistent findings is that attractive defendants are at an advantage compared to unattractive ones with respect to being acquitted, receiving a light sentence, and gaining the sympathy of the jurors.' They suggest that evidence indicates this effect is due to the 'beautiful-is-good stereotype' whereby attractive physical features seem to be associated with attractive or positive psychological characteristics. In a similar way stereotypes relating to criminals being physically unattractive may also have an effect on legal decision-making.

- Michelini and Snodgrass (1980) found that physically attractive defendants were more likely to be acquitted.
- Sigall and Ostrove (1975) found experimental participants shown an attractive photograph of a defendant charged with burglary recommended almost half the average sentence of those shown no photo or an unattractive one.
- Stewart (1980) conducted an observational study of American judges' decisions regarding 74 male defendants and found that attractive defendants tended to receive lighter sentences and were less likely to receive prison sentences than unattractive ones (Lippa, 1990). Downs and Lyons (1991) found a similar effect on the setting of bail or fines by 40 judges in 1500 court cases involving misdemeanours (Baron and Byrne, 1997).

Factors that influence the effect of the defendant's physical attractiveness include:

- **The seriousness of the crime** – the attractiveness effect is strongest with serious but nonfatal crimes such as burglary, but ceases to have an effect with extremely serious crimes.
- **The nature of the crime** – Sigall and Ostrove's (1975) experiment also found attractive defendants charged with fraud received higher average recommended sentences than unattractive defendants and those with no photo, perhaps because they used their looks to accomplish their crime.
- **The gender of the defendant** – physical attractiveness seems to have a stronger effect with female defendants, perhaps because women are judged as attractive on a more physical basis then men, especially by men (see the evolution of sex differences in mate choice).
- **The attractiveness of the victim** – Castellow et al (1990) found that in cases of sexual harassment the relative level of attractiveness between the defendant and victim was important. For example, an unattractive male defendant was more likely to be judged guilty of harassing an attractive female, than an attractive male defendant was of harassing an unattractive female (Baron and Byrne, 1997). Kerr's (1978) mock jury experiment found that an attractive victim of theft was more likely to provoke a guilty verdict for the defendant than an unattractive victim.

RACE / ETHNICITY

Race or ethnicity is another characteristic of defendants that could influence judge and jury decision-making due to stereotyping and prejudice. However the effect of defendant ethnicity upon verdicts is less consistent than that of physical attractiveness, and depends upon many factors, e.g.:

- **The race of the jurors** – variable effects have been found here and depend on the degree of prejudice.
  Baldwin and McConville's (1979) study of British real-life trials revealed that a black defendant was more likely to be perversely convicted than perversely acquitted, even by mostly black juries.
  Pfeifer and Ogloff (1991) found that white university students were more likely to rate black defendants as more guilty than white defendants. Skolnick and Shaw (1997) found little difference between black and white student mock jurors in their verdicts concerning black defendants, however compared to white jurors, the black jurors were significantly more likely to find a white defendant guilty, but half as likely to find them not guilty, than black defendants (Brewer, 2000)
- **The nature of the crime** – Gordon et al (1988) found that defendants charged with burglary were given longer sentences if they were black rather than white, but the reverse was true if the crime was embezzlement (Coolican, 1996).
- **The race of the victim** – Pfeifer and Ogloff (1991) found that white students were even more likely to rate black defendants as guilty if the victim was white. However, Henderson and Taylor (1985) report that, regardless of a defendant's race, those who kill a white victim are more likely to be sentenced to death than those who kill a black victim.

Evaluation

In some studies on defendant race and attractiveness, if an emphasis is put on proving the facts beyond a reasonable doubt the effects are reduced or disappear completely.

Social influences on crime

THE JUST WORLD HYPOTHESIS

What is the just world hypothesis?

The just world hypothesis (Lerner, 1966) refers to the belief that the world is essentially a fair and just place where people get what they deserve, i.e. good things happen to good people, while bad things happen to bad people. It is a learnt belief, probably originating from early childhood, and provides comfort by making the world seem safe, predictable and controllable.

What effect does it have?

The belief in a just world has important consequences for the **attribution of blame** and **attitudes** concerning the victims of crime. Severe and upsetting crimes that seriously challenge the belief that the world is a fair place create **cognitive dissonance** (a state of tension resulting from holding two contradictory beliefs) that people can only reduce by:

1 Changing their belief in a just world – however, people are often afraid of doing so.
2 Changing their social perception of the crime – to make the crime more predictable and understandable in the light of their just world belief by:
   • Attributing the cause of the crime, and thus the blame, to the victim.
   • Derogating the victim to make them seem more deserving of the crime.

Who does it affect?

- For offenders or outside observers considering the crime, blaming the victim in some way is a 'simple' internal attribution of causes to consistent personality factors which makes the crime seem less unpredictable and unfair. The victim could therefore be more likely to be perceived as provoking, careless or irresponsible, or they may even be dehumanised and have their character attacked to make them seem more deserving of their awful experience. Additionally, attention will often be directed towards finding confirming evidence of these assumptions. There are many examples of such behaviour, from suggesting that a rape victim was wearing provoking clothes or had a 'reputation', to the dehumanisation of the Jews by the Nazis in World War Two to 'justify' the Holocaust. In a legal context the just world hypothesis may affect the judgements of juries and judges.
- For the victims of the crime, especially traumatic and violent crimes, self-blame may occur as the victim 'can experience a strong and debilitating sense that the world is no longer stable, meaningful, controllable and just. One way to reinstate an illusion of control is by taking some responsibility for the event (Miller and Porter, 1983)' (Hogg and Vaughan, 1995).

Evidence for the just world hypothesis

- Lerner and Simmons (1966) found that experimental participants rated victims who continued to receive experimental electric shocks as less socially attractive than victims whom they could stop the shocks for. Seeing victims continue to suffer resulted in their derogation.
- Jones and Aronson (1973) found that participants asked their opinions on rape scenarios attributed more blame to the victims of the crimes they regarded as most deserving of punishment (in terms of length of sentence for the rapist).

SELF-FULFILLING PROPHECY AND ANTI-SOCIAL BEHAVIOUR

What is the self-fulfilling prophecy?

A self-fulfilling prophecy (Merton, 1948) is where an **observer's beliefs or expectations** about a person or group **influences their social interactions** with them and thus actually **elicits or creates the expected behaviour**.

How does it occur?

- The observer's beliefs or expectations – these involve the observer's **schemas** or **stereotypes** relating to the individual or group. They may be applied to others on an entirely **false** basis to begin with or be based on **misleading** first impressions, but are relatively persistent beliefs that lead to **confirmatory bias**.
- The observer's influencing social interaction – this refers to the **conveying of** the beliefs and **expectations** to the observed and the **effects of confirmatory bias**. Observers will selectively attend to (and thus notice more frequently), seek (i.e. through questioning) and react to (i.e. positively or negatively) behaviour from the observed that matches their expectations.
- The creation of expected behaviour – this occurs as the observer's social interactions **change** the **cognition** (i.e. sense of self-esteem, self-belief in abilities, attitudes towards the observer, etc.) and the **behaviour** (i.e. due to selective reinforcement/punishment of behaviour, conformity or other reactions, e.g. resentment, to expectations etc.) **of the observed**. These reactions of the observed act to **confirm** the expectations of the observers, creating the ever-increasing **feedback** that creates the self-fulfilling prophecy.

Evidence for the self-fulfilling prophecy

- The effects of the self-fulfilling prophecy have been experimentally demonstrated in the areas of education (see Rosenthal and Jacobson, 1968) and interpersonal attraction (Snyder et al, 1977), although not always replicated.
- Ecologically valid research on the creation of anti-social behaviour via self-fulfilling prophecy is difficult to conduct because of the many variables involved, ways in which the expectations can have their effect, and ethical problems.
- Jahoda (1954, cited in Gross, 1996) reported that the Ashanti tribe of West Africa believe that those born on a Wednesday are naturally aggressive while those born on a Monday are naturally calm, and are given names which reflect this. Police records there show a higher percentage of juvenile delinquents have Wednesday than Monday names.

The observers:
- Expect anti-social behaviour from certain individuals or groups, e.g. criminal behaviour from the children of criminal parents or higher levels of aggression in boys than girls.
- Convey expectations of anti-social behaviour and seek confirmation of examples of such behaviour, e.g. ignoring pro-social behaviour, but selectively reprimanding or tolerating criminal or aggressive behaviour compared to other individuals/groups.

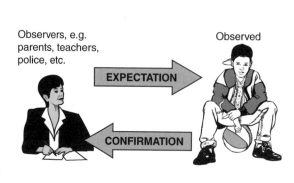

Observers, e.g. parents, teachers, police, etc.

EXPECTATION

Observed

CONFIRMATION

The observed will respond to expectations and selective social interaction by behaving in anti-social ways due to:
- The encouragement provided for such behaviour.
- Believing they are only capable of such behaviour and less capable of pro-social actions.
- Pressure to conform and live up to expectations.
- Feeling that other behaviour is not noticed so why bother showing it.

Treating crime

CONTROLLING AGGRESSION

There are many means of controlling aggression that can be derived from psychological research, for example psychodynamic or humanist researchers would suggest insight-based counselling, whereas social psychologists would propose social skills training. Two other approaches are:

BEHAVIOURAL MEANS OF CONTROLLING AGGRESSION

Many methods aim to alter aggressive **behaviour** through **learning theory** principles such as classical and operant conditioning and social learning theory, e.g.:

Punishment of aggression – applied in a variety of contexts and ways, from school punishments such as detention, expulsion, extra work etc., to societal punishments, such as victim reparation, prison sentences for criminal aggression and within-prison sanctions for violent behaviour.

Rewarding non-violent behaviour – through the use of token economy systems, praise, privileges, sometimes encouraged through the imitation of role models.

Evaluation

* There are a number of problems with the punishment of behaviour (see behavioural principles applied to problem behaviour in the classroom) such as the creation of hostility and revenge, the displacement of aggression and the modelling effect of punishing aggression with aggression.
* Rewarding non-aggressive behaviour is more desirable and effective, but difficult to employ in the justice system.
* Punishment and reward usually have to be administered promptly for maximum effect although this does not always happen in the criminal justice system for violent behaviour.
* Punishment for aggression in one context (i.e. in prison) may not always be generalised to other settings, thus token economy systems that are successful in prison may not prevent violent re-offending in the community.

COGNITIVE-BEHAVIOURAL MEANS OF CONTROLLING AGGRESSION

Other methods aim to alter the **thought processes** that underlie or trigger aggressive behaviour through **cognitive theoretical** principles such as attribution of intentions, e.g.:

Attribution training – involves helping violent offenders overcome their over-attribution of hostile intentions to others.

Cognitive preparation – involves training in recognising social stimuli, and responses to them, that trigger aggression and identifying negative trains of thought that lead to anger and aggressive behaviour.

Self-instructional training – involves acquiring aggression-reducing inner dialogues and strategies, e.g. saying 'stop' or 'calm down' to oneself, or counting to ten before acting. Cognitive techniques can then be tested in role-play situations to see whether thought and reason can control the behaviour.

Evaluation

* Many successful anger treatment programmes (e.g. Novaco, 1975) are cognitive-behavioural - addressing maladaptive thought processes as well as teaching non-aggressive or assertive behavioural techniques.
* Such multi-modal approaches that target specific responses such as aggression have been more successful in preventing violent re-offending. Lipsey (1992) conducted a meta-analysis of over 400 studies of juvenile delinquency treatment programmes and concluded that cognitive-behavioural methods were at least 20% more successful at preventing re-offending than approaches like counselling.

ZERO TOLERANCE

What is zero tolerance?

Zero tolerance refers to a policing strategy that involves a high profile crack down on all types of crimes, including the most 'minor' offences such as littering, graffiti and vandalism, rather than prioritising only the most serious crimes.

How effective is zero tolerance?

Zero tolerance certainly seems to be associated with reduced crime. For example, it was introduced in New York in 1992 and resulted in a 25% increase in arrests but a steady drop in serious crime over the following six years (e.g., homicides had decreased by around two-thirds by 1997).

Why is zero tolerance thought to be effective?

1 *Psychological factors* – the original idea behind zero tolerance (Wilson and Kelling, 1982) was that acting against and reducing minor crimes would help reduce major crimes. Allowing minor crimes encourages criminals to progress to more serious offences and encourages crime in others by establishing a climate of disorder that:
   * Models criminal behaviour (social learning theory)
   * Sets norms of crime (that may be conformed to)
   * Reduces inhibitions to commit criminal acts (through diffusion of responsibility and lack of punishment)
   * Desensitises people to everyday crime (making it more acceptable and likely to escalate to higher/more serious levels, but less likely to be reported)

   Thus zero tolerance may be an effective method of crime **prevention** by addressing the above psychological principles.

2 *Policing and apprehension factors* – zero tolerance also has the effect of reducing serious crime through non-psychological measures, e.g.:
   * Increasing the apprehension of serious criminals, e.g. through arresting them for minor offences and linking them to major offences through their fingerprints, or increasing police funding and effort in general, e.g. in terms of greater numbers of police officers (New York received an extra 7000).
   * Increasing the removal from society of criminals who commit serious offences through their incarceration for minor offences.

Criticisms of zero tolerance effectiveness

* The evidence for zero tolerance effectiveness is based on natural experimentation and correlational data – there are many other factors that could have decreased crime levels in cities where zero tolerance was introduced, for example natural demographic and criminal trends or other police or community crime initiatives.
* There may be negative consequences of zero tolerance, such as higher costs and poorer police-community relations.
* Other approaches to policing may be more cost effective and perceived as less 'oppressive', e.g. targeting police resources towards violent crime rather than minor offences, increasing crime detection through the use of surveillance cameras and neighbourhood watch schemes, or crime prevention through community education schemes, property marking, etc.

Behaviourist learning theory applied to education 1

BEHAVIOURAL PRINCIPLES AND THE DELIVERY OF EDUCATION

- The behaviourists focused on **observable**, **stimulus and response** interactions between the environment and the individual. They believed that **learning by association** from the **environment** was the most important influence upon behaviour, and developed the **theories** of **classical** and **operant conditioning** to explain how experience could change observable behaviour without the need to refer to the cognitive workings of the mind.
- Their contribution to education therefore involves guidelines on how to **alter environmental stimuli**, e.g. classroom conditions, presentation of information, performance consequences and teacher behaviour, to produce repeated behavioural responses that reflect educational requirements. For example, providing a pleasant classroom environment and atmosphere may create *positive conditioned emotional responses* (feelings or attitudes) towards the subject matter or learning in general through association via the process of classical conditioning. Clearly *emphasising* important aspects of information (stimuli) to be attended to, providing positive consequences (*reinforcement*) for correct responses and *pointing out associations* between old and new stimuli, will encourage the correct responses to be made, repeated and generalised to new situations.
- Skinner suggested that the application of behavioural principles could be optimised through *programmed learning*.

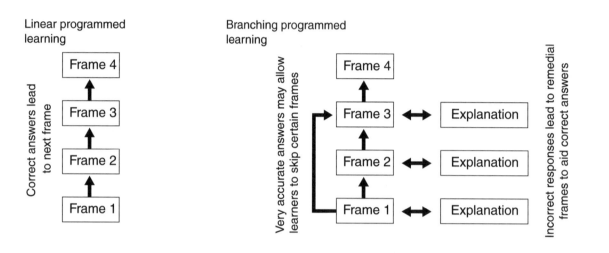

PROGRAMMED LEARNING

How does programmed learning work?

1 Information is broken down into manageable units (known as **frames**) which are presented in a logical order. In **linear** programmes very **small** amounts of information are presented. **Branching** programmes present **larger** frames.
2 Questions are asked in each frame. In **linear** programmes very **simple** questions with helpful prompts are asked (making it difficult to get the answer wrong) and the correct response leads to the next frame. **Branching** programmes present a **range of alternative answers** and learners have to select the correct one, which enables them to proceed more quickly or receive help depending upon the accuracy of their answers.
3 Each learner proceeds through the programme **individually** and is **immediately informed** of whether they have answered correctly. Knowledge of achieving the correct answer is presumed to be reinforcing.

Why is programmed learning needed?

- Many points of information are presented but it is often difficult to distinguish between them.
- The classroom contains many sources of distraction and reinforcement for behaviour that is not conducive to learning desired responses.
- The learner has to progress at the same speed as the rest of the class, which may be too fast or slow – leading to frustration.
- The learner in a class is often passive and has to compete with others for reinforcement – many may know the answer but only one is praised for getting it correct.
- Wrong answers may be punished leading to a fear of responding.

What are the strengths of programmed learning?

- Breaking the information down into manageable units clarifies which responses have to be learnt and does not overload the memory.
- The individualistic nature of programmed learning means it can occur without the distracting presence of others and provides each learner with their own task to focus on.
- Each learner can progress at their own pace through the material. Branching programmes provide extra support.
- The learner is actively involved in the learning process and is individually reinforced for their responses.
- In linear programmes the small amount of information and the ease of the questions presented ensures few mistakes are made and therefore most feedback is positive reinforcement.

What are the weaknesses of programmed learning?

- Not all topics can be broken down into small chunks or taught effectively in this way. The method may be more suitable for learning information rather than skills.
- The presence of others in a class may be a necessary part of education, e.g. for group discussion, task co-operation, social skills and motivation to learn.
- The speed of progress through the programme depends upon the motivation of the learner.
- Not all learners find mere progression through the programme (especially the really easy linear ones) sufficiently interesting or fulfilling.
- The programmes can not be sufficiently flexible to answer all the questions a learner may have, which may stifle curiosity and independence.

Behaviourist learning theory applied to education 2

BEHAVIOURAL PRINCIPLES AND THE REDUCTION OF PROBLEM BEHAVIOUR IN THE CLASSROOM

The behaviourist would first identify the problem behaviour, e.g. lack of attention, disruptive behaviour, insufficient work rate or quality, etc. and then alter environmental stimuli to change its frequency.

PUNISHMENT

According to behaviourist principles, **problem behaviour** can be **reduced in frequency** by associating it with **negative consequences**. These can take the form of:

Applying negative stimuli, e.g.:

- Verbal reprimands – these can be made publicly or privately, harshly or softly, and with or without giving the reasoning behind the reprimand.
- Non-verbal reprimands – such as expressions of facial disapproval, eye contact glaring, negative head-shaking.
- Unpleasant activities – like extra homework or line writing.
- Physical punishment – such as extra push-ups/running laps (in physical education lessons!) or smacking/caning (where legal).

Removing positive stimuli, e.g.:

- Exclusion – such as exclusion from classroom activities (time-outs) or break/home time (detention).
- Penalties – (or response cost punishments) are where a certain amount of already gained credits or privileges are removed per undesirable behaviour.

Evaluation

Strengths

- Punishment brings undesirable behaviour to the attention of both the offender and witnesses, who may then act to avoid future punishment (see negative reinforcement).
- Certain behaviours have to be seen to be unacceptable.
- Non-physical reprimands, made privately and with justification, can be very effective in managing problem behaviour, as can penalty systems, especially if provided by a warm and otherwise accepting authority figure.

Weaknesses

- Physical punishment is ethically objectionable and can be counter-productive (punishing violence with violence only serves to model aggressive behaviour).
- Punishment on its own does not inform those receiving it of what desirable behaviour they should be showing.
- Punishment only inhibits undesirable behaviour and creates further negative feelings and resentment towards authority.
- Exclusion from class may increase the extent to which the excluded individual gets behind and their sense of alienation from normal classroom behaviour.
- Punishment methods have variable effects – reprimands may reinforce undesirable behaviour in those who crave attention, 'psychopaths' may not learn from punishment.

REINFORCEMENT

Reinforcement attempts to reduce the problem behaviour by *encouraging* or gradually **shaping** the opposite, **desirable responses**. Reinforcement can take a number of forms:

Positive reinforcement, e.g.:

- Socially rewarding stimuli – such as attention and praise from the teacher (or classmates) for desirable behaviour.
- Educational feedback – like good grades and, in the longer term, examination success.
- Token systems – such as merit points, star charts, etc. These tokens can reflect social praise or be exchanged at a later time for other reinforcers (see below).
- The Premack principle – using behaviour / activities that are liked (frequently shown) to reward desirable, educational behaviour (that may be less frequent / liked!).

Selective positive reinforcement – the same as positive reinforcement above, but in combination with ignoring and withholding reinforcement from problem behaviour to encourage its extinction.

Negative reinforcement – involves maintaining good behaviour by allowing the negative consequences associated with problem behaviour to be avoided, e.g. warnings or threats of punishments for bad behaviour.

Evaluation

Strengths

The behaviourist, Skinner, argued that reinforcement was more effective than punishment in education, since:

- Rewards provide information on desirable behaviour, increase motivation to perform it rather than other behaviour and are associated with pleasant emotions.
- Reinforcement is a very flexible form of behaviour control – selective reinforcement can shape many different types of behaviour and reinforcement schedules mean rewards do not have to be given for every desirable behaviour.

Weaknesses

- Lepper and Greene (1975) found that providing too much extrinsic reinforcement (external rewards) for behaviour can undermine the intrinsic (internal) satisfaction for it, which can reduce self-motivation and produce 'mercenary' attitudes (only behaving when rewarded).
- Reinforcement is most effective if provided immediately, but this is not always possible or practical.
- Rewards can be costly in terms of time (and sometimes expense) to set up and administer.

EVALUATION OF THE USEFULNESS OF THE BEHAVIOURAL APPROACH TO LEARNING

Practically – Many behaviourist principles have been shown to be highly successful in controlling problem behaviour, e.g. O'Leary and Becker (1967), and programmed learning has been found to be at least as successful as normal classroom methods for some topics. However, behaviourists ignore individual differences – different learners find different stimuli punishing and reinforcing and show different levels of intrinsic motivation to learn. Teachers can never control all the competing sources of punishment and reinforcement in the learning environment, e.g. from peers and influences outside the classroom.

Theoretically – behaviourists neglect cognitive influences upon learning – e.g. punishment and reinforcement are most effective if explanations are also given, and the learner's cognitive attributions are important in the decision over whether they are performing behaviour for its own sake or for a reward, whether praise given is genuine, etc.

Key application – of cognitive developmental theories to education

APPLICATIONS OF PIAGET'S THEORY TO EDUCATION

Piaget did not apply his theory to the classroom himself and most of the following recommendations are what other researchers have proposed based on Piagetian principles. Overall Piaget's theory has applications for *when* and *how* to teach.

WHEN TO TEACH
- Because of Piaget's ideas on stages of development, the notion of '**readiness**' is important – children show qualitatively different kinds of thinking at different ages and should only be taught concepts suitable for their underlying level of cognitive development.

CURRICULUM IMPLICATIONS
- Some researchers have suggested that because of the notion of readiness certain concepts should be taught before others or even in a specific *order* – for example, conservation of number, followed by conservation of weight, followed by conservation of volume.
- New knowledge should be *built on pre-existing schemas*, which should be expanded through accommodation. Concrete operational children should therefore start with concrete examples before progressing onto more abstract tasks.
- However there should be a *balance* between accommodation (learning new concepts) and assimilation (practising and utilising those concepts).

LIMITATIONS ON PROGRESS
- Piaget proposed that cognitive development should *not* be speeded up because of its dependence on biological maturation. Teaching children a concept before they are biologically ready prevents them from discovering it for themselves – resulting in incomplete understanding.
- Piaget disagreed with Bruner over the ability of *language training* to advance cognitive reasoning.

HOW TO TEACH
Because of Piaget's emphasis on the individual child's self construction of its cognitive development, education should be *student centred* and accomplished through **active discovery learning**.

THE ROLE OF THE TEACHER
The role of the teacher in the Piagetian classroom is as a *facilitator*. Teachers should be involved in the indirect imparting of knowledge, not direct tuition and should therefore:
1. Focus on the *process* of learning rather than the end product of it.
2. Assess the *level* of the child's development so suitable tasks can be set.
3. Choose tasks that are *self-motivating* for the child, to engage its interest and further its own development.
4. Set tasks that are challenging enough to put the child into *disequilibrium* so it can accommodate and create new schemas.
5. Introduce abstract or formal operational tasks through *concrete* examples.
6. Encourage *active interaction* not just with task materials but with other children. In small group work children can learn from each other.

THE THEORIES OF BRUNER AND VYGOTSKY APPLIED TO EDUCATION
- Bruner and Vygotsky both disagreed with Piaget's strict notion of readiness and argued that the teacher should *actively intervene* to help the child develop its understanding - instruction *is* an important part of the learning process. The teacher, or more knowledgeable other, provides the 'tools' or 'loan of consciousness' required for the child to develop cognitively by providing structure, direction, guidance and support, not just facts. The following concepts are therefore important in education according to the theories of both Bruner and Vygotsky:

THE SPIRAL CURRICULUM
The '*spiral curriculum*' involves material being structured so that complex ideas can be presented at simplified levels first and then *re-visited* at more complex levels later on. This opposes Piaget's idea of readiness.
Children should be made aware of the structure and direction of the subjects they study, and progression should proceed via an *active problem solving* process.

SCAFFOLDING
'*Scaffolding*' is a kind of hypothetical support structure around the child's attempt to understand new ideas and complete new tasks. The scaffolding allows the child to climb to the higher levels of development in manageable amounts by
1. Reducing degrees of freedom (simplifying the tasks)
2. Direction maintenance (motivating and encouraging the child)
3. Marking critical features (highlighting relevant parts or errors)
4. Demonstration (providing model examples for imitation)

THE ZONE OF PROXIMAL DEVELOPMENT AND EDUCATION
- Tharp and Gallimore (1988) propose the following definition of teaching according to Vygotsky's ideas – "*Teaching consists in assisting performance through the ZPD. Teaching can be said to occur when assistance is offered at points in the ZPD at which performance requires assistance*" and go on to quote Vygotsky (1956) who said that teaching was only good when it "*awakens and rouses to life those functions which are in a stage of maturing, which lie in the zone of proximal development*".
- Teachers should assist performance by working sensitively and *contingently* within the ZPD. Bruner developed this idea of contingency (responding appropriately and flexibly to the child's individual needs only when required) in his own work, and Wood and Middleton (1975) have investigated contingency by watching mothers help their children build a puzzle. The mothers showed contingency by offering different levels of help depending on how much difficulty the child was having.

Cognitive information-processing theory applied to education

COGNITIVE PSYCHOLOGY AND EDUCATION

- The cognitive approach assumes that it is important to study inner mental processes such as attention and memory because such processes actively filter, organise and manipulate the information we receive. It is also assumed that humans, like computers, are information-processors, and that their processing of information can be modelled and scientifically tested.
- What does this mean for education? It means that cognitive psychologists would argue that their scientific models make a sound basis for informing teachers how they can **best adapt teaching to suit the way humans filter, organise, store and manipulate information**, and the **limitations** of their information processing abilities.

AUSUBEL – SUBSUMPTION THEORY

Ausubel's ideas on education are linked to cognitive psychological research on schemas and the organisation of memory.

How does Ausubel think we learn?

- Ausubel suggests that new information is only meaningful if it can be related to previous knowledge / concepts. This means that for learning to occur a new concept must be **subsumed under** (be related to, or a new or slightly different example of) a previously learned concept.
- Because **more specific concepts become subsumed under more general ones**, knowledge is gradually **represented** (stored) in a **hierarchical** way in the mind. This means a cognitive (mental) structure is formed which is arranged so that the most general concepts are at the top and increasingly specific sub-concepts are found beneath.
- Although subsumption involves finding **similarities** between past concepts and new ones, new concepts will only be **remembered** if they are separated or distinguished in some way from previous concepts (Ausubel calls this **dissociative subsumption**). Forgetting occurs, according to Ausubel, when there is **zero dissociability** (or **obliterative subsumption**) because new learning cannot be distinguished from the old.
- Obviously new concepts will vary in how different they are from previous ones and therefore cause different amounts of change in the underlying cognitive structure. 'Derivative subsumption occurs when new material is so similar to what is already known that it could have been derived from it; correlative subsumption involves material that is sufficiently novel that it requires some change in existing cognitive structure' (Lefrancois 1994).

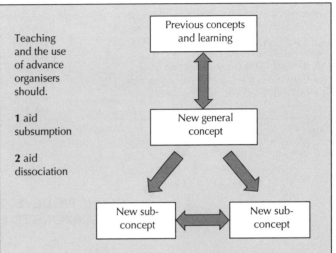

Teaching and the use of advance organisers should.

1 aid subsumption

2 aid dissociation

What should teachers do?

- New material should be **integrated** with previously acquired knowledge through comparison and contrast.
- **General ideas** should be presented first, then more detailed subsumed concepts should be taught and **dissociated** (shown to be different in some way) from each other.

Teachers should therefore present **advance organisers** before teaching new material to create an explicit **link** between what has been learned and what is about to be learned, and to provide an **general** (subsuming) **framework** for understanding new sub-concepts. When the information to be learned is completely new, the advance organisers are termed **expository** organisers, whereas when familiar material is about to be presented, they are termed **comparative** organisers.

GAGNE – CONDITIONS OF LEARNING

Gagne's research has many implications for education since it describes:

What is learned – by identifying the different **outcomes of learning** that can be achieved. Gagne sees the **five main categories** of learning as being: verbal information, intellectual skills, cognitive strategies, motor skills and attitudes.

How learning occurs – by identifying the different **conditions of learning** or **instructional events** that are needed to achieve each kind of learning. Often these instructional events can be sequenced or ordered hierarchically to show how teaching should best progress.

Why learning occurs – by identifying the **cognitive processes** that underlie and explain the success of the instructional events.

Example: Learning outcome = intellectual skill (learning a new concept, e.g. what is a duck?)

Nine instructional events required (in order), with examples.		Cognitive process involved
1	Gain attention	*OK, everyone, let's start the lesson...*	Reception
2	Identify objective	*Today we are going to learn about ducks...*	Expectancy
3	Recall prior learning	*What do you remember about our lesson on birds?*	Retrieval
4	Present stimulus	*A duck can be defined and described as...*	Selective perception
5	Guide learning	*Here are several examples of pictures of ducks...*	Semantic encoding
6	Elicit performance	*Now, all of you draw your own picture of a duck...*	Responding
7	Provide feedback	*Correct, correct, no that is wrong I'm afraid...*	Reinforcement
8	Assess performance	*Good, 10/10, looks like a chicken – adjust the beak...*	Retrieval
9	Enhance retention/transfer	*Now, out of all these bird pictures, identify the ducks...*	Generalisation

Evaluating cognitive applications to education

PIAGET'S APPLICATIONS TO EDUCATION

- Bruner agreed with Piaget that discovery learning was important in teaching.
- Criticisms of Piaget's applications to education have been made both of the notion of readiness and discovery learning.
- Meadows (1988) in her review of the research finds that 'the behaviours typical of different stages ... can certainly be accelerated by training... Contrary to the predictions of the Piagetian account, training does produce improvement in performance which can be considerable, long-lasting and pervasive. A variety of training methods have been seen to succeed...' .
- Brainerd (1983) has concluded that while 'self-discovery training can produce learning, it is generally *less* effective than tutorial training'.

BRUNER AND VYGOTSKY'S APPLICATIONS TO EDUCATION

- Bruner and Vygotsky were correct in assuming that teachers can assist performance by working sensitively and ***contingently*** within the ZPD and training children to understand concepts.
- Wood and Middleton (1975) have supported the idea of contingency by watching mothers help their children build a puzzle. The mothers showed contingency by offering different levels of help depending on how much difficulty the child was having.
- Sonstroem et al (1966) encouraged children who failed conservation of substance tests to use all of their modes of representation to increase their ability to conserve. The children who rolled the plasticine into a ball themselves (enactive mode) while watching their own actions (iconic mode) and verbally describing what was happening, e.g. 'it's getting longer but thinner' (symbolic mode) showed the greatest improvement in conservation.
- Ausubel's ideas support Bruner's on the value of organisational hierarchies and the spiral curriculum method of presenting more general and simple concepts before proceeding to more specific and complex ones.

COGNITIVE DEVELOPMENTAL APPLICATIONS TO EDUCATION

HOW GOOD ARE COGNITIVE APPLICATIONS TO EDUCATION?

INFORMATION PROCESSING THEORY APPLICATIONS TO EDUCATION

AUSUBEL'S APPLICATIONS TO EDUCATION

- Ausubel's ideas are mainly limited to the learning of meaningful verbal / textual information in the classroom.
- Bruner suggests that students should discover and construct their own meaningful hierarchies from the components given them, Ausubel thinks this is a waste of time for older children because teachers can outline complex cognitive structures more efficiently through expository teaching.
- Advance organisers have been shown to facilitate learning.
- Research consistently supports the idea that the more background knowledge a learner has on a particular topic, the greater their ability to learn and understand new information concerning it (Alexander and Judy, 1988).

GAGNE'S APPLICATIONS TO EDUCATION

- Gagne's ideas apply to a range of different kinds of learning and recognise the importance of different learning strategies for different learning outcomes.
- In line with cognitive psychological principles, Gagne's ideas are specific in their suggestions and their effects are scientifically verifiable.
- Gagne may have identified which conditions of learning or instructional events are most suitable for certain learning outcomes, but not which are most suitable for certain students. The theory therefore neglects individual differences in learning style and ability.

Teaching styles and attitudes

DIDACTIC TEACHING

Refers in general to teacher-centred methods, which tend to be associated with:

Formal style (Bennett, 1976) – e.g. controlling the seating, associations and movement of the students, focusing on student-teacher rather than student-student interactions, and emphasising teacher assessment and motivation of achievement.

Direct style (Flanders, 1970) – e.g. using lecturing, expository and authority based methods of relaying information and opinions. Students are told what to think and do.

How might these affect student performance?

Research suggests that a formal style is associated with greater academic achievement, lower noise levels and suitability for insecure/anxious students than an informal style. The success of a direct style depends upon the subject matter, conditions of leaning (i.e. time-constraints) and student learning style.

STUDENT-CENTRED TEACHING

Refers in general to methods, which tend to be associated with:

Informal style (Bennett, 1976) – e.g. allowing greater student freedom of choice over conditions of learning and emphasising internal motivation and satisfaction over external teacher-based assessment.

Indirect style (Flanders, 1970) – e.g. encouraging student ideas, opinions and behaviour through question asking and the acceptance of student contributions.

Discovery learning (e.g. Piaget and Bruner) – e.g. student self-construction of learning based upon teacher-provided materials.

How might these affect student performance?

Bennett (1979) suggests that an informal style is associated with greater communication between students, but not always higher creativity compared to formal methods. Discursive subject matter may benefit more from an indirect style, while discovery learning may be unsuitable for less-motivated students, learning very complex material under time constraints.

TEACHING STYLES AND THEIR EFFECT ON STUDENT PERFORMANCE

TEACHERS' ATTITUDES/EXPECTATIONS AND THEIR EFFECT ON STUDENT PERFORMANCE

LABELLING AND STEREOTYPING

- Labelling concerns the attachment of a descriptive term onto an individual or group by others. Such descriptive labels for students can be positive, e.g. 'hardworking', 'clever', 'attentive', 'well-behaved', etc, or negative, e.g. 'lazy', 'slow', 'distractible', 'troublemaking', etc.
- Labels may be based upon past experience or an assessment of some kind with the individual or group, or may be attached based upon stereotypes.
- Stereotypes are pre-formed opinions of groups or categories of people that are presumed to share similar typical characteristics. Stereotyping involves allocating people to certain categories based on little more than visible cues (e.g. gender, dress, and skin colour) and assuming they possess the same general descriptive characteristics as the other category members. Stereotyping can exaggerate the differences between groups and cause the prejudgement of student behaviour and performance.

What are the possible effects of labelling and stereotyping?

1. **The creation of lasting and fairly stable impressions** of the labelled individual or group, which take fairly dramatic changes in behaviour to cause a re-assessment. For example, a student's initial bad behaviour, poor performance or group stereotype may create a lasting impression in their teacher of them being a 'troublemaker' or a 'less-able' student.
2. **The creation of distortions in the perception of behaviour** in the light of the attached label. For example, a teacher may become more vigilant for bad behaviour in a labelled 'troublemaker' or have lower expectations for a 'less-able' student. This may lead the teacher to remember the 'troublemaker's' misbehaviour more than good behaviour, and regard the 'less-able' student's poorer performance as normal/more acceptable, thus strengthening the negative opinions.
3. **The creation of self-fulfilling prophecies** in the behaviour of the labelled, through reactions to the behaviour and expectations of the labeller. A labelled 'troublemaker' may stop trying to be good since it does not seem to be noticed and behave as expected out of resentment. The labelled 'less-able' student may develop a negative self-image of their ability, think they are incapable of producing higher quality work, and stop trying to. The teacher may set less demanding work, thus slowing their progress. Marking and assessment may become biased.

Evaluation – Rosenthal and Jacobson's (1968) study is the classic support for the effects of labelling in the classroom – randomly selected students improved in intellectual and academic ability because their teachers were given the mistaken impression that they had been identified as (labelled) intellectual 'spurters'. This study has been criticised (e.g. by Smith and Cowie, 1994) and not always replicated, however Good and Brophy's (1991) review of research suggests teacher expectations do influence student behaviour. Similarly, teacher prejudice based on stereotypes has also been shown to affect students.

It is not always clear whether self-fulfilling prophecy effects result more from teacher reinforcement/neglect/punishment, teacher assessment bias, student reactions to expectation, or changes in student self-image. Positive teacher expectations may actually result in worse performance if more teacher attention is devoted to those perceived as more needy.

Student variables in learning

INDIVIDUAL LEARNING
- Refers to students learning and completing tasks on their own without regard for others' performance.
- The rewards of learning are independent of those received by others.
- The rewards of learning gained reflect one's own effort and are not limited by other people's performance.
- Self-esteem is based on one's own actions.
- Is less likely to involve social distractions.
- Does not require or provide social skills, may suit the shy.
- Individuals can employ their own learning style and work at their own rate.
- Receives no emotional and intellectual support from peers.

CO-OPERATIVE LEARNING
- Refers to students learning the same material together and completing the same tasks as a group.
- The rewards of learning are the same for each group member and may depend upon the success of the group.
- Rewards may not always reflect one's own effort and be limited by the group's performance, but quality may increase.
- Self-esteem is based on the group's actions. May increase liking of others.
- Is more likely to involve sources of social distraction.
- Requires and provides social skills, may not suit the shy.
- Individuals may have to compromise on their preferred learning style and work at other's rate.
- Receives more emotional and cognitive support from peers.

COMPETITIVE LEARNING
- Refers to students learning on their own, but with regard to other's performance.
- The rewards of learning depend on the success of the individual relative to the success of others.
- Rewards may not always reflect one's own effort and be limited by other's performance.
- Self-esteem is based on one's own actions relative to other's. May decrease liking of others.
- Involves some social distraction.
- Does not require or provide social skills, may not suit the shy.
- Individuals can employ their own learning style and but may feel pressure to work at other's rate.
- Receives little emotional and intellectual support from peers.

WHAT LEARNING CONDITIONS MIGHT DIFFERENT STUDENTS PREFER?

STUDENT VARIABLES IN LEARNING

WHAT LEARNING/COGNITIVE STYLES MIGHT DIFFERENT STUDENTS PREFER?

TYPES OF LEARNING/COGNITIVE STYLE
Learning or cognitive styles are preferred ways of acquiring information that are characteristic of different students. They involve differences in students' cognition, emotion, physiology and behaviour that influence how they perform and react when exposed to different methods of teaching. Students are presumed to feel more comfortable and learn/achieve better when the teacher's method of presentation and instruction matches their preferred style. Differences may be found in:
- Cognitive factors – the student's typical way of processing (perceiving, storing, thinking, problem-solving and remembering) information, e.g. whether they prefer to receive information through visual, auditory or tactile (learning by doing) presentation.
- Emotional factors – the way the student feels about their own ability or different teaching and assessment methods, e.g. based upon their confidence, self-image, sociability and levels of (intrinsic or extrinsic) motivation.
- Physiological factors – the differences relating to activity levels, sex, physical handicap, and even body rhythms.

The effectiveness of sex related differences in learning style
Some have suggested that the increasing under-achievement of boys in British schools is due to average differences in their learning style because of their:
- higher physiological arousal levels
- competitive need for immediate feedback
- preference for visual or tactile presentation.

These aspects of learning style do not always suit educational methods, although more negative, culturally produced attitudes towards learning are probably more responsible.

The effectiveness of mastery-orientated and failure-avoiding styles
Greater academic success is usually experienced by those with mastery-orientated rather than failure-avoiding styles.
- Mastery-orientated students are intrinsically motivated to improve their ability to overcome new challenges. Failure motivates them to modify their strategies.
- Failure-avoiding students see their ability as fixed and thus only attempt tasks they feel they can achieve. Their dependence on external assessment and motivation means failure is usually blamed on external factors and may lead to acceptance of failure.

Assessment and education

ASSESSMENT AND IQ IN EDUCATION
- Assessment in education provides individual and comparative measures of ability and feedback on performance and progress.
- Where assessment is used for comparative purposes, it has especially important implications for selection and the relative awarding of rewards, and so it is important that the assessment method should valid, reliable and unbiased.
- IQ tests are a common method of comparative assessment in education, but have generated some controversy regarding their validity, reliability, and the extent to which they might be biased towards certain groups.
- This has led some to question the value of IQ tests in education, despite the fact that IQ test results do seem to be associated with academic achievement.

VALIDITY AND RELIABILITY OF IQ TESTS
Validity – refers to whether an assessment measures what it is supposed to, i.e. do IQ tests really measure intelligence, and can be examined in terms of its:
- **Face Validity** – Does the test appear to measure what it is supposed to measure? Does the IQ test look like it measures intelligence?
- **Content Validity** – Do the test items measure every necessary aspect of the concept? Do the IQ questions measure all types of behaviour that is regarded as important in reflecting intelligence? Although intelligence is generally thought of as a general intellectual ability, many psychologists have identified sub-components of intelligence, e.g. verbal, mathematical, logical etc.
- **Construct Validity** – Does the test reflect its underlying theoretical constructs/assumptions? Do the IQ questions distinguish the measurement of intelligence from the measurement of other concepts?
- **Predictive Validity** – Do the test results predict later performance? Do the results of IQ tests predict future intellectual achievement?
- **Concurrent Validity** – Do the test results correlate positively with the results of other tests designed to measure the same concept? Do the results of one IQ test match those of others?

Reliability – refers to whether a test measures consistently and fairly, i.e. do IQ tests accurately and fairly measure intelligence of and between individuals?
- **External Reliability** – Does the test measure in the same way every time it is used? Do IQ tests record the same level of intelligence for the same individuals over time provided no change in intelligence has occurred?
- **Internal Reliability** – Does the test measure consistently within itself? Do IQ tests provide accurate and standardised measurements and discriminations of and between individuals' intelligence?

THE EDUCATIONAL IMPLICATIONS OF IQ TESTS
Validity – It is not always clear what the concepts that make up intelligence actually are. Different researchers put a different emphasis on the number of aspects to intelligence and the factors that contribute to it (e.g. the relative influence of nature and nurture). This may have the following educational implications:
- IQ tests that have obvious face validity give away the purpose of the test and allow practise and preparation for similar items on subsequent tests. Test practice may therefore vary between students.
- IQ tests may measure general aspects of intelligence that are related to academic performance in general, i.e. speed of processing and comprehension of new concepts, as well as some specific aspects of intelligence that are related to performance in particular subjects, e.g. verbal ability and English. However, IQ tests may not measure all abilities and variables associated with academic success, and may be associated with some subjects more than others.
- It is not always clear whether IQ tests measure concepts that are unique to intelligence. The motivation and attitudes of a student towards IQ tests and education, as well as their 'intelligence' may account for their performance.
- Intelligence and IQ results may not be perfectly stable over time therefore reducing the predictive validity of IQ tests.
- Other methods of measuring intelligence, ability and attainment in education also have problems, so concurrent validity may not be very useful.

Reliability – IQ tests may not measure fairly since:
- To prevent practice effects, a different IQ test should be used for each subsequent measure of intelligence, however these may differ in terms of their difficulty or standardisation.
- Tests may be administered under different conditions for different students, allowing many variables other than 'intelligence' to influence the IQ test results.

BIAS IN ASSESSMENT
- What is regarded as intelligent or the most important aspects of intelligence may differ across cultures and genders, e.g. in terms of conceptual grouping or the relative number of spatial and verbal items (males on average perform better on the former, females on the latter items).
- Test construction may be biased in terms of the wording of questions (e.g. the complexity of the language used) or the educational experience required to answer them.
- Gould's 'Nation of Morons' article illustrates the problems of cultural bias in IQ tests.
- Some researchers have attempted to produce culture-free or culture-specific intelligence tests to combat these difficulties. Nevertheless comparison between the IQs of students in education remains a problematic issue given that the results of such tests have been used to select certain students for special treatment, either consciously, i.e. streaming of classes, special education etc. or unconsciously, in terms of teacher attention, reinforcement and expectations.

Special needs assessment

THE INITIAL IDENTIFICATION OF SPECIAL EDUCATIONAL NEEDS

The special needs of students in education are usually noted by parents and doctors at a young age in obvious cases and by teachers when subtler or later manifesting needs become apparent in school through classroom behaviour and performance. The child is then referred to an educational psychologist for assessment.

Children may be referred to an educational psychologist without a clear idea of what is causing educational problems and precise identification of educational difficulties will often only occur at this stage.

Difficulties in initial identification

Special educational needs may go unidentified for a number of reasons:
- Subtle learning difficulties may be attributed to laziness or carelessness with work.
- The frustration produced by learning difficulties may cause anti-education attitudes and disruptive behaviour, which may draw attention away from the source of the problem.
- Highly creative individuals may be perceived as non-conforming troublemakers.
- The highly intelligent may not have the opportunity to show their full ability when having to complete the same work at the same pace as other class members.
- Those gifted with particular talents may not have the opportunity to show them when faced with a narrow curriculum.

THE ASSESSMENT OF SPECIAL EDUCATIONAL NEEDS

The assessment of special educational needs is based on:
- The definition of special needs as those where the student is experiencing **greater educational difficulty than the majority of children of the same age** and which **requires special educational provision in addition to, or different from, other students.**
- The **use of assessment techniques** such as **observation** (e.g. of classroom behaviour), **interviews** (e.g. with teachers, student and parents), **physical and psychiatric diagnosis** (e.g. where a physical cause or mental illness is suspected), **attainment tests** (e.g. the analysis of reading, speaking, writing, comprehension and numeracy achievement) and **ability tests** (e.g. intelligence tests).
- **Psychometric techniques** such as norm referencing and standardisation may also be applied to assess the frequency and severity of the need relative to other children of the same age. Such analysis usually involves the use of normal distribution curves.
- The **allocation** of the student to an **assessment category** and the **recommendation for remedial action**.

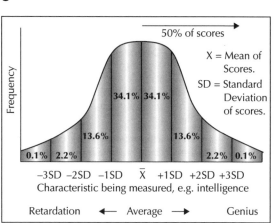

50% of scores

X = Mean of Scores.
SD = Standard Deviation of scores.

Frequency

34.1% 34.1%
13.6% 13.6%
0.1% 2.2% 2.2% 0.1%

−3SD −2SD −1SD X̄ +1SD +2SD +3SD
Characteristic being measured, e.g. intelligence

Retardation ← Average → Genius

Problems in the assessment of special needs
- Assessment of special needs may be value-based and is usually applied to those with learning problems rather than the gifted.
- Every assessment technique has its weaknesses as well as its strengths. Problems in the validity and reliability of the methods may result from their construction (e.g. imprecise observational definitions or culturally biased IQ tests), application (e.g. from who conducts them under what conditions) and interpretation (e.g. expectations may bias the interpretation of the results).
- The definitions of certain categories/concepts can be a little vague at times, e.g. what exact characteristics constitute 'giftedness' (an exceptional IQ, achievement or single talent?) and how rare (as a percentage of the population) do they have to be?

THE CATEGORISATION OF SPECIAL NEEDS

There are many different categories of special needs, e.g.:
Physical difficulties – including physical and sensory impairments such as loss of limb and motor control and visual/hearing impairments.
Social, emotional and behavioural difficulties – due, for example, to ADHD, autism, anxiety, aggression, shyness, delinquency, depression or schizophrenia.
Cognitive difficulties – including general intellectual disability (different levels of mental retardation) and specific learning difficulties, e.g. dyslexia.
Gifted and talented – e.g. those of general exceptional ability, aptitude and achievement, or those with a specific area of expertise, i.e. musical, artistic, creative or athletic ability.

Problems with the categorisation of special needs
1 Labelling of the categorised may occur, which may lead to:
   - ignoring individual differences between category members
   - underestimating abilities the labelled do possess
   - interpreting all behaviour as a consequence of their categorisation (thus ignoring other internal and external factors i.e. motivation)
   - exaggerating the differences between those categorised and the rest of the population
   - discrimination against the labelled
2 Special treatment may have certain consequences, e.g.:
   - Special schools may provide important academic and emotional support but increase feelings of isolation and rejection by society
   - Acceleration (rather than enrichment) of gifted children may cause social maladjustment, pressure and equal opportunity problems

Traits and sport

THE TRAIT APPROACH TO PERSONALITY

Personality traits refer to the **characteristics of individuals** (such as how they typically think, feel and behave) that are supposed to remain reasonably **consistent across situations** and **over time**, but that may **vary between individuals** in degree. Two major personality trait theories established through statistical factor analysis (although using slightly different approaches) have been proposed by **Eysenck** and **Cattell**:

- Eysenck suggested three basic personality types that vary between people along dimensions and are mostly biologically based. The extremes of the dimensions are introversion / extraversion, neuroticism / stability, and psychoticism, and can be measured using the EPI or EPQ (Eysenck Personality Inventory/Questionnaire).
- Cattell suggested 16 basic source personality traits, again varying between people along dimensions and measured using the 16PF (Sixteen-Personality Factor Questionnaire).

Eysenck's personality types:

- **Extraverts** – are sociable, crave excitement and change, take chances, and are impulsive. They tend to be carefree, optimistic, unreliable and lose their temper fairly quickly. Eysenck suggests they get bored more quickly, are less responsive to pain and are poor at extended periods of concentration if change and excitement is not involved.
- **Introverts** – are reserved, socially retiring, plan their actions and control their emotions. They tend to be serious, reliable and pessimistic, and do not lose their temper easily.
- **Neurotics** – are anxious, worrying, moody and overly emotional and reactive, finding it difficult to calm after upset.
- **Stables** – are emotionally calm, unreactive and unworried.
- **Psychotics** – are unempathetic, solitary and often uncaring, troublesome, aggressive or cruel towards others.

SPORTING CHOICE AND SUCCESS

TRAITS AND SPORT CHOICE AND SUCCESS

Much research has been devoted to trying to link specific personality traits to the choice of sport in general, different sports in particular, and sporting success. The research was undertaken in the hope that individuals could be selected for their potential for different sports or their suitability for training.

Traits and sport choice

- Kroll and Crenshaw (1970) – assessed the personality profiles of individuals highly skilled in American football, wrestling, gymnastics and karate using Cattell's 16PF questionnaire. Similar profiles were gained for the American footballers and wrestlers, but distinct profiles were found for those involved in gymnastics and karate (Woods, 1998).
- Kirkcaldy (1982) – assessed 199 team athletes and 124 individual sport athletes aged 22–24 using the EPI, but found no significant differences between those involved in team or individual sports (unlike previous research that has found team players to be more anxious and extravert). However, on analysing the within-team differences, males in offensive positions scored significantly higher on psychoticism and extraversion than midfield players, while defenders tended to score slightly higher than forwards on stability (Banyard and Hayes, 1994).
- Daino (1985, also cited in Banyard and Hayes, 1994) found 66 teenage tennis players scored higher on extraversion and lower on neuroticism, psychoticism and anxiety than an age matched control group who played no sport.

Traits and sporting success

- Williams and Parkin (1980) found the 16PF profiles of international standard male hockey players were different from those of club standard players (Woods, 1998).
- Garland and Barry (1990, cited in Jarvis, 1999) found that the 16PF traits of tough-mindeness, extraversion, group dependency and emotional stability accounted for 29% of the variance in the skill ratings of American college athletes.

EVALUATION OF THE TRAIT APPROACH TO SPORT PSYCHOLOGY

- Despite hundreds of studies, there have been many contradictory findings and the effects of personality traits on sport choice and success seem to range from none to minor.
- Researchers such as Ogilvie and Tutko (1972) have argued that personality profiles emerge most consistently at elite levels of competition, while Fisher et al (1978) report that personality traits appear in general to explain no more than 10% of the behavioural variability in sporting situations.
- Personality profiles may have better success at predicting more extreme sporting activities (e.g. rock-climbing and sensation-seeking).
- Personality traits appear to be better at predicting sport choice rather than success. This may be due to studying individuals who have stuck at a sport because they were more successful at it compared to unsuccessful players who gave it up, thus obscuring a significant proportion of the success.
- There are many methodological problems in trait research. Correlational data means that sporting choice and success could cause or shape, rather than result from, personality traits. Longitudinal research is needed to measure whether traits lead to sport activity and remain stable through sporting careers.
- There are many other more important factors than personality that influence sporting choice and success, e.g. interests, abilities, motivation, and experience. Interactionism of personality and situation is a more likely explanation.
- Personality traits may not actually remain stable across situations and time, and personality tests have many problems with their reliability and validity, e.g. mood and motivation may affect the results.
- There are better ways of predicting sporting performance and suitability, e.g. actual performance trials.

Sport and socialisation 1

SOCIAL LEARNING THEORY AND INDIVIDUAL DIFFERENCES IN BEHAVIOUR

Social Learning Theory (Bandura, 1962, Mischel, 1973), proposes that individual differences in behaviour result from different environmental experience. It suggests that in addition to behaviour being learned through personal experience (via the behaviourist processes of classical and operant conditioning), individual differences may be acquired by just observing others' modelled behaviour and its consequences, via the following processes:

- **Observation learning** – being able to automatically learn behaviour from just observing models, without the need for reinforcement. Models provide information about **behaviour** (actions, statements, skills etc.) and its **consequences** (whether it leads to positive or negative outcomes).
- **Cognitive processes** – such as **attention** and **memory** abilities that allow the person to focus on relevant models and behaviour, e.g. based on past memories of who and what is most useful and appropriate to imitate in a given environment. A memory representation of how to reproduce what was said or done is stored with information concerning the past consequences of the behaviour. Models most likely to be imitated are those who are rewarded for their behaviour (e.g. high status and successful models) or regarded as socially appropriate, relevant and similar to the observer (e.g. those of similar gender, age and interests).
- **Imitation** – involves the motor reproduction (copying) of previously witnessed and stored actions with varying degrees of accuracy.
- **Motivation** – the imitation of behaviour depends upon the expected consequences of behaviour, based upon whether it was seen to be rewarded in others (vicarious or indirect reinforcement) or punished, whether individuals were rewarded or punished for it themselves, or if they felt good about it last time (self-reinforcement).

Thus each person will have a unique actual and vicarious reinforcement history depending upon the particular set of environmental and social interactions they have experienced and witnessed, although common life events and a shared culture will mean individuals will also show marked similarities in behaviour.

EVALUATION

- The theory incorporates many important social, cognitive and learning influences upon the development of sport behaviour.
- The theory neglects the role of innate, biological factors upon abilities and personality traits that may affect sport choice and behaviour.

Social learning theory and sport behaviour

Individual difference in sporting behaviour may result, according to Social Learning Theory, from:

- **Exposure** to sport and sporting models – the interest in and opportunity to attend or watch sporting events determines the degree of attention paid to sport behaviour and skills.
- **Observation of models** who are:
  1 highly successful, famous or well paid in sport (especially if attention is drawn to them through media exposure)
  2 similar to the observer in gender and sporting interests (this has implications for gender differences in imitation of certain athlete role models and sports).
- **Cognitive ability** to represent and store sport related skills (this perhaps relates to procedural and visuo-spatial memory encoding and retrieval abilities).
- **Motor skill** and strength to reproduce stored sport-related actions – a mixture of innate capacity, age and practice determines this.
- **The degree of encouragement** for imitated or personally acquired (through trial and error) sporting performance. This depends upon the relative degrees of positive reinforcement (e.g. praise, success), negative reinforcement (e.g. avoidance of criticism, failure) and punishment (e.g. criticism and failure) actually or vicariously received.

Note. Social learning theorists would also accept that positive or negative emotional responses (e.g. due to enjoyment) can be associated with sporting activity through classical conditioning, thus affecting attitudes to sport.

THE EFFECT OF SOCIALISATION ON SPORTING BEHAVIOUR

Socialisation refers to the process of acquiring the behaviour, beliefs, values and attitudes of one's society. As indicated above, Social Learning Theory suggests that environmental experience can shape sporting attitudes and behaviour, and that different patterns of reinforcement history result from different kinds of environmental influence. Three major socialising influences that can affect sport participation, choice, attitudes and behaviour include family, culture and gender.

- **Family influences** – socialisation begins in the home and parental or sibling interest and participation in sport act as important first role models and sources of reinforcement. Children often attempt to emulate and compete with their sibling peers; success may lead to a similar choice of sport, while failure may result in switching to other sports or a lack of further participation. Parental encouragement of children's sporting participation and performance often triggers a life-long interest and is vital for sport participation outside of school.
- **Cultural influences** – it has long been accepted, at least since Roman gladiatorial times, that the general norms and values of a society can affect attitudes toward sport and the kind of sports indulged in. Sipes (1973) in an observational anthropological study found that 9 of 10 warlike societies had combative sports, but only 2 of 10 peaceful societies did. Sipes also found a positive correlation between military activity and the popularity of combative sports in the United States. Individualistic cultures like the USA tend to emphasise individual achievement and competition more than collectivistic cultures, perhaps socialising their children to be competitive but less willing to be good team players. This socialisation actually appears to cause many American children to drop out of sport due to the emphasis on winning, since interviews with young children typically reveal that their initial participation in sport is due to the desire to make or maintain friendships and have fun rather than to win.

Gender socialisation and sporting behaviour

The way boys and girls are socialised in general can have a profound influence on their attitudes towards, and performance in, sport.

- Duquin (1978) reports 'support for the notion that parents, other adults, teachers, textbooks, and the media all affirm the idea that sport, vigorous physical activity, and risk-taking are all appropriate behaviours for males [but not] for females' (Oglesby, 1984).
- Many studies (e.g. Fagot, 1977) indicate that females are reinforced for dependency, passivity, low competitiveness, and less aggression and rough-and-tumble play.
- Gill and Deeter (1988) found males scored higher than females on competitiveness and win orientation using the Sport Orientation Questionnaire, while females scored a little higher on goal orientation (reaching personal goals) in sport (Woods, 1998).
- Coolican (1996) reports that, compared to boys, girls have been found to prefer non-competitive activities (Weinberg and Jackson, 1979), value sport less (Eccles and Harold, 1991) and be perceived as less physically competent when matched on performance (Brawley et al, 1979).

Sport and socialisation 2

THE EFFECT OF SPORT ON SOCIAL DEVELOPMENT

- Rather than just reflecting socialisation, sport may actually be an important socialising influence itself.
- Sports people are, in social learning theory terms, widely publicised and admired role models, while sporting activities and games effectively represent the goals, norms and personal qualities found in, or desired by, a society.
- Since socialisation refers to the process of acquiring the behaviour, beliefs, values and attitudes of one's society, we should not necessarily expect this influence to be entirely positive, as is often thought.
- A society's sports and role models may, unwittingly or otherwise, portray, communicate and reinforce the socially undesirable behaviour and attitudes of a society to its children.

SPORT AND AGGRESSION

Psychologists have argued that sport legitimises aggression that would otherwise be prosecuted, e.g. boxing, and socially sanctions, expects and rewards it. The socialising effect of sport to create aggression has been found in many studies:

- Smoll and Smith conducted extensive field studies of Little League teams in North America and found that the coaches they interviewed reported little in the way of character building in the children they coached. However, the researchers concluded that competitive sport could have a beneficial effect on the children depending on the coach's behaviour and the degree to which adult pressure to win affected the children.
- Silva (1981) found that while the constitutive (official or formal) rules of sport were designed to promote pro-social behaviour, the normative (informal or unwritten) rules of some team sports socialised children to be violent, cheat, foul and negatively stereotype injure, intimidate and dehumanise their opponents. Silva argues that anti-social normative behaviour is reinforced by success, praise and social pressure, and cites the study of McMurtry (1974) who found that ice hockey players who refused to conform to normative rules concerning aggression against the opposition were negatively labelled and sometimes ostracised from the team.

Viewers and fans of sport may also be affected by the aggression it contains and sanctions, as well as falling prey to the inter-group identity, competition and conflict it creates (thus the violence of football hooliganism, for example).

- Phillips (1983) found homicide rates increased by over 12% on average following heavyweight boxing championship prize fights, especially highly publicised ones (Lippa, 1990). Goldstein and Arms (1971) found the contact sports of wrestling and ice hockey increased aggression in viewers, whereas competitive but non-contact sports such as gymnastics and swimming did not.

THE POSSIBLE EFFECTS OF SPORT

POSITIVE EFFECTS OF SPORT

Character building
- Self-reliance, assertiveness, courage, sportsmanship.
- Dedication, self-discipline and perseverance.

Cognitive skills
- Decision-making skills, moral cognitive development.
- Mastery, competence and self-efficacy.

Social skills
- Co-operation, friendship and communication skills.

Emotional effects
- Positive self-esteem, pride and a sense of accomplishment.

Pro-social effects
- Delinquency avoidance via provision of a sense of purpose and productive use of time.
- Prejudice reduction though the portrayal of positive images of minorities, inter-group contact, super-ordinate team goals and shared in-group identity.
- Transmission of socially desired values (e.g. individual achievement and competitiveness in individualistic societies, teamwork and respect in collectivist societies).
- Transmission of society's norms of acceptable and unacceptable behaviour and rules of fair play.
- Punishment of anti-social behaviour and rule breaking, e.g. via yellow and red cards or fines.

NEGATIVE EFFECTS OF SPORT

Character deterioration
- Selfishness, self-absorption, arrogance, over-competitiveness, and aggressiveness / combativeness.
- Lack of dedication and perseverance if consistent failure.

Cognitive skills
- Lower moral cognitive development, lack of guilt.
- Lack of competence / self-efficacy if consistent failure.

Social skills
- Lack of teamwork or co-operation and social isolation if individual achievement is emphasised or rewarded.

Emotional effects
- Negative self-esteem, fear of failure as a result of failure.

Anti-social effects
- Prejudice reinforcement though the selective media reporting and exposure of majority group sporting events, e.g. male rather than female football, or stereotypes.
- The creation of frustration and inter-group conflict, competition, stereotyping, dehumanisation and violence.
- Transmission of socially undesirable values (e.g. gamesmanship, aggression, cheating without discovery, and disrespect of rules and authority, i.e. referees).
- Encouragement of anti-social behaviour and rule breaking (e.g. through the ineffective use of punishment or the higher rewards of winning over offending).

Intrinsic and extrinsic motivation and sport

WHAT IS MOTIVATION?
As Silva and Weinberg (1984) point out, "Like many other psychological constructs, *motivation* has been defined in a variety of ways, but in general it refers to the intensity and direction of behaviour. The direction of behaviour indicates whether an individual approaches or avoids a particular situation, and the intensity of behaviour relates to the degree of effort put forth to accomplish the behaviour. Thus, motivation can affect the selection, intensity, and persistence of an individual's behaviour, which in sport can obviously have a strong impact on the quality of an athlete's performance."

INTRINSIC MOTIVATION AND SPORT
- Intrinsic motivation comes from, or is perceived to come from, **within** the individual.
- In the context of sport it may refer to the spontaneous enjoyment of sporting activities, the sense of mastery and competence in acquiring skills, the inner need to achieve, and the feelings of self-worth at having achieved **personal** standards or goals.
- When not being controlled by external goals or limits, the above intrinsic influences are self-perpetuating and remarkably persistent forms of motivation.
- A sense of voluntary, self-determining choice and control over one's sporting activities is central to the individual regarding their sporting activity as intrinsically motivated.
- Intrinsic motivation occurs spontaneously in individuals and is evident from very young ages.
- Intrinsic motivation and inner standards, rewards and punishments are incorporated into psychodynamic, humanistic, cognitive and social learning psychological theories.

EXTRINSIC MOTIVATION AND SPORT
- Extrinsic motivation comes from, or is perceived to come from, **outside** the individual.
- In the context of sport it may refer to the positive or negative reinforcement of sporting achievement through physical means, such as the possibility of gaining or losing prizes (e.g. trophies and money), or social means, such as praise or the avoidance of criticism. Extrinsic motivation may also involve competition with others to achieve **external** standards or goals.
- External rewards or goals may set limits on motivation and need to be maintained to keep motivation persistent.
- A sense of lack of voluntary, self-determining choice and control over one's sporting activities is central to regarding sporting activity as extrinsically motivated.
- Extrinsic motivation may be applied at any age depending upon the type of reinforcer used, e.g. very young children are not readily motivated by competition with others.
- Extrinsic motivation and reinforcement is a key assumption of behaviourist learning theory psychology.

INTRINSIC AND EXTRINSIC MOTIVATION AND SPORT PSYCHOLOGY
Psychologists originally assumed that providing extrinsic motivators for an interesting activity would add to the intrinsic motivation. However Deci's (1975) Cognitive Evaluation Theory suggests that extrinsic motivation can undermine intrinsic motivation if it:
- Removes the individual's sense of voluntary control or choice over performing an activity.
- Provides information that decreases the individual's sense of competence or self-worth in the activity.

Competition can also undermine intrinsic interest by reducing enjoyment and 'turning play into work'. Coaches should therefore:
- Use extrinsic rewards to encourage activities not originally found intrinsically interesting, then gradually phase them out.
- Use extrinsic motivators carefully, e.g. praise rather than punish, and reinforce the athlete's sense of competence rather than control their performance.
- Emphasise intrinsic motivations in competitive sports, e.g. enjoyment, mastery and personal goals, especially after losing.
- Take into account that different athletes (e.g. genders) may find different stimuli reinforcing.

STUDIES OF INTRINSIC AND EXTRINSIC MOTIVATION
Deci (1971) found that participants paid to conduct an intrinsically interesting activity (puzzle-solving) later spent almost half the time on it than participants who had not previously been paid for it.

Lepper and Greene (1975) – their field experiment tested nursery school children who had shown a high intrinsic interest in picture drawing. They found those children told to expect a certificate and gold star for their drawing before actually receiving this external 'reward' later showed lower interest in the activity, implying their intrinsic interest had been undermined. Children unexpectedly given the same reward, or those who were neither told about or received it, showed higher levels of interest than the first group in a free-choice situation.

Smith, Smoll and Curtis (1979) – found American children showed greater enthusiasm and enjoyment of sport if their coaches encouraged and reinforced them rather than stressing winning and competition, thus reinforcing rather than undermining their intrinsic motivation.

Deci et al (1981) – found participants given an intrinsically interesting task and told to compete with others were later found to show less motivation in the task than those not instructed to compete.

Deci et al (1977) – found males who competed for a reward showed more intrinsic interest than those who competed for no reward, but females showed the opposite tendency.

Weinberg (1979) – found higher levels of intrinsic motivation in participants after they had won in an activity than lost in it.

Achievement motivation and sport

WHAT IS ACHIEVEMENT MOTIVATION?

'Achievement' refers to a measure of ability or attainment that reflects progress or an accomplished goal. 'Motivation' refers to the impulse or desire to behave in certain ways. 'Achievement motivation' therefore concerns the desire to do well, succeed and reach standards in one's own eyes and the eyes of others, and reflects a willingness to persist in behaviour that enables higher standards to be reached despite the possibility of failure.

Researchers such as McClelland et al (1953) and Atkinson (1964) extensively studied achievement motivation, the latter suggesting that it could be precisely formulated and calculated by measuring the **desire to succeed** of an individual and **subtracting** from it a measurement of that person's **fear of failure**.

In most early studies, achievement motivation was measured by *projective testing* – for example, people were asked to create a story on a particular topic and their responses were analysed to reveal how much the themes of their stories reflected desires to succeed or fear of failure.

Atkinson regarded achievement motivation as a **personality trait** – differing between individuals but remaining fairly consistent within each person and thus stable across different situations they might encounter. However, it was recognised that achievement motivation *interacted* with **situational factors**, in particular:

- The difficulty of the tasks faced – measured in terms of the probability of success or failure
- The incentive value of success – measured in terms of the importance to the individual of success or failure in a particular task.

ACHIEVEMENT MOTIVATION AND SPORT

Achievement motivation has many implications for sporting attitudes, training and performance. For example, those showing high levels tend to show:

- **Desire for challenge** – seeking challenging opponents (i.e. those of equal or slightly higher ability) or tasks, and demanding but achievable standards or goals. Those scoring low on achievement motivation will either not seek sporting challenge at all or will choose either very easy or very hard opponents, tasks and goals (especially if high on fear of failure) so success is guaranteed or failure justifiable.
- **Concern for excellent standards and value of feedback** – meaning they may respond better to constructive criticism in coaching, training for skill acquisition and practice for skill refinement.
- **Lower fear of failure and more positive internal attributions regarding failure and success** – leading to greater persistence in sport endeavours.
- **Positive attitudes towards evaluation** – in combination with all the above factors may lead to higher standards of performance.

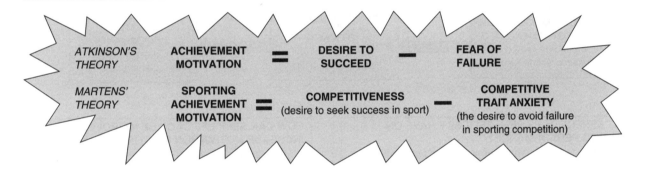

| ATKINSON'S THEORY | ACHIEVEMENT MOTIVATION | = | DESIRE TO SUCCEED | − | FEAR OF FAILURE |

| MARTENS' THEORY | SPORTING ACHIEVEMENT MOTIVATION | = | COMPETITIVENESS (desire to seek success in sport) | − | COMPETITIVE TRAIT ANXIETY (the desire to avoid failure in sporting competition) |

EVALUATING ACHIEVEMENT MOTIVATION IN SPORT

Achievement motivation does not reliably predict performance in sport. Contradictory findings have been produced, probably because research shows that those high in achievement motivation are likely to choose tasks of 0.5 probability (50:50) of success (e.g. equally matched opponents), while those low in achievement motivation are more likely to choose tasks of very high or low probability of success (e.g. very easy or very difficult opponents). Factors like relative ability and attribution may be more important in predicting persistence and performance in sport.

Measures of achievement motivation often lack reliability and validity. Projective tests are of doubtful reliability and validity because of the often subjective nature of their interpretation – different interpreters can arrive at different conclusions (poor inter-rater reliability) and may in fact project their own characteristics on to others' responses (poor validity). There is also the problem of relying on self-report data (which also applies to the use of questionnaires) to measure achievement motivation since people's responses and reported attitudes may not actually reflect how they behave.

Achievement motivation is too general and complex as a concept Cassidy and Lynn (1989, cited in Rolls and Eysenck, 1998) suggest it consists of six components: work ethic (the notion that work is 'good' in itself), pursuit of excellence, status aspiration (will to dominate others), competitiveness, acquisitiveness (desire for money), and mastery (competitiveness against set standards rather than against other people). This means that:

- People high in achievement motivation may possess these components to differing extents
- These intrinsic motives will respond differently to different extrinsic motivating factors or rewards (see intrinsic and extrinsic motivation)
- Achievement motivation may vary across different situations and sports.

- Horner (1972) suggested that *fear of success* is another important factor in achievement motivation, which can explain gender differences. Horner gave female undergraduates projective tests by asking them to create stories about successful female or male figures, and found around two-thirds invented negative consequences for the female figure. Because they did not tend to do this for male story figures, Horner concluded that women have a higher fear of success than men do. However, the research was based on a limited sample (a minority of women) and other studies have found men show equal (Robbins and Robbins, 1973) or higher (Pyke and Kahill, 1983) fear of success (cited in Tavris and Wade, 1990).

- Martens (1977) attempted to make achievement motivation more sport specific by suggesting that sporting motivation and performance can be more precisely predicted by comparing competitiveness (e.g. measured by Gill and Deeter's Sport Orientation Questionnaire) with competitive trait anxiety (which can be measured by Martens's Sport Competition Anxiety Test).

Sports men and women scoring high in competitive trait anxiety are more likely to show cognitive and physical state anxiety in competitive situations that will affect their performance (see **Effects of Anxiety/Arousal**).

Improving motivation in sport – self-efficacy

WHAT IS SELF-EFFICACY?

Bandura (1977b) regarded self-efficacy as the **cognitive belief** that one **is competent** at a **particular task**. As a concept, it is thus **distinct from** (although it may be linked to):

- Self-esteem because this relates to positive or negative *feelings* about one's ability, rather than the **thought processes** of self-efficacy.
- Achievement motivation because this concerns one's desire or need to be competent and do well, rather than the **actual self-perception of current competence** of self-efficacy.
- General self-confidence because self-efficacy is **situation-specific** (one may have self-efficacy in football but not other sports).

As a measure, self-efficacy refers to the **strength of conviction** that behaviour can be **successfully executed** to produce a certain outcome. It can be regarded as an important **mediating variable** between past and future performance.

WHAT CAUSES SELF-EFFICACY?

Several sources of information can form the basis of the self-efficacy belief, some more valid or important than others, for example:

- **One's own past performance** – the most influential and valid influence on the strength of self-efficacy. The relative levels of past success and failure in the particular sport, skill or task provide *probability information* on the likelihood of future success or failure. Repeated failure, for example, will lead to very low self-efficacy, especially for beginners.
- **Verbal feedback and persuasion** – coaches or other observers may provide positive or negative information on competence or performance in sporting tasks that may modify, favourably or otherwise, the individual's own beliefs. Observers' perceptions and information may be less or more accurate than the performer's, however, and depend upon attributions of cause.
- **The observation of others' performance** – Bandura's Social Learning Theory suggests that other people act as models that provide information regarding the consequences of actions. Through observational learning of models' actions, and their success or failure, the learner may vicariously experience competence, which may affect their own sense of efficacy. Such self-efficacy may be illusory, short-term and easily contradicted by their own ability-based performance, however, as observers find it is not as easy or hard as it looks.

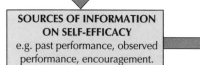

| SOURCES OF INFORMATION ON SELF-EFFICACY e.g. past performance, observed performance, encouragement. | → | SELF-EFFICACY Strength of current competence belief | → | SPORTING PERFORMANCE Quality of future performance |

WHAT EFFECT DOES SELF-EFFICACY HAVE ON SPORTING PERFORMANCE?

Self-efficacy affects **expectations of success** and performance via:

- **Task motivation** – influencing how much effort and persistence is shown in a task by affecting tolerance of defeat and fear of failure (consistent past success makes self-efficacy and motivation more resistant to a defeat or two). Those high in self-efficacy are also likely to attribute the cause of performance to internal factors that they can work on to improve.
- **Arousal and anxiety** – perceived competence can reduce negative arousal, distracting worrying or negative self-statements. Arousal that is experienced may be interpreted more positively with higher self-efficacy (thinking one is 'psyched up' not 'stressed out'!).
- **Tactical confidence** – self-efficacy might influence the confidence to employ skilful or daring (but productive) tactics, or intimidate / cause self-doubt in the opposition with displays of confidence.

HOW CAN SELF-EFFICACY BE IMPROVED TO INCREASE MOTIVATION IN SPORT?

- **Appropriate goal setting** – since the most important influence on self-efficacy is past experience, coaches should give plenty of opportunity for players to actually practise skills and tasks and to experience success by setting achievable goals, especially for beginners (Bandura and Schunk, 1981). McAuley (1985, cited in Woods, 1998) found guiding gymnasts through a task was more successful than having them watch a model do it, and was more effective at reducing anxiety than verbal persuasion.
- **Positive and constructive feedback** – coaches should provide and reinforce skill, competence and confidence.
- **False feedback** – exaggerating success can increase performance within limits. Wells et al (1993, cited in Jarvis, 1999) found weightlifters duped into thinking they had lifted more weight than they had, later did lift more than weightlifters given accurate feedback.

EVALUATION OF SELF-EFFICACY IN SPORT

- Bandura realised that many other factors are important in influencing sport performance and has applied his ideas to *team* self-efficacy too.
- Self-efficacy does seem associated with increased performance, but it is not always clear exactly how it has its effect, and measures of it are not as good as past performance at predicting future performance.
- The correlational nature of many studies on self-efficacy means it is not always certain how much it is a cause rather than effect of performance.

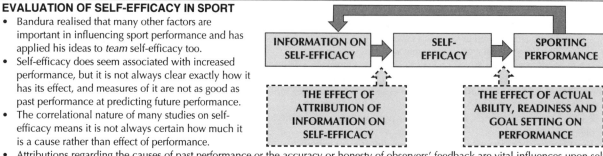

- Attributions regarding the causes of past performance or the accuracy or honesty of observers' feedback are vital influences upon self-efficacy. Dweck (1975) demonstrated that the *attribution* of success, not just success itself, is important for improved performance.

Improving motivation in sport – attribution

WHAT IS ATTRIBUTION?
- Attribution refers to how individuals **explain the cause of behaviour**.

HOW ARE ATTRIBUTIONS MADE?
Weiner's (1972) model of attribution points out that depending upon a *logical cognitive assessment* of
- whether behaviour is caused by factors relating to the actor or the situation they are in
- whether the cause is stable or unstable over time

an individual will attribute behaviour to one of four kinds of cause (see below). Various theories have been proposed (e.g. Jones and Davis, 1965, Kelley, 1967) to explain how factors like intention, ability, distinctiveness, social desirability, consistency and comparison with others, can be used to rationally derive such attributions.

However, humans often show **biases or errors** in attribution, for example based on their access to, or perception, of information, or for motivational reasons (such as to maintain self-esteem).

Biases or errors in attribution include:
- The fundamental attribution error (Ross, 1977) is the general tendency people have *to make internal attributions for others' behaviour* rather than external, situational ones, when there may be equally convincing evidence for both types of cause.
- The actor-observer effect (Jones and Nisbett, 1972) refers to the tendency of people to attribute internal / dispositional causes when observing others' behaviour (as in the fundamental attribution error), but *attribute external / situational causes to their own behaviour* (when they are the actors).
- The self-serving bias effect (Miller and Ross, 1975) refers to the tendency of **actors** to *attribute successful behaviour to internal causes*, but *unsuccessful behaviour to external ones*, thus qualifying the actor-observer effect.

Attributional bias tends to increase with the *seriousness of the consequences* of the behaviour and its *personal (hedonic) relevance*.

WEINER'S MODEL OF ATTRIBUTION

		LOCUS OF CAUSE	
		INTERNAL	EXTERNAL
STABILITY OF CAUSE	STABLE	**ABILITY** e.g. natural level of talent in a particular task	**TASK DIFFICULTY** e.g. ability of opposition
	UNSTABLE	**EFFORT** e.g. level of concentration and preparation	**LUCK** e.g. weather conditions, opponent mistakes

HOW CAN ATTRIBUTIONS BE IMPROVED TO INCREASE MOTIVATION IN SPORT?
Attributional retraining – coaches should not just provide opportunities for success rather than failure, but should encourage players to attribute those experiences favourably or appropriately (Dweck, 1975). More specifically:
- Beginners should be encouraged to attribute success to internal factors, with an emphasis on stability to draw attention to their natural ability and potential in the sport. This should encourage choice and persistence of sporting activities by increasing self-efficacy.
- Established athletes should be encouraged to attribute success to internal factors, with an emphasis on instability to draw attention to their ability to improve through increasing their own effort (appealing to their intrinsic mastery and achievement motivation).
- Athletes should be encouraged to attribute failure to a mixture of unstable internal factors, to encourage responsibility and further effort, and external factors to maintain self-esteem.

EVALUATION OF ATTRIBUTION IN SPORT
- Some of the research has been contradictory, for example Roberts (1975) found baseball teams as a group attributed more logically than individuals (who used the self-serving bias), whereas Brawley (1980) found hockey teams were just as likely to show the same bias as individuals. Attribution is affected by many factors.
- Although Weiner has added controllability to his model, the kinds of attribution shown may be more complex and integrated than suggested.
- Focus just on the effects of winning or losing on attributions may neglect the athlete's perception of success and failure. A narrow loss against a significantly superior opponent may be regarded as a success, and a team loss may not have the same effect if the individual played well.

WHAT EFFECT DO ATTRIBUTIONS HAVE ON SPORTING PERFORMANCE?
Attributions of sporting success and failure are very important in explaining future expectations of success and performance (and thus for achievement motivation and self-efficacy).
- Consistent failure can lead to negative internal attributions. A sense of learned helplessness may result where failure is attributed to stable internal factors such as lack of ability, rather than unstable internal factors (meaning individuals will think effort will make no difference, so it is not even worth trying). This will lead to a self-fulfilling prophecy effect of the athlete's attitudes on their performance.
- Fortunately, both laboratory and field research generally indicates that athletes tend to make both individual and team attributions in line with the self-serving bias to help maintain their self-esteem – attributing success to internal factors (such as their ability or effort) and failure to external ones (such as strong opposition or bad luck).
- The self-serving bias can lead to false impressions of one's ability or even self-handicapping behaviour, e.g. deliberately choosing difficult opponents or insufficiently preparing to justify or excuse defeat.
- Successful athletes adopt an internal unstable attribution leading them to feel they are responsible for their performance but can also strive to improve it.
- Gender differences in attributions have emerged in some studies, indicating that females are more likely to attribute success to luck, but failure to lack of ability, while males show roughly the opposite tendency.
- The actor-observer effect and self-serving bias can be important in understanding how athletes and coaches perceive the causes of sporting behaviour. Disagreement is more likely over the causes of failure – the athlete will be more likely to blame external factors, while the coach will focus on internal factors of the athlete. Observers and actors are more likely to show agreement on internal attributions when a victory is gained.

Social facilitation

WHAT IS SOCIAL FACILITATION?

Social facilitation refers to **the effect that the mere presence of other people has on performance**. The effect can be:

- **Positive** – increasing / facilitating performance,
- **Negative** – decreasing / inhibiting performance.

Performance appears to be *facilitated* by the presence of others when *easy* or *well known* tasks are attempted, but *inhibited* with *difficult* or *new tasks*. Social facilitation research has focused on two kinds of situation:

- **Coaction** – when people work individually, side by side on similar tasks
- **Audiences** – when people are watching an individual performing a task.

Triplett (1897) – Performed the earliest experiments on cyclists in cycling trials under three conditions. In the first condition cyclists were told to race *individually* against the clock, in the second condition they were told to race *together* but *not* to *compete*, and in the third condition they were sent off together and asked to *compete*. The fastest time was recorded for the competing group, but importantly the non-competing group was significantly faster than the individuals.

ZAJONC'S (1965) DRIVE THEORY

Zajonc's drive theory suggests that the *mere presence* of others triggers an innate response of *increased drive* or *arousal*, which *energises the performance of dominant responses*. The theory is based on Clarke Hull's ideas on drives and behavioural responses, which suggests that dominant responses are those most learned and habitual. Zajonc proposed that in *easy* or well-known tasks the *most frequently available (dominant)* responses of an organism *are correct* ones - so these are energised to increase performance. With *complex* or unpractised tasks however, the *most likely or dominant* responses that an organism could make are incorrect ones – and when these are energised performance is bound to decrease!

Zajonc proposed that arousal in the presence of others is a biologically *innate* response, thus accounting for his cockroach results, but other researchers have suggested different (and more cognitive) reasons for this arousing effect.

Zajonc reviewed many studies conducted up to 1965 and concluded that his theory could explain the fairly consistent finding that easy/well-practised tasks tend to be facilitated while difficult/novel ones were inhibited by the presence of others. Later research also tended to confirm this finding:

Zajonc et al (1969) – Tested *cockroaches* in easy and difficult mazes and found that they escaped more quickly in the easy maze if two cockroaches ran the maze or an audience of cockroaches watched, but took longer to escape in the more difficult maze under the same conditions.

Michaels et al (1982) – Rated *pool players* as either good or below average, and then stood around and pool table in a small group to watch them play. The *best players* showed an *increase* in shot accuracy by 9%, while the *poor players* showed a *decrease* of 11%, suggesting that tasks which are easy or well known are facilitated, while difficult or unpractised tasks are inhibited by audiences.

Bell and Yee (1989) – Tested 16 skilled and 17 unskilled subjects in karate, both in front of an expert audience and on their own. The task was to kick a target as many times as possible in 15 seconds over four trials. The skilled karate kickers performed equally well under both conditions whereas the *unskilled* performed significantly less kicks in front of the audience.

EVALUATION APPREHENSION THEORY

Cottrell (1968) accepted Zajonc's drive theory of social facilitation but argued that the arousal is triggered by a learned rather than instinctive source – evaluation. Evaluation apprehension theory proposes that social facilitation effects only occur when individuals feel they are under evaluation from, and thus will receive positive or negative outcomes for their performance from, other people, either when working together (coaction) or being directly watched (audience).

Dashiell (1930, 35) – Found social facilitation just by telling subjects that others were performing the same task *elsewhere*. In a later experiment Dashiell carefully arranged the coaction experiment so that the subjects could *not compete*, rather than just telling them not to, and found no coaction facilitation effect.

Paulus and Murdock (1971) – Found that audience effects are stronger in front of *experts* than non-experts.

Cottrell (1968) – *Blindfolded* the audience and found no social facilitation. However, Schmitt et al's (1986) study (see below) contradicts this finding.

DISTRACTION CONFLICT THEORY

Baron (1986) suggests that others have an arousing effect simply because they are a *source of distraction*, regardless of whether they are evaluating us or not. The presence of others puts people into a state of *attentional conflict* over whether to allocate attention to the task or others, and this conflict may raise their drive / arousal level. In addition, *well-known* or simple tasks require *less attention* and so will be less distracted by the presence of others as they are more automatic, whereas difficult tasks require much more attention to be effectively performed and so are more open to distraction from other sources.

Baron, Moore and Saunders (1978) – Found *non-social* stimuli, e.g. noise and lights also produce distraction arousal and social facilitation effects.

Schmitt et al (1986) – Asked subjects to type their name into a computer (easy task) or to type their name backwards (difficult) under one of three conditions – alone, with the experimenter watching, or in the same room with a blindfolded and ear-muffed subject whose back was turned (supposedly waiting for another experiment). The times in seconds revealed that the *mere presence* of another was sufficient to increase the performance of easy tasks and decrease the performance of more difficult ones.:

Results	Alone	Experimenter	Mere presence
Easy task	15 sec	7 sec	10 sec
Difficult task	52 sec	63 sec	73 sec

- The research and theory in this area have tended to *oversimplify* the number of factors at work. In real life, the *reactions of the audience* vary considerably, e.g. the home crowd advantage. *Hostile* audiences may impair the performance of even the simplest tasks and there is often more than one recipient of an audience, individuals may be affected more than teams.
- Each of the above theories relies to some extent on the notion of psychological drive or arousal, however physiological signs of this activation have not been consistently found or linked to performance across subjects. The kind and level of arousal (see optimal arousal theory) also needs to be considered. Other, more purely cognitive, theories of social facilitation have been proposed.

Teams and performance

TEAM COHESION AND PERFORMANCE
What is team cohesion?
Team cohesion refers to the total field of forces causing members to remain with a group (Festinger et al, 1950), or its resistance to disruptive forces (Gross and Martin, 1952), that keep members together to achieve team goals (Carron, 1982). Rather than being fixed, cohesion undergoes dynamic changes in sports teams and consists of two main forms:
* **Task cohesion** – the level of commitment to work together as a team to achieve common objectives
* **Social cohesion** – the level of friendship and mutual trust and support between team members.

Many factors influence the cohesion of sports teams, some of the most important being:
* *The size and stability of the group* – large groups or constantly fluctuating membership decreases cohesion.
* *The satisfaction of members* – successful teams that enjoy their sport are more cohesive.
* *The similarity of members* – members with similar values and goals are more cohesive.
* *Clarity of roles, goals and communication* – clear understanding of responsibilities and objectives, and conformity to roles, increases cohesion.
* *Leadership* – managers and captains can encourage team unity by adopting strategies designed to improve the above factors.

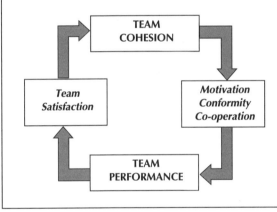

THE EFFECTS OF COHESION ON PERFORMANCE
Possible positive effects
* Increases conformity to team roles, values and goals and thus co-ordination.
* Increases motivation to do well for the team.

Possible negative effects
* Increases conformity to behaviour and attitudes more conducive to social cohesion than task cohesion.
* Socially cohesive sub-groups within a team (cliques) may reduce overall task cohesiveness, e.g. by only passing to friends rather than better-placed individuals.
* Increases team self-deception over weaknesses to avoid conflict.
* Reduces rivalry and competition over standards between team members, and therefore weakens motivation.

These effects probably depend upon the nature of the sport.
* According to Carron (1982), in 'group situations in which the individual's task is either carried out independently (e.g. rifle shooting, bowling) or is under external control for initiation and overall co-ordination (e.g. rowing), group tension, rivalry and intragroup competitiveness can serve to motivate the individual toward better performance'. In each of these sports, lower interpersonal attraction (social cohesion) has been associated with performance success.
* Where teams have to co-operate and co-ordinate themselves more to achieve success, e.g. basketball or hockey, cohesion teamwork and closeness has been associated with increased performance (Arnold and Straub, 1972, Ball and Carron, 1976).

THE EFFECTS OF PERFORMANCE ON COHESION
* Ruder and Gill (1981) found team ratings of cohesiveness in women's volleyball markedly increased after a victory whereas losers' ratings of cohesion decreased slightly (Carron, 1982).

Cohesion and performance can be highly correlated but it is difficult to infer their cause and effect.
* Hacker and Williams (1981), based on their study of women's field hockey teams, suggested that there is a circular relationship between cohesion, performance and satisfaction. This means, for example, that greater cohesion may lead to greater success, which leads to greater satisfaction, which in turn leads to greater cohesion.

THE NEGATIVE EFFECT OF TEAM MEMBERSHIP ON INDIVIDUAL PERFORMANCE
When individuals work in a team with others on a *shared or additive task* **social loafing** can occur. This is where individuals put in less effort than they would alone (a decrease in individual performance), even on the simplest collective tasks (e.g. pulling on a rope or shouting with others). Social loafing could occur for a number of reasons.

Physical factors – such as performance losses due to:
* problems in co-ordination of effort or production-blocking (where group members restrict each others' access to the task and output, causing a certain degree of turn-taking).

Motivational losses – a reduction of actual effort put into the task due to:
* Reduction of evaluation – if a task is not intrinsically motivating and individual performance can not be identified or assessed in a group, then members may think they can get away with putting in less effort.
* Output equity – people expect others will loaf and so put in less effort themselves so as not to become a 'sucker'.
* Lack of common standards – members of a team may not have a clear idea of the standard they are capable of achieving and thus not work to peak performance.

Social loafing can therefore be reduced by improving co-ordination, ensuring individuals know that their performance will be identified, making tasks more intrinsically interesting, giving feedback from other members of high performance and setting high standards.

STUDIES OF SOCIAL LOAFING
* Ringlemann, 1913) had young men pull on a rope (horizontally, as in tug-of-war) individually and together in groups of two, three or eight, and found the force exerted per person decreased as group size increased.

	Average force of pull in kilograms		
	Pull exerted	Pull expected	Force lost
Lone person	63		
Two pulling	118	126	8 (6%)
Three pulling	160	189	29 (15%)
Eight pulling	248	504	256 (51%)

* Ingham et al (1974) replicated Ringlemann's study using pseudo-groups (with confederates who did not actually pull) and found the group force loss was due to both motivation and co-ordination losses.
* Latane et al (1979) found the amount of noise produced per person in shouting and clapping groups was reduced by 29% in groups of two, 49% in groups of four and 60% in groups of six.

Arousal, anxiety and performance

WHAT ARE AROUSAL AND ANXIETY?

- Arousal refers to the state of *general physiological and psychological activation and alertness* experienced by an individual that varies in degree over time. Increased levels of arousal are associated with greater activity of the sympathetic autonomic nervous system (preparing the body for action) and higher levels of attention and mental processing activity. Arousal levels vary naturally with biological rhythms but also in response to a range of environmental triggers (see **Social Facilitation**, for example).
- Anxiety refers to **arousal that is experienced as a negative emotional state** and is associated with **feelings and thoughts of worry, apprehension and nervousness**. Anxiety has a significant cognitive as well as somatic (physiological) aspect – anxiety is particularly likely to result under 'stressful conditions' when individuals perceive that they may be unable to meet or cope with the demands of a situation, or cognitively interpret and label their arousal as 'distressing' rather than 'exciting'.

Arousal and anxiety both significantly influence behaviour and so have important implications for sporting performance.

HOW DO AROUSAL AND ANXIETY AFFECT PERFORMANCE?

DRIVE THEORY

Drive theory, developed by Hull (1943) and Spence (1956), suggests that increasing levels of drive (arousal) will increasingly energise the performance of habitual (well-learned), dominant responses in a **linear manner**.

PERFORMANCE = DRIVE AROUSAL × HABIT STRENGTH

If these responses are correct ones, as is likely in simple or well-practised tasks, then the greater the drive arousal, the better the performance. If the habitual responses are incorrect, as is likely with new or complex tasks, then increased drive will worsen performance by energising them. Thus beginners should practise with low arousal.

Evaluation

- Performance does not always improve with ever-increasing amounts of arousal, too much can inhibit performance (see optimal arousal theory).
- Drive theory ignores the kind of arousal (anxiety may have a negative impact upon performance) and it is difficult to measure how habitual responses are.

Arousal and the performance of simple or habitual tasks

OPTIMAL AROUSAL THEORY

Optimal arousal theory (the inverted-U hypothesis) suggests that **up to a certain optimal level** arousal will increasingly energise performance, but beyond this point higher levels of arousal will only serve to interfere with and reduce performance. The theory has been developed in several ways:

- Different sporting tasks will require different optimal levels of arousal. Tasks requiring fine motor movements, precision and control (e.g. golf, snooker and shooting) will have lower optimal levels than those requiring speed and strength (e.g. weight lifting, shot-putt and rugby tackling).
- Different athletes will have different zones of optimal functioning (Hanin, 1986) that reflect individual differences in how much arousal is required to reach peak performance and how improved that performance can be (depending on skill and practice levels).
- Performance will not always smoothly change with arousal levels – the inverted-U may only apply to performance under conditions of low cognitive anxiety. If high levels of cognitive anxiety accompany physiological arousal, then a small increase in arousal beyond the optimum may result in a catastrophic drop in performance. Cognitive anxiety may have its negative effect by distracting or inappropriately focusing attention in sporting tasks (Nideffer, 1976b).

Evaluation

Martens and Landers (1970) found boys exposed to moderate levels of stress and with moderate trait anxiety scores (which affects state anxiety levels during performance) performed significantly better than boys with low or high stress and trait anxiety. Klavora (1978) found 95 male basketball players' pre-game state anxiety levels showed an inverted-U pattern with their coach's post-game ratings of their performance – very high or low levels of anxiety were associated with worse performance than moderate levels. Coaches and trainers can use optimal arousal theory to help athletes reach their optimal level either by 'psyching' them up or calming them down depending upon their current state of arousal and anxiety and the nature of the task they are attempting. More specifically, muscle relaxation can be used for somatic over-anxiety/arousal, whereas cognitive self-instructional techniques can be used to stop negative thinking and distracting worry when athletes are high in cognitive anxiety. In practice, however, arousal and anxiety levels will fluctuate during a sporting event and current performance may depend upon how well a sports person has performed up to that point.

Optimal level

Optimal levels for different tasks or athletes

Point of catastrophe

Synapses, neurotransmitters and drugs

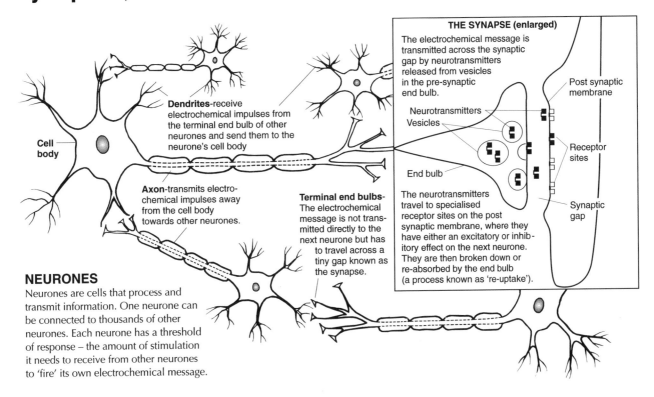

Dendrites-receive electrochemical impulses from the terminal end bulb of other neurones and send them to the neurone's cell body

Cell body

Axon-transmits electro-chemical impulses away from the cell body towards other neurones.

Terminal end bulbs-The electrochemical message is not trans-mitted directly to the next neurone but has to travel across a tiny gap known as the synapse.

THE SYNAPSE (enlarged)
The electrochemical message is transmitted across the synaptic gap by neurotransmitters released from vesicles in the pre-synaptic end bulb.

Neurotransmitters
Vesicles
End bulb

Post synaptic membrane
Receptor sites
Synaptic gap

The neurotransmitters travel to specialised receptor sites on the post synaptic membrane, where they have either an excitatory or inhib-itory effect on the next neurone. They are then broken down or re-absorbed by the end bulb (a process known as 're-uptake').

NEURONES
Neurones are cells that process and transmit information. One neurone can be connected to thousands of other neurones. Each neurone has a threshold of response – the amount of stimulation it needs to receive from other neurones to 'fire' its own electrochemical message.

NEUROTRANSMITTERS AND THEIR EFFECTS
Neurotransmitters are the body's natural chemical messengers that transmit information from one neurone to another in the brain.

NEUROTRANSMITTER	EFFECTS	EVALUATION
• ACETYLCHOLINE (ACh)	• Excitatory effect at synapse with voluntary muscle, causing contraction. • Role in hippocampus of brain in memory consolidation.	• Curare blocks ACh from receptor sites causing muscular paralysis. • Loss of ACh producing neurones in Alzheimer's disease may cause memory loss.
• DOPAMINE	• Mainly inhibitory – involved in voluntary movement, learning, arousal, and feelings of pleasure.	• Deficiency causes Parkinson's disease, over activity is involved in schizophrenia
• GAMMA-AMINO BUTYRIC ACID (GABA)	• Mainly inhibitory – involved in motor control and anxiety.	• Valium increases GABA and has a calming effect on anxiety.
• NOREPINEPHRINE	• Excitatory – involved in the experience of a range of emotions and acts as a hormone to stimulate the sympathetic nervous system.	• Injections cause accelerated heart rate which may be labelled as certain emotions. Deficiencies are involved in depression.
• SEROTONIN	• Mainly inhibitory – involved in sleep, arousal levels and emotional experience.	• Deficiencies can lead to mood, anxiety, and sleep disorders.

DRUG EFFECTS ON NEUROTRANSMITTERS AND SYNAPTIC FUNCTIONING
Drugs have their effects on neurotransmitters and synaptic functioning in a number of ways, for example by:
• Influencing the amount of brain neurotransmitters produced (by increasing or decreasing production, storage and release).
• Simulating or mimicking the effect of natural neurotransmitters (by acting as artificial *agonists* that activate the same synaptic receptor sites).
• Influencing the rate of transmission across the synapse (by affecting the rate of re-uptake and breakdown by enzymes).
• Blocking the effects of neurotransmitters (by acting as an *antagonist* that competes for, but does not activate, synaptic receptor sites).

Examples of drugs and their possible mode of action
• ALCOHOL – possibly increases the sensitivity of neurones to the inhibitory neurotransmitter GABA by increasing the sensitivity of GABA receptors.
• COCAINE – slows the re-uptake and increases the firing rate of neurones that produce norepinephrine (giving energy) and dopamine (giving euphoria).
• HEROIN – acts as an agonist by binding with and activating the brain's natural pain-killing enkephalin and endorphin receptor sites. Naloxone nullifies its effect.
• LSD – inhibits serotonin activity, thus possibly reducing serotonin's inhibition of acytlcholine in cells involved in the initiation of dreaming.

Substance abuse

SHORT-TERM Physiological and psychological effects of drugs	LONG-TERM Physiological and psychological effects of drugs
These refer to the *immediate* effects of the drug at different doses on: • The brain – the inhibition or activation of neurotransmitters and brain areas. • Subjective experience – how thoughts, feelings and perceptions are changed. • Behaviour – how the person is likely to act.	Prolonged and excessive use of drugs (substance abuse) can lead to addiction (substance dependency). According to the DSM IV substance dependency is defined in terms of psychological dependency, either with or without physical dependency: **PHYSICAL DEPENDENCY** – when the body adapts to a drug to the extent that it shows: • **Tolerance** – increasing amounts of the substance are needed to achieve the same desired effect. • **Withdrawal** – the body is affected when the substance is *not* taken. Abstinence causes severe and unpleasant physical and psychological symptoms (usually the reverse of the drug's effects) and a craving and compulsion to use the drug to relieve or avoid the withdrawal effects. **PSYCHOLOGICAL DEPENDENCY** – occurs when the user feels and behaves as if the substance is necessary for their well being. Use of the drug is continued despite knowledge of its negative health or social consequences, despite efforts to reduce consumption, and even despite remission of physical dependency (it thus provokes relapse). • **Relapse** – when substance use begins again after a period of abstinence or remission.

SHORT-TERM EFFECTS ALCOHOL	DEPENDENCY AND TOLERANCE	WITHDRAWAL AND RELAPSE
• Physiological effects – possibly increases the inhibitory effects of the neurotransmitter GABA, first in the brain's inhibitory areas (thus suppressing their inhibitory effects on behaviour) then throughout the brain-depressing arousal centres, slowing cognitive functions and affecting movement and balance in the cerebellum. • Psychological effects – lowers: ➤ Social inhibitions (facilitating behaviour such as sociability, enjoyment or aggression). ➤ Reaction time, co-ordination, memory and alertness (the overall depressant effect can increase sleepiness or anxious and depressive thinking).	• Physiological effects – long-term abuse produces many negative physical conditions, e.g. cirrhosis, memory loss, increased vulnerability to infection, physical dependence, increased tolerance (up to about 200%), and severe withdrawal symptoms. Physical dependency is fairly slow to develop, but repeated consumption of over 8 ounces of strong whisky a day is sometimes sufficient to produce addiction in humans (Davidson, 1985). • Psychological effects – alcohol causes psychological dependence that can cause major disruption to normal social, occupational and recreational activities, depression, and increased risk of accidental death (of others too). It is estimated that more than 10% of all drinkers in the US abuse alcohol, more than half of whom may be physically dependent (Sarafino, 1994).	• After-effects of excessive use of alcohol are familiar to many (i.e. hangovers). However, abstinence for those highly physically dependent on alcohol can produce delirium tremens ('the DTs') – a withdrawal syndrome associated with intense anxiety, irritability, nausea, headaches, body tremors and frightening hallucinations. In severe cases death may result from withdrawal. • The alcoholic will attempt to maintain the habit to avoid withdrawal symptoms, and the long-term psychological dependency produces strong cravings and impulses to drink (especially in social situations) when abstinence is attempted or remission experienced, leading to frequent relapse.
HEROIN • Physiological effects – Heroin powerfully binds with the brain's natural pain-killing enkephalin and endorphin receptor sites due to its similar structure, then breaks down into morphine, which has similar but less powerful effects. • Psychological effects – produces short-term but intense feelings of euphoria and pleasure, followed by longer-lasting pain-dulling and numbing effects.	• Physiological effects – single use may not result in addiction, but prolonged use quickly leads to physical dependence (due to the brain adapting and producing less of its own natural endorphins), intense withdrawal symptoms and the rapid development of extreme tolerance. Experienced users can tolerate up to 5000% of the dose tolerable by a naïve, first-time user (Kendall and Hammen, 1995). Sharing among users leads to an increased risk of death by overdose (due to differences in tolerance) and infection with HIV or hepatitis. • Psychological effects – causes psychological dependence that can cause life disruption, increased and persistent anti-social behaviour to gain the drug in order to avoid the onset of withdrawal, and depression and anxiety.	• Abstinence for those physically dependent on heroin produces withdrawal symptoms within 6 to 8 hours of the last dose, typically peaking within 2 days and remitting within a week. Symptoms depend upon the tolerance reached (since the brain has been producing insufficient levels of natural pain killers) and include severe physical discomfort, diarrhoea, chills and goosebumps on the skin ('cold turkey') twitching of the extremities (e.g. kicking of legs), irritability, hallucinations and intense craving for the drug (Kendall and Hammen, 1995). • When remission is experienced, relapse is fairly common.
Evaluation The short-term effects of drugs may vary across individuals according to their body weight, personality, moods, expectations, and natural or acquired tolerance.	**Evaluation** The potential for long-term use and abuse of drugs, and thus the severity of their physiological and psychological effects, depends upon many conditions and may vary across individuals (see **Social and psychological Factors affecting addiction**, next page).	**Evaluation** The risk of relapse after withdrawal or physical dependency on alcohol or heroin: • Decreases with age. • Is triggered by high-risk situations, e.g. negative emotional states, social pressure, modelling of use or conflict.

Social and psychological factors affecting addiction

SOCIAL FACTORS

Cultural norms, attitudes and availability create the environment in which drug use is exposed, initiated, maintained and abused. Social psychological processes such as conformity and in-group identities operate to transmit cultural norms of behaviour and positive or negative attitudes towards substances, e.g. the norms for drinking at parties or celebrations. However, differences in these factors will occur across different cultures, and within the same culture over time and at any one time (e.g. in sub-cultural groups).

- **Cross-cultural differences** – the extent of use of different substances varies across cultures due to *legal*, *social* and *religious* sanctions and prohibitions. These factors affect the availability, exposure and attitudes towards drugs (e.g. in terms of its recreational, medicinal or spiritual use). Thus some cultures (many Western ones) abuse alcohol for recreation, while others (e.g. Muslim) forbid it on religious grounds. Some cultures take drugs medicinally (e.g. coca leaf chewing to improve stamina in South America), while others take them for spiritual reasons (e.g. Peyote in Native Americans for 'visions').

- **Cultural change over time** – the same substances differ in their availability and acceptability over time within the same culture (thus the prohibition periods in America and the fluctuating use of opiates, cocaine and nicotine over time in Western cultures). Legal controls are often based upon moral or religious grounds rather than physiological, thus the wide acceptability of highly unhealthy alcohol and nicotine compared to the relatively healthy effects of cannabis.

- **Subcultures** – Vaz (1967) pointed out how peer groups, especially adolescent ones, form cohesive sub-cultural units that operate away from adult/official supervision and may have norms regarding drug use that differ from the majority in society. Subtle competition in risk-taking behaviour (usually defined by defying social norms and laws) may result in 'peer pressure' to seek and experiment with drugs, often to excessive extents, to gain in-group prestige and status (Kendall and Hammen, 1995).

LEARNING THEORY

Learning theory can be applied to addiction in many ways:

- **Classical conditioning** – cues present in the environment during drug taking may become associated with the pleasure and physiological changes caused by the substances (e.g. a bar may be associated with the pleasure from alcohol). These cues may thereafter act as prompts by creating a craving for the drug in its absence (see classical conditioning processes) and are key factors in psychological dependence and relapse (e.g. walking back into a familiar bar or seeing a friend with a cigarette after giving up alcohol or nicotine).

- **Operant conditioning** – once drugs are taken, the short-term pleasure they provide is obviously a major positive reinforcer of drug seeking and taking behaviour, compared to the longer-term negative effects (punishment). Avoidance of unpleasant withdrawal symptoms acts as a potent source of negative reinforcement for these behaviours. In terms of more psychological negative reinforcement, Tension Reduction Theory (Conger, 1956) argues that drugs may help escape from stress or fear arousal (e.g. of social situations by reducing inhibitions).

- **Social learning theory** – children may see many influential role models (e.g. parents, peers and media celebrities) taking drugs like alcohol and, because they often selectively see the positive consequences of enjoyment rather than the negative ones (unless they live with long-term alcoholic and abusive family members), they develop positive expectations and wish to use them too (see below).

PERSONALITY FACTORS

- **Personality** – people with certain behavioural traits may be more disposed to drug use, e.g. drug abusers have been found to be more rebellious, impulsive and sensation-seeking than non-users (Stein et al , 1987). This could be a cause rather than effect of drug use, however longitudinal studies have been conducted (e.g. Shedler and Block, 1990) that found those with poor impulse control, social alienation and emotional distress at ages 7 and 11 were more likely to use marijuana once a week and have tried at least one other drug at age 18.

- **Genetic vulnerability** – some people may be more responsive to drugs or prone to develop addictive personalities or physiological dependency for genetic reasons. For example, a twin is twice as likely to become an alcoholic if an identical rather than non-identical twin is one, and adopted children are around four times more likely to become problem drinkers than other adoptees if their biological parents were alcoholics, regardless of the drinking habits of their adoptive parents (Sarafino, 1994).

COGNITIVE FACTORS

Smith's (1980) Perceived Effects Theory suggests that **expectancies** regarding the effects of psychoactive substances play a major role in the initiation, maintenance and excessive use of drugs. Brown et al (1980, cited in Kendall and Hammen, 1995) found drinkers subscribed to six separate positive expectations about the effects of drinking, namely that it:

- Helps to perceive events in a positive and pleasurable way.
- Increases social and physical pleasure.
- Enhances sexual performance.
- Increases feelings of personal dominance.
- Encourages assertiveness.
- Relieves tension.

Taking drugs may even become a self-handicapping strategy to provide an excuse for failure in people who lack confidence in their abilities.

Cognitive expectations have been found:

- In children before they actually start drinking, probably acquired through social learning imitation of role models (Adesso, 1985).
- To be associated with the purpose and frequency of social drinking – Hansen et al (1991) found that those who abuse alcohol are more likely to perceive fewer negative consequences. However, those who expect strong negative effects of alcohol (often on a more moral and behavioural basis than medical one) are less likely to use and abuse drugs.
- To be associated with the actual effects of the drugs themselves. By using placebos, many researchers have demonstrated that expectancies about a drug's effect can sometimes have more of an influence upon its effects than the physiological changes it produces. Wilson and Lawson (1976) found subjects who expected sexual arousal effects from alcohol did indeed show more arousal if they were given a placebo and told it was alcohol than if they received alcohol but were told it was only a placebo. Thus users of LSD may have a good or bad trip depending upon their mood and expectations before taking it and their cognitive interpretation of the symptoms as they occur.

Sources of stress

THE CONCEPT OF STRESS

The concept of stress has been viewed in different ways. Stress has been regarded as:

1 An ***internal bodily response*** – an essentially automatic biological ***reaction*** to external stimuli. This neglects the type of stimuli that causes the reaction.

2 An ***external stimuli*** that exerts a destructive force upon the organism. This neglects the fact that the same external stimuli will not always produce the same reaction.

3 An ***interaction or transaction*** between stimulus and response that depends upon ***cognitive appraisal*** of the situation – the stress reaction will only result if individuals ***perceive*** a mismatch between the demands of the situation and their ability to cope with it (regardless of actual demands and coping ability). This is currently the most common view and thus a widely used definition of stress is: "A pattern of negative physiological states and psychological responses occurring in situations where people perceive threats to their well being which they may be unable to meet" Lazarus and Folkman (1984).

Stress can result from:

- changeable or continuous causes (e.g. life-events or steady occupational demands)
- predictable or unpredictable causes (e.g. depending on the experience of control)
- biological sources (e.g. disruption of bodily rhythms, illness, fatigue), social sources (e.g. interpersonal and work related), environmental sources (e.g. noise and pollution) or psychological causes (e.g. locus of control and personality type).

LIFE CHANGES AS A CAUSE OF STRESS

STRESSFUL LIFE EVENTS: Holmes and Rahe (1967) suggested that stress is caused by ***change*** and may lead to greater susceptibility to physical and mental health disorders. They compiled the 'Social Readjustment Rating Scale' (SRRS) – a list of 47 life events involving stressful change and rated them for their severity out of one hundred (e.g. death of a spouse = 100, marriage = 50, change in school = 20 etc.). Scores of over 300 life change units in a year would represent a high risk for stress-related health problems.

Evaluation – The SRRS has been criticised for its over-generalised approach. There are many individual differences in what events people find most stressful and how they react to them. Positive and predictable changes may be less stressful than negative and unpredictable ones. The evidence for the scale relating to health is mostly correlational, illness may have contributed towards the development of stressful life events such as losing employment, rather than vice versa.

HASSLES & UPLIFTS: Researcher such as Lazarus and Kanner have proposed that more ***everyday problems*** or pleasant occurrences were more likely to affect stress levels and health. They designed the 'Hassles and Uplifts Scale' to measure these incidents and their effects.

Evaluation – The 'Hassles and Uplifts Scale' has been found to be a better predictor of health. Continuous diary monitoring of everyday stresses has enabled a causal link to be made with later illness (Stone et al, 1987).

CATASTROPHIC STRESS: ***Single traumatic events*** such as natural disasters, warfare or violent assault can provoke long lasting stress and health problems. Mental disorder classification systems term this Post Traumatic Stress Disorder. (**Evaluation** – see PTSD research).

BIOLOGICAL CAUSES: SRRS items relating to changing work and sleep patterns could cause stress through biological changes like the desynchronisation of body rhythms with new zeitgebers, e.g. activity and light levels. (**Evaluation** – see shift work and jet lag research).

THE WORKPLACE AS A SOURCE OF STRESS

WORKPLACE STRESSORS: Occupational stress can result from factors relating to the nature of the job (e.g. its security, clarity of purpose, workload and intensity of skill use) and the social and environmental conditions in which it takes place (e.g. the co-worker relationships, organisational management, control of workload, career progression, physical workspace and noise). Workplace stressors therefore tend to result from stable characteristics rather than change (although changes in job and working conditions can also causes stress).

A common example is ***work overload/underload*** which involves stress resulting from a perceived mismatch between the time and skills the job requires and the time and skills available to complete it. Such a mismatch may cause feelings of unfairness, resentment and lack of control – especially in overload circumstances where the deadlines are important, there is external pressure to meet them and they are set by external sources. Relief from work overload stress is reduced by the lack of time left for other activities and the fatigue felt during such time.

Occupational burnout results from continual levels of stress due to highly demanding work requiring consistently high levels of concentration, responsibility, frustration or exposure to suffering, e.g. air traffic controllers or nurses. (see **Stress at work**.)

CONTROL AND STRESS

The inability to control life event changes, everyday hassles, work schedules/deadlines and unexpected traumatic events etc. is a major cause of stress and consequent ill health. Weiss (1972) found rats that could **control** electric shocks were less likely to develop gastric ulceration than those who could not, despite receiving an identical number of shocks. Workers with little control at the bottom of organisational hierarchies are often found to suffer the most ill health from stress. Rotter (1966) suggested that an 'external locus of control' leads people to think they have a lack of control over their lives and can result in less active coping strategies and greater stress-related illness. Even the illusion or possibility of control in humans can reduce the effects of stress. Feelings of control are thus important in increasing the perception that one has an ability to cope that is sufficient to match the demands of the situation (see definition of stress above). Very high levels of control however can also be stressful, especially when one is responsible for decisions and many choices are available – which may account for the executive stress of some managers.

Stress as a bodily response

Selye (1976) identified the **General Adaptation Syndrome** (GAS) – a **non-specific** physiological response that occurs to a **variety** of stressful stimuli. Much research has investigated the 3 phases of the GAS.

PHASE 1
ALARM REACTION
The physiological response triggered by stressful stimuli.

Perception of stressful stimuli

↓

HYPOTHALAMUS

Activates pituitary gland to release adrenocorticotrophic hormone (ACTH)

Activates the sympathetic branch of the autonomic nervous system

↓

ADRENAL GLAND

Activates adrenal cortex to release corticosteroids

Activates adrenal medulla to release adrenaline and noradrenaline

Inhibits immune system response, inhibits tissue inflammation, releases energy from the liver, etc.

Activates fight or flight reactions of increased heart and breathing rate, blood pressure, muscle tension, etc.

PHASE 2
STAGE OF RESISTANCE
If the stressor persists or is not dealt with, the body seeks to maintain arousal at a constant if lower level.

Individual differences may modify stress effects.
Factors that could mediate in the resolving or continuation of stress arousal or even modify its effects, include:

1 Behavioural coping style
Stress arousal will often not persist if fight or flight behaviours *deal with* the stressful stimuli. Optimal arousal theory states that up to a certain level stress can provide a beneficial motivating effect on behaviour (Selye called this 'eustress') that helps deal with the source of stress. However, although not all modern-day problems can be solved through physical means, different people use different **coping strategies** – some adopt **problem-focused strategies** and deal with the source of stress, others adopt **emotion-focused strategies** and try to deal with its effects.

2 Personality factors and cognitive style
Friedman and Rosenman (1974) argued that some people have '**Type A' personalities** that create and maintain high levels of stress in their life styles. These people are often aggressive, competitive and highly driven perfectionists who will not delegate and are impatient towards others. Kobasa (1979) suggests people with '**Hardy personalities'** are less vulnerable to the effects of stress because they have a greater sense of control over, and a more positive attitude towards, stressful events and a stronger sense of purpose. Rotter agrees that cognitive style, like a sense of control over stressful events (i.e. an *internal* rather than *external* locus of control) will moderate the effects of stress.

3 Gender and cultural factors
Genders and cultures may differ in the amount and type of stress experienced (e.g. discrimination in society and the workplace) or even physiological susceptibility. Men and those from capitalist / individualistic cultures may be more socialised into aggressive and competitive Type A behaviour towards stressful situations, and have different coping styles and levels of social support.

PHASE 3
STAGE OF EXHAUSTION
Eventually continued high arousal levels exhaust bodily resources producing negative physiological & psychological effects.

1 Physiological effects:

a Reduced resistance to infection
Studies on both animals and humans have shown that stress, especially in the long-term, can adversely affect the immune system as corticosteroids suppress its activity and thus increase vulnerability to infection. Stress has been associated with many illnesses, ranging from headaches (Gannon et al, 1987) and asthma (Miller and Strunk, 1979), to colds (Stone et al, 1987), stomach ulcers (Brady, 1958) and cancer (Jacobs and Charles, 1980).

b Heart and circulatory disorders
Stress-triggered increases in heart rate and blood pressure, as well as levels of glucose/fatty acids released into the blood stream, may result in the deterioration and blocking of blood vessels and thus increased cardiovascular disorder. Rosenman et al (1975) found in a 9 year study involving over 3 thousand men that type A personalities were more prone to suffer heart disease. However, there is debate over whether the personality traits are a cause or result of stress, and which traits are the most important since some studies have not replicated Rosenman et al's results.
Stress may also indirectly cause physiological effects since it leads to unhealthy behaviour, e.g. lack of exercise, drinking and smoking.

2 Psychological effects:

a Anger and frustration – Can cause a vicious circle of stress production as they contribute to a more stressful environment. Hostility may be a key stress-provoking factor in type A behaviour.

b Depression and helplessness – Seligman (1975) found continual and unavoidable stress caused learned helplessness and depression which would be inappropriately generalised to different situations.

c Anxiety – Different types of stressful situation can produce different types of anxiety disorder, e.g. persistent, unresolvable stress could lead to generalised anxiety disorder, whereas 'one-off' traumatic events could cause post-traumatic stress disorder.

Managing and reducing stress

HOW CAN STRESS BE REDUCED?
There are really only two ways that stress can be reduced:

1 DEAL WITH THE CAUSES OF STRESS
Those strategies that focus on removing or coping with stressful *stimuli* or *situations* before they produce a stress reaction are known as '**problem-focused strategies**'. This is obviously the best way to deal with potential stress, but may not be possible since:

- there are a huge variety of sources for stress, it may therefore be impossible to deal with them all
- the individual may be unaware of the source of stress or may only realise after the stress reaction has occurred
- not all sources of stress can be avoided, some may be an inevitable part of living and working life, others may be mental worries that physical action cannot deal with. Problem-focused strategies become counter-productive under such conditions.

2 DEAL WITH THE EFFECTS OF STRESS
Those strategies that focus on removing or coping with stress *reactions* once they have occurred are known as '**emotion-focused strategies**'. This is the approach that most methods employ.

People use a variety of coping strategies in everyday life, however specific physiological and psychological techniques have also been developed to help manage stress that individuals feel unable to deal with sufficiently on their own. Most of these techniques are emotion-focused strategies but some aim to incorporate elements of problem-focused strategy as well.

NATURAL COPING STRATEGIES FOR STRESS
Appropriate behaviour – These range from dealing with the source of stress, e.g. time management planning and avoiding stressful situations, to natural behavioural reactions that combat its effects, e.g. rest and relaxation (holidays), laughter, arguments, exercise and sport.

Defence mechanisms – Freud would argue that many of the above natural stress reduction methods are in fact the products of ego defence mechanisms. Stress-related psychic energy can be given cathartic expression through displacement and sublimation, e.g. aggression towards scapegoats, laughter and physical exercise, or alternatively repressed into the unconscious and/or dissociated from consciousness through denial (which could lead to anxiety or even dissociative disorders if long-term stress was experienced).

Social support – individuals who perceive they have social support (e.g. reassurance, advice and practical aid) suffer less physiological stress effects than those without such support, e.g. those with no intimate friends (Brown and Harris, 1978) or partners (Tache et al, 1979).

EVALUATION
Natural coping strategies are not always sufficient on their own and some, e.g. arguments and aggression, may actually contribute towards further stress. Freudian defence mechanisms have not always been supported by empirical evidence and may be counter productive – only providing short-term solutions while creating long-term problems. Social support is significantly correlated with lower mortality rates, but causation is difficult to determine.

BIOLOGICAL TECHNIQUES FOR STRESS MANAGEMENT
Anti-stress drugs
Beta-blockers – act on the autonomic nervous system to reduce physiological stress arousal.
Anxiolytic drugs – minor tranquillisers, e.g. Valium, combat anxiety without causing sleepiness.
Anti-depressant drugs – less often used, but can be appropriate for severe anxiety.

Other drugs
Alcohol is an often sought remedy for stress, its sedative effects slow down neural and bodily functions and its effect on loosening inhibitions can lead to cathartic behaviour.

Biofeedback
Feedback signals on body processes can help control the adverse physiological effects of stress such as increased heart rate and blood pressure.

EVALUATION
Anti-anxiety drugs can cause psychological and physical dependence and other unpleasant side effects. Drugs are only short-term stress remedies that temporarily reduce its effects but may make dealing with its causes more difficult or even create further sources (especially alcohol).
Although there is debate over how it works, biofeedback can lower heart rate and blood pressure, but again it only treats the symptoms not causes of stress.

PSYCHOLOGICAL TECHNIQUES FOR STRESS MANAGEMENT
Therapy - *Stress inoculation training* (Meichenbaum, 1977) and *Hardiness training* (Kobasa, 1986) are both cognitive behavioural techniques designed to increase stress resistance or 'hardiness' by:

1 Analysing – Getting clients to learn to analyse sources and physical signs of stress.
2 Teaching coping strategies and techniques to combat stressful situations - e.g. relaxation, positive self-instructional statements and specific skills with stress inoculation therapy, or the re-living and reconstruction of stressful situations in hardiness training.
3 Changing behaviour – e.g. practising skills in simulated and real situations so a successful change is produced (with stress inoculation) or reinforcing a sense of control through performing manageable tasks (with hardiness training).

Mental state relaxation – Meditation and hypnosis (including self-hypnosis) reduce stress effects through mentally inducing relaxation.

EVALUATION
Cognitive behavioural therapies are effective although it is unsure whether the behavioural aspects (successfully dealing with a stressful situation) are more important than the cognitive ones (stress reducing statements and a sense of control). The techniques aim to deal with the source as well as the effects of stress and so are potentially more effective in the long term.
Meditation and hypnosis do not have the side effects and equipment needs of physiological methods but also focus on the effects and ignore causes.

Primary prevention and health education programmes

WHAT IS PRIMARY PREVENTION?

Primary prevention refers to activities that attempt to avoid disease and ill health by improving the health environment or human behaviour. The latter involves:

- **Prevention** – to stop the development of unhealthy behaviour (that which leads to a high risk of disease and ill health) *before* it occurs and to encourage health promoting behaviour from an early age.
- **Change** – to stop, reduce or alter unhealthy behaviour that has *already* developed but not yet triggered health problems, the less desirable but more common and easily employed of the two approaches.

Primary prevention that targets human behaviour can be attempted through:

- **Behaviour modification** – the attempt to directly change health-related behaviour through altering its reinforcement consequences. This may involve positive reinforcement (e.g. parental praise for children brushing their teeth) or punishment (e.g. making cigarettes more expensive to buy). However, since most aspects of health are generally regarded as matters of choice (in adults at least), the more voluntary method below is often used.
- **Attitude change** – the attempt to change the attitudes and beliefs that are presumed to underlie actions to create healthy, and prevent unhealthy, behaviour. This involves the provision of medical information that aims to inform people of the advantages and risks of certain actions and thus alter behaviour by providing choices that have a high probability of improving health. Such information could concern inherited disorders (genetic counselling), immunisation, and health-related behaviour, e.g. regarding hygiene, nutrition, exercise, substance use and activities that could lead to contagious infection, based on epidemiological and mortality rate studies of risk (Sarafino, 1994).

WHY IS PRIMARY PREVENTION DIFFICULT TO ACHIEVE?

- Behaviour modification often needs monitoring and rewards and punishments need to be of sufficient intensity and applied promptly for maximum effect, although this is not always possible.
- Changes in behaviour do not always last or produce changes in underlying attitudes since mere compliance, resentment, hostile attitudes and reactance may result from punishment and perceived control.
- Many people are not interested in changing their health-related behaviour or may not perceive the need to because they are currently healthy, still underestimate the risks to themselves if informed, and prefer the short-term pleasures of some unhealthy behaviours (immediate reinforcement) while being less influenced by the long-term disadvantages (punishment).
- Official sources of primary prevention may have a less powerful influence on attitudes and behaviour than the family or peer group.

CHANGE ATTITUDES → **PRIMARY PREVENTION** Changing health-related behaviour to prevent ill health ← **CHANGE BEHAVIOUR**

HEALTH EDUCATION PROGRAMMES

Health education programmes aim to transmit the information required for primary prevention (and sometimes secondary prevention to improve chances of early detection and treatment of health problems). The information provides *knowledge* about the positive and negative effects of health-related behaviour, health or social *skills*, and prompts or *reminders* for those who already know. Repeated prompts and reminders also help establish *social consensus* and so gradually change the norms of a society and encourage *conformity* to them.

Different methods have been attempted to convey the information in the most effective manner possible:

- **Mass communication** – e.g. using the mass media to transmit health messages via television, radio, newspapers etc. This has the advantage of reaching a wide number and variety of people but has a diffused impact.
- **Direct instruction** – e.g. targeting particular sections of the population at high risk and providing face-to-face instruction and training on specific health behaviour. This has a greater effect, perhaps because it is more individual (being specific to exact health needs and avoiding diffusion of responsibility effects) and involves greater opportunity for monitoring, evaluation and a degree of reinforcement.
- **Social role modelling** – e.g. encouraging parents to set healthy examples for children or using media celebrities as role models to establish norms and encourage identification. This increases attention to and imitation of behaviour according to social learning theory. However, role models have to be salient to the targets since they vary in their importance and appeal among different populations.
- **Use of emotion** – e.g. fear appeals that use frightening warnings of the effects of unhealthy behaviour to increase attention and healthy behaviour (possibly through negative reinforcement). Research shows fear appeals can work but that very high fear levels can sometimes interfere with processing the message, cause denial and only have short-term effects.

HEALTH EDUCATION PROGRAMMES FOR AIDS AND SMOKING

- Evans et al (1981) employed social learning principles in an attempt to inoculate students against social influences to smoke and provide coping skills to aid refusal by using films and posters to explain the effects of peer, family and media pressure and model ways of resisting. There was moderate success over 3 years in terms of reduced smoking and intentions to smoke in experimental compared to control groups (Gatchel et al, 1989).
- Change in sexual and drug-habit-related behaviour can be difficult because of the privacy and reinforcement pleasures involved. However, AIDS education targeted at gay men in American cities has produced 'the most profound modifications of personal health-related behaviours ever recorded' (according to Stall et al, 1988, quoted in Sarafino, 1994). There is a danger that by targeting populations, people will perceive that the threat only applies to certain groups, e.g. thinking AIDS is only a gay disease.
- Abraham and Sheeran (1994) report that health education programmes that provide social skills and assertiveness training for young people, e.g. practising dialogues relevant to purchasing and negotiating condom use, are self-empowerment techniques that may increase self-efficacy.

Health promotion and the health belief model

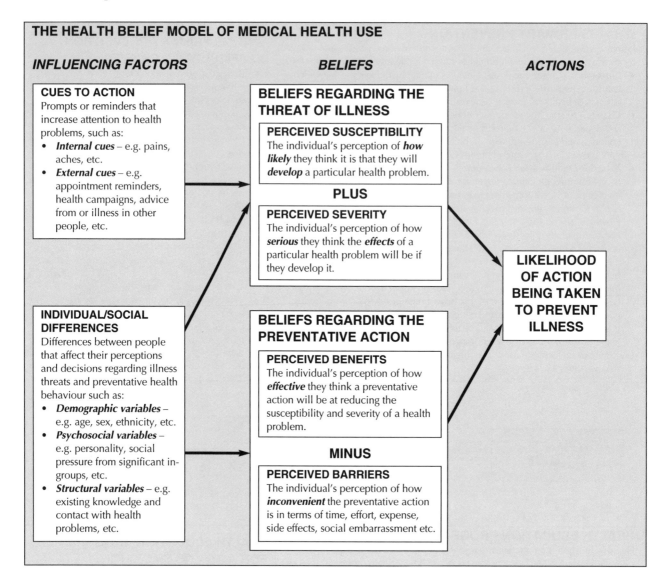

THE HEALTH BELIEF MODEL OF MEDICAL HEALTH USE

INFLUENCING FACTORS • *BELIEFS* • *ACTIONS*

CUES TO ACTION
Prompts or reminders that increase attention to health problems, such as:
- *Internal cues* – e.g. pains, aches, etc.
- *External cues* – e.g. appointment reminders, health campaigns, advice from or illness in other people, etc.

BELIEFS REGARDING THE THREAT OF ILLNESS

PERCEIVED SUSCEPTIBILITY
The individual's perception of *how likely* they think it is that they will *develop* a particular health problem.

PLUS

PERCEIVED SEVERITY
The individual's perception of how *serious* they think the *effects* of a particular health problem will be if they develop it.

INDIVIDUAL/SOCIAL DIFFERENCES
Differences between people that affect their perceptions and decisions regarding illness threats and preventative health behaviour such as:
- *Demographic variables* – e.g. age, sex, ethnicity, etc.
- *Psychosocial variables* – e.g. personality, social pressure from significant in-groups, etc.
- *Structural variables* – e.g. existing knowledge and contact with health problems, etc.

BELIEFS REGARDING THE PREVENTATIVE ACTION

PERCEIVED BENEFITS
The individual's perception of how *effective* they think a preventative action will be at reducing the susceptibility and severity of a health problem.

MINUS

PERCEIVED BARRIERS
The individual's perception of how *inconvenient* the preventative action is in terms of time, effort, expense, side effects, social embarrassment etc.

LIKELIHOOD OF ACTION BEING TAKEN TO PREVENT ILLNESS

THE HEALTH BELIEF MODEL
- The health belief model (Rosenstock, 1966, Becker and Rosenstock, 1984) helps explain and predict people's preventative health behaviour and compliance to medical advice. The model has undergone some elaboration over the years, for example by adding a general health motivation component – how important health in general is to the individual (not included above) – that has led some to argue that the model is increasingly hard to test.
- For example, the likelihood of people using a condom to prevent sexually transmitted diseases such as AIDS could depend upon factors such as:
  - How likely they think they are to acquire HIV and AIDS from unprotected sex with a particular individual.
  - How severe they believe the symptoms or risk of death from AIDS are.
  - How effective they think condoms are at preventing transmission of HIV.
  - How inconvenient they believe condoms are to use, e.g. in terms of reduced pleasure or remembering to carry them.
  - Whether they have been recently exposed to cues to action, e.g. AIDS awareness publicity campaigns or contact with those suffering from AIDS.
  - The nature of the person, e.g. their existing knowledge regarding AIDS or exposure to peer group social pressure or norms to use them.
- The health belief model has been applied to many preventative health behaviours and although each key variable does seem to be significantly correlated with the behaviour studied, they typically only account for around 10% of the variance in behaviour when combined (Marks et al, 2000).

USING THE HEALTH BELIEF MODEL IN HEALTH PROMOTION
By specifying the factors involved in why people do or do not follow health advice and behaviour, health promoters can work out how to better implement their interventions. For example, health education on a particular topic may benefit from targeting certain:
- Perceptions (e.g. by providing clear, accurate and up-to-date information on the prevalence and effects of certain health problems and the prevention methods available).
- Populations (e.g. some populations may be less willing to adopt health behaviour or respond to different techniques).
- Medical procedures (e.g. providing postcard reminders for screening tests).
- Barriers to use (e.g. by challenging social embarrassment or providing social skills to negotiate the use of condoms between sexual partners).

Health promotion and the theory of reasoned action

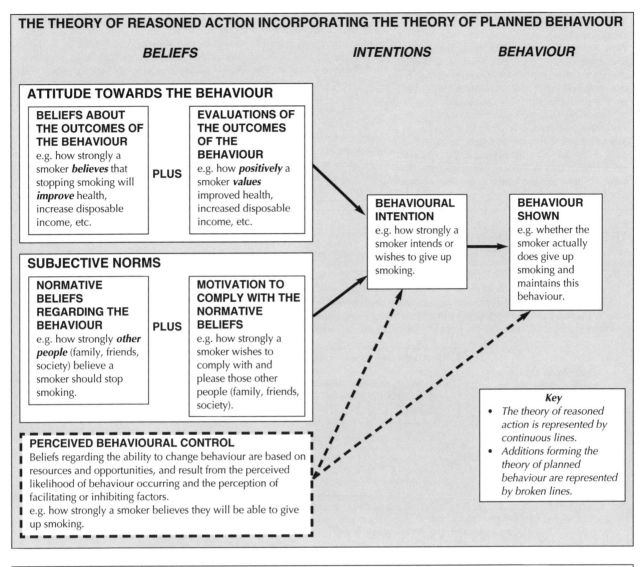

THE THEORY OF REASONED ACTION INCORPORATING THE THEORY OF PLANNED BEHAVIOUR

BELIEFS　　　　　　*INTENTIONS*　　　　*BEHAVIOUR*

ATTITUDE TOWARDS THE BEHAVIOUR

BELIEFS ABOUT THE OUTCOMES OF THE BEHAVIOUR
e.g. how strongly a smoker **believes** that stopping smoking will **improve** health, increase disposable income, etc.

PLUS

EVALUATIONS OF THE OUTCOMES OF THE BEHAVIOUR
e.g. how **positively** a smoker **values** improved health, increased disposable income, etc.

SUBJECTIVE NORMS

NORMATIVE BELIEFS REGARDING THE BEHAVIOUR
e.g. how strongly **other people** (family, friends, society) believe a smoker should stop smoking.

PLUS

MOTIVATION TO COMPLY WITH THE NORMATIVE BELIEFS
e.g. how strongly a smoker wishes to comply with and please those other people (family, friends, society).

PERCEIVED BEHAVIOURAL CONTROL
Beliefs regarding the ability to change behaviour are based on resources and opportunities, and result from the perceived likelihood of behaviour occurring and the perception of facilitating or inhibiting factors.
e.g. how strongly a smoker believes they will be able to give up smoking.

BEHAVIOURAL INTENTION
e.g. how strongly a smoker intends or wishes to give up smoking.

BEHAVIOUR SHOWN
e.g. whether the smoker actually does give up smoking and maintains this behaviour.

Key
- *The theory of reasoned action is represented by continuous lines.*
- *Additions forming the theory of planned behaviour are represented by broken lines.*

THE THEORY OF REASONED ACTION AND HEALTH

- The theory of reasoned action (Fishbein and Ajzen, 1975), later modified into the theory of planned behaviour (Ajzen, 1985, 1991), is another social cognition model that has been applied to health beliefs and behaviour.
- The theory suggests that health behaviours are based upon intentions, which are formed by a mixture of personal attitudes towards, and social pressure to adopt, a particular health behaviour. Based upon Bandura's (1977) work on self-efficacy, perceptions of the ability to actually implement behavioural changes are also important in explaining and predicting the likelihood that preventative health measures will be taken.
- Marks et al (2000) report two particularly relevant studies.
  - Rise (1992) used a questionnaire based upon the theory of reasoned action to test the behavioural intentions of over a thousand 17–19-year-old Norwegians to use a condom during their next intercourse. Both attitudes and subjective norms were significantly positively correlated with behaviour intentions (0.29 and 0.55 respectively). However, a variable not included in the theory of reasoned action, past behaviour (previous/habitual condom use), was even more significantly positively correlated (at 0.75). This indicates that the theory is incomplete in explaining health behaviour.
  - Conner and Sparks (1995) supported this conclusion, reporting that while the variables of the theory of reasoned action accounted for between 43% and 46% of the variance in the intention to perform health related behaviour, and those of the theory of planned behaviour accounted for up to 50% of the variance, there is still a good deal of behavioural intention unaccounted for by these models. In addition, it must be remembered that intentions to behave in a certain way only correlate between 0.45 and 0.62 with actual behaviour.

EVALUATION OF SOCIAL COGNITION MODELS OF HEALTH BEHAVIOUR

The health belief model, theory of reasoned action and theory of planned behaviour are all regarded as social cognition models that aim to predict health-related behaviour from an analysis of people's beliefs and attitudes. They have been shown to explain and predict health behaviour to varying degrees of precision, however they have also been criticised on a number of grounds:

- They assume that behaviour is rationally thought out and regulated and so ignore the emotional, irrational and habitual influences upon health behaviour.
- They cannot sufficiently measure and incorporate all of the variables that influence health behaviours. These variables may differ depending upon the health behaviour concerned.
- They underestimate the role of external physical and social factors that are unpredictable and act to counteract or facilitate behavioural intentions, e.g. the variations in the availability of cigarettes and condoms.
- The measurement and testing of attitudes and intentions is based upon self-report techniques, which can lack reliability and validity.

The concept and importance of work

THE CONCEPT OF WORK
What is work?
Work is difficult to define and is often contrasted with leisure (which is not much help since this is also difficult to define!). A variety of definitions have been offered throughout history. Economists tend to see work as paid employment and leisure as consumption, while Marxism tends to regard work as any productive, creative activity and leisure as free time to recover from work. Religion has looked upon work as alternatively a moral ideal (e.g. the Puritan Work Ethic of Max Weber) or God's punishment for Man's Original Sin, and leisure as frivolity or grateful reprieve respectively.

Definitions of work and their problems
- *Work as paid activity* – this neglects maintenance activity such as housework and childcare and, of course, unpaid voluntary work. The focus on pay as an extrinsic (external) motivation neglects the intrinsic gains (see below).
- *Work as obligation* – work is often perceived as involving a lack of choice and pleasure, a necessary activity to remain alive. However, people still continue working or return to work after becoming financially liberated (e.g. continuing work after retirement or winning the lottery) and enjoy their work.
- *Work as productive activity* – but this does not always distinguish the concept from leisure activities, which can also be productive, but not regarded as work.

THE IMPORTANCE OF WORK IN ADULT LIFE
Work serves a variety of very important functions involving, broadly speaking, the following individual and social ones:

INDIVIDUAL FUNCTIONS
Work is directly involved in satisfying a number of individual needs or goals, best represented by Maslow's (1954) hierarchy of needs. These needs range from necessary survival ones at the bottom of the hierarchy, to self-actualisation ones at the top. While the *economic, extrinsic function of work* to 'earn a living' (e.g. money) is necessary to satisfy the basic needs, the *intrinsic functions of work* satisfy needs higher up the hierarchy (although material wealth may act to facilitate the achievement of them).

Examples of Maslow's needs and the function and importance of work

Self-actualisation – the need to achieve one's full potential and to 'become everything that one is capable of becoming' (Maslow, 1943).
- Work can provide a sense of purpose, challenge, mastery, creativity, usefulness and meaningful achievement, or sufficient wealth to pursue such self-actualisation outside of work.

Esteem – the need to achieve the esteem and respect of others and of oneself.
- Work allows one's abilities to be proven to the self and others through achievement, promotion, positive feedback, the earning of wealth/resources/power and social status.

Love and belongingness – the need to give and receive affection and love, and to be accepted by and feel part of social groups.
- Work provides regular contact with groups beyond the family, the opportunity to develop friendships, intimate relationships and social skills, and social / emotional support, e.g. against stress. Argyle (1983) reports that contact with others is one of the most commonly reported sources of job satisfaction.

Safety – the need to feel protected from social or environmental threats, stable and secure from the unpredictable.
- Work may create a steady source of income, savings, insurance and pension to protect against threats and provide stability and security. It also provides structure, organisation, routine and predictability to life.

Physiological – the need for basic survival factors such as food, water, activity, rest, shelter, sex, etc.
- Work provides money/resources for the basic survival needs and acts as a major source of social stimulation and activity.

SOCIAL FUNCTIONS
- Work represents an important form of **social organisation** that reflects the *power structure*, *roles* and *norms* of a society. The organisation of work regulates and structures social interactions by providing individuals with *occupational* (doctor, teacher, accountant, salesperson, refuse collector, etc) and *power-based* (e.g. employer/employee, buyer/seller) **roles** and **status** within a society, and is thus an important source of **self-identity** and **self-esteem**.
- However, the social organisation of work means that individuals may not always be able to achieve their needs equally. According to Marxist theorists, rather than directly serving the needs of the individual, work in capitalistic societies may frequently benefit the rich. When work is determined by private ownership and possession of wealth and resources rather than ability, social classes are created and some members of society will have restricted access to certain jobs, identity and status. If work is a person's identity, then a salary means that identity is sold and may serve the purposes of others.
- The idea that work regulates social interactions and serves the power structures of society means that work may serve to maintain order and the status quo in society rather than individual needs – work is the best police!

Theories of work motivation

HERZBERG'S (1966) TWO-FACTOR THEORY

Herzberg argued that humans have two types of need, which means that dissatisfaction and satisfaction are created by two different sets of factors:

Motivator factors

- These factors result, according to Herzberg, from the particular human *need for psychological growth*.
- They include intrinsic aspects of the work itself, especially **responsibility** (which provides the opportunity and challenge for psychological growth), **achievement** (the attainment of growth) and **recognition** (the reinforcement of achievement).
- Herzberg argued that the *presence* of these 'motivators' would *produce satisfaction* in workers, but their *absence* would *not* necessarily lead to *dissatisfaction*.

Hygiene or context factors

- These factors result, according to Herzberg, from the *need* humans share with animals *to avoid pain*.
- They include extrinsic aspects of the job, such as salary, social and working conditions, especially company policy, administration and supervision.
- Herzberg argued that the positive *presence* of these factors would *not produce satisfaction* in workers but that insufficiency or problems regarding them would create *dissatisfaction* (because they represent sources of discomfort or 'pain' that humans wish to avoid).

Herzberg therefore suggested that companies could avoid worker dissatisfaction by only adequately providing hygiene factors but that worker satisfaction would require the presence of motivational factors.

EVALUATION

- Herzberg et al (1959) interviewed around 200 engineers and accountants in Pittsberg, USA, and asked them 'critical incident' questions. These involved recalling events that made them feel particularly good or bad about their work and how these incidents had affected their satisfaction, performance, work relations and general well–being. From a content analysis of the incidents, Herzberg et al found the factors that led to satisfaction were generally different from those that led to dissatisfaction.
- Herzberg et al's study has been criticised for its unrepresentative sample (other occupations, with different wages in different countries may be more motivated by hygiene factors like wages) and interviewer bias (interviews were conducted by researchers aware of Herzberg's need theory). Kline (1975) reports 9 supporting replications of Herzberg et al's study that, although also possibly suffering from interviewer bias, involved 16 different occupations and two other countries. Herzberg (1987) reported that his findings generalised well over many cultures but may not apply to some unskilled and poorly paid jobs.
- Studies of companies using Herzberg's factors for job enrichment report increased worker satisfaction and reduced labour turnover.
- Herzberg may have been right in emphasising salary as a hygiene rather than motivating factor. Harpaz (1989), for example, found that the majority of people in seven different countries reported that they would continue working if they won the lottery (although people do not always behave in reality as they say they would!).
- However, other research has indicated that Herzberg's hygiene factors such as salary and working conditions (e.g. relations with other workers) *are* important motivators and sources of satisfaction, while lack of 'motivators' like achievement and recognition *can* cause dissatisfaction.

HACKMAN & OLDHAM'S (1975, 1976) JOB CHARACTERISTICS MODEL

Hackman and Oldham identified five **core job characteristics** that lead to **critical psychological states** for **positive work outcomes**.

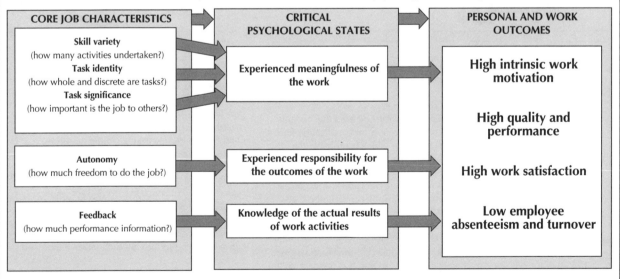

EVALUATION

Precisely defined concepts and job assessment – a *motivating potential score* can be calculated for any job by assessing it though employee questionnaires on dimensions for each core characteristic, then multiplying the autonomy score, the feedback score and the average of the skill variety / task identity / task significance scores (these latter three are weighted with less importance).

Identification of implementing concepts – the model has led to applied techniques for improving motivation, such as combining tasks (to provide skill variety), forming natural work units (to provide a meaningful sequence of tasks), allowing client contact (e.g. to increase variety, responsibility and feedback) or vertical loading (to give greater responsibility, self-supervision).

Individual differences – people differ in their need for growth, thus the model may be less successfully applied to some workers.

Personnel selection and assessment 1

METHODS OF SELECTING PERSONNEL
Selecting personnel involves first analysing the job requirements and then assessing candidates to find the right person for the job.

JOB ANALYSIS
Job analysis involves the systematic study of job requirements to provide a job description and/or person specification, and verifiable predictors (test samples or signs) to assess the suitability of candidates to perform the job.

JOB DESCRIPTIONS
A job description is arrived at through **task-orientated** job analysis. A detailed task-analysis is conducted to specify:
- *What* is actually *done* in a job (e.g. the organisation, motivation and supervision of workers in a manager's job, or building walls for a bricklayer's job).
- The *results* or end performance required from the job (e.g. the production of a certain amount of a product in a certain amount of time).
- Test *samples* of the job that candidates can be asked to perform to assess their suitability (e.g. candidates could be asked to lay some bricks or organise a work roster).

Evaluation
- Task analysis is more objective, specific, easily sampled and less prone to error with clearly defined tasks.
- Getting candidates to actually perform the job has face validity (but limited samples may be unrepresentative).
- Task analysis accepts that in some jobs people with different abilities can achieve the same results.
- However, task analysis is less suitable for jobs that are very complex, not easily defined, or changeable. Representative samples of the job may not be easily selected or there may be too many aspects to sample.

PERSON SPECIFICATIONS
A person specification is arrived at through **worker-orientated or functional** job analysis, to specify:
- The *behaviour, skills, knowledge and abilities* required to successfully perform a job (e.g. the intelligence, social or physical skills, relevant knowledge, personality and attitudes required for effective management or building).
- Test *signs* of the above qualities that candidates can be assessed for to measure their suitability for the job (e.g. scores on relevant ability, aptitude, personality and motivational tests, qualifications, past experience, etc.).

Evaluation
- Functional or worker analysis is more suitable for ill-defined or changeable jobs that require abilities that will generalise well over a variety of tasks or shifting situations and indicate potential for promotion.
- Methodologically, identifying required qualities for a job is difficult and often based on intuition, especially with new jobs. The qualities of current employees doing the same job may not actually reflect the job requirements (e.g. they may be over-qualified or inefficient).
- Measuring suitability using indirect testing methods raises problems of the reliability and validity of the tests.

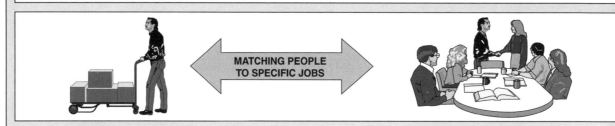

MATCHING PEOPLE TO SPECIFIC JOBS

INTERVIEWS
Selection interviews involve a verbal, face-to-face assessment of prospective candidates where employers ask questions, of varying specificity, in order to:
- elicit self-report data and signs of ability
- elaborate upon, verify or seek additional information from that already possessed (e.g. from personnel records, references and application forms).
Kline (1975) states 'It is ironic that the interview which is probably the least effective form of assessment is in fact the most widely used', and suggests:
- The interview method is so common since 'It is easy to give, needs no equipment, appears to need no specialised training and is a technique in which many people feel themselves exceptionally competent'. It also has 'considerable face validity'.
- Studies show that 'interviews are unreliable, hence invalid. Even when this unreliability can be reduced, as it sometimes can, there is still little evidence for their validity'. Magson (1926) found business interviewers' ratings of interviewees' intelligence only had a 0.16 correlation with the IQ test results. Hartog and Rhodes (1935) only found a 0.41 correlation between two civil service interview boards rating the same people.
- Interviews can be made more reliable and valid if interviewers are very specific about the qualities they are looking for, are trained to avoid sources of bias, make use of objective data, and use the interview to check and confirm facts or amplify the findings of psychological tests.
However, Huffcutt and Arthur's (1994) meta-analysis found that **structured** and **standardised** interviews produce a mean validity coefficient of 0.56.

Sources of bias in interviews
Interviewer biases – distortions of judgement and assessment may come from the interviewer's stereotypes, expectations and first impressions regarding the interviewee that may cause confirmation bias by asking certain questions and reacting in certain ways that support those opinions.
Pingitore et al (1994) showed interviewers were biased against overweight interviewees (especially female ones) when all other factors were kept constant, while Dougherty et al (1994) found interviewers reacted more positively towards candidates who looked good on paper (Baron and Byrne, 1997).
Interviewee biases – self-report and impression management may result in distorted self-presentation due to deception, socially desirable responding, problems with verbal expression or nervousness. Riggio and Throckmorton (1988) found that merely leaning forward, nodding and smiling could produce higher ratings from interviewers.

Personnel selection and assessment 2

THE USE OF PSYCHOMETRIC TESTS FOR RECRUITMENT, PROMOTION AND 'DEMOTION'

WHAT ARE PSYCHOMETRIC TESTS AND WHY ARE THEY USED?

A psychometric test is one that *measures* some aspect of a person's psychological functioning to provide a score that can then:

- Enable **comparisons** to be made with the scores of other people (some tests are standardised around a population average or norm, so scores can be more accurately compared).
- Enable **predictions** to be made concerning future behaviour and performance.

Psychometric tests are thus obviously of use for selection purposes to distinguish between individuals and to predict which will be the most suited to job requirements in terms of recruitment, promotion, redeployment and training potential.

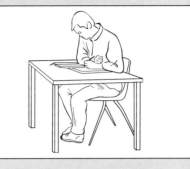

PERSONALITY TESTS

Personality refers to the **stable** and **distinctive characteristics** of a person that determine how they think, feel and behave in the environment. Certain characteristics possessed by certain individuals may match specific job requirements and thus be of use to employers as indicators of employee efficiency, job satisfaction and motivation.

Although personality tests can be idiographic (focusing in detail on unique aspects of the individual), in practice most selection tests are nomothetic – they seek to measure **types** or **traits** that are found in varying degrees across all individuals to facilitate comparison and aid selection.

Examples

Eysenck's EPQ (Eysenck Personality Questionnaire) measures 3 personality types as dimensions – introversion/extraversion, neuroticism/stability, and psychoticism.

Cattell's 16PF (Sixteen Personality Factor Questionnaire) claims to measure 16 basic source traits.

The Saville and Holdsworth consultancy firm's OPQ (Occupational Personality Questionnaire) measures 30 traits as dimensions with scoring norms from 4000 British managers.

Evaluation

- Nelson and Wedderburn (1988) report that personality tests on their own are only 2.5% better than chance at selecting personnel.
- Blinkhorn and Johnson's (1990) review of studies found that fewer than 10% of correlations between personality traits and job performance were statistically significant.
- Schmitt et al's (1984) meta-analysis found personality tests only had a mean (uncorrected) correlation with performance of 0.15.
- Although personality questionnaires aim to obscure the nature of the variables tested and include lie scales, they are still self-report measures prone to faults such as socially desirable responding.

APTITUDE TESTS

Aptitude refers to the capacity to acquire general or specific types of knowledge or skill (in contrast to attainment or achievement which refers to knowledge and skills already gained). Aptitude informs an employer of the individual's potential to benefit from training for jobs in general or certain tasks or occupations in particular.

IQ tests are thought to measure general cognitive aptitude by some. However, since different jobs require different knowledge and skills, many more specific aptitude tests have been developed. Aptitude scores are compared between candidates or with those currently performing the job successfully.

Examples

Wechsler's WAIS-R (Wechsler Adult Intelligence Scale, revised 1981) is a widely used test of general cognitive aptitude.

Bennet et al's (1962) DAT (Differential Aptitude Test) measures verbal, numerical, abstract and mechanical reasoning, clerical aptitude, space relations, spelling and grammar, based upon a normative sample of over 50,000 American high school students. More specific tests measure artistic, musical or creative aptitude.

Evaluation

- Ghiselli's (1966) review of tests from 1919 to 1964 found intelligence correlates at least 0.42 with training success for all jobs and 0.22 for professional success.
- Hunter and Hunter's (1984) meta-analysis found IQ tests correlated well (0.53) with later job success (except with very simple jobs).
- Quereshi (1972) found that while the DAT had high reliability and concurrent validity (it correlated well with other aptitude tests), it only had predictive validity for employment selection in terms of its average scores across all aptitudes. For example, the clerical items on their own did not predict who became clerks, but general aptitude was correlated with job success. This implies that the test does not 'differentiate' between jobs but measures intelligence.

EVALUATION OF PSYCHOMETRIC TESTS FOR RECRUITMENT/SELECTION

- If the tests are well constructed, they can be more objective and fairer for selection than the subjective views of an interviewer.
- The suitable use of psychometric testing may help efficient job selection and save employers and employees time, money, training effort and frustration, even if the benefits of some tests are only marginal.
- Researchers such as Mischel (1968) point out that behaviour may not always be consistently distinct across situations, meaning that personality tests may not be able to reliably and validly select between candidates and predict behaviour at work.
- In practice aptitude tests can never purely measure aptitude rather than attainment, since all tests assume some sort of past learning or experience with certain words, concepts, objects and situations. The difference between aptitude and attainment tests is therefore mainly one of intended use – to predict future learning potential and performance or reflect past learning respectively. Aptitude should not therefore be regarded as completely fixed (see IQ nature/nurture debate) and testers should guard against discrimination in terms of, for example, pre-existing levels of cultural knowledge to prevent cultural bias (see Gould, 1982).
- Many other important factors, unrelated to personality and aptitude, affect job performance and suitability, e.g. motivation and experience. Personality and aptitude tests are not generally better than qualifications at predicting vocational success.
- Since psychometric tests have various problems with their validity, reliability and standardisation, and may cause labelling and self-fulfilling prophecy, their strengths and limitations need to be properly understood by both employers and employees.

Leadership effectiveness

LEADERSHIP STYLES AND EFFECTIVENESS

Lewin, Lippitt and White (1939) researched the effects of autocratic, democratic and laissez-faire leadership styles on group behaviour.

AUTOCRATIC STYLE
- Leader organised activities, gave orders, praised or punished without explanation, was aloof and task-orientated.

Effects
- Leaders were liked less.
- Groups were leader-dependent, lacking in initiative and rebellious.
- Productivity was high when the leader was present, low when absent.

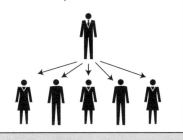

DEMOCRATIC STYLE
- Leader consulted and discussed plans with the group, factually explained praise or criticism and participated in the group.

Effects
- Leaders were liked more.
- Groups were friendly, group-centred and task-orientated.
- Productivity was fairly high whether the leader was present or not.

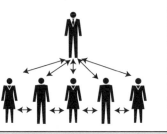

LAISSEZ-FAIRE STYLE
- Leader let the group organise and make decisions, did not initiate help or give praise or criticism, but helped if asked.

Effects
- Leaders liked, but not as leaders.
- Groups asked for more information but were play-orientated.
- Productivity was fairly low but increased if the leader was absent.

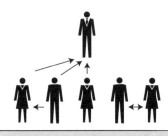

EVALUATION
- Lewin, Lippitt and White (1939) studied the effects of autocratic, democratic and laissez-faire leadership styles on group effectiveness and atmosphere in 10–11-year-old boys making models in after-school activity clubs. The same leadership styles were played by different confederates to control for personality effects. The groups of five were matched in intelligence, social behaviour (e.g. obedience, participation, quarrelling and physical energy, rated by teachers), social relations (i.e. patterns of friendship, rated by sociometric questionnaires), setting, equipment and activity interests. Over several months, 11 trained observers continually monitored all behaviour, interactions and conversations with an average inter-observer reliability of 0.84.
- There are problems with generalising the results from a limited sample of recreational activities in children, to the variety of work activities shown by adults in different occupations.

FIEDLER'S CONTINGENCY THEORY OF LEADERSHIP EFFECTIVENESS

Fiedler argued that the effectiveness of a particular type of leadership style was contingent (dependent) upon the degree of situational control or favourableness of leadership conditions.

Leadership style
Measured by the leader's rating on 18 dimensions of their least preferred co-worker (LPC):
- ***Task-orientated leaders*** – have low LPC scores which indicates more concern with directing and controlling workers to achieve tasks regardless of worker relations.
- ***Relationship-orientated leaders*** – have high LPC scores, indicating a willingness to maintain positive group relationships.

Situational control or favourableness
Rated on an 8-point scale depending upon the degree of:
- ***Leader/member relations*** – high when leaders and group members trust and like each other.
- ***Task structure*** – high when clarity of tasks is high and complexity of decisions is low.
- ***Position power*** – high when leader has support and control of rewards and punishments.

Fiedler found task-orientated leaders were most effective in very favourable or unfavourable situations, while relationship-orientated leaders were most suited to average situations.

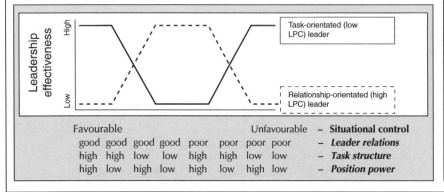

EVALUATION
- Fiedler's theory takes into account aspects of both leaders and situations and is thus a more realistic and practical theory of leadership.
- Fiedler conducted a number of studies in both the laboratory and field, e.g. on American Airforce bomber crews and board chairmen of small companies (Pennington, 1986) that supported his theory.
- The theory has received meta-analytic support from other researchers (e.g. Peters et al, 1985) from many studies conducted on a wide range of occupations.
- The assessment of leaders into just two main types is rather simplistic, although many other researchers have made similar distinctions, e.g. autocratic/democratic, task specialist/socio-emotional specialist etc.
- The least preferred co-worker scale has been criticised as an unreliable and invalid measure of leadership style.

Leadership, group dynamics and decision-making

GROUP INFLUENCES AND DECISION-MAKING

- Groups are collections of individuals who possess a shared set of interests or goals. In order to achieve their goals, groups have to make **decisions** and researchers have investigated how **group dynamics** (the identity, structure, communication and influence of group members) and **leadership** (the influence of a particular individual with the power to organise groups) can affect the decision-making process.

Research on groups in many applied settings (see, for example, jury decision-making) has revealed that social influences within the group (**intra-group** influence), such as those below, can significantly affect the efficiency and rationality of decision-making, often for the worse (see examples opposite).

- **Group polarisation** – (based on Stoner's risky-shift phenomenon) refers to the tendency for groups to make more extreme decisions than individuals.
- **Groupthink** – refers to 'a deterioration of mental efficiency, reality testing, and moral judgement that results from in-group pressures' (Janis, 1972).
- **Social loafing** – refers to individual group members putting in less effort than they would alone on a shared task (e.g. less thought into decision-making).
- **Evaluation-apprehension** – refers to the willingness and ability to perform or contribute to group tasks depending on the difficulty of the task and the degree to which the individual feels their contribution can be assessed. Contributions may decrease with increasing difficulty and anonymity.

DIFFERENTIATION OF ROLES WITHIN A GROUP

- This refers to the various identity, task and status roles within a group that represent the group's structure.
- Each role has norms (expected ways of behaving) that must be conformed to and effectively conducted if group goals are to be achieved.
- Group roles may be formally assigned by employers or emerge informally. Problems with decision-making and efficient performance are experienced if role identities, tasks and status are unclear or contested.
- Tuckman and Jensen (1977) suggested that newly formed groups go through five stages of forming, storming, norming, performing and adjourning. If conflicts over approaches, responsibilities and leadership are not properly resolved after the storming stage, then efficient group norms and decision-making may not develop to allow the group to direct its energy towards performing its task to reach its goals.

CONFORMITY

- Group pressure to agree with majority opinions in group decision-making may result in a lack of consideration for alternative, minority opinions and **group polarisation**. The group tends to make more extreme decisions (either riskier or more cautious) through a process of **social comparison** and ever-increasing conformity to the group's initial majority decision.
- The social pressure to make such comparisons and yield to the majority may result from uncertainty over the best decision and the need to refer to others for knowledge guidance (**informational social influence**) or from the need to behave in socially approved of ways (**normative social influence**) to avoid disapproval and sanctions from the group.

MERE PRESENCE OF OTHERS

- Can either inhibit or increase the performance and decision-making of groups depending upon the degree to which the individuals feel they can be individually evaluated and the complexity of the task or decision.
- If group members feel they cannot be individually evaluated, **social loafing** may occur due to a **diffusion of responsibility** between members.
- Group members may perform worse on difficult tasks than easy ones for a variety of reasons (see **Social facilitation and inhibition**), for example due to **evaluation apprehension** (not wanting to lose face by being wrong).
- These factors may account for the inferior brainstorming (the uncritical expression of suggestions and ideas to increase the number of options in decision-making) of groups compared to the same number of individuals working independently (Taylor et al, 1958) and the willingness of individuals to yield to other opinions.

GROUP COHESIVENESS

- Refers to how positive and co-operative group members are towards each other. Cohesiveness in groups increases when group goals are more clear and shared, when workers' attitudes and status are similar, and when groups are stable, small and (sometimes) under perceived threat.
- Cohesive groups are more likely to reach Tuckman and Jensen's performing stage and thus reach decisions more quickly.
- However, very highly cohesive and isolated groups can produce inferior decisions due to **groupthink** – 'the psychological drive for consensus at any cost that suppresses dissent and appraisal of alternatives in cohesive decision-making groups' (Janis, 1982).

MINORITY INFLUENCE

- Moscovici (1976) suggests that minorities can sometimes influence majority decision-making by conversion over a longer period of time, if they are consistent, committed, act on principle and are not overly rigid and unreasonable in their opinions and arguments.
- **Leaders** are the most important source of minority influence. Their greater levels of reward, coercive, legitimate, and often expert and referent power, mean they can exert considerable influence upon group decision-making.
- Effective leaders can monitor and organise groups to clarify goals and roles, **prevent social loafing**, create cohesiveness, but **avoid groupthink** and **polarisation** by encouraging alternative opinions.

The psychological implications of unemployment

THE CONCEPT OF UNEMPLOYMENT

Unemployment is a general term for not being in paid work. There may be different reasons for this, e.g. a person may:

- Have voluntarily left employment, e.g. due to illness or financial independence.
- Work without direct payment, e.g. a voluntary worker or houseperson.
- Not yet have entered employment, i.e. a school leaver yet to find a job.
- Have been made redundant, often losing employment on a sudden and involuntary basis.
- Have retired, usually losing employment with some advanced warning.

Unemployment has a number of psychological implications for those who experience it, particularly relating to people's ability to make productive use of their **increased 'leisure' time**. Although research into the general implications of unemployment has been conducted, there are often important differences in the effects depending upon the kind of unemployment experienced, e.g. between **redundancy** and **retirement**.

WHAT MIGHT THE PSYCHOLOGICAL IMPLICATIONS OF UNEMPLOYMENT BE?

Since work serves a variety of very important individual and social functions, unemployment may well be expected to have a number of effects based upon the deprivation of these:

INDIVIDUAL EFFECTS OF UNEMPLOYMENT

Examples of Maslow's needs and the psychological implications of unemployment

Self-actualisation – Unemployment may cause a loss of sense of purpose, challenge, mastery, creativity, usefulness and meaningful achievement, or a lack of wealth to pursue self-actualisation in increased leisure time.

Esteem – Unemployment may cause a loss of achievement, positive feedback, self-esteem, wealth/resources/power and social status. Leisure activities may not provide these factors.

Love and belongingness – The unemployed may lose regular contact with groups beyond the family, work friendships, and the stimulation and social / emotional support they provide. Much of the increased leisure time may not be shared with employed friends.

Safety and stability – Unemployment may cause a loss of steady income, savings and insurance leading to feelings of instability and insecurity. The unemployed may feel aimless and lack structure, routine and predictability in their lives. Increased 'leisure' activities may not provide the same externally provided structure as employment.

Physiological – The unemployed may lack money and thus have fewer sources of social stimulation/activity, becoming bored or apathetic. The unemployed may therefore lack the motivation and resources to make the best use of increased 'leisure' time.

SOCIAL EFFECTS OF UNEMPLOYMENT

- Since work employment represents an important source of **roles** and **status** within a society, unemployment may thus affect **self-identity** and **self-esteem**.
- The norms and expectations of people to be employed may result in the stigmatisation of the unemployed.
- Social beliefs in a 'just world' may cause the unemployed to be blamed for their unemployment (see **Just world hypothesis**).

THE EFFECTS OF UNEMPLOYMENT ON HEALTH

- Argyle (1989) reported that unemployment is associated with higher levels of ill health, mortality rates, mental disorder (e.g. depression), distress and suicide, that increase with its duration.

This may result from:

- A kind of bereavement response to loss of work.
- Learned helplessness or lack of rewards (learning theory).
- Social stigmatisation of the unemployed.
- Internal attributions of blame and negative self-image.

EVALUATION

INDIVIDUAL DIFFERENCES IN THE EFFECTS OF UNEMPLOYMENT

Unemployment does not have universal effects, e.g.:

- Individuals adjust better to unemployment if they have time-structuring hobbies, other sources of non-work identity, financial security, good health, a lack of dependants, social support and strong interests outside of work or can maintain some kind of continuity with it.
- Warr (1984) found 27% of 954 British unemployed people reported a decrease in health, but 11% reported an increase (Gross, 1996). Some studies have failed to find negative effects of unemployment on mental or physical health.

DIFFERENCES BETWEEN RETIREMENT AND REDUNDANCY

Different types of unemployment may have different effects, e.g.:

- Kelvin and Jarrett (1985) found involuntary redundancy led to shock, optimism, pessimism then fatalism, while Atchley (1985) found planned retirement led to euphoria, disenchantment, reorientation and stability.
- Argyle (1989) reports that, compared to the redundant, the retired are generally happier, in better health, and can make better use of their leisure time (since, for example, they do not have to seek employment, feel they have earned their leisure time and are not made to feel socially guilty).

Stress at work

WHY STUDY STRESS AT WORK?
According to Frese (1998) 'Work is interesting because it can contribute not only to well-being (consider the fact that depressed unemployed people become well again, when they find a job) but also to ill health.... Stress at work is a major factor contributing to ill health, to human suffering and to productivity loss. Rosch and Pelletier (1989) have estimated the costs of stress at work to be US$150 billion in the USA because of increased absenteeism, diminished productivity, compensation claims, health insurance and medical expenses.'

WHAT CAUSES STRESS AT WORK?
Many *physical*, *organisational* and *social* factors in the workplace can become sources of stress, usually exerting a relatively *long-term*, *stable* and *chronic* influence. Work overload or underload, lack of control, role ambiguity or conflict, job insecurity or poor interpersonal relations at work may all contribute to distress, ill health and eventual burnout (physical, emotional and mental/attitudinal exhaustion, depersonalisation, and perceived inadequacy/low personal accomplishment).

WORK OVERLOAD/UNDERLOAD
Work overload or underload refers to the *demands* of a job in terms of its *workload*, *complexity* and *responsibilities*.
Work overload can be:
- *Quantitative* (too much to do in too little time), or
- *Qualitative* (the work itself is too demanding on cognitive and emotional abilities, e.g. requiring high levels of concentration, complexity or responsibility).

Stress often depends upon individuals perceiving a mismatch between the demands of the situation and their ability to cope with it, but not always. Work underload can also be:
- *Quantitative* (too little work to do in too much time), or
- *Qualitative* (the work itself is too undemanding on cognitive and emotional abilities, e.g. requiring too little concentration, complexity or responsibility).

The above factors may lead to a number of distressing physical, emotional and cognitive effects, e.g. exhaustion, frustration, fear, resentment, feelings of inadequacy, boredom, uselessness and low self-esteem.

Research evidence
Haynes and Feinleib (1980) compared working women, who had been employed outside the home for more than half their adult years, with housewives and men. They found that working women with children (high family and work demand) were more likely to develop coronary heart disease (CHD) – a tendency that increased with the number of children – whereas the incidence of CHD actually decreased with more children for housewives (cited in Gatchel et al, 1989).

CONTROL
Control or job autonomy refers to the level of control workers have over the speed, nature and conditions of work. Control increases as the power to make work decisions and alter work conditions increases.
Control can cause stress if:
- There is far too little job control – the inability to control work schedules, deadlines, the pace of work or the organisation of work tasks is a major cause of stress. Workers with little control at the bottom of organisational hierarchies may therefore suffer the most ill health from stress.
- There is far too much job control – (see **Complexity and responsibility work overload**). Very high levels of control can also be stressful if decision responsibility and importance is extremely high and many choices are available, which may explain executive stress in the highest-ranking managers.

Feelings of control are important in increasing the perception that one has an ability to cope that is sufficient to match the demands of the situation.

Research evidence
Marmot et al (1997) found civil service clerical and office support employees on the lowest grades were four times more likely to die of a heart attack than those on the most senior grades. They were also more likely to suffer from cancers, strokes and gastrointestinal disorders (cited in Eysenck and Flanagan, 2000). Marmot et al identified lower levels of control triggering greater stress as the most important influencing factor.

SPECIFICALLY STRESSFUL OCCUPATIONS
The job strain model
Karasek et al (1982) argues that a **combination** of **low levels of control** and **excessive workload** create **job strain**, which is particularly associated with *high levels* of job-related stress. An analysis of specifically stressful occupations reveals that job strain does result from a combination of work overload and low control.
- Medical personnel such as doctors and nurses have heavy workloads, high levels of responsibility and exposure to suffering, and are required to maintain high levels of concentration over many hours. Control is often lacking, particularly with regard to patient admissions (work rate) and variety of cases (work complexity) in accident and emergency departments, or relating to the ability to improve health in terminal patients.
- 'Production line workers' in factories or the catering industry (e.g. cooks and waiting personnel) may also be subjected to high workloads that that they are unable to control, such as machinery pace or influx of customer demands.

Research evidence
- Wolfgang (1988, cited in Cox, 2000), using self-report questionnaires, found the highest levels of stress to be among nurses.
- Karasek et al (1979, cited in Huczynski and Buchanan, 1991) surveyed American and Swedish workers from a variety of occupations using questionnaires and found that stress was strongly associated with high workload and low job discretion (control) over how the work was done. Those in high-stress jobs with these characteristics included assembly workers, nurses' aids and orderlies, and telephone operators. The main symptoms were exhaustion, sleep problems, depression and anxiety, with a strong link between work stress and the consumption of tranquillisers and sleeping pills.
- Karasek et al (1981) found the job strain model predicted cardiovascular disease and mortality in Swedish workers.
- Theorell et al (1985, cited in Gatchel et al, 1989) reported 'greater systolic blood pressure elevations among those in high demand-low control occupations (e.g. waiters, drivers and cooks) than among those in more controllable or less demanding settings'.

Personal space

WHAT IS PERSONAL SPACE?

Personal space refers to the *social boundaries* surrounding a person's body that regulate *how closely interpersonal interactions are conducted*. The boundaries determine *how comfortable* individuals feel about approaching, and being approached by, *other people* at *different distances*. Personal space varies according to the:

- nature of those interacted with
- nature of the individual
- purpose of the interaction
- part of body/direction of approach.

HALL'S FOUR ZONES OF PERSONAL SPACE

Hall (1963, 1966) identified four zones of personal space based upon a white American sample:

- **Intimate distance** (0 to 18 inches / 0 to .5 metres) – normally reserved for emotionally intimate relationships involving contact (i.e. comforting or sexual), although norm/rule governed (e.g. sport or medically related) or norm/rule breaking (e.g. argument or violence related) interactions also involve this degree of proximity and contact. This distance allows the communication of very detailed and discrete sensory information.
- **Personal distance** (18 inches to 4 feet / .5 to 1.25 metres) – normally allowed for friends in everyday conversation. Allows detailed and fairly discrete communication via verbal, visual and sometimes tactile means.
- **Social distance** (4 to 12 feet / 1.25 to 4 metres) – usually for more formal or unfamiliar relationships or interactions. Allows visual scanning of whole body posture.
- **Public distance** (12 to 25 feet / 4 to 8 metres) – for very formal (e.g. public speaking) or defensive interactions. Requires exaggerated verbal and non-verbal communication.

INDIVIDUAL DIFFERENCES IN PERSONAL SPACE

- **Degree of liking/attraction** – physical proximity appears to increase in parallel with the emotional closeness, attraction, and self-disclosure of interpersonal relationships. Thus people feel more comfortable at close proximity with family and partners than friends, who in turn are allowed closer than casual acquaintances, disliked others, etc. Conversely hostility and dislike increases interpersonal distance.
- **Status** – the greater the status or rank difference between adults the greater the interpersonal distance between them.
- **Personality** – violent criminals appear to need greater personal space, especially to the front and back. Mentally disturbed individuals show greater variation in personal space. Extraverts appear to have smaller personal spaces than anxious individuals.
- **Gender** – females show closer interactions with females, while men maintain greater personal space zones with other men, and tend to show more discomfort when it is invaded.
- **Age** – personal space increases with age until the early teens.

CULTURAL DIFFERENCES IN PERSONAL SPACE

Hall (1966) suggested that cultures differ in their norms of personal space so that 'contact cultures' (e.g. Arabic and Mediterranean) show closer proximity in personal and social space zones than 'non-contact cultures' (e.g. white Northern Europeans and Americans). Watson and Graves (1966) found such differences in personal space between American and Arabic participants, which may make interpersonal contact between the two somewhat uncomfortable, however research is complicated by many sub-cultural norms and differences.

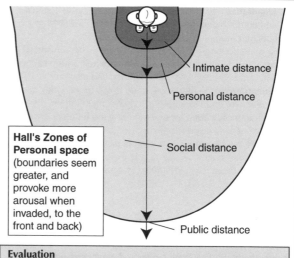

Hall's Zones of Personal space (boundaries seem greater, and provoke more arousal when invaded, to the front and back)

Intimate distance

Personal distance

Social distance

Public distance

Evaluation

There is a nature/nurture debate over what causes such differences in personal space.

- Age and cultural differences seem to imply a degree of environmental learning of what distances are appropriate.
- Ethologists and evolutionary theorists, however, would point out the universal existence of some form of personal space in humans, its presence in some other species and its survival functions (e.g. defence and communication).

THE CONSEQUENCES OF INVASION OF PERSONAL SPACE

Many studies have illustrated the effects of personal space invasion, e.g.:

- Felipe and Sommer (1966) had a female researcher sit at various distances from female subjects who sat on their own at a table in a library. When the subjects' intimate zone of personal space was invaded (without actual contact) they were observed to build barriers of books between themselves and the intruder, to turn or lean away from them and were significantly more likely than control subjects (who sat completely alone) to leave within 10 minutes.
- Sommer (1969) reported similar signs of discomfort from personal space invasion in different locations (e.g. park benches) and with different samples (e.g. men and mentally disordered patients).
- Middlemist et al (1976) suggested that personal space invasion increases physiological tension or arousal. By observing and timing men in public urinals (via periscope from an adjacent toilet stall) they found signs of this in terms of delayed onset, but faster completion, of micturation with a confederate standing in the next urinal compared to two away or when alone (Pennington, 1986).

Evaluation

There are a number of practical and ethical methodological difficulties in researching personal space and the effects of invading it.

- Field studies sometimes lack control over all the variables and the accuracy of recorded data.
- Laboratory studies and self-report data are more controlled but have their own methodological problems. Physiological responses can be recorded (e.g. through galvanic skin conductance) but such measures show a lack of reliability across subjects and thus validity as measures of arousal or anxiety.
- There are also ethical problems in invading personal space or privacy and causing discomfort and worry.

Territory

WHAT IS A TERRITORY?

Unlike personal space, a territory refers to a *relatively fixed geographical area* that is:

- Usually larger than one's personal space, but also provides a sense of ownership and privacy
- Often *habitually* used by an individual or group.
- Often visibly **marked out** through **personalisation** (e.g. decoration, signs or personal belongings) to establish **boundaries** and **ownership**.
- **Defended** against intrusion by others with varying degrees of effort.

ALTMAN'S (1975) THREE TYPES OF HUMAN TERRITORY

- **Primary territory** – e.g. homes, private offices. Primary territories concern our primary groups (e.g. family), are the most habitually occupied, and are the most important for privacy regulation, self-identity and self-esteem. They therefore have the most clear boundary markers and personalisation, invoke the strongest feelings of ownership, and will be the most vigorously defended from intruders. Individuals have the most control over primary territories, especially regarding others' access, and societies have official legislation to reinforce a citizen's rights regarding them.
- **Secondary territory** – e.g. shared apartment entry halls, classroom seats, local pubs where one is a 'regular' and other semi-public areas. Secondary territories are used on a regular basis but for variable lengths of time and provide moderate levels of control, privacy and sense of ownership. Access and defence is mostly governed by social norms.
- **Public territory** – e.g. seats on a train, in a restaurant or library, and places on a beach. Public territories are occupied less regularly and for limited periods of time. Temporary markers, e.g. bags, coats and beach towels, may be used to indicate occupancy and boundaries. However, the levels of control, privacy and ownership are fairly weak.

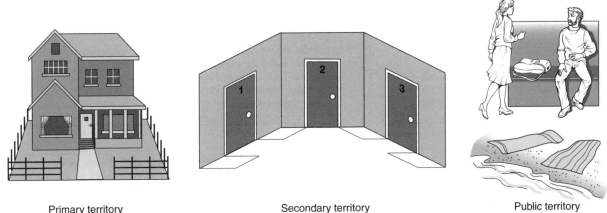

Primary territory   Secondary territory   Public territory

THE FUNCTIONS OF TERRITORY

THE ORIGINS OF TERRITORIALITY

Research on the acquisition, marking and defence of territories originated from ethological and evolutionary studies of non-human animal behaviour. Many species expend considerable time and effort upon establishing territories for vital food, protection and mating survival purposes, which led researchers such as Ardrey (1966) to suggest that humans too have evolved a territorial instinct to become attached to and defend geographical areas. Certainly many wars have been fought over territory for the resources and space they contain, however psychologists have also been interested in the possible *psychological functions* of territorial behaviour in humans.

SOCIAL ORGANISATION

Altman (1975) suggested that territories, once established, regulate social interactions with others and actually serve to reduce further social conflict and aggression. The marking of boundaries and personalisation serves to communicate ownership and establish norms of behaviour for different geographical locations.

Territories are important sources of self and group identity and esteem, which also influences social organisation (e.g. social class) and interaction between members of a society.

Evaluation

- Sundstrom and Altman (1974) found that the establishment of stable territories among institutionalised boys, especially the dominant ones, reduced the amount of further conflict between them.
- The establishment of favourable territories based on dominance or wealth may reduce conflict in the short term, but represent long-term sources of dissatisfaction and inter-group conflict.

PRIVACY REGULATION

Altman (1975) also suggested that territorial behaviour, particularly relating to primary territory, served to regulate privacy levels. Privacy refers to the optimal level of social and environmental stimulation received or sought, for example, in terms of the degree of noise, interaction or information disclosure desired with others. Too much or too little privacy can be psychologically distressing, so establishing and controlling the access to territories is an important means of adjusting to, and coping with, the environment.

Evaluation

- The above functions of privacy are revealed by the negative effects of territory invasion (e.g. burglary), lack of privacy (e.g. in hospitals and open-plan offices) and social isolation (too much privacy).
- Cross-cultural differences are found in the degree of communal sharing of primary territories and in the forms of privacy and territorial behaviour shown, but the need for a certain level of privacy seems universal.

Architectural effects on communication and residential satisfaction

ARCHITECTURE AND RESIDENTIAL SATISFACTION

ARCHITECTURAL VARIABLES
Generally speaking research has found that residential satisfaction is most associated with:

Physical functionality
- *Size* – for adequate personal space in rooms (particularly living/dining rooms) and storage. Some garden space is preferred.
- *Repair* – i.e. working heating / plumbing.
- *Location* – in terms of access to workplace, shops, schools etc. and noise levels.

Social functionality
- *Optimal privacy* – detached, single-family homes are most preferred in the USA and Britain (Cooper, 1972) probably because they provide greater control over privacy levels (Cave, 1998).
- *Social communication* – associated semi-private or secondary territories nearby.
- *Security* – for possessions and personal safety as well as low fear of crime.

Aesthetic appeal
- *Attractiveness* – of architecture, repair and location, although this depends to a greater extent on mediating variables, e.g. needs.

MEDIATING VARIABLES
Needs
Krupat (1985), based on work by Zeisel (1975), has argued that residential satisfaction is dependent upon the degree to which six common needs are satisfied by architecture:
- *Security* – the need to feel safe.
- *Clarity* – for ease of navigation.
- *Convenience* – for optimal access to resources.
- *Social interaction* – for stimulation and support.
- *Privacy* – to regulate stimulation.
- *Identity* – for social recognition and status.

However, needs vary according to:

Hierarchical demands –
Maslow (1970) argues security needs have to be met before identity needs.

Individual / cultural preferences –
e.g. in what locations or architectural features are perceived as important or attractive, and how space is used.

EFFECTS
Research has shown that architectural factors are associated with:

Overall life satisfaction – Rent and Rent (1978) found that overall life satisfaction was associated with liking one's residence.

Physical / mental health – Duvall and Booth (1978) found poor housing was associated with greater problems in physical and mental health (Bell et al, 1990).

However, it is important to remember such findings are correlational, so cause and effect is difficult to determine, e.g. those with poorer health may have been less able to work and thus afford better housing.

Sociopetal arrangement

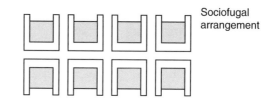

Sociofugal arrangement

ARCHITECTURE AND COMMUNICATION
When Winston Churchill said 'we shape our buildings, and thereafter our buildings shape us' he was referring to his belief that the shape of the House of Commons, with its two sets of opposing seating, had influenced British politics to a certain extent through its confrontational effect on communication (Ornstein and Carstensen, 1991).

Although the extent of architectural influences upon political behaviour is open to question, environmental psychologists have found that the architectural design of buildings and rooms does affect the degree of social communication and interaction shown.

- **Sociopetal architecture** – brings people together and encourages social communication by promoting face-to-face interactions. Examples include shared, communal or semi-private meeting spaces, especially those that are centrally located, or close, inward-facing seating.
- **Sociofugal architecture** – keeps people apart and encourages social isolation, separateness and lack of eye-contact by orientating individuals away from each other. Examples include buildings with a lack of shared communal space, or with such spaces located in out-of-the-way places or so open and public that they are regarded as no man's land. Fixed, parallel or outward-facing seating arrangements also discourage communication.

Appropriate levels of social communication, interaction and neighbourhood friendship formation have been consistently reported as major influences upon a sense of community and residential satisfaction in interviews and surveys.

Studies of architecture, communication and residential satisfaction
- Jacobs (1961) described how social communication, neighbour and extended family friendships, sense of community and identity, social support, and neighbourhood satisfaction were all higher in certain areas regarded as 'slums' than in most high-rise housing projects. This was probably in part due to the prevalence of semi-public or secondary territories in the former compared to the latter architectural environments.
- Fried (1963) reported that members of Boston's West End community were so attached to the area that many suffered symptoms of grief, depression and physical illness after it was destroyed and rebuilt, and they were re-housed (Bell et al, 1990).
- Sommer (1969) in 'Personal Space: the behavioural basis of design' reported that re-arranging the furniture in an old people's hospital ward from sociofugal to sociopetal formations increased 'brief interactions' by 55% and 'sustained interactions' by 69% (Hewstone et al, 1996).
- Howell et al (1976) found that a central location of a lounge near entrances or on main hallways encouraged greater social use of it compared to more distant locations, probably due to its greater access and social ease of visiting and leaving it (Hogg and Vaughan, 1995).
- Brolin (1972) illustrated how the Indian city of Chantigarh in the Punjab, that was built according to the Western architectural design assumptions of Le Corbusier, was not suited to the culture of its residents in terms of city or residential house layout. Social communication with relatives in the city was inhibited, parks were not used, and the design of rooms made traditional sleeping, eating and entertaining arrangements awkward (Krupat, 1985).

Defensible space, crime and residential satisfaction

DEFENSIBLE SPACE AND ITS EFFECTS

Oscar Newman (1972) in his book 'Defensible Space: Crime Prevention through Urban Design' suggested that defensible space is a **clearly marked** or bounded **semi-private area** or secondary territory that **appears to belong** to someone and allows **visual surveillance**.

Newman proposed that defensible space invokes 'latent territoriality and a sense of community in the inhabitants' for an area, which encourages a sense of ownership and responsibility. Crime will therefore be inhibited due to increased:

- **territorial behaviour**, such as surveillance and defence by residents.
- **use of the space**, leading to greater recognition of residents, intruders and normal behaviour, social cohesion, and thus ability to intervene.
- **deterrence** due to perception by criminals that the area is watched and actively guarded.

Newman argues that residential areas lacking in defensible space will suffer from more crime and fear of crime, and less residential satisfaction, than properties whose physical architectural design creates such spaces.

Evaluation

- Studies of the effect of defensible space upon crime levels have received some support, although the results have sometimes been inconsistent and many studies have failed to exactly identify which factors produce the changes.
- There are many strong influences upon residential crime levels apart from defensible space, which itself seems to have variable effects across different cultures and subcultures (Taylor et al, 1980). This has led researchers such as Merry (1981a) to concluded that defensible space is a necessary but not sufficient condition for crime reduction.

HOW CAN DEFENSIBLE SPACE BE DESIGNED?

Architectural adjustments should be made to:

1 Increase residents' care over semi-private or secondary territories in their environment through:
- Providing boundary markers to indicate zones of territorial influence and privacy to residents and outsiders, e.g. using fences and paving changes.
- Allocating responsibility for zones to residents, e.g. by sub-dividing areas adjacent to particular residences / primary territories.
- Improving the image and individuality of properties to increase identification and pride, e.g. by regular maintenance, improving appearance or providing more individual decoration.

2 Increase residents' surveillance ability over outside and inside secondary territories by:
- Exposing entrances and communal areas to greater and unobstructed view, e.g. providing overlooking windows, orientating them towards public scrutiny from the roads, designing outdoor balconies and stairwells, and improving lighting.
- Restricting entryways, throughways and number of residents per property to encourage a sense of community and to identify intruders more easily.

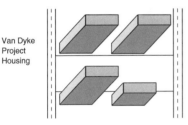

Van Dyke
Project
Housing

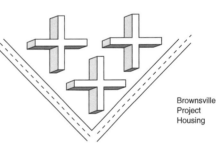

Brownsville
Project
Housing

EXAMPLES OF GOOD AND BAD PRACTICE IN ARCHITECTURAL DESIGN AND DEFENSIBLE SPACE

THE PRUITT-IGOE PROJECT

Yancey (1971) studied the Pruitt-Igoe housing project in St Louis, USA, which was built in 1954 for poor urban families relocated from 'slum' areas. It consisted of 43, 11-storey blocks housing 12,000 people. The blocks were designed so there would be no 'wasted space' but in effect the large population, long narrow corridors, secluded stairwells, and over-large public open spaces, resulted in:

- A lack of sociopetal and semi-private areas to socialise in, causing lack of recognition, isolation and anonymity.
- Problems with surveillance and control over intruders and children.
- Discontent with the neighbourhood.
- High levels of crime, drug abuse, vandalism and rape.

Sixteen years after it was built almost two-thirds of the blocks were uninhabited and two years after this all were demolished.

THE VAN DYKE PROJECT

Newman (1972) studied crime in two housing projects in New York. The Brownsville project (built in 1947) consisted of 3- to 6-storey buildings containing fewer families in each, with reasonable surveillance of stairways, smaller outside areas, and entrances that were mostly orientated to face the road.

The Van Dyke project (built in 1955) had 76% of its population housed in 14-storey buildings, with entrances serving over 100 families that opened onto much larger public areas on the interior of the project.

Although the total number and type of residents were roughly similar, crime in the Van Dyke project was 66% higher, with 2.5 times more robberies, and greater maintenance repair costs due to vandalism, than the Brownsville project (Krupat, 1985).

FOWLER ET AL (1979)

Fowler et al implemented physical and social changes to increase defensible space in a housing project in Hartford, Connecticut, USA, by creating cul-de-sacs to reduce through traffic and increase surveillance, visual entrances to the estate to mark boundaries, and forming neighbourhood organisations to foster a sense of community.

Residents reported feeling safer, were more likely to recognise strangers and had fewer burglaries than other similar projects.

PERKINS ET AL (1993)

Studied 48 London street blocks in detail comparing crime rates with defensible space characteristics. They found physical features of the built environment such as wide streets, with obstructed views and non-residential buildings, were better predictors of higher crime rates than the demographic nature (e.g. age, income) of the residents, their watchfulness or the dilapidation of their property (Hewstone et al, 1996).

Sources of environmental stress and their effects on behaviour

NOISE AND ITS EFFECTS

ENVIRONMENTAL NOISE
Noise can be defined as unwanted sound that creates a negative affective response (Baron, 1984). Generally research shows sound is evaluated as unpleasant and a source of stress if it is:
- **Loud** – daytime sound above 60 decibels can become annoying and inconvenient, and there are legal duration limits beyond 90 decibels.
- **Unpredictable** – random or erratic sound distracts attention and is harder to habituate to than constant or regular sound.

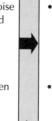

MEDIATING VARIABLES
The following influence noise effects:
- **Context** – sound may be perceived as noise depending upon context and background levels, e.g. in a disco, library or when sleeping. Noise irritates more if it seems unnecessary or if made without respect for others.
- **Control** – noise emitted by oneself or even under one's perceived control has fewer negative effects.
- **Individual differences** – some people are more noise-sensitive than others. Around 30% of variability in the response to noise is accounted for by people's attitudes (Tracor, 1971, cited by Cave, 1998), which may result from their perception of risk or experience of negative noise effects.

EFFECTS
Noise has been associated with:
- **Health problems** – e.g. hearing loss and an increased risk of immune system suppression, hypertension, cardiovascular disease, fatal strokes, stomach ulceration, and mental health problems/psychiatric admissions.
- **Disturbed learning and performance** – e.g. in occupational and educational task achievement and reading ability.
- **Anti-social behaviour** – e.g. in terms of increased aggression when provoked due to greater frustration and less social interaction, inter-personal attraction and helping behaviour.

EVALUATION
There is much research evidence for the negative effects of noise as a stressor, however the results of studies conducted in the environment rather than laboratory are often difficult to assess since:
- The effects are mediated by many different variables, which makes field study results on airport or motorway noise complex to interpret.
- All of the proposed effects can themselves generate additional stress, so it is difficult to evaluate the degree of influence of noise itself.
- The effects of noise can influence the mediating variables and thus the perception further noise.
- Correlation studies are open to doubt over cause and effect, e.g. rather than noise causing mental disorder, those with mental problems may be more sensitive to, or irritated by, noise.

Glass et al (1969) studied types, mediating variables and effects of noise as a stressor in the laboratory.

GLASS, SINGER AND FRIEDMAN (1969)
Participants were first asked to work for 30 minutes on simple numerical and verbal tasks while being exposed to:
- No noise, *soft* noise or *loud* (108-decibel) noise.

However, the experimenters also manipulated:
- Whether the noise was *predictable* or *unpredictable* (random).
- Whether the noise was *controllable* by pressing a button (that they were asked not to do if possible) or *uncontrollable*.

The noise had little immediate effect on the performance of the tasks and the physiological arousal provoked by the noise (measured via electrodes) decreased somewhat as the participants managed to adapt. However, when the participants were then taken to a quiet room and given four puzzles (two of which were insoluble) and a proof-reading task, those exposed to the *loud, unpredictable* and *uncontrollable* noise showed the greatest *stress after-effect* on *performance*. They showed least persistence on the puzzles (indicating increased frustration) and most errors in proof-reading (Hogg and Vaughan, 1995). Other studies have supported the stressful effects of lack of control and predictability.

TEMPERATURE
Research has found many links between environmental weather conditions or laboratory manipulated temperature and negative thoughts, feelings and behaviour. In particular uncomfortable:
- High temperatures and humidity have been associated with greater arousal and frustration levels that increase the likelihood of anti-social behaviour, e.g. aggression, riots, crime and reduced helping behaviour.
- High or low temperatures have been associated with increased rates of illness, e.g. coronary heart disease, or colds in winter and allergies in summer, that themselves increase stress levels.

Evaluation
Studying the effects of natural weather conditions upon behaviour can be difficult because of the many variables involved, e.g.:
- Increased vulnerability to illness in winter could result from changes in temperature, light levels (seasonal affective disorder) or increased indoor activity.
- Aggression shows a curvilinear but complex relationship with temperature such that extremes may increase aggressive thoughts and feelings but lower aggressive behaviour. Cold and snowy weather can sometimes actually increase co-operation, while hot, dry winds have been linked with greater suicide, crime, and industrial and traffic accident rates because they create more positively charged atmospheric ions (Sulman et al 1974) rather than just higher temperatures.

POLLUTION
Research upon pollution has shown that it can create stress and negative effects and increase vulnerability to the effects of other stressors, e.g.:
- High pollution has been associated with increased respiratory and cardiovascular illness and mortality rates.
- Researchers such as Rotton and Frey (1984, 1985) have found odour and bad air are associated with negative interpersonal behaviour, family disturbances reported to the police and psychiatric problems.

Evaluation
- However, residents sometimes habituate to bad air quality and report being less bothered about it than newcomers to an area.
- Effects depend on the kind of pollution – different varieties and amounts of air toxins can have different types and degrees of influence.
- Cause and effect is again difficult to disentangle since those with health or mental problems may have reduced income and therefore be forced to live in polluted areas.

Strategies for coping with environmental stressors

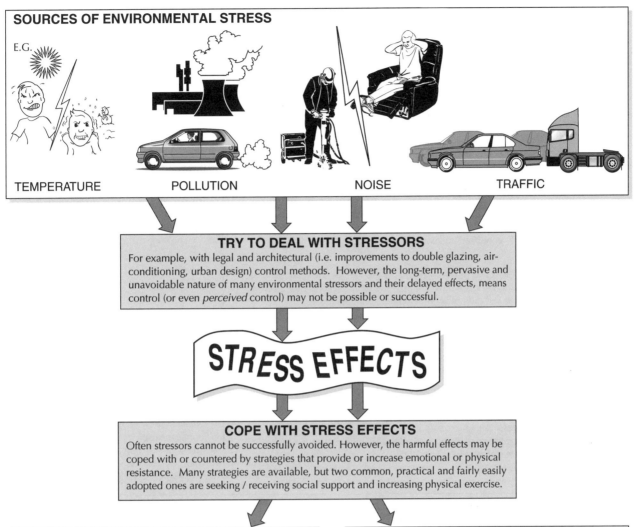

SOURCES OF ENVIRONMENTAL STRESS

E.G.

TEMPERATURE   POLLUTION   NOISE   TRAFFIC

TRY TO DEAL WITH STRESSORS

For example, with legal and architectural (i.e. improvements to double glazing, air-conditioning, urban design) control methods. However, the long-term, pervasive and unavoidable nature of many environmental stressors and their delayed effects, means control (or even *perceived* control) may not be possible or successful.

STRESS EFFECTS

COPE WITH STRESS EFFECTS

Often stressors cannot be successfully avoided. However, the harmful effects may be coped with or countered by strategies that provide or increase emotional or physical resistance. Many strategies are available, but two common, practical and fairly easily adopted ones are seeking / receiving social support and increasing physical exercise.

SEEKING SOCIAL SUPPORT

Social support has been associated with increased resistance to and recovery from a very wide range of stressors and stress-related illnesseses. Other people may have either a direct or stress-buffering effect to help avoid or cope with stressors by providing (according to Wills, 1985, cited in Gatchel et al, 1989) different kinds of social support:

- *Esteem support* – by praising, comforting, or protecting our ego.
- *Informational support* – by providing useful knowledge to help deal with stressors.
- *Companionship support* – to increase positive stimulation and activities. Some research suggests social events like celebrations and friendly get-togethers can sometimes have a more positive effect on health than negative events have a negative effect, and that a decrease in positive events can have a worse effect than an increase in negative events (Baron and Byrne, 1997).
- *Instrumental support* – by increasing physical aid, e.g. money.

Evaluation
- It is *difficult to measure* social support since the quality as well as the number of friendship bonds is involved and self-reports of friendship may be biased by socially desirability.
- There are important *individual differences* in *willingness* (e.g. due to personality) and *ability* (e.g. due to lack of sociopetal and semi-private architecture in high-rise blocks) to *seek support*.
- Social support may be more effective for social stressors (e.g. unemployment and bereavement) than environmental ones.

INCREASING PHYSICAL EXERCISE

Regular exercise, in combination with suitable diet and sleep, not only provides strength and endurance but also increases:

- *resistance to illness* (e.g. cardiovascular and respiratory)
- *faster recovery* from illness
- *positive moods*, a sense of well-being and ability to cope.

Brown (1991) found beneficial long-term effects (fewer health centre visits despite high levels of stress) in undergraduates who reported engaging in more physical exercise and showed better heart rate recovery at the beginning of term.

Exercise may have its effects through improving circulation and the immune system, generating a sense of self-efficacy and control, providing enjoyment or even (according to some) by reducing frustration, anger and aggression through catharsis.

Evaluation
- Retrospective and correlation studies based on real life measures do not tell us whether increased exercise really reduces stress or if those with less stress are just able to exercise more. However, more controlled field experiments, e.g. by Goldwater and Collis (1985) and Jennings et al (1986), have shown increased exercise does have positive effects on reported anxiety levels and cardiovascular health by directly manipulating exercise levels in young adults (Sarafino, 1994).
- However, exercise can be more unpleasant, difficult and less effective in noisy, hot and polluted environments.

High-density living

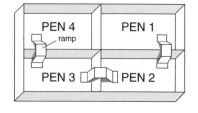

CALHOUN'S (1962) STUDY ON RAT POPULATION DENSITY
Method
- In a series of studies, groups of either 32 or 56 rats were placed in a 10-by-14-foot (3 x 4.2 metre) enclosure designed to comfortably accommodate 48 rats, and allowed to breed until a moderately severe over-population of 80 rats was reached (thereafter surviving young were removed to maintain this level).
- The enclosure was divided into four pens (the species of rat usually live in colonies of 12) that were partitioned by electrified barriers but with interconnecting ramps except between pens 1 and 4 (which turned them into more defensible end pens).
- Adequate levels of, and access to, food, water and nest-building materials were provided in all pens. The rats' behaviour was observed over 16 months.

Results
Population distribution
- A dominant male rat was better able to restrict access to and defend territories in end pens 1 and 4 and was therefore able to maintain a harem of 8–12 females.
- The majority of rats (up to around three-quarters) were found in pens 2 and 3 which became highly densely populated and was termed the 'behavioural sink'.

Population behaviour
- Behaviour in the end pens was relatively normal, although the dominant male had to be constantly vigilant and sleep by the ramp. Any other males permitted entry were extremely passive and did not attempt to breed with the females.
- Behaviour in the *middle pens* was highly abnormal in both males and females:
  Male rats divided into types, showing increased and often indiscriminate:
  Aggression – attacking females and juveniles, ignoring appeasement responses and fighting to the death, biting the tails of other rats and showing cannibalism.
  Sexual activity – including homosexuality and forced copulation with females (even those not in oestrus) and juveniles.
  Passivity – showing avoidance and lack of any social interaction with either sex.
  Female rats – showed a lack of sexual, nest-building and maternal behaviour.

Health and mortality rates
- Greater physical deterioration, e.g. enlarged adrenal glands occurred, especially in the middle pens and the females who lived there.
- The mortality rate was around 50% for unweaned young in the end pens, but between 80 to 96% (and around 50% for adult females) in the middle pens.

EVALUATION
Strengths
- Many of the negative effects found have been confirmed in naturalistic observations and field studies of overpopulation in the wild, e.g. in deer (Christian et al, 1960).
- Laboratory-based studies on animals have greater control and ease of accurate data recording than field studies, and are more ethical and practical (e.g. in terms of duration, control of escape, faster breeding and life cycles) than human studies.

Weaknesses
- The study lacked ecological validity due to the unusual apparatus and complete lack of escape, and was still unethical.
- It is uncertain if the negative effects result from high density or territoriality (both may be population limitation mechanisms).
- The study cannot be generalised to humans, due to methodological and psychological differences.

THE EFFECTS OF HIGH-DENSITY LIVING ON HUMANS
Definitions
Since humans are thought to be more influenced by cognitive perceptions, psychologists distinguish between population density and crowding.
Density = objective measure of people per unit of space. However different effects may result depending upon the whether the density measured is:
- *Outside density* – the number of people within a geographic area.
- *Inside density* – the number of people within a contained space.
- *Social density* – increased by adding greater numbers of people.
- *Spatial density* – increased by reducing the size of the space.

Crowding = the subjective psychological experience of density that reflects differences in perception, tolerance and coping due to:
- *Individual, social* and *cultural* factors, e.g. due to gender or cultural differences in personal space, sociability or experience of density.
- *Contextual factors*, e.g. due to control, ability to escape, enjoyment of density (i.e. in a rock concert or subway train), and expectations.

Effects of high-density living
- *Arousal* – high inside density is associated with greater physiological arousal, which may increase levels of aggression (particularly in males) or social withdrawal (less social interaction and helping behaviour) as coping responses, depending upon individual and contextual factors.
- *Illness* – long-term, inside high-density living is associated with increased blood pressure, infection (possibly due to ease of transmission as well as stress effects on the immune system) and mortality rates.

Explanations of high-density effects
There are many theories of population density effects. For example, density may become crowding when other people:
- Interfere with our goals and perception of control.
- Overload us with physical or social stimulation / invade our privacy.
- Increase competition for territory and resources.

Studies of high-density living on humans
Laboratory studies – have found higher social and spatial inside density increases arousal and aggression, with men finding spatial density more disturbing than women do. This may be due to greater personal space requirements in men (especially with other men) or the tendency for women to talk about the discomfort with others and make less internal hostile attributions about the situation. However, although laboratory studies have greater control and ability to measure physiological and behavioural responses, they are often short-term and artificial (e.g. people know they can escape to greater space at some point).
Field studies – e.g. studies on student housing and prisons. Cox et al (1984) reported that a 20% increase in prison population was associated with a 36% increase in assaults, while a 30% drop was followed by a 60% decrease. Blood pressure and illness has been found to positively correlate with fluctuating prison densities, while Paulus et al (1978) found a positive correlation of .81 between population density and (non-violent) death. However field studies lack control over many variables, e.g. unrepresentative samples.
Correlation studies – e.g. based on sociological and demographic surveys. Freedman et al (1975) found no significant correlation between population outside density and violent assaults in areas of New York City. Similar results are found with illness when variables like income and housing quality are taken into account.

Crowd behaviour in humans 1

Crowd psychology has largely focused on the nature of crowd action – whether it is:
1 Wild, unruly and irrational, involving a loss of identity, or
2 Purposeful, rational and rule governed (i.e. understandable in terms of precipitating factors or the crowd's identity and goals).

Wild and unruly

Rational and rule-governed

CROWDS AS WILD AND UNRULY

COLLECTIVE UNCONSCIOUS THEORY

Le Bon's (1895) book *The Crowd* argued that individuals in a crowd lose their conscious individual personalities to the primitive, animalistic, spirit of the crowd. Individuals in a crowd descend 'several rungs in the ladder of civilisation' showing impulsive, irritable, highly suggestible and overly emotional behaviour and an incapacity to reason.

Milgram (1977) in describing Le Bon's theory states:

'Le Bon's fundamental idea is that men undergo a radical transformation in a crowd. Once in the grip of the 'law of mental unity of crowds', primitive, irrational elements emerge. Immersed in the crowd, a man loses self-control and may act in a bestial fashion. He can be cruel, savage, irrational, a Jekyll turned Hyde with the crowd itself as the elixir. He performs actions that would shock him if carried out when alone... . Crowd characteristics appear as emergent properties not predictable from an acquaintance with solitary man. The overarching emergent is nothing less than a collective mind.'

Le Bon (1903) (quoted in Milgram, 1977) himself states:

'Whoever be the individuals that compose it, however like or unlike be their mode of life, their occupations, their character, or their intelligence, the fact that they have been transformed into a crowd puts them in possession of a sort of collective mind which makes them feel, think, and act in a manner quite different from that in which each individual of them would feel, think, and act were he in a state of isolation.'

Through the mechanisms of:
- **Anonymity** (due to sheer numbers the individual in the crowd feels a sense of invincible power along with a lack of responsibility).
- **Contagion** (crowd behaviour spreads amongst its members like an involuntary disease).
- **Suggestibility** (the suggestions of crowd members or leaders are accepted uncritically due to a loss of conscious personality).

The crowd has the following effect upon its members:
- **Homogeneity of personality** – all members behave in the same way.
- **Intellectual retardation** – crowds are intellectually inferior to the individuals who compose it, showing rapid shifts of attention and acceptance of ideas in the absence of evidence.
- **Violent action** – with a loss of constraints, savage and destructive behaviour is shown.
- **Exaggerated emotionalism** – crowd members become excited and impulsive.

EVALUATION
- Le Bon's style of reporting his ideas was not very scientific (they are presented in a disorganised and exaggerated manner) and the theory itself is based largely on anecdotal rather than first hand systematic evidence. As Milgram (1977) suggests, 'One senses that, at best, he drew the drapes of his apartment window enough to peek at the rabble below, then closed the velour, ran tremulously to his desk, and dashed off his classic'!
- Le Bon contrasts the irrationality of crowds with a model of the normal, isolated individual. However, lone individuals can be just as irrational, stupid and emotional. Indeed in complete contradiction to his ideas convergence theory argues that habitually aggressive and impulsive people are attracted to, and make up the majority in, mobs.
- Le Bon does not distinguish between types of crowds – all are tarred with the same brush. Crowds are often peaceful and gathered together for the purpose of enjoyment and celebration, e.g. at concerts, football matches, parties etc.
- Explanations of mobs as being unruly and irrational serve the political purpose of denying that crowd action can be caused by legitimate social concerns.
- Although Le Bon's ideas have been very influential (Freud used them to support his own ideas on crowds, as did Hitler and Mussolini), other psychologists have pointed out the vagueness of some of his notions, e.g. contagion and loss of identity, and have developed their own theories to replace them (see below).
- Others completely disagree with his theory on crowds, suggesting that crowd behaviour is not wild and unruly and does not involve a loss of individual identity.

Crowd behaviour in humans 2

CROWDS AS WILD AND UNRULY (continued)
Later research focused on two main aspects of crowd behaviour outlined by Le Bon: contagion and the loss of individual identity.

CONTAGION OF BEHAVIOUR

LOSS OF INDIVIDUAL IDENTITY

EARLY THEORIES OF CONTAGION
McDougall (1920) suggested that the facial and bodily expressions of an emotion instinctively arouses the same emotion in the viewer. Thus anger or laughter will be perceived, imitated and naturally spread through a group. Allport (1924) argued that emotion is perpetuated and exaggerated by the feedback responses of others – producing a circular reaction. When someone imitates your expression it reinforces and stimulates your own emotion, and so on until ever-higher levels of excitement are reached.

Evaluation
Instinctual responses suggest that crowd behaviour is beyond conscious control, but people do not always become angry just by seeing other people angry and not everyone follows the laughter of a group. Contagion theory does not explain the limits or restraints of crowd behaviour.

EMERGENT NORM THEORY
Turner and Killian (1972) explain behavioural contagion in crowds by proposing that collective crowd action is triggered off by the first people to show a clear pattern of behaviour. Their actions define the norm of behaviour – the appropriate thing to do, since social comparison theory and informational social influence suggests that people in a crowd are uncertain how to react and look to others for information. Thus if the emergent norm becomes 'applaud the performance', 'run for the fire escape' or 'throw bricks' then crowd members follow the established pattern.

Evaluation
Reicher (1982) disagrees with the idea that norms are only established by a small number of initial actors because this ignores pre-existing whole group identities.

DEINDIVIDUATION THEORY
Zimbardo and other researchers suggest that individuals may lose their sense of individual identity and control over behaviour in a crowd for many social psychological reasons such as sensory overload, arousal, anonymity and reduced self-awareness. These factors may lead to loosened inhibitions and thus uncharacteristic behaviour not in line with usual internal standards.

Evaluation
Since deindividuation in crowds is difficult to test experimentally, researchers such as Zimbardo have looked at the effect of deindividuation in the laboratory through the use of uniforms which increase anonymity, e.g. Zimbardo's electrocution experiment (1969) and his prison simulation experiment (1973). Diener et al (1976) also looked at deindividuation with children at Hallowe'en. These experiments all have their methodological problems however and we cannot be certain how far we can generalise the results to real life crowd behaviour.

CROWDS AS RULE-GOVERNED AND RATIONAL

SOCIAL IDENTITY THEORY
Reicher (1982a) argues that traditional crowd psychology ignores the social causation of crowd behaviour and regards only individuals as capable of directly planned and rational behaviour. Rather than losing their identity (as collective unconscious theory suggests), social identity theory argues that individuals in a crowd often have a common identity and purpose, and will act in a rule governed and coherent manner in line with the values and norms of such an identity. Reicher used social identity theory and the St Paul's riot in Bristol to show how crowd behaviour was not wild and irrational, but defined and directed by the group identity assumed by the individuals. Violence was spontaneous and uniform (e.g. collective brick throwing), but governed and limited by the aims of being a member of the St Paul's community (crowd aggression was directed at the police only and restricted to St Paul's geographic area). Rather than wild, mindless mob violence, the crowd directed traffic flow through the area and families shopped during the riot.
Reicher also rejects contagion theory, which suggests *any* behaviour will be transmitted throughout a crowd and that irritability or aggression is inevitable, since behaviour that is not in line with a crowd's identity will be frowned upon and discouraged. When in the St Paul's riot stones hit targets other than the police, the individuals responsible were ridiculed and stopped by crowd members.

Evaluation
* Reicher admits it can be difficult to gain objective data from interviews, despite using the method of triangulation (using separate sources to confirm accounts).
* Interviews suffer from the problems of self-report statements – there is a limit to the amount of disclosure rioters are willing to give about their law breaking behaviour and participants may wish to present themselves in a positive light.
* Social identity theory may underestimate the effects of fear and confusion on the crowd's ability to reason and control their behaviour.

NORM THEORY
Marsh (1978) found that regularly occurring crowds develop implicit roles and norms that guide and regulate behaviour. From studying football crowds on the terraces Marsh distinguished and named different groups among the supporters (e.g. 'novices', 'rowdies' and 'nutters') each with their own identities, rules and norms of behaviour. Violence was not wild and undirected, but tended to have constraints and be more verbal and ritualised than physically damaging.

SOCIAL CONDITIONS FOR RIOTS
Most psychologists agree that crowds do not riot without reason. Schneider (1988) gives four conditions necessary for a riot to occur:
1 A long-standing suppressed impulse of hostility (often due to perceived social injustice / oppression).
2 A precipitating incident (e.g. the beating of Rodney King in the Los Angeles riots).
3 The translation of impulse into behaviour (this usually occurs as the incident and anger it causes focuses and energises behaviour).
4 The relaxation of usual inhibitions against violence (due to anonymity and social sanction as rioting becomes normative).

Why behaviour is often not environmentally friendly

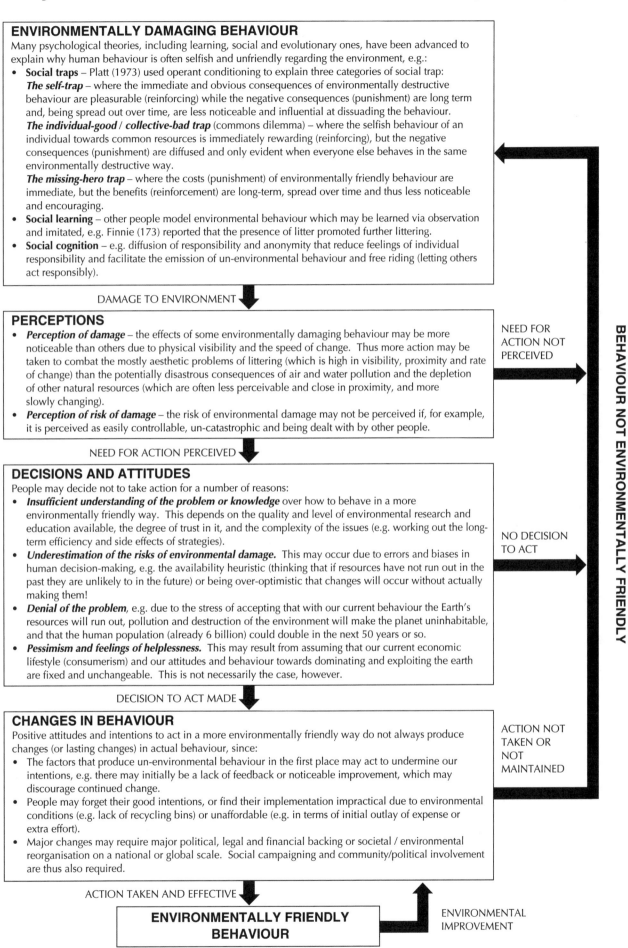

ENVIRONMENTALLY DAMAGING BEHAVIOUR

Many psychological theories, including learning, social and evolutionary ones, have been advanced to explain why human behaviour is often selfish and unfriendly regarding the environment, e.g.:

- **Social traps** – Platt (1973) used operant conditioning to explain three categories of social trap:

  The self-trap – where the immediate and obvious consequences of environmentally destructive behaviour are pleasurable (reinforcing) while the negative consequences (punishment) are long term and, being spread out over time, are less noticeable and influential at dissuading the behaviour.

  The individual-good / collective-bad trap (commons dilemma) – where the selfish behaviour of an individual towards common resources is immediately rewarding (reinforcing), but the negative consequences (punishment) are diffused and only evident when everyone else behaves in the same environmentally destructive way.

  The missing-hero trap – where the costs (punishment) of environmentally friendly behaviour are immediate, but the benefits (reinforcement) are long-term, spread over time and thus less noticeable and encouraging.

- **Social learning** – other people model environmental behaviour which may be learned via observation and imitated, e.g. Finnie (173) reported that the presence of litter promoted further littering.

- **Social cognition** – e.g. diffusion of responsibility and anonymity that reduce feelings of individual responsibility and facilitate the emission of un-environmental behaviour and free riding (letting others act responsibly).

DAMAGE TO ENVIRONMENT

PERCEPTIONS

- **Perception of damage** – the effects of some environmentally damaging behaviour may be more noticeable than others due to physical visibility and the speed of change. Thus more action may be taken to combat the mostly aesthetic problems of littering (which is high in visibility, proximity and rate of change) than the potentially disastrous consequences of air and water pollution and the depletion of other natural resources (which are often less perceivable and close in proximity, and more slowly changing).

- **Perception of risk of damage** – the risk of environmental damage may not be perceived if, for example, it is perceived as easily controllable, un-catastrophic and being dealt with by other people.

NEED FOR ACTION PERCEIVED

DECISIONS AND ATTITUDES

People may decide not to take action for a number of reasons:

- **Insufficient understanding of the problem or knowledge** over how to behave in a more environmentally friendly way. This depends on the quality and level of environmental research and education available, the degree of trust in it, and the complexity of the issues (e.g. working out the long-term efficiency and side effects of strategies).

- **Underestimation of the risks of environmental damage.** This may occur due to errors and biases in human decision-making, e.g. the availability heuristic (thinking that if resources have not run out in the past they are unlikely to in the future) or being over-optimistic that changes will occur without actually making them!

- **Denial of the problem**, e.g. due to the stress of accepting that with our current behaviour the Earth's resources will run out, pollution and destruction of the environment will make the planet uninhabitable, and that the human population (already 6 billion) could double in the next 50 years or so.

- **Pessimism and feelings of helplessness.** This may result from assuming that our current economic lifestyle (consumerism) and our attitudes and behaviour towards dominating and exploiting the earth are fixed and unchangeable. This is not necessarily the case, however.

DECISION TO ACT MADE

CHANGES IN BEHAVIOUR

Positive attitudes and intentions to act in a more environmentally friendly way do not always produce changes (or lasting changes) in actual behaviour, since:

- The factors that produce un-environmental behaviour in the first place may act to undermine our intentions, e.g. there may initially be a lack of feedback or noticeable improvement, which may discourage continued change.

- People may forget their good intentions, or find their implementation impractical due to environmental conditions (e.g. lack of recycling bins) or unaffordable (e.g. in terms of initial outlay of expense or extra effort).

- Major changes may require major political, legal and financial backing or societal / environmental reorganisation on a national or global scale. Social campaigning and community/political involvement are thus also required.

ACTION TAKEN AND EFFECTIVE

ENVIRONMENTALLY FRIENDLY BEHAVIOUR

NEED FOR ACTION NOT PERCEIVED

NO DECISION TO ACT

ACTION NOT TAKEN OR NOT MAINTAINED

BEHAVIOUR NOT ENVIRONMENTALLY FRIENDLY

ENVIRONMENTAL IMPROVEMENT

Changing attitudes towards environmental issues

PROMOTIONAL LITERATURE

This strategy aims to cause attitude change that will **prevent** destructive behaviour and **create** environmentally friendly behaviour. Promotional literature may change attitudes, particularly in the young, by:

- **Increasing knowledge** regarding the **negative effects** of behaviour upon the environment. This should focus on the immediacy and urgency of the problem as well as the money and resources lost rather than the gains made, since human risk-taking seems more motivated to avoid losses than improve gains (Cave, 1998).
- **Increasing knowledge** regarding methods of **conservation, re-use, recycling and safe disposal**. This should increase awareness, self-efficacy and the ability to make ethical choices regarding environmentally friendly behaviour.
- **Encouraging individual responsibility** and the need for persistence and **commitment** to overcome diffusion of responsibility and the social traps.
- **Acting as a reminder**, cue and prompt to maintain attitude change, to reinforce environmentally friendly behaviour and establish social consensus.

Research shows that environmental education programmes on their own do not often produce large and lasting changes in reported attitudes (Lingwood, 1971), and that when attitude change is produced it does not necessarily lead to large and lasting changes in behaviour. However, their effectiveness can be improved by taking into account persuasive communication variables (see opposite) and in combination with legal enforcement, community support and behavioural reinforcement and punishment (see below).

Evaluation

Changing attitudes may not change behaviour.

- Bickman (1972) found that 94% of students agreed that everyone should pick up litter when they saw it, but when tested 98.6% of them failed to do so (Bell et al, 1990).
- There may be barriers to action, such as set attitudes, high costs and inconvenience.
- The degree of attitude change produced by persuasive communication depends upon many important variables. For example, the **Yale Persuasive communication model** (Janis and Hovland, 1959) suggests:

  Attention to information is affected by *source factors*, e.g. expertise, trustworthiness, likeability, status and race.

  Comprehension of information is affected by *message factors*, e.g. the presentation of the arguments.

  Acceptance of information is affected by *audience factors*, e.g. persuasibility, initial attitudes, intelligence and personality.

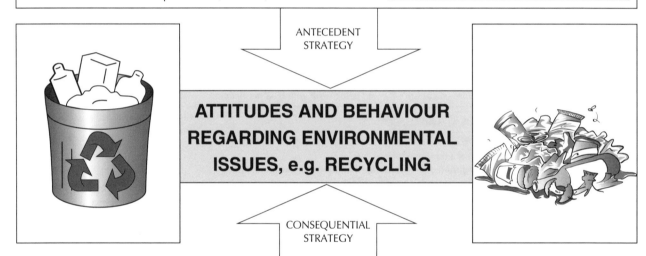

ANTECEDENT STRATEGY

ATTITUDES AND BEHAVIOUR REGARDING ENVIRONMENTAL ISSUES, e.g. RECYCLING

CONSEQUENTIAL STRATEGY

REWARDS AND PUNISHMENTS

This strategy aims to inhibit destructive behaviour and reinforce environmentally friendly behaviour in order to change attitudes towards the environment and thus maintain the behavioural change (since attitudes often follow from and reflect actions).

Clear laws, controls, regulations and informal social agreements or norms should be established and regulated by the **government** or **social community** through:

- **Punishment** for environmentally selfish and damaging behaviour – by fines, imprisonment, reparation (e.g. environmental community service) and social sanctions/disapproval (to encourage conformity). This brings the long-term costs closer to the present and makes them more conspicuous and individually applicable, thus reducing the social traps and diffusion of responsibility.
- **Negative reinforcement** for environmentally friendly behaviour – by clear threats and warnings of punishment, e.g. publicity and notices (see promotional literature).
- **Positive reinforcement** for co-operative and environmentally friendly behaviour – by providing polite and specific prompts and cues followed by feedback, financial rewards and incentives, and social approval. This reduces the missing-hero social trap.

Research has shown, for example, that providing laws, feedback and financial incentives regarding waste disposal and recycling has increased the return of bottles, collection of litter, use of recycling facilities, and the compaction and reduction of trash (Cave, 1998)

Evaluation

- Environmental behaviour needs to be monitored and acted upon which can be time consuming, difficult to achieve and financially costly.
- Short-term costs will bring long-term savings and rewards, however individuals, communities and governments need to persist and invest for the pay off and to avoid the social trap.
- Rewards and punishments need to be of sufficient intensity and applied promptly and individually for maximum effect although this is not always possible.
- Positive reinforcement strategies are more socially desirable, effective and economically viable than punishment strategies.
- Changes in behaviour do not always produce the desired changes in attitudes since:
  1 Mere compliance may result from punishment (leading to cheating wherever possible).
  2 Resentment, hostile attitudes and reactance may result from the threats and perceived control of negative reinforcement strategies.
  3 Mercenary behaviour may result from extrinsic rewards that undermine intrinsic motivation, ideals and satisfaction (leading to only showing environmentally friendly behaviour when a reward is provided).

INDEX